THE *unofficial* GUIDE®
™Washington, D.C.
9TH EDITION

THE
unofficial GUIDE®
TO Washington, D.C.

9TH EDITION

EVE ZIBART *with* JOE SURKIEWICZ

WILEY

Please note that prices fluctuate in the course of time and that travel information changes under the impact of many factors that influence the travel industry. We therefore suggest that you write or call ahead for confirmation when making your travel plans. Every effort has been made to ensure the accuracy of information throughout this book, and the contents of this publication are believed to be correct at the time of printing. Nevertheless, the publishers cannot accept responsibility for errors or omissions, for changes in details given in this guide, or for the consequences of any reliance on the information provided by the same. Assessments of attractions and so forth are based upon the authors' own experiences; therefore, descriptions given in this guide necessarily contain an element of subjective opinion, which may not reflect the publisher's opinion or dictate a reader's own experience on another occasion. Readers are invited to write the publisher with ideas, comments, and suggestions for future editions.

Published by:
John Wiley & Sons, Inc.
111 River Street
Hoboken, NJ 07030-5774

Produced by Menasha Ridge Press

Cover design by Michael J. Freeland

Interior design by Vertigo Design

For information on our other products and services or to obtain technical support, please contact our Customer Care Department within the United States at 800-762-2974, outside the United States at 317-572-3993, or by fax at 317-572-4002.

John Wiley & Sons, Inc. also publishes its books in a variety of electronic formats. Some content that appears in print may not be available in electronic formats.

ISBN 978-0-470-04208-3

Manufactured in the United States of America

5 4 3 2

CONTENTS

LIST *of* MAPS

ABOUT *the* AUTHOR *and* CONTRIBUTORS

Eve Zibart, AUTHOR OF SEVERAL BOOKS, INCLUDING *The Unofficial Guide to New Orleans, The Unofficial Guide to New York, The Unofficial Guide to Walt Disney World for Grown-ups,* and *The Ethnic Food Lover's Companion,* is a feature writer and restaurant critic for the "Weekend" section of the *Washington Post;* as the former nightlife columnist, she drew on her intimate knowledge of D.C.'s diverse after-hours scene as well as the area's vast array of dining spots when writing our entertainment and restaurant sections. Eve also scoped out where to find the best deals for our chapter on shopping and gently reminded Joe that biking is only one form of exercise.

THE CONTRIBUTOR OF MUCH OF THE ORIGINAL WORK on this guide, **Joe Surkiewicz** has coauthored five titles in the *Unofficial Guides* series and written two guides to the best places to ride a mountain bike in the Mid-Atlantic states. Joe is communications director at the Legal Aid Bureau of Maryland. He lives in Baltimore with his best friend and counselor, Ann Lembo. When not traveling or bicycling, they enjoy evenings curled up on the sofa with their black-and-white feline companions, Molly and Trixie, to watch black-and-white movies starring 1930s film divas Kay Francis, Norma Shearer, and Miriam Hopkins.

A NATIVE OF THE BALTIMORE SUBURBS, **Alisa Bralove** is a legal-affairs writer for Maryland's business and legal daily newspaper, *The Daily Record.* She and her husband, Rich Scherr, live in Owings Mills, Maryland. Alisa personally inspected more than 140 hotels and inns for our Accommodations chapter.

PREFACE

GEORGE WASHINGTON MAY HAVE BEEN, famously, "first in the hearts of his countrymen," but no such claim could have been made for the city that bore his name. In fact, strange as it may sound, Washington, D.C. has spent most of its history suffering from a serious inferiority complex.

It has never been given much respect, or at least not until fairly recently. Charles Dickens called it "the City of Magnificent Intentions," filled with "spacious avenues that begin in nothing and lead nowhere." In 1809, the British minister Francis Jackson called it "scantily and rudely cultivated." Washington Irving called it a "forlorn . . . desert town." Even John F. Kennedy famously described it a "city of Northern charm and Southern efficiency," although the massive beautification programs launched by Lady Bird Johnson in the mid-1960s and committed to the National Park Service have done much to change that. Pierre L'Enfant, who planned the city, died penniless and brokenhearted; his vision was considered too grandiose and was repeatedly amended.

It wasn't the first or second or even fifth city to serve as the capital. Philadelphia was first and foremost: The Continental Congress briefly adjourned to Baltimore when the British threatened, but quickly returned, only to retreat again to York, Pennsylvania, with an overnight session in Lancaster. The representatives returned to Philadelphia in 1778, but an uprising five years later by not British but their own troops (who were still awaiting their promised pay) sent them first to Princeton, New Jersey; then to Annapolis; then to Trenton, New Jersey; then to New York; and—inevitably—back to Philadelphia. (There's a good reason that the city's main boulevard is named Pennsylvania Avenue.)

When the nation's capital was finally established (in 1790), its site was highly problematic—a "foggy bottom," still the nickname given to the Department of State. It had to borrow land from Maryland

and Virginia, only to have the latter state renege and request its acreage back. While New York grandly swept to Gilded Age grandeur and Chicago awarded itself the title of "Second City," the seat of the national government couldn't even settle on a name: designer L'Enfant called it the Capital City. Jefferson referred to it as Federal Town. It was officially dubbed Washington City in 1791, but modest George never used that name himself, continuing to refer to it the Federal City. (He did, however, allow the city to use his coat of arms as a basis for its flag and to place him on its seal.) Even Annapolis outshone Washington as a social center in its early days, as did Alexandria and Georgetown.

Worse, as Washingtonians frequently point out, it is still more like a colony of the United States, because residents have no voting Representative in Congress (only a nonvoting seat) and no Senator at all—which is why you will see license plates bearing the ironic slogan "Taxation without Representation." (The District's motto, *Justitia omnibus,* or "Justice for all," might also be considered somewhat ironic.) Residents of the District couldn't even vote for President until 1961. Washington was briefly under the administration of a territorial governor after the Civil War, but the office was abolished soon thereafter, and the city remained under the direct rule of Congress until 1975, when the city was allowed to elect a mayor and city council. And although the House of Representatives passed a measure in 1992 approving statehood for "New Columbia," the Senate has consistently refused to consider it.

Perhaps it's appropriate, then, that Washington is a more international city than an American one, housing as it does the scores of embassies and consulates, the headquarters of the World Bank and International Monetary Fund, the Organization of American States, and so on. And of course, repeated waves of immigration have made it if not the melting pot of America, a sizeable and simmering one.

In another way, however, Washington is among the oldest areas to have been developed. The first Europeans to explore the Washington region were Spanish; Admiral Pedro Menendez, who also founded St. Augustine, may have sailed up the Potomac River (which he dubbed the Espiritu Santo) as far as Occoquan, Virginia. Captain John Smith of Pocahontas fame came even farther, to what is now Great Falls, Virginia, in 1608, though it is not clear whether he actually landed. Foragers from the Jamestown colony raided an Indian village in Anacostia in 1622; a few years later, George Calvert, Lord Baltimore, was granted the tract of Virginia north and east of the river—henceforth to be known as Maryland—as a refuge for British Catholics. By the middle of the 17th century, the entire area had been staked out as great tracts and manor seats.

The question of whether the nation's capital should be built in the North or the South was a subject of much debate, and in fact, while the Congress was in Trenton, some members made an attempt to lay out a site on the Delaware River. Vice President John Adams, voting as president of the Senate, favored Germantown, Pennsylvania. A compromise was finally struck, so the legend goes, at a private dinner Thomas Jefferson hosted for Alexander Hamilton and "Light Horse" Harry Lee, former governor of Virginia and father of Robert E. Lee.

The specific site was selected by Washington himself, probably because the former surveyor believed the Potomac River would become a major waterway. The initial design was a diamond shape, 10 miles by 10 miles, or 100 square miles; many of the mile markers around the perimeter, which were laid by Andrew Ellicott and Benjamin Banneker—a farmer, mathematician, astronomer, inventor, and probably the most famous black man in Colonial America—still stand, though badly deteriorated. (The "zero milestone" on the Ellipse refers not to the boundaries but to the distance markers of U.S. highways.)

Like New York, the District was originally a confederation of smaller towns: Washington City, which ended at Rock Creek Park on the west and Florida Avenue and Benning Road on the north; Georgetown, or the Port of Georgetown; Alexandria County, which included parts of the city of Alexandria as well as present-day Arlington County; and the unincorporated County of Washington. (Florida Avenue was then called Boundary Street, which explains why the streetcar exhibit in the American History Museum shows cars with that destination.)

But in 1846 the residents of Alexandria, who feared that the capital would outlaw slavery and thus strangle the slave trade in that busy port, voted to ask Congress to return the portion of the District across the river to the state of Virginia, and in July the request was granted. It was just short of a third of the 100 square miles; you can clearly see on a map how the original diamond is cut off at the southwestern corner by the Potomac. Eventually the city charters for Washington and Georgetown were revoked and their duties given over to the District of Columbia—in fact, the sector outside Washington City, termed the County of Washington, remains in historical, if not practical, limbo.

The cornerstone of the White House was laid on October 13, 1792, the day after the 300th anniversary of Columbus's arrival in the New World, but Washington never resided there; in fact, the building was still under construction in 1800 when President John Adams moved in. Congress finally convened later that year, too, in the one wing of the Capitol that had been finished. And Washington was officially declared the nation's capital on December 1, 1800.

Even so, the Capitol and White House had barely been finished in 1814 when British troops set both on fire, along with nearly every other public building. A temporary Capitol, at which James Monroe took his oath of office, was built where the Supreme Court Building is now. The President's house was restored in 1817 and the Capitol reopened at the end of 1819. (Incidentally, although the map directions of the District—Northwest, Northeast, Southwest, and Southeast—are taken from the Capitol building, the geographical center of the city is near Fourth Street, L Street, and New York Avenue NW.)

The city would be invaded once more, in 1864, by Confederate troops under the command of General Jubal A. Early; that raid, which culminated in the battle at Fort Stevens in Northwest Washington, marks the only time in American history that a President of the United States was present at a battle. Abraham Lincoln was reportedly so fascinated that he kept standing up to watch, oblivious to the bullets flying around him. (The young captain who finally yelled, "Get down, you damned fool!" to the civilian he did not recognize was future Supreme Court Justice Oliver Wendell Holmes Jr.)

At the beginning of the Civil War, Washington held only about 75,000 residents; the war and the subsequent expansion of federal agencies boosted that number to nearly 132,000. The population peaked at more than 800,000 in 1950, making the city the ninth largest in the country; it's now about 583,000.

Today, early in its third century, Washington is again at a cultural, and architectural, crossroads, considering a massive new Mall development plan, expanding public transportation and embracing the suburbs, balancing national dignity with "security" barriers. The astounding revitalization of the Pennsylvania Avenue neighborhood and reuse of historical buildings is a testament to the vision of L'Enfant (who, by the way, was finally reinterred in Arlington National Cemetery). Washington has clearly taken its place among the world's great cities as the crossroads of international policy. Soon, perhaps, Washingtonians will feel lucky to live here.

—*Eve Zibart*

INTRODUCTION

WELCOME *to* WASHINGTON

I LIVE IN WASHINGTON NOW, but I came first as a tourist—and later as a sort of Tennessean in exile.

I must have been about 6 the first time I laid eyes on the Washington Monument. My parents and older brother were equally delighted—we are a sentimental clan—but they were rather more sensible: I begged to be allowed to walk up all those 897 steps; my mother quite intelligently brokered a deal whereby we took the elevator up and walked down. Still, I can recall quite clearly that seemingly endless, mesmerizing downward-spiraling trek; the vision a few hours later of that flood-lit spire—it was reflected in the river—from a restaurant along the Southwest Waterfront; the towering gravity of Lincoln's great visage; and the gleaming width of the Mall itself.

When later I moved here to work, I made myself into a sort of professional tourist: I took two months off between jobs to learn my way around, to find my place in the neighborhood (Capitol Hill was my immediate first love), and to luxuriate in the myriad riches of the Smithsonian museums. I also determined to discover the secrets to negotiating traffic—a process that is much easier now thanks to the increased reach of the Metrorail subway but which then forced me to become an intimate of the city's unique and sometimes mysterious layout.

I never really expected to become a Washingtonian, but I eventually succumbed to the strange, almost hybrid spell: a city with Southern charm and manners but New Yorkian attractions, and a life rhythm somewhere in between. I was stubborn, though: It was at least five years before I realized I had shifted allegiance. I was flying in down the Potomac River and past the Mall when I suddenly became aware that I was feeling the "coming home" sensation, not the "back to work" one. I began to feel proud, almost possessive of the city's beauty, of the friezes and the statuary and the gardens (and the flower

washington at a glance

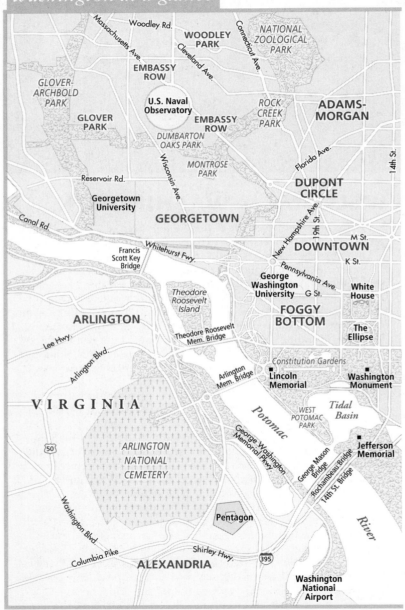

Woodley Rd.

Massachusetts Ave.

WOODLEY PARK

Cleveland Ave.

Connecticut Ave.

NATIONAL ZOOLOGICAL PARK

EMBASSY ROW

GLOVER-ARCHBOLD PARK

U.S. Naval Observatory

GLOVER PARK

EMBASSY ROW

DUMBARTON OAKS PARK

ROCK CREEK PARK

ADAMS-MORGAN

MONTROSE PARK

14th St.

Reservoir Rd.

Wisconsin Ave.

Florida Ave.

DUPONT CIRCLE

Georgetown University

Canal Rd.

GEORGETOWN

New Hampshire Ave.

19th St.

M St.

DOWNTOWN

K St.

Francis Scott Key Bridge

Whitehurst Fwy.

Pennsylvania Ave.

Theodore Roosevelt Island

George Washington University

G St.

White House

FOGGY BOTTOM

ARLINGTON

Lee Hwy.

Theodore Roosevelt Mem. Bridge

The Ellipse

Arlington Blvd.

Arlington Mem. Bridge

Constitution Gardens

■ **Lincoln Memorial**

■ **Washington Monument**

VIRGINIA

50

Potomac

WEST POTOMAC PARK

Tidal Basin

George Washington Memorial Pkwy.

ARLINGTON NATIONAL CEMETERY

George Mason Bridge

■ **Jefferson Memorial**

Rochambeau Bridge

14th St. Bridge

Washington Blvd.

Pentagon

River

Columbia Pike

Shirley Hwy.

395

ALEXANDRIA

Washington National Airport

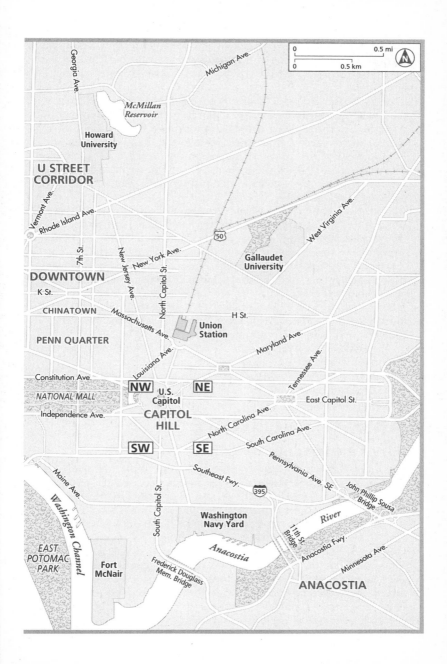

plantings in every leftover bit of ground, a permanent tribute to the graciousness of Lady Bird Johnson), of the cemeteries and cathedrals and historic homes. I walked, and continue to walk, its broad avenues and winding paths; I sit at sidewalk cafes and watch the passersby just as if I were in Paris—and frankly, the celebrity spotting's better here.

Sure, Washington can be hot, but isn't that the point of most of the beach vacations people take? It can be cold, too, which might be more of a surprise: the first week I lived here, it was too cold to recaulk the replacement windows for two that had been taken out. (I spent most of the time with my feet in the fireplace.) The traffic's extraordinary, but so is the scenery. Washington is a living multicultural festival, with infinite chances to make new friends and experience new customs.

Even more astoundingly, Washington has blossomed in the 21st century, the 9/11 chill more than offset by the boom in first-rate restaurants, theater and performing arts, and museum exhibits. And unlike the ones in New York, nearly all the museums here are free!

Sure, Washingtonians make jokes about the tourists, but rarely are they serious. In fact, most Washingtonians came from somewhere else, just as I did, and chose to stay. We're actually pretty friendly: you'll find us smiling at the people on the sidewalk, turning the confused around toward the White House, explaining the intricacies of the Metro farecard machines, and recommending favorite watering holes.

So welcome to Washington. Whether you think of it as the nation's capital, "Hollywood on the Potomac," Power Central, the center of the free world, or just a beautiful city, it's well worth the time. This time, and the next.

ABOUT *this* GUIDE

WHY "UNOFFICIAL"?

MOST "OFFICIAL" GUIDES TO WASHINGTON, D.C., tout the well-known sights, promote the local restaurants and accommodations indiscriminately, and leave out a lot of good stuff. This one is different.

Instead of pandering to the tourist industry, we'll tell you if the food is bad at a well-known restaurant, we'll complain loudly about D.C.'s notorious high prices, and we'll guide you away from the crowds and lines for a break now and then.

Visiting Washington requires wily strategies not unlike those used in the sacking of Troy. We sent in a team of evaluators who toured each site, ate in the city's best restaurants, performed critical evaluations of its hotels, and visited Washington's wide variety of nightclubs. If a museum is boring, or standing in line for two hours to view a famous attraction is a waste of time, we say so—and, in the process, hopefully make your visit more fun, efficient, and economical.

CREATING A GUIDEBOOK

WE GOT INTO THE GUIDEBOOK BUSINESS because we were unhappy with the way travel guides force the reader to work to get any usable information. Wouldn't it be nice, we thought, if we were to make guides that are easy to use?

Most guidebooks are compilations of lists. This is true regardless of whether the information is presented in list form or artfully distributed through pages of prose. There is insufficient detail in a list, and prose can present tedious helpings of nonessential or marginally useful information. Not enough wheat, so to speak, for nourishment in one instance, and too much chaff in the other. Either way, these types of guides provide little more than departure points from which readers initiate their own quests.

Many guides are readable and well researched, but they tend to be difficult to use. To select a hotel, for example, a reader must study several pages of descriptions with only the boldface hotel names breaking up large blocks of text. Because each description essentially deals with the same variables, it is difficult to recall what was said concerning a particular hotel. Readers generally must work through all the write-ups before beginning to narrow their choices. The presentation of restaurants, nightclubs, and attractions is similar except that even more reading is usually required. To use such a guide is to undertake an exhaustive research process that requires examining nearly as many options and possibilities as starting from scratch. Recommendations, if any, lack depth and conviction. These guides compound rather than solve problems by failing to narrow travelers' choices down to a thoughtfully considered, well-distilled, and manageable few.

HOW *UNOFFICIAL GUIDES* ARE DIFFERENT

READERS CARE ABOUT THE AUTHORS' OPINIONS. The authors, after all, are supposed to know what they are talking about. This, coupled with the fact that the traveler wants quick answers (as opposed to endless alternatives), dictates that authors should be explicit, prescriptive, and above all, direct. The authors of the *Unofficial Guide* try to be just that. They spell out alternatives and recommend specific courses of action. They simplify complicated destinations and attractions and allow the traveler to feel in control in the most unfamiliar environments. The objective of the *Unofficial Guide* authors is not to give the most information or all of the information, but to offer the most accessible, useful information.

An *Unofficial Guide* is a critical reference work; it focuses on a travel destination that appears to be especially complex. Our experienced authors and research team are completely independent from the attractions, restaurants, and hotels we describe. *The Unofficial Guide to Washington, D.C.* is designed for individuals and families traveling for the fun of it, as well as for business travelers and conventioneers, especially those visiting D.C. for the first time. The guide is directed at value-conscious, consumer-oriented adults who seek a cost-effective, though not spartan, travel style.

SPECIAL FEATURES

THE *UNOFFICIAL GUIDE* OFFERS the following special features:

- Friendly introductions to Washington's most fascinating neighborhoods.
- "Best of" listings, giving our well-qualified opinions on things ranging from bagels to baguettes, 4-star hotels to 12-story views.
- Listings that are keyed to your interests, so you can pick and choose.
- Advice to sightseers on how to avoid the worst of the crowds; advice to business travelers on how to avoid traffic and excessive costs.
- Recommendations for lesser-known sights that are away from the huge monuments of the Mall but are no less spectacular.
- A neighborhood system and maps to make it easy to find places you want to go to and avoid places you don't.
- Expert advice on avoiding Washington's notorious street crime.
- A Hotel Information Chart that helps you narrow down your choices fast, according to your needs.
- Shorter listings that include only those restaurants, clubs, and hotels we think are worth considering.
- A detailed index to help you find things fast.
- Insider advice on crowds, lines, best times of day (or night) to go places, and our secret weapon, Washington's stellar subway system.

What you *won't* get:

- Long, useless lists where everything looks the same.
- Information that gets you somewhere you want to go at the worst possible time.
- Information without advice on how to use it.

HOW THIS GUIDE WAS RESEARCHED AND WRITTEN

WHILE A LOT OF GUIDEBOOKS have been written about Washington, D.C., very few have been evaluative. Some guides come close to regurgitating the hotels' and tourist offices' own promotional material. In preparing this work, nothing was taken for granted. Each museum, monument, federal building, hotel, restaurant, shop, and attraction was visited by a team of trained observers who conducted detailed evaluations and rated each according to formal criteria. Team members conducted interviews with tourists of all ages to determine what they enjoyed most and least during their Washington visit.

While our observers are independent and impartial, they did not claim to have special expertise. Like you, they visited Washington as tourists or business travelers, noting their satisfaction or dissatisfaction.

The primary difference between the average tourist and the trained evaluator is the evaluator's skills in organization, preparation, and observation. The trained evaluator is responsible for much more than simply observing and cataloging. While the average tourist is gazing in awe at stacks of $20 bills at the Bureau of Engraving and Printing, for instance, the professional is rating the tour in terms of the information provided, how quickly the line moves, the location of restrooms, and how well children can see the exhibits. He or she also checks out things like other attractions close by, alternate places to go if the line at a main attraction is too long, and the best local lunch options. Observer teams use detailed checklists to analyze hotel rooms, restaurants, nightclubs, and attractions. Finally, evaluator ratings and observations are integrated with tourist reactions and the opinions of patrons for a comprehensive quality profile of each feature and service.

In compiling this guide, we recognize that a tourist's age, background, and interests will strongly influence his or her taste in Washington's wide array of attractions and will account for a preference for one sight or museum over another. Our sole objective is to provide the reader with sufficient description, critical evaluation, and pertinent data to make knowledgeable decisions according to individual tastes.

LETTERS, COMMENTS, AND QUESTIONS FROM READERS

WE EXPECT TO LEARN FROM OUR MISTAKES, as well as from the input of our readers, and to improve with each new book and edition. Many of those who use the *Unofficial Guides* write to us asking questions, making comments, or sharing their own discoveries and lessons learned in Washington. We appreciate all such input, both positive and critical, and encourage our readers to continue writing. Readers' comments and observations will frequently be incorporated into revised editions of the *Unofficial Guide* and will contribute immeasurably to its improvement.

How to Write the Author:

Eve Zibart
The Unofficial Guide to Washington, D.C.
P.O. Box 43673
Birmingham, AL 35243
UnofficialGuides@menasharidge.com

When you write by mail, be sure to put your return address on your letter as well as on the envelope—sometimes envelopes and letters get separated. And remember, our work takes us out of the office for long periods of time, so forgive us if our response is delayed.

Reader Survey

At the back of the guide you will find a short questionnaire that you can use to express opinions about your Washington visit. Clip out the questionnaire along the dotted line and mail it to the address on page 7.

The *Unofficial Guide* Web Site

The Web site of the *Unofficial Guide* Travel and Lifestyle Series, providing in-depth information on all *Unofficial Guides* in print, is at **www.theunofficialguides.com.**

HOW INFORMATION IS ORGANIZED: BY SUBJECT AND BY LOCATION

TO GIVE YOU FAST ACCESS to information about the *best* of Washington, we've organized material in several formats.

ACCOMMODATIONS Since most people visiting Washington stay in one hotel for the duration of their trip, we have summarized our coverage of hotels in charts, maps, ratings, and rankings that allow you to quickly focus your decision-making process. We do not go on, page after page, describing lobbies and rooms which, in the final analysis, sound much the same. Instead, we concentrate on the specific variables that differentiate one hotel from another: location, size, room quality, services, amenities, and cost. The accommodations are compared by rankings in a concise table (pages 48–55), and the vital information for all accommodations is provided in an extensive chart (pages 60–75).

ATTRACTIONS Attractions—historic buildings, museums, art galleries— draw visitors to Washington, but it's practically impossible to see them all in a single trip. We list them by type as well as location (see pages 176–181) and then evaluate each one, including its appeal to various age groups. These descriptions are the heart of this guidebook and help you determine what to see, and when.

RESTAURANTS We provide a lot of detail when it comes to restaurants. Since you will probably eat a dozen or more restaurant meals during your stay, and since not even you can predict what you might be in the mood for on Saturday night, we provide detailed profiles of the best restaurants in and around Washington. They are also listed by cuisine and location (see pages 276–283).

ENTERTAINMENT AND NIGHTLIFE Visitors frequently try several different clubs or nightspots during their stay. Since clubs and nightspots, like restaurants, are usually selected spontaneously after arriving in Washington, we believe detailed descriptions are warranted. The best nightspots and lounges in Washington are profiled as well (see profiles starting on page 382).

NEIGHBORHOODS Once you've decided where you're going, getting there becomes the issue. To help you do that, we have divided the city into neighborhoods:

- The National Mall and Arlington Memorials
- Capitol Hill
- Downtown
- Foggy Bottom
- Georgetown
- Dupont Circle/Adams-Morgan
- Upper Northwest
- Northeast
- Southeast
- Maryland Suburbs
- Virginia Suburbs

All hotel charts, as well as profiles of restaurants and nightspots, include the neighborhood. If you are staying at the Carlyle Suites, for example, and are interested in Japanese restaurants within walking distance, scanning the restaurant profiles for restaurants in Dupont Circle/Adams-Morgan will provide you with the best choices.

PART ONE

PLANNING *Your* VISIT *to* WASHINGTON

■ WHEN *to* GO

GOING WHEN THE WEATHER IS GOOD

THE BEST TIMES TO VISIT WASHINGTON are in the spring and fall, when the weather is most pleasant and nature puts on a show. The city's fabled cherry blossoms bloom in late March or early April—not necessarily coinciding with the Cherry Blossom Parade or festivities but luring a lot of pedestrian and vehicular traffic, which don't always coexist peacefully—while fall brings crisp, cool weather and, by mid-October, a spectacular display of gold, orange, and red leaves.

The summers—mid-June through September—can be brutally hot and humid. Visitors in July and August not only contend with the heat as they sprint from building to building, but also must endure the city's heavy reliance on air-conditioning that often reaches meat-locker chill. August, with its predictably oppressive heat, is the month when Washingtonians leave town in droves.

On the other hand, if you don't mind the humidity, or like an early-and-late schedule with a break in the afternoon, August has its good side: far less traffic (shorter lines), easy restaurant reservations, extended museum hours, and—because Congress is in recess and many federal employees on vacation—less-oppressive security. It's so much less crowded, in fact, that August is when Washington area chefs hold the year's second Restaurant Week, offering bargain-priced three-course lunch and dinner menus at about $20 and $30, respectively.

Washington's winter weather, on the other hand, is erratic. Balmy, mid-60s days are possible through December. While it often gets into the teens in January and February, midday temperatures can climb into the 40s and 50s. This is the season to beat the crowds.

March is tricky. While warm daytime temperatures are frequent, sometimes a large, moist air mass moving north from the Gulf of Mexico will collide with a blast of frigid air from Canada. The result is a big, wet snowfall that paralyzes the city for days. (It should be further noted that the mere *prediction* of snow can paralyze D.C.)

Washington weather can run the gamut from subzero (rarely), to mild (most of the winter, some of the summer, and most of the spring and fall), to scorchingly hot and unbearably humid (most of July and August). The table below lists the city's average monthly temperatures, in degrees Fahrenheit.

WASHINGTON'S AVERAGE MONTHLY TEMPERATURES

	HIGH	LOW		HIGH	LOW
January	42° F	27° F	July	87° F	68° F
February	44° F	28° F	August	84° F	66° F
March	53° F	35° F	September	78° F	60° F
April	64° F	44° F	October	67° F	48° F
May	75° F	54° F	November	55° F	38° F
June	83° F	64° F	December	45° F	30° F

AVOIDING CROWDS

IN GENERAL, POPULAR TOURIST SITES are busier on weekends than weekdays, Saturdays are busier than Sundays, and summer is busier than winter. The best days for avoiding big crowds at Washington's most popular attractions are Monday through Wednesday. Crowds begin to increase as the week progresses, with the volume of visitors peaking on Saturday. During the busiest tourist seasons—spring and summer—major Washington tourist attractions are always crowded between 9:30 a.m. and 3 p.m. For people in town on business, this tourist influx means heavier traffic, congested airports, a packed Metro . . . and a tough time finding a convenient hotel room.

Driving in weekday rush hours (featuring at least 100,000 frantic, short-tempered bureaucrats clawing their way to office or home) should be avoided at all costs. On weekends, the same government workers and their families become tourists, often creating midday traffic snarls during the warmer months.

TO BEAT THE CROWDS . . .

- Avoid the worst tourist seasons: the Cherry Blossom Festival (early spring) and midsummer.
- Hit major Mall attractions on weekdays or Sunday.
- Avoid driving in rush hour (which in D.C. means 6:30 to 10 a.m. and 2 to 7 p.m.).
- Get off the Mall and visit Georgetown, Dupont Circle, or downtown attractions.

If you're driving to Washington, try to time your arrival on a weekend or during a non–rush hour time—before 7 a.m. or during a rather narrow window that opens around 10 a.m. and starts to close quickly around 2 p.m. Afternoon traffic doesn't begin to clear up until 7:30 p.m. Friday afternoon rush hours are the worst: don't even think of driving near D.C. until after 8 p.m.

TRYING TO REASON WITH THE TOURIST SEASON

WHETHER YOU'RE IN TOWN ON BUSINESS or pleasure, it's a good idea to be aware of when the big crowds of tourists are likely to be jamming up the Metro, the sidewalk, or the place you've picked for lunch.

The best time to avoid crowds entirely is in winter. On weekdays especially, the Mall is nearly deserted and museums, monuments, and normally crowd-intensive hot spots like the Capitol are nearly empty—except for the people who work there. Furthermore, the relative scarcity of tourists in the off-season eliminates the worst of D.C.'s traffic gridlock, except during peak rush hours.

After the winter doldrums, crowds begin picking up in late March and peak in early April, when the Japanese cherry trees along the Tidal Basin bloom and Washington is flooded with visitors. Mammoth throngs pack the Mall, and it's elbow to elbow in the National Air and Space Museum. Because of the crowded conditions, we do not recommend touring Washington in the early spring.

Instead, if at all possible, delay your visit until late May or early June. Crowds are more manageable for a few weeks, and the weather is usually delightful.

The tourist pace begins picking up again in mid-June as schools let out. July through mid-August are very crowded—and usually the weather is brutally hot and humid. Popular museums such as the Museum of Natural History, the National Air and Space Museum, and the National Museum of American History (which is currently closed for an extensive renovation) fill up with masses of people; eating in restaurants becomes a stress-inducing ordeal; and the entire experience becomes exhausting. Driving conditions, never good in Washington, degenerate into gridlock—even on weekends—and the Metro is packed to rush-hour levels all day.

The throngs begin to thin during the last two weeks of August, when kids start returning to school. After Labor Day, the volume of visitors drops off significantly during the week, but weekends remain packed through October—though not as packed as in spring and summer. In November, tourist activity slows down dramatically.

After May and June, the best time to visit Washington is in the late fall and winter. While Thanksgiving Day brings hordes of visitors to popular sights on the Mall, car traffic is light and getting around town from November through March is easy. Winter visitors can't count on balmy weather, but crowds are virtually nonexistent and Washington's elaborate cultural season kicks into full swing. Plays, music, opera, and ballet fill the city's theaters and halls—the Kennedy Center, Arena Stage, the Shakespeare Theater at the Folger, the National Theater, Ford's Theatre, and the Library of Congress. Both business visitors and folks in town to tour the sights will find Washington a lot easier to get around in during the late fall and winter.

A CALENDAR of
FESTIVALS and EVENTS

January

WASHINGTON RESTAURANT WEEK Early to mid-January. More than 150 area restaurants offer fixed-price lunch ($20) and dinner ($30) menus. For more information go to **www.washington.org/restaurantwk.**

ROBERT E. LEE'S BIRTHDAY CELEBRATION Mid-January. The birthdays of Confederate General Robert E. Lee (January 19) and of his father, Revolutionary War Colonel Henry "Light Horse Harry" Lee (January 29) are celebrated with period music, refreshments, and house tours at the Lee-Fendell House in Old Town Alexandria, home to members of the family from 1885 to 1903; for more information call ☎ 703-548-1789. (Ongoing renovation will prevent the 2007 celebration.)

February

CHINESE NEW YEAR PARADE Early February to early March. Marching bands, lion and dragon dancers, clowns, and other performers celebrate through Chinatown and around Verizon Center; ☎ 202-393-7838.

ABRAHAM LINCOLN'S BIRTHDAY February 12. A wreath-laying ceremony, music, and a dramatic reading of the Gettysburg Address at the Lincoln Memorial; ☎ 202-619-7222.

FREDERICK DOUGLASS'S BIRTHDAY February 14. A wreath-laying ceremony, musical tributes, and other activities honor the birthday anniversary of the abolitionist leader at Cedar Hill, the Frederick Douglass National Historic Site; ☎ 202-426-5961.

EAST COAST JAZZ FESTIVAL Mid- to late February. Workshops, recitals, and concerts by top local and national jazz artists sponsored by the Fish Middleton Jazz Scholarship Fund; ☎ 301-933-1822; **www.fmjseastcoastjazz.com.**

GEORGE WASHINGTON BIRTHDAY CELEBRATION Third weekend. Mount Vernon celebrates the first president's birthday anniversary with parades and a sample of Washington's favorite breakfast, "hoecakes swimming in butter and honey"; music; a wreath-laying ceremony; and free admission; ☎ 703-780-2000.

WASHINGTON'S BIRTHDAY PARADE Third Sunday. The nation's largest, with marching bands, floats, military reenactors, and other units, on the streets of Old Town Alexandria; ☎ 703-838-4200 or 703-991-4474.

AMERICAN CRAFT COUNCIL CRAFT FAIR Late February. More than 700 craft artists display their works during this annual edition of Maryland's largest indoor craft show at the Baltimore Convention Center; ☎ 410-649-7000 or 800-836-3470.

March

WASHINGTON ANTIQUARIAN BOOK FAIR About 75 exhibitors from across the United States offer rare books, manuscripts, documents, maps, and other memorabilia in this annual benefit for Concord Hill School, March 3 and 4, at the Holiday Inn Rosslyn, 1900 North Fort Myer Drive, Arlington; ☎ 301-654-2626; **www.wabf.com.**

SPRING ANTIQUES FAIR First weekend. More than 100 dealers offer furniture, folk art, jewelry, and other goods at the D.C. Armory; ☎ 301-933-9433.

ALEXANDRIA ST. PATRICK'S DAY PARADE First Saturday. The annual parade of floats, bands, Irish dancers, and other units through the streets of Old Town Alexandria; ☎ 703-838-4200 or 703-237-2199.

AMERICAN PIANO FESTIVAL Mid-March. A dozen public events, including concerts, lectures, videos, and symposiums, at the Clarice Smith Performing Arts Center, University of Maryland in College Park; ☎ 301-405-2787.

WASHINGTON ST. PATRICK'S DAY PARADE Sunday before March 17. Dancers, bagpipers, and marching bands salute Ireland and all things Irish along Constitution Avenue NW from Seventh to 17th streets; ☎ 202-619-7222.

ENVIRONMENTAL FILM FESTIVAL Mid- to late March. Nearly 100 international documentary, feature, animated, archival, and children's films on environmental issues are screened at museums, universities, and other Washington venues; ☎ 202-342-2564 or **www.dcenvironmental filmfest.org.**

EQUINE EVENT EAST Mid-March. An all-breed, all-discipline horse expo with equestrian demonstrations, clinics by experts, and displays by vendors of related goods at Dulles Expo Center Road off Route Chantilly, Virginia; ☎ 410-321-9559 or 703-378-0910.

SMITHSONIAN KITE FESTIVAL Late March. The Smithsonian Institution hosts a free annual festival on the Mall with competitions in design, performance, and other categories; ☎ 202-619-7222 or 202-357-3030; **www.kitefestival.org.**

 NATIONAL CHERRY BLOSSOM FESTIVAL Late March into early April. The blooming cherry trees surrounding the Tidal Basin are the centerpiece of this annual festival that culminates in the annual National Cherry Blossom Festival Parade along Constitution Avenue NW and the Sakura Matsuri Street Festival on Pennsylvania Avenue; ☎ 202-547-1500 or 202-619-7222; **www.nationalcherryblossom festival.org.**

WHITE HOUSE EASTER EGG ROLL Late March to mid-April (April 8 in 2007, March 23 in 2008, April 12 in 2009, and April 4 in 2010). Colored egg collectings and entertainment held Easter Monday, rain or shine. Open to children ages 3 to 6 accompanied by adults. Free tickets are distributed at Ellipse Visitors Center, 15th and E streets, on the Saturday before Easter, beginning at 7:30 a.m.; ☎ 202-456-2200; **www.whitehouse.gov/easter.**

AFRICAN AMERICAN FAMILY CELEBRATION Late March to mid-April. The annual Easter Monday jubilee, with an Easter egg hunt, gospel music, storytellers, and food vendors, at the National Zoo; ☎ 202-633-4800.

April

THOMAS JEFFERSON'S BIRTHDAY Speakers, a military honor guard, and a wreath-laying ceremony mark the birthday anniversary of the third president, noon at the Jefferson Memorial; ☎ 202-619-7222.

MOUNT VERNON GARDEN PARTY Mid-April. Celebrate spring at the first president's estate with music, wagon rides, and gardening demonstrations at Mount Vernon, at the southern end of the George Washington Memorial Parkway; ☎ 703-780-2000; **www.mount vernon.org/calendar.**

WHITE HOUSE SPRING GARDEN TOURS Mid-April (weather permitting). Free, timed tickets distributed each day on first-come basis at Ellipse Visitors Pavilion at 15th and E streets NW at 7:30 a.m.; ☎ 202-456-2200.

SHAKESPEARE'S BIRTHDAY Third Sunday. Annual open house with free cake, children's activities, theater tours, dramatic readings, medieval crafts, and entertainment at the Folger Shakespeare Library; ☎ 202-544-4600; **www.folger.edu.**

WASHINGTON INTERNATIONAL FILM FESTIVAL Mid- to late April. Scores of new American and foreign films are screened in theaters across town during the annual Filmfest DC; ☎ 202-628-3456; **www.filmfestdc.org.**

SMITHSONIAN CRAFT SHOW Third weekend. About 120 artists and artisans display their museum-quality creations in 12 juried media categories at the National Building Museum; ☎ 202-357-4000 or 888-832-9554; **www.smithsoniancraftshow.com.**

MARYLAND DAY Last Saturday. The University of Maryland holds an open house with exhibits, lectures, demonstrations, tours, and performances throughout the campus in College Park; ☎ 877-868-3777 or 301-405-1000; **www.marylandday.umd.edu.**

GEORGETOWN HOUSE TOUR Last Saturday. Tour private homes in Washington's Georgetown district; ☎ 202-338-1796; **www.george townhousetour.com.**

May

VIRGINIA GOLD CUP First Saturday. Annual running of the international steeplechase classic at Great Meadow in The Plains, Virginia; ☎ 540-347-1215; **www.vagoldcup.com.**

CHESAPEAKE BAY BRIDGE WALK First Sunday (weather permitting). 4.3-mile Chesapeake Bay Bridge is closed to vehicles for pedestrian crossing; ☎ 877-229-7726.

MARY LOU WILLIAMS WOMEN IN JAZZ FESTIVAL Second weekend. At multiple sites at the Kennedy Center for the Performing Arts; ☎ 202-467-4600; **www.kennedy-center.org/programs/jazz/womeninjazz.**

PREAKNESS PARADE Second Saturday. The Preakness Parade, with floats, marching bands, and giant balloons in Baltimore's Inner Harbor, kicks off a week-long celebration culminating in the running of the Preakness Stakes at Pimlico; ☎ 877-225-8466.

NATIONAL ZOO ZOOFARI Mid-May. This annual fund-raising gala features tastings by more than 100 area restaurants, international wines, entertainment, animal demonstrations, and a silent auction at the National Zoo; ☎ 202-633-4800; **www.nationalzoo.si.edu.**

MOUNT VERNON SPRING WINE FESTIVAL AND SUNSET TOUR Mid- to late May. Taste wines from Virginia vineyards, learn more about George Washington's winemaking efforts, and enjoy live jazz at the first president's estate. Tickets are required; ☎ 202-397-7328 (tickets) or 703-780-2000 (information); **www.mountvernon.org.**

D.C. CHILI COOK-OFF Third Saturday. The area's leading chili chefs compete for a place in the International Chili Society's world championships, with music on multiple stages and other foods and refreshments around 12th and C streets SW; ☎ 202-244-7900.

PREAKNESS STAKES Third Saturday. Running of the middle jewel in thoroughbred horse racing's Triple Crown at Pimlico Race Course in Baltimore; ☎ 410-542-9400; **www.preakness.com.**

JOINT SERVICE OPEN HOUSE AND AIR SHOW Mid- to late May. Aerial demonstrations by precision flying teams and other aircraft, a mass paratroop drop, sky diving by the Golden Knights, and ground displays of vintage and modern warplanes are featured at Andrews Air Force Base; ☎ 301-981-4424; **public.andrews.amc.af.mil/jsoh/schedule.html.**

SHAKESPEARE THEATRE "FREE FOR ALL" Late May to early June. The Shakespeare Theatre presents free outdoor performances of Shakespeare plays at Carter Barron Amphitheatre. Free tickets are distributed day of show; ☎ 202-547-1122 or 202-334-4790; **www .shakespearetheatre.org/about/free.aspx.**

ROCKVILLE HOMETOWN HOLIDAYS Last weekend. Three-day street festival in Rockville includes Memorial Day parade, Rockville restaurant vendors, children's activities, and local and national entertainers; **www.rockvillemd.gov.**

NSO MEMORIAL DAY CONCERT Last Sunday. The National Symphony Orchestra and guest performers from Broadway, pop, and country music in a free concert on the West Lawn of the U.S. Capitol; ☎ 202-619-7222.

MEMORIAL DAY CEREMONIES Last Monday. Commemorative events and wreath layings are scheduled at Arlington National Cemetery, the Vietnam Veterans Memorial, National Law Enforcement Officers Memorial, the Air Force Memorial, and the Women in Military Service for America Memorial; ☎ 202-619-7222.

MEMORIAL DAY PARADE Last Monday. Marching bands and veteran units from all 50 states parade down Constitution Avenue, beginning at noon.

MEMORIAL DAY NAVY BAND CONCERT The U.S. Navy Band performs a free concert at the U.S. Navy Memorial; ☎ 202-433-2525 or 202-433-2525.

June

UPPERVILLE COLT AND HORSE SHOW More than 1,000 horse-and-rider teams compete at the show grounds in Upperville; ☎ 540-253-5760 or 540-592-3858; **www.upperville.com.**

COLUMBIA FESTIVAL OF THE ARTS Mid-June. International, national, and regional music, stage, and dance stars perform over two weeks at venues throughout Columbia; ☎ 410-715-3044; **www.columbia festival.com.**

CAPITAL PRIDE FESTIVAL Second weekend. A parade Saturday in the Dupont Circle area and a street festival Sunday along Pennsylvania Avenue with crafts and food vendors wind up week-long celebration by the area's gay, lesbian, bisexual, and transgender residents; ☎ 202-797-3510; **www.capitalpride.org.**

ANTIQUE AND CLASSIC BOAT FESTIVAL Mid-June. Displays of antique and classic boats, wooden boat building demonstrations, a crafts fair, music, and food vendors at the Chesapeake Bay Maritime Museum in St. Michaels, Maryland; ☎ 410-745-2916; **www.chesapeakebayacbs.net.**

ALEXANDRIA WATERFRONT FESTIVAL Third weekend. Music on multiple stages, an arts-and-crafts fair, ship tours, exhibits, rides, food vendors, and more at Oronoco Bay Park on the Potomac; ☎ 703-549-8300; **www.waterfrontfestival.org.**

BOOZ/ALLEN CLASSIC Third week. The world's top golfers compete at this PGA Tour event at Congressional Country Club in Bethesda; ☎ 301-469-3737.

WASHINGTON INTERNATIONAL WINE AND FOOD FESTIVAL Late June. Sample thousands of wines from around the world and watch demonstrations by celebrity chefs; tickets required; ☎ 800-343-1174.

NATIONAL CAPITAL BARBECUE BATTLE Late June. Teams from across the country compete to represent the United States in the World Barbecue Championship, with entertainment on multiple stages, cooking demonstrations by celebrity chefs, children's activities, and food vendors, along Pennsylvania Avenue between Ninth and 14th streets NW; ☎ 202-828-3099; **www.barbecuebattle.com.**

CARIBBEAN CARNIVAL Late June. Parade along Georgia Avenue on Saturday winds up near Howard University with food, dance, arts and crafts, and entertainment; festival continues Sunday; ☎ 202-726-2204.

SMITHSONIAN AMERICAN FOLKLIFE FESTIVAL Late June to early July. Annual festival celebrates the food, music, arts, and culture of at least one state or territory and one foreign country, on the Mall between Seventh and 14th streets; ☎ 202-633-1000; **folklife.si.edu/ center/festival.html.**

July

FOURTH OF JULY CELEBRATION Independence Day is commemorated with the National Independence Day Parade along Constitution Avenue NW, the "Capitol Fourth" concert by the National Symphony Orchestra, and guest celebrities on the West Lawn of the U.S. Capitol, culminating in fireworks over the Washington Monument grounds; ☎ 202-619-7222.

CONTEMPORARY AMERICAN THEATER FESTIVAL Second weekend through the rest of the month. New American plays are performed in rotating repertory at Shepherd University in Shepherdstown, West Virginia; ☎ 304-876-3473; **www.catf.org.**

USA/ALEXANDRIA BIRTHDAY CELEBRATION First Saturday. The Alexandria Symphony Orchestra celebrates the City of Alexandria's birthday (it's older) and America with a concert that includes Tchaikovsky's *1812 Overture* with cannon followed by fireworks at Oronoco Bay Park on the Potomac; ☎ 703-883-4686.

BASTILLE DAY CELEBRATION July 14. Live entertainment and a race by tray-bearing waiters and waitresses down Pennsylvania Avenue from 12th Street to the U.S. Capitol and back; ☎ 202-347-6848.

SCREEN ON THE GREEN Mid-July to mid-August. Monday night outdoor screenings of classic movies on the West Lawn of the U.S. Capitol; ☎ 202-619-7222.

CHINCOTEAGUE PONY SWIM Late July. Wild ponies are rounded up and swum across the channel for auction in Chincoteague, Virginia, the event made famous by *Misty of Chincoteague;* ☎ 757-336-6161.

LEGG MASON TENNIS CLASSIC First week. The U.S. Open men's tennis tour (and young women pros) stop at FitzGerald Tennis Center in Rock Creek Park; ☎ 202-397-7328 (tickets), ☎ 202-721-9500 (information); **www.leggmasontennisclassic.com.**

August

COMCAST OUTDOOR FILM FESTIVAL Mid-month. Watch free family feature films on a giant outdoor screen nightly on the lawn of the Music Center at Strathmore in North Bethesda; ☎ 301-581-5100; **www.filmfestnih.org.**

WASHINGTON RESTAURANT WEEK Early- to mid-August. More than 150 area restaurants offer fixed-price lunch ($20) and dinner ($30) menus; **www.washington.org/restaurantwk,** or contact the DC Convention and Tourism Corporation.

MARYLAND STATE FAIR Late August to Labor Day. Huge old-fashioned fair features livestock displays, home and garden exhibits, thoroughbred racing, carnival rides, and entertainment at the Maryland State Fairgrounds in Timonium; ☎ 410-252-0200; **www.marylandstatefair.com.**

MARYLAND RENAISSANCE FESTIVAL Late August to late October. Entertainment, food, crafts, and jousting in a re-creation of a 16th-century English village; weekends and Labor Day in Crownsville, outside Annapolis; ☎ 800-296-7304 or 410-266-7304; **www.rennfest.com.**

September

LABOR DAY CONCERT First Sunday. Broadway, pop, country, and armed-forces bands join the National Symphony Orchestra for a free concert on the West Lawn of the U.S. Capitol; ☎ 202-619-7222.

NAVY BAND CONCERT First Monday. The U.S. Navy Band and Sea Chanters commemorate Labor Day with a free concert at the U.S. Navy Memorial; ☎ 202-433-2525 or 202-433-2525.

ALEXANDRIA FESTIVAL OF THE ARTS Second weekend. An outdoor festival features sculptures, paintings, photography, fused glass, jewelry, and other works by more than 150 artists and artisans along King Street in Old Town Alexandria; ☎ 703-838-5005 or 703-838-4200.

NATIONAL CAPITAL CAT SHOW Second weekend. More than 500 cats compete in nation's largest feline show at Dulles Expo Center in Chantilly, Virginia; ☎ 703-378-0910; **www.nationalcapitalcatshow.com.**

BLACK FAMILY REUNION Second weekend. Annual cultural celebration of the African American family, with live entertainment, exhibits, an arts-and-crafts marketplace, and food vendors on the Mall; ☎ 202-737-0120.

KENNEDY CENTER OPEN HOUSE Mid-September. Free daylong celebration of music, ballet, theater, and other performance arts on multiple indoor and outdoor stages at the Kennedy Center for the Performing Arts; ☎ 202-467-4600; **www.kennedy-center.org/openhouse.**

ROSSLYN JAZZ FESTIVAL Mid-September. Daylong free outdoor concerts by local and national jazz stars at Gateway Park (near the Rosslyn Metro station); ☎ 703-228-1850; **www.rossren.com/ ros_arts_jazzfest.cfm.**

SILVER SPRING JAZZ FESTIVAL Mid-September. Daylong free outdoor concerts by local and national jazz stars downtown (near Silver Spring Metro station); ☎ 301-565-7300.

ADAMS-MORGAN DAY Second Saturday. Daylong celebration of Washington's most famous multicultural neighborhood with entertainment, children's activities, food vendors, and sports; ☎ 202-232-1960; **www.adamsmorganday.org.**

ARTS-ON-FOOT FESTIVAL Mid-September. Free performances, artist demonstrations, cooking lessons, open rehearsals, and theatrical events in Washington's Penn Quarter; ☎ 202-482-7271; **www.artsonfoot.org.**

18TH-CENTURY FAIR Mid-September. Crafts displays and demonstrations by artisans in Colonial attire, 18th-century entertainment, and children's activities at Mount Vernon; ☎ 703-780-2000; **www.mount vernon.org.**

KALORAMA HOUSE AND EMBASSY TOUR Mid-September. Visit embassies, ambassadors' residences, and other sites; ☎ 202-387-4062.

MOUNTAIN HERITAGE CRAFTS FESTIVAL Third weekend. Displays by about 200 artists and artisans, music by bluegrass bands, and food vendors; between Harpers Ferry and Charles Town, West Virginia; ☎ 304-725-2055 or 800-624-0577; **www.jeffersoncounty.com/festival.**

INTERNATIONAL CHILDREN'S FESTIVAL Third weekend. Children's performers from around the world entertain on multiple stages at Wolf Trap Park in Vienna; ☎ 703-642-0862 or 703-255-1860; **www.artsfairfax.org/festival/index.shtml.**

COLUMBIA CLASSIC GRAND PRIX Late September. World-class and Olympic team riders compete in this annual equestrian event at Howard Community College in Columbia; ☎ 410-772-4450; **www .howardcc.edu/grandprix.**

NATIONAL BOOK FESTIVAL Last Saturday. More than 70 authors of all types gather for readings, signings, and literacy exhibits along the Mall; **www.loc.gov/bookfest.**

October

MOUNT VERNON FALL WINE FESTIVAL AND SUNSET TOUR October 6 to 8. Taste wines from Virginia vineyards, learn more about George Washington's winemaking efforts, and enjoy live jazz at the first president's estate; at the southern end of the George Washington Memorial Parkway. Tickets are required, and advance purchase is recommended. For tickets, ☎ 202-397-7328; for information, call ☎ 703-780-2000 or visit **www.mountvernon.org.**

DUKE ELLINGTON JAZZ FESTIVAL First weekend. Over 60 concerts at venues around town, including the Kennedy Center and the Mall; **www.dejazzfest.org.**

WATERFORD FAIR First weekend. The 62nd annual festival on the streets of this 1733 village, with music, a crafts fair, crafts demonstrations, and tours of Colonial homes in Waterford, Virginia; ☎ 540-882-3018 or 540-882-3085; **www.waterfordva-wca.org/waterford-fair.htm.**

TASTE OF BETHESDA First Saturday. This street festival features samples from area restaurants, entertainment on multiple stages, and kids' activities in downtown Bethesda; ☎ 301-215-6660; **www.bethesda .org/specialevents/taste/taste.htm.**

ART ON THE AVENUE First Saturday. A multicultural arts festival, with exhibits by more than 300 artists, entertainment, and food vendors, along Mount Vernon Avenue in Alexandria; ☎ 703-683-3100; **www.artontheavenue.org.**

ALEXANDRIA SEAPORT DAY First Saturday. Boat-building demonstrations, model boat–building workshops, exhibits, and boat rides at Waterfront Park in Old Town Alexandria; ☎ 703-549-7078; **www.alexandriaseaport.org.**

FESTIVAL OF THE BUILDING ARTS First Saturday. Hands-on activities for all ages illustrate the skills used in the building arts at the National Building Museum; ☎ 202-272-2448; **www.nbm.org.**

COLUMBUS DAY CEREMONY A celebration of the explorer's achievements at the Columbus Memorial Statue at Union Station; ☎ 202-619-7222.

WHITE HOUSE FALL GARDEN TOURS Mid-October. Free, timed tickets distributed each day on first-come basis at Ellipse Visitors Pavilion at 15th and E streets NW at 7:30 a.m.; ☎ 202-456-2200.

INTERNATIONAL GOLD CUP Third Saturday. Annual running of this fall classic steeplechase race at Great Meadow in The Plains, Virginia; ☎ 540-347-1215; **www.vagoldcup.com.**

GRAND MILITIA MUSTER Third weekend. Competitions and pageantry by St. Maries City Militia and other 17th-century military reenactment units in Historic St. Mary's City, Maryland's first capital, in St. Mary's County; ☎ 800-762-1634.

BETHESDA ROW ARTS FESTIVAL Third weekend. More than 180 artists and artisans display their creations along four blocks in downtown Bethesda; ☎ 301-816-6958; **www.bethesdarowarts.org.**

WASHINGTON INTERNATIONAL HORSE SHOW Late October. Hundreds of horses and riders from around the world compete in hunter and jumper events at the Verizon Center. For tickets, ☎ 202-397-7328; for information, ☎ 202-628-3200 or 301-987-9400; **www.wihs.org.**

"BOO AT THE ZOO" Last weekend. Halloween trick-or-treating, animal demonstrations, and zookeeper talks at the National Zoo; ☎ 202-633-4800; **www.nationalzoo.si.edu.**

MARINE CORPS MARATHON Last Sunday in October. Tens of thousands of runners start at the Iwo Jima Memorial in Arlington and follow a course into Washington, along the Mall and back to the Memorial; ☎ 800-786-8762; **www.marinemarathon.com.**

November

VETERANS DAY CEREMONIES November 11. Commemorations and wreath-laying ceremonies at Arlington National Cemetery, the U.S. Navy Memorial, the Vietnam Veterans Memorial, the Vietnam Women's Memorial, and the Women in Military Service for America Memorial; ☎ 202-619-7222.

WATERFOWL FESTIVAL Mid-November. The annual festival celebrates ducks and geese in photographs, paintings, carvings, sculpture, and other media, with music, duck-calling contests, children's activities, and food vendors in Easton, Maryland; ☎ 410-822-4567; **www.water fowlfestival.org.**

WASHINGTON CRAFT SHOW Mid-November. Nearly 200 artists from across the country display their glassworks, furniture, textiles, and other creations at the Washington Convention Center; ☎ 202-249-3000 or 203-254-0486; **www.craftsamericashows.com.**

MOUNT VERNON BY CANDLELIGHT Thanksgiving weekend though early December. Tour the first president's estate, including the usually closed third-floor Cupola; ☎ 703-780-2000; **www.mountvernon.org.**

December

KENNEDY CENTER HOLIDAY FESTIVAL All month. The Kennedy Center celebrates the holidays with free performances and ticketed concerts; ☎ 202-467-4600; **www.kennedy-center.org.**

D.C. WINTER ANTIQUES FAIR First weekend. More than 100 dealers offer fine art, furniture, jewelry, and other goods at the D.C. Armory; ☎ 301-933-9433.

SCOTTISH CHRISTMAS WALK First Saturday. More than 100 Scottish clan units parade through Old Town Alexandria; ☎ 703-549-0111 or 703-838-4200; **www.scottishchristmaswalk.com.**

HOLIDAY SING-A-LONG First Sunday. Free family carol-sing at Wolf Trap Park in Vienna; ☎ 877-965-3872 or 703-255-1860; **www.wolftrap.org.**

PAGEANT OF PEACE Early December. The lighting of the National Christmas Tree on the Ellipse, usually by the President and First Lady, kicks off a month of free holiday activities, including nightly choral performances and a display of lighted trees representing the state and territories; ☎ 202-208-1631 or 202-619-7222; **www.pageant ofpeace.org.**

PEARL HARBOR DAY December 7. A ceremony commemorates the 1941 attack on Pearl Harbor at the U.S. Navy Memorial; ☎ 202-737-2300.

HISTORICAL ALEXANDRIA CANDLELIGHT TOUR Second Sunday. Sites include the Lloyd House, Lee-Fendell House, Gadsby's Tavern Museum, and the Carlyle House in Old Town Alexandria, with music, colonial dancing, period decorations, and light refreshment; ☎ 703-838-4242.

NEW YEAR'S EVE Family-oriented, alcohol-free "First Night" festivals with concerts, children's entertainers, and other activities are in Alexandria (☎ 703-838-4200), Annapolis (☎ 410-268-8553), Fredericksburg (☎ 800-260-3646), Leesburg (☎ 703-777-6306), Warrenton (☎ 703-777-6306), and Baltimore's Inner Harbor (☎ 877-225-8466).

The Longest Lines

Unlike Disney World, a tourist destination with which Washington shares some similarities, D.C. has only a handful of attractions that require enduring long queues—most notably, the U.S. Capitol and the FBI (currently closed to tourists). Even at these, a little judicious planning can virtually guarantee you won't spend hours standing in line.

If your visit to Washington must coincide with the heavy tourist season, read on: There are ways to make it more tolerable, in spite of the record crowds jamming the Mall, the popular museums, eateries, public transportation, and highways. Check Part Five (page 113) for detailed information on transportation and Part Six (page 133) for sightseeing tips.

THE LOCAL PRESS

WASHINGTON IS A CITY OF NEWS JUNKIES, and the *Washington Post* is the opiate of choice. Visitors should make a point of picking up Friday's edition, which includes the paper's "Weekend" section. It's loaded with information on things to do in and around Washington; if you can, grab a copy of a Friday Post on your way into town for the weekend.

The *Washington Times,* D.C.'s other major daily newspaper, offers a more conservative slant on national and world events.

City Paper, a free weekly "alternative" newspaper, is another good source of information on arts, theater, clubs, popular music, and movie reviews. It's available from street-corner vending machines and stores all over town.

The *Washingtonian,* a monthly magazine, is strong on lists (top 10 restaurants, etc.) and provides a calendar of events, dining information, and feature articles.

Where/Washington is one of several free publications that list popular things to do around town; it's usually available in your hotel or at airport racks.

Visitors looking for the latest information on Washington theater, nightlife, restaurants, special exhibitions, and gallery shows in advance of their trip should call or write:

Where/Washington Magazine, 1225 19th Street NW, Suite 510, Washington, D.C. 20036-2411, ☎ 202-463-4550.

The *Washingtonian,* 1828 L Street NW, Suite 200, Washington, D.C. 20036, ☎ 202-331-0715.

■ **WHAT** *to* **PACK**

WASHINGTON MAY BE A TOURIST TOWN, but it's also an old Southern city, and a cosmopolitan center to boot. Which means you'll be tolerated in shorts during the day—and Lord knows you'll be one of hundreds—but you might feel a social chill if you wear that Hawaiian shirt to a moderately upscale restaurant for dinner. (Everyone will be too polite to actually comment unless you're a celebrity, in which case you'll be assumed to be making a fashion statement.) After all, most people will still be in work clothes—at least long pants if not suits.

This doesn't mean you have to pack a tuxedo, unless you have a formal engagement. But it never hurts to dress up rather than down. A nice sports jacket or even sweater, for either sex, is not only a way of looking nice but of usefully offsetting either air-conditioning or off-season chill. (Plus, sweaters pack thinner than sweatshirts.)

In general, shorts and polo shirts are fine for day close to half the year (spring and fall are temperate times); a sundress or reasonably neat pair of khakis will make you look downright respectable. A rainproof top of some sort, a lightweight jacket and/or sweater may be all you'll need in the summer; not only will you probably be going in and out of air-conditioning or showers, but if you're flying into Washington, you'll have that on-and-off-the-airplane chill.

Something along the lines of a trench coat with a zip-in lining or a wool walking coat with a sweater will usually do in winter. Fur coats are not a moral issue in Washington but are only likely to be necessary in January or February, and the hassle of dealing with them on planes these days makes them unpleasant unless you're staying for some time.

Women will find a heavy scarf or shawl a good interim layer in fall, and it will stand in as a sweater (or throw) in emergencies. Men should take not just polite little pocket squares but decent-sized handkerchiefs: they make good seat covers and sun protectors as well as forehead moppers.

With the ever-shifting regulations about packing on-board items, we would recommend you pack only the amount of any prescription medicines you really need for 12 hours of so, but carry photocopies of the prescription or numbers in case your packed bag gets lost. Zippered plastic bags are one of the great inventions of humanity: they

unofficial **TIP**
A penlight and magnifying reading glasses may come in handy for perusing small or dimly lit art or museum captions.

keep dry clothes dry and wet clothes separated, keep your underwear together so the luggage inspector doesn't have to sort through them, prevent jewelry from tarnishing, and prevent shampoos and lotions from leaking. Those stain-removing pens or packets can be very helpful, too.

Frankly, the most important thing to consider when packing is comfortable shoes, and more than one pair of them. This is a culture of concrete and marble, and even if you are using one of the trolleys or shuttles, you're likely to be standing about at monuments and in museums quite a bit. Wearing walking or running shoes during the day is fine, but don't think you're necessarily going to want to pull on those high heels or shiny lace-ups at the end of a long day of sightseeing. Pick your evening shoes (or boots) with reasonable comfort in mind.

Finally, as longtime travelers, we can assure you that the most common mistake tourists make is packing too much—expecting to wear a different outfit every day (and evening). Nobody is going to know if you wear the same shirt twice, or the same jeans or khakis. Little black dress? Think little black skirt—something thin that folds flat. If you do overpack, you're just going to have to lug a heavier suitcase around. (Why do you think they call it luggage?) And besides, you're probably going to buy a souvenir T-shirt anyway.

PEOPLE *with* SPECIAL NEEDS

WASHINGTON IS ONE OF THE MOST accessible cities in the world for folks with disabilities. With the equal-opportunity federal government as the major employer in the area, Washington provides a good job market for disabled people. As a result, the service sector—bus drivers, waiters, ticket sellers, retail clerks, cab drivers, tour guides, and so on—are somewhat more attuned to the needs of people with disabilities than service-sector employees in other cities. It doesn't hurt that a number of organizations that lobby for physically challenged people are headquartered in Washington.

The Metro, for example, was designed to meet federal standards for accessibility. As a result, the stations and trains provide optimal services to a wide array of people with special requirements. Elevators provide access to the mezzanine, or ticketing areas platform, and street level; call the Metro's 24-hour elevator hot line at ☎ 202-962-1825 to check if the elevators at the stations you plan to use are operating.

The edge of the train platform is built with a 14-inch smooth, light-gray granite strip that's different in texture from the rest of the station's flooring so that visually impaired passengers can detect the platform edge with a foot or cane. Flashing lights embedded in the granite strip alert hearing-impaired passengers that a train is entering the station. Handicapped-only parking spaces are placed close to station entrances. While purchasing a farecard is a strictly visual process (unless the station is equipped with the talking vending machines), visually impaired passengers can go to the nearby kiosk for assistance. Priority seating for senior citizens and passengers with disabilities is located next to doors in all cars.

Visitors with disabilities who possess a transit ID from their home city can pick up a courtesy Metro ID that provides substantial fare discounts; the ID is good for a month. Go to Metro Headquarters, 600 Fifth Street NW, from 7:30 a.m. to 3 p.m. weekdays to pick one up; call ☎ 202-962-1245 for more information. If you want to ride the Metro to get there, the nearest station is Judiciary Square (F Street exit), a half-block away. For a free guide with information on Metro's rail and bus system for the elderly and physically disabled, call ☎ 202-637-1328. "Metro Mobility Link" is a help line for people with disabilities. Call ☎ 202-962-6464 for basic as well as more specialized information on Metro stations.

The Smithsonian and the National Park Service, agencies that run the lion's share of popular sights in Washington, offer top-notch services to people with disabilities. Museums are equipped with entrance ramps, barrier-free exhibits, elevator service to all floors, and accessible restrooms and water fountains. Visually impaired visitors can pick up large-print brochures, audio tours, and raised-line drawings of museum artifacts at many Smithsonian museums. The National Air and Space Museum offers special tours that let visitors touch models and artifacts; call ☎ 202-357-2700 for information.

unofficial **TIP**
Designated handicapped parking spaces are located along Jefferson Drive on the Mall.

Hearing-impaired visitors to the National Air and Space Museum can arrange tours with an interpreter by calling ☎ 202-357-2700. Public telephones in the museum are equipped with amplification, and the briefing room is equipped with audio loop. For a copy of the Smithsonian's "A Guide for Disabled Visitors," call ☎ 202-357-2700 or ☎ 202-357-1729 (TDD).

The Lincoln and Jefferson memorials and the Washington Monument are equipped to accommodate disabled visitors. Most sightseeing attractions have elevators for seniors and others who want to avoid a lot of stair climbing. The White House, for example, has a special entrance on Pennsylvania Avenue for visitors arriving in wheelchairs, and White House guides usually allow visually handicapped visitors to touch some of the items described on tours.

Tourmobile offers a special van equipped with a wheelchair and scooter lift for disabled visitors. The van visits all the regular sites on the tour; in fact, visitors can usually specify what sites they want to see in any order, and the van will wait until they are finished touring. The service is the same price as the standard Tourmobile rate, $20 for adults and $10 for children. Call ☎ 202-554-7020 at least a day in advance to reserve a van. Information is available at **www.tourmobile.com.**

In spite of all the services available to disabled visitors, it's still a good idea to call ahead to any facility you plan to visit and confirm that services are in place and that the particular exhibit or gallery you wish to see is still available.

Foreign visitors to Washington who would like a tour conducted in their native language can contact the **Guide Service of Washington** (see "Get Up Close and Personal" on page 155).

GETTING *to* WASHINGTON

FOLKS PLANNING A TRIP to our nation's capital have some options when it comes to getting there: by car, train, or plane. Your distance from Washington—and your tolerance for hassles such as Capital Beltway gridlock and inconveniently located airports—will probably determine which mode of transportation you ultimately take. (See also Part Four, Arriving and Getting Oriented, page 87.)

DRIVING

A LOT OF PEOPLE WHO LIVE in the populous Eastern Seaboard or anywhere else within a 12-hour drive of D.C. automatically jump in the family car when embarking on a vacation to Washington. And no wonder: even though gasoline prices have increased, a nearly complete interstate highway system makes the car trip both easy and inexpensive. The problem, however, is when you arrive in Washington . . . or, to be more exact, when you hit the notorious Capital Beltway that surrounds the city in the Maryland and Virginia suburbs. Arrive on a weekday morning between 6:30 a.m. and 10 a.m. or in the afternoon from 2 p.m. to 7 p.m. and you'll discover why Washington has a reputation for traffic congestion rivaled only by New York and Los Angeles: traffic inches along during rush hours and is astonishingly heavy the rest of the day and on warm-weather weekends as well. It only gets worse the closer you get to the Mall. Washington's peculiar geography and 18th-century street layout, coupled with unremitting urban and suburban growth, makes touring by car almost impossible. Street parking near popular tourist sights is severely limited, and parking garages, while plentiful in downtown D.C., are expensive and often inconvenient. Our recommendation: If at all possible, leave the car at home. Washington's air-and-rail connections are excellent, and its Metro subway system is one of the best in the world. And where the Metro won't take you—Georgetown, Mount Vernon, and the Washington National Cathedral come to mind—plentiful cabs, shuttle buses, and commercial touring outfits will. If you do drive, arrive on a weekend to miss the worst traffic, or very early or late on a weekday. Stay at a hotel with off-street parking and within easy walking distance to a Metro station. Use public transportation and leave the car parked through most of your stay.

TAKING THE TRAIN

WASHINGTON'S GLEAMING UNION STATION, recently refurbished and the city's most visited tourist attraction (the National Air and Space Museum is number two), is only one of the reasons that taking the train to D.C. is an excellent idea. Another is convenience: Folks living along the East Coast from Boston to Miami are served daily by Amtrak, and lots of people living east of the Mississippi are

Amtrak Passenger-train Service to Washington

REGION/CITY	DISTANCE	TRAVEL TIME	FREQUENCY
NORTHEAST			
Philadelphia	115 miles	1.5–2 hours	more than 1 per hour
New York City	225 miles	3–4.5 hours	more than 1 per hour
Boston	400 miles	8–9.75 hours	11 per day
SOUTH			
Richmond	110 miles	2 hours	8 per day
Newport News	187 miles	4 hours	2 per day
Raleigh-Durham	305 miles	6 hours	2 per day
Charlotte	376 miles	8.5–10 hours	2 per day
Charleston, S.C.	503 miles	9–9.5 hours	2 per day
Atlanta	633 miles	13.5 hours	1 per day
Birmingham	799 miles	18 hours	1 per day
New Orleans	1,155 miles	25–36 hours	1 per day
Jacksonville	753 miles	13.5–15 hours	3 per day
Tampa	996 miles	18 hours	1 per day
Orlando	1,129 miles	16.5–18.5 hours	2 per day
Miami	1,166 miles	22.5–24 hours	3 per day
WEST			
Pittsburgh	300 miles	7.5 hours	1 per day
Cleveland	440 miles	11 hours	1 per day
Toledo	550 miles	13 hours	1 per day
Cincinnati	602 miles	14 hours	3 per week
Chicago	780 miles	18 hours	10 per week

close to direct rail service into the nation's capital. In some cases you can board the train in the evening and arrive in Washington in the morning. From Union Station you're only minutes from a downtown hotel by subway—the Union Station Metro is right alongside the tracks and covered from the weather—or, if your hotel isn't near a Metro stop, you can easily hail a cab. Because of the city's exasperating traffic—and a public-transportation system that virtually eliminates the need for a car—it's the smart way to travel to Washington. We've provided a listing of some major cities with direct Amtrak passenger train service to Washington's Union Station (the frequency of service indicates the number of trains running in both directions). For schedules and reservations, call Amtrak at ☎ 800-872-7245 or visit **www.amtrak.com.**

FLYING

WASHINGTON, THE SEAT OF THE FEDERAL GOVERNMENT and probably the world's most powerful city, is understandably well served by the airline industry. The town boasts three airports, each with its own peculiarities. **Ronald Reagan Washington National Airport** is by far the most convenient, located a few miles south of D.C. on the Virginia side of the Potomac River. Yet its closeness to the city has resulted in some odd restrictions: planes aren't allowed to fly over the White House and other sensitive places, so all approaches and takeoffs are routed over the Potomac River; no planes are allowed to take off or land late at night; only 37 large jets are allowed to land or take off in an hour; and a "perimeter rule" restricts nonstop flights to and from National to a distance of 1,250 miles or less. With virtually no international connections, think of National as the "East Coast short-hop" airport. If you can't get a direct flight into National from your hometown, consider making a connection that will get you into National. It will probably be faster—and certainly more convenient—than flying into either of the other two airports that serve Washington. While the recently refurbished (for about $1 billion) National is our first choice for travelers flying into D.C., its close proximity to the bustling city can create problems for the unwary flyer: it's often congested by heavy traffic; parking is expensive; long-term parking is a long bus ride away; and renting a car and driving into D.C. can be a drawn-out, frustrating experience. The good news: cab fares to downtown are reasonable; free shuttles can get you to your hotel in a half-hour or so; and National has its own Metro stop.

Dulles International Airport is 45 minutes to an hour from the city by car and with no direct public transportation downtown (although a light-rail connection to the Vienna Metro is being studied). Dulles is primarily known as an international hub, although domestic flights are on the increase (spurring a construction project that in 1996 doubled the main terminal's size to 1.1 million square feet).

In a sly marketing move a few years back, Baltimore's Friendship Airport became **Baltimore-Washington International Airport (BWI),** and eventually Thurgood Marshall Baltimore-Washington International (whew!). It worked: 2000 was a record-breaking year for this ever-expanding air hub. Southwest Airlines, for example, has increased its low-cost service to 65 flights a day, attracting a lot of travelers to Washington who would otherwise drive. BWI is also aggressively pursuing an international market and in 1997 opened a $110-million international pier. Yet this busy airport is still closer to Baltimore than to Washington, which means D.C.-bound tourists face at least a 50-minute car or van ride before the Washington Monument comes into view. Another option for folks arriving at BWI is to take the train: Maryland commuter rail service (called MARC) and Amtrak connect BWI to D.C.'s Union Station. The train ride takes almost an hour, though—hardly convenient for tourists itching to explore the marble edifices lining the Mall.

PART TWO

ACCOMMODATIONS

▌ DECIDING *where to* STAY

ON WEEKDAYS, DRIVING AND PARKING in downtown Washington are nightmarish. On weekends there is less traffic congestion, but parking is extremely difficult, particularly in the area of the Mall. Because the best way to get around Washington is on the Metro, we recommend a hotel within walking distance of a Metro station. With two rather prominent exceptions, all of Washington's best areas, as well as most of the Virginia and Maryland suburbs, are safely and conveniently accessible via this clean, modern subway system. In fact, the **Penn Quarter,** which lies between the U.S. Capitol and the White House and is Washington's most rapidly revitalizing neighborhood, is served by a handful of stations, with several more (if you don't want to bother to transfer) only a few more blocks away. Only historic **Georgetown** and the colorful, ethnically diverse **Adams-Morgan** neighborhood are off-line (and even they are only a few blocks' walk from a stop or connector bus; see Part Five, Getting around Washington, page 113).

Unless you plan to spend most of your time in Georgetown, we suggest that you pick a hotel elsewhere in the city. If you lodge in Georgetown, you will be reduced to driving or cabbing to get anywhere else. Adams-Morgan, a great neighborhood for dining and shopping, does not offer much in the way of lodging though there are increasing numbers of B&B options in Logan Circle and Dupont Circle. If you go to Adams-Morgan, especially at night, take a cab.

SOME CONSIDERATIONS

1. When choosing your Washington lodging, make sure your hotel is situated in a location convenient to your recreation or business needs, and that it is in a safe and comfortable area. Please note that while it is not practical to walk to the Washington Convention Center (the major

convention venue) from many of the downtown hotels, larger conventions and trade shows provide shuttle service.

2. Find out how old the hotel is and when the guest rooms were last renovated. Request that the hotel send you its promotional brochure. Ask if brochure photos of guest rooms are accurate and current.

3. If you plan to take a car, inquire about the parking situation. Some hotels offer no parking at all; some charge dearly for parking; and a few offer free parking.

4. If you are not a city dweller, or if you are a light sleeper, try to book a hotel on a more quiet side street. Ask for a room off the street and high up.

5. Much of Washington is quite beautiful, as is the Potomac River. If you are on a romantic holiday, ask for a room on a higher floor with a good view.

6. When you plan your budget, remember that there is a 14.5% hotel tax (including sales tax) in the District of Columbia.

7. Washington is one of the busiest convention cities in the United States. If your visit to Washington coincides with one or more major conventions or trade shows, hotel rooms will be both scarce and expensive. If, on the other hand, you are able to schedule your visit to avoid big meetings, you will have a good selection of hotels at reasonably competitive prices. If you happen to be attending one of the big conventions, book early and use some of the tips listed on the following pages to get a discounted room rate. To assist in timing your visit, we have included a convention and trade-show calendar (see pages 84–85).

GETTING *a* GOOD DEAL *on a* ROOM

THOUGH WASHINGTON, D.C., is a major tourist destination, the economics of hotel room pricing is driven by business, government, and convention trade. This translates to high "rack rates" (a hotel's published room rate) and very few bargains. The most modest Econo Lodge or Days Inn in Washington charges from $84 to $139 a night, and midrange chains, such as Holiday Inn and Radisson, ask from $129 to $229.

The good news is that Washington, D.C., and its Virginia and Maryland suburbs offer a staggering number of unusually fine hotels, including a high percentage of suite properties. The bad news, of course, is that you can expect to pay dearly to stay in them.

In most cities, the better and more expensive hotels are located close to the city center, with less expensive hotels situated farther out. There is normally a trade-off between location and price: if you are willing to stay out off the interstate and commute into downtown, you can expect to pay less for your suburban room than you would for a downtown room. In Washington, D.C., unfortunately, it very rarely works this way.

In the greater Washington area, every hotel is seemingly close to something. No matter how far you are from the Capitol, the Mall, and downtown, you can bank on your hotel being within spitting distance of some bureau, agency, airport, or industrial complex that funnels platoons of business travelers into guest rooms in a constant flow. Because almost every accommodation has its own captive market, the usual proximity/price trade-off doesn't apply. The Marriott at the Beltway and Wisconsin Avenue, for example, is 30 to 40 minutes away by car from the Mall but stays full with visitors to the nearby National Institutes of Health.

WHERE THE HOTEL DISCOUNTS ARE

Special Weekend Rates

Although well-located Washington hotels are tough for the budget-conscious, it's not impossible to get a good deal, at least relatively speaking. For starters, some hotels that cater to business, government, and convention travelers offer special weekend discount rates that range from 15 to 40% below normal weekday rates. You can find out about weekend specials by calling individual hotels or by consulting your travel agent.

Getting Corporate Rates

Many hotels offer discounted corporate rates (5 to 20% off rack). Usually you do not need to work for a large company or have a special relationship with the hotel to obtain these rates. Simply call the hotel of your choice and ask for their corporate rates. Many hotels will guarantee you the discounted rate on the phone when you make your reservation. Others may make the rate conditional on your providing some sort of bona fides, for instance a fax on your company's letterhead requesting the rate, or a company credit card or business card on check-in. Generally, the screening is not rigorous.

Preferred Rates

If you cannot book the hotel of your choice through a half-price program, you and your travel agent may have to search for a lesser discount, often called a preferred rate. A preferred rate could be a discount made available to travel agents to stimulate their booking activity, or a discount initiated to attract a certain class of traveler. Most preferred rates are promoted through travel industry publications and so are often accessible only through an agent.

We recommend sounding out your travel agent about possible deals. Be aware that the rates shown on travel agents' computerized reservations systems are not always the lowest rates obtainable. Zero in on a couple of hotels that fill your needs in terms of location and quality of accommodations, and then have your travel agent call for the latest rates and specials.

Hotel reps are almost always more responsive to travel agents because the latter represent a source of additional business. There are certain specials that hotel reps will disclose *only* to travel agents. Travel agents also come in handy when the hotel you want is supposedly booked. A personal appeal from your agent to the hotel's director of sales and marketing will get you a room more than half of the time.

Half-price Programs

The larger discounts on rooms (35 to 60%), in Washington or anywhere else, are available through half-price hotel programs, often called travel clubs. Program operators contract with an individual hotel to provide rooms at deep discounts, usually 50% off rack rate, on a space-available basis. Space available in practice generally means that you can reserve a room at the discounted rate whenever the hotel expects to be at less than 80% occupancy. A little calendar sleuthing to help you avoid city-wide conventions and special events will increase your chances of choosing a time when the discounts are available.

Most half-price programs charge an annual membership fee or directory subscription charge of $25 to $125. Once enrolled, you are mailed a membership card and a directory listing participating hotels. Examining the directory, you will notice immediately that there are many restrictions and exceptions. Some hotels, for instance, "black out" certain dates or times of year. Others may only offer the discount on certain days of the week or require you to stay a certain number of nights. Still others may offer a much smaller discount than 50% off rack rate.

D.C. HALF-PRICE HOTEL PROGRAMS	
Encore	☎ 800-638-0930; **www.preferredtraveller.com**
Entertainment Publications	☎ 800-285-5525; **www.entertainment.com**
International Travel Card	☎ 800-342-0558
Quest	☎ 800-638-9819

Programs specialize in domestic travel, international travel, or both. More established operators offer members between 1,000 and 4,000 hotels to choose from in the United States. All of the programs have a heavy concentration of hotels in California and Florida, and most have a very limited selection of participating properties in New York City or Boston. Offerings in other cities and regions of the United States vary considerably. The programs with the largest selections of Washington hotels are Encore, Travel America at Half Price (Entertainment Publications), International Travel Card, and Quest. Each of these programs lists between 4 and 50 hotels in the greater Washington area.

One problem with half-price programs is that not all hotels offer a full 50% discount. Another slippery problem is the base rate against which the discount is applied. Some hotels figure the discount on an exaggerated rack rate that nobody would ever have to pay. A few participating hotels may deduct the discount from a supposed "superior" or "upgraded" room rate, even though the room you get is the hotel's standard accommodation. Though hard to pin down, the majority of participating properties base discounts on the published rate in the *Hotel & Travel Index* (a quarterly reference work used by travel agents) and work within the spirit of their agreement with the program operator. As a rule, if you travel several times a year, your room-rate savings will easily compensate you for program membership fees.

A noteworthy addendum: Deeply discounted rooms through half-price programs are not commissionable to travel agents. In practical terms this means that you must ordinarily make your own inquiry calls and reservations. If you travel frequently, however, and run a lot of business through your travel agent, he or she will probably do your legwork, lack of commission notwithstanding.

Wholesalers, Consolidators, and Reservation Services

If you do not want to join a program or buy a discount directory, you can take advantage of the services of a wholesaler or consolidator. Wholesalers and consolidators buy rooms, or options on rooms (room blocks), from hotels at a low, negotiated rate. They then resell the rooms at a profit through travel agents and tour packagers, or directly to the public. Most wholesalers and consolidators have a provision for returning unsold rooms to participating hotels, but they are disinclined to do so. The wholesaler's or consolidator's relationship with any hotel is predicated on volume. If they return rooms unsold, the hotel might not make as many rooms available to them the next time around. Thus, wholesalers and consolidators often offer rooms at bargain rates, at anywhere from 15 to 50% off rack, occasionally sacrificing their profit margin in the process, to avoid returning the rooms to the hotel unsold.

HOTEL DISCOUNTERS	
Accommodations Express	☎ 800-444-7666
Capitol Reservations	☎ 800-847-4832; **www.hotelsdc.com**
Hotel Discounts	☎ 800-715-7666; **www.hoteldiscounts.com**
Hotels.com	☎ 800-964-6835; **www.hotels.com**
Quikbook	☎ 800-789-9887; **www.quikbook.com**
Washington, D.C., Accommodations	☎ 800-503-3338

When wholesalers and consolidators deal directly with the public, they frequently represent themselves as "reservation services." When you call, you can ask for a rate quote for a particular hotel, or, alternatively, ask for their best available deal in the area where you prefer to stay. If there is a maximum amount you are willing to pay, say so. Chances are, the service will find something that will work for you, even if they have to shave a dollar or two off their own profit. Sometimes you will have to pay for your room in advance, with a credit card, when you make your reservation. Other times you will pay at the usual time, when you check out.

Bed and Breakfasts (B&Bs)

B&Bs offer a lodging alternative based on personal service and hospitality that transcend the sterile, predictable product of chain hotels; however, they can be quirky. Most, but not all, B&Bs are open year-round. Some accept only cash or personal checks, while others take all major credit cards. Not all rooms come with private baths. Some rooms with private baths may have a tub but not a shower, or vice versa. Some allow children but not pets, others pets but not children. Many B&Bs provide only the most basic breakfast, while some provide a sumptuous morning feast. Still others offer three meals a day. Most B&Bs are not wheelchair accessible, but it never hurts to ask.

unofficial **TIP**
Because staying at a B&B is like visiting someone's home, reservations are recommended, though B&Bs with more than ten rooms usually welcome walk-ins.

To help you sort out your B&B options, we recommend the following guides. Updated regularly, these books describe B&Bs in more detail than is possible in the *Unofficial Guide.*

Inspected, Rated, and Approved, Bed & Breakfasts and Country Inns, by Beth Burgreen Stuhlman, published by the American Bed & Breakfast Association. Covers the entire United States. Visit **www .abba.com**.

Bed & Breakfasts—Country Inns and The Official Guide to American Historic Inns, by Deborah Sakach, published by American Historic Inns, Inc. Covers the entire United States. To order, phone ☎ 949-499-8070.

Recommended Country Inns, Mid-Atlantic and Chesapeake Region, by Suzi Forbes Chase, published by The Globe Pequot Press. Covers Virginia, Delaware, Maryland, Pennsylvania, New Jersey, New York, and West Virginia. To order, phone ☎ 800-243-0495.

For Washington-area B&B reservations, check the Web site **www .bedandbreakfastdc.com,** or call **Bed and Breakfast Accommodations, Ltd.** at ☎ 202-328-3510.

HELPING YOUR TRAVEL AGENT HELP YOU

WHEN YOU CALL YOUR TRAVEL AGENT, ask if he or she has been to Washington. If the answer is no, be prepared to give your travel agent some direction. Do not accept any recommendations at face value.

Check out the location and rates of any suggested hotel and make certain that the hotel is suited to your itinerary.

Because some travel agents are unfamiliar with Washington, your agent may try to plug you into a tour operator's or wholesaler's preset package. This essentially allows the travel agent to set up your whole trip with a single phone call and still collect an 8 to 10% commission. The problem with this scenario is that most agents will place 90% of their Washington business with only one or two wholesalers or tour operators. In other words, it's the line of least resistance for them, and not much choice for you.

Travel agents will often use wholesalers who run packages in conjunction with airlines, like Delta's Dream Vacations or American's Fly-Away Vacations. Because of the wholesaler's exclusive relationship with the carrier, these trips are very easy for travel agents to book. However, they will probably be more expensive than a package offered by a high-volume wholesaler who works with a number of airlines in a primarily Washington market.

To help your travel agent get you the best possible deal, do the following:

1. Determine where you want to stay in Washington and, if possible, choose a specific hotel. This can be accomplished by reviewing the hotel information provided in this guide and by writing or calling hotels that interest you.

2. Check out the hotel deals and package vacations advertised in the Sunday travel section of the *Washington Post*. Often you will be able to find deals that beat the socks off anything offered in your local paper. See if you can find specials that fit your plans and include a hotel you like.

3. Call the hotels, wholesalers, or tour operators whose ads you have collected. Ask any questions you have concerning their packages, but do not book your trip with them directly.

4. Tell your travel agent about the deals you find and ask if he or she can get you something better. The deals in the paper will serve as a benchmark against which to compare alternatives proposed by your travel agent.

5. Choose from among the options that you and your travel agent uncover. No matter which option you elect, have the agent book it. Even if you go with one of the packages in the newspaper, it will probably be commissionable (at no additional cost to you) and will provide the agent some return on the time invested on your behalf. Also, as a travel professional, your agent should be able to verify the quality and integrity of the deal.

IF YOU MAKE YOUR OWN RESERVATION

AS YOU POKE AROUND trying to find a good deal, there are several things you should know. First, always call the specific hotel as opposed to the hotel chain's national toll-free number. Quite often, the reservationists at the national toll-free number are unaware of local specials. Always ask about specials before you inquire about corporate rates. Do not be reluctant to bargain. If you are buying a hotel's weekend package, for example, and want to extend your stay into the following week, you can often obtain at least the corporate rate for the extra days. Do your bargaining, however, before you check in, preferably when you make your reservations.

HOW TO EVALUATE A TRAVEL PACKAGE

HUNDREDS OF WASHINGTON PACKAGE VACATIONS are offered to the public each year. Packages should be a win-win proposition for both the buyer and the seller. The buyer has to make only one phone call and deal with just one salesperson to set up the whole vacation: transportation, rental car, lodging, meals, tours, attraction admissions, and even golf and tennis. The seller, likewise, has to deal with the buyer only once, eliminating the need for separate sales, confirmations, and billing. In addition to streamlining sales, processing, and administration, some packagers also buy airfares in bulk on contract like a broker playing the commodities market. Buying a large number of airfares in advance allows the packager to buy them at a significant savings from posted fares. The same practice is also applied to hotel rooms. Because selling vacation packages is an efficient way of doing business, and because the packager can often buy individual package components (airfare, lodging, etc.) in bulk at a discount, savings in operating expenses realized by the seller are sometimes passed on to the buyer. In addition to being convenient, such packages can be exceptional values. In any event, that is the way it is supposed to work.

All too often, in practice, the seller cashes in on discounts and passes none on to the buyer. In some instances, packages are loaded up with extras that cost the packager next to nothing but inflate the retail price sky-high. As you may expect, the savings to be passed along to customers evaporate.

When considering a package, choose one that includes features you are sure to use. Whether you use all the features or not, you will certainly pay for them. Second, if cost is of greater concern than convenience, make a few phone calls and see what the package would cost if you booked its individual components (airfare, rental car, lodging, etc.) on your own. If the package price is less than the à la carte cost, the package is a good deal. If the costs are about the same, the package is probably worth buying just for the convenience.

If your package includes a choice of rental car or "airport transfers" (transportation to and from the airport), take the transfers unless you are visiting Washington for the weekend and don't plan to visit the Mall. During the weekend, it is relatively easy to get around by car as long as you don't visit the dreaded "Monument Alley." During the week, forget it—a car is definitely *not* the way to go. If you do take the car, be sure to ask if the package includes free parking at your hotel.

TIPS *for* BUSINESS TRAVELERS

THE PRIMARY CONSIDERATIONS for business travelers are afford-ability and proximity to the site or area where you will transact your business. Identify the areas where your business will take you on the maps on pages 78–81, and then use the Hotel Information Chart on pages 60–75 to cross-reference the hotels located in that area. Once you have developed a short list of possible hotels that are conveniently located, fit your budget, and offer the standard of accommodations you require, you (or your travel agent) can make use of the cost-saving suggestions discussed earlier to obtain the lowest rate.

LODGING CONVENIENT TO WASHINGTON CONVENTION CENTER

IF YOU ARE ATTENDING A MEETING OR TRADE SHOW at **Washington Convention Center,** look for convenient lodging in downtown Washington, where at least a half-dozen hotels are within walking distance. From most downtown hotels, Washington Convention Center is a five- to eight-minute cab or shuttle ride away. Parking is available at the convention center, but it is expensive and not terribly conve-nient. We recommend that you leave your car at home and use shuttles and cabs.

The Washington Convention Center is served directly by the Mount Vernon Square/Seventh Street–Convention Center Metro Station and is only about five blocks from Metro Center. The walk passes through a section of town that is safe during daylight hours.

Commuting to Washington Convention Center from the suburbs or the airports during rush hour is something to be avoided if possible. If you want a room downtown, book early—very early. If you screw up and need a room at the last minute, try a wholesaler or reservation service, or one of the strategies that follow.

CONVENTION RATES: HOW THEY WORK AND HOW TO DO BETTER

IF YOU ARE ATTENDING A MAJOR CONVENTION or trade show, it is probable that the meeting's sponsoring organization has negotiated "convention rates" with a number of hotels. Under this arrangement, hotels agree to "block" a certain number of rooms at an agreed-upon price for convention-goers. Sometimes, as in the case of a small meet-ing, only one hotel is involved. In the event of a large citywide conven-tion at Washington Convention Center, however, almost all downtown and airport hotels will participate in the room block.

Because the convention sponsor brings a lot of business to the city and reserves a large number of rooms, it usually can negotiate a vol-ume discount on the room rates, a rate that should be substantially below rack rate. The bottom line, however, is that some conventions and trade shows have more clout and negotiating skill than others.

Hence, your convention sponsor may or may not be able to obtain the lowest possible rate.

Once a convention or trade show sponsor has completed negotiations with participating hotels, it will send its attendees a housing list that includes all the hotels serving the convention, along with the special convention rate for each. When you receive the housing list, you can compare the convention rates with the rates obtainable using the strategies covered in the previous section. If the negotiated convention rate doesn't sound like a good deal, you can try to reserve a room using a half-price club, a consolidator, or a tour operator. Remember, however, that many of the deep discounts are available only when the hotel expects to be at less than 80% occupancy, a condition that rarely prevails when a big convention is in town.

Here are some tips for beating convention rates:

1. Reserve early. Most big conventions and trade shows announce meeting sites one to three years in advance. Get your reservation booked as far in advance as possible using a half-price club. If you book well before the convention sponsor sends out its hotel list, chances are much better that the hotel will have space available.

2. If you've already got your convention's housing list, compare it with the list of hotels presented in this guide. You might be able to find a hotel not on the convention list that better suits your needs.

3. Use a local reservation agency or consolidator. This strategy is useful even if, for some reason, you need to make reservations at the last minute. Local reservation agencies and consolidators almost always control some rooms, even in the midst of a huge convention or trade show. (See our section on wholesalers and consolidators on page 37.)

4. Book a hotel somewhat distant from the convention center but situated close to the Metro. You may save money on your room rate, and your commuting time underground to the convention center will often be shorter than if you take a cab or drive from a downtown hotel.

5. Stay in a bed and breakfast, either downtown or near a Metro line. Bed and Breakfast Accommodations, Ltd., at ☎ 202-328-3510; **www.bedandbreakfastdc.com**, can help you locate one.

HOTEL AND MOTEL TOLL-FREE NUMBERS

FOR YOUR CONVENIENCE, we've listed on page 44 the toll-free phone numbers, including TDDs (Telecommunication Device for the Deaf) for many hotel and motel chains.

ACCOMMODATIONS:
Rated and Ranked

WHAT'S IN A ROOM?

EXCEPT FOR CLEANLINESS, state of repair, and décor, most travelers do not pay much attention to hotel rooms. There is, of course, a discernible standard of quality and luxury that differentiates Motel 6 from Holiday Inn, Holiday Inn from Marriott, and so on. In general, however, hotel guests fail to appreciate that some rooms are better engineered than others.

Contrary to what you might suppose, designing a hotel room is (or should be) a lot more complex than picking a bedspread to match the carpet and drapes. Making the room usable to its occupants is an art, a planning discipline that combines both form and function.

Décor and taste are important, certainly. No one wants to spend several days in a room where the décor is dated, garish, or even ugly. But beyond the décor, certain variables determine how livable a hotel room is. In Washington, D.C., we have seen some beautifully appointed rooms that are simply not well designed for human habitation. The next time you stay in a hotel, pay attention to the details and design elements of your room. Even more than décor, these are the things that will make you feel comfortable and at home.

It takes the *Unofficial Guide* researchers about 40 minutes to inspect a hotel room. Here are a few of the things we check that you may want to start paying attention to:

ROOM SIZE While some smaller rooms are cozy and well designed, a large and uncluttered room is generally preferable, especially for a stay of more than three days.

TEMPERATURE CONTROL, VENTILATION, AND ODOR The guest should be able to control the temperature of the room. The best system, because it's so quiet, is central heating and air-conditioning, controlled by the room's own thermostat. The next best system is a room module heater and air-conditioner, preferably controlled by an automatic thermostat, but usually by manually operated button controls. The worst system is central heat and air without any sort of room thermostat or guest control.

The vast majority of hotel rooms have windows or balcony doors that have been permanently secured shut. Though there are some legitimate safety and liability issues involved, we prefer windows and balcony doors that can be opened to admit fresh air. Hotel rooms should be odor-free and smoke-free and should not feel stuffy or damp.

ROOM SECURITY Better rooms have locks that require a plastic card instead of the traditional lock and key. Card-and-slot systems allow the hotel to change the combination or entry code of the lock with

Hotel and Motel Toll-free Numbers

Best Western	☎ 800-780-7234 U.S. and Canada	☎ 800-528-2222 TDD
Comfort Inn	☎ 877-424-6423 U.S. and Canada	☎ 800-228-3323 TDD
Courtyard by Marriott	☎ 800-321-2211 U.S. and Canada	☎ 800-228-7014 TDD
Days Inn	☎ 800-325-2525 U.S.	☎ 800-329-7155 TDD
DoubleTree and DoubleTree Guest Suites	☎ 800-222-8733 U.S. and Canada	☎ 800-528-9898 TDD
Econo Lodge		☎ 800-424-4777 U.S.
Embassy Suites	☎ 800-362-2779 U.S. and Canada	☎ 800-458-4708 TDD
Fairfield Inn by Marriott	☎ 800-228-2800 U.S. and Canada	
Hampton Inn	☎ 800-426-7866 U.S. and Canada	☎ 800-451-4833 TDD
Hilton	☎ 800-445-8667 U.S	☎ 800-368-1133 TDD
Holiday Inn	☎ 800-465-4329 U.S. and Canada	☎ 800-238-5544 TDD
Howard Johnson	☎ 800-654-2000 U.S. and Canada	☎ 800-544-9881 TDD
Hyatt	☎ 800-233-1234 U.S. and Canada	☎ 800-228-9548 TDD
Loews		☎ 800-235-6397 U.S. and Canada
Marriott	☎ 800-228-9290 U.S. and Canada	☎ 800-228-7014 TDD
Quality Inn	☎ 800-228-5151 U.S. and Canada	☎ 800-228-3323 TDD
Radisson	☎ 800-333-3333 U.S. and Canada	☎ 800-906-2200 TDD
Ramada Inn	☎ 800-228-3838 U.S.	☎ 800-228-3232 TDD
Renaissance	☎ 800-468-3571 U.S. and Canada	☎ 800-228-7014 TDD
Residence Inn by Marriott	☎ 800-331-3131 U.S. and Canada	☎ 800-228-7014 TDD
Ritz-Carlton	☎ 800-241-3333 U.S. and Canada	☎ 800-228-7014 TDD
Sheraton	☎ 800-325-3535 U.S. and Canada	
Wyndham		☎ 800-822-4200 U.S.

each new guest who uses the room. A burglar who has somehow acquired a room key to a conventional lock can afford to wait until the situation is right before using the key to gain access. Not so with a card-and-slot system. Though the largest hotels and hotel chains with lock-and-key systems usually rotate their locks once each year, they remain vulnerable to hotel thieves much of the time. Many smaller or independent properties rarely rotate their locks.

In addition to an entry-lock system, the door should have a dead-bolt and preferably a chain that can be locked from the inside. A chain by itself is not sufficient. Doors should also have a peephole. Windows and balcony doors should have secure locks.

SAFETY Every room should have a fire or smoke alarm, clear fire instructions, and preferably a sprinkler system. Bathtubs should have a nonskid surface, and shower stalls should have doors that either open outward or slide side-to-side. Bathroom electrical outlets should be positioned high on the wall and not too close to the sink. Balconies should have sturdy, high rails.

NOISE Most travelers have been kept awake by the television, partying, or amorous activities of people in the next room, or by traffic on the street outside. Better hotels are designed with noise control in mind. Wall and ceiling construction are substantial, effectively screening out routine noise. Carpets and drapes, in addition to being decorative, also absorb and muffle sounds. Mattresses mounted on stable platforms or sturdy bed frames do not squeak even when challenged by the most passionate lovers. Televisions enclosed in cabinets, and with volume governors, rarely disturb guests in adjacent rooms.

In better hotels, the air-conditioning and heating system is well maintained and operates without noise or vibration. Likewise, plumbing is quiet and positioned away from the sleeping area. Doors to the hall, and to adjoining rooms, are thick and well fitted to better keep out noise.

DARKNESS CONTROL Ever been in a hotel room where the curtains would not quite come together in the middle? In cities where many visitors stay up way into the wee hours, it's important to have a dark, quiet room where you can sleep late without the morning sun blasting you out of bed. Thick, lined curtains that close completely in the center and extend beyond the dimensions of the window or door frame are required. In a well-planned room, the curtains, shades, or blinds should almost totally block light at any time of day.

LIGHTING Poor lighting is an extremely common problem in American hotel rooms. The lighting is usually adequate for dressing, relaxing, or watching television, but not for reading or working. Lighting needs to be bright over tables and desks and alongside couches or easy chairs. Since many people read in bed, there should be a separate light for each person. A room with two queen beds should have an individual light for four people. Better bedside reading lights illuminate a small area, so if you want to sleep and someone else prefers to stay up and read, you will not be bothered by the light. The worst situation by far is a single lamp on a table between the beds. In each bed, only the person next to the lamp will have sufficient light to read. This deficiency is often compounded by light bulbs of insufficient wattage.

In addition, closet areas should be well lit, and there should be a switch near the door that turns on lights in the room when you enter. A seldom seen but desirable feature is a bedside console that allows a guest to control all or most lights in the room from the bed.

FURNISHINGS At bare minimum, the bed(s) must be firm. Pillows should be made with nonallergenic fillers and, in addition to the sheets and spread, a blanket should be provided. Bedclothes should be laundered with a fabric softener and changed daily. Better hotels usually provide extra blankets and pillows in the room or on request and sometimes use a second top sheet between the blanket and the spread.

There should be a dresser large enough to hold clothes for two people during a five-day stay. A small table with two chairs, or a desk with a chair, should be provided. The room should be equipped with a luggage rack and a three-quarter- to full-length mirror.

The television should be cable-connected and should ideally have a volume governor and remote control. It should be mounted on a swivel base and preferably enclosed in a cabinet. Local channels should be posted on the set, and a local TV program guide should be supplied.

The telephone should be touch-tone, conveniently situated for bedside use, and should have, on or near it, easily understood dialing instructions and a rate card. Local white and yellow pages should be provided. Better hotels have phones in the bath and equip room phones with long cords; even better ones have Internet connections or wireless access in every room.

Well-designed hotel rooms usually have a plush armchair or a sleeper sofa for lounging and reading. Better headboards are padded for comfortable reading in bed, and there should be a nightstand or table on each side of the bed(s). Nice extras in any hotel room include a small refrigerator, a digital alarm clock, and a coffeemaker.

BATHROOM Two sinks are better than one, and you cannot have too much counter space. A sink outside the bath is a great convenience when one person dresses as another bathes. Sinks should have drains with stoppers.

Better bathrooms have both a tub and a shower with a nonslip bottom. Tub and shower controls should be easy to operate. Adjustable shower heads are preferred. The bath needs to be well lit and should have an exhaust fan and a guest-controlled bathroom heater. Towels should be large, soft, and fluffy and provided in generous quantities, as should hand towels and washcloths. There should be an electrical outlet for each sink, conveniently and safely placed.

Complimentary shampoo, conditioner, and lotion are a plus, as are robes and bathmats. Better hotels supply their bathrooms with tissues and extra toilet paper. Luxurious baths feature a phone, a hair dryer, sometimes a small television or a jacuzzi.

VENDING There should be complimentary ice and a drink machine on each floor. Welcome additions include a snack machine and a sundries (combs, toothpaste) machine. The latter are seldom found in large hotels that have 24-hour restaurants and shops.

ROOM RATINGS

TO SEPARATE PROPERTIES according to the relative quality, tasteful-ness, state of repair, cleanliness, and size of their standard rooms, we have grouped the hotels and motels into classifications denoted by stars:

★★★★★	Superior Rooms	Tasteful and luxurious by any standard
★★★★	Extremely Nice Rooms	What you would expect at a Hyatt Regency or Marriott
★★★	Nice Rooms	Holiday Inn or comparable quality
★★	Adequate Rooms	Clean, comfortable, and functional without frills (like a Motel 6)
★	Super-Budget	

Star ratings in this guide do not necessarily correspond to ratings awarded by Mobil, AAA, or other travel critics. Because stars have lit-tle relevance when awarded in the absence of commonly recognized standards of comparison, we have tied our rating to expected levels of quality established by specific American hotel corporations.

Star ratings apply to *room quality only* and describe the property's standard accommodations. For most hotels and motels a "standard accommodation" is a hotel room with either one king bed or two queen beds. In an all-suite property, the standard accommodation is a one- or two-room suite. In addition to standard accommodations, many hotels offer luxury rooms and special suites that are not rated in this guide. Star ratings for rooms are assigned without regard to whether a property has restaurant(s), recreational facilities, enter-tainment, or other extras.

In addition to stars (which delineate broad categories), we also employ a numerical rating system. Our rating scale is 0 to 100, with 100 the best possible rating and 0 the worst. Numerical ratings are presented to show the difference we perceive between one property and another that may be in the same star category. Rooms at the Mor-rison House, the Embassy Suites Tysons Corner, and the Marriott Crystal Gateway, for instance, are all rated as ★★★★ (four stars). In the supplemental numerical ratings, the Morrison House and the Embassy Suites Tysons Corner are rated 87 and 86, respectively, while the Marriott Crystal Gateway is rated 83. This means that within the four-star category, the Morrison House and the Embassy Suites Tysons Corner are comparable, and that both have somewhat nicer rooms than the Marriott Crystal Gateway.

The location column identifies the greater Washington area (by neighborhood) where you will find a particular property.

How the Hotels Compare in Washington, D.C.

HOTEL	OVERALL RATING	QUALITY RATING	COST ($ = $50)	LOCATION
Ritz-Carlton Washington, D.C.	★★★★★	98	$$$$$$$	Dupont Circle/ Adams-Morgan
Ritz-Carlton Pentagon City	★★★★½	95	$$$$$–	Virginia Suburbs
Hotel George	★★★★½	94	$$$$–	Downtown
River Inn	★★★★½	94	$$$$$–	Foggy Bottom
Watergate Hotel	★★★★½	94	$$$$–	Foggy Bottom
Westin Grand	★★★★½	94	$$$$$$$$–	Georgetown
Hay-Adams Hotel	★★★★½	93	$$$$$$$$$–	Downtown
Mandarin Oriental	★★★★½	93	$$$$$$$$$$$–	National Mall
Park Hyatt	★★★★½	93	$$$$$$$$	Georgetown
Ritz-Carlton Georgetown	★★★★½	92	$$$$$$$$	Georgetown
Willard Inter-Continental	★★★★½	92	$$$$$$$$+	Downtown
Four Seasons Hotel	★★★★½	91	$$$$$$$$$$$+	Georgetown
Hamilton Crowne Plaza	★★★★½	90	$$$$	Downtown
Hotel Palomar	★★★★½	90	$$$$$$$$$–	Dupont Circle/ Adams-Morgan
Hotel Topaz	★★★★½	90	$$$$$$$	Dupont Circle/ Adams-Morgan
Jefferson Hotel	★★★★½	90	$$$$$$$$$	Downtown
Renaissance Mayflower Hotel	★★★★½	90	$$$$$	Downtown
Sheraton Premiere Tysons Corner	★★★★½	90	$$$$$$$$–	Virginia Suburbs
Sofitel Lafayette	★★★★½	90	$$$$$$+	Downtown
St. Regis (closed for renovations)	★★★★½	90	$$$$$$$$	Downtown

HOW THE ACCOMMODATIONS COMPARE

COST ESTIMATES ARE BASED ON THE HOTEL'S published rack rates for standard rooms. Each "$" represents $50. Thus, a cost symbol of "$$$" means a room (or suite) at that hotel will cost about $150 a night.

Below is a hit parade of the nicest rooms in town. We've focused strictly on room quality and excluded any consideration of location, services, recreation, or amenities. In some instances, a one- or two-room suite can be had for the same price or less than that of a regular hotel room.

If you used previous editions of this guide, you may notice that many of the ratings and rankings have changed. These changes reflect the inclusion of new properties, as well as guest-room renovations or

HOTEL	OVERALL RATING	QUALITY RATING	COST ($ = $50)	LOCATION
Westin Embassy Row	★★★★½	90	$$$$$$	Dupont Circle/ Adams-Morgan
Hotel Helix	★★★★	89	$$−	Upper Northwest
Hotel Madera	★★★★	89	$$$$	Dupont Circle/ Adams-Morgan
Hyatt Regency Crystal City	★★★★	89	$$$$$$	Virginia Suburbs
DoubleTree Washington, D.C.	★★★★	88	$$$$$+	Upper Northwest
Fairmont Washington, D.C.	★★★★	88	$$$$$+	Georgetown
Grand Hyatt Washington	★★★★	88	$$$$$$$$$−	Downtown
J.W. Marriott Pennsylvania Ave.	★★★★	88	$$$$$$$$$−	Downtown
Morrison-Clark Inn	★★★★	88	$$$$$$−	Upper Northwest
Sheraton Suites Alexandria	★★★★	88	$$$$$$$$	Virginia Suburbs
Washington Renaissance Hotel	★★★★	88	$$$$−	Downtown
Wyndham Washington	★★★★	88	$$$$$	Downtown
Hyatt Arlington	★★★★	87	$$−	Virginia Suburbs
Madison Hotel	★★★★	87	$$$$$−	Downtown
Morrison House	★★★★	87	$$$$$$+	Virginia Suburbs
Omni Shoreham Hotel	★★★★	87	$$$$$$$$+	Upper Northwest
One Washington Circle Hotel	★★★★	87	$$$$$$$$$$	Foggy Bottom
Washington Suites Georgetown	★★★★	87	$$$$$$$+	Georgetown
Carlyle Suites Hotel	★★★★	86	$$$$$+	Dupont Circle/ Adams-Morgan
Crowne Plaza Silver Spring	★★★★	86	$$$$−	Maryland Suburbs

improved maintenance and housekeeping in previously listed properties. A failure to properly maintain guest rooms or a lapse in housekeeping standards can negatively affect the ratings.

Finally, before you begin to shop for a hotel, take a hard look at this letter we received from a couple in Hot Springs, Arkansas:

> We cancelled our room reservations to follow the advice in your book [and reserved a hotel room highly ranked by the Unofficial Guide]. We wanted inexpensive, but clean and cheerful. We got inexpensive, but [also] dirty, grim, and depressing. I really felt disappointed in your advice and the room. It was the pits. That was the one real piece of information I needed from your book! The room spoiled the holiday for me aside from our touring.

How the Hotels Compare (continued)

HOTEL	OVERALL RATING	QUALITY RATING	COST ($ = $50)	LOCATION
Embassy Suites Alexandria	★★★★	86	$$$$	Virginia Suburbs
Embassy Suites Tysons Corner	★★★★	86	$$$$	Virginia Suburbs
Hotel Monaco	★★★★	86	$$$$$–	Downtown
Hotel Rouge	★★★★	86	$$$$$$–	Dupont Circle/ Adams-Morgan
L'Enfant Plaza Hotel	★★★★	86	$$$$$	National Mall
Melrose Hotel & Suites	★★★★	86	$$$$$$$$–	Georgetown
St. Gregory Luxury Hotel	★★★★	86	$$$$$+	Dupont Circle/ Adams-Morgan
Embassy Row Hilton	★★★★	85	$$$$$	Dupont Circle/ Adams-Morgan
Embassy Suites Downtown	★★★★	85	$$$$+	Dupont Circle/ Adams-Morgan
Georgetown Inn	★★★★	85	$$$	Georgetown
Hyatt Regency Bethesda	★★★★	85	$$$$$$–	Maryland Suburbs
Beacon Hotel	★★★★	84	$$$$$$	Dupont Circle/ Adams-Morgan
Churchill Hotel	★★★★	84	$$$$	Dupont Circle/ Adams-Morgan
Courtyard Washington Northwest	★★★★	84	$$$$$	Dupont Circle/ Adams-Morgan
Embassy Suites Chevy Chase	★★★★	84	$$$$–	Upper Northwest
Embassy Suites Crystal City	★★★★	84	$$$$$–	Virginia Suburbs

Needless to say, this letter was as unsettling to us as the bad room was to our reader. Our integrity as travel journalists, after all, is based on the quality of the information we provide our readers. Even with the best of intentions and the most conscientious research, however, we cannot inspect every room in every hotel. What we do, in statistical terms, is take a sample: We check out several rooms selected at random in each hotel and base our ratings and rankings on those rooms. The inspections are conducted anonymously and without the knowledge of the management. Although it is unusual, it is certainly possible that the rooms we randomly inspect are not representative of the majority of rooms at a particular hotel. Another possibility is that the rooms we inspect in a given hotel are representative but that by bad luck a reader

HOTEL	OVERALL RATING	QUALITY RATING	COST ($ = $50)	LOCATION
Hilton Arlington and Towers	★★★★	84	$$$$$–	Virginia Suburbs
Hyatt Regency Capitol Hill	★★★★	84	$$$$$$$$	Downtown
Marriott Wardman Park Hotel	★★★★	84	$$$$$$$$–	Upper Northwest
Residence Inn Pentagon City	★★★★	84	$$$	Virginia Suburbs
Washington Court Hotel	★★★★	84	$$$$$$$$$–	Downtown
Bethesda Court Hotel	★★★★	83	$$$$–	Maryland Suburbs
DoubleTree Hotel Crystal City	★★★★	83	$$$$–	Virginia Suburbs
Georgetown Suites Hotel	★★★★	83	$$$$–	Georgetown
Marriott Crystal Gateway	★★★★	83	$$$$$$	Virginia Suburbs
Marriott Hotel Bethesda	★★★★	83	$$+	Maryland Suburbs
Residence Inn Bethesda	★★★★	83	$$$$$$$–	Maryland Suburbs
Washington National Airport Hilton	★★★★	83	$$$	Virginia Suburbs
Washington Suites Alexandria	★★★★	83	$$$$+	Virginia Suburbs
Courtyard Crystal City	★★★½	82	$$–	Virginia Suburbs
DoubleTree Bethesda	★★★½	82	$$$$$$	Maryland Suburbs
DoubleTree Hotel Tysons Corner	★★★½	82	$$$$+	Virginia Suburbs
Hilton Alexandria at Mark Center	★★★½	82	$$–	Virginia Suburbs
Hotel Monticello	★★★½	82	$$$$$$	Georgetown
Hotel Washington	★★★½	82	$$$$$–	Downtown
M Street Hotel	★★★½	82	$$$$+	Dupont Circle/ Adams-Morgan

is assigned a room that is inferior. When we rechecked the hotel our reader disliked, we discovered that our rating was correctly representative but that he and his wife had unfortunately been assigned to one of a small number of threadbare rooms scheduled for renovation.

The key to avoiding disappointment is to snoop around in advance. We recommend that you ask for a photo of a hotel's standard guest room before you book, or at least get a copy of the hotel's promotional brochure. Be forewarned, however, that some hotel chains use the same guest room photo in their promotional literature for all hotels in the chain; a specific guest room may not resemble the brochure photo. When you or your travel agent call, ask how old the property is and when your guest room was last renovated. If you

How the Hotels Compare (continued)

HOTEL	OVERALL RATING	QUALITY RATING	COST ($ = $50)	LOCATION
Old Town Hotel	★★★½	82	$$–	Virginia Suburbs
Phoenix Park Hotel	★★★½	82	$$$$+	Capitol Hill
Sheraton National Hotel	★★★½	82	$$$$$$	Virginia Suburbs
Washington Marriott Hotel	★★★½	82	$$$$+	Dupont Circle/ Adams-Morgan
Capitol Hilton	★★★½	81	$$$$$	Downtown
Radisson Hotel Reagan National	★★★½	81	$$–	Virginia Suburbs
Residence Inn Dupont Circle	★★★½	81	$$$$$$+	Dupont Circle/ Adams-Morgan
Best Western Georgetown Suites	★★★½	80	$$–	Dupont Circle/ Adams-Morgan
Hilton Washington	★★★½	80	$$$$$$	Dupont Circle/ Adams-Morgan
Holiday Inn on the Hill	★★★½	80	$$$$$	Downtown
Marriott Crystal City	★★★½	80	$$$	Virginia Suburbs
Marriott Hotel Key Bridge	★★★½	80	$$$$$$	Virginia Suburbs
Radisson Plaza Hotel Old Town	★★★½	80	$$$$$–	Virginia Suburbs
Tysons Corner Marriott	★★★½	80	$$	Virginia Suburbs
Comfort Inn Pentagon	★★★½	79	$$$$–	Virginia Suburbs
Sheraton Crystal City	★★★½	79	$$$$$$$$–	Virginia Suburbs

arrive and are assigned a room that does not live up to the brochure's promises, demand to be moved to another room.

GOOD DEALS AND BAD DEALS

HAVING LISTED THE NICEST ROOMS IN TOWN, first by quality, then by location, let's reorder the list to rank the best combinations of quality and price in a room—in other words, its value. Using a mathematical formula that factors in a hotel's quality and star ratings as well as the rack rate, we derive a list of hotels ranked by value. As before, the rankings are made without consideration of location or the availability of restaurants, recreational facilities, entertainment, or amenities. We list only the top 30 hotel values because, as consumers, value-conscious readers are simply concerned with finding the best deals.

We use the hotels' rack rates as a level playing field, so to speak, when calculating value. However, most hotels offer special rates and incentives; they also increase rates to capitalize on periods of peak

HOTEL	OVERALL RATING	QUALITY RATING	COST ($ = $50)	LOCATION
Courtyard Embassy Row	★★★½	78	$$$$$$$	Dupont Circle/ Adams-Morgan
Courtyard Rosslyn	★★★½	78	$$$$$	Virginia Suburbs
Hampton Inn Alexandria	★★★½	78	$$–	Virginia Suburbs
Hawthorn Suites	★★★½	78	$$$+	Virginia Suburbs
Hilton of Silver Spring	★★★½	78	$$$	Maryland Suburbs
Holiday Inn Arlington	★★★½	78	$$$$–	Virginia Suburbs
Holiday Inn Georgetown	★★★½	78	$$$	Upper Northwest
Hotel Lombardy	★★★½	78	$$$$$–	Foggy Bottom
Latham Hotel	★★★½	78	$$$$	Georgetown
Residence Inn Vermont Avenue	★★★½	78	$$$$$$+	Downtown
Courtyard New Carrollton	★★★½	77	$$$$–	Maryland Suburbs
Hilton Garden Inn Washington Downtown	★★★½	77	$$$$$	Downtown
Marriott Metro Center	★★★½	77	$$$$$$$$	Downtown
Quincy Suites	★★★½	77	$$$$–	Downtown
Savoy Suites Hotel	★★★½	77	$$$$$$	Upper Northwest
Courtyard Alexandria	★★★½	76	$$	Virginia Suburbs
Crowne Plaza National Airport	★★★½	76	$$$$–	Virginia Suburbs
State Plaza Hotel	★★★½	76	$$$$	Foggy Bottom

demand. If you're looking for a room on short notice most times of the year, then the value chart on page 56 should serve you well. If, however, you're planning a value-conscious vacation well in advance, use the chart as a guide but by no means as a substitute for the advice listed under "Getting a Good Deal on a Room," on page 34.

A reader recently complained to us that he had booked one of our top-ranked rooms in terms of value and had been very disappointed in the room. We noticed that the room the reader occupied had a quality rating of ★★½. We remind you that the value ratings are intended to give you some sense of value received for dollars spent. A ★★½ room at $90 may have the same value rating as a ★★★★ room at $200, but that does not mean the rooms will be of comparable quality. Regardless of whether it's a good deal or not, a ★★½ room is still a ★★½ room.

Listed on page 56 are the best room buys for the money, ordered without regard to quality or star ratings. Note that sometimes a suite can cost less than a hotel room.

How the Hotels Compare (continued)

HOTEL	OVERALL RATING	QUALITY RATING	COST ($ = $50)	LOCATION
Holiday Inn Rosslyn at Key Bridge	★★★½	75	$$$$–	Virginia Suburbs
Jurys Normandy	★★★½	75	$$$$$–	Dupont Circle/ Adams-Morgan
Four Points Sheraton Downtown	★★★	74	$$$$$$$–	Downtown
Kalorama Guest House	★★★	74	$$–	Dupont Circle/ Adams-Morgan
Best Western Pentagon Hotel	★★★	73	$$$+	Virginia Suburbs
Channel Inn Hotel	★★★	72	$$$	National Mall
Clarion Hotel Bethesda	★★★	72	$$$$+	Maryland Suburbs
Courtyard Alexandria Pentagon South	★★★	72	$$$$	Virginia Suburbs
Holiday Inn Hotel and Suites	★★★	72	$$$$	Virginia Suburbs
Holiday Inn National Airport	★★★	72	$$$$	Virginia Suburbs
Holiday Inn Capitol	★★★	71	$$$$	Capitol Hill
Holiday Inn Central	★★★	71	$$$$$–	Upper Northwest
Quality Inn Iwo Jima	★★★	70	$$$$$–	Virginia Suburbs
Holiday Inn Chevy Chase	★★★	68	$$–	Maryland Suburbs
Quality Inn College Park	★★★	68	$$–	Maryland Suburbs
Washington Plaza Hotel	★★★	67	$$$+	Downtown
Best Western Tysons Westpark	★★★	65	$$$$–	Virginia Suburbs

HOTEL	OVERALL RATING	QUALITY RATING	COST ($ = $50)	LOCATION
Comfort Inn Tysons Corner	★★★	65	$$+	Virginia Suburbs
Comfort Inn Washington Gateway	★★★	65	$$$	Virginia Suburbs
Holiday Inn Alexandria	★★★	65	$$$	Virginia Suburbs
Comfort Inn Landmark	★★½	64	$$+	Virginia Suburbs
Tabard Inn	★★½	64	$$$	Dupont Circle/ Adams-Morgan
Days Inn Connecticut Avenue	★★½	63	$$−	Upper Northwest
Comfort Inn Downtown	★★½	62	$$$	Upper Northwest
Comfort Inn Ballston/Arlington	★★½	61	$$−	Virginia Suburbs
Adam's Inn	★★½	60	$$+	Upper Northwest
American Inn of Bethesda	★★½	60	$$$$$	Maryland Suburbs
Embassy Inn	★★½	60	$$$$−	Dupont Circle/ Adams-Morgan
Red Roof Inn Downtown	★★½	60	$$$+	Downtown
Pentagon Lodge	★★½	58	$$+	Virginia Suburbs
Windsor Park Hotel	★★½	56	$$$	Dupont Circle/ Adams-Morgan
Days Inn Alexandria	★★	54	$$+	Virginia Suburbs
Hotel Harrington	★★	50	$$+	Downtown

The Top 30 Best Deals in Washington, D.C.

HOTEL	OVERALL RATING	ROOM RATING	COST ($ = $50)	LOCATION
1. Tysons Corner Marriott	★★★½	80	$$	Virginia Suburbs
2. Marriott Hotel Bethesda	★★★★	83	$$+	Maryland Suburbs
3. Hyatt Arlington	★★★★	87	$$–	Virginia Suburbs
4. Hotel Helix	★★★★	89	$$–	Upper Northwest
5. Courtyard Alexandria	★★★½	76	$$	Virginia Suburbs
6. Watergate Hotel	★★★★½	94	$$$$–	Foggy Bottom
7. Residence Inn Pentagon City	★★★★	84	$$$	Virginia Suburbs
8. Hotel George	★★★★½	94	$$$$–	Downtown
9. Old Town Hotel	★★★½	82	$$–	Virginia Suburbs
10. Hampton Inn Alexandria	★★★½	78	$$–	Virginia Suburbs
11. Georgetown Inn	★★★★	85	$$$	Georgetown
12. Washington National Airport Hilton	★★★★	83	$$$	Virginia Suburbs
13. Hamilton Crowne Plaza	★★★★½	90	$$$$	Downtown
14. Best Western Georgetown Suites	★★★½	80	$$–	Dupont Circle/ Adams-Morgan
15. Courtyard Crystal City	★★★½	82	$$–	Virginia Suburbs
16. Hilton Alexandria at Mark Center	★★★½	82	$$–	Virginia Suburbs
17. Radisson Hotel Ronald Reagan National	★★★½	81	$$–	Virginia Suburbs
18. Washington Renaissance	★★★★	88	$$$$–	Downtown
19. Holiday Inn Georgetown	★★★½	78	$$$	Upper Northwest
20. Bethesda Court Hotel	★★★★	83	$$$$–	Maryland Suburbs
21. Embassy Suites Chevy Chase	★★★★	84	$$$$–	Upper Northwest
22. Crowne Plaza Silver Spring	★★★★	86	$$$$–	Maryland Suburbs
23. River Inn	★★★★½	94	$$$$$–	Foggy Bottom
24. Embassy Suites Alexandria	★★★★	86	$$$$	Virginia Suburbs
25. Georgetown Suites Hotel	★★★★	83	$$$$–	Georgetown
26. Ritz-Carlton Pentagon City	★★★★½	95	$$$$$–	Virginia Suburbs
27. Kalorama Guest House	★★★	74	$$–	Dupont Circle/ Adams-Morgan
28. Marriott Crystal City	★★★½	80	$$$	Virginia Suburbs
29. DoubleTree Hotel Crystal City	★★★★	83	$$$$–	Virginia Suburbs
30. Embassy Suites Tysons Corner	★★★★	86	$$$$	Virginia Suburbs

dupont circle accommodations

■ ACCOMMODATIONS

1. Beacon Hotel
2. Best Western Georgetown Suites
3. Comfort Inn Downtown
4. Courtyard by Marriott Northwest
5. Courtyard Embassy Row
6. Embassy Suites Hotel Downtown
7. Hilton Washington
8. Hotel Madera

9. Hotel Palomar
10. Hotel Topaz
11. Jefferson Hotel
12. Jurys Normandy
13. Kalorama Guest House
14. Madison Hotel
15. Omni-Shoreham Hotel
16. Park Hyatt
17. Renaissance Mayflower

18. Residence Inn Vermont Avenue
19. Ritz-Carlton DC
20. Saint Gregory Luxury Hotel
    and Suites
21. Tabard Inn
22. Washington Marriott Hotel
23. Washington Plaza Hotel
24. Westin Grand
25. Wyndham Washington

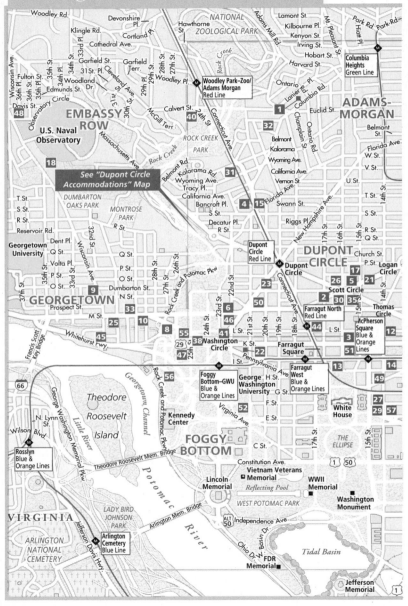

washington, d.c., accommodations

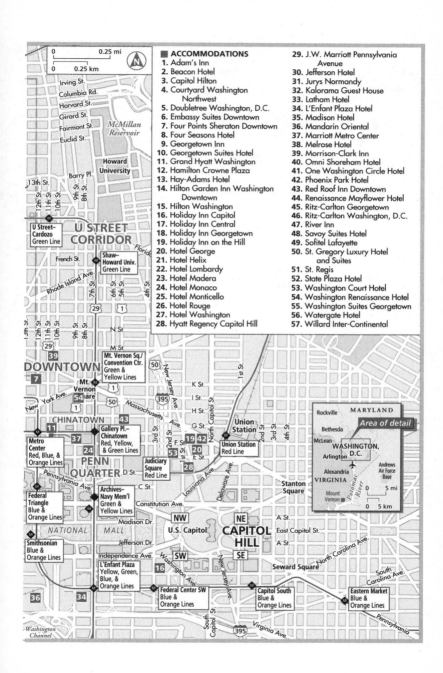

■ ACCOMMODATIONS

1. Adam's Inn
2. Beacon Hotel
3. Capitol Hilton
4. Courtyard Washington Northwest
5. Doubletree Washington, D.C.
6. Embassy Suites Downtown
7. Four Points Sheraton Downtown
8. Four Seasons Hotel
9. Georgetown Inn
10. Georgetown Suites Hotel
11. Grand Hyatt Washington
12. Hamilton Crowne Plaza
13. Hay-Adams Hotel
14. Hilton Garden Inn Washington Downtown
15. Hilton Washington
16. Holiday Inn Capitol
17. Holiday Inn Central
18. Holiday Inn Georgetown
19. Holiday Inn on the Hill
20. Hotel George
21. Hotel Helix
22. Hotel Lombardy
23. Hotel Madera
24. Hotel Monaco
25. Hotel Monticello
26. Hotel Rouge
27. Hotel Washington
28. Hyatt Regency Capitol Hill
29. J.W. Marriott Pennsylvania Avenue
30. Jefferson Hotel
31. Jurys Normandy
32. Kalorama Guest House
33. Latham Hotel
34. L'Enfant Plaza Hotel
35. Madison Hotel
36. Mandarin Oriental
37. Marriott Metro Center
38. Melrose Hotel
39. Morrison-Clark Inn
40. Omni Shoreham Hotel
41. One Washington Circle Hotel
42. Phoenix Park Hotel
43. Red Roof Inn Downtown
44. Renaissance Mayflower Hotel
45. Ritz-Carlton Georgetown
46. Ritz-Carlton Washington, D.C.
47. River Inn
48. Savoy Suites Hotel
49. Sofitel Lafayette
50. St. Gregory Luxury Hotel and Suites
51. St. Regis
52. State Plaza Hotel
53. Washington Court Hotel
54. Washington Renaissance Hotel
55. Washington Suites Georgetown
56. Watergate Hotel
57. Willard Inter-Continental

Hotel Information Chart

Adam's Inn ★★½
1746 Lanier Place NW
Washington, DC 20009
☎ 202-745-3600
FAX 202-319-7958
TOLL FREE ☎ 800-578-6807
www.adamsinn.com

ROOM QUALITY	60
COST ($ = $50)	$$+
LOCATION	Upper Northwest
NO. OF ROOMS	26
PARKING	Garage $10
ROOM SERVICE	—
BREAKFAST	Continental
ON-SITE DINING	—
POOL	—
SAUNA	—
EXERCISE FACILITIES	—

American Inn of Bethesda ★★½
8130 Wisconsin Avenue
Bethesda, MD 20814
☎ 301-656-9300
FAX 301-656-2907
TOLL FREE ☎ 800-323-7081
www.american-inn.com

ROOM QUALITY	60
COST ($ = $50)	$$$$$
LOCATION	Maryland Suburbs
NO. OF ROOMS	76
PARKING	Free lot
ROOM SERVICE	—
BREAKFAST	Continental
ON-SITE DINING	•
POOL	•
SAUNA	—
EXERCISE FACILITIES	—

Beacon Hotel ★★★★
1615 Rhode Island Avenue NW
Washington, DC 20036
☎ 202-296-2100; FAX 202-331-0227; TOLL FREE ☎ 800-821-4367
www.capitalhotelswdc.com/
BeaconHotelWDC

ROOM QUALITY	84
COST ($ = $50)	$$$$$$
LOCATION	Dupont Circle/ Adams-Morgan
NO. OF ROOMS	199
PARKING	Valet $25
ROOM SERVICE	•
BREAKFAST	—
ON-SITE DINING	•
POOL	Access
SAUNA	—
EXERCISE FACILITIES	•

Bethesda Court Hotel ★★★★
7740 Wisconsin Avenue
Bethesda, MD 20814
☎ 301-656-2100
FAX 301-986-0375
TOLL FREE ☎ 800-874-0050
www.bethesdacourtwashdc.com

ROOM QUALITY	83
COST ($ = $50)	$$$$–
LOCATION	Maryland Suburbs
NO. OF ROOMS	75
PARKING	Self $12
ROOM SERVICE	—
BREAKFAST	Continental
ON-SITE DINING	—
POOL	—
SAUNA	•
EXERCISE FACILITIES	•

Capitol Hilton ★★★½
1001 16th Street NW
Washington, DC 20036
☎ 202-393-1000
FAX 202-639-5784
TOLL FREE ☎ 800-HILTONS
www.hilton.com

ROOM QUALITY	81
COST ($ = $50)	$$$$$
LOCATION	Downtown
NO. OF ROOMS	544
PARKING	Valet $28
ROOM SERVICE	•
BREAKFAST	—
ON-SITE DINING	•
POOL	—
SAUNA	•
EXERCISE FACILITIES	•

Carlyle Suites Hotel ★★★★
1731 New Hampshire Avenue NW
Washington, DC 20009
☎ 202-234-3200
FAX 202-387-0085
TOLL FREE ☎ 866-468-3532
www.carlylesuites.com

ROOM QUALITY	86
COST ($ = $50)	$$$$$+
LOCATION	Dupont Circle/ Adams-Morgan
NO. OF ROOMS	170
PARKING	Free lot
ROOM SERVICE	—
BREAKFAST	—
ON-SITE DINING	•
POOL	—
SAUNA	—
EXERCISE FACILITIES	Free access

Comfort Inn Ballston/ Arlington ★★½
1211 North Glebe Road
Arlington, VA 22201
☎ 703-247-3399
FAX 703-524-8739
TOLL FREE ☎ 877-424-6423
www.comfortinn.com

ROOM QUALITY	61
COST ($ = $50)	$$–
LOCATION	Virginia Suburbs
NO. OF ROOMS	126
PARKING	Free lot
ROOM SERVICE	•
BREAKFAST	Continental
ON-SITE DINING	•
POOL	—
SAUNA	—
EXERCISE FACILITIES	•

Comfort Inn Downtown ★★½
1201 13th Street NW
Washington, DC 20005
☎ 202-682-5300
FAX 202-408-0830
TOLL FREE ☎ 877-424-6423
www.comfortinn.com

ROOM QUALITY	62
COST ($ = $50)	$$$
LOCATION	Upper Northwest
NO. OF ROOMS	100
PARKING	Self $27
ROOM SERVICE	—
BREAKFAST	Continental
ON-SITE DINING	—
POOL	—
SAUNA	—
EXERCISE FACILITIES	•

Comfort Inn Landmark ★★½
6254 Duke Street
Alexandria, VA 22312
☎ 703-642-3422
FAX 703-642-1354
TOLL FREE ☎ 877-782-1981
www.comfortinn.com

ROOM QUALITY	64
COST ($ = $50)	$$+
LOCATION	Virginia Suburbs
NO. OF ROOMS	150
PARKING	Free lot
ROOM SERVICE	—
BREAKFAST	Continental
ON-SITE DINING	•
POOL	•
SAUNA	—
EXERCISE FACILITIES	—

Best Western Georgetown Suites ★★★½

1121 New Hampshire Avenue NW
Washington, DC 20037
☎ 202-457-0565; FAX 202-331-9421; TOLL FREE ☎ 800-762-3777
www.bestwesternwashingtondc.com

ROOM QUALITY	80
COST ($ = $50)	$$–
LOCATION	Dupont Circle/ Adams-Morgan
NO. OF ROOMS	76
PARKING	Self $18
ROOM SERVICE	—
BREAKFAST	Continental
ON-SITE DINING	—
POOL	—
SAUNA	—
EXERCISE FACILITIES	—

Best Western Pentagon Hotel ★★★

2480 South Glebe Road
Arlington, VA 22206
☎ 703-979-4400
FAX 703-979-0189
TOLL FREE ☎ 800-426-6886
www.bestwestern.com

ROOM QUALITY	73
COST ($ = $50)	$$$+
LOCATION	Virginia Suburbs
NO. OF ROOMS	205
PARKING	Free lot
ROOM SERVICE	—
BREAKFAST	Continental
ON-SITE DINING	•
POOL	•
SAUNA	—
EXERCISE FACILITIES	•

Best Western Tysons Westpark ★★★

8401 Westpark Drive
McLean, VA 22102
☎ 703-734-2800
FAX 703-734-0521
TOLL FREE ☎ 800-336-3777
www.bestwestern.com

ROOM QUALITY	65
COST ($ = $50)	$$$$–
LOCATION	Virginia Suburbs
NO. OF ROOMS	301
PARKING	Free lot
ROOM SERVICE	•
BREAKFAST	•
ON-SITE DINING	•
POOL	•
SAUNA	•
EXERCISE FACILITIES	•

Channel Inn Hotel ★★★

650 Water Street SW
Washington, DC 20024
☎ 202-554-2400
FAX 202-863-1164
TOLL FREE ☎ 800-368-5668
www.channelinn.com

ROOM QUALITY	72
COST ($ = $50)	$$$
LOCATION	National Mall
NO. OF ROOMS	100
PARKING	Self, free
ROOM SERVICE	•
BREAKFAST	—
ON-SITE DINING	•
POOL	•
SAUNA	—
EXERCISE FACILITIES	Access

Churchill Hotel ★★★★

1914 Connecticut Avenue NW
Washington, DC 20009
☎ 202-797-2000
FAX 202-462-0944
TOLL FREE ☎ 800-424-2464
www.thechurchillhotel.com

ROOM QUALITY	84
COST ($ = $50)	$$$$
LOCATION	Dupont Circle/ Adams-Morgan
NO. OF ROOMS	144
PARKING	Valet $28
ROOM SERVICE	•
BREAKFAST	•
ON-SITE DINING	•
POOL	—
SAUNA	—
EXERCISE FACILITIES	•

Clarion Hotel Bethesda ★★★

8400 Wisconsin Avenue
Bethesda, MD 20814
☎ 301-654-1000
FAX 301-654-0751
TOLL FREE ☎ 877-795-7842
www.ichotelsgroup.com

ROOM QUALITY	72
COST ($ = $50)	$$$$+
LOCATION	Maryland Suburbs
NO. OF ROOMS	163
PARKING	Self $11
ROOM SERVICE	•
BREAKFAST	—
ON-SITE DINING	•
POOL	—
SAUNA	—
EXERCISE FACILITIES	•

Comfort Inn Pentagon ★★★½

2480 South Glebe Road
Arlington, VA 22206
☎ 703-682-5500
FAX 703-682-5505
TOLL FREE ☎ 800-325-3535
www.comfortinn.com

ROOM QUALITY	79
COST ($ = $50)	$$$$–
LOCATION	Virginia Suburbs
NO. OF ROOMS	120
PARKING	Free lot
ROOM SERVICE	•
BREAKFAST	Continental
ON-SITE DINING	•
POOL	•
SAUNA	—
EXERCISE FACILITIES	•

Comfort Inn Tysons Corner ★★★

1587 Spring Hill Road
Vienna, VA 22182
☎ 703-448-8020
FAX 703-448-0343
TOLL FREE ☎ 800-228-5150
www.comfortinnfallschurch.com

ROOM QUALITY	65
COST ($ = $50)	$$+
LOCATION	Virginia Suburbs
NO. OF ROOMS	250
PARKING	Free lot
ROOM SERVICE	—
BREAKFAST	Continental
ON-SITE DINING	•
POOL	•
SAUNA	•
EXERCISE FACILITIES	—

Comfort Inn Washington Gateway ★★★

6111 Arlington Boulevard
Falls Church , VA 22044
☎ 703-534-9100
FAX 703-534-5589
TOLL FREE ☎ 800-228-5150
www.comfortinn.com

ROOM QUALITY	65
COST ($ = $50)	$$$
LOCATION	Virginia Suburbs
NO. OF ROOMS	111
PARKING	Free lot
ROOM SERVICE	—
BREAKFAST	Continental
ON-SITE DINING	—
POOL	•
SAUNA	—
EXERCISE FACILITIES	•

Hotel Information Chart (continued)

Courtyard Alexandria

★★★½
2700 Eisenhower Avenue
Alexandria, VA 22314
☎ 703-329-2323
FAX 703-329-6853
TOLL FREE ☎ 800-321-2211
www.marriott.com

ROOM QUALITY	76
COST ($ = $50)	$$
LOCATION	Virginia Suburbs
NO. OF ROOMS	176
PARKING	Free lot
ROOM SERVICE	—
BREAKFAST	—
ON-SITE DINING	•
POOL	—
SAUNA	—
EXERCISE FACILITIES	•

Courtyard Alexandria Pentagon South ★★★

4641 Kenmore Avenue
Alexandria, VA 22304
☎ 703-751-4510
FAX 703-751-9170
TOLL FREE ☎ 888-298-2054
www.marriott.com

ROOM QUALITY	72
COST ($ = $50)	$$$$
LOCATION	Virginia Suburbs
NO. OF ROOMS	203
PARKING	Self $10
ROOM SERVICE	—
BREAKFAST	—
ON-SITE DINING	•
POOL	•
SAUNA	•
EXERCISE FACILITIES	•

Courtyard Crystal City

★★★½
2899 Jefferson Davis Highway
Arlington, VA 22202
☎ 703-549-3434
FAX 703-549-7440
TOLL FREE ☎ 800-847-4775
www.marriott.com

ROOM QUALITY	82
COST ($ = $50)	$$–
LOCATION	Virginia Suburbs
NO. OF ROOMS	272
PARKING	Self $12
ROOM SERVICE	•
BREAKFAST	•
ON-SITE DINING	•
POOL	•
SAUNA	•
EXERCISE FACILITIES	—

Courtyard Washington Northwest ★★★★

1900 Connecticut Avenue NW
Washington, DC 20009
☎ 202-332-9300
FAX 202-328-7039
TOLL FREE ☎ 800-321-2211
www.marriott.com

ROOM QUALITY	84
COST ($ = $50)	$$$$$
LOCATION	Dupont Circle/ Adams-Morgan
NO. OF ROOMS	147
PARKING	Valet $20
ROOM SERVICE	•
BREAKFAST	—
ON-SITE DINING	•
POOL	•
SAUNA	—
EXERCISE FACILITIES	•

Crowne Plaza National Airport ★★★½

1489 Jefferson Davis Highway
Arlington, VA 22202
☎ 703-416-1600
FAX 703-416-1651
TOLL FREE ☎ 800-2-CROWNE
www.cpnationalairport.com

ROOM QUALITY	76
COST ($ = $50)	$$$$$–
LOCATION	Virginia Suburbs
NO. OF ROOMS	308
PARKING	Self $15
ROOM SERVICE	•
BREAKFAST	•
ON-SITE DINING	•
POOL	•
SAUNA	—
EXERCISE FACILITIES	•

Crowne Plaza Silver Spring ★★★★

8777 Georgia Avenue
Silver Spring, MD 20910
☎ 301-589-0800
FAX 301-587-4791
TOLL FREE ☎ 800-972-3159
www.ichotelsgroup.com

ROOM QUALITY	86
COST ($ = $50)	$$$$$–
LOCATION	Maryland Suburbs
NO. OF ROOMS	220
PARKING	Self $9, valet $12
ROOM SERVICE	•
BREAKFAST	•
ON-SITE DINING	•
POOL	•
SAUNA	—
EXERCISE FACILITIES	•

DoubleTree Hotel Crystal City ★★★★

300 Army Navy Drive
Arlington, VA 22202
☎ 703-416-4100
FAX 703-416-4126
TOLL FREE ☎ 800-222-TREE
www.doubletree.com

ROOM QUALITY	83
COST ($ = $50)	$$$$–
LOCATION	Virginia Suburbs
NO. OF ROOMS	632
PARKING	Self $17, valet $22
ROOM SERVICE	•
BREAKFAST	—
ON-SITE DINING	•
POOL	•
SAUNA	—
EXERCISE FACILITIES	•

DoubleTree Hotel Tysons Corner ★★★½

7801 Leesburg Pike
Falls Church, VA 22043
☎ 703-893-1340
FAX 703-847-9520
TOLL FREE ☎ 800-222-TREE
www.doubletree-tysons.com

ROOM QUALITY	82
COST ($ = $50)	$$$$+
LOCATION	Virginia Suburbs
NO. OF ROOMS	409
PARKING	Self-Free
ROOM SERVICE	—
BREAKFAST	—
ON-SITE DINING	•
POOL	•
SAUNA	•
EXERCISE FACILITIES	•

DoubleTree Washington, D.C. ★★★★

1515 Rhode Island Avenue NW
Washington, DC 20036
☎ 202-232-7000
FAX 202-521-7103
TOLL FREE ☎ 800-222-TREE
www.doubletree.com

ROOM QUALITY	88
COST ($ = $50)	$$$$$+
LOCATION	Upper Northwest
NO. OF ROOMS	219
PARKING	Valet $26
ROOM SERVICE	•
BREAKFAST	•
ON-SITE DINING	•
POOL	—
SAUNA	—
EXERCISE FACILITIES	•

Courtyard Embassy Row ★★★½
1600 Rhode Island Avenue NW
Washington, DC 20036
☎ 202-293-8000
FAX 202-293-0085
TOLL FREE ☎ 800-321-2211
www.courtyardembassyrow.com

ROOM QUALITY	78
COST ($ = $50)	$$$$$$$
LOCATION	Dupont Circle/ Adams-Morgan
NO. OF ROOMS	156
PARKING	Valet $20
ROOM SERVICE	•
BREAKFAST	—
ON-SITE DINING	—
POOL	•
SAUNA	—
EXERCISE FACILITIES	•

Courtyard New Carrollton ★★★½
8330 Corporate Drive
Landover, MD 20785
☎ 301-577-3373
FAX 301-577-1780
TOLL FREE ☎ 800-321-2211
www.marriott.com

ROOM QUALITY	77
COST ($ = $50)	$$$$–
LOCATION	Maryland Suburbs
NO. OF ROOMS	150
PARKING	Free lot
ROOM SERVICE	•
BREAKFAST	—
ON-SITE DINING	•
POOL	•
SAUNA	—
EXERCISE FACILITIES	•

Courtyard Rosslyn ★★★½
1533 Clarendon Boulevard
Rosslyn, VA 22209
☎ 703-528-2222
FAX 703-528-1027
TOLL FREE ☎ 800-321-2211
www.marriott.com

ROOM QUALITY	78
COST ($ = $50)	$$$$$
LOCATION	Virginia Suburbs
NO. OF ROOMS	162
PARKING	Self $10
ROOM SERVICE	•
BREAKFAST	—
ON-SITE DINING	—
POOL	•
SAUNA	—
EXERCISE FACILITIES	•

Days Inn Alexandria ★★
110 S. Bragg Street
Alexandria, VA 22312
☎ 703-354-4950
FAX 703-642-2873
TOLL FREE ☎ 800-241-7382
www.daysinnalexandria.com

ROOM QUALITY	54
COST ($ = $50)	$$+
LOCATION	Virginia Suburbs
NO. OF ROOMS	200
PARKING	Free lot
ROOM SERVICE	—
BREAKFAST	Continental
ON-SITE DINING	—
POOL	•
SAUNA	—
EXERCISE FACILITIES	—

Days Inn Connecticut Avenue ★★½
4400 Connecticut Avenue NW
Washington, DC 20008
☎ 202-244-5600
FAX 202-244-6794
TOLL FREE ☎ 800-952-3060
www.choicehotels.com

ROOM QUALITY	63
COST ($ = $50)	$$–
LOCATION	Upper Northwest
NO. OF ROOMS	155
PARKING	Self $10
ROOM SERVICE	•
BREAKFAST	—
ON-SITE DINING	•
POOL	—
SAUNA	—
EXERCISE FACILITIES	•

DoubleTree Bethesda ★★★½
8120 Wisconsin Avenue
Bethesda, MD 20814
☎ 301-652-2000
FAX 301-664-7317
TOLL FREE ☎ 800-222-8733
www.doubletreebethesda.com

ROOM QUALITY	82
COST ($ = $50)	$$$$$$
LOCATION	Maryland Suburbs
NO. OF ROOMS	267
PARKING	Self $14
ROOM SERVICE	•
BREAKFAST	•
ON-SITE DINING	•
POOL	•
SAUNA	•
EXERCISE FACILITIES	•

Embassy Inn ★★½
1627 16th Street NW
Washington, DC 20009
☎ 202-234-7800
FAX 202-234-3309
TOLL FREE ☎ 800-423-9111
www.windsorembassyinns.com

ROOM QUALITY	60
COST ($ = $50)	$$$$–
LOCATION	Dupont Circle/ Adams-Morgan
NO. OF ROOMS	38
PARKING	Self $15
ROOM SERVICE	—
BREAKFAST	Continental
ON-SITE DINING	—
POOL	—
SAUNA	—
EXERCISE FACILITIES	—

Embassy Row Hilton ★★★★
2015 Massachusetts Avenue NW
Washington, DC 20036
☎ 202-265-1600
FAX 202-328-7526
TOLL FREE ☎ 800-HILTONS
www.hilton.com

ROOM QUALITY	85
COST ($ = $50)	$$$$$
LOCATION	Dupont Circle/ Adams-Morgan
NO. OF ROOMS	196
PARKING	Valet $30
ROOM SERVICE	•
BREAKFAST	—
ON-SITE DINING	•
POOL	•
SAUNA	—
EXERCISE FACILITIES	•

Embassy Suites Alexandria ★★★★
1900 Diagonal Road
Alexandria, VA 22314
☎ 703-684-5900
FAX 703-684-1403
TOLL FREE ☎ 800-EMBASSY
www.embassysuites.com

ROOM QUALITY	86
COST ($ = $50)	$$$$
LOCATION	Virginia Suburbs
NO. OF ROOMS	268
PARKING	Self $16
ROOM SERVICE	•
BREAKFAST	Cooked to order
ON-SITE DINING	•
POOL	•
SAUNA	—
EXERCISE FACILITIES	•

Hotel Information Chart *(continued)*

Embassy Suites Chevy Chase ★★★★
4300 Military Road NW
Washington, DC 20015
☎ 202-362-9300
FAX 202-686-3405
TOLL FREE ☎ 800-EMBASSY
www.embassysuitesdcmetro.com

ROOM QUALITY	84
COST ($ = $50)	$$$$-
LOCATION	Upper Northwest
NO. OF ROOMS	198
PARKING	Self $15
ROOM SERVICE	–
BREAKFAST	Cooked to order
ON-SITE DINING	•
POOL	•
SAUNA	–
EXERCISE FACILITIES	•

Embassy Suites Crystal City ★★★★
1300 Jefferson Davis Highway
Arlington, VA 22202
☎ 703-979-9799
FAX 703-920-5947
TOLL FREE ☎ 800-EMBASSY
www.embassysuites.com

ROOM QUALITY	84
COST ($ = $50)	$$$$$-
LOCATION	Virginia Suburbs
NO. OF ROOMS	267
PARKING	Self $17
ROOM SERVICE	•
BREAKFAST	Cooked to order
ON-SITE DINING	•
POOL	•
SAUNA	–
EXERCISE FACILITIES	•

Embassy Suites Downtown ★★★★
1250 22nd Street NW
Washington, DC 20037
☎ 202-857-3388
FAX 202-293-3173
TOLL FREE ☎ 800-EMBASSY
www.embassysuites.com

ROOM QUALITY	85
COST ($ = $50)	$$$$+
LOCATION	Dupont Circle/Adams-Morgan
NO. OF ROOMS	318
PARKING	Self $20
ROOM SERVICE	•
BREAKFAST	Cooked to order
ON-SITE DINING	•
POOL	•
SAUNA	–
EXERCISE FACILITIES	•

Four Seasons Hotel ★★★★½
2800 Pennsylvania Avenue NW
Washington, DC 20007
☎ 202-342-0444
FAX 202-944-2076
TOLL FREE ☎ 800-819-5053
www.fourseasons.com

ROOM QUALITY	91
COST ($ = $50)	$$$$$$$$$$$+
LOCATION	Georgetown
NO. OF ROOMS	183
PARKING	Valet $26
ROOM SERVICE	•
BREAKFAST	–
ON-SITE DINING	•
POOL	•
SAUNA	•
EXERCISE FACILITIES	•

Georgetown Inn ★★★★
1310 Wisconsin Avenue NW
Washington, DC 20007
☎ 202-333-8900
FAX 202-625-1744
TOLL FREE ☎ 888-587-2388
www.georgetowncollection.com

ROOM QUALITY	85
COST ($ = $50)	$$$
LOCATION	Georgetown
NO. OF ROOMS	96
PARKING	Valet $32
ROOM SERVICE	•
BREAKFAST	–
ON-SITE DINING	•
POOL	–
SAUNA	–
EXERCISE FACILITIES	•

Georgetown Suites Hotel ★★★★
1111 30th Street NW
Washington, DC
☎ 202-298-7800
FAX 202-333-5792
TOLL FREE ☎ 800-348-7203
www.georgetownsuites.com

ROOM QUALITY	83
COST ($ = $50)	$$$$-
LOCATION	Georgetown
NO. OF ROOMS	220
PARKING	Self $18
ROOM SERVICE	–
BREAKFAST	Continental
ON-SITE DINING	–
POOL	–
SAUNA	–
EXERCISE FACILITIES	•

Hawthorn Suites ★★★½
420 North Van Dorn Street
Alexandria, VA 22304
☎ 703-370-1000
FAX 703-751-1467
TOLL FREE ☎ 800-368-3339
www.hawthorn.com

ROOM QUALITY	78
COST ($ = $50)	$$$+
LOCATION	Virginia Suburbs
NO. OF ROOMS	185
PARKING	Free lot
ROOM SERVICE	–
BREAKFAST	Buffet
ON-SITE DINING	–
POOL	•
SAUNA	–
EXERCISE FACILITIES	•

Hay-Adams Hotel ★★★★½
One Lafayette Square NW
Washington, DC 20006
☎ 202-638-6600
FAX 202-638-2716
TOLL FREE ☎ 800-853-6807
www.hayadams.com

ROOM QUALITY	93
COST ($ = $50)	$$$$$$$$$-
LOCATION	Downtown
NO. OF ROOMS	145
PARKING	Valet $30
ROOM SERVICE	•
BREAKFAST	–
ON-SITE DINING	•
POOL	–
SAUNA	–
EXERCISE FACILITIES	–

Hilton Alexandria at Mark Center ★★★½
5000 Seminary Road
Alexandria, VA 22311
☎ 703-845-1010
FAX 703-845-7662
TOLL FREE ☎ 800-HILTONS
www.hilton.com

ROOM QUALITY	82
COST ($ = $50)	$$-
LOCATION	Virginia Suburbs
NO. OF ROOMS	496
PARKING	Self $13, valet $15
ROOM SERVICE	–
BREAKFAST	–
ON-SITE DINING	•
POOL	•
SAUNA	–
EXERCISE FACILITIES	•

Embassy Suites Tysons Corner ★★★★
8517 Leesburg Pike
Vienna, VA 22182
☎ 703-883-0707
FAX 703-760-9842
TOLL FREE ☎ 800-EMBASSY
www.embassysuites.com

ROOM QUALITY	86
COST ($ = $50)	$$$$
LOCATION	Virginia Suburbs
NO. OF ROOMS	232
PARKING	Free lot
ROOM SERVICE	•
BREAKFAST	Cooked to order
ON-SITE DINING	•
POOL	•
SAUNA	—
EXERCISE FACILITIES	•

Fairmont Washington, D.C. ★★★★
2401 M Street NW
Washington, DC 20037
☎ 202-429-2400
FAX 202-457-5010
TOLL FREE ☎ 800-257-7544
www.fairmont.com/washington

ROOM QUALITY	88
COST ($ = $50)	$$$$$+
LOCATION	Georgetown
NO. OF ROOMS	415
PARKING	Valet $27
ROOM SERVICE	•
BREAKFAST	—
ON-SITE DINING	•
POOL	•
SAUNA	•
EXERCISE FACILITIES	Fee $10

Four Points Sheraton Downtown ★★★
1201 K Street NW
Washington, DC 20005
☎ 202-289-7600
FAX 202-349-2215
TOLL FREE ☎ 888-625-5144
www.fourpointswashingtondc.com

ROOM QUALITY	74
COST ($ = $50)	$$$$$$—
LOCATION	Downtown
NO. OF ROOMS	265
PARKING	Valet $28
ROOM SERVICE	•
BREAKFAST	—
ON-SITE DINING	•
POOL	•
SAUNA	•
EXERCISE FACILITIES	•

Grand Hyatt Washington ★★★★
1000 H Street NW
Washington, DC 20001
☎ 202-582-1234
FAX 202-637-4781
TOLL FREE ☎ 800-233-1234
www.grandwashingtonhyatt.com

ROOM QUALITY	88
COST ($ = $50)	$$$$$$$$$—
LOCATION	Downtown
NO. OF ROOMS	888
PARKING	Self $20, valet $26
ROOM SERVICE	•
BREAKFAST	—
ON-SITE DINING	•
POOL	•
SAUNA	•
EXERCISE FACILITIES	•

Hamilton Crowne Plaza ★★★★½
1001 14th Street NW
Washington, DC 20005
☎ 202-682-0111
FAX 202-682-9525
TOLL FREE ☎ 800-980-6429
www.crowneplaza.com

ROOM QUALITY	90
COST ($ = $50)	$$$$
LOCATION	Downtown
NO. OF ROOMS	318
PARKING	Valet $28
ROOM SERVICE	•
BREAKFAST	—
ON-SITE DINING	•
POOL	—
SAUNA	—
EXERCISE FACILITIES	•

Hampton Inn Alexandria ★★★½
4800 Leesburg Pike
Alexandria, VA 22302
☎ 703-671-4800
FAX 703-671-2442
TOLL FREE ☎ 800-HAMPTON
www.hamptoninn.com

ROOM QUALITY	78
COST ($ = $50)	$$—
LOCATION	Virginia Suburbs
NO. OF ROOMS	130
PARKING	Free lot
ROOM SERVICE	•
BREAKFAST	Full
ON-SITE DINING	—
POOL	•
SAUNA	—
EXERCISE FACILITIES	•

Hilton Arlington and Towers ★★★★
950 North Stafford Street
Arlington, VA 22203
☎ 703-528-6000
FAX 703-528-4386
TOLL FREE ☎ 800-HILTONS
www.hilton.com

ROOM QUALITY	84
COST ($ = $50)	$$$$$$—
LOCATION	Virginia Suburbs
NO. OF ROOMS	208
PARKING	Self $15
ROOM SERVICE	•
BREAKFAST	—
ON-SITE DINING	•
POOL	—
SAUNA	—
EXERCISE FACILITIES	—

Hilton Garden Inn Washington Downtown ★★★½
815 14th Street NW
Washington, DC 20005
☎ 202-783-7800
FAX 202-783-7801
TOLL FREE ☎ 800-HILTONS
www.hiltongardeninn.com

ROOM QUALITY	77
COST ($ = $50)	$$$$$
LOCATION	Downtown
NO. OF ROOMS	300
PARKING	Valet $24
ROOM SERVICE	•
BREAKFAST	—
ON-SITE DINING	•
POOL	•
SAUNA	—
EXERCISE FACILITIES	•

Hilton of Silver Spring ★★★½
8727 Colesville Road
Silver Spring, MD 20910
☎ 301-589-5200
FAX 301-588-1841
TOLL FREE ☎ 800-445-8667
www.hilton.com

ROOM QUALITY	78
COST ($ = $50)	$$$
LOCATION	Maryland Suburbs
NO. OF ROOMS	263
PARKING	Valet $10
ROOM SERVICE	•
BREAKFAST	—
ON-SITE DINING	•
POOL	—
SAUNA	—
EXERCISE FACILITIES	•

Hotel Information Chart (continued)

Hilton Washington ★★★½
1919 Connecticut Avenue NW
Washington, DC 20009
☎ 202-483-3000
FAX 202-232-0438
TOLL FREE ☎ 800-HILTONS
www.hilton.com

ROOM QUALITY	80
COST ($ = $50)	$$$$$$
LOCATION	Dupont Circle/ Adams-Morgan
NO. OF ROOMS	1,119
PARKING	Self $23
ROOM SERVICE	•
BREAKFAST	—
ON-SITE DINING	•
POOL	•
SAUNA	—
EXERCISE FACILITIES	•

Holiday Inn Alexandria ★★★
2460 Eisenhower Avenue
Alexandria, VA 22314
☎ 703-960-3400
FAX 703-329-0953
TOLL FREE ☎ 800-972-3159
www.holidayinn.com

ROOM QUALITY	65
COST ($ = $50)	$$$
LOCATION	Virginia Suburbs
NO. OF ROOMS	196
PARKING	Free lot
ROOM SERVICE	•
BREAKFAST	—
ON-SITE DINING	•
POOL	•
SAUNA	—
EXERCISE FACILITIES	•

Holiday Inn Arlington ★★★½
4610 North Fairfax Drive
Arlington, VA 22203
☎ 703-243-9800
FAX 703-527-2677
TOLL FREE ☎ 800-HOLIDAY
www.hiarlington.com

ROOM QUALITY	78
COST ($ = $50)	$$$$–
LOCATION	Virginia Suburbs
NO. OF ROOMS	221
PARKING	Self $7, free on Fri. and Sat.
ROOM SERVICE	•
BREAKFAST	•
ON-SITE DINING	•
POOL	•
SAUNA	—
EXERCISE FACILITIES	•

Holiday Inn Georgetown ★★★½
2101 Wisconsin Avenue, NW
Washington, DC 20007
☎ 202-338-4600
FAX 202-338-4458
TOLL FREE ☎ 800-HOLIDAY
www.higeorgetown.com

ROOM QUALITY	78
COST ($ = $50)	$$$
LOCATION	Upper Northwest
NO. OF ROOMS	285
PARKING	Self $17
ROOM SERVICE	•
BREAKFAST	—
ON-SITE DINING	•
POOL	•
SAUNA	•
EXERCISE FACILITIES	•

Holiday Inn Hotel and Suites ★★★
625 First Street
Alexandria, VA 22314
☎ 703-548-6300
FAX 703-548-8032
TOLL FREE ☎ 800-972-3159
www.holidayinn.com

ROOM QUALITY	72
COST ($ = $50)	$$$$
LOCATION	Virginia Suburbs
NO. OF ROOMS	178
PARKING	Self $12
ROOM SERVICE	•
BREAKFAST	—
ON-SITE DINING	•
POOL	•
SAUNA	•
EXERCISE FACILITIES	•

Holiday Inn National Airport ★★★
2650 Jefferson Davis Highway
Arlington, VA 22202
☎ 703-684-7200
FAX 703-684-3217
TOLL FREE ☎ 800-972-3159
www.holidayinn.com

ROOM QUALITY	72
COST ($ = $50)	$$$$
LOCATION	Virginia Suburbs
NO. OF ROOMS	280
PARKING	Self $14
ROOM SERVICE	•
BREAKFAST	•
ON-SITE DINING	•
POOL	•
SAUNA	—
EXERCISE FACILITIES	Access with fee

Hotel Harrington ★★
436 11th Street
Washington, DC 20004
☎ 202-628-8140
FAX 202-393-2311
TOLL FREE ☎ 800-424-8532
www.hotel-harrington.com

ROOM QUALITY	50
COST ($ = $50)	$$+
LOCATION	Downtown
NO. OF ROOMS	242
PARKING	Self $10
ROOM SERVICE	—
BREAKFAST	—
ON-SITE DINING	•
POOL	—
SAUNA	—
EXERCISE FACILITIES	—

Hotel Helix ★★★★
1430 Rhode Island Avenue NW
Washington, DC 20005
☎ 202-462-9001
FAX 202-332-3519
TOLL FREE ☎ 800-706-1202
www.hotelhelix.com

ROOM QUALITY	89
COST ($ = $50)	$$–
LOCATION	Upper Northwest
NO. OF ROOMS	178
PARKING	Valet $29
ROOM SERVICE	•
BREAKFAST	Continental
ON-SITE DINING	•
POOL	—
SAUNA	—
EXERCISE FACILITIES	•

Hotel Lombardy ★★★½
2019 Pennsylvania Avenue NW
Washington, DC 20006
☎ 202-828-2600
FAX 202-872-0503
TOLL FREE ☎ 800-424-5486
www.hotellombardy.com

ROOM QUALITY	78
COST ($ = $50)	$$$$$–
LOCATION	Foggy Bottom
NO. OF ROOMS	134
PARKING	Valet $28
ROOM SERVICE	•
BREAKFAST	—
ON-SITE DINING	•
POOL	—
SAUNA	—
EXERCISE FACILITIES	•

Holiday Inn Capitol ★★★
550 C Street SW
Washington, DC 20024
☎ 202-479-4000
FAX 202-479-4353
TOLL FREE ☎ 800-972-3159
www.holidayinn.com

ROOM QUALITY	71
COST ($ = $50)	$$$$
LOCATION	Capitol Hill
NO. OF ROOMS	532
PARKING	Self $22
ROOM SERVICE	•
BREAKFAST	—
ON-SITE DINING	•
POOL	•
SAUNA	—
EXERCISE FACILITIES	•

Holiday Inn Central ★★★
1501 Rhode Island Avenue NW
Washington, DC 20005
☎ 202-483-2000
FAX 202-797-1078
TOLL FREE ☎ 800-972-3159
www.holidayinn.com

ROOM QUALITY	71
COST ($ = $50)	$$$$$–
LOCATION	Upper Northwest
NO. OF ROOMS	212
PARKING	Self $25
ROOM SERVICE	•
BREAKFAST	—
ON-SITE DINING	•
POOL	•
SAUNA	—
EXERCISE FACILITIES	•

Holiday Inn Chevy Chase ★★★
5520 Wisconsin Avenue
Chevy Chase, MD 20815
☎ 301-656-1500
FAX 301-656-5045
TOLL FREE ☎ 800-972-3159
www.holidayinn.com

ROOM QUALITY	68
COST ($ = $50)	$$–
LOCATION	Maryland Suburbs
NO. OF ROOMS	214
PARKING	Free lot and garage
ROOM SERVICE	•
BREAKFAST	•
ON-SITE DINING	•
POOL	•
SAUNA	—
EXERCISE FACILITIES	•

Holiday Inn on the Hill ★★★½
415 New Jersey Avenue NW
Washington, DC 20001
☎ 202-638-1616
FAX 202-638-0707
TOLL FREE ☎ 800-638-1116
www.hionthehilldc.com

ROOM QUALITY	80
COST ($ = $50)	$$$$$
LOCATION	Downtown
NO. OF ROOMS	343
PARKING	Self $25
ROOM SERVICE	•
BREAKFAST	—
ON-SITE DINING	—
POOL	•
SAUNA	—
EXERCISE FACILITIES	•

Holiday Inn Rosslyn at Key Bridge ★★★½
1900 North Fort Myer Drive
Arlington, VA 22209
☎ 703-807-2000
FAX 703-522-8864
TOLL FREE ☎ 888-465-4329
www.holidayinn.com

ROOM QUALITY	75
COST ($ = $50)	$$$$–
LOCATION	Virginia Suburbs
NO. OF ROOMS	307
PARKING	Self, free
ROOM SERVICE	•
BREAKFAST	—
ON-SITE DINING	•
POOL	•
SAUNA	—
EXERCISE FACILITIES	•

Hotel George ★★★★½
15 E Street NW
Washington, DC 20001
☎ 202-347-4200
FAX 202-346-4213
TOLL FREE ☎ 800-576-8331
www.hotelgeorge.com

ROOM QUALITY	94
COST ($ = $50)	$$$$–
LOCATION	Downtown
NO. OF ROOMS	139
PARKING	Valet $32
ROOM SERVICE	•
BREAKFAST	—
ON-SITE DINING	•
POOL	—
SAUNA	•
EXERCISE FACILITIES	•

Hotel Madera ★★★★
1310 New Hampshire Avenue NW
Washington, DC 20036
☎ 202-296-7600
FAX 202-293-2476
TOLL FREE ☎ 800-368-5691
www.hotelmadera.com

ROOM QUALITY	89
COST ($ = $50)	$$$$
LOCATION	Dupont Circle/ Adams-Morgan
NO. OF ROOMS	82
PARKING	Valet $28
ROOM SERVICE	•
BREAKFAST	—
ON-SITE DINING	•
POOL	—
SAUNA	—
EXERCISE FACILITIES	—

Hotel Monaco ★★★★
700 F Street NW
Washington, DC 20004
☎ 202-628-7177
FAX 202-628-7277
TOLL FREE ☎ 800-649-1202
www.monaco-dc.com

ROOM QUALITY	86
COST ($ = $50)	$$$$$–
LOCATION	Downtown
NO. OF ROOMS	184
PARKING	Valet $34
ROOM SERVICE	•
BREAKFAST	—
ON-SITE DINING	•
POOL	—
SAUNA	—
EXERCISE FACILITIES	•

Hotel Monticello ★★★½
1075 Thomas Jefferson Street NW
Washington, DC 20007
☎ 202-337-0900
FAX 202-333-6526
TOLL FREE ☎ 800-388-2410
www.monticellohotel.com

ROOM QUALITY	82
COST ($ = $50)	$$$$$$
LOCATION	Georgetown
NO. OF ROOMS	47
PARKING	Valet $25
ROOM SERVICE	—
BREAKFAST	Continental
ON-SITE DINING	—
POOL	—
SAUNA	—
EXERCISE FACILITIES	—

Hotel Information Chart (continued)

Hotel Palomar ★★★★½
2121 P Street NW
Washington, DC 20037
☎ 202-293-3100
FAX 202-857-0134
TOLL FREE ☎ 800-333-3333
www.hotelpalomar-dc.com

ROOM QUALITY	90
COST ($ = $50)	$$$$$$$$$–
LOCATION	Dupont Circle/Adams-Morgan
NO. OF ROOMS	325
PARKING	Valet $32
ROOM SERVICE	•
BREAKFAST	—
ON-SITE DINING	•
POOL	•
SAUNA	—
EXERCISE FACILITIES	•

Hotel Rouge ★★★★
1315 16th Street NW
Washington, DC 20036
☎ 202-232-8000
FAX 202-667-9827
TOLL FREE ☎ 800-738-1022
www.rougehotel.com

ROOM QUALITY	86
COST ($ = $50)	$$$$$$–
LOCATION	Dupont Circle/Adams-Morgan
NO. OF ROOMS	137
PARKING	Valet $27
ROOM SERVICE	•
BREAKFAST	—
ON-SITE DINING	•
POOL	—
SAUNA	—
EXERCISE FACILITIES	•

Hotel Topaz ★★★★½
1733 N Street NW
Washington, DC 20036
☎ 202-393-3000
FAX 202-785-9581
TOLL FREE ☎ 800-775-1202
www.topazhotel.com

ROOM QUALITY	90
COST ($ = $50)	$$$$$$$
LOCATION	Dupont Circle/Adams-Morgan
NO. OF ROOMS	99
PARKING	Valet $27
ROOM SERVICE	•
BREAKFAST	Buffet
ON-SITE DINING	•
POOL	—
SAUNA	—
EXERCISE FACILITIES	•

Hyatt Regency Capitol Hill ★★★★
400 New Jersey Avenue NW
Washington, DC 20001
☎ 202-737-1234
FAX 202-737-5773
TOLL FREE ☎ 800-233-1234
www.washingtonregency.hyatt.com

ROOM QUALITY	84
COST ($ = $50)	$$$$$$$
LOCATION	Downtown
NO. OF ROOMS	834
PARKING	Valet $33
ROOM SERVICE	•
BREAKFAST	—
ON-SITE DINING	•
POOL	•
SAUNA	—
EXERCISE FACILITIES	•

Hyatt Regency Crystal City ★★★★
2799 Jefferson Davis Highway
Arlington, VA 22202
☎ 703-418-1234
FAX 703-418-1289
TOLL FREE ☎ 800-233-1234
www.crystalcity.hyatt.com

ROOM QUALITY	89
COST ($ = $50)	$$$$$$
LOCATION	Virginia Suburbs
NO. OF ROOMS	685
PARKING	Valet $23
ROOM SERVICE	•
BREAKFAST	—
ON-SITE DINING	•
POOL	•
SAUNA	•
EXERCISE FACILITIES	•

J.W. Marriott Pennsylvania Avenue ★★★★
1331 Pennsylvania Avenue NW
Washington, DC 20004
☎ 202-393-2000
FAX 202-626-6991
TOLL FREE ☎ 800-228-9290
www.jwmarriottdc.com

ROOM QUALITY	88
COST ($ = $50)	$$$$$$$$$–
LOCATION	Downtown
NO. OF ROOMS	772
PARKING	Self $28
ROOM SERVICE	—
BREAKFAST	•
ON-SITE DINING	•
POOL	•
SAUNA	•
EXERCISE FACILITIES	•

L'Enfant Plaza Hotel ★★★★
480 L'Enfant Plaza SW
Washington, DC 20024
☎ 202-484-1000
FAX 202-646-4456
TOLL FREE ☎ 800-635-5065
www.lenfantplazahotel.com

ROOM QUALITY	86
COST ($ = $50)	$$$$$
LOCATION	National Mall
NO. OF ROOMS	370
PARKING	Valet $28
ROOM SERVICE	•
BREAKFAST	—
ON-SITE DINING	•
POOL	•
SAUNA	—
EXERCISE FACILITIES	•

Latham Hotel ★★★½
3000 M Street NW
Washington, DC 20007
☎ 202-726-5000
FAX 202-348-1800
TOLL FREE ☎ 800-LATHAM-1
www.georgetowncollection.com

ROOM QUALITY	78
COST ($ = $50)	$$$$
LOCATION	Georgetown
NO. OF ROOMS	143
PARKING	Valet $25
ROOM SERVICE	•
BREAKFAST	—
ON-SITE DINING	•
POOL	•
SAUNA	—
EXERCISE FACILITIES	•

M Street Hotel ★★★½
1143 New Hampshire Avenue NW
Washington, DC 20037
☎ 202-775-0800
FAX 202-331-9491
TOLL FREE ☎ 888-803-1298
www.marriott.com

ROOM QUALITY	82
COST ($ = $50)	$$$$+
LOCATION	Dupont Circle/Adams-Morgan
NO. OF ROOMS	352
PARKING	Valet $28
ROOM SERVICE	•
BREAKFAST	—
ON-SITE DINING	•
POOL	—
SAUNA	—
EXERCISE FACILITIES	•

Hotel Washington ★★★½
Pennsylvania Avenue NW at 15th
Washington, DC 20004
☎ 202-638-5900
FAX 202-638-1594
TOLL FREE ☎ 800-424-9540
www.hotelwashington.com

ROOM QUALITY	82
COST ($ = $50)	$$$$$–
LOCATION	Downtown
NO. OF ROOMS	345
PARKING	Self $28
ROOM SERVICE	•
BREAKFAST	—
ON-SITE DINING	•
POOL	•
SAUNA	•
EXERCISE FACILITIES	•

Hyatt Arlington ★★★★
1325 Wilson Boulevard
Arlington, VA 22209
☎ 703-525-1234
FAX 703-908-4790
TOLL FREE ☎ 800-233-1234
www.hyatt.com

ROOM QUALITY	87
COST ($ = $50)	$$–
LOCATION	Virginia Suburbs
NO. OF ROOMS	304
PARKING	Self $12, valet $14, weekends free
ROOM SERVICE	•
BREAKFAST	—
ON-SITE DINING	•
POOL	—
SAUNA	—
EXERCISE FACILITIES	•

Hyatt Regency Bethesda ★★★★
One Bethesda Metro Center
Bethesda, MD 20814
☎ 301-657-1234
FAX 301-657-6453
TOLL FREE ☎ 800-233-1234
www.bethesda.hyatt.com

ROOM QUALITY	85
COST ($ = $50)	$$$$$$–
LOCATION	Maryland Suburbs
NO. OF ROOMS	381
PARKING	Self $12–$15, valet $17–$20
ROOM SERVICE	•
BREAKFAST	•
ON-SITE DINING	•
POOL	•
SAUNA	—
EXERCISE FACILITIES	•

Jefferson Hotel ★★★★½
1200 16th Street NW
Washington, DC 20036
☎ 202-347-2200
FAX 202-331-7982
TOLL FREE ☎ 866-270-8102
www.thejeffersonwashingtondc.com

ROOM QUALITY	90
COST ($ = $50)	$$$$$$$$$
LOCATION	Downtown
NO. OF ROOMS	100
PARKING	Valet $28
ROOM SERVICE	•
BREAKFAST	—
ON-SITE DINING	•
POOL	—
SAUNA	—
EXERCISE FACILITIES	•

Jurys Normandy ★★★½
2118 Wyoming Avenue NW
Washington, DC 20008
☎ 202-483-1350
FAX 202-387-8241
TOLL FREE ☎ 800-424-3729
www.juryswashingtondc.com/
normandy_inn.htm

ROOM QUALITY	75
COST ($ = $50)	$$$$$–
LOCATION	Dupont Circle/ Adams-Morgan
NO. OF ROOMS	75
PARKING	Self $20
ROOM SERVICE	—
BREAKFAST	—
ON-SITE DINING	—
POOL	—
SAUNA	—
EXERCISE FACILITIES	—

Kalorama Guest House ★★★
1854 Mintwood Place NW
Washington, DC 20009
☎ 202-667-6369
FAX 202-319-1262
TOLL FREE ☎ 800-974-6450
www.kaloramaguesthouse.com

ROOM QUALITY	74
COST ($ = $50)	$$–
LOCATION	Dupont Circle/ Adams-Morgan
NO. OF ROOMS	29
PARKING	Self $15–$28
ROOM SERVICE	—
BREAKFAST	Continental
ON-SITE DINING	—
POOL	—
SAUNA	—
EXERCISE FACILITIES	—

Madison Hotel ★★★★
1177 15th Street NW
Washington, DC 20005
☎ 202-862-1600
FAX 202-785-1255
TOLL FREE ☎ 800-424-8578
www.loewshotels.com

ROOM QUALITY	87
COST ($ = $50)	$$$$$–
LOCATION	Downtown
NO. OF ROOMS	353
PARKING	Valet $28
ROOM SERVICE	•
BREAKFAST	—
ON-SITE DINING	•
POOL	—
SAUNA	•
EXERCISE FACILITIES	•

Mandarin Oriental ★★★★½
1330 Maryland Avenue SW
Washington, DC 20024
☎ 202-554-8588
FAX 202-787-6161
TOLL FREE ☎ 888-888 1778
www.mandarinoriental.com

ROOM QUALITY	93
COST ($ = $50)	$$$$$$$$$$–
LOCATION	National Mall
NO. OF ROOMS	400
PARKING	Valet $39
ROOM SERVICE	•
BREAKFAST	•
ON-SITE DINING	•
POOL	•
SAUNA	•
EXERCISE FACILITIES	•

Marriott Crystal City ★★★½
1999 Jefferson Davis Highway
Arlington, VA 22202
☎ 703-413-5500
FAX 703-413-0192
TOLL FREE ☎ 800-228-9290
www.marriott.com

ROOM QUALITY	80
COST ($ = $50)	$$$
LOCATION	Virginia Suburbs
NO. OF ROOMS	343
PARKING	Self $16
ROOM SERVICE	—
BREAKFAST	—
ON-SITE DINING	•
POOL	•
SAUNA	•
EXERCISE FACILITIES	•

Hotel Information Chart (continued)

Marriott Crystal Gateway ★★★★
1700 Jefferson Davis Highway
Arlington, VA 22202
☎ 703-920-3230
FAX 703-271-5212
TOLL FREE ☎ 800-228-9290
www.crystalgatewaymarriott.com

ROOM QUALITY	83
COST ($ = $50)	$$$$$$
LOCATION	Virginia Suburbs
NO. OF ROOMS	697
PARKING	Self $16, valet $22
ROOM SERVICE	•
BREAKFAST	Continental
ON-SITE DINING	•
POOL	•
SAUNA	—
EXERCISE FACILITIES	•

Marriott Hotel Bethesda ★★★★
5151 Pooks Hill Road
Bethesda, MD 20814
☎ 301-897-9400
FAX 301-897-0192
TOLL FREE ☎ 800-228-9290
www.marriott.com

ROOM QUALITY	83
COST ($ = $50)	$$+
LOCATION	Maryland Suburbs
NO. OF ROOMS	399
PARKING	Self $8, valet $12
ROOM SERVICE	•
BREAKFAST	—
ON-SITE DINING	•
POOL	•
SAUNA	•
EXERCISE FACILITIES	•

Marriott Hotel Key Bridge ★★★½
1401 Lee Highway
Arlington, VA 22209
☎ 703-524-6400
FAX 703-524-8964
TOLL FREE ☎ 800-228-9290
www.marriott.com

ROOM QUALITY	80
COST ($ = $50)	$$$$$$
LOCATION	Virginia Suburbs
NO. OF ROOMS	582
PARKING	Self $12
ROOM SERVICE	—
BREAKFAST	—
ON-SITE DINING	•
POOL	•
SAUNA	•
EXERCISE FACILITIES	•

Morrison House ★★★★
116 South Alfred Road
Alexandria, VA 22314
☎ 703-838-8000
FAX 703-684-6283
TOLL FREE ☎ 866-834-6628
www.morrisonhouse.com

ROOM QUALITY	87
COST ($ = $50)	$$$$$$+
LOCATION	Virginia Suburbs
NO. OF ROOMS	45
PARKING	Valet $20
ROOM SERVICE	•
BREAKFAST	—
ON-SITE DINING	•
POOL	—
SAUNA	—
EXERCISE FACILITIES	—

Morrison-Clark Inn ★★★★
1015 L Street NW
Washington, DC 20001
☎ 202-898-1200
FAX 202-289-8576
TOLL FREE ☎ 800-222-8474
www.morrisonclark.com

ROOM QUALITY	88
COST ($ = $50)	$$$$$$–
LOCATION	Upper Northwest
NO. OF ROOMS	54
PARKING	Valet $22
ROOM SERVICE	•
BREAKFAST	—
ON-SITE DINING	•
POOL	—
SAUNA	—
EXERCISE FACILITIES	•

Old Town Hotel ★★★½
480 King Street
Alexandria, VA 22314
☎ 703-549-6080
FAX 703-684-6508
TOLL FREE ☎ 800-368-5047
www.hotel-ot.com

ROOM QUALITY	82
COST ($ = $50)	$$–
LOCATION	Virginia Suburbs
NO. OF ROOMS	201
PARKING	Self $12
ROOM SERVICE	•
BREAKFAST	Continental
ON-SITE DINING	•
POOL	•
SAUNA	•
EXERCISE FACILITIES	•

Pentagon Lodge ★★½
2485 South Glebe Road
Arlington, VA 22206
☎ 703-979-4100
FAX 703-979-6120

ROOM QUALITY	58
COST ($ = $50)	$$+
LOCATION	Virginia Suburbs
NO. OF ROOMS	160
PARKING	Free lot
ROOM SERVICE	—
BREAKFAST	Continental
ON-SITE DINING	—
POOL	•
SAUNA	—
EXERCISE FACILITIES	—

Phoenix Park Hotel ★★★½
520 N. Capitol Street NW
Washington, DC 20001
☎ 202-638-6900
FAX 202-393-3236
TOLL FREE ☎ 800-824-5419
www.phoenixparkhotel.com

ROOM QUALITY	82
COST ($ = $50)	$$$$+
LOCATION	Capitol Hill
NO. OF ROOMS	149
PARKING	Valet $30
ROOM SERVICE	•
BREAKFAST	—
ON-SITE DINING	•
POOL	—
SAUNA	—
EXERCISE FACILITIES	•

Quality Inn College Park ★★★
7200 Baltimore Boulevard
College Park, MD 20740
☎ 301-276-1000
FAX 301-276-1111
TOLL FREE ☎ 877-424-6423
www.qualityinn.com

ROOM QUALITY	68
COST ($ = $50)	$$–
LOCATION	Maryland Suburbs
NO. OF ROOMS	154
PARKING	Free lot
ROOM SERVICE	—
BREAKFAST	Continental
ON-SITE DINING	—
POOL	•
SAUNA	•
EXERCISE FACILITIES	•

Marriott Metro Center ★★★½
775 12th Street NW
Washington, DC 20005
☎ 202-737-2200
FAX 202-347-5886
TOLL FREE ☎ 800-228-9290
www.metrocentermarriott.com

ROOM QUALITY	77
COST ($ = $50)	$$$$$$$$
LOCATION	Downtown
NO. OF ROOMS	456
PARKING	Self $22–$27, valet $22–$29
ROOM SERVICE	—
BREAKFAST	—
ON-SITE DINING	•
POOL	•
SAUNA	—
EXERCISE FACILITIES	•

Marriott Wardman Park Hotel ★★★★
2660 Woodley Road NW
Washington, DC 20008
☎ 202-328-2000
FAX 202-234-0015
TOLL FREE ☎ 800-228-9290
www.marriott.com

ROOM QUALITY	84
COST ($ = $50)	$$$$$$$$–
LOCATION	Upper Northwest
NO. OF ROOMS	1,335
PARKING	Self $23, valet $28
ROOM SERVICE	•
BREAKFAST	—
ON-SITE DINING	•
POOL	•
SAUNA	—
EXERCISE FACILITIES	•

Melrose Hotel ★★★★
2430 Pennsylvania Avenue NW
Washington, DC 20037
☎ 202-955-6400
FAX 202-955-5765
TOLL FREE ☎ 800-635-7673
www.melrosehotelwashington
dc.com

ROOM QUALITY	86
COST ($ = $50)	$$$$$$$$–
LOCATION	Georgetown
NO. OF ROOMS	240
PARKING	Valet $28
ROOM SERVICE	•
BREAKFAST	—
ON-SITE DINING	—
POOL	—
SAUNA	—
EXERCISE FACILITIES	•

Omni Shoreham Hotel ★★★★
2500 Calvert Street NW
Washington, DC 20008
☎ 202-234-0700
FAX 202-265-7972
TOLL FREE ☎ 888-444-6664
www.omnihotels.com

ROOM QUALITY	87
COST ($ = $50)	$$$$$$$$+
LOCATION	Upper Northwest
NO. OF ROOMS	834
PARKING	Self $23, valet $28
ROOM SERVICE	•
BREAKFAST	—
ON-SITE DINING	•
POOL	•
SAUNA	•
EXERCISE FACILITIES	Fee $10

One Washington Circle Hotel ★★★★
One Washington Circle NW
Washington, DC 20037
☎ 202-872-1680
FAX 202-887-4989
TOLL FREE ☎ 800-424-9671
www.onewashcirclehotel.com

ROOM QUALITY	87
COST ($ = $50)	$$$$$$$$$$
LOCATION	Foggy Bottom
NO. OF ROOMS	149
PARKING	Valet $21
ROOM SERVICE	•
BREAKFAST	—
ON-SITE DINING	•
POOL	•
SAUNA	—
EXERCISE FACILITIES	•

Park Hyatt ★★★★½
24th Street at M Street NW
Washington, DC 20037
☎ 202-789-1234
FAX 202-419-6795
TOLL FREE ☎ 800-233-1234
www.parkwashington.hyatt.com

ROOM QUALITY	93
COST ($ = $50)	$$$$$$$$
LOCATION	Georgetown
NO. OF ROOMS	223
PARKING	Valet $35
ROOM SERVICE	•
BREAKFAST	—
ON-SITE DINING	•
POOL	•
SAUNA	•
EXERCISE FACILITIES	•

Quality Inn Iwo Jima ★★★
1501 Arlington Boulevard
Arlington, VA 22209
☎ 703-524-5000
FAX 703-522-5484
TOLL FREE ☎ 877-424-6423
www.qualityinn.com

ROOM QUALITY	70
COST ($ = $50)	$$$$$–
LOCATION	Virginia Suburbs
NO. OF ROOMS	141
PARKING	Free lot
ROOM SERVICE	•
BREAKFAST	—
ON-SITE DINING	•
POOL	•
SAUNA	—
EXERCISE FACILITIES	•

Quincy Suites ★★★½
1823 L Street NW
Washington, DC 20036
☎ 202-223-4320
FAX 202-223-4320
TOLL FREE ☎ 800-424-2970
www.quincysuites.com

ROOM QUALITY	77
COST ($ = $50)	$$$$–
LOCATION	Downtown
NO. OF ROOMS	99
PARKING	Self $28
ROOM SERVICE	•
BREAKFAST	—
ON-SITE DINING	—
POOL	—
SAUNA	—
EXERCISE FACILITIES	—

Radisson Hotel Reagan National ★★★½
2020 Jefferson Davis Highway
Arlington, VA 22202
☎ 703-920-8600
FAX 703-920-2840
TOLL FREE ☎ 800-333-3333
www.radisson.com/arlingtonva

ROOM QUALITY	81
COST ($ = $50)	$$–
LOCATION	Virginia Suburbs
NO. OF ROOMS	251
PARKING	Self $10
ROOM SERVICE	•
BREAKFAST	—
ON-SITE DINING	•
POOL	•
SAUNA	—
EXERCISE FACILITIES	•

Hotel Information Chart (continued)

Radisson Plaza Hotel
Old Town ★★★½
901 North Fairfax Street
Alexandria, VA 22314
☎ 703-683-6000
FAX 703-683-7597
TOLL FREE ☎ 800-333-3333
www.radisson.com

ROOM QUALITY	80
COST ($ = $50)	$$$$$–
LOCATION	Virginia Suburbs
NO. OF ROOMS	253
PARKING	Self $12
ROOM SERVICE	•
BREAKFAST	—
ON-SITE DINING	—
POOL	•
SAUNA	—
EXERCISE FACILITIES	•

Red Roof Inn
Downtown ★★½
500 H Street NW
Washington, DC 20001
☎ 202-289-5959
FAX 202-682-9152
TOLL FREE ☎ 800-RED-ROOF
www.redroofinn.com

ROOM QUALITY	60
COST ($ = $50)	$$$+
LOCATION	Downtown
NO. OF ROOMS	197
PARKING	Self $20
ROOM SERVICE	—
BREAKFAST	—
ON-SITE DINING	•
POOL	—
SAUNA	•
EXERCISE FACILITIES	•

Renaissance Mayflower
Hotel ★★★★½
1127 Connecticut Avenue NW
Washington, DC 20036
☎ 202-347-3000
FAX 202-776-9182
TOLL FREE ☎ 800-228-7697
www.marriott.com

ROOM QUALITY	90
COST ($ = $50)	$$$$$
LOCATION	Downtown
NO. OF ROOMS	657
PARKING	Valet $28
ROOM SERVICE	•
BREAKFAST	—
ON-SITE DINING	—
POOL	—
SAUNA	—
EXERCISE FACILITIES	•

Residence Inn Vermont
Avenue ★★★½
1199 Vermont Avenue NW
Washington, DC 20005
☎ 202-898-1100
FAX 202-898-1110
TOLL FREE ☎ 800-331-3131
www.marriott.com

ROOM QUALITY	78
COST ($ = $50)	$$$$$$+
LOCATION	Downtown
NO. OF ROOMS	202
PARKING	Valet $20
ROOM SERVICE	—
BREAKFAST	Buffet
ON-SITE DINING	—
POOL	—
SAUNA	—
EXERCISE FACILITIES	•

Ritz-Carlton
Georgetown ★★★★½
3100 South Street NW
Washington, DC 20007
☎ 202-912-4100
FAX 202-912-4199
TOLL FREE ☎ 800-241-3333
www.ritzcarlton.com

ROOM QUALITY	92
COST ($ = $50)	$$$$$$$$
LOCATION	Georgetown
NO. OF ROOMS	86
PARKING	Valet $32
ROOM SERVICE	•
BREAKFAST	—
ON-SITE DINING	•
POOL	—
SAUNA	•
EXERCISE FACILITIES	•

Ritz-Carlton
Pentagon City ★★★★½
1250 South Hayes Street
Arlington, VA 22202
☎ 703-415-5000
FAX 703-415-5061
TOLL FREE ☎ 800-241-3333
www.ritzcarlton.com

ROOM QUALITY	95
COST ($ = $50)	$$$$$–
LOCATION	Virginia Suburbs
NO. OF ROOMS	366
PARKING	Valet $15
ROOM SERVICE	•
BREAKFAST	—
ON-SITE DINING	•
POOL	•
SAUNA	•
EXERCISE FACILITIES	•

Sheraton Crystal City
★★★½
1800 Jefferson Davis Highway
Arlington, VA 22202
☎ 703-486-1111
FAX 703-769-3970
TOLL FREE ☎ 888-625-5144
www.sheraton.com/crystalcity

ROOM QUALITY	79
COST ($ = $50)	$$$$$$$$–
LOCATION	Virginia Suburbs
NO. OF ROOMS	210
PARKING	Self $15
ROOM SERVICE	•
BREAKFAST	—
ON-SITE DINING	•
POOL	•
SAUNA	•
EXERCISE FACILITIES	•

Sheraton
National Hotel ★★★½
900 South Orme Street
Arlington, VA 22204
☎ 703-521-1900
FAX 703-271-6626
TOLL FREE ☎ 888-625-5144
www.sheratonnational.com

ROOM QUALITY	82
COST ($ = $50)	$$$$$
LOCATION	Virginia Suburbs
NO. OF ROOMS	408
PARKING	Self $16, valet $25
ROOM SERVICE	•
BREAKFAST	—
ON-SITE DINING	•
POOL	•
SAUNA	—
EXERCISE FACILITIES	•

Sheraton Premiere
Tysons Corner ★★★★½
8661 Leesburg Pike
Vienna, VA 22182
☎ 703-448-1234
FAX 703-610-8293
TOLL FREE ☎ 888-625-5144
www.starwoodhotels.com

ROOM QUALITY	90
COST ($ = $50)	$$$$$$$$–
LOCATION	Virginia Suburbs
NO. OF ROOMS	437
PARKING	Free lot
ROOM SERVICE	•
BREAKFAST	—
ON-SITE DINING	•
POOL	•
SAUNA	•
EXERCISE FACILITIES	•

Residence Inn Bethesda ★★★★
7335 Wisconsin Avenue
Bethesda, MD 20814
☎ 301-718-0200
FAX 301-718-0679
TOLL FREE ☎ 800-331-3131
www.residenceinnbethesda
hotel.com

ROOM QUALITY	83
COST ($ = $50)	$$$$$$$–
LOCATION	Maryland Suburbs
NO. OF ROOMS	187
PARKING	Self and valet $17
ROOM SERVICE	—
BREAKFAST	Buffet
ON-SITE DINING	—
POOL	•
SAUNA	•
EXERCISE FACILITIES	•

Residence Inn Dupont Circle ★★★½
2120 P Street NW
Washington, DC 20037
☎ 202-466-6800
FAX 202-466-9630
TOLL FREE ☎ 800-331-3131
www.marriott.com

ROOM QUALITY	81
COST ($ = $50)	$$$$$$+
LOCATION	Dupont Circle/ Adams-Morgan
NO. OF ROOMS	107
PARKING	Self $23
ROOM SERVICE	•
BREAKFAST	Buffet
ON-SITE DINING	•
POOL	•
SAUNA	—
EXERCISE FACILITIES	•

Residence Inn Pentagon City ★★★★
550 Army Navy Drive
Arlington, VA 22202
☎ 703-413-6630
FAX 703-418-1751
TOLL FREE ☎ 800-331-3131
www.marriott.com

ROOM QUALITY	84
COST ($ = $50)	$$$
LOCATION	Virginia Suburbs
NO. OF ROOMS	299
PARKING	Self $16
ROOM SERVICE	•
BREAKFAST	Buffet
ON-SITE DINING	•
POOL	•
SAUNA	—
EXERCISE FACILITIES	•

Ritz-Carlton Washington, D.C. ★★★★★
1150 22nd Street NW
Washington, DC 20037
☎ 202-835-0500
FAX 202-835-1588
TOLL FREE ☎ 800-241-3333
www.ritzcarlton.com

ROOM QUALITY	98
COST ($ = $50)	$$$$$$$
LOCATION	Dupont Circle/ Adams-Morgan
NO. OF ROOMS	300
PARKING	Valet $20
ROOM SERVICE	•
BREAKFAST	—
ON-SITE DINING	•
POOL	•
SAUNA	•
EXERCISE FACILITIES	Access $12

River Inn ★★★★½
924 25th Street NW
Washington, DC 20037
☎ 202-337-7600
FAX 202-337-6520
TOLL FREE ☎ 888-874-0100
www.theriverinn.com

ROOM QUALITY	94
COST ($ = $50)	$$$$$–
LOCATION	Foggy Bottom
NO. OF ROOMS	126
PARKING	Valet $23
ROOM SERVICE	•
BREAKFAST	—
ON-SITE DINING	—
POOL	—
SAUNA	—
EXERCISE FACILITIES	•

Savoy Suites Hotel ★★★½
2505 Wisconsin Avenue NW
Washington, DC 20007
☎ 202-337-9700
FAX 202-337-3644
TOLL FREE ☎ 800-944-5377
www.savoysuites.com

ROOM QUALITY	77
COST ($ = $50)	$$$$$
LOCATION	Upper Northwest
NO. OF ROOMS	150
PARKING	Free garage
ROOM SERVICE	•
BREAKFAST	—
ON-SITE DINING	•
POOL	•
SAUNA	•
EXERCISE FACILITIES	Access

Sheraton Suites Alexandria ★★★★
801 North St. Asaph Street
Alexandria, VA 22314
☎ 703-836-4700
FAX 703-548-4518
TOLL FREE ☎ 888-625-5144
www.starwoodhotels.com

ROOM QUALITY	88
COST ($ = $50)	$$$$$$$$
LOCATION	Virginia Suburbs
NO. OF ROOMS	247
PARKING	Self $18
ROOM SERVICE	•
BREAKFAST	—
ON-SITE DINING	•
POOL	•
SAUNA	•
EXERCISE FACILITIES	•

Sofitel Lafayette ★★★★½
806 15th Street NW
Washington, DC 20005
☎ 202-730-8800
FAX 202-730-8500
TOLL FREE ☎ 800-763-4835
www.sofitel.com

ROOM QUALITY	90
COST ($ = $50)	$$$$$$+
LOCATION	Downtown
NO. OF ROOMS	237
PARKING	Valet $35
ROOM SERVICE	•
BREAKFAST	•
ON-SITE DINING	•
POOL	—
SAUNA	—
EXERCISE FACILITIES	•

St. Gregory Luxury Hotel & Suites ★★★★
2033 M Street, Washington, DC 20036 ☎ 202-530-3600; FAX 202-446-6770; TOLL FREE ☎ 800-829-5034; www.capitalhotelswdc.com/ StGregoryHotelWDC_com

ROOM QUALITY	86
COST ($ = $50)	$$$$$+
LOCATION	Dupont Circle/ Adams-Morgan
NO. OF ROOMS	154
PARKING	Valet $18.50 weekday, $25 weekend
ROOM SERVICE	•
BREAKFAST	•
ON-SITE DINING	•
POOL	—
SAUNA	—
EXERCISE FACILITIES	•

Hotel Information Chart (continued)

St. Regis ★★★★½
923 16th Street & K Street NW
Washington, DC 20006
☎ 202-638-2626
FAX 202-683-4231
TOLL FREE ☎ 800-562-5661
www.starwoodhotels.com

ROOM QUALITY	90
COST ($ = $50)	$$$$$$$$$
LOCATION	Downtown
NO. OF ROOMS	193
PARKING	Valet $28
ROOM SERVICE	•
BREAKFAST	—
ON-SITE DINING	•
POOL	•
SAUNA	—
EXERCISE FACILITIES	•

State Plaza Hotel ★★★½
2117 E Street NW
Washington, DC 20037
☎ 202-861-8200
FAX 202-659-8601
TOLL FREE ☎ 800-424-2859
www.stateplaza.com

ROOM QUALITY	76
COST ($ = $50)	$$$$
LOCATION	Foggy Bottom
NO. OF ROOMS	279
PARKING	Self $30
ROOM SERVICE	•
BREAKFAST	—
ON-SITE DINING	•
POOL	—
SAUNA	—
EXERCISE FACILITIES	•

Tabard Inn ★★½
1739 N Street NW
Washington, DC 20036
☎ 202-785-1277
FAX 202-785-6173
www.tabardinn.com

ROOM QUALITY	64
COST ($ = $50)	$$$
LOCATION	Dupont Circle/Adams-Morgan
NO. OF ROOMS	40
PARKING	Free lot
ROOM SERVICE	—
BREAKFAST	Continental
ON-SITE DINING	•
POOL	—
SAUNA	—
EXERCISE FACILITIES	Free access

Washington National Airport Hilton ★★★★
2399 Jefferson Davis Highway
Arlington, VA 22202
☎ 703-418-6800
FAX 703-418-3763
TOLL FREE ☎ 800-HILTONS
www.hilton.com

ROOM QUALITY	83
COST ($ = $50)	$$$
LOCATION	Virginia Suburbs
NO. OF ROOMS	386
PARKING	Valet $20
ROOM SERVICE	•
BREAKFAST	—
ON-SITE DINING	•
POOL	•
SAUNA	—
EXERCISE FACILITIES	•

Washington Plaza Hotel ★★★
10 Thomas Circle NW
Washington, DC 20005
☎ 202-842-1300
FAX 202-371-9602
TOLL FREE ☎ 800-424-1140
www.washingtonplazahotel.com

ROOM QUALITY	67
COST ($ = $50)	$$$+
LOCATION	Downtown
NO. OF ROOMS	340
PARKING	Self $23
ROOM SERVICE	•
BREAKFAST	—
ON-SITE DINING	•
POOL	•
SAUNA	—
EXERCISE FACILITIES	•

Washington Renaissance Hotel ★★★★
999 Ninth Street NW
Washington, DC 20001
☎ 202-898-9000
FAX 202-289-0947
TOLL FREE ☎ 888-236-2427
www.marriott.com

ROOM QUALITY	88
COST ($ = $50)	$$$$–
LOCATION	Downtown
NO. OF ROOMS	807
PARKING	Self $22, valet $27
ROOM SERVICE	•
BREAKFAST	•
ON-SITE DINING	•
POOL	•
SAUNA	•
EXERCISE FACILITIES	•

Westin Embassy Row ★★★★½
2100 Massachusetts Avenue NW
Washington, DC 20008
☎ 202-293-2100
FAX 202-293-0641
TOLL FREE ☎ 866-716-8117
www.westin.com

ROOM QUALITY	90
COST ($ = $50)	$$$$$$
LOCATION	Dupont Circle/Adams-Morgan
NO. OF ROOMS	206
PARKING	Valet $28
ROOM SERVICE	•
BREAKFAST	—
ON-SITE DINING	•
POOL	—
SAUNA	—
EXERCISE FACILITIES	•

Westin Grand ★★★★½
2350 M Street NW
Washington, DC 20037
☎ 202-429-0100
FAX 202-429-9759
TOLL FREE ☎ 888-937-8461
www.westin.com

ROOM QUALITY	94
COST ($ = $50)	$$$$$$$–
LOCATION	Georgetown
NO. OF ROOMS	263
PARKING	Valet $28
ROOM SERVICE	•
BREAKFAST	—
ON-SITE DINING	•
POOL	•
SAUNA	•
EXERCISE FACILITIES	•

Willard Inter-Continental ★★★★½
1401 Pennsylvania Avenue NW
Washington, DC 20004
☎ 202-628-9100
FAX 202-637-7326
TOLL FREE ☎ 800-980-6429
www.intercontinental.com

ROOM QUALITY	92
COST ($ = $50)	$$$$$$$$+
LOCATION	Downtown
NO. OF ROOMS	334
PARKING	Valet $28
ROOM SERVICE	•
BREAKFAST	—
ON-SITE DINING	•
POOL	—
SAUNA	—
EXERCISE FACILITIES	•

Tysons Corner Marriott ★★★½
8028 Leesburg Pike
Vienna, VA 22182
☎ 703-734-3200
FAX 703-734-5763
TOLL FREE ☎ 800-228-9290
www.marriott.com

ROOM QUALITY	80
COST ($ = $50)	$$
LOCATION	Virginia Suburbs
NO. OF ROOMS	390
PARKING	Free lot
ROOM SERVICE	—
BREAKFAST	—
ON-SITE DINING	•
POOL	•
SAUNA	•
EXERCISE FACILITIES	•

Washington Court Hotel ★★★★
525 New Jersey Avenue NW
Washington, DC 20001
☎ 202-628-2100
FAX 202-879-7918
TOLL FREE ☎ 800-321-3010
www.washingtoncourthotel.com

ROOM QUALITY	84
COST ($ = $50)	$$$$$$$$$–
LOCATION	Downtown
NO. OF ROOMS	267
PARKING	Valet $26
ROOM SERVICE	•
BREAKFAST	—
ON-SITE DINING	•
POOL	•
SAUNA	—
EXERCISE FACILITIES	•

Washington Marriott Hotel ★★★½
1221 22nd St. and M Street NW
Washington, DC 20037
☎ 202-872-1500
FAX 202-872-1424
TOLL FREE ☎ 800-393-3053
www.marriottwashington.com

ROOM QUALITY	82
COST ($ = $50)	$$$$+
LOCATION	Dupont Circle/ Adams-Morgan
NO. OF ROOMS	417
PARKING	Self $23
ROOM SERVICE	•
BREAKFAST	—
ON-SITE DINING	•
POOL	•
SAUNA	•
EXERCISE FACILITIES	•

Washington Suites Alexandria ★★★★
100 South Reynolds Street
Alexandria, VA 22304
☎ 703-370-9600
FAX 703-370-0467
TOLL FREE ☎ 877-736-2500
www.washingtonsuitesalexandria.com

ROOM QUALITY	83
COST ($ = $50)	$$$$+
LOCATION	Virginia Suburbs
NO. OF ROOMS	225
PARKING	Free lot
ROOM SERVICE	•
BREAKFAST	Continental
ON-SITE DINING	•
POOL	•
SAUNA	—
EXERCISE FACILITIES	•

Washington Suites Georgetown ★★★★
2500 Pennsylvania Avenue
Washington, DC 20037
☎ 202-333-8060; FAX 202-955-5765; TOLL FREE ☎ 877-736-2500
www.washingtonsuitesgeorgetown.com

ROOM QUALITY	87
COST ($ = $50)	$$$$$$$+
LOCATION	Georgetown
NO. OF ROOMS	124
PARKING	Valet $25
ROOM SERVICE	—
BREAKFAST	Continental
ON-SITE DINING	—
POOL	—
SAUNA	—
EXERCISE FACILITIES	•

Watergate Hotel ★★★★½
2650 Virginia Avenue NW
Washington, DC 20037
☎ 202-965-2300
FAX 202-337-7915
TOLL FREE ☎ 800-289-1555
www.watergatehotel.com

ROOM QUALITY	94
COST ($ = $50)	$$$$–
LOCATION	Foggy Bottom
NO. OF ROOMS	250
PARKING	Valet $26
ROOM SERVICE	•
BREAKFAST	—
ON-SITE DINING	•
POOL	•
SAUNA	•
EXERCISE FACILITIES	•

Windsor Park Hotel ★★½
2116 Kalorama Road NW
Washington, DC 20008
☎ 202-483-7700
FAX 202-332-4547
TOLL FREE ☎ 800-247-3064
www.windsorparkhotel.com

ROOM QUALITY	56
COST ($ = $50)	$$$
LOCATION	Dupont Circle/ Adams-Morgan
NO. OF ROOMS	43
PARKING	Street, free
ROOM SERVICE	—
BREAKFAST	Continental
ON-SITE DINING	—
POOL	—
SAUNA	—
EXERCISE FACILITIES	—

Wyndham Washington ★★★★
1400 M Street NW
Washington, DC 20005
☎ 202-429-1700
FAX 202-785-0786
TOLL FREE ☎ 800-WYNDHAM
www.wyndham.com

ROOM QUALITY	88
COST ($ = $50)	$$$$$
LOCATION	Downtown
NO. OF ROOMS	400
PARKING	Valet $26
ROOM SERVICE	•
BREAKFAST	—
ON-SITE DINING	•
POOL	•
SAUNA	—
EXERCISE FACILITIES	—

PART THREE

VISITING WASHINGTON *on* BUSINESS

NOT ALL VISITORS ARE HEADED *for the* MALL

WHILE MOST OF THE 21 MILLION people who come to Washington each year are tourists, not everyone visiting the city has an itinerary centered around the National Mall. In fact, almost 1.5 million visitors are convention-goers attending shows at the **Washington Convention Center,** located in downtown Washington. In addition, as the seat of the United States government, the city draws another 4.5 million visitors from around the world who fly in to conduct business with both federal agencies and a wide array of private organizations headquartered here.

The city is also a center of higher education. The District is home to **George Washington University, Georgetown University, American University, Howard University,** and the **Catholic University of America,** among others. As a result, Washington attracts a lot of visiting academics, college administrators, and students and their families.

In many ways, the problems facing business visitors on their first trip to Washington don't differ much from the problems of folks in town intent on hitting the major tourist attractions. People visiting on business need to locate a hotel that's convenient, want to avoid the worst of the city's traffic, face the same problems getting around an unfamiliar city, must figure out how to buy a Metro ticket, and want to know the locations of the best restaurants. This book can help.

For the most part, though, business visitors aren't nearly as flexible about the timing of their visit as folks who pick Washington as a vacation destination. While we advise that the best times for coming to D.C. are spring and fall, the necessities of business may dictate that January is when you pull into town—or, even worse, early April, when the city is mobbed for the Japanese-cherry-blossom festivities.

convention center concourses a, b, and c

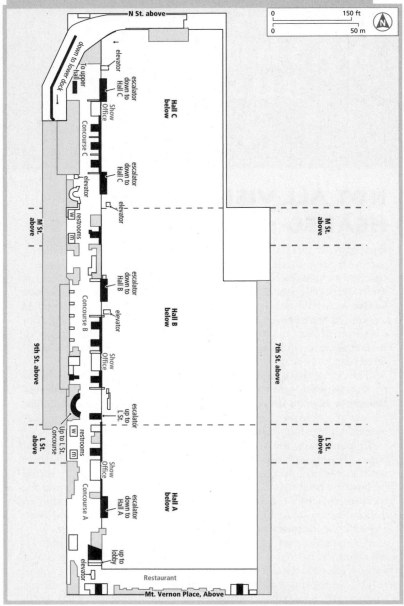

convention center level two

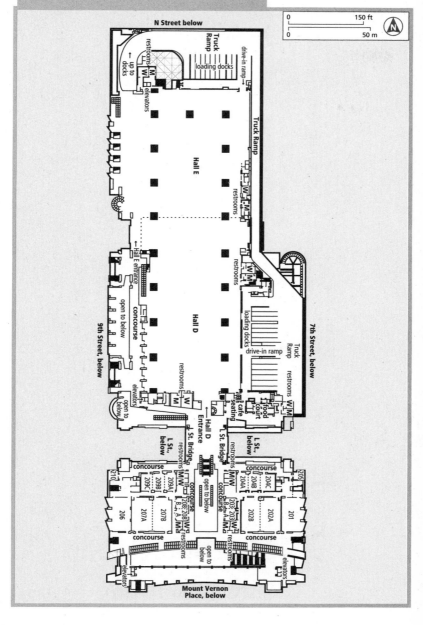

convention center level three

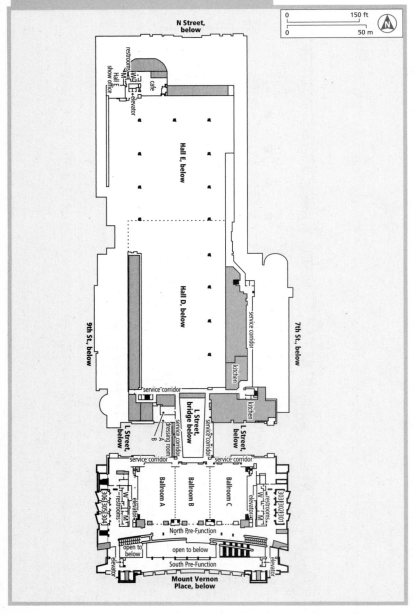

convention center street level

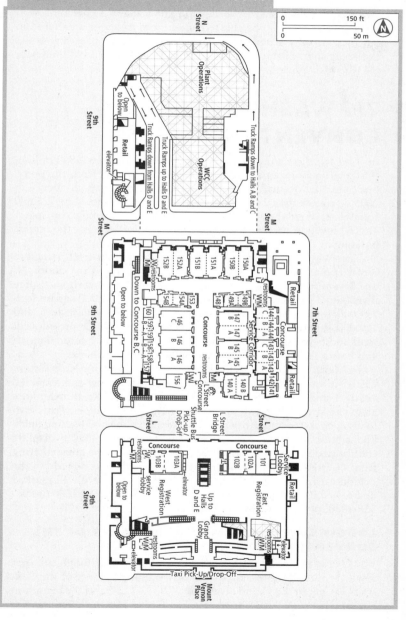

Yet much of the advice and information presented in the *Unofficial Guide* is as valuable to business visitors as it is to tourists. As for our recommendations on seeing the city's many sights . . . who knows? Perhaps you'll be able to squeeze a morning or an afternoon out of your busy schedule, grab this book, and spend a few hours exploring some of the attractions that draw the other 15 million people who visit Washington each year.

The WASHINGTON CONVENTION CENTER

IN THE FALL OF 1998, ground was broken for a new $800-million Washington Convention Center, located two blocks from the previous center at Mount Vernon Square. The building, which opened in 2003, has more than 2 million square feet of space, including 725,000 square feet of exhibit space, 500,000 square feet of contiguous space, and 70 meeting rooms totaling 150,000 square feet. It's the largest building in D.C.

The Washington Convention Center is a four-level structure located on a 17-acre site bounded by Mount Vernon Place, Ninth, N, and Seventh streets NW. The center contains 56 meeting rooms (some divisible), 3 ballrooms, and 5 exhibit halls with 151,000 square feet, 194,000 square feet, 128,000 square feet, 111,000 square feet, and 119,000 square feet of space, respectively. The Center provides all food and beverage services on the premises, including catered meals and brand restaurants like Wolfgang Puck's and Starbucks.

For both exhibitors and attendees, the Washington Convention Center is an excellent site for a meeting or trade show and attracted nearly 1 million visitors in its first year. Large and small exhibitors alike can set up their exhibits with a minimum of effort. Forty-two loading docks and huge bay doors make unloading and loading quick and simple for large displays arriving by truck. Smaller displays transported in vans and cars are unloaded in the same area, entering from N Street. Equipment can be carried or wheeled directly to the exhibit area. The exhibit areas and meeting rooms are well marked and easy to find. For more information, call ☎ 202-789-1600 or 800-368-9000, or visit **www.dcconvention.com.**

LODGING WITHIN WALKING DISTANCE OF THE CONVENTION CENTER

WHILE PARTICIPANTS IN CITYWIDE conventions lodge all over town, a couple of hotels are within easy walking distance of the Convention Center: the Grand Hyatt (☎ 202-582-1234) and the Hamilton Crowne Plaza (☎ 202-682-0111). The Grand Hyatt, directly across the street from the Center, features 900 rooms and 65 suites. The Hamilton Crowne Plaza, two blocks away at Metro Center, has 318 rooms, each supplied with a minibar, and 40 suites.

Other hotels within a few blocks of the Washington Convention Center are:

HOTEL	ROOMS	SUITES	DISTANCE
Marriott at Metro Center	456	3	1 block
Red Roof Inn Downtown	197	none	3 blocks
J.W. Marriott Hotel	772	23	4 blocks
Willard InterContinental	307	33	8 blocks

See "Tips for Business Travelers" on page 41 for more information on lodging.

PARKING AT THE CONVENTION CENTER

WHILE THERE'S NO PARKING in the Washington Convention Center itself, the surrounding area offers 15 parking lots and garages within a three-block walk. Daily rates run as high as $10 but average around $7.

The Mount Vernon Square/Seventh Street–Convention Center Metro stop is on the Yellow Line and connects directly with Ronald Reagan Washington National Airport. The Metro Center stop on the Red Line is three stops from Union Station, making it convenient for people coming in by train. Metro Center can be entered from the Grand Hyatt Hotel's lobby, directly across the street from the Convention Center.

CABS AND SHUTTLES TO THE CONVENTION CENTER

LARGE, CITYWIDE CONVENTIONS OFTEN PROVIDE complimentary bus service from major hotels to the Convention Center. If you are staying at a smaller hotel and wish to use the shuttle bus, walk to the nearest large hotel on the shuttle route. In addition, cabs are relatively cheap and plentiful in Washington. The Metro, D.C.'s subway system, is clean, safe, and fast; the nearest stations are Metro Center and Mount Vernon Square–Convention Center, both about two blocks from the Convention Center. See Part Five, Getting Around Washington (page 113), for more.

LUNCH ALTERNATIVES FOR CONVENTION AND TRADE-SHOW ATTENDEES

PRICES OF FOOD FROM THE CONVENTION CENTER'S food service are on the high side, but convention attendees needn't feel trapped: plenty of good eating establishments are within a few blocks. Among those near and nice enough to entertain a prospective client are: **Bobby Van's Grill**

A Convention Calendar

The city's considerable convention business (1.5 million delegates in 2004) can make it hard to get a hotel room in and around the city. Use the following list of major 2007 and 2008 convention dates to plan your trip to Washington.

2007

DATES	CONVENTION/EVENT	ATTENDEES
Jan 13–14	NBC4 Health and Fitness Expo	72,000
Jan 23–28	Washington Auto Show	Public
Feb 3–6	American Academy of Dermatology	15,000
Feb 15–19	Washington Boat Show	Public
Feb 20–22	Satellite 2007	6,000
Feb 25–28	Washington Gift Show	6,000
Mar 8–11	Washington Home and Garden Show	Public
Mar 17	JAMFest Cheer and Dance Event	5,000
Mar 20–22	FOSE	20,000
Mar 25–28	National Postal Forum	8,000
Mar 30–Apr 1	International Franchise Show	9,000
Apr 12–14	International Window Coverings Expo	8,000
Apr 16–18	American Association of Neurological Surgeons	6,000
Apr 29–May 2	Federation of American Societies for Experimental Biology	13,000
May 9–13	GovSec, U.S. Law and Ready!	5,500
May 19–24	Digestive Disease Week	15,000
May 26–27	United House of Prayer Memorial Service	5,000
May 27	Black Lesbian and Gay Pride Day	10,000
June 3–6	Society of Nuclear Medicine	7,000
June 23–26	American Library Association	26,000
June 29–July 2	American Baptist Churches USA	4,500
July 6–7	Telugu Association of North America Biennial Convention	10,000
July 14–17	American Veterinary Medical Association Annual Convention	7,500
July 24–25	Cable and Television Telecommunications Association for Marketing	4,000
Aug 5–8	Washington Gift Show	6,000

DATES	CONVENTION/EVENT	ATTENDEES
Sept 16–19	American Academy of Otolaryngology	10,000
Sept 26–29	Congressional Black Caucus Foundation	5,000
Oct 8–10	Association of the United States Army	20,000
Oct 15–17	American Society for Reproductive Medicine	5,500
Oct 21–22	Transcatheter Cardiovascular Therapeutics Annual Meeting	13,000
Oct 28–30	American Academy of Periodontology	5,500
Nov 4–7	American Public Health Association	14,000
Nov 14–15	Government Video Technology Expo	7,000
Dec 2–5	American Society for Cell Biology Annual Convention	8,000
2008		
Mar 4–6	Credit Union National Association	4,000
Mar 16–19	Society of Interventional Radiology	4,000
Apr 11–13	International Franchise Show	Public
May 4–8	American Psychiatric Association	15,000
May 15–17	Internal Medicine 2008	12,000
May 27–29	NAFSA: Association of International Educators Annual Convention	5,800
June 2–4	American Israel Public Affairs Committee	4,000
June 30–July 4	National Education Association	17,000
July 13–18	Alpha Kappa Alpha Sorority	10,000
July 29–31	American Association for Clinical Chemistry	17,000
Aug 6–9	American Association of Diabetes Educators	7,000
Sept 4–6	AARP National Member Conference	8,000
Sept 17–20	National Black MBA Association	15,000
Sept 24–27	Congressional Black Caucus Foundation	5,000
Oct 6–8	Association of the United States Army	20,000
Oct 13–16	Transcatheter Cardiovascular Therapeutics Annual Meeting	12,000
Oct 26–28	Infectious Diseases Society of America and American Society for Microbiology Joint Meeting	20,000
Nov 16–18	Society for Neuroscience	23,000

(201 New York Avenue NW; ☎ 202-589-1504), the New Orleans–style **Acadiana** (901 New York Avenue NW; ☎ 202-719-8848), and the surf-and-turf **Finn and Porter** (900 Tenth Street NW; ☎ 202-719-1600). However, if you have a little more time to walk (or jump the subway), the Convention Center is only five or six blocks from the many choices of Penn Quarter; see the list in Part Eight, Dining and Restaurants, for more suggestions.

PART FOUR

ARRIVING *and* GETTING ORIENTED

◄ COMING *into the* CITY

BY CAR

IF YOU DRIVE, you will most likely arrive on one of three freeways: Interstate 95 (I-95) from the north, I-95 from the south, or I-70 from the northwest. Other routes that converge in Washington are I-66 from the west (which links with I-81 in Virginia's Shenandoah Valley), US 50 (which hooks up with Annapolis, Maryland, US 301, and Maryland's Eastern Shore), and the Baltimore-Washington Parkway, which parallels I-95 between the two cities' beltways.

All these routes have one common link: they connect with Washington's Capital Beltway, a ribbon of concrete encircling the city. Now for an introduction to how unfriendly D.C. freeways can be to unsuspecting motorists: Part of the Beltway is numbered both I-95 and I-495. Why? Since I-95 doesn't cut directly through Washington (the way it does in Richmond to the south and Baltimore to the north), it's rerouted along the southern half of the Beltway. It's quite confusing to visitors, and it's only the first of many Washington driving horrors you'll encounter.

Drivers coming from the north and I-70 and headed downtown should take the Beltway to the Baltimore-Washington Parkway and exit south. Bear right onto New York Avenue where the Parkway splits; it goes straight to downtown, near Union Station.

From the south and west, motorists can take either I-66 or I-395 (what I-95 becomes after it crosses inside the Beltway). Both get you across the Potomac and into D.C. near the center of the tourist hubbub.

Our advice to drivers unfamiliar with Washington: Sit down with a map before you leave home and carefully trace out the route to your destination. If you need to make a phone call or two for directions, do it then. And don't try to fight the weekday rush-hour traffic (6:30 to 10 a.m. and 2:30 to 7 p.m.).

washington, d.c., and vicinity

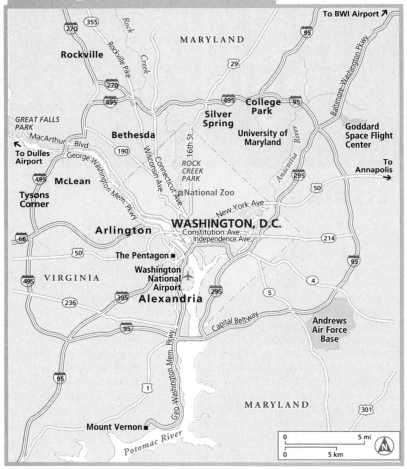

BY PLANE

RONALD REAGAN WASHINGTON NATIONAL AIRPORT While Washington officially has three major airports, this is the most convenient by far for domestic flyers, just a few miles south of the city on the Virginia side of the Potomac. Don't ask a friend to pick you up—parking is terrible at this cramped facility. A courtesy van service can whisk you into town from the Virginia side of the Potomac.

A $1-billion, 1-million-square-foot main terminal that opened in the summer of 1997 wiped out National's notorious reputation as a cramped, hard-to-get-in-and-out-of airport. The terminal features seamless connection between ground transportation, parking, buses, and D.C.'s subway. It also boasts a Legal Sea Foods, Ruby Tuesday, and Matsutake Japanese Restaurant as well as many quick-stop eateries, 32 elevators, 26 escalators, 12 baggage carousels, dozens of retail stores, and a great view of the nation's capital across the Potomac River. Along with 6,500 new parking spaces, new roadways, and expanded curb space and travel lanes (eight lanes for lower-level baggage claims, five lanes for upper-level ticket counters), this newest facility makes things much easier for travelers.

Nearly 5,000 parking spaces are housed in the parking garage directly across from the terminal and are reached via moving sidewalks. Two Metro mezzanines connect D.C.'s subway system to the terminal via two pedestrian bridges spanning the airport's roads. Two ground-transportation centers located on the baggage claim level provide information on Metro, taxi service, SuperShuttle vans, and rental cars.

Cab fares to nearby downtown Washington are reasonable ($9 to $19). **SuperShuttle** shared-service vans leave every 15 (or fewer) minutes to any destination in the D.C. area. Fares range from $18 to $22 to any address in Washington and from $12 to more than $30 in the Virginia and Maryland suburbs. Three SuperShuttle ticket counters are located at National; look for the "Washington Flyer/SuperShuttle" signs posted throughout the airport. For more information, exact fares, and reservations for return pick-up to National, call ☎ 800-BLUE VAN (258-3826) or go to **www.supershuttle.com.**

WASHINGTON-DULLES INTERNATIONAL AIRPORT Foreign flights arrive at Dulles, although AirTran (formerly ValuJet) and Western Pacific have increased the airport's domestic traffic volume considerably in the last few years. Reflecting that growth is Dulles's expansion of the main terminal, which doubled the size of the building to 1.1 million square feet. Yet Dulles remains the least convenient of the three airports serving Washington. Located in the rolling Virginia countryside beyond the suburbs, Dulles is about a 45-minute drive from downtown—longer during rush hour. Use the Dulles Access Road, which connects with the Capital Beltway and I-66.

From the gate, go to the lower level and claim your baggage at the baggage carousels. Then proceed out of the terminal on the ground

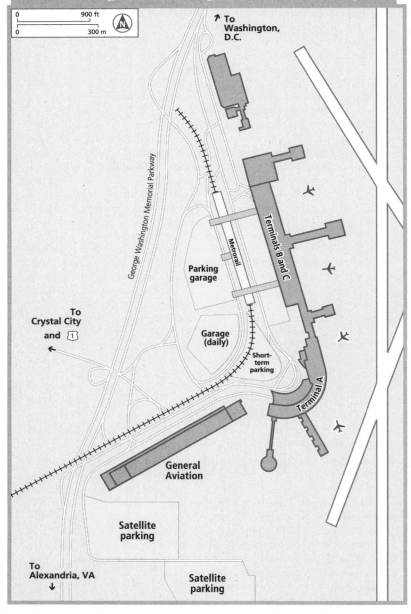

ronald reagan washington national airport

0   900 ft
0   300 m

To
Washington,
D.C.

George Washington Memorial Parkway

Metrorail

Parking
garage

Terminals B and C

To
Crystal City
and 1

Garage
(daily)

Short-
term
parking

Terminal A

General
Aviation

Satellite
parking

To
Alexandria, VA

Satellite
parking

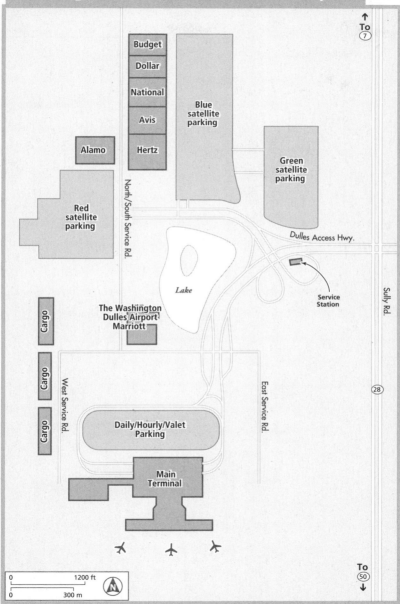

washington-dulles international airport

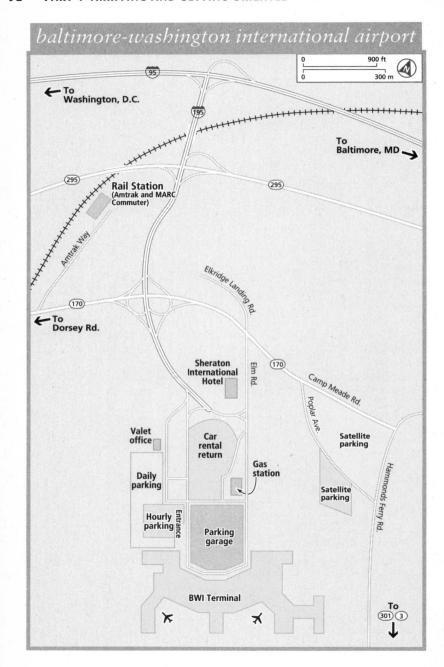

baltimore-washington international airport

level to the curb, where you can meet someone picking you up or find ground transportation out of the airport. The **Washington Flyer** shuttle to the West Falls Church Metro station leaves about every 30 minutes weekdays ($8 one-way, $14 round-trip) and every 30 minutes on weekends; it's a 22-minute bus trip to the subway station. SuperShuttle shared-ride vans will take you anywhere in the D.C. metropolitan area; there's usually about a 30-minute wait and fares range from $7 to more than $40 to the downtown area (typically $22 for the first person and $10 for each additional person). For more information, exact fares, and reservations for pickup for your return trip to Dulles, call SuperShuttle at ☎ 800-BLUE VAN (258-3826) or go to **www.supershuttle.com.** Cab fare to downtown D.C. can run more than $50 one-way.

THURGOOD MARSHALL BALTIMORE-WASHINGTON INTERNATIONAL
BWI, as it's generally referred to, is located ten miles south of Baltimore's Inner Harbor. It's about a 50-minute drive from downtown Washington; allow lots more time during rush hour. From the gate area, descend to the luggage pickup belts, which are located next to the ground-level doors. If someone is picking you up, they can meet you outside the baggage claim area at the curb. SuperShuttle offers van service to the Washington Convention Center in downtown Washington. Vans leave on the hour from 6 a.m. to 7 p.m. daily; the fare is $31 per person one-way (children under age 6 ride free). Tickets are sold at the ground transportation desk on the lower level in Pier C. No reservations are required for service from the airport to downtown D.C.; for reservations for the return trip to BWI or for more information, call ☎ 800-BLUE VAN (258-3826) or go to **www .supershuttle.com.** Cab fares to downtown D.C. start at around $55 one-way. In addition, BWI offers train service to Washington's Union Station via MARC commuter trains on weekdays (cheap) and Amtrak on weekends and holidays (expensive).

BY TRAIN

UNION STATION, LOCATED NEAR CAPITOL HILL, is the central Amtrak connecting point in Washington. From here, trains go out all over the country. For most routes you can choose either a speedy Acela Express, Metroliner, or a regular train. Once inside the newly restored train station, you can jump on the Metro, located on the lower level. But not so fast! The station itself is full of delights—small shops, cafes, and even a cinema complex. To reach cabs, limousines, buses, and open-air tour trolleys, walk through Union Station's magnificent Main Hall to the main entrance.

A GEOGRAPHIC OVERVIEW
of WASHINGTON

CITY AND TWO STATES

WASHINGTON, D.C., IS A CITY of more than 500,000 people, located near the southern end of the East Coast megalopolis stretching from Boston to Richmond. George Washington chose the city's site where the Anacostia River flows into the Potomac, upriver from his Mount Vernon plantation. Maryland and Virginia donated wedges of land from both sides of the Potomac to make the 100-square-mile diamond called the District of Columbia. In 1846, Virginia snatched its lands back; today, the planned city of Washington sits on the former Maryland acreage on the river's east bank.

Washington proper is surrounded by bustling, congested suburbs. Across the Potomac, Arlington County, the town of Alexandria, and Fairfax County crowd D.C. from the south and west, while the Maryland counties of Montgomery and Prince Georges surround Washington's northwestern and eastern borders. All the suburbs surrounding D.C. are experiencing exponential growth. Rockville, for example, a few miles north of the D.C. line, has become Maryland's second-largest city, after Baltimore. Loudoun County, west of Fairfax County, is the fastest-growing and, by some estimates, wealthiest county in the nation.

Washington's most important geographical feature, the Potomac River, is a natural impediment to both tourists and suburban commuters. The few bridges that cross the river from Virginia to Washington are rush-hour bottlenecks. While driving across the border to the Maryland suburbs is nominally easier, D.C.'s intense traffic and concentration of government and tourist sites near the river make for a long trek into Maryland.

D.C.'S STREET PLAN

WHILE WASHINGTON'S REPUTATION as a tough city to get around in is well deserved—at least for first-time visitors—the city's layout is actually fairly logical. Downtown streets are arranged in a grid, with numbered streets running north–south and lettered streets going east–west. The loose cannons in the scheme are streets named after states, which cut across the grid diagonally and meet in traffic circles that are the nemesis of Washington drivers.

Our advice: Ignore the state-named streets on your map and you'll discover the underlying logic of the system. If your destination is, in fact, on a street named after a state, the underlying grid of number- and letter-named streets will get you there and can even help you locate your block. An example: A popular destination for both tourists

unofficial **TIP**
The two blocks of Pennsylvania Avenue immediately in front of the White House are closed to vehicles.

NAVIGATING THE CITY. . .

- Confused by Washington's quadrant street addresses—Northeast, Southeast, Northwest, Southwest? Relax. Virtually everything that interests tourists is in Northwest.

- If it looks like you'll be riding Metro twice or more a day, purchase a one-day pass for $6.50, and you won't have to worry about figuring out fares (you'll save money, too). If you plan to use both the subway and bus system—or if you intend to park a car at a Metro station (except on weekends or federal holidays)—get a SmarTrip card instead.

- Is Georgetown or Adams-Morgan on your itinerary? Metro doesn't go there, and parking is beyond lousy—so take a cab instead. They're cheap and plentiful in D.C.

- If you ignore our advice and drive to Washington, do yourself a favor: Map out your route in advance, avoid rush hour on weekdays, and arrive early on weekends.

and power seekers is 1600 Pennsylvania Avenue NW. Because this well-known street snakes a course from the poor neighborhoods of Southeast Washington through downtown and into Georgetown, pinpointing an exact address is tough. The clue, however, is in the street address: the White House is near the intersection of Pennsylvania Avenue and 16th Street.

FINDING YOUR WAY

ONCE YOU GET THE HANG OF IT, finding your way around Washington is a snap. You'll have a head start if you know the basics of how D.C. is arranged. The roughly diamond-shaped city's four corners point north, south, east, and west. Inside the diamond, Washington is laid out in a rectilinear, gridlike plan and divided into four pie-wedge-shaped quadrants: Northwest (NW), Northeast (NE), Southwest (SW), and Southeast (SE); in the center of the pie is the U.S. Capitol building. Separating the quadrants and running in compass directions from the Capitol are North Capitol Street, East Capitol Street, and South Capitol Street. What happened to West Capitol Street? It's the Mall, which runs west from the Capitol to the Potomac River.

Within each quadrant, numbered streets run north–south, and lettered streets run east–west. Addresses on lettered streets give a clue to the numbered cross street at the end of the block. For example, the National Building Museum, at 401 F Street NW, is located on F Street between Fourth and Fifth streets NW.

Surprise: Washington has four First Streets, four E Streets, and so on, one for each quadrant. As a result, addresses must bear designations such as NW to prevent utter confusion. The good news for short-term visitors is that they can ignore the quadrants: virtually all tourist sights, hotels, restaurants, and nightlife are in Northwest Washington. Northeast and Southeast Washington, with the exception of the middle-class enclave of Capitol Hill, are predominantly poor and less commercially developed, while tiny Southwest is mostly middle class.

Avenues are named after states (Connecticut, Massachusetts, Wisconsin, etc.) and cut diagonally across the street grid. Some are major thoroughfares and do a good job of disrupting the traffic pattern. Downtown, the avenues meet at circles and squares, the most noteworthy of which are:

- **Dupont Circle** (Connecticut, Massachusetts, and New Hampshire avenues)

- **Washington Circle** (New Hampshire and Pennsylvania avenues)

- **Scott Circle** (Massachusetts and Rhode Island avenues, and 16th Street)

- **Mount Vernon Square** (Massachusetts and New York avenues)

Here's a rundown of some major roads that visitors will encounter in the city:

- **Pennsylvania Avenue** runs from Southeast and Capitol Hill through downtown and into Georgetown. The two blocks of Pennsylvania Avenue immediately in front of the White House are closed to vehicles.

- **Wisconsin Avenue** starts in Georgetown and leads north to the Maryland suburbs.

- **Connecticut Avenue** runs from Lafayette Square, in front of the White House, through Dupont Circle, past the National Zoo, and into Chevy Chase, Maryland.

- **16th Street NW** heads due north from the White House through Adams-Morgan and merges with Georgia Avenue in the Maryland suburbs.

- **K Street NW** is a major east–west downtown business artery running from the Convention Center area to the Georgetown waterfront.

- **Constitution** and **Independence avenues** run east–west on either side of the Mall.

- **New York Avenue** is a major artery that runs from the White House to Northeast Washington and turns into US 50 and the Baltimore-Washington Parkway.

- **14th Street SW** is a major point of access to and egress from the Virginia suburbs.

- **Massachusetts Avenue** runs from east of Union Station through Dupont Circle, up Embassy Row, and past Washington National Cathedral and American University on its way to Maryland.

THINGS *the* NATIVES ALREADY KNOW

WHERE THERE'S SMOKE, THERE'S THE FEDS

IF YOU HAVEN'T ALREADY REALIZED IT, WASHINGTON—that is, the District of Columbia—is predominantly public territory. And since the federal government has finally figured out that indoor tobacco smoke is as hard on art, archival materials, and even infrastructure and support services as it is on the human body, smoking is prohibited in all public facilities, including, but not limited to: federal buildings, including all the Smithsonian museums (and all other museums as well), memorials, and federal offices; Metrorail and Metrobus, as well as most smaller transit services, including tour buses and trolleys; performing-arts venues and educational facilities, cinemas, the Verizon Center, and other indoor arenas; airports and train terminals; stores and shopping malls; restaurants; and hotel lobbies (and most hotel restrooms). Most open-air facilities—football and baseball stadiums, for instance—have restricted, designated smoking areas.

Consequently, if you are a habitual smoker, you'll need to factor that in to your itineraries, or at least calculate where and when you can take a butt break. And that's not a bathroom joke.

THE METRO: AN INTRODUCTION

The first section of Washington's clean, modern, safe, and efficient subway system opened in 1976, just in time for the nation's bicentennial celebrations. As the five-line system has expanded over the years, the rave reviews keep coming. All of the stations follow the same brown-and-beige color scheme, with high, curved ceilings made of square concrete panels that fade into the distance. Monotonous, maybe, but the stations are safe and make the lives of visitors infinitely easier.

unofficial **TIP**
In contrast to New York's subway system, food and drink are prohibited on the Metro.

The trains themselves are clean, quiet, carpeted, virtually crime free (except for those kids who can't resist noshing on board), and air-conditioned. They run so often that carrying a schedule isn't really necessary; just remember that trains run more frequently at rush hours (5 to 10 a.m. and 2:30 to 7 p.m. than at other times—as much as ten minutes more frequently). With two notable exceptions (trendy Georgetown and hip Adams-Morgan), the Metro delivers visitors within a comfortable walking distance of everywhere they might want to go inside the city and into the suburbs.

Even if, like a lot of Americans, you're not comfortable with the idea of relying on public transportation, Washington provides a strong argument for seriously reconsidering your love affair with your car. The

Metro system is easy, even fun, to ride. There's really no excuse *not* to use it. Later, in Part Five (page 113), we include a chapter on how.

TAXIS

WASHINGTON'S CAB FARES ARE LOW, but the fare system is weird: fares are based on zones, not a meter. You can go two blocks from one zone to another and be charged more than for a 12-block ride within one zone. It helps to know the zones.

Washington has more cabs per capita than any other American city. But other than for schlepping your luggage to and from National Airport or Union Station, or dining out in subway-free Georgetown and Adams-Morgan, cabs are superfluous, thanks to the Metro. Take the train instead.

In our experience, Washington cabbies are polite and friendly. Yet it's a good idea to ask for a receipt at the beginning of the ride, just to let the driver know that you're not some inexperienced out-of-towner and you won't tolerate being charged for a roundabout route through many zones. Most sightseeing attractions and hotels are in Zone 1. (The strange hows, whats, and wheres of taxi travel in D.C. are discussed in more detail in Part Five, Getting around Washington, page 113.)

TRAFFIC

IF AT ALL POSSIBLE, AVOID DRIVING during your stay in Washington. If you arrive by car, make sure your hotel has parking and is either within walking distance to a Metro station (more on that in Part Five) or offers convenient shuttles to one. Park your car and, with few exceptions, don't plan on moving it until you leave.

Here's why: driving in Washington is infuriating, and trying to park your car near major tourist sites and government buildings is usually hopeless. The city is a bewildering mix of traffic circles, diagonal boulevards, and one-way streets that change direction depending on the time of day. To make matters worse, some avenues change names for no apparent reason. And the volume of traffic? The *Washington Post* doesn't call its regular traffic column "Dr. Gridlock" for nothing.

One last note: You'll see a lot of cars with cute red, white, and blue license plates imprinted with the word "Diplomatic." The driver of such a car is associated with a foreign embassy and has diplomatic immunity from many local laws—including traffic violations. Give these cars a wide berth. (We cover driving in more detail in Part Five, Getting around Washington, page 113.)

THE NEIGHBORHOODS

ARGUABLY, WASHINGTON IS THE MOST important city in the world. When most people think of D.C., they conjure up an image of the Mall, anchored by the U.S. Capitol at the east end and the Lincoln

Memorial on the other. On its east end alone, the Mall features at least 11 major museums and attractions. In the center is the Washington Monument, with the White House just to the north.

While there's much to see and do on the Mall, visitors who don't get beyond the two-mile strip of green are missing a lot of what this vibrant, international city has to offer: brick sidewalks in front of charming colonial-era row houses in Georgetown, the bohemian cafes of Adams-Morgan, the stately town houses and mansions near Dupont Circle, the glitter and overflowing street life in the "new downtown" of Penn Quarter, or the "New U," U Street NW around 14th Street. At the very least, a foray off the Mall can elevate your trip beyond the level of an educational grade-school field trip and give you a taste of the lively city itself. All the neighborhoods that follow are safe for visitors to explore on foot, except where noted. For more information on neighborhoods, see page 8.

The Southwest Waterfront

A fascinating array of private yachts is on view in Washington's waterfront area, a stretch along Maine Avenue that features marinas, seafood restaurants, and the Wharf Seafood Market, where visitors can sample fresh fish and Chesapeake Bay delicacies such as oysters on the half shell. Here's where you can take a scenic river cruise to Mount Vernon on the *Potomac Spirit*. It's easy to get to the waterfront: take the subway to the Waterfront Metro station.

Capitol Hill

The neighborhood surrounding the Capitol is a mix of residential and commercial, with plenty of restored town houses and trendy bars. Called "The Hill" by natives, here congressional staffers, urban homesteaders, and lower-middle-class people commingle—sometimes not so successfully: street crime can be a problem in the northeast parts in particular. Blocks can change character abruptly from one end to the other, but if you don't wander far from the busier commercial areas you'll be okay.

Downtown

Directly north of the Mall is "old downtown," an area undergoing a renaissance symbolized by the Verizon Center and the popular International Spy Museum. In recent years, spiffed up and promoted as the Penn Quarter, it has experienced an unimaginable renaissance. It's a neighborhood full of department stores, government office buildings (including the FBI), shops, street vendors, hotels, restaurants, two Smithsonian museums, Ford's Theatre, a tiny Chinatown, and the Washington Convention Center. To the west is "new downtown," the glittery glass-and-steel office buildings where D.C.'s legions of lobbyists and lawyers do their thing. Both areas offer visitors plenty of choices for shopping, dining, and sightseeing.

Foggy Bottom

Located west of the White House, Foggy Bottom got its name from the swampy land on which it was built. Today, it's home to George Washington University, the U.S. Department of State ("Foggy Bottom" is journalese for "State"), the Kennedy Center, and the Watergate. Closer to the Mall, massive government office complexes such as the Department of the Interior and the Federal Reserve crowd the White House.

Georgetown

A river port long before Washington was built, Georgetown is now the epitome of swank. From a distance, Georgetown is immediately identifiable by its skyline of spires. The neighborhood of restored town houses is filled with crowded bars and shops, and the streets pulse with crowds late into the night. An overflow of suburban teens on weekends makes for traffic congestion that's intense, even by Washington standards; but it also makes for fabulous people-watching and late-night shopping. Georgetown University marks the neighborhood's western edge. The Chesapeake & Ohio Canal and its famous towpath begin in Georgetown (at the east end, behind the Four Seasons Hotel) and follow the Potomac River upstream for 184 miles to Cumberland, Maryland, with many options for recreation (see Part Eleven, Exercise and Recreation, for suggestions).

Adams-Morgan

An ethnic neighborhood with a heavy emphasis on the Hispanic and African, Adams-Morgan is where young and cool bohemians migrated after the price of real estate zoomed around Dupont Circle in the 1970s and 1980s. While it doesn't offer much in the way of large museums or monuments, the neighborhood is full of ethnic restaurants, eclectic shops, and nightclubs. Parking, alas, is a severe problem. But since the nearest subway stop is Woodley Park–National Zoo–Adams-Morgan—an eight- to ten-minute walk over the Rock Creek Park bridge—your best bet might be to take a cab.

Dupont Circle

Dupont Circle is the center of one of the city's most fashionable neighborhoods, where you'll find elegantly restored town houses, boutiques, restaurants, cafes, bookstores, and art galleries. A stroll down Embassy Row (along Massachusetts Avenue) leads past sumptuous embassies and chancelleries, as well as some of Washington's best visitor attractions: Anderson House, the Phillips Collection, Woodrow Wilson House, and the Islamic Center. You can recognize an embassy by the national coat-of-arms or flag; a pack of reporters and TV cameras may indicate that international unrest has erupted somewhere in the world.

Rock Creek Park

It's not a neighborhood but a managed forest in the heart of Washington well worth knowing about. Hikers, joggers, inline skaters, equestrians, mountain bikers, and anyone wishing an escape from the city can get away here. In the summer, it's ten degrees cooler than the rest of the city.

Upper Northwest

Here's where the Washington National Cathedral, the National Zoo, the Hillwood Museum, the city's best private schools, and its wealthiest citizens are found. Without clear boundaries to separate them, Tenleytown, Glover Park, Woodley Park, and Cleveland Park are full of Victorian houses that are homes to members of Congress, rich lobbyists, and attorneys.

unofficial **TIP**
Attention, joggers: Upper Northwest is where you go for a nighttime run.

Anacostia

The city's first suburb today sits in the midst of a war zone of drive-by shootings, drug dealing, and random violence. When Washington was labeled the "Murder Capital of the U.S.," the reference was to a large swath of Northeast and Southeast Washington across the Anacostia River from downtown. While Anacostia is well off the beaten tourist path, there are two attractions visitors should take the time to explore: Cedar Hill, the home of 19th-century abolitionist Frederick Douglass (scheduled to emerge from a lengthy restoration in 2007); and the Smithsonian's Anacostia Museum. Either drive or ride special tourist buses (not public transportation) to visit these attractions. There are ambitious plans underway for the Anacostia riverfront, including a new professional soccer arena that will face the new baseball stadium on the opposite shore.

CUSTOMS AND PROTOCOL

DRESS In spite of its status as a world capital, Washington is a fairly relaxed town under the surface. The city's laid-back Southern heritage and the vestiges of an inferiority complex relative to older East Coast cities mean that Washingtonians, by the way they dress and socialize, aren't an ostentatious crowd. While it's becoming a little more fashion conscious, it's still fairly conservative.

Tourists have diplomatic immunity from this dreary dress code, however, so long as they stick to tourist territory. In daytime and around the major tourist areas, it's perfectly okay to look apart: if it's hot, wear a T-shirt and bermudas as you stroll the Mall with three cameras around your neck.

For forays up Connecticut Avenue and into Georgetown, though, leave the cameras and loud Hawaiian print shirts in your hotel room. The crowds are better dressed and hipper, and if you don't follow suit, you'll really stand out in the crowd. And even if your dinner restaurant doesn't require a jacket, you'll look less the rube if you wear one. Likely enough, you'll appreciate it once the AC kicks in.

EATING IN RESTAURANTS Washington, as an international city, is full of inexpensive ethnic restaurants—Ethiopian, Thai, Vietnamese, Chinese, Japanese, West African, Lebanese, Greek, Afghani . . . the list goes on. Most are casual and you needn't feel intimidated about unfamiliar menus—just ask the waiter or waitress for a recommendation. Since Washington doesn't take itself as seriously as, say, New York, you won't be made to feel uncomfortable in a Japanese restaurant if you request a spoon for your miso soup. Expect to be elbow to elbow with other diners in the crowded eateries, since dining out seems to be a full-time activity for a lot of Washingtonians.

TIPPING Is the tip you normally leave at home appropriate in Washington? The answer is yes. Just bear in mind that a tip is a reward for good service. Here are some guidelines:

Porters, redcaps, and bellmen	At least $1–$2 per bag and $5 for a lot of baggage
Cab drivers	15%–20% of the fare; add an extra dollar if the cabbie does a lot of luggage handling
Valet parking	$1–$2
Waiters	15–20% of the pretax bill
Bartenders	10–15% of the pretax bill
Chambermaids	$1–$2 per day
Checkroom attendants in restaurants or theaters	$1 per garment

GOING WHERE THE LOCALS GO During the week, you'll have to get away from the Mall or the Washington Convention Center if you want to rub shoulders with native Washingtonians. But not too far— Capitol Hill bars and restaurants are crowded with congressional aides, lobbyists, secretarial staff, and even the odd congressperson or two. During the lunch hour on weekdays (but not weekends and holidays), L'Enfant Plaza is jammed with bureaucrats from the myriad concrete-enclosed agencies located south of Independence Avenue.

North of the White House, the "new downtown" (roughly from 15th Street NW west to Rock Creek Park) is an area of glass-enclosed office buildings where lawyers, lobbyists, and other professionals ply their trades—and take their clients to lunch. Dupont Circle, formerly Washington's bohemian quarter, remains headquarters to Washington's artist, international, and gay communities.

But the hottest neighborhood these days is sort of halfway between downtown and Capitol Hill: the Penn Quarter, served by several subway stops, home to several museums, the Verizon Center sports arena, and a dozen of Washington's most popular restaurants. For more on Penn Quarter, see Part Eight, Dining and Restaurants (page 261).

TIPS FOR THE DISABLED

WASHINGTON IS ONE OF THE MOST ACCESSIBLE cities in the world for the disabled. The White House, for example, has a special entrance on Pennsylvania Avenue for visitors arriving in wheelchairs, and White House guides usually allow visually handicapped visitors to touch some of the items described on tours. All federal buildings are handicapped accessible (and nonsmoking). Each Metro station is equipped with an elevator, complete with Braille number plates.

All Smithsonian museum buildings are accessible to wheelchair visitors, as are all museum floors. For a copy of "Smithsonian Access," call ☎ 202-357-2700 or 202-357-1729 (TDD). Folks headed to the National Zoo can get a copy of the Zoo Guide for Disabled Visitors by calling ☎ 202-673-4717 or 202-673-4823 (TDD). The Lincoln and Jefferson memorials and the Washington Monument are equipped to accommodate disabled visitors. Most sightseeing attractions have elevators for others who want to avoid a lot of stair climbing. See our section "People with Special Needs" on page 26 in Part One, Planning Your Visit to Washington, to find additional information.

TELEPHONES

THE WASHINGTON AREA IS SERVED BY SEVERAL AREA CODES: ☎ 202 inside the District; ☎ 703 in the Northern Virginia suburbs across the Potomac River; ☎ 504 in the outer Virginia suburbs; ☎ 401 in Baltimore and Annapolis; and ☎ 301 and ☎ 240 for the Maryland suburbs. To dial out of D.C. to suburbs beyond the city's limits, it's necessary to dial the right area code. While calls to Arlington, Alexandria, and most of Fairfax County in Virginia and to Montgomery and Prince George counties in Maryland are dialed as if they're long distance, they are charged as local calls (50¢ from most pay phones).

RESTROOMS

FIELD RESEARCHERS FOR THE *Unofficial Guide* are selected for their reporting skills, writing ability . . . and sympathy for travelers with small bladders. When we enter a marble edifice, you can be sure we're not just scrutinizing the layout, the flow of the crowd, and the aesthetics: we're also nervously eyeing the real estate for the nearest public facility where we can unload that second cup of coffee.

So how does Washington rate in the restroom department? Actually, pretty well. That's because of the huge number of museums, monuments, federal office buildings, restaurants, bars, department stores, and hotels that cover the city. Most rest rooms are clean and conveniently located.

Leading any list of great restroom locations should be the National Air and Space Museum on the Mall. For women who claim there's no justice in the world when it comes to toilet parity, consider this: there are three times as many women's restrooms as there are men's restrooms. "And the men don't seem to notice," says a female Smithsonian employee who works at the information desk.

Other facilities of note on the Mall include those at the National Gallery of Art, the Arthur M. Sackler Gallery, the Hirshhorn Museum and Sculpture Garden, and the National Museum of African Art. The restrooms in the National Museum of Natural History are inconveniently located on a lower level. At the Arts and Industries Building, facilities are located far away from the front entrance. On the other hand, the restrooms in The Castle, the Smithsonian's visitor center, are easy to find and usually not very crowded.

Virtually all the monuments are restroom equipped, including the Lincoln and Jefferson memorials and the Washington Monument. The new restrooms at the National World War II Memorial on the

unofficial **TIP**
The restrooms off the huge lobby of the Stouffer Mayflower Hotel on Connecticut Avenue are both convenient and elegant.

Mall are very nice. More facilities will be available as the visitors centers at the U.S. Capitol, White House, and Washington Monument are completed. Downtown, hotels, restaurants, and bars are good bets. Avoid the few public restrooms, such as the ones beneath Dupont Circle; they're usually dirty. You won't find restrooms in Metro stations, although a few stations are located in complexes that do provide restrooms, including Union Station, Metro Center, Farragut North, and L'Enfant Plaza.

HOW *to* AVOID CRIME *and* KEEP SAFE *in* PUBLIC PLACES

CRIME IN WASHINGTON

THE COMBINATION OF A WIDESPREAD crack epidemic and the availability of high-powered weaponry put Washington on the map for a dubious distinction: "Murder Capital of the United States." Much of 2006 was spent on what the D.C. Metropolitan Police called a "crime emergency state"; and statistics put the per capita crime rate as the second worst in the country—about one for every 16 persons, more than twice as bad as New York. Anyone who watches the evening news or reads a newspaper knows about Washington's grim murder rate. So the question arises, as you contemplate a trip to D.C.: Just how safe is Washington anyway? Am I going to end up just another statistic?

"It's very safe," says Officer Rod Ryan of D.C.'s Metropolitan Police Department, as long as you stay in proscribed areas. Ryan, a veteran of the force who has worked special anticrime details around the Mall and popular tourist sites, explains, "Washington patrols its main visitor areas very strongly, because tourism is all the city has for income." And sadly, those per capita figures skew the real tragedy—that certain housing developments or neighborhoods are devastated by gang violence, while more affluent areas have relatively little (and less serious) crime.

To get an idea of how much protection the average tourist or business visitor gets, consider this fact: it's not just Officer Ryan and the rest of D.C.'s finest patrolling the city. Contributing to the task are a number of other law enforcement agencies whose jobs include protecting visitors: the U.S. Park Police patrols the monuments, the U.S. Capitol Police protects the Capitol and the 20-square-block area around it, and the Secret Service patrols the area around the White House. Plus, the Metro has its own police force for protecting people riding public transportation. That's not all: post-Sept. 11, a new network of security cameras has been added on the Mall by the Park Police, and the Metropolitan Police has installed a network of security cameras in high-traffic areas such as Georgetown, Union Station, and around the White House.

"Police are patrolling on bicycles, on horseback, on small motorcycles, on foot, and in unmarked cars," explains Officer Ryan. "And the Smithsonian has its own police force—highly trained federal officers—who patrol inside the buildings and around the grounds. Anyone who knows what he's looking for can spot five police patrols from anywhere on the Mall."

So, who's on the receiving end of all that automatic weapons fire? Most of the victims are either young drug dealers in shootouts with competitors or people involved in violent domestic disputes. Random murders are rare events in D.C., despite its reputation, and police say the odds here are about the same as anywhere else. Furthermore, the mayhem usually occurs in sections of the city visitors do not normally frequent: low-income residential areas that are removed from the city center and business/tourist districts. The worst areas are in Northeast and Southeast Washington, across the Anacostia River from downtown and the major visitor areas. You'd have to go to quite an effort to get there, even by mistake.

"Tourists should never wander across the bridge over the Anacostia River," says Officer Ryan, who should know—he leads a mountain bike patrol that has helped reduce street crime by 75% in one of the worst sections of Southeast Washington. "Visitors should stay within the boundaries of the Mall, Georgetown, upper Northwest, Dupont Circle, Adams-Morgan, and downtown."

Even Capitol Hill, which gained notoriety when a legislative aide was murdered on the street, is as safe for visitors as any other area that out-of-towners frequent. Ryan explains, "Too many powerful congressmen live in Capitol Hill for it not to be well patrolled."

Over the last decade a new force of uniformed city employees has been making Washington both safer and cleaner: downtown SAM (Safety and Maintenance) Teams, easily recognized by their bright red attire. By cleaning streets and sidewalks, removing graffiti, and assisting visitors, SAM Teams are creating a safer environment downtown. Visitors are encouraged to stop a SAM Team member and ask for directions, get a restaurant recommendation, or obtain directions to a landmark.

HAVING A PLAN

RANDOM VIOLENCE AND STREET CRIME are facts of life in any large city. You've got to be cautious and alert and plan ahead. When you are out and about, you must work under the assumption that you must use caution because you are on your own; if you run into trouble, it's unlikely that police or anyone else will be able to come to your rescue. You must give some advance thought to the ugly scenarios that might occur, and consider both preventive measures that will keep you out of harm's way and an escape plan just in case. Not being a victim of street crime is sort of a survival-of-the-fittest thing. Just as a lion stalks the weakest member of the antelope herd, muggers and thieves target the easiest victim. Simply put, no matter where you are or what you are doing, you want potential felons to think of you as a bad risk.

ON THE STREET For starters, you always present less of an appealing target if you are with other people. Second, if you must be out alone, act alert, be alert, and always have at least one of your arms and hands free. Felons gravitate toward preoccupied people—the kind found plodding along staring at the sidewalk, with both arms encumbered by briefcases or packages. Visible jewelry (on either men or women) attracts the wrong kind of attention. Men, keep your billfolds in your front trouser or coat pocket. Women, keep your purses tucked tightly under your arm; if you're wearing a coat, put it on over your shoulder bag strap.

Here's another tip: Men can carry two wallets, including one inexpensive one, carried in your hip pocket, containing about $20 in cash and some expired credit cards. This is the one you hand over if you're accosted. Your real credit cards and the bulk of whatever cash you have should be in either a money clip or a second wallet hidden elsewhere on your person. Women can carry a fake wallet in their purse and keep the real one in a pocket or money belt.

IF YOU'RE APPROACHED Police will tell you that a felon has the least amount of control over his intended victim during the few moments of his initial approach. A good strategy, therefore, is to short-circuit the crime scenario as quickly as possible. If a felon starts by demanding your money, for instance, quickly take out your billfold (preferably your fake one) and hurl it in one direction while you run shouting for help in the opposite direction. The odds are greatly in your favor that the felon will prefer to collect your silent billfold rather than pursue you. If you hand over your wallet and just stand there, the felon will likely ask for your watch and jewelry next. If you're a woman, the longer you hang around, the greater your vulnerability to personal injury or rape.

SECONDARY CRIME SCENES Under no circumstance, police warn, should you ever allow yourself to be taken to another location—a "secondary crime scene" in police jargon. This move, they explain, provides the felon more privacy and consequently more control. A felon can rob you on the street very quickly and efficiently. If he tries to remove you to another location, whether by car or on foot, it is a certain indication that he has more in mind than robbery. Even if the felon has a gun or knife, your chances are infinitely better running away. If the felon grabs your purse, let him have it. If he grabs your coat, come out of the coat. Hanging onto your money or coat is not worth getting mugged, raped, or murdered.

Another maxim: Never believe anything a felon tells you, even if he's telling you something you desperately want to believe, for example, "I won't hurt you if you come with me." No matter how logical or benign he sounds, assume the worst. Always, always break off contact as quickly as possible, even if that means running.

IN PUBLIC TRANSPORT When riding a bus, always take a seat as close to the driver as you can; never ride in the back. Likewise, on the subway, sit near the driver's or attendant's compartment. These people have a phone and can summon help in the event of trouble.

IN CABS While it is possible to hail a cab on the street in Washington any time of day, after dark you are better off doing so along the busier commercial routes or even approaching the doorman of a hotel with a dollar or so and asking him to summon one for you. Otherwise, call a reliable cab company and stay inside while they dispatch a cab to your door. When your cab arrives, check the driver's certificate, which must, by law, be posted on the dashboard. Address the cabbie by his last name (Mr. Jones or whatever) or mention the number of his cab. This alerts the driver to the fact that you are going to remember him and/or his cab. Not only will this contribute to your safety, it will also keep your cabbie from trying to run up the fare.

If you are comfortable reading maps, familiarize yourself with the most direct route to your destination ahead of time. If you can say, "Georgetown via Wisconsin Avenue, please," the driver is less likely to run up your fare by taking a circuitous route so he can charge you for three zones instead of two.

If you need to catch a cab at the train station or at one of the airports, always use the taxi queue. Taxis in the official queue are properly licensed and regulated. Never accept an offer for a cab or limo made by a stranger in the terminal or baggage claim. At best, you will be significantly overcharged for the ride. At worst (though it's unlikely), you may be abducted.

PERSONAL ATTITUDE

WHILE SOME AREAS OF EVERY CITY are more dangerous than others, never assume that any area is completely safe. Never let down your guard. You can be the victim of a crime, and it can happen to you anywhere. If you go to a restaurant or nightspot, use valet parking or park in a well-lit lot. Women leaving a restaurant or club alone should never be reluctant to ask to be escorted to their car.

Never let your pride or sense of righteousness and indignation imperil your survival. This is especially difficult for many men, particularly for men in the presence of women. It makes no difference whether you are approached by an aggressive drunk, a mentally ill street person, or an actual felon, the rule is the same: Forget your pride and break off contact as quickly as possible. Who cares whether the drunk insulted you if everyone ends up back at the hotel safe and sound? When you wake up in the hospital with a concussion and your jaw sewn shut, it's too late to decide that the drunk's filthy remark wasn't really all that important.

Felons, druggies, some street people, and even some drunks play for keeps. They can attack with a bloodthirsty hostility and hellish abandon that is beyond the imagination of most people. Believe us, you are not in their league (nor do you want to be).

SELF-DEFENSE

IN A SITUATION WHERE IT IS IMPOSSIBLE to run, you'll need to be prepared to defend yourself. Most policemen insist that a gun or knife is not much use to the average person. More often than not, they say, the weapon will be turned against the victim. Additionally, concealed firearms and knives are illegal in most jurisdictions. The best self-defense device for the average person is Mace defense spray. Not only is it legal in most states, it is nonlethal and easy to use. (However, it must be registered with the D.C. Police Department.)

When you shop for Mace, look for two things: it should be able to fire about eight feet, and it should have a protector cap so it won't go off by mistake in your purse or pocket. Carefully read the directions that come with your device, paying particular attention to how it should be carried and stored, and how long the active ingredients will remain potent. Wearing a rubber glove, test-fire your Mace, making sure that you fire downwind.

When you are out about town, make sure your Mace is someplace easily accessible, say, attached to your keychain. If you are a woman and you keep your Mace on a keychain, avoid the habit of dropping your keys (and the Mace) into the bowels of your purse when you leave your hotel room or your car. The Mace will not do you any good if you have to dig around in your purse for it. Keep your keys and your Mace in your hand until you have safely reached your destination.

CARJACKINGS

ALTHOUGH CARJACKING EPISODES HAVE FALLEN OFF, drivers still need to take special precautions. "Keep alert when you're driving in D.C. traffic," Officer Ryan warns. "Keep your doors locked, with the windows rolled up. In traffic, leave enough space in front of you so that you're not blocked in and can make a U-turn. That way, if someone approaches your car and starts beating on your windshield, you can drive off." Store your purse or briefcase under your knees when you are driving, rather than on the seat beside you.

RIPOFFS AND SCAMS

FIRST-TIME VISITORS TO THE MALL stepping off the escalator at the Smithsonian Metro are often confronted by fast-talking men who try to sell them museum brochures. Don't fall for it; the brochures are free in Smithsonian museums—and the fast talkers are trying to rip you off.

Another scam that visitors need to watch out for is the well-dressed couple who claim their car broke down and they need $5 for train fare. Refer them to a cop for help and move on.

MORE THINGS TO AVOID

WHEN YOU DO GO OUT, walk with a minimum of two people whenever possible. If you have to walk alone, stay in well-lit areas that have plenty of people around. And don't walk down alleys. It also helps not to look like a tourist when venturing away from the Mall. Don't wear a camera around your neck, and don't gawk at buildings and unfold maps on the sidewalk. Be careful about whom you ask for directions. (When in doubt, shopkeepers are a good bet.) Don't count your money in public, and carry as little cash as possible. At public phones, if you must say your calling card number to make a long-distance call, don't say it loud enough for strangers around you to hear. And, with the exception of the Mall, avoid public parks after dark. In particular, don't go to Rock Creek Park at night.

HELP MAY BE CLOSER THAN YOU THINK

WHILE WALKING IN WASHINGTON, try to be aware of public and federal facilities. If, despite your precautions, you are attacked, head for any federal office building for help. The entrances are all patrolled by armed guards who can offer assistance.

While this litany of warnings and precautions may sound grim, it's really just commonsense advice that applies to visitors in any large American city. Keep in mind that Washington's reputation for crime is enhanced by the worldwide media attention the city gets—local news in Washington is really national news. Finally, remember that 21 million visitors a year still flock to the nation's capital, making it one of the most visited destinations in the United States. The overwhelming majority encounter no problems with crime during their Washington visit.

THE HOMELESS

IF YOU'RE NOT FROM A BIG CITY or haven't visited one in a while, you're in for a shock when you come to Washington. It seems that every block in the city is filled with shabbily dressed people asking for money. Furthermore, along the Mall, near the national monuments, on downtown sidewalks, and in parks and gardens, you will see people sleeping in blankets and sleeping bags, their possessions piled up next to them. On crowded Georgetown streets filled with opulent shops, homeless women with small children beg for money. Drivers are approached at stoplights by men carrying Magic Marker–on–cardboard signs reading "Homeless—Will Work for Food." Virtually every Metro exit is choked with clusters of people begging for money.

WHO ARE THESE PEOPLE? "Most are lifelong D.C. residents who are poor," according to Joan Alker, assistant director of the National Coalition for the Homeless, an advocacy group headquartered in Washington. "The people you see on the streets are primarily single men and women. A disproportionate number of them are minorities and people with disabilities—they're either mentally ill, or substance abusers, or have physical disabilities."

ARE THEY A THREAT TO VISITORS? "No," Ms. Alker says. "Studies done in Washington show that homeless men have lower rates of conviction for violent crimes than the population at large. We know that murders aren't being committed by the homeless. I can't make a blanket statement, but most homeless people you see are no more likely to commit a violent crime than other people."

SHOULD YOU GIVE THE HOMELESS MONEY? "That's a personal decision," Ms. Alker says. "But if you can't, at least try to acknowledge their existence by looking them in the eye and saying, 'No, I can't.' " While there's no way to tell if the guy with the Styrofoam cup asking for a handout is really destitute or just a con artist, no one can dispute that most of these people are what they claim to be: homeless. We tend to carry a few dollar bills in outside pockets so that it's not necessary to open a purse or wallet. And again, a smile is well spent.

WAYS TO HELP It's really a matter for your own conscience. We confess to being both moved and disturbed by these unfortunate people: moved by their need and disturbed that the nation's capital should be home to so many needy men and women. In the final analysis, we found that it is easier on the conscience and spirit to keep some extra $1 bills in the outer snap pocket of your purse. The cost of giving those homeless who approach you a dollar really does not add up to all that much in the great scheme of things—how much was that double latte you had at Starbucks?—and it is much better for the psyche to respond to their plight than to deny or ignore their presence.

There is a notion, perhaps valid in some instances, that money given to a homeless person generally goes toward the purchase of alcohol or drugs. If this bothers you excessively, carry granola bars for distribution or buy some inexpensive gift coupons that can be redeemed at a McDonald's or other fast-food restaurant for coffee or a sandwich.

We have found that a little kindness regarding the homeless goes a long way, and that a few kind words delivered along with your quarter or granola bar brighten the day for both you and your friend in need. We are not suggesting a lengthy conversation or prolonged involvement, just something simple like, "Sure, I can help a little bit. Take care." You will probably receive more blessings than you deserve.

Those moved to get more involved in the nationwide problem of homelessness can send inquiries—or a check—to the National Coalition for the Homeless, 1012 14th Street NW, Suite 600, Washington, D.C. 20005-3471; ☎ 202-737-6444; **www.nationalhomeless.org.**

KEEP IT BRIEF Finally, don't play psychologist. All the people you encounter on the street are strangers. They may be harmless, or they may be dangerous. Either way, maintain distance and keep any contact or encounter brief. Be prepared to handle street people in accordance with your principles, but mostly, just be prepared. If you happen to run into the one druggie who gets in your face wanting a handout, the last thing you want to do is pull out your wallet and thumb through the twenties looking for a one-dollar bill. As the sergeant on *Hill Street Blues* used to say, "Be careful out there!"

PART FIVE

GETTING
around
WASHINGTON

DRIVING YOUR CAR:
A Really Bad Idea

TRAFFIC HOT SPOTS

HERE'S SOME BAD NEWS for anyone considering driving to our nation's capital: Washington is legendary for its traffic congestion. Let's start with the Capital Beltway (I-495 and I-95), which encircles the city through the Virginia and Maryland suburbs: it's guaranteed to be log-jammed on weekdays from 6:30 a.m. to 9:30 a.m. and again from 3 p.m. to 7:30 p.m. Unremitting suburban growth and geography confound the best efforts of traffic engineers to alleviate the congestion.

Inside the Beltway, the situation only gets worse. The few bridges that connect Washington and Virginia across the Potomac River are rush-hour bottlenecks. Interstates 66 and 395 in Virginia have restricted car-pool lanes inbound in the morning and outbound in the evening. Inside the District, Rock Creek Parkway becomes one-way during rush hour, and major thoroughfares such as Connecticut Avenue switch the direction of center lanes to match the predominant flow of traffic at different times of day. Downtown, the city's traffic circles can trap unwary motorists and reduce drivers to tears or profanity. Pierre L'Enfant's 18th-century grand plan of streets and avenues that intersect in traffic circles is a nightmare for 21st-century motorists.

First-time drivers to Washington should map out their routes in advance, avoid arriving and departing during rush hour, and leave the car parked throughout their stay. Lunch-hour traffic can be equally ferocious, and don't think that weekends are immune from traffic snarls: Washington's popularity as a tourist mecca slows Beltway traffic to a crawl on Saturdays and Sundays in warm weather. If there's any good news about driving in Washington, it's this: after evening rush hour subsides, getting around town by car is pretty easy.

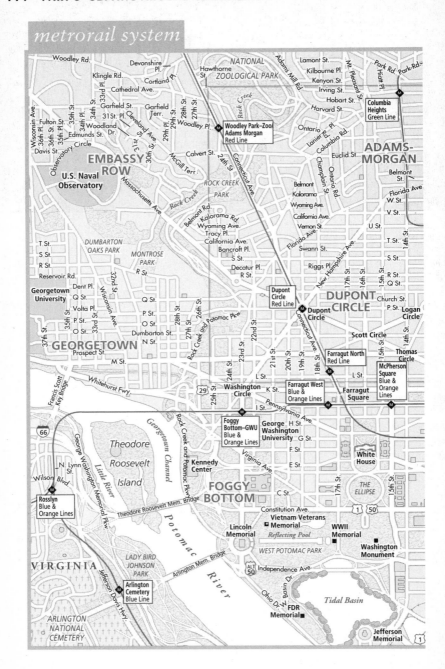

metrorail system

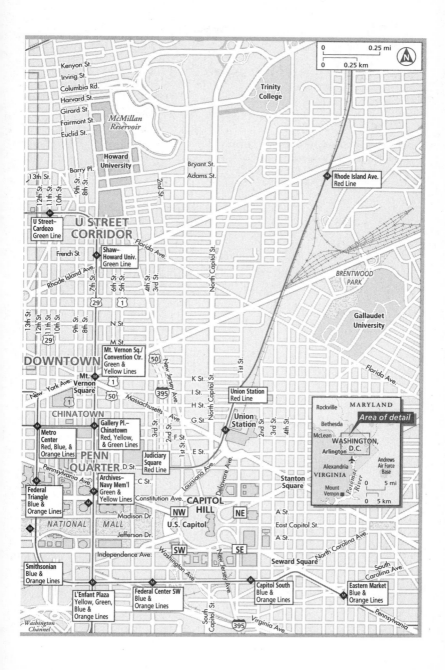

BRONZE PYLONS (*right*) identify Metro stations; colored stripes at top show the line or lines served by that station.

METRO SYSTEM AND NEIGHBORHOOD MAPS (*above*) are located in the mezzanine of each station, as are automated Farecard vending machines (*below*).

PARKING

IF YOU IGNORE OUR ADVICE about driving in Washington (we repeat, *don't*) and battle your way downtown by car, you'll find yourself stuck in one of those good news/bad news scenarios. The good news: there are plenty of places to park. The bad news: virtually all the spaces are in parking garages that charge an arm and a leg. Figure on $12 a day or $5 an hour, minimum.

Think you can beat the system by finding street parking? Go ahead and try, but bring a lot of quarters—and plenty of patience. Most metered parking is restricted to two hours—not a long time if you're intent on exploring a museum or attending a business meeting. And D.C. cops are quick to issue tickets for expired meters. Also, a lot of legal spaces turn illegal during afternoon rush hour.

In popular residential neighborhoods such as Georgetown and Adams-Morgan, parking gets even worse at night. Unless you've got a residential parking permit—not likely if you're from out of town—street parking is limited to two or three hours, depending on the neighborhood. The parking permits are prominently displayed in the cars of area residents.

Also, be sure to check the times on parking signs; they may not be right alongside the money box. But if your car is in a traffic lane at rush hour, no matter how much you put in that box, you're outta there.

If you're tempted to park illegally, be warned: D.C. police are grimly efficient at whisking away cars parked in rush-hour zones, and the fines are hefty. If your car is towed, call the D.C. Department of Public Works at ☎ 202-727-1010; if you're not sure if it was towed, call ☎ 202-727-5000. Incredibly, there's free parking along the Mall beginning at 10 a.m. weekdays; the limit is three hours. Needless to say, competition for the spaces is fierce.

RIDING *the* METRO:
A Really Good Idea

A CLEAN, SAFE ALTERNATIVE

IT SHOULD BE CLEAR BY NOW that visitors who would prefer to spend their time doing something productive rather than sit in traffic jams shouldn't drive in or around Washington. Thanks to the Metro, visitors can park their cars and forget them—just remember you need a Metro farecard or SmarTrip to exit the parking lots; cash or paper tickets are not accepted. It might be easier to buy your Metro pass in advance; if you go to **www.wmata.com/riding/passes,** you can purchase any of them online. Five color-coded subway lines connect downtown Washington to the outer reaches of the city and beyond to the Maryland and Virginia suburbs. It's a clean, safe, and efficient system that saves visitors time, money, and shoe leather as it whisks them around town. Visitors to Washington should use the Metro as their primary mode of transportation.

The trains are well maintained and quiet, with carpeting, cushioned seats, and air-conditioning. The stations are modern, well lit, and usually spotless, and they are uniformly constructed with high, arching ceilings paneled with sound-absorbing, lozenge-shaped concrete panels.

The wide-open look of the stations has been criticized as sterile and monotonous, but the design may explain why the Metro has maintained a crime-free reputation: there's no place for bad guys to hide. In addition, the entire system is monitored by closed-circuit TV cameras, and each car is equipped with passenger-to-operator intercoms, as are rail platforms and elevators. And cars and stations are nearly graffiti free.

The Metro (nobody calls it Metrorail, its real name) transports more than 700,000 passengers a day along 115 miles of track and through 86 stations (more extensions and a Purple Line are under consideration). It's a world-class engineering marvel.

Trains operate so frequently that carrying a schedule is unnecessary. During peak hours (weekdays 5 a.m. to 9:30 a.m. and 3 p.m. to 7 p.m.), trains enter the stations every three to six minutes. During off-peak hours, the interval increases to an average of 12 minutes; it can go to 20 minutes on weekends. To maintain the intervals throughout the year, the Metro adds and deletes trains to compensate for holidays and peak tourist season. Hours of operation are 5 a.m. to midnight Monday through Thursday, and 7 a.m. to 3 a.m. on weekends and holidays.

HOW TO RIDE THE METRO

Finding the Stations

Many (but, unfortunately, not all) street signs in Washington indicate the direction and number of blocks to the nearest Metro station. Station entrances are identified by brown columns or pylons with an "M" on all four sides and a combination of colored stripes in red, yellow, orange, green, or blue that indicate the line or lines serving that station. Since most stations are underground, users usually descend on escalators to the mezzanine or ticketing part of the station. At above-ground and elevated stations outside of downtown Washington, the mezzanine is most often on the ground level. At the kiosk located there, pick up a system map with quick directions on how to use the Metro.

Purchasing a Farecard

If you are making only one or two trips, you might want to determine your destination and your fare ahead of time because the ticketing system is automated. Walk up to the backlit, color-coded

STEP 1: (*left*)
To purchase a farecard, insert bills and/or coins.

STEP 2 (*left*): Use toggle switches to add or decrease the farecard's value. Plug in enough cash to buy at least a round-trip ticket (or more, if desired).

STEP 3 (*right*): Press the "Push for Farecard" button; the farecard appears at the "Used Farecard Trade-in" slot.

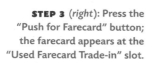

RUSH HOUR AND NON-RUSH HOUR FARES are listed alphabetically at each station's kiosk.

AUTOMATED FAREGATES, which control access in and out of spacious Metro stations, are located near the kiosk. The woman pictured here is exiting the station.

map located in each mezzanine and find the station nearest your ultimate destination. Then look on the bottom of the map, where an alphabetized list of stations reveals both the fare (peak and off-peak) and the estimated travel time to each. Peak fares, usually more expensive, are in effect from 5 a.m. to 9:30 a.m. and from 3 p.m. to 7 p.m. weekdays (and again from 2 a.m. to 3 a.m. on weekends). Unless you're traveling from a suburban station to downtown, or from one suburb to another, one-way fare is $3.90 maximum at rush hour and $1.35 at non-rush hour. Check with the station agent about your return trip. Some lines have shorter routes within them at rush hour, so that the busiest stations get more service. If you are staying in Bethesda, for example, you can take a Red Line train marked either Grosvenor-Strathmore or Shady Grove; both are beyond Bethesda. If you're going to Rockville, however, you'd have to disembark at Grosvenor-Strathmore and wait for a Shady Grove–bound train—not unpleasant in nice weather but chilly in the snow!

If you have time to purchase a pass in advance, you might benefit by choosing a one-day pass for $3 or a weekly pass for $11 ($6 for seniors or passengers with disabilities); for information, go to **www .wmata.com/riding/passes.**

Farecard Vending Machines

Those big vending machines lining the walls of the mezzanine don't dispense sodas. Instead, they swallow your money and issue farecards with magnetic stripes that get you in and—this is crucial—out of Metro stations. (If you are expecting to use the system very much, or to park at a Metro station, you must have a SmarTrip card instead; see the explanation on the next page.) Once you get your card, hang onto it.

Buying a farecard works like this: Walk up to the farecard vending machine and look for the numeral "1" on the left side at eye level. (We'll call this **Step 1.**) This is where you insert bills and/or coins. If your destination is, say, a $1.35 fare, and you're making a round-trip, insert $2.70 into the machine. As the money slides in, look at the middle of the machine for the numeral "2" (**Step 2**), where a digital readout registers the amount you've shoved into the contraption.

Machines that accept paper money invariably screw up, and these machines are no exception. They often spit back bills they don't like, so try smoothing wrinkled bills before inserting them and choose new, unfrayed greenbacks over bills that are worn. Inserting coins is nearly foolproof, but not very practical if you're riding the Metro a lot.

Our advice is to cut down on using these infernal machines as much as possible by plugging in $5, $10, or even $20 at once, which means you're buying a ticket that can last several days or longer. The computerized turnstiles print the remaining value on the farecard after each use, which lets you know when it's time to buy a new one. If you are sure of the exact fare, however, and don't intend to use the card again, you can get change: Below the digital readout at Step 2 are white "plus" and "minus" buttons that let you adjust the readout to the exact fare you wish to purchase. For example, if your round-trip fare is $2.70 and you inserted a $5 bill, toggle the readout from $5 down to $2.70 by repeatedly pushing the "minus" button. (If you overshoot, push the "plus" button to increase the value.) Then look to the right side of the machine and the numeral "3" (**Step 3**), and press the button that reads "Press for Farecard." If all goes well (and, in all fairness, it usually does), out pops your farecard and your change—in this case, $2.30 in change; the machines don't dispense bills.

But even if the farecard machine accepts $20 bills, keep in mind that the maximum amount of change the machine can spit out is $4.95—which means you're stuck buying a farecard with a minimum value of $15.05.

SmarTrip Cards

For the past several years, Washington-area transit authorities have been working toward a unified system for paying fares, like the one in New York. **SmarTrip,** as the pass is called, is already a mainstay of the subway system; is required for exiting any Metro-station parking lot (except on weekends, when parking is free); can be used on any Metro bus; and is being phased in for use on the regional bus and shuttle systems. You can buy the passes in Metro stations at the same machines that sell paper tickets, and if you expect to do any extensive traveling by public transportation, they are both sturdier and faster than paper passes. Instead of inserting them and waiting for them to reemerge, you simply press the face of the SmarTrip card to the large round plate so marked, and it calculates the fare electronically.

All Metrobuses are equipped with SmarTrip readers that work the same way—touch and go—except that you only touch it once and the fare is automatically counted. If you have used the card at a Metrorail station or other Metrobus within the past two hours, the SmarTrip box automatically registers your fare as a transfer. If you are going from the Metrobus to yet another related shuttle, such as the DC Circulator (see page 129) or a regional Ride On bus that may not yet have a SmarTrip register installed, ask the driver for a paper transfer. Once you become really comfortable with the system, you can add money to the SmarTrip card at the bus as well as at the subway-station machines.

There are two drawbacks to the SmarTrip concept. The card costs $5 in the beginning (but can be recharged and reused indefinitely, which could be a great convenience to business travelers who return frequently); plus, some of the bus and shuttle machines can be a little balky, so you might want to hang on to a couple of dollars just in case.

For more information about SmarTrip, visit **www.wmata.com/riding/smartrip.cfm.**

WHEN ENTERING OR EXITING, INSERT THE FARECARD (*face up with the magnetic strip on the right*) into the slot on the front of the faregate.

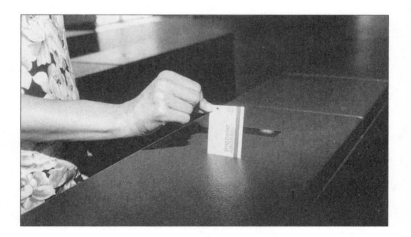

THE FARECARD REAPPEARS AT THE TOP OF THE FAREGATE; remove it and the faregate opens. On faregates for disabled people, the farecard reappears at the front of the gate.

NOTE: Remember to hang on to the farecard—you need it to exit the system.

WHEN THE VALUE OF A FARECARD DROPS BELOW $1,
trade it in for a new one at a farecard machine.

EMERGENCY INTERCOMS are located on all station platforms.

Talking Fare Machines

Metro has installed talking express farecard vending machines at 46 mezzanines in the system's busiest stations; look for the name *Passes/Farecards* across the top. An optional audio button lets you hear a voice guide you through the steps to purchase farecards, which removes much of the confusion and is a real boon to visually impaired riders.

The machines let you buy up to $200 worth of farecards with a top denomination of $45. You can also purchase the $6.50 one-day pass, valid for unlimited rides after 9:30 a.m. weekdays and all day on weekends and holidays (a very good deal that we recommend most visitors take advantage of). Currently, you can charge your farecard purchases to VISA, Discover, and MasterCard.

Entering the Station

With your farecard firmly in hand, you are now authorized to enter the Metro station. Hold the card in your right hand with the brown magnetic stripe facing up and on the right. Walk up to one of the waist-high faregates with the green light and white arrow near the kiosk (not the faregates that read "Do Not Enter"—they are for passengers exiting the station) and insert your card into the slot, where it is slurped into the bowels of the Metro. As the gate opens, walk through and grab your card as it is regurgitated from the slot at the top of the gate. All this happens in less than a second. Place the farecard in a safe place; if you lose it, you must pay the maximum fare when you exit.

The SmarTrip card is not inserted into the machine but presses onto the magnetic reader (clearly marked). When you exit, you press again; when the gate opens, the machine will read out your remaining balance. You can add onto the SmarTrip at the same machines as the farecards.

Finding the Train Platform

Once you're past the faregate, look for signs with arrows and the name of your intended line's end station that point toward the platform where your train will arrive. At an underground station, you will descend on an escalator or stairs to the train platform; at an aboveground station, you will ascend to the platform. You can reconfirm that you're on the correct side of the platform by reading the list of stations printed on the pylon located there and finding your destination. If your destination is listed, you're on the right track; departing trains go in one direction only; as you face forward, the "out" lane is to your right, as if you were driving a car. Stand in the red-tiled area to wait for the next train.

Boarding the Train

As a train approaches a station, lights embedded in the floor along the granite edge of the platform begin flashing. As the train comes out of the tunnel, look for a sign over the front windshield that states the train's destination and line (Blue, Red, Green, Orange, or Yellow). The destination, but not the color, is also shown on the side of the train. Double-check to make sure the approaching train is the one you want.

If it's the right train, approach the doors, but stand clear to let departing passengers exit the train. Then move smartly; the train stops for only a few seconds, then chimes will indicate that the doors are about to close. If you're rushing to catch a train and hear the chimes, don't attempt to board. Unlike elevator doors, the train doors won't pop open if you lean on them—and they exert a lot of pressure. Wait for the next train.

Inside, take a seat or, if you're a first-time Metro user, study the system map located near the doors. The trains all have real operators who announce the next station over a PA system and give information for transferring to other lines (sometimes you can even hear them over the din); the newer cars have electronic signs at the front and rear that list the next station. It's better to study the map and read the signs mounted on the cavernous station walls at each stop.

Exiting the Station

As the train enters your station, move toward the doors. When you step off the train, look for stairs or escalators on the platform and walk toward them. Some stations have two or more exits, but the signs on the walls of the stations aren't always clear about where each exit goes. If you know which exit you want (for example, at the Smithsonian station most tourists want the Mall exit, not Independence Avenue), look for that sign and follow the arrow.

At the top of the escalator or stairs, walk toward the mezzanine area, get your farecard ready, and repeat the same procedure you used to enter the Metro system (card in right hand, magnetic stripe up and on the right, insert in slot). If you bought exact fare, you won't get your card back, but the gate will open and a little sign will flash "Exact Fare." You're on your way. If your farecard still has money left on it, it pops up as the gate opens and the sign flashes "Take Farecard." Do same; exit station.

If your farecard doesn't have enough value to cover your trip, the gate won't open and the card will pop back out. You need to take it to an "Exitfare" machine somewhere just behind you. (Invariably, ten people are lined up behind you when this happens, creating the equivalent of a minor Beltway backup.) The reddish-colored Exitfare machines look like their brothers, the farecard machines. Insert your card and immediately the digital readout displays the exact amount of moolah it needs so you can exit the station—which is all it will allow you to add: if the machine asks for 40 cents and you stick a $5 bill into it, you'll get $4.60 in change back.) Plug in the coins; the farecard reappears; grab it; insert same into the faregate, which swallows it and sets you free.

Remember: A paper farecard will not get your car out of the parking lot. You must have a SmarTrip card. Parking is $4 except on Saturday and Sunday, when you can get out of jail (so to speak) for free.

Changing from One Line to Another

Sooner or later—probably sooner—you will need to transfer from one Metro line to another. Metro Center is the Big Enchilada of the transfer stations, where the Red, Orange, and Blue lines converge in downtown Washington. Other transfer stations tourists are likely to hit are Gallery Place–Chinatown (Red, Yellow, and Green); L'Enfant Plaza (Yellow, Blue, Orange, Green); Rosslyn (Orange and Blue); and Pentagon (Yellow and Blue).

To transfer, you don't use your farecard. Simply exit your train, take the escalator to the correct platform, and reboard. Try to listen to the PA system as your train enters the station: the driver recites where the different lines are located in the approaching station (for example, "Transfer to the Red Line on the lower level"). If you can't hear the driver's instructions, look for the color-coded pylons with arrows that point toward the platforms, and look for the one with your destination listed on it.

The Gallery Place–Chinatown station is especially complicated. Frequently, you're routed down and up escalators to reach your platform. Keep your eyes up for signs overhead that state reassuring messages such as "Red Line–Wheaton Straight Ahead."

METRO FOIBLES AND HOW TO COPE

Boarding the Wrong Train

Unless you're concerned about being ten minutes or so late for your meeting with the president, boarding a train going in the wrong direction isn't a big problem. Simply get off at the next station, and if the platform is located between the tracks, go to the other side of the platform to wait for the next train running in the opposite direction, and board it. If both sets of tracks run down the center of the station, take the escalator or stairs and cross the tracks to the other side, where you can catch the next train going the other way.

If you realize you've boarded the wrong *color* train (say, the Orange Line to Vienna, Virginia, instead of the Blue Line to Van Dorn Street), just get off at the next station, stay on the same platform, and take the next Blue Line train.

What to Do with Farecards Worth 50 Cents

After a few days in Washington, you may start accumulating farecards that don't have enough value for even a one-way trip. Don't throw them away! Instead, next time you're using the Metro go up to a farecard vending machine in the mezzanine and insert the old farecard into the slot on the right side of the machine where it says "Trade In Used Farecard." Its value will be displayed on the digital readout at Step 2. Feed the machine money at Step 1, futz with the "plus" and "minus" buttons, and press the white "Push for Farecard" button to get a new card that includes the value on your old card.

If, Like Joe, You're Color Blind . . .

Unofficial Guide coauthor Joe Surkiewicz's heart sank the first time he tried to figure out Washington's Metro system: like a few other men, he is afflicted with red-green color blindness. To his eyes, the Metro's Red and Green Lines look nearly identical in color, and the Orange Line looks a lot redder than it ought to. The only lines on the system map he could distinguish by color were the Blue and Yellow ones.

The solution is to fixate on the names of the stations at the ends of the lines. That way, the Red Line becomes the "Wheaton–Shady Grove" line, while the Green Line is the "U Street–Cardozo/Anacostia" line. It's harder at first, but you'll end up with a distinct advantage over those who blindly follow colored signs: knowing a line's end station is helpful when you've got to make a split-second decision on whether or not to board a train that's almost ready to depart the station. For instance, if you enter the Dupont Circle Metro and want to go to Union Station, you need to board the Red Line train heading toward Wheaton, not Shady Grove. So, sooner or later, you'll get familiar with the end stations anyway.

DISCOUNTS AND SPECIAL DEALS

CHILDREN Up to two children aged 4 or younger can ride free when accompanied by a paying passenger.

SENIOR CITIZENS AND PEOPLE WITH DISABILITIES Reduced fares are available for qualified senior citizens; call ☎ 202-637-7000 for more information. People with disabilities can call ☎ 202-962-1245 for information on reduced fares. A new service called "Metro Mobility Link" supplies people with disabilities with specialized information about Metro stations, including general features of each station, the location of Braille signs, whether the station has a center or side platform, and other disabled-accessible features. The number is ☎ 202-962-6464.

The Metro is a tourist attraction in its own right, featuring the Western Hemisphere's longest escalator: the 230-foot, mezzanine-to-platform-level behemoth at the Wheaton Metro in suburban Maryland. If that's a little out of the way, the Dupont Circle Metro's escalator is nearly as long. If escalators terrify you or you are wheelchair bound, all stations are equipped with elevators. But it's a good idea to check at a station kiosk and confirm that the elevator at your destination station is in operation. To find the elevator, look for the wheelchair symbol near the station entrance.

FARE DISCOUNTS If you plan on using the Metro more than once or twice a day, call Metrorail at ☎ 202-637-7000 to find out what discounts are in effect during your visit. A high-value farecard of $20 or more garners a 10% bonus. A Metrorail One-day Pass lets you ride from 9:30 a.m. till midnight for $6.50 weekdays, and all day on weekends and holidays; it's the way to go if you plan to ride the subway to several locations in one day. Commuters can save money by purchasing passes that let them ride anywhere, anytime, for two weeks. Discount passes are available at the Metro Center sales office and from the new talking farecard machines installed in busier Metro Stations. Discount passes are also sold at many Safeway, Giant, and SuperFresh grocery stores.

FREE INFORMATION For a free visitor information kit that includes a Metro system map, specific information on getting to Smithsonian museums and other attractions, and information on driving to suburban Metro stations, call this number: ☎ 202-637-7000. The computer literate can get up-to-the-minute Metro information on the Internet at **www.wmata.com.** You can also purchase tickets in $10, $15, and $20 increments.

METROBUS AND OTHER BUS SYSTEMS

WASHINGTON'S EXTENSIVE BUS SYSTEM, known as Metrobus, serves Georgetown, downtown, and the suburbs. Racks recently installed on metro buses as part of the new Bike-on-Bus program further increase commuter flexibility. There is no additional charge for passengers with bicycles. However, with 400 routes and more than 1,500 buses, Metrobus is an extremely complicated system to figure out how to use. As a result, we feel that visitors to Washington should leave Metrobus to the commuters and stick to the Metro except when the route is fairly simple—the 30s from downtown to Georgetown—or your concierge has written it down for you.

If you plan to transfer from the Metro to a Metrobus in D.C. or Virginia, get a free transfer before you board the Metro train from the machine located next to the escalator in the mezzanine of the station that you entered; one from your exit point will not be validated. Most of Washington's suburbs have good subsidiary bus or shuttle systems that connect to the subway (and then into the District of Columbia), and if you are staying with friends, they'll probably show you the nearest stop; otherwise, these systems are probably too complicated for most tourists. But there are two restricted shuttle routes that may be useful to tourists, especially those staying downtown or doing sustained sightseeing.

The **DC Circulator** runs three useful routes: one connecting Union Station to Georgetown by way of the Washington Convention Center and K Street NW; a second running east and west around the National Mall between Fourth and 17th streets NW; and a third north and south from above the Convention Center to the Southwest Waterfront and back, so that it also crosses the Mall at Seventh Street. There are ticket machines all along the way (and also at the

Gallery Place, Waterfront, and Mount Vernon Square–Convention Center Metro stations).

The bright-red Circulator buses, with a distinctive fish-shaped gold route map on the side, run from 7 a.m. to 9 p.m. daily. Tickets are $1 or 35¢ with a Metrorail transfer; 50¢ for seniors or riders with disabilities (free with Metrorail transfers). Anyone with a Metrobus or Circulator transfer can reboard for free within two hours of the transfer stamp time. You can pay cash (exact change) at the front driver's door, and if you're boarding with a transfer you can enter at any of the doors, but be sure to hold on any passes, because systems officials get on buses and make random checks. Circulator stops are marked with a fish-shaped red-and-gold logo. Metrobus stop markers are red, white, and blue.

You can also get an all-day pass for $3 from one of the machines, which take change or credit cards but no paper bills. For route maps and more information go to **www.dccirculator.com.**

The **Georgetown Metro Connection** has an even more restricted route, but depending on where you are staying or plan to dine or shop, it may be cheap and easy. It also has two mini-circuits, one that goes between the Foggy Bottom–GWU Metro station and Georgetown via K Street (along the Georgetown waterfront) to Wisconsin Avenue NW and up through the main commercial strip before turning back down. The other route circulates between Dupont Circle, picking up about a block south of the Dupont Circle Metro station's south entrance, and the Rosslyn Metro Station, hooking up there to any of the Virginia subway stops. Along the way, it traverses M Street, the main chain-shopping strip of Georgetown.

The buses run about every ten minutes from 7 a.m. to midnight Monday through Thursday; 7 to 2 a.m. Fridays; 8 to 2 a.m. Saturdays; and 8 a.m. to midnight on Sundays. Fares are $1 or 35¢ with a subway transfer slip. (Remember, you have to punch the transfer machine as you go into the subway system, not when you exit.) For more information, go to **www.georgetowndc.com/shuttle.** You also need to pick up a bus transfer at the White Flint, Twinbrook, and New Carrollton suburban stations to qualify for reduced parking fees on weekdays; look for signs in the station.

TAXIS

WASHINGTON TAXIS ARE PLENTIFUL and relatively cheap. They're also strange. Instead of a metered fare system, fares are figured on a map that splits the city into 5 zones and 27 subzones; the base fare for one zone is $5. A zone map and fare chart are posted in all legal cabs but probably won't mean much to first-time visitors—or most residents, for that matter. If you're concerned about getting ripped

MAJOR D.C. TAXI COMPANIES	
Capitol	☎ 202-546-2400
Diamond	☎ 202-387-6200
Yellow Cab	☎ 703-522-2222

off, request a receipt before you start the ride. That way the driver knows he's got no defense in an overcharging claim.

The cab system has other quirks. Drivers can pick up other fares as long as the original passenger isn't taken more than five blocks out of the way of the original destination. That's good news if you're the second or third rider and it's raining; it's not so hot if you're the original passenger and trying to catch a train.

To eliminate the possibility of a ride in a poorly maintained cab or one driven by a recent immigrant who is as unfamiliar with the city as you are, stick to the major cab companies. Some of the independents are illegal yet still carry the markings and roof light of a seemingly legitimate cab. One way to spot a fly-by-night taxi is to check for hubcaps. If there aren't any, pass that one by.

PART SIX

SIGHTSEEING
TIPS *and* TOURS

▮ PLAN *before* YOU LEAVE HOME

THERE ARE SEVERAL GOOD REASONS why you should take the time to do some planning before coming to Washington to tour its sights. First of all, Washington is a big, sprawling city that covers a lot of real estate. The National Mall, for example, is two miles long—and there's more to Washington beyond that long expanse of green. Spending a poorly planned day traipsing back and forth from monument to museum to federal building to monument can waste a lot of time, energy, and shoe leather.

But it's not only Washington's physical size that makes planning a must: it's the mind-boggling number of tourist attractions that are available. Even if your vacation is a week long, be prepared to make some hard choices about how many sights you can fit into your itinerary. If your visit is shorter, say only two or three days, it's even more imperative that you have a firm idea of what you want to see. Attempting to see too much during your allotted time is exhausting: your visit becomes a blur of marble monuments and big rooms (and at press time, there were at least another half-dozen memorials and attractions in the making). As with most large-scale projects, a little research can go a long way in making your trip more pleasurable.

Our recommendation is to do some soul-searching and try to reach some decisions about what your interests are before you leave for Washington. Are you curious about how the government spends all your tax money? Have you always wanted to gaze up at the solemn figure of Lincoln in his marble memorial? Do you love antiques? Are you a military buff? Does technology fascinate you? Do you love exploring art museums? Gardens? Historical houses? Washington offers places to explore for people with all these interests. Yet neither this guide nor any other can tell you what your interests are. You gotta do your homework.

Some more advice: To help winnow your choices, get as much written information as you can before you leave—and read it. To supplement this guide, you can get information concerning Washington tourist attractions, hotels, and recreation at the public library and travel agencies, or by calling or writing any of the profiled attractions.

Web surfers and the computer literate will be glad to know that Washington now has several Web sites listing D.C. hotels by location and price, restaurants searchable by neighborhood, tour information, and calendars of special events and festivals, and so on. Among the best are **www.washington.org, www.dcvisit.com,** and **www.washingtondc.com.**

THINKING IN CATEGORIES

VISITORS TO WASHINGTON ARE OFTEN thrown into large groups of tourists as they visit famous and popular edifices such as the Washington Monument, the U.S. Capitol, and the White House. Unless you've made prior arrangements for a VIP tour or Uncle Milt is a congressional staffer, you'll be craning your neck under the Capitol dome with 49 other tourists as you listen to your tour guide's spiel. Our advice: Go with the flow, relax, and enjoy the tour. But not everything you do while in Washington has to turn into a group traipse.

Question: How do you avoid the big crowds that clog the major tourist attractions?

Answer: By organizing your visit around things that interest you.

By charting your own course, you get off the beaten track and visit places that offer higher-quality tours than the canned presentations given in the better-known attractions. Often, you find yourself visiting places with small groups of people who share your interests. In short, you have more fun.

By following your own interests, you can make some intriguing discoveries as you visit Washington:

- A collection of miniature Revolutionary soldiers fighting a mock battle (Anderson House);
- A four-sided colonial-era mousetrap that guillotines rodents (Daughters of the American Revolution building);
- A tropical rain forest located just off the Mall (Organization of American States building);
- A space capsule you can climb into (Navy Museum);
- Fabergé eggs encrusted with diamonds (Hillwood Museum);
- The tomb of the only president buried in Washington (National Cathedral);
- A garden filled with flowers mentioned in the plays of William Shakespeare (the Folger Shakespeare Library);
- A pub that shows how typical colonial-era Americans lived (Gadsby's Tavern).

AFRICAN AMERICAN

African American Civil War
  Memorial

Anacostia Museum

Bethune Museum and Archives

Black Revolutionary War Patriots
  Memorial

Frederick Douglass House
  (Cedar Hill)

Dr. Martin Luther King Jr. Memorial
  (under construction)

National Museum of African Art

National Museum of American Art

ARCHITECTURE

Constitution Hall

Daughters of the American
  Revolution Museum

Hirshhorn Museum

House of the Temple

Kennedy Center

Library of Congress
  (Jefferson Building)

Meridian International Center

National Archives

National Building Museum

National Gallery of Art: East Building

National Postal Museum

Old Post Office Pavilion

Ronald Reagan Building

U.S. Capitol

U.S. Supreme Court

Union Station

Washington Monument

Washington National Cathedral

ART MUSEUMS

Art Museum of the Americas (at the
  Organization of American States)

National Museum of African Art

National Museum of Women in the
  Arts

Corcoran Gallery of Art

Dumbarton Oaks

National Portrait Gallery

Phillips Collection

Freer Gallery of Art

Renwick Gallery

Hirshhorn Museum and Sculpture
  Garden

Sackler Gallery

Kreeger Museum

Smithsonian American Art Museum

kids GOOD FOR CHILDREN

Bureau of Engraving and Printing

Federal Bureau of Investigation

International Spy Museum

National Air and Space Museum
  National Zoological Park

National Aquarium

National Geographic Society's
  Explorers Hall

National Museum of American History

National Museum of Natural
  History

National Postal Museum

National Wildlife Visitor Center

Old Post Office Pavilion

Washington Monument

Washington Navy Yard

DECORATIVE ARTS AND ANTIQUES

Anderson House

Christian Heurich Mansion

Daughters of the American Revolution Museum and Period Rooms

Decatur House

Dumbarton Oaks

Hillwood Museum

Mount Vernon

The Octagon

Textile Museum

Tudor Place

U.S. Department of State Diplomatic Reception Rooms

GARDENS

Bishops Garden at Washington National Cathedral

Constitution Gardens

Dumbarton Oaks

Folger Shakespeare Library

Franciscan Monastery

Enid A. Haupt Garden

Hillwood Museum

Kenilworth Aquatic Gardens

Meridian International Center

Mount Vernon

National Arboretum

National Gallery of Art (behind the Castle on the Mall)

Sculpture Garden

Tudor Place

U.S. Botanic Gardens

GOVERNMENT

Bureau of Engraving and Printing

Federal Bureau of Investigation

National Archives

U.S. Capitol

U.S. Department of the Treasury

U.S. Supreme Court

Voice of America

GREAT VIEWS

Arlington House (Arlington National Cemetery)

Iwo Jima Memorial

Kennedy Center

Lincoln and Jefferson memorials

Mount Vernon

Old Post Office Pavilion

Washington Monument

Washington National Cathedral

GREAT PLACES TO WALK

Cathedral Avenue between Connecticut Avenue and Washington National Cathedral

Dupont Circle

Embassy Row (Massachusetts Avenue northwest of Dupont Circle)

Fort McNair and the Southwest

Georgetown

Kenilworth Aquatic Gardens

The Mall

National Arboretum

National Zoo

Pennsylvania Avenue from the Capitol to the White House

the bike path along the Potomac from the Kennedy Center to Georgetown

HISTORICAL BUILDINGS AND SITES

Arlington House

Chesapeake & Ohio Canal

Decatur House

Frederick Douglass House

Ford's Theatre

Georgetown House

Gunston Hall

Mount Vernon

The Octagon

Old Stone House

Old Town Alexandria

U.S. Capitol

Woodrow Wilson

HISTORY

Anacostia Museum

Arlington House

Bethune Museum and Archives

Chesapeake & Ohio Canal

Decatur House

Folger Shakespeare Library

Georgetown House

Gunston Hall

International Spy Museum

Lincoln Museum (in Ford's Theatre)

Mount Vernon

National Air and Space Museum

National Archives

National Cryptologic Museum

National Museum of American
    History

National Museum of the
    American Indian

National Portrait Gallery

Old Town Alexandria

U.S. Holocaust Memorial Museum

MILITARY

Air Force Memorial

Anderson House

Arlington National Cemetery

Black Revolutionary War Patriots
    Memorial

Fort Ward

Iwo Jima Memorial

National Air and Space Museum

National Cryptologic Museum

Smithsonian's Udvar-Hazy Center*

U.S. Navy Memorial

Vietnam Veterans Memorial

Washington Navy Yard

Women in Vietnam Memorial

A National Air and Space Museum that houses aircraft from both World Wars, located at Washington Dulles International Airport.

MONUMENTS AND MEMORIALS

African American Civil War Memorial

Air Force Memorial

Arlington Cemetery

Black Revolutionary War

Franklin Delano Roosevelt Memorial

George Mason Memorial

Iwo Jima Memorial

Vietnam Veterans Memorial

Lincoln and Jefferson memorials

Kennedy Center

Dr. Martin Luther King Jr. Memorial
    (under construction)

Korean War Veterans Memorial

National Law Enforcement

National World War II Memorial
    Patriots Memorial

Navy Memorial

9/11 Memorial (under construction)

MONUMENTS AND MEMORIALS (CONTINUED)

Officers Memorial

U.S. Holocaust Memorial

Washington Monument Museum

Women in Vietnam Memorial

OUTDOORS

Chesapeake & Ohio Canal

Great Falls Park

Mount Vernon Trail

National Wildlife Visitor Center

Potomac Park

Rock Creek Park

Roosevelt Island

PLACES OF WORSHIP

Adas Israel Synagogue at the Lillian
 and Albert Small Jewish Museum

Franciscan Monastery

Islamic Center

National Shrine of the Immaculate
 Conception

Pope John Paul II Cultural Center

St. John's Episcopal Church (across
 from the White House)

Washington National Cathedral

TECHNOLOGY

Arts and Industry Building

Goddard Space Flight Center

International Spy Museum

Koshland Science Museum

National Air and Space Museum

National Building Museum

National Museum of American History

National Cryptologic Museum

National Museum of Health and
 Medicine

National Postal Museum

Washington Navy Yard

As you travel around Washington, you'll discover sights like these and many others that most visitors miss. To help you on your way, we've selected major categories and listed the best destinations for visitors to explore. As you read the list, keep in mind that many attractions overlap. For example, the National Air and Space Museum appeals to both technology and military buffs, while the Woodrow Wilson House is interesting to history fans, lovers of the decorative arts, and folks curious about how the high and mighty conducted their day-to-day lives in the 1920s.

PUTTING YOUR CONGRESSPERSON TO WORK

A LETTER TO A REPRESENTATIVE OR SENATOR well in advance of your trip (six months is not too early) can bring a cornucopia of free goodies your way: admittance to the limited White House tours, reservations on VIP tours of the Supreme Court and the Bureau of Engraving and Printing that can save you hours of time waiting in line, as well as getting you on longer, more informative tours. In addition, your eager-to-please congressperson (he or she wants your vote) can provide timely information about hotels, restaurants, shopping, and special events. It's all free. Just be sure to include the exact dates of your visit.

Here's why you must send off your letter as soon as you know the dates that you'll be in Washington: senators and House members are limited in the number of spaces on VIP tours they can provide to constituents. Since all the legislators get the same number of passes, reason dictates that the farther away your state is from Washington, D.C., the better chance you have of getting on a coveted VIP tour. For example, Maryland legislators, some of whose constituents can literally jump on the Metro to reach D.C., are often booked five and six months in advance for the popular White House VIP tours. But if you're from South Dakota, chances are your congressperson will be able to get you reservations during your visit.

There is a downside to the VIP tours: some of them take place very early, usually before the regular, nonreserved tours begin. For example, Bureau of Engraving and Printing VIP tours depart at 8:15 a.m. and 8:45 a.m. Monday through Friday. The upside: if you're touring in the spring and summer, you've already resigned yourself to early starts to beat the worst of the crowds anyway. Another myth shattered: the VIP tours still require waiting in line. But the tours are longer and, unlike the unreserved version, guided.

How do you reserve a VIP tour? Write a letter to your senator or representative at his or her home office or the one in Washington. For senators, the Washington address is U.S. Senate, Washington, D.C. 20510. For House members, address your letter to the U.S. House of Representatives, Washington, D.C. 20515. Again, don't forget to include the dates you'll be visiting Washington.

A Sample Letter

25 January 2007

The Honorable [*your congressperson or senator's name*]
U.S. House of Representatives (or U.S. Senate)
Washington, D.C. 20515 (or 20510 for the Senate)

Dear Mr. or Ms. [*your congressperson or senator's name*]:

During the week of [*fill in your vacation date*] my family and I will be visiting Washington to tour the major attractions on the Mall, Capitol Hill, and downtown. I understand your office can make reservations on VIP tours for constituents.

Specifically, I would like tours for the White House, the Treasury Department, and the U.S. Capitol during that week. I'll need four reservations for each tour. If at all possible, please schedule our tours in the middle of our week.

In addition, I'd appreciate any other touring information on Washington you can send me. Thanks in advance for your help.

Yours truly,
[*Your name*]

OPERATING HOURS

BY AND LARGE, WASHINGTON'S MAJOR ATTRACTIONS keep liberal operating hours, making it easy for visitors to plan their itineraries without worrying about odd opening and closing times. There are, however, a few exceptions. Of all the major tourist attractions, the Bureau of Engraving and Printing keeps the weirdest hours: closed in the afternoon and not open seven days a week. In that sense, it's the most European institution in town.

Smithsonian museums are open every day from 10 a.m. to 5:30 p.m. During the summer, hours may be extended into the evening if operating budgets allow. The Bureau of Engraving and Printing allows visitors to view its money-printing operation Monday through Friday from 9 to 10:45 a.m., from 12:30 to 2 p.m., and again from 5 to 7:30 p.m. in the summer (a free time-ticket system is in effect in the spring and summer but you have to get in line early).

Most monuments, on the other hand, are open 24 hours a day. Our recommendation is to visit the Lincoln and Jefferson memorials after dark. Lit up by floodlights, the marble edifices appear to float in the darkness, and the Reflecting Pool and Tidal Basin dramatically reflect the light. It's much more impressive than by day—and a lot less crowded, and Park Rangers are on duty as late as midnight to answer questions. The Washington Monument now has a time-ticket system that eliminates long lines.

While many sights are open every day, a lot of Washington attractions close on federal holidays: January 1, Martin Luther King Jr. Day (the third Monday in January), Presidents' Day, Memorial Day, Independence Day, Labor Day (the first Monday in September), Columbus Day (the second Monday in October), Veterans Day, Thanksgiving, and Christmas Day (when virtually everything except outdoor monuments and Mount Vernon is closed).

RHYTHMS OF THE CITY

ALTHOUGH IT'S IMPOSSIBLE TO BE SPECIFIC, the ebb and flow of crowds follows a pattern throughout the day and the week at major tourist attractions. By being aware of the general patterns, you can sometimes avoid the worst of the crowds, traffic congestion, and long lines.

Mornings are slow, and the quietest time to visit most museums and sights is when they open. As lunchtime approaches, the number of people visiting a popular attraction begins to pick up, peaking around 3 p.m. Then the crowds begin to thin, and after 4 p.m. things start to get quiet again. It follows that the best times to visit a wildly popular place like the National Air and Space Museum is just after it opens and just before it closes. Conversely, when the crowds are jamming the Museum of Natural History during the middle of the day, expand your cultural horizons with a visit to the Sackler and Freer Galleries, or the National Museum of African Art. They are rarely, if ever, crowded.

Among days of the week, Monday, Tuesday, and Wednesday see the lowest number of visitors. If you plan to visit the Washington Monument, the Bureau of Engraving and Printing, the National Air and Space Museum, the National Museum of American History (currently under renovation), or the National Museum of Natural History, try to do so early in the week. Attempt to structure your week so that Thursday, Friday, and the weekend are spent visiting sights that are away from the Mall.

IF YOU VISIT DURING PEAK TOURIST SEASON

THE KEY TO MISSING THE WORST OF THE CROWDS in spring and summer is to get a hotel close to a Metro station, park the car, and leave it. Then decide what is most important for you to see, and get to those places early.

An example: You've miraculously secured a convenient D.C. hotel room in early April. From your in-town window, Washington is laid out before you—and for most of the day, it's a view of gridlocked motor coaches, school buses, families in cars, angry commuters, and jammed sidewalks. Everyone but the commuters is drawn by the Japanese cherry trees in bloom along the Tidal Basin and the Reflecting Pool on the Mall.

But don't rush out the door and join the throngs on their way to see the trees. Because it's early (say, 7 a.m.), your plan is to hit the sights that you want to see before the crowds arrive. So walk to the nearby Metro station and take the train to the Smithsonian station: there's a coffee kiosk that opens early at the Castle, among other places. From there, it's a ten-minute stroll to the Washington Monument—and at 7:30, you're near the front of the line when the kiosk that distributes time tickets opens. By 9 a.m., you're out of the marble obelisk and on your way to the nearby Bureau of Engraving and Printing. At the ticket office on Raoul Wallenberg Place, pick up a time ticket for a tour of the money-printing facility that begins at 1:30 p.m. From there, it's a short walk to the Jefferson Memorial and those famous trees.

At 10 a.m, you stroll toward the Mall for a visit to the National Air and Space Museum as it opens. At 10:15, you join a free guided tour. At 11 a.m., you're back on your own again to explore some corners of the museum that interest you.

By noon, you're ready to grab a bite of lunch—you and several hundred of your closest friends. Many of the museums have attractive dining options; see "The Best Museum Restaurants on the Mall" in Part Eight, Dining and Restaurants (page 261). Then it's an easy walk to the Bureau of Engraving and Printing to see the stacks of money.

By 2 p.m., you have already visited three of the world's most popular attractions during peak season with almost no waiting in line. Now you can spend the afternoon exploring a wide range of attractions that never get crowded, even when Washington is besieged by tourists in the spring: the Freer Gallery, the Hirshhorn Museum, the Vietnam Veterans Memorial, the Corcoran Gallery, or the DAR Museum, just to name a few.

WASHINGTON *with* CHILDREN

MOST ADULT VISITORS TO WASHINGTON experience a rush of thrill and pride on viewing the U.S. Capitol, the Washington Monument, and the White House. And, for most of us, those are feelings that hold up well over repeat visits to the nation's capital. In fact, a fascination for the city often begins on a first visit to Washington in grade or high school and can continue through adulthood.

So it follows that Washington is one of the most interesting, beautiful, and stimulating cities in the world for children and young people. Where else can kids see the president's house, touch a moon rock, feed a tarantula, and view a city from the top of a 555-foot marble obelisk?

Luckily, most popular Washington tourist destinations for kids offer a lot to hold an adult's attention, too—which means you don't have to worry about parking the kids someplace while you tour a museum. For example, as your kids marvel at the dinosaur skeletons in the Museum of Natural History or feed that giant spider, you can be fantasizing over the Hope Diamond. Even so, on a Washington vacation with small children, anticipation is the name of the game. Here are some things you need to consider:

AGE Although the big buildings, spaciousness, and thrill of Washington excite children of all ages, and while there are specific sights that delight toddlers and preschoolers, Washington's attractions are generally oriented to older kids and adults. We believe that children should be a fairly mature 8 years old to get the most out of popular attractions

THE TEN MOST POPULAR SIGHTS FOR CHILDREN

1. National Air and Space Museum
2. National Zoological Park
3. International Spy Museum
4. National Museum of Natural History
5. Bureau of Engraving and Printing
6. Federal Bureau of Investigation (scheduled to reopen in 2007)
7. National Museum of American History (closed for renovation)
8. National Geographic Society's Explorers Hall
9. Washington Navy Yard
10. Washington Monument

THE TEN LEAST POPULAR SIGHTS FOR CHILDREN

1. National Gallery of Art
2. Library of Congress
3. U.S. Supreme Court
4. Pentagon
5. Kennedy Center
6. Dumbarton Oaks mansion and museum
7. National Portrait Gallery
8. Folger Shakespeare Library
9. Textile Museum
10. Renwick Gallery

such as the National Museum of Natural History and the Air and Space Museum, and a year or two older to get much out of the art galleries, monuments, and other federal buildings around town.

TIME OF YEAR TO VISIT If there is any way to swing it, avoid the hot, crowded summer months. Try to go in late September through November, or mid-April through mid-June. If you have children of varying ages and your school-age kids are good students, consider taking the older ones out of school so you can visit during the cooler, less-congested off-season. Arrange special study assignments relating to the many educational aspects of Washington. If your school-age children can't afford to miss any school, take your vacation as soon as the school year ends in late May or early June. Nothing, repeat, nothing will enhance your Washington vacation as much as avoiding the early spring—Spring Break traditionally means long lines of high-school kids and tour buses—and summer months.

BUILDING NAPS AND REST INTO YOUR ITINERARY Washington is huge and offers more attractions than you can possibly see in a week, so don't try to see everything in one day. Tour in the early morning and return to your hotel midday for a swim (if your hotel has a pool; see next page) and a nice nap. Even during the fall and winter, when the crowds are smaller and the temperature more pleasant, the sheer size of D.C. will exhaust most children under 8 by lunchtime. Go back and visit more attractions in the late afternoon and early evening.

WHERE TO STAY The time and hassle involved in commuting to and from downtown Washington and its surrounding neighborhoods will be lessened if you can afford to stay inside the District and near a Metro station. But even if, for financial or other reasons, you lodge outside of Washington, it remains imperative that you get small children off the Mall for a few hours to rest and recuperate. Neglecting to relax and unwind is the best way we know to get the whole family in a snit and ruin the day (or the entire vacation).

With small children, there is simply no excuse for not planning ahead. Make sure you get a hotel, in or out of Washington, within a few minutes' walk to a Metro station. Naps and relief from the frenetic pace of touring Washington, even in the off-season, are indispensable. While it's true that you can gain some measure of peace by finding a quiet spot near the Tidal Basin to relax, there is no substitute for returning to the familiarity and security of your own hotel. Regardless of what you have heard or read, children too large to sleep in a stroller will not relax and revive unless you get them back to your room.

Another factor in choosing a hotel is whether or not it has a swimming pool. A lot of visitors to D.C. assume that, like those in most destinations, Washington hotels automatically come with a pool. Alas, it ain't necessarily so. A swimming pool, especially in warmer weather, can be a lifesaver for both you and your kids. So if a refreshing dip is important to your family, be sure to ask before making hotel reservations or check the list of public pools in Part Eleven, Exercise and Recreation (page 397).

EVERYTHING IN MODERATION While we acknowledge that a Washington vacation can be a capital investment (pardon the pun), remember that having fun is not necessarily the same as seeing everything. When you and your children start getting tired and irritable, call time out and regroup. What would really work best right now? Another museum; a rest break with some ice cream; going back to the room for a nap? *The way to protect your investment is to stay happy and have a good time, whatever that takes.* You do not have to meet a quota for experiencing every museum on the Mall, seeing every branch of government, walking through every monument, or anything else. It's your vacation; you can do what you want.

SETTING LIMITS AND MAKING PLANS The best way to avoid arguments and disappointments is to develop a game plan before you go. Establish some general guidelines for the day and get everybody committed in advance. Be sure to include:

1. Wake-up time and breakfast plans.
2. What time you need to depart for the part of Washington you plan to explore.
3. What you need to take with you.
4. A policy for splitting the group up or for staying together.
5. A plan for what to do if the group gets separated or someone is lost.
6. How long you intend to tour in the morning and what you want to see, including fall-back plans in the event an attraction is too crowded.
7. A policy on what you can afford for snacks, lunch, and refreshments.
8. A target time for returning to your hotel for a rest.
9. What time you will return to touring D.C. and how late you will stay.
10. Plans for dinner.
11. A policy for shopping and buying souvenirs, including who pays: Mom and Dad or the kids.

BE FLEXIBLE Having a game plan does not mean forgoing spontaneity or sticking rigidly to the itinerary. Once again, listen to your intuition. Alter the plan if the situation warrants. Be prepared to roll with the punches.

OVERHEATING, SUNBURN, AND DEHYDRATION In the worst of Washington's hot and humid summers, the most common problems of smaller children are overheating, sunburn, and dehydration. A small bottle of sunscreen carried in a pocket or fanny pack will help you take precautions against overexposure to the sun. Be sure to put some on children in strollers, even if the stroller has a canopy. Some of the worst cases of sunburn we have seen were on the exposed foreheads and feet of toddlers and infants in strollers. To avoid overheating, rest at regular intervals in the shade or in an air-conditioned museum, hotel lobby, or federal building.

Do not count on keeping small children properly hydrated with soft drinks and water-fountain stops. Long lines often make buying refreshments problematic, and water fountains are not always handy. What's more, excited children may not inform you or even realize that they're thirsty or overheated. We recommend using a stroller for children 6 years old and under, and carrying plastic water bottles.

BLISTERS Blisters and sore feet are common for visitors of all ages, so wear comfortable, well-broken-in shoes and two pairs of thin socks (preferable to one pair of thick socks). If you or your children are unusually susceptible to blisters, carry some precut Moleskin bandages; they offer the best possible protection, stick great, and won't sweat off. When you feel a hot spot, stop, air out your foot, and place a Moleskin over the area before a blister forms. Moleskin is available by name at all drugstores. Sometimes small children won't tell their parents about a developing blister until it's too late. We recommend inspecting the feet of preschoolers two or more times a day.

IF YOU BECOME SEPARATED Before venturing out of your hotel room, sit down with your kids and discuss what they should do if they get separated from you while touring a museum, monument, or federal building. Tell them to find a uniformed guard and ask for help. Point out that the main entrance of most Washington attractions has an information desk where they should go if they temporarily get separated.

We suggest that children under age 8 be color-coded by dressing them in purple T-shirts or equally distinctive attire. It is also a good idea to sew a label into each child's shirt that states his or her name, your name, and the name of your hotel. The same thing can be accomplished less elegantly by writing the information on a strip of masking tape: hotel security professionals suggest that the information be printed in small letters and that the tape be affixed to the outside of the child's shirt five inches or so below the armpit.

RAINY DAYS Rainy days and Mondays can get you down—even while on vacation—and cooped-up children suffer even worse. Museums and galleries are obvious choices during inclement weather (as you can tell from the crowds), but don't rule out some other options to keep children entertained when the sun doesn't shine or you're museumed out. Let the kids catch a movie at Union Station's nine-screen cinema complex while you explore the shops, or take the Metro to Alexandria's Torpedo Factory, where 150 craftsmen work and sell their creations Tuesday through Sunday. And don't forget that age-old panacea for boredom— shopping. The Old Post Office Pavilion, the Shops at National Place, and Georgetown Park are other indoor shopping centers with interesting specialty stores. If you run out of ideas, check the *Washington Post* "Weekend" section for inspiration.

Of course, some attractions can bore active kids to tears—even if it's raining outside. An entire afternoon in the National Gallery of Art can be deadly to 8-year-olds. The best plan is to reward your youngsters for their patience with a trip to someplace really special when the weather clears. The National Zoo should top the list. And you'll enjoy it, too.

The BEST *inside* TOURS *in* TOWN

IF YOU'RE MORE INCLINED TO ENJOY a few places in depth than to try to make the Big Circuit, you can pretty much have your pick. Many museums, historic homes, and religious sites offer guided tours or detailed brochures and recordings that you can use. Or you can just wander about at your pleasure. Of course, in the post-9/11 era, fewer government agencies are so open: tours of the **U.S. Capitol** are guided and by ticket only, though free; the Pentagon no longer offers tours at all. At press time, the popular tours of the FBI's **Hoover Building** were still suspended but officially attributed to renovation delays. The **Bureau of Printing and Engraving** has resumed tours, however, and the **White House** has expanded its tours to include any group of ten—but you'll have to put your request in through a member of Congress at least 30 days in advance. Self-guided tours are available Tuesday through Saturday, from 7:30 to 11:30 a.m.; for more information, call the White House Visitors Center at ☎ 202-465-7041. The **National Portrait Gallery–Smithsonian Museum of American Art** has reopened in glorious form after six years, but the **National Museum of American History** has begun its own complex renovation that should keep it closed at least through 2008.

Meanwhile, here are some of our favorite places:

The **Thomas Jefferson Building of the Library of Congress** is a stunning example of lavish public construction, with its mythological murals and sculptures, gilded ceilings, stained-glass skylights, mosaics, allegorical friezes, and grand staircases—and that's not even counting the Gutenberg Bible or the great dome of the main reading room made famous by that vertiginous tracking shot in *All the President's Men*. It's not just a library, it's a work of art (First Street SE facing the Capitol; ☎ 202-707-8000; **www.loc.gov**).

The **Daughters of the American Revolution Museum** is one of Washington's underrated beauties. It has 33 period rooms, and even though you can peek in from the doors, the wealth of decorative pieces, ceramics, paintings, silver, costumes, and oddities is wonderful. It may not sound kid-friendly, but in fact there is a space upstairs where children can play with real 18th- and 19th-century toys and flags (1776 D Street NW; ☎ 202-879-3241; **www.dar.org**).

The **U.S. State Department's Diplomatic Reception Rooms** are another lesser-known delight, a stunning geode of 18th- and 19th-century decorative arts—worth close to $100 million—hidden inside that boulder of an office building. You have to reserve a spot well in advance, but it's worth it. Use common sense: this is the State Department, so don't pack pointed objects; also, no strollers are allowed, but this attraction isn't recommended for kids younger than 12 anyway (22nd and C streets NW; ☎ 202-647-3241; **receptiontours.state.gov**).

The **Society of the Cincinnati at Anderson House** in Dupont Circle is a turn-of-the-20th-century fantasia of Florentine architecture, built for an American diplomat whose patriotic fervor extended to hiring muralists and decorators to install historic scenes and symbols throughout the house. The upper floors have their original furnishings and tapestries—check out the crystal chandeliers in the two-story ballroom and the Gilbert Stuart painting in the billiards parlor—while the first floor holds displays of Revolutionary War artifacts (2118 Massachusetts Avenue NW; ☎ 202-785-2040; **www .thesocietyofthecincinnati.addr.com**).

Anderson House cost $750,000 in 1905; the formal gardens alone at **Hillwood Museum,** the home of cereal heiress, socialite, and collector Marjorie Merriweather Post, probably cost that much. (One of Post's husbands was the equally wealthy E. F. Hutton, and another was ambassador to the Soviet Union, so they came in handy when she began collecting art and confiscated Romanov treasures.) If you love exquisite silver, ornate Imperial china, impressive portraits with crowns, and, oh yes, Fabergé eggs, this is the place. The bedrooms and closets are pretty astounding, too; even the earliest photos of Post's daughter, actress Dina Merrill, look like Hollywood studio stills. Have a glass of wine or high tea and play aristocrat. Reservations are required (4155 Linnean Avenue NW; ☎ 202-686-8507; **www.hillwoodmusuem.org**).

It's not an easy tour, but the **U.S. Holocaust Memorial Museum** is one of the most powerful experiences in Washington and an astounding example of how visionary architecture can magnify that power.

Just don't try to squeeze this one into a multistop itinerary—it will leave you emotionally drained (100 Raoul Wallenberg Place; ☎ 202-488-0400; **www.ushmm.org**).

There's a lot more to **Mount Vernon** than two hours' worth, including a view over the Potomac so fine it explains why Washington was so eager to retire. In fact, there's now even more: to the mansion, stables, greenhouses, working farm, and slave quarters has been added an orientation center and a museum education center. The lavish new complex, which opened October 27, 2006, offers state-of-the-art interactive displays; films; life-size forensic re-creations of Washington at three points in his life; and rooms full of china, jewelry, rare books and private letters, Revolutionary War artifacts, and family effects that were not previously on display. If you go around Christmas, you get to tour the cupola, which isn't always open (☎ 703-780-2000; **www.mountvernon.org**).

There are a couple of docent-led tours of **Washington National Cathedral** every day, and you can certainly wander about on your own. But the most fun tours combine an in-depth review of all the gargoyles and buttresses with afternoon tea high in the tower, which affords a stunning view (Tuesdays and Wednesdays at 1:30 p.m., $22; ☎ 202-537-8993; **www.cathedral.org**). If you come early on Wednesdays, you can hear a free demonstration of the great organ at 12:30 p.m.

The **U.S. Department of the Treasury,** alongside the White House, is a fabulous, almost palatial building that has been renovated to its pre–Civil War state, but access is very limited. You'll have to enlist the help of your senator or representative to get a reservation here as well, expect to show photo IDs, and so on. The hour-long guided tours are free but offered only on Saturdays at 9, 9:45, 10, and 11:15 a.m.—and don't even think about being late. Enter on the south side of the building facing the Washington Monument (1500 Pennsylvania Avenue NW; ☎ 202-622-2000; **www.ustreas.gov**).

TAKING *an* ORIENTATION TOUR

FIRST-TIME VISITORS TO WASHINGTON can't help but notice the regular procession of open-air, multicar tour buses—"motorized trolleys" is probably a more accurate term—that prowl the streets along the Mall, the major monuments, Arlington Cemetery, downtown, Georgetown, and Upper Northwest Washington. These regularly scheduled shuttle buses drop off and pick up paying customers along a route that includes the town's most popular attractions. Between stops, passengers listen to a tour guide talk about the city's monuments, museums, and famous buildings.

We recommend the big charter companies mostly for those who need some orientation to begin with stage, for those with children, those with a somewhat short time frame, or those who have mobility or breathing problems such as allergies or asthma. (Check with your hotel staff about air quality; Washington is prone to pollution and irritant buildup, especially in the summer, and health officials will issue alerts on those days.) Chartered tours are also handy if you haven't bought a travel guide, since each comes with some sort of narration, often a conductor or miked driver (but sometimes just a recording) who passes along the primary facts about each building or memorial and tosses in a few jokes and, not infrequently, some intriguing trivia.

If you're already pretty familiar with the major monuments, you should look into the special-interest tours, whether guided or do-it-yourself. Several good online resources can help you customize your own route. What's more, many of the national monuments have park rangers on site who know everything—and who talk for free. Government buildings, religious sites, and historic houses are likely to offer docent-led tours and/or detailed recorded versions.

Certain types of tours are more common at particular seasons: ghost tours around Halloween, candlelight tours from Thanksgiving to New Year's, garden tours in early summer, and the like; check newspapers or local Web sites. And, obviously, some types of tours— kayaks, Segways, open-air vessels—are likely to be warmer-weather options. Call well ahead if you plan to try one of those.

GET ON THE BUS, GUS

PAUL REVERE WOULD HAVE A HARD TIME signaling for a Washington monuments tour, whether by land or by sea (at least if you count the Potomac River). You can tour by day or by night; get around via bike or Segway (or wheelchair); hire a horse-drawn carriage or hoof it yourself. There was a time when you could sightsee by air, too, but most of official Washington is under restricted airspace these days.

If you choose one of the big drive-around tours, you can either stick to the bus for the whole circuit or hop on and off at more than a dozen hot spots. These on–off tours circulate every 20 to 30 minutes, so you can pretty much set your own rhythm. On the other hand, even tour operators suggest not trying to see more than a half-dozen sites in a day, so you might want to make a list of the ones you really care about. Also note that if you are buying tickets from the driver on the bus, you'll probably need to pay cash, so be prepared.

Among the major land operators are **Tourmobile,** which has the franchise for operating on National Park Service territory and shuttles open-air buses around the Mall from Capitol Hill past the Tidal Basin and to Arlington National Cemetery ($20 adults, $10 ages 3 to 11 at any red-and-white route marker along the way; ☎ 202-554-5100); the **L'il Red Trolley,** an on–off service that makes a two-hour loop around the Mall and Penn Quarter attractions between 8:30 a.m. and 4:30 p.m. (☎ 202-832-9800); and **Old Town Trolley** ($32 adults, $16 ages 3 to 11;

washington old town trolley

34th St.

Cathedral Ave.

National Zoological Park

12

Cleveland Ave.

Calvert St.

11

Euclid St.

Georgia Ave.

Adams-Morgan

Florida Ave.

1

Wisconsin Ave.

Mass. Ave.

Conn. Ave.

New Hampshire Ave.

16th St.

Florida Ave.

Rhode Island Ave.

N.J. Ave.

Florida Ave.

N. Capitol St.

Rock Creek

P St.

10

Mass. Ave.

N.Y. Ave.

50

Georgetown

13

M St.

9

Mass. Ave.

K   St.

H   St.

Key Bridge

14

Penn. Ave.

8

4

White House

5

E St.

1

66

Theodore Roosevelt Is.

Virginia Ave.

19th St.

7

14th St.

6

Penn. Ave.

2

50

Theodore Roosevelt Bridge

15

Reflecting Pool

3

Constitution Ave

The Mall

Independence Ave.

U.S. Capitol

19

Arlington Memorial Bridge

17

18

16

Potomac River

Arlington National Cemetery

S. Capitol St.

395

1

●●●● Trolley Route

1 Trolley Stops and Ticket Sales

0 ——— 1 mi
0 ——— 1 km

● TROLLEY STOPS AND TICKET SALES
1. Union Station
2. Capitol Arboretum
3. Old Post Office/American and National History Museums
4. Museum of Women in the Arts
5. Chinatown
6. FBI Building/Ford's Theatre
7. Freedom Plaza/National Aquarium
8. The White House
9. National Geographic Society
10. Dupont Circle Neighborhood

11. Kalorama/Adams-Morgan Neighborhoods
12. Washington National Cathedral
13. Georgetown
14. Washington Harbour
15. Lincoln Memorial/Vietnam Veterans Memorial
16. Arlington National Cemetery
17. Washington Monument/Holocaust Museum
18. Air and Space Museum/Smithsonian Mall
19. U.S. Capitol/Library of Congress

☎ 202-289-1995), which runs from 9 a.m. to 5:30 p.m. (until 4:30 p.m. in winter). Both trolley lines make stops at Washington National Cathedral—which, unlike most of the other sites, is not near a Metro stop, so you may want to work that in. Old Town Trolley also offers a two-and-a-half-hour "Monuments by Moonlight" version that leaves Union Station at 7:30 p.m. (6:30 p.m. in fall and winter) and includes a few ghostly anecdotes.

The **Circulator** bus is not a tour shuttle per se, and you won't hear any stories, but the tour routes will carry you to more than a dozen attractions along the Mall as well as to Penn Quarter (Verizon Center, National Portrait Gallery–Smithsonian American Art Museum, International Spy Museum), the Convention Center, and the Waterfront, so it may serve you just as well. Fares are 50¢ to $1, and you can get off and back on within two hours at no charge with a transfer (or get a day pass for $3). See more information on the Circulator in Part Five, Getting Around Washington (page 113).

If you're willing to devote more time to the tour, **Gray Line** offers a four-hour coach tour that takes in Old Town Alexandria as well as downtown and another tour that combines Old Town and Mount Vernon ($37, $18 ages 3 to 11; ☎ 202-289-1995).

DC Party Shuttle Tours (☎ 202-756-1983) has a hop-on–hop-off system with a difference: the tour guide gets off with you and continues the narration. And it's unusually extensive, stopping at a dozen points and passing two dozen more. If you have the time—it's a six-hour, $60 circuit with a lunch stop at the Pentagon City Mall food court—this tour will get you far better situated than the others. It also offers a three-hour "nightlights" tour starting at 7 p.m. ($30).

Scandal Tours takes a slightly different tack. It covers much of the same geography—the Tidal Basin (remember Fanne Foxe and Wilbur Mills?), the White House (specifically, the Lincoln Bedroom, favorite haunt of Friends of Bill and of Abraham Lincoln's ghost), the U.S. Capitol (John and Rita Jenrette's not-so-private trysting spot)—but with "celebrity" guides (members of the local comedy troupe Gross National Product). Tours leave Saturdays at 1 p.m., April through Labor Day, from the Warehouse Theater in the Penn Quarter (reservations required; ☎ 202-783-7212).

On Location Tours runs a three-hour tour of about 40 locales used in *The Exorcist, The West Wing, Wedding Crashers,* and other productions. Actors are scheduled to do the narration (although Linda Blair's head-turning part hasn't been cast). Tours depart from Union Station at 2 p.m., Friday through Sunday ($32; ☎ 800-979-3370; **www.screentours.com**).

GET YOUR FEET WET

WATER TOURS GO IN BASICALLY TWO DIRECTIONS: up and down the Potomac. Many are floating restaurants, with pretty but passing views of the Capitol, the Washington Monument, the Kennedy Center, Georgetown, the Southwest Waterfront, and Old Town Alexandria. If you're going to drink, dine, and dance, the scenery is just a backdrop.

Spirit Cruises offers a ride to Mount Vernon and back that includes admission over a two-hour break to Washington's home ($38, $36 seniors, and $31 ages 6 to 11; ☎ 202-554-8000). Many cruises are seasonal, especially those on the smaller open-air boats. Tours leave from Pier 4 at the Southwest Waterfront.

Potomac Riverboat Company (☎ 703-548-9000 or 877-511-2628) offers a "Washington by Water" cruise that goes up to the Capitol and back down toward Alexandria; go round-trip or get off and wander. Round-trips are $22 adults, $19 seniors, and $11 ages 2 to 12; one-way fares are $11 adults and $7 children. The same company operates photo cruises past Mount Vernon ($9 adults, $5 ages 6 to 10) and an Old Town–Mount Vernon excursion with mansion access ($32 and $19). All Potomac Riverboat vessels are nonsmoking.

Smaller, quicker trips take off from the open-air bar area at the foot of Wisconsin Avenue in Georgetown. From April through October, **Capitol River Cruises** leave on the hour from Washington Harbour for a 50-minute narrated cruise past the Kennedy Center, the Capitol building, the LBJ and Maritime memorials, the Custis-Lee Mansion, and other points of interest ($12 adults, $6 ages 3 to 12; ☎ 301-460-7447). **Potomac Pintails** (☎ 202-369-7077) runs a quick, pleasant 50-minute pontoon tour from Washington Harbour to the Jefferson Memorial every hour from 12:45 to 7:45 p.m. Tuesday through Thursday and 11:45 a.m. to 8:45 p.m. Friday through Sunday, April through October. Tours carry a maximum of 20 passengers and include complimentary beverages and live narration.

If you can stand the "wise quacks," or if your party includes kids, take the **DC Ducks** tour aboard renovated WWII amphibious vehicles ($29 adults, $14 ages 4 to 12; ☎ 202-832-9800). Ducks leave Union Station every hour, roll through the Mall, then plop into the Potomac River near Georgetown and cruise down to Gravely Point, under the National Airport flight path. These are seasonal tours, running only from mid-March to the end of October, and only if the weather permits.

If you love the water, try the **American Spirit** schooner tour. This three-hour sail aboard a 62-footer goes along the Anacostia and Potomac rivers and past Fort McNair and Bolling Air Force Base, the Alexandria waterfront, and so on. Tours leave from Union Station at 5:30 p.m. (you take a bus to the boat), July through mid-September ($69; ☎ 301-386-8300).

And if you *really* love the water, you can book a weekend kayaking tour and get right down into it with **Atlantic Kayaks** ($44; ☎ 301-292-6455; **www.atlantickayak.com**). Daytime or sunset tours start from Jack's Boathouse on K Street at the foot of Key Bridge and paddle down past Memorial Bridge; even first-timers are allowed.

They're a little more limited in focus and season (warm weather), but the **National Park Service**'s hour-long barge trips, drawn 19th-century–style by mules through the locks of the C&O Canal between Georgetown and Great Falls, Virginia (and leaving from either end), are wonderful family excursions. Park Service guides in costume explain the workings of the lock system and the history of the canal. In Georgetown, board at the landing near Foundry Mall on Thomas Jefferson Street ($8 adults, $6 ages 62 and over, $5 ages 4 to 14; ☎ 202-653-5190). For information about the Great Falls stop, call ☎ 301-767-3714. These trips are particularly fun on summer weekends, when there are sometimes free canal-side concerts.

Personally, we think drinking–dining cruises aren't the way to go, only because the sights tend to be mere window dressing (you're glassed in most of the time). But if you're touring for more than one day or you've been to Washington before, you might like them. *Odyssey III* offers lunch, brunch, dinner, and sometimes midnight cruises from two to three hours long, departing from the Gangplank Marina at Sixth and Water streets SW ($38 to $92 adults, $16 children lunch only; ☎ 800-946-7245 or 202-488-6000; **www.odysseycruises.com**). The *Cruise Ship Dandy* is berthed at Old Town Alexandria and comes up for lunch or for dinner and dancing (lunch $32 to $40, dinner $75 and up; ☎ 703-683-6076; **www.dandydinnerboat.com**).

WHEELING AROUND WASHINGTON

BIKE TOURS HAVE A FEW ADVANTAGES, and getting on and off in a second is just one. And it's certainly closer than a drive-by ("Every seat is a window seat," goes the sales pitch). You get some exercise, you don't have to get your old bike in order (rental and helmets are included), and you can bring the kids—tandem trailers are available—so long as they're old enough to wear helmets and hold their heads up. On the other hand, bike tours are subject to the whims of weather (closed January and February) and require advance bookings.

Bike the Sites offers three-hour tours of the monuments by day and sometimes by night, plus a larger Capitol Hill–Mall tour and, by prior arrangement, group rides down to Mount Vernon. Tours depart from the Old Post Office Pavilion at 10 a.m. and 2:30 p.m., with occasional evening tours at 6:30 p.m. ($40 adults, $30 for kids; includes mountain bike and helmet rental; ☎ 202-842-2453; **www.bikethesites.com**). The three-hour "Wild Washington" tour of animal sculptures rolls from the National Zoo through Rock Creek and the Mall, with views of the friezes and sculptures and decorations around town.

Bike the Sites also rents wheelchairs and mobility scooters: wheelchairs, $15 for two hours, then $5 per hour to $35 maximum; scooters, $35 for two hours and then $10 per hour to $65 maximum.

Segways are great fun, but you do have to learn how to drive one first, so tours begin with training sessions and safety checks. (Segways are not suited to children under age 16 or anyone over 260 pounds.) Tours are also somewhat seasonal, obviously, as the surfaces are weather susceptible.

City Segway Tours leads four-hour tours that leave from the courtyard of the Willard Hotel at 9:30 a.m. and 2 p.m. ($70; ☎ 202-349-4060 or 877-734-8689). **Segs in the City,** which shares a kiosk behind the Old Post Office Pavilion with Bike the Sites, offers two-hour tours at 10 a.m. and 2 p.m., a one-hour "mini-tour" at 12:30 and 5 p.m., and a two-hour tour of Embassy Row on Sundays only ($45 for the one-hour tours and $70 for the two-hour tours; ☎ 800-734-7393). **Capital Segway** runs its own tours that leave from its showroom at 14th and I streets NW at noon and 3 p.m., Monday through Saturday and Sunday by appointment ($65; ☎ 202-333-2586). Capital is an authorized Segway dealership, and if you fall so in love with your ride that you want to buy it, your tour fee will be shifted to the bill.

WHEELS WITH HORSEPOWER

WHILE THEY MAY NOT BE AS FAMOUS OR UBIQUITOUS as the carriages of Central Park, horse-drawn buggy tours are available in Washington. Six people is usually the limit, but it would be a prime possibility for romance. **Charley Horse Carriage Company** ($125 and up; ☎ 202-801-2333; **charleyhorse@earthlink.net**) usually picks up outside the Hyatt Regency Hotel on Capitol Hill between 7 and 11 p.m.; at Christmas rides depart from near the National Christmas Tree on the Ellipse, and you might see a buddy lurking near the ice-skating rink at the National Galley of Art. **Carriages of the Capitol** ($150 per hour and up; ☎ 202-841-4135; **www.carriagesofthecapitol.com**) generally depart from the Willard Hotel at 6:30 p.m. (other hours by reservation) or from Capitol Hill.

HOOFING IT YOURSELF

THERE ARE PLENTY OF REGULARLY SCHEDULED WALKING TOURS you can hook up with. **Washington Walks** (☎ 202-484-1565; **www .washingtonwalks.com**), founded by Carolyn Crouch, who moved to Washington and walked it on her own, is an established organization whose most popular subjects include "Memorials by Moonlight"; the "I've Got a Secret" tour (more trivia game than Scandal Tours, it includes a onetime brothel and the severed leg of a Civil War general); various neighborhood tours; and the new "Bus, Camera, Action!" tour of local sites that appear in movies and television, giving the usually dull Monday night a good name. (If you don't know yet that there is no Georgetown subway station, it's time you learned.) The "Moveable Feast" tours, held the first and third Saturdays of the month, add a touch of ethnic fare to the mix, but the food is extra. Some Washington Walks are seasonal, some are scheduled for particular dates rather than weekly, and a few are for younger audiences; check the Web site for a full list. You can also book any Washington Walks tour for times and/or days other than the regularly scheduled ones.

Once you have a feel for the area, you may want to do it alone, taking it one attraction or area at a time. One extensive online resource is **Cultural Tourism DC** (**www.culturaltourismdc.org**), which offers information on local attractions by neighborhood (Barracks Row, U Street, the Southwest Waterfront); by cultural niche (religious sites, art museums, and so on); by historical themes such as black history and the Civil War; and by a few specialized interests, including outdoor sculpture, cemeteries, and historic houses. Some pages include route maps as well as walking itineraries.

If you're iPod literate, you can download a free tour of the monuments and the Mall from **Ten Toe Tours** (**www.tentoetours.com**) and wander at your own pace. If you go the MP3 route, you can download tour files with printable maps for the Mall or historic Georgetown from **Audio Steps Tours** ($12; **www.audiosteps.com**).

GET UP CLOSE AND PERSONAL

IF YOU'RE SERIOUS ABOUT A PARTICULAR FIELD OF INTEREST, you may want to hire an expert. Customized tours are likely to be expensive, probably starting at close to $75 an hour for the guide alone, not counting any transportation, admission fees, or gratuities (plus, most tours last three or four hours). But rates are generally the same for a solo or a small group, so if you have a friend who shares your passion, it might help with the bill. Be sure your guide is licensed by the District government—it's the law.

With a personal guide, you can set your own timetable and mode of transportation, so there's more flexibility. The **Guide Service of Washington** (☎ 202-628-2842; **www.dctourguides.com**) and the **Guild of Professional Tour Guides of Washington** (☎ 202-298-1474; **www .washingtondctourguides.com**) can steer you to former government employees, professors, historians, and even ex-spies who will spill the beans on Washington history and gossip.

One of Washington's better-known tour guides, who calls his walks "anecdotal history tours," is History Channel narrator and historian **Anthony Pitch** (☎ 301-294-9514; **www.dcsightseeing.com**). Tour locations and themes include Georgetown, Adams-Morgan, the Capitol Hill neighborhood ("Skirting the Capitol" points up some Congressional bloopers), "Spooks of Lafayette Square," Lincoln's assassination, and the burning of the capital during the War of 1812.

Jeanne Fogel (☎ 703-525-2948; **www.atourdefource.com**), a writer and adjunct professor of regional history and tour guiding at Northern Virginia Community College, also takes a raconteur's approach to Washington history. Her "Tour de Force" itineraries are all customized, but she prefers to explore the social history and architectural evolution of the neighborhoods.

Author **Mary Kay Ricks** specializes in Georgetown (spies and scandals, cemeteries, the Underground Railroad); Dupont Circle and Embassy Row; and Striver's Row, the homes of Washington's black elite. Ninety-minute group tours are $350, her public Saturday walks $15 apiece (☎ 202-588-8999; **www.tourdc.com**).

Carole Bessette (☎ 703-569-1875; **www.spiesofwashingtontour .com**) is a retired Air Force intelligence officer and Vietnam veteran who's a walking, talking, one-woman international spy museum. She leads group walks ($12 per person) and customized private driving tours. Carole also leads walks for tourists with dogs and for families.

Historic Strolls (☎ 301-588-9255; **www.historicstrolls.com**) takes a more dramatic approach, using for the most part professional actors who assume historical identities at key spots along the way. A character from *A Christmas Carol* leads the "Charles Dickens in Washington" tour; "Gussie the Government Gal" adjusts to life in World War II D.C.; a hoop-skirted gossip explores the Civil War sites. And one of the most intriguing tours brings out the pickpockets, con men, cardsharps, and "soiled doves" of 19th-century Washington. All tours ($10 adults, $5 under age 16) partly benefit nonprofit groups.

UC Tours specializes in African American history and multicultural tours, and one focusing on the Washington residences and memorabilia of Jacqueline Bouvier Kennedy; who also attended prep school here (☎ 202-526-3384 or **www.uctour.com**).

Children's Concierge is more of a middleman (or -woman) that helps design itineraries for family groups but would also be a good resource for something like a reunion or multigenerational gathering (☎ 301-948-3312).

OPTIMUM ADULT TOURING PLAN

AN OPTIMUM TOURING PLAN IN WASHINGTON, D.C., requires a thoughtful itinerary, a minimum of five days in town (not including travel time), a surprisingly modest amount of money (most attractions are free), and a comfortable pair or two of walking shoes. It also requires a fairly prodigious appetite for marble edifices, huge museums, and historical trivia. We suggest one basic, but it's only an outline; fill in the sites that matter to you.

With an Optimum Touring Plan, you can see the various attractions in and around Washington without facing huge crowds on the Mall, sitting in restaurants and shops that are jammed to capacity, or trudging through heat and humidity during sweltering afternoons.

Since an Optimum Touring Plan calls for seeing a lot of different parts of D.C., it makes for easier logistics if you stay at a hotel that's in the city and close to a Metro station. But even if your hotel is in the suburbs, you can still use the day-by-day plan as long as you can walk to the Metro. You'll lose some time commuting, but you may save some money on hotel rates. You'll lose even more time if you have to drive to a Metro station and park, which requires a SmarTrip card except on weekends (see page 122). Once you get in your car and start driving around in D.C., you're defeating the purpose of the Optimum Touring Plan, and you'll know it. *We repeat:* Don't drive in the city.

If you plan to visit Washington during the busiest months (which are discussed on page 13), you need to get up early to beat the crowds. Getting free "time tickets" for the Washington Monument and Bureau of Engraving and Printing is basically incompatible with sleeping in. If you want to sleep late and enjoy your touring experience, visit Washington in the fall or winter, when crowds are smaller; or go to the less crowded art museums or historic homes. The Optimum Touring Plan assumes your visit is during the busy season.

We do not believe there is one ideal itinerary. Tastes, levels of energy, and basic perspectives on what is interesting or edifying vary. This understood, what follows is our personal version of an optimum Washington vacation week.

Before You Go

1. Write your congressperson as far in advance as possible for VIP tour reservations and a packet of free information on visiting Washington.

2. Determine which of the attractions that appeal to you require advance reservations, select one or two that most interest you, and make them for the afternoon of Day 3 at the same time you write your congressperson.

3. Read through all your information and make an informal list of sights that you and your family want to see during your Washington stay.

4. If you like theater or music, look into the Kennedy Center Schedule (www.kennedycenter.org) to see if something there attracts you; you can get your tickets online or by phone. Go early and wander around or have a cocktail on the terrace overlooking the Potomac River.

On Site

DAY 0

1. Arrive and get settled. Explore the features and amenities of your hotel.

2. If you get checked in by 3 p.m., go to the Mall and visit the Castle, the Smithsonian's visitor center. (If you're not within walking distance, this is an opportunity to get familiar with the Metro. Read our chapter on how it works and take the Blue Line to the Smithsonian station.) Since crowds start to thin in the late afternoon, you may have time to duck into the National Air and Space Museum or the National Museum of Natural History after viewing the orientation film in the Castle.

3. Take the Metro to Dupont Circle for dinner at the Thai, Japanese, Italian, or Greek restaurant of your choice. When you get back to your

hotel, check with the desk to find the nearest stop for boarding either the L'il Red Trolley or Tourmobile sightseeing tours. This will save you time in the morning.

DAY 1

1. After breakfast at your hotel, board one of the sightseeing buses for an orientation tour of Washington. The driver sells tickets.

2. Stay on the bus for a complete circuit, which takes about an hour and a half (two hours for L'il Red Trolley; Old Town Trolley tickets are only good for one complete tour). You'll gain a good overview of Washington's huge number of attractions, which will help you decide what sights you want to see on this trip—and which ones can wait for another visit.

3. For lunch, get off the tour bus at Union Station, an architectural masterpiece, and head for the lower-level food court. Over lunch, decide what stops you want to make from the bus this afternoon.

4. Reboard your tour bus at Union Station. In deciding where to get off next, consider an attraction that's not convenient to your hotel. On L'il Red Trolley, both Georgetown and Washington National Cathedral are good choices. On Tourmobile, consider the Arlington National Cemetery tour. Another hint: Some of the guides on the buses really know their stuff regarding sights, restaurants, and strategies on how to tour D.C. Ask them for suggestions. Plan to get off at either Georgetown or the Kennedy Center.

5. If you aren't going to the Kennedy Center for a sit-down show, take advantage of the free show every night at 6 p.m. in the main concourse at the Millennium Stage. Then for dinner, walk the riverfront to Georgetown. After dinner, take in a stroll and some nightlife. If you are going to the Kennedy Center another time, go down to the Georgetown Waterfront, called Washington Harbour; there are several restaurants with outdoor bars and seating, or indoor water views if you're overheated.

DAY 2

1. An early start: Get to 15th Street by 7 a.m. and pick up "time tickets" to the White House, the Washington Monument (15th and E NW), and the Bureau of Engraving and Printing (15th and C SW).

2. After lunch, return to your hotel for a nap or a dip in the pool.

3. Around 3 p.m. take the Metro to Dupont Circle, where you can window-shop, stroll down Embassy Row, and stop in Anderson House, a sumptuous mansion and museum. Then have dinner in one of the many restaurants nearby.

DAY 3

1. Get in line for the International Spy Museum tour by 8:30 a.m. After breakfast, hit one of the popular Mall museums: Air and Space, American History, or Natural History.

2. After lunch, concentrate on some of the best art galleries in the world—the National Gallery of Art, The Freer and Sackler, and the Hirshhorn Museum and Sculpture Garden. Or take the tour of the U.S. Department of State Diplomatic Reception Rooms or one of the other reservation-only tours that you set up before the trip. If a few hours off your feet sounds attractive, consider taking in a movie at the five-story IMAX screen at the Air and Space Museum.

3. Take the Metro to Gallery Place or Archives–Navy Memorial–Penn Quarter for dinner at one of the many restaurants in that booming neighborhood. Then take the Metro to the Federal Triangle station and go to the Old Post Office Pavilion for dessert and a spectacular night view of Washington from the 315-foot-high clock tower. Afterward, go to a jazz or blues club.

DAY 4

1. Tour Capitol Hill: the U.S. Capitol (arrive at the kiosk by 8 a.m. to pick up tickets), the Supreme Court, and the Library of Congress. Eat lunch at a Capitol Hill cafe.

2. If it's a scorching summer day, consider one of these options after lunch: downtown's American Art Museum and the National Portrait Gallery (at Gallery Place) or the DAR Museum. Around 4 p.m., take the Metro to Woodley Park and walk or take a cab to the National Zoo. For dinner, pick from the many restaurants in Woodley Park or Cleveland Park, both of which are within walking distance, and both of which have some late-night music and bar scene options.

DAY 5

1. Either drive or take the 8:30 a.m. Gray Line bus or the 10 a.m. Tourmobile to Mount Vernon, George Washington's estate on the Potomac River. If you drive, leave before 7:30 a.m. or after 9:30 a.m. to avoid the worst rush-hour traffic.

2. Visit Old Town Alexandria for lunch and more 18th-century Americana. Stop in the Torpedo Factory to shop for unique arts and crafts.

3. If you're visiting in the summer, start your evening with a free military-band concert. These are held on a rotating basis at 8 p.m. at either the U.S. Navy Memorial (Archives–Navy Memorial–Penn Quarter Metro), the steps of the U.S. Capitol (Capitol South Metro), or the Sylvan Theatre, located on the grounds of the Washington Monument (Smithsonian Metro). Afterward, take the Metro to the Waterfront station and walk to a Maine Avenue seafood restaurant for dinner.

TOURING STRATEGIES

ATTRACTIONS GROUPED BY METRO STATION

WITH THE EXCEPTION OF THE RED LINE TOUR, we don't recommend structuring your visit around attractions located near Metro stations. But we do think a list of tourist attractions located within walking distance of Metro stations can help make a last-minute touring selection to fill in part of a morning or afternoon—and maybe save you a buck or two in Metro fares. *A warning:* Although this list shows what attractions are closest to a Metro station, some sights could be as far as 20 minutes away by foot. For example, while the Foggy Bottom–GWU Metro is the closest to the Lincoln Memorial, it's still about a three-quarter-mile hike.

Red Line

BROOKLAND-CUA The National Shrine of the Immaculate Conception, the Franciscan Monastery (10- and 20-minute walks, respectively)

UNION STATION National Postal Museum, the U.S. Supreme Court, the U.S. Capitol, Senate office buildings, Folger Shakespeare Library, Library of Congress

JUDICIARY SQUARE National Building Museum, National Law Enforcement Officers Memorial, the Lillian and Albert Small Jewish Museum

GALLERY PLACE–CHINATOWN National Portrait Gallery, Smithsonian American Art Museum, Chinatown, National Building Museum, Washington Convention Center, Ford's Theatre, the FBI (tours scheduled to resume in 2007), International Spy Museum, Koshland Science Museum

METRO CENTER National Museum of Women in the Arts, U.S. Department of the Treasury, the Washington Convention Center, the Shops at National Place

FARRAGUT NORTH Swank shops on Connecticut Avenue, National Geographic Society's Explorers Hall

DUPONT CIRCLE Shops and restaurants, Embassy Row, the Phillips Collection, Anderson House, the Islamic Center, Woodrow Wilson House, the Textile Museum, House of the Temple

WOODLEY PARK–ZOO/ADAMS-MORGAN National Zoo, Washington National Cathedral, Adams-Morgan (the Zoo is about a ten-minute walk; Adams-Morgan is about 15 minutes away on foot; and the Cathedral is a half-hour stroll.)

CLEVELAND PARK National Zoo (this way you're walking down hill rather than up), trendy restaurants, lounges

VAN NESS–UDC Intelsat, Hillwood Museum (20-minute walk)

TENLEYTOWN-AU Kreeger Museum

Blue and Orange Lines

CAPITOL SOUTH Library of Congress, House office buildings,

Capitol Hill restaurants, the U.S. Capitol, Folger Shakespeare Library, the U.S. Supreme Court

FEDERAL CENTER SW U.S. Botanic Garden, the National Air and Space Museum, National Museum of the American Indian

L'ENFANT PLAZA Shops and restaurants, the National Air and Space Museum, the Hirshhorn Museum and Sculpture Garden, the Arts and Industries Building (closed for renovation), National Museum of the American Indian

SMITHSONIAN The National Mall, the Freer and Sackler Galleries, the National Museum of African Art, the Bureau of Engraving and Printing, the National Museum of Natural History, the National Museum of American History (closed for renovation), the Washington Monument, the Smithsonian Castle visitor center, the Tidal Basin, the Jefferson Memorial (15-minute walk), FDR Memorial (15-minute walk), Korean War Veterans' Memorial (20-minute walk), Lincoln Memorial (20-minute walk), Martin Luther King Jr. Memorial (under construction), the U.S. Holocaust Memorial Museum, National World War II Memorial, National Museum of the American Indian

FEDERAL TRIANGLE The Old Post Office Pavilion, the National Aquarium, the FBI (tours to resume in 2007), Pennsylvania Avenue, National Museum of American History, National Museum of Natural History, the White House Visitors Center, Visitor Information Center (in the Ronald Reagan Building)

MCPHERSON SQUARE The White House, the *Washington Post* building, Lafayette Park

FARRAGUT WEST Decatur House, Renwick Gallery, the Old Executive Office Building, the White House, the Corcoran Gallery of Art, the DAR Museum, the Ellipse, the Octagon

FOGGY BOTTOM–GWU The Kennedy Center, the U.S. Department of State Diplomatic Reception Rooms, Vietnam Veterans Memorial, Korean War Veterans Memorial, National World War II Memorial, the Reflecting Pool, the Lincoln Memorial, the FDR Memorial, Georgetown (20- to 30-minute walk)

ARLINGTON CEMETERY Arlington National Cemetery, the Lincoln and FDR memorials (across Memorial Bridge)

PENTAGON The Pentagon (closed to visitors)

RONALD REAGAN WASHINGTON NATIONAL AIRPORT Ronald Reagan Washington National Airport

KING STREET Old Town Alexandria (15-minute walk), shops and restaurants, the Torpedo Factory (20-minute walk), the Stabler-Leadbetter Apothecary Museum (15-minute walk), the George Washington National Masonic Memorial

Yellow Line

GALLERY PLACE–CHINATOWN National Portrait Gallery and Smithsonian, American Art Museum, Chinatown, National Building Museum, Washington Convention Center, Ford's Theatre, the FBI (tours temporarily suspended), International Spy Museum, Koshland Science Museum

ARCHIVES–NAVY MEMORIAL–PENN QUARTER The National Archives, the U.S. Navy Memorial, the National Gallery of Art, the National Museum of Natural History

Green Line

WATERFRONT-SEU Washington's Potomac River waterfront area (restaurants, marinas, and river cruises), Fort McNair, Arena Stage

SEEING WASHINGTON ON A TIGHT SCHEDULE

MANY VISITORS DO NOT HAVE FIVE DAYS to devote to visiting Washington. They may be en route to other destinations, or may live within a day's drive, making later visits practical. Either way, efficient, time-effective touring is a must. Such visitors cannot afford long waits in line to see attractions or spend hours trying to find a place to park the family car.

Even the most efficient touring plan will not allow the visitor to visit the Mall, Capitol Hill, and Georgetown in one day, so plan on allocating at least an entire day to the Mall (but not just museums), and devoting your remaining days to other parts of Washington that appeal to you.

ONE-DAY TOURING

A COMPREHENSIVE TOUR OF WASHINGTON is literally impossible in a day. But a day trip to Washington can be a fun, rewarding experience. Pulling it off hinges on following some basic rules.

Determine in Advance What You Really Want to See

What are the categories that appeal to you most? If it's government, spend your day on Capitol Hill. If it's exploring museums, visit the Mall. If you like trendy shops and a sophisticated ambience, go to Georgetown or Dupont Circle.

Select an Area to Visit

For example, if visiting the U.S. Capitol is your goal, look at what other nearby attractions on Capitol Hill or the east end of the Mall interest you. That way you won't waste time and steps.

Arrive Early! Arrive Early! Arrive Early!

This is the single most important key to efficient touring and avoiding big crowds. First thing in the morning, lines are short at the

Bureau of Engraving and Printing and the Washington Monument's ticket kiosk. You can visit three famous Washington attractions in one or two hours that would take an entire afternoon if you arrived at noon. Eat breakfast before you arrive so you will not have to waste your prime touring time sitting in a crowded restaurant.

Avoid Bottlenecks

Helping you avoid bottlenecks and big crowds is what this guide is all about. Bottlenecks occur as a result of crowd concentrations in the absence of crowd management. Concentrations of hungry people create bottlenecks at restaurants during the lunch and dinner hours; concentrations of visitors heading toward the best-known monuments, memorials, museums, and government buildings create elbow-to-elbow crowds during afternoons. Avoiding bottlenecks involves knowing when and where large concentrations of visitors begin to occur.

In addition, day-trippers need to avoid the agony of driving in D.C. traffic if they expect to have any fun and see enough Washington attractions to make the trip worthwhile. There are two ways to do it:

PARK YOUR CAR IN THE SUBURBS In suburban Maryland and Virginia, the Metro extends to the Beltway and beyond, eliminating the need for you to battle Washington traffic, as well as saving you time, money, and stomach acid. On weekends, Metro users park for free at any suburban station. During the week, unless you arrive before 7 a.m. (or right at 10 a.m., when the unused "reserved" slots are freed up), your choice of suburban Metro stations is limited to six: Vienna (on I-66 in Virginia); New Carrollton (on the Beltway in Maryland); Greenbelt (also on the Beltway in Maryland); Shady Grove (off I-270 in Maryland); Grosvenor-Strathmore (just outside the Beltway in Maryland); and Silver Spring (inside the Beltway in Maryland). We recommend that you park at a Maryland station, unless you can make it to a Virginia station very early. From the outermost suburbs, it's about a 20-minute stress-free train ride to the Mall. (*Note:* Payment must be made by using a SmarTrip fare card, sold in vending machines in Metro stations or online at **www.wmata.com**).

New Carrollton has plenty of parking, plus a parking garage for overflow. Take Beltway Exit 19B (US 50 west) and follow the signs to the Metro. Go to the second parking lot, where you can park all day for $6.75 (free on weekends). If it's filled, park in the five-level garage for $7.50 all day. On weekdays, make sure to pick up a bus transfer in the station on your return trip to qualify for the low parking rate.

Greenbelt is an easy Metro station to reach for day-trippers from Baltimore and other points north. Take I-95 or the Baltimore-Washington Parkway south to the Capital Beltway, go south about two miles, and get off at Exit 24, which goes to the Greenbelt Metro station. All-day parking is $3.50 during the week, free on weekends. Take the train to the Fort Totten station (which is temporarily the end of the line) and transfer to the Red Line train to Shady Grove, which takes you downtown.

Shady Grove also has plenty of parking for day-trippers. From I-270 near Gaithersburg, take Exit 9 (marked "Sam Eig Highway/Metro Station") to I-370 East, which takes you directly to the station. Metro parking is $4 for the day (free on weekends); if the Metro lots are filled, park in the nearby garage for $2.50.

Thanks to the construction of a new garage, there is much more space than previously at Grosvenor-Strathmore, but it's very popular, and also serves as the parking lot for the Strathmore Music Center, so its still best to go there early. Enter from Route 355/Rockville Pike just north of the Beltway; parking is $4 (free on weekdays).

Silver Spring is a somewhat less convenient option for day-trippers because it means a short drive inside the Beltway. But there's plenty of commercial parking close by. Take US 29/Colesville Road south from the Beltway and turn left onto Georgia Avenue in downtown Silver Spring; follow the signs to the Metro, loop past it, and park in one of the big parking garages. Parking is around $6 for the day.

2. TAKE THE TRAIN Taking the train to Washington is a snap for day visitors who live along the Eastern Seaboard from Richmond to Philadelphia. Amtrak, Maryland commuter (MARC), and Virginia Railway Express trains arrive at gleaming Union Station, located on the Metro's Red Line. You can be on the Mall minutes after getting off your train. From Union Station, visitors are only a few blocks' walk from the U.S. Capitol, the U.S. Supreme Court, the Library of Congress, the Folger Shakespeare Library, and the newest Smithsonian facility, the National Postal Museum.

From Virginia, Virginia Railway Express operates two commuter lines connecting Fredericksburg (to the south) and Manassas (to the west) with Union Station in downtown Washington. The 18-station system offers inbound service in the mornings and outbound service in the afternoons, Monday through Friday. For more information, call ☎ 703-684-1001 or 800-RIDE VRE (743-3873) or visit **www.vre.org.**

MARC train service operates three lines connecting Washington with the Maryland suburbs: one to BWI airport, another to downtown Baltimore, and the third going northwest along the Potomac River into western Maryland. For information and schedules for Amtrak, the national passenger train service, call ☎ 800-872-7245 or visit **www.amtrak.com.** For express Metroliner information, call ☎ 800-523-8720. By the way, Amtrak also provides weekend and holiday service along several of the lines used by MARC and Virginia Railway Express (but at a higher cost than the commuter services).

EXCURSIONS *beyond* the **BELTWAY**

IF YOU'VE GOT THE TIME OR IF YOUR VISIT to Washington is a repeat trip, consider exploring some places outside the city. From the mountains to the west and the Chesapeake Bay to the east, there's plenty to see. Furthermore, a look at something that's not made of marble or granite can be a welcome relief to eyes wearied by the constant onslaught of Washington edifices and office buildings. Here are a few suggestions for day trips that Washington visitors can make beyond the Beltway.

Annapolis

Maryland's capital for more than 300 years, Annapolis is more than a quaint little town on the Chesapeake Bay—it's one of the biggest yachting centers in the United States. Acres and acres of sailboats fill its marinas. A steady parade of sailboats moves past the City Dock during the sailing season, April through late fall. You'll see oyster and crab boats that work the bay, in addition to pleasure boats, cruise ships, and old sailing ships. Annapolis has a fine old state-office building and is home to the U.S. Naval Academy.

Annapolis has been discovered and is now a major bedroom community for well-off Washingtonians. The town boasts fine restaurants, fancy shops, bars, and jazz clubs, many in the historic district and down to the harbor. On weekends during the summer, Annapolis is packed with visitors. The town is about a one-hour drive from Washington on US 50.

Baltimore

Steamed crabs, H. L. Mencken, the Orioles baseball team, and the National Aquarium are just a few of the reasons Washingtonians trek north one hour on a regular basis to this industrial city on the Chesapeake Bay. Washington's visitors have good reason to detour and discover the charms of Baltimore.

Day-trippers can explore the Inner Harbor, dominated by a bilevel shopping mall that's heavy on restaurants and boutiques. The National Aquarium features a tropical rain forest and a sea mammal pavilion—and it's a much larger attraction than the National Aquarium in Washington.

kids Kids will love the Maryland Science Center and nearby Fort McHenry, where Francis Scott Key wrote the national anthem from a ship anchored offshore. If you've got the time, explore some other Baltimore attractions: the B&O Railroad Museum, the Edgar Allan Poe House, and the Babe Ruth House.

Shenandoah National Park

Although it makes for a long day, a drive to Shenandoah National Park in Virginia is a treat for outdoors lovers, featuring some of the prettiest mountain scenery in the eastern United States. A drive along a portion of the 105-mile-long Skyline Drive takes visitors to a nearly endless series of mountain overlooks where you can get out of the car and walk on well-maintained trails. In early June, the mountain laurel blooms in the higher elevations, and in the fall, it's bumper-to-bumper as hordes of Washingtonians rush to see the magnificent fall foliage. It's about a two-hour drive from Washington, one-way.

Harpers Ferry National Historical Park

This restored 19th-century town at the confluence of the Shenandoah and the Potomac rivers in West Virginia offers visitors history and natural beauty in equal doses. At the park's visitor center you can see a film about radical abolitionist John Brown's 1859 raid on a U.S. armory here, an event that was a precursor to the Civil War. Then you can tour a renovated blacksmith's shop, ready-made clothing store, and general store. A short hike to Jefferson Rock is rewarded with a spectacular mountain view of three states (Maryland, Virginia, and West Virginia) and two rivers (the Potomac and the Shenandoah). Thomas Jefferson said the view was "worth a voyage across the Atlantic." Luckily, the trip by car from Washington is only about 90 minutes.

A Tour of Civil War Battlefields

From the number of battlefield sites there, it would seem that the entire Civil War was fought in nearby Virginia, Maryland, and Pennsylvania—which is nearly the truth. Visitors with an interest in history and beautiful countryside can tour a number of Civil War sites within a day's drive of Washington. Several of the larger touring companies such as Gray Line offer bus excursions to some of these sites.

One of the closest Civil War museums is at **Fort Ward**, a 40-acre site just south of King Street and I-395 in Alexandria (4801 West Braddock Street; ☎ 703-838-4848), which is often staffed by volunteer reenactors.

Gettysburg, where the Union turned the tide against the South, is about two hours north of D.C. While the overdeveloped town is a testament to tourist schlock gone wild, the National Battlefield Park features a museum, a tower that gives sightseers an aerial view of the battlefield, and many acres of rolling countryside dotted with monuments, memorials, and stone fences. It's a popular tourist destination and worth the drive.

The first battle of the Civil War took place at Bull Run near Manassas, on the fringe of today's Virginia suburbs. The **Manassas National Battlefield Park** features a visitor center, a museum, and miles of trails on the grounds.

The Confederate victory set the stage for the next major battle, at Antietam, across the Potomac River in Maryland. **Antietam National Battlefield,** near Sharpsburg, is the site of the bloodiest day of the Civil War: on September 17, 1862, there were 12,410 Union and 10,700 Confederate casualties in General Robert E. Lee's failed attempt to penetrate the North. The battlefield, about a 90-minute drive from Washington, is 15 miles west of Frederick, Maryland.

A number of later Union campaigns are commemorated at Fredericksburg and **Spotsylvania National Military Park** in Virginia, halfway between Washington and Richmond. Included in the park are the battlefields of Fredericksburg, Chancellorsville, the Wilderness, and Spotsylvania. The park is about an hour's drive south of D.C.

HELPFUL HINTS

A WORST-CASE TOURING SCENARIO

HERE'S HOW NOT TO VISIT WASHINGTON: On a weekday, load the kids in the family car, and arrive around 8 a.m.—the worst part of rush hour. Then battle your way downtown through bumper-to-bumper traffic, arriving at the Mall about 9:30, your nerves thoroughly frayed. Waste a half-hour looking for a parking space before giving up and shelling out $12 for a space in a parking garage. Next, troop over to the Washington Monument, where a sign in the window of the time-ticket kiosk informs you that the day's allotment of tickets has already been given out. Then go to the National Air and Space Museum, where it's packed shoulder-to-shoulder around the most popular exhibits.

Later, at the National Museum of Natural History, little Jimmy disappears into the bowels of the paleontological exhibits, and since you didn't agree on a designated meeting place, it takes 45 minutes to track him down. At 5 p.m., you and your family stagger back to the car, just in time to join the afternoon rush hour.

Amazingly, people do this all the time. But it doesn't have to be this way. Instead of hitting Beltway traffic at 8 a.m., leave a half hour earlier, go to any suburban Metro station, and park. Then it's a 20-minute trip by train downtown. You can be at the Washington Monument by 8 a.m. and pick up a time ticket while the line is short. Then pick up tickets for a tour of the Bureau of Engraving and Printing later in the morning at the ticket booth on Raoul Wallenberg Place. Next, visit the National Air and Space Museum.

After watching money being printed, eat lunch at the Old Post Office Pavilion, then take the Metro to Dupont Circle. There, you can visit the Phillips Collection, a really classy art gallery, and tour Anderson House, a sumptuous mansion. Next, go to the National Zoo in the late afternoon or early evening, when the temperature begins to drop and the animals get more active. Eat dinner at a restaurant near the Woodley Park Metro on Connecticut Avenue and then take the Metro back to your car.

The second scenario takes advantage of two things: an early start and no time wasted in traffic or searching for a parking space. It lets you visit at a leisurely pace and gives you the freedom to explore out-of-the-way and unusual sights you normally wouldn't take the time to see. It's the smart way to visit Washington.

TRAVEL TIPS FOR TOURISTS

THE IDEA BEHIND VISITING ANY MAJOR TOURIST attraction is to have fun, and you can't do that if you're getting fatigued or crabby. Here are some touring tips you should review before your visit. They're really no more than commonsense rules for any type of outing:

1. **Drink water.** You'll need to drink plenty, especially on hot, humid, sunny Washington afternoons. Dehydration can sneak up on you and cause physical problems which might ruin your vacation plans. So don't hesitate to drink more water than you think you'll need.

2. **Avoid sunburn.** Protect sun-sensitive areas of your body. Shade your head and eyes with a hat. Wear sunglasses. Treat exposed skin with a sunscreen lotion—especially your face. And if you're wearing sandals, don't forget your feet. You don't have to go to the beach to get a really nasty burn on the tops of your feet!

3. **Pace yourself.** Washington is filled with good places to sit in the shade and rest, and people-watching is part of the fun. Hunger, overheating, tension from fighting the crowds for hours, fatigue—each of these realities of touring and all of them together can combine to produce fussy kids and grumpy adults. You'll notice if someone else in your party is getting unpleasant to be around, but you may not recognize the symptoms in yourself unless you periodically make an effort to run a little self-check and think about your behavior. If you and your party can't salvage things with a rest and a food break, cut your day short and go back to your hotel for a swim, a nap—or a drink in the bar. Visiting Washington is not meant to be a test of your temper and patience, after all. You're here to have fun.

4. **Wear comfortable clothes.** This especially goes for shoes—shoes that cushion, shoes that are broken in, shoes that won't make your feet too hot—and carry a couple of Band-Aids, just in case. Wear clothing that protects you from the sun and permits the air to circulate around your skin and doesn't bind or chafe. Elastic waistbands, or at least forgiving ones, make the clambering in-and-out of shuttle buses a lot easier, as well.

5. **Use food strategies.** Keep on good terms with your stomach, but don't let it dictate your trip. Eat a good breakfast before you set out for the day, then snack a lot while touring. Avoid predictable midday lunch lines, especially those at overpriced museum cafeterias, by eating a little later in the afternoon.

6. **Travel smart with teens.** Do yourself and them a favor: send them off
   on their own for at least part of a day during your D.C. visit. Arrange to
   meet them at a specific time and place, and elicit a very firm and definite
   understanding about this meeting time and place. Give them a watch if
   they don't have one, a map, and the hotel number for emergencies.

Getting Touring Information When in Washington

The Visitor Information Center in the **Ronald Reagan Building and
International Trade Center** at 1300 Pennsylvania Avenue NW is the place
to go for up-to-date information on attractions, hotels, restaurants,
shops, cultural venues, and tourist services. The center is staffed by
knowledgeable personnel and is stocked with free brochures and maps.
Also on-hand are interactive information kiosks, and visitors can make
hotel and restaurant reservations, as well as purchase souvenirs.

The 3,200-square-foot center is located on street level at the
Wilson Plaza entrance of the Ronald Reagan Building, across
the street from the Federal Triangle Metro station. This newest of
huge federal buildings offers an extensive food court, public phones,
and restrooms, and is centrally located between the Mall and downtown. Hours of operation for the Visitor Information Center are
Monday through Saturday, 8 a.m. to 6 p.m. The phone number for
the D.C. Chamber of Commerce is ☎ 202-DC VISIT.

Designated Meeting Places

Families and groups touring together should designate a meeting spot
in case members get separated. On the Mall, good places to link
up are in front of the Castle (the Smithsonian visitor center), the
Carousel in the Center of the Mall, or in front of the domed National
Museum of Natural History. The information desks located in most
main museum lobbies are logical meeting places if the group separates. Downtown, it's easy to lose your sense of direction due to a
scarcity of landmarks. A good designated meeting place would be
a hotel lobby, a department store entrance, or a Metro station.

A Money-saving Tip for Lunch

Where *not* to have lunch: the sidewalk food vendors on the Mall, the
kiosk in front of the National Museum of Natural History, and
the small restaurant down the hill from the Washington Monument
charge about a dollar more for a hot dog than the street vendors you
see everywhere off the Mall. Unless you're dying of hunger, walk to
either Constitution or Independence Avenue, find a street vendor, and
save yourself some dough. The hot dogs, by the way, are pretty good.

Where's the Smithsonian?

It's a common question fielded by the folks who staff the information
desk in the Castle, the main visitor center for the Smithsonian Institution (☎ 202-357-2700; **www.si.edu**). The query is posed by first-time

THE SMITHSONIAN'S FACILITIES	
The National Mall	**Downtown**
Air and Space Museum	American Art Museum
American History Museum	National Portrait Gallery–
Arts and Industries Building	Museum of American Art
Freer and Sackler Galleries	Renwick Gallery
Hirshhorn Museum and Sculpture Garden	**Upper Northwest**
	National Zoo
National Museum of African Art	**Northern Virginia**
National Museum of the American Indian	Anacostia Museum and Center for African American History and Culture
National Museum of Natural History	
National Postal Museum	Air and Space Museum (Steven F. Udvar-Hazy Center)
Smithsonian Institution Building (the Castle)	

visitors who have the mistaken notion that the renowned museum complex is located in one building somewhere along the Mall. In reality, the Smithsonian is a complex of 14 museums and a world-class zoo, scattered around the city. In 2004, the Smithsonian opened the $110-million National Museum of the American Indian on the Mall. In addition, the Institution operates the Cooper-Hewitt National Design Museum and the National Museum of the American Indian, both located in New York City. (Some folks are also surprised when they learn that the National Gallery of Art and the Holocaust Memorial Museum are not part of the Smithsonian complex. Nor is the International Spy Museum, an incredibly successful but commercial venture.) The great thing—well, one of them—about the Smithsonian institutions are that they are all free to the public, although these days a small donation is very welcome. Here is an alphabetical rundown of the Smithsonian's Washington facilities by location.

unofficial **TIP**
Across from the Mall near the Lincoln Memorial is the stately National Academy of Sciences on Constitution Avenue. Outside, Albert Einstein's statue is waiting for you to crawl into its lap so you can have your picture taken; it's a D.C. tradition.

A Photography Tip

Washington, D.C., with its impressive memorials and federal buildings, is a photographer's mecca. But for a really spectacular shot of downtown Washington, go across the Potomac River to the Iwo Jima Memorial in Arlington, Virginia. Stand on the hill near the Netherlands Carillon and look toward the Lincoln Memorial. At dawn, the sun rises almost directly behind the U.S. Capitol. At dusk, the panorama of twinkling lights includes the Jefferson and

Lincoln memorials, the Washington Monument, and, more than two miles away, the U.S. Capitol.

How to Sneak on a Reservation-only Tour at the National Archives

For the behind-the-scenes tour of the National Archives, most people call weeks in advance for reservations. If you didn't, however, take a chance and show up at the Pennsylvania Avenue entrance (across from Eighth Street) at tour time. If there's a cancellation or a no-show, you're in. The free reserved tours begin at 10:15 a.m. and 1:15 p.m. daily and last about an hour and a half. On the reserved tour, you'll explore the building, including book stacks, the microfilm viewing rooms, and the exhibits and models that show how researchers preserve documents. The tour ends in the magnificent Rotunda, where the great documents are on display. For more information, call ☎ 866-272-6272.

Getting a Free Pass to a National Gallery of Art Show

Most people call or stop by weeks in advance to get free "time tickets" that admit them to the wildly popular art exhibits regularly held in the National Gallery of Art's East Building. What most of them don't know is that hundreds of tickets per half-hour are reserved for folks like you. Tickets can be picked up any day a show is in progress. Just show up by noon on weekends or by 2 p.m. on weekdays at the ticket counter in the main lobby and come back later in the day to see the show.

An Informal Georgetown Tour of JFK Residences

Structure an informal walking tour around Georgetown by viewing—from the outside only, please—a few places where a great American statesman once lived. As a congressman and senator, John F. Kennedy lived in four different houses in Georgetown: **1528 31st Street NW, 1400 34th Street NW, 3271 P Street NW,** and **3307 N Street NW.** The last address is where the Kennedys lived just before moving to 1600 Pennsylvania Avenue NW. For more information, call Tour D.C. at ☎ 301-588-8999.

D.C. on the Air

Aside from the usual babble of format rock, talk, easy listening, and country music radio stations, Washington is home to a few radio stations that really stand out for high-quality broadcasting. Tune in to what hip Washingtonians listen to, as listed on the next page.

How to Tell if the President Is Home

A flag flies over the White House when the president is in Washington. At night, one of the facades on the White House stays lit for the benefit of trench coat–clad TV news reporters who intone to the camera, "Live, from the White House . . ."

FORMAT	FREQUENCY	STATION
Adult contemporary	107.3	WRQX-FM
All news	103.5	WTOP-FM
Alternative rock	101.1	WWDC-FM
Bluegrass, folk, talk	88.5	WAMU-FM
Christian music	91.9	WGTS-FM
Classic rock	94.7	WARW-FM
Classic rock	100.3	WBIG-FM
Classical	103.5	WGMS-FM
Country	98.7	WMZQ-FM
Conservative talk/news	630	WMAL-AM
Jazz	89.3	WPFW-FM
News analysis	1500	WTWP-AM
NPR	90.9	WETA-FM
Urban	95.5	WPGC-FM

How to Tell if the House or Senate Is in Session

Look for a flag flying over the respective chamber of the U.S. Capitol to determine which, if either, house of Congress is in session. From the Mall, the Senate is to the left of the dome; the House of Representatives is on the right. At night, a light burns on top of the Capitol dome if Congress is in session.

Avoiding the Heat on a Sweltering Afternoon

On the Mall, one solution to touring on a hot day is to visit this trio of museums: the National Museum of African Art, the Arthur M. Sackler Gallery, and the Freer Gallery. The first two museums are built underground, so they're probably cool even during a power failure (dark, too). The three museums are connected by tunnels, eliminating the need to venture outside.

unofficial **TIP**
On hot, humid D.C. afternoons, it's imperative to avoid long walks between sights; in fact, you shouldn't leave an air-conditioned building at all, if you can help it.

More good choices that will reduce the possibility of heatstroke include the Corcoran Gallery of Art, the Phillips Collection, and the National Gallery of Art. Another strategy is to visit museums next to each other (the National Museum of the American Indian and the Air and Space Museum, for instance). And don't plan any ambitious treks like a walk to the Jefferson Memorial from the Capitol, or from one end of the Mall to the other, when it's scorchingly hot outside.

D.C. after Dark

Touring Washington's monuments and memorials after dark offers dramatic views of both famous marble edifices and Washington itself. At night, the Jefferson and Lincoln memorials float in pools of light; from the steps of the Lincoln Memorial, the Eternal Flame at the John F. Kennedy gravesite shimmers across the river in Arlington National Cemetery. The scene at the Vietnam Veterans Memorial is a moving experience as people hold flickering matches up to the reflective black marble surface, searching for names.

Capitol Hill: A Family Affair

Rather than just getting in line to tour the U.S. Capitol, give yourself and your kids a real civics lesson you'll all remember: visit your congressperson or senator.

"Go to your member's office and get a pass to see the House and Senate in session," suggests a guard at the Capitol. "It's a real experience—and the kids will love it. And while you're there, ask for a special tour of the Capitol given by a member's staff person." House office buildings are across Independence Avenue from the Capitol building; Senate office buildings are across Constitution Avenue. Offices are open weekdays during normal business hours, and you don't need an appointment. If you don't know the name of your representative, go to either one of your senators' offices.

Where the Real Work of Congress Is Done

Most visitors who obtain gallery passes to the House or Senate in session are mildly disappointed: the scene is usually one member giving a speech to a nearly empty chamber, unless you happen to stumble in during a vote. Everyone else is at committee meetings, where the real work is done.

unofficial **TIP**
Check the *Washington Post* "A" section for a list of legislative hearings open to the public, along with their times and locations (always in one of the buildings near the Capitol).

Speeding Through the Ubiquitous Metal Detectors

Walk-through metal detectors staffed by no-nonsense guards are standard equipment in virtually every federal building in Washington, including the U.S. Capitol, the Supreme Court, all Senate and House office buildings, Mall museums, and the National Archives. Men: To speed your way through, you should get in the habit of carrying all your change and keys in one place. When your turn comes to pass through the metal detector, dump it all into one of the bowls provided, and you'll avoid the tedious drill of passing through the door-sized detector a half-dozen times. (You'll also find out which metal-buckled belt not to wear when visiting government buildings.) Women may be asked to place their purses on a conveyor that shoots it through the X-ray machine, then walk through the detector; or to open the bag and its compartments for visual inspection. Backpacks and briefcases are treated the same way.

PART SEVEN

WASHINGTON'S ATTRACTIONS

WHERE *to* GO

VISITORS COME TO WASHINGTON from all over the world—and for a lot of different reasons. Some want to see how the U.S. government works (or, as some cynics say, *doesn't* work); others want to see the places where history happened; and many are drawn by the city's magnificent monuments and museums.

It's tough for a guidebook to decree to such a diverse group where they should spend their time. Is the National Gallery of Art better than the Air and Space Museum? The answer is yes—but only if your interests and tastes range more toward Van Gogh than von Braun.

Because we can't read your mind and tell *you* the top places you should visit on your trip to Washington, we'll do the next best thing: give you enough information so that you can quickly choose the places you want to see—with enough detail so that you can plan your visit logically—without spending a lot of time (and energy) retracing your steps and standing in line.

Armed with enough information to make informed choices about how to spend your valuable time, you can avoid a common mistake a lot of visitors to D.C. make: hitting the Mall for a death march through a blur of Smithsonian museums, federal buildings, and monuments.

TIME-SAVING CHARTS

BECAUSE OF THE WIDE RANGE of attractions in and around the city—from a 500-foot marble obelisk on the Mall to collections of modern art—we've provided the following charts to help you prioritize your touring at a glance. In the first, you'll find attractions listed by type, allowing you to locate a particular attraction easily even if you don't know its location. In the second, attractions are listed by neighborhood, allowing you to plan efficient touring in a given area. In each

Attractions by Type

CEMETERIES

Arlington National Cemetery ★★★★   NATIONAL MALL
LARGEST U.S. MILITARY CEMETERY

CHURCHES/HOUSES OF WORSHIP

Basilica of the National Shrine of the Immaculate Conception ★   NORTHEAST
LARGEST CATHOLIC CHURCH IN U.S.

Franciscan Monastery and Gardens ★★   NORTHEAST
RESTORED CHURCH, CATACOMBS, GARDEN

Islamic Center ★★   DUPONT CIRCLE/ADAMS-MORGAN
EXOTIC MOSQUE

Washington National Cathedral ★★★★★   UPPER NORTHWEST
6TH LARGEST CATHEDRAL IN THE WORLD

GOVERNMENT BUILDINGS OPEN FOR TOURS

Bureau of Engraving and Printing ★★   NATIONAL MALL
WHERE U.S. DOLLARS AND STAMPS ARE PRINTED

National Archives ★★★   NATIONAL MALL
HOME TO OUR NATION'S MOST IMPORTANT DECLARATIONS

U.S. Capitol ★★★★★   CAPITOL HILL
WHERE CONGRESS MEETS

U.S. Department of State Diplomatic Reception Rooms ★★★★★   FOGGY BOTTOM
DECORATIVE ARTS; RESERVATION ONLY

U.S. Supreme Court ★★★★   CAPITOL HILL
NATION'S HIGHEST COURT

Voice of America ★★★   NATIONAL MALL
RADIO STUDIOS

Washington Navy Yard ★★★   SOUTHEAST
3 MILITARY MUSEUMS AND U.S. NAVY DESTROYER; RESERVATIONS ONLY

HISTORIC BUILDINGS AND HOMES

Christian Heurich House Museum ★★★   DUPONT CIRCLE/ADAMS-MORGAN
LAVISH GILDED AGE HOME

Decatur House ★★★   NATIONAL MALL
EARLY D.C. RESIDENCE NEAR THE WHITE HOUSE

Ford's Theatre/Petersen House ★★★   DOWNTOWN
WHERE LINCOLN WAS ASSASSINATED AND DIED

Frederick Douglass National Historic Site ★★★★   SOUTHEAST
PRESERVED VICTORIAN MANSION

Gunston Hall ★★★   VIRGINIA SUBURBS
GEORGE MASON'S PLANTATION

House of the Temple ★   DUPONT CIRCLE/ADAMS-MORGAN
MASONIC TEMPLE MODELED ON AN ANCIENT WONDER

Meridian International Center ★★★   DUPONT CIRCLE/ADAMS-MORGAN
2 MANSIONS, GALLERIES, GARDENS

Mount Vernon ★★★★★   VIRGINIA SUBURBS
GEORGE WASHINGTON'S RIVER PLANTATION

The Octagon ★★★   NATIONAL MALL
EARLY D.C. HOME AND MUSEUM

Old Town Alexandria ★★★★   VIRGINIA SUBURBS
RESTORED COLONIAL PORT TOWN

Society of the Cincinnati Museum at Anderson House ★★★★ DUPONT CIRCLE/ADAMS-MORGAN
LAVISH MANSION AND REVOLUTIONARY WAR MUSEUM

Union Station ★★★★   CAPITOL HILL
BEAUX ARTS PALACE; FOOD COURT, SHOPPING MALL

White House ★★   NATIONAL MALL
THE EXECUTIVE MANSION, RESERVATION ONLY

Woodrow Wilson House ★★★★   DUPONT CIRCLE/ADAMS-MORGAN
FINAL HOME OF THE 28TH PRESIDENT

LIBRARIES

Folger Shakespeare Library ★★½   CAPITOL HILL
BARD MUSEUM AND THEATER

Library of Congress ★★★★   CAPITOL HILL
WORLD'S LARGEST LIBRARY

MONUMENTS AND MEMORIALS

Franklin Delano Roosevelt Memorial ★★★★   NATIONAL MALL
OPEN-AIR MEMORIAL TO FDR

Jefferson Memorial ★★★   NATIONAL MALL
CLASSICAL-STYLE MONUMENT ON TIDAL BASIN

Korean War Veterans Memorial ★★★   NATIONAL MALL
"WALKING" PLATOON MEMORIAL

Lincoln Memorial ★★★   NATIONAL MALL
MEMORIAL TO 16TH PRESIDENT ON REFLECTING POOL

Martin Luther King Jr. National Memorial NA   NATIONAL MALL
MEDITATION GARDEN AND WALK (UNDER CONSTRUCTION)

National World War II Memorial ★★★   NATIONAL MALL
TRIBUTE TO "THE GREATEST GENERATION"

Old Post Office Tower and Pavilion ★★★★   NATIONAL MALL
A GREAT VIEW AND A FOOD COURT

U.S. Air Force Memorial ★★   NATIONAL MALL
MEMORIAL WALK AND SCULPTURE

Vietnam Veterans Memorial ★★★★   NATIONAL MALL
U.S. SOLDIER MEMORIAL ON THE MALL

Washington Monument ★★★★★   NATIONAL MALL
500-FOOT MEMORIAL TO FIRST U.S. PRESIDENT

MUSEUMS AND GALLERIES

Anacostia Museum N/A   SOUTHEAST
AFRICAN AMERICAN HISTORY AND CULTURE

Arts and Industries N/A   NATIONAL MALL
(CLOSED FOR RENOVATION)

Arthur M. Sackler Gallery ★★★   NATIONAL MALL
ASIAN ART

Corcoran Gallery of Art ★★★   NATIONAL MALL
MODERN AND CLASSICAL ART AND ANTIQUES

DAR Museum ★★★★   NATIONAL MALL
DECORATIVE U.S. ARTS AND ANTIQUES

Freer Gallery of Art ★★★★   NATIONAL MALL
ASIAN AND AMERICAN ART

Attractions by Type (continued)

MUSEUMS AND GALLERIES (CONTINUED)

Hillwood Museum and Gardens ★★★★★ MANSION WITH FABULOUS ART TREASURES, RESERVATION ONLY	UPPER NORTHWEST
Hirshhorn Museum and Sculpture Garden ★★★★★ MODERN ART	NATIONAL MALL
International Spy Museum ★★½ SPOOK EXHIBITS	DOWNTOWN
Koshland Science Museum ★½ FOR BUDDING RESEARCHERS	DOWNTOWN
Kreeger Museum ★★★ MODERN-ART MUSEUM	DUPONT CIRCLE/ADAMS-MORGAN
NASA/Goddard Space Flight Visitors Center ★★★ SPACE-FLIGHT MUSEUM	MARYLAND SUBURBS
National Air and Space Museum ★★★★★ CHRONICLES MANNED FLIGHT	NATIONAL MALL
National Aquarium ★★ FISH TANKS IN A BASEMENT	NATIONAL MALL
National Building Museum ★★★★ ARCHITECTURAL MARVEL AND EXHIBITS	DOWNTOWN
National Cryptologic Museum ★½ NSA SPOOK MUSEUM	MARYLAND SUBURBS
National Gallery of Art: East ★★★★★ 20TH-CENTURY ART	NATIONAL MALL
National Gallery of Art: West ★★★★★ EURO AND AMERICAN CLASSICAL ART	NATIONAL MALL
National Geographic Society's Explorers Hall ★★ HIGH-TECH EXHIBITION FOR KIDS	DOWNTOWN
National Museum of African Art ★★ TRADITIONAL ARTS OF AFRICA	NATIONAL MALL
National Museum of American History ★★★★★ (CLOSED FOR RENOVATION)	NATIONAL MALL
National Museum of the American Indian ★★★ NATIVE ART AND ARTIFACTS	NATIONAL MALL
National Museum of Health and Medicine ★★ MEDICAL MUSEUM	UPPER NORTHWEST
National Museum of Natural History ★★★★★ TREASURE CHEST OF NATURAL SCIENCES	NATIONAL MALL

you'll find an authors' rating from one star (skip it) to five stars (not to be missed), and a brief description of the attraction. (Some, like the Smithsonian's Anacostia Museum—which doesn't have permanent collections—weren't rated because exhibits change.) Remember that these are not necessarily comments on the quality of a particular collection. Occasionally, the attraction's relative accessibility has weighed in its rating. In other cases it is a matter of how narrow or general the institution's attraction may be, so read the entire profile if

National Museum of Women in the Arts ★★★★   DOWNTOWN
MODERN AND CLASSICAL ART BY WOMEN

National Portrait Gallery–Smithsonian American Art Museum ★★★★   DOWNTOWN
TWO IMPORTANT ART COLLECTIONS IN ONE BEAUTIFULLY RESTORED BUILDING

National Postal Museum ★★★   CAPITOL HILL
PHILATELY AND EXHIBITS

Phillips Collection ★★★★   DUPONT CIRCLE/ADAMS-MORGAN
FIRST U.S. MODERN-ART MUSEUM

Renwick Gallery ★★   NATIONAL MALL
AMERICAN CRAFTS AND DECORATIVE ARTS

Smithsonian Institution Building (The Castle) ★★★★   NATIONAL MALL
MUSEUM INFORMATION AND DISPLAY

Textile Museum ★★   DUPONT CIRCLE/ADAMS-MORGAN
TEXTILE ARTS

U.S. Department of the Interior ★½   FOGGY BOTTOM
OLD-FASHIONED MUSEUM OF PARKS AND OUTDOORS

U.S. Holocaust Memorial Museum ★★★½   NATIONAL MALL
GRAPHIC MEMORIAL TO WWII HOLOCAUST

PARKS, GARDENS, AND ZOOS

Dumbarton Oaks and Gardens ★★★★   GEORGETOWN
MANSION/MUSEUM AND A BEAUTIFUL GARDEN

Kenilworth Park and Aquatic Gardens ★★★   SOUTHEAST
NATIONAL PARK FOR WATER PLANTS

National Wildlife Visitor Center ★★★   MARYLAND SUBURBS
MUSEUM ON 13,000-ACRE WILDLIFE REFUGE

National Zoological Park ★★★★★   UPPER NORTHWEST
WORLD-CLASS ZOO IN A WOODED

U.S. Botanic Garden ★★★   CAPITOL HILL
HUGE GREENHOUSE AND LIVING MUSEUM ON MALL

U.S. National Arboretum ★★★   NORTHEAST
444-ACRE COLLECTION OF TREES, FLOWERS, HERBS

THEATERS/PERFORMANCES

JFK Center for Performing Arts ★★   FOGGY BOTTOM
STUNNING PERFORMING-ARTS CENTER ON THE POTOMAC

you're undecided. Also note that a few of the attractions require advance reservations. Each attraction is individually profiled later in this section. But there are dozens of "attractions" we haven't listed, partly because they are stand-alone memorials (all those statues in traffic circles), parks, cemeteries with fine statuary; or simply buildings or bridges with elaborate facades, friezes, and carvings. Washington is a city worth seeing; so don't find yourself walking with your nose glued to a book, even this one. Art is all around.

Attractions by Location

THE NATIONAL MALL

Arlington National Cemetery
Arts and Industries
Bureau of Engraving and Printing
Corcoran Gallery of Art
DAR Museum
Decatur House
Freer Gallery of Art
Hirshhorn Museum and Sculpture
   Garden
Jefferson Memorial
Martin Luther King Jr. National
   Memorial
Korean War Veterans Memorial
Lincoln Memorial
National Air and Space Museum
National Aquarium
National Archives
National Gallery of Art: East
National Gallery of Art: West
National Museum of African Art
National Museum of American
   History
National Museum of the American
   Indian
National Museum of Natural History
National World War II Memorial
Old Post Office Tower and Pavilion

The Octagon
Renwick Gallery
Franklin Delano Roosevelt Memorial
Arthur M. Sackler Gallery
Smithsonian Institution Building
   (The Castle)
U.S. Air Force Memorial
U.S. Holocaust Memorial Museum
Vietnam Veterans Memorial
Voice of America
Washington Monument
White House

NORTHEAST

Basilica of the National Shrine of the
   Immaculate Conception
Franciscan Monastery and Gardens
U.S. National Arboretum

DUPONT CIRCLE/
ADAMS-MORGAN

Christian Heurich House Museum
House of the Temple
Islamic Center
Kreeger Museum
Meridian International Center
Phillips Collection
Society of the Cincinnati Museum at
   Anderson House

The NATIONAL MALL *and*
ARLINGTON MEMORIALS

AS THE EAST HALF OF THE MALL is to museums, so the west side
is to monuments. Many of them are smallish and open-air, some
classical, some modern. And while the older memorials tend to be

valedictory and emotionally elevating, if solemn—Washington's Egyptian-Masonic monolith, Jefferson's Pantheon, and Lincoln's impressive Parthenon—those erected in the late 20th century are somewhat grimmer and more realistic. The **Korean War Veterans Memorial,** with its platoon of dogged, almost antiheroic grunts, and the two sculptural appendages to the otherwise-stark **Vietnam Veterans Memorial**—one honoring soldiers and the other the female medical and

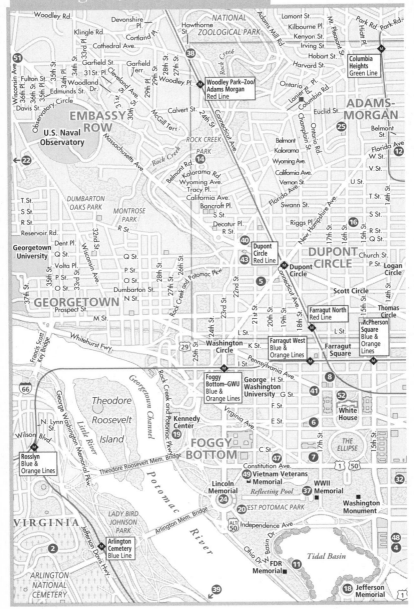

washington, d.c., attractions

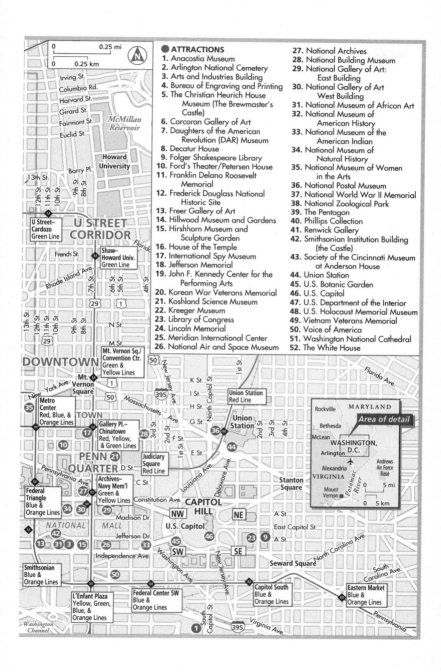

● ATTRACTIONS

1. Anacostia Museum
2. Arlington National Cemetery
3. Arts and Industries Building
4. Bureau of Engraving and Printing
5. The Christian Heurich House Museum (The Brewmaster's Castle)
6. Corcoran Gallery of Art
7. Daughters of the American Revolution (DAR) Museum
8. Decatur House
9. Folger Shakespeare Library
10. Ford's Theater/Petersen House
11. Franklin Delano Roosevelt Memorial
12. Frederick Douglass National Historic Site
13. Freer Gallery of Art
14. Hillwood Museum and Gardens
15. Hirshhorn Museum and Sculpture Garden
16. House of the Temple
17. International Spy Museum
18. Jefferson Memorial
19. John F. Kennedy Center for the Performing Arts
20. Korean War Veterans Memorial
21. Koshland Science Museum
22. Kreeger Museum
23. Library of Congress
24. Lincoln Memorial
25. Meridian International Center
26. National Air and Space Museum

27. National Archives
28. National Building Museum
29. National Gallery of Art: East Building
30. National Gallery of Art West Building
31. National Museum of African Art
32. National Museum of American History
33. National Museum of the American Indian
34. National Museum of Natural History
35. National Museum of Women in the Arts
36. National Postal Museum
37. National World War II Memorial
38. National Zoological Park
39. The Pentagon
40. Phillips Collection
41. Renwick Gallery
42. Smithsonian Institution Building (the Castle)
43. Society of the Cincinnati Museum at Anderson House
44. Union Station
45. U.S. Botanic Garden
46. U.S. Capitol
47. U.S. Department of the Interior
48. U.S. Holocaust Memorial Museum
49. Vietnam Veterans Memorial
50. Voice of America
51. Washington National Cathedral
52. The White House

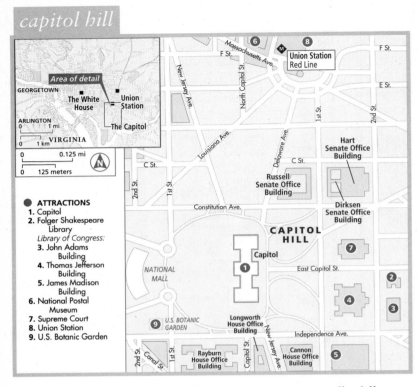

capitol hill

Area of detail

GEORGETOWN

The White House

Union Station

ARLINGTON

0   1 mi

0   1 km   **VIRGINIA**

The Capitol

0   0.125 mi

0   125 meters

● **ATTRACTIONS**
1. Capitol
2. Folger Shakespeare Library
  Library of Congress:
3. John Adams Building
4. Thomas Jefferson Building
5. James Madison Building
6. National Postal Museum
7. Supreme Court
8. Union Station
9. U.S. Botanic Garden

Union Station Red Line

Hart Senate Office Building

Russell Senate Office Building

Dirksen Senate Office Building

CAPITOL HILL

Capitol

East Capitol St.

NATIONAL MALL

U.S. BOTANIC GARDEN

Longworth House Office Building

Independence Ave.

Rayburn House Office Building

Cannon House Office Building

support troops who tended them—provoke an essentially different emotional response from visitors than do the great temples of the Founding Fathers.

In addition to the monuments and memorials profiled later are two others you should stop to examine as you stroll from Washington to Lincoln, so to speak. Notable for its restrained elegance, the **District of Columbia War Memorial** is an open-sided Doric temple with the names of D.C. residents killed in World War I engraved upon its outer walls. Above the circular colonnade is another inscription, subtle but striking in its irony: a reference to "*the* World War"—the one after which Americans believed there would be no other. President Herbert Hoover and General John Pershing both took part in the dedication ceremony in 1931, and the bandleader, John Phillip Sousa, played not only his own "Stars and Stripes Forever" but also "The Star-spangled Banner," which had just been named the U.S. national anthem by an act of Congress. As befits a monument to what in some ways was the last 19th-century war, the memorial is about halfway between the Lincoln and World War II memorials, on the south side of Constitution Gardens facing Independence Avenue.

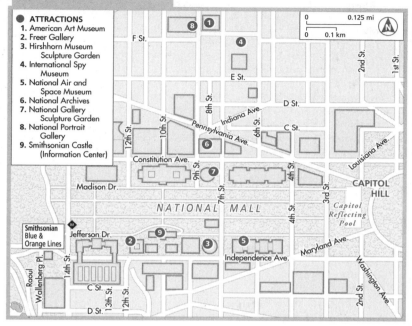

the national mall

ATTRACTIONS
1. American Art Museum
2. Freer Gallery
3. Hirshhorn Museum
   Sculpture Garden
4. International Spy
   Museum
5. National Air and
   Space Museum
6. National Archives
7. National Gallery
   Sculpture Garden
8. National Portrait
   Gallery
9. Smithsonian Castle
   (Information Center)

Almost directly opposite, between 17th and 20th streets just south of Constitution Avenue, is a pretty figure eight–shaped lake, at one side of which is a small island that houses the **56 Signers of the Declaration of Independence Memorial.** The memorial itself is simply designed, with the final phrase of the Declaration, "We pledge to each other our Lives, our Fortunes, and our sacred Honor," engraved in the base and the 56 signatures reproduced in the granite blocks of a semicircle. Something of the signers' varied personalities seems evident in their handwriting—the self-consciously elegant Thomas Jefferson, the expansive John Hancock, the plain John Adams, and the even plainer Samuel Adams. Dedicated to mark the bicentennial in 1976, the island is also a waterfowl refuge. It is so often overlooked by tour companies that you're more likely to see locals than visitors reading or resting beneath one of its weeping willows.

And there is more to come: the **Martin Luther King Jr. National Memorial** is being constructed on the northwest shore of the Tidal Basin in a direct line between the Lincoln and Jefferson memorials, emphasizing the long, historic "line of freedom" in America. Much like the FDR Memorial, the King Memorial will combine a meditation walk with statuary and plaques bearing quotations from the civil-rights leader.

Across the Potomac River, partly in the District and partly in Virginia, are several armed-forces and war memorials. Though not within the Mall proper, they are certainly connected to it, and so we have included them here.

At the opposite end of the Memorial Bridge from the Lincoln Memorial, just outside the entrance to Arlington National Cemetery, is the little island comprising **Lady Bird Johnson Park.** Though not technically a memorial, it is a fittingly green tribute to the First Lady who turned her energies to the beautification of the capital. About a mile south of the Memorial Bridge along the George Washington Parkway is the **Lyndon Baines Johnson Memorial Grove,** which consists of a commemorative monolith and a grove of 500 white pines. (The stream between Lady Bird Johnson Park and the cemetery is **Boundary Channel,** which marks the border between D.C. and Virginia.) The **U.S. Marine Corps Memorial,** popularly known as the Iwo Jima Memorial and recently the subject of a major motion picture, *Flags of Our Fathers,* is about a 20-minute walk from the Arlington Cemetery subway stop. The 32-foot-long sculpture, capped by a 60-foot-tall flagpole, was dedicated by President Eisenhower on Veterans Day, November 11, 1954. Alongside the memorial is the **Netherlands Carillon,** a gift from the Dutch people in gratitude for American aid during and after World War II. It plays recorded music—mostly armed-forces themes, marches, "The Star-spangled Banner," and the like—hourly from 10 a.m. to 6 p.m. every day, with some longer concerts in the summer.

The **U.S. Air Force Memorial,** which opened in mid-October 2006, is a triad of soaring (270-foot tall) stainless-steel arcs that are illuminated at night and are visible from many of the approaches to Washington. The actual site includes an inscribed glass contemplation wall that represents those who have been killed in action, along with a curving wall that one follows up to the sculpture—at its foot there is a great view of the Washington Monument—and back down. Keep in mind that you'll need a car or taxi to get there: the memorial entrance is off Columbia Pike/Route 244.

ATTRACTION PROFILES

Anacostia Museum (*a Smithsonian museum*)

APPEAL BY AGE *Because the museum features special exhibitions that change throughout the year, it's not really possible to rate this Smithsonian facility's appeal by age group.*

Location 1901 Fort Place SE, in Anacostia; Nearest Metro station Anacostia; ☎ 202-633-4820; anacostia.si.edu

Type of attraction A museum focusing on African American history and culture (self-guided tour). **How to get there** For specific information on where to board the buses and for the schedule, stop at any museum information desk on the Mall or call ☎ 202-287-3382. **To drive** From the Mall, take Independence Avenue east past the Capitol to Second Street SE, where it is intersected by Pennsylvania

Avenue. Bear right onto Pennsylvania Avenue, go to 11th Street SE, and turn right. Cross the 11th Street Bridge and follow signs to Martin Luther King Jr. Avenue (left lanes). Follow MLK Avenue to Morris Road (3rd traffic signal) and turn left. Go up the hill to 17th Street SE, where Morris Road becomes Erie Street. In about 5 blocks, Erie Street becomes Fort Place; the museum is on the right. Because this part of Southeast Washington is unsafe for pedestrians, we don't recommend taking public transportation. **Admission** Free. **Hours** Daily, 10 a.m.– 5 p.m.; closed Christmas Day. **When to go** Anytime. But either call first or pick up a brochure at the Castle on the Mall to find out what's on view before making the trip. **Special comments** This "neighborhood" museum features temporary special exhibits, which makes rating impossible; between shows, there is often very little to see, so call first. **How much time to allow** 1 hour.

DESCRIPTION AND COMMENTS Located on the high ground of old Fort Stanton, the Anacostia Museum features changing exhibits on black culture and history and the achievements of African Americans. Unfortunately for out-of-town visitors, it's in a location that's difficult to reach.

TOURING TIPS To save yourself the frustration of arriving between major shows, either call the museum first or pick up a flyer at the Castle on the Mall.

OTHER THINGS TO DO NEARBY Frederick Douglass National Historic Site is a short drive, but you should call in advance to make reservations for the house tour. Anacostia is a high-crime area. It's okay to drive through during daylight, but it's not an area we advise visitors to visit on foot or at night.

 ## Arlington National Cemetery ★ ★ ★ ★

APPEAL BY AGE	PRESCHOOL ★	GRADE SCHOOL ★ ★	TEENS ★ ★ ★
YOUNG ADULTS ★ ★ ★ ★		OVER 30 ★ ★ ★ ★	SENIORS ★ ★ ★ ★

Location **Across the Potomac from Washington via Arlington Memorial Bridge, which crosses the river near the Lincoln Memorial;** Nearest Metro station **Arlington Cemetery; ☎ 703-607-8000; www.arlingtoncemetery.org**

Type of attraction The largest military cemetery in the United States (guided and self-guided tours). **Admission** Free. **Hours** Daily, April–September, 8 a.m.– 7 p.m.; October–March, 8 a.m.–5 p.m. **When to go** Before 9 a.m. in spring and summer. **Special comments** Beyond tourism; don't underestimate the ferocity of Washington summer afternoons; in hot weather, get here early. **How much time to allow** 2 hours.

DESCRIPTION AND COMMENTS It's not fair to call a visit to Arlington National Cemetery mere sightseeing; as Americans, our lives are too intimately attached to the 200,000 men and women buried here. They include the famous, the obscure, and the unknown: John F. Kennedy, General George C. Marshall, Joe Louis, Abner Doubleday, and Oliver Wendell Holmes are among them. Sights located in the cemetery's 612 rolling acres include the Tomb of the Unknowns (guarded 24 hours a day; witness the changing of the guard on the hour from October to March, and on the half-hour the

arlington national cemetery

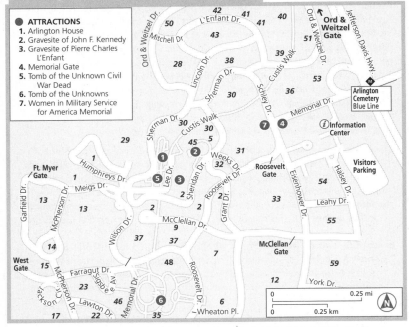

● **ATTRACTIONS**
1. Arlington House
2. Gravesite of John F. Kennedy
3. Gravesite of Pierre Charles
   L'Enfant
4. Memorial Gate
5. Tomb of the Unknown Civil
   War Dead
6. Tomb of the Unknowns
7. Women in Military Service
   for America Memorial

rest of the year); memorials to the crew of the space shuttle *Challenger;* the Iran Rescue Mission Memorial; and Arlington House, built in 1802. With the ease of touring provided by Tourmobile, Arlington Cemetery should be on every first-time visitor's list of things to see.

TOURING TIPS To avoid the worst of Washington's brutal summer heat and humidity, plan to arrive as early as possible. Private cars are not allowed inside, but there's plenty of parking near the visitor center at $1.25 an hour for the first three hours, then $2 an hour. Take the Metro instead. Although you can wander around the cemetery on your own, the narrated Tourmobile tour is informative and saves wear and tear on your feet—and at $6 for adults and $3 for children under age 12, it's a good deal. The ticket allows you to get off at all the major sites and reboard at your leisure. The shuttle tours leave the visitor center (where tickets are sold) about every 15 to 20 minutes. If you're touring the Mall by Tourmobile, transferring to the cemetery tour is free for that day only. If you want to tour the cemetery by shuttle bus on a different day, don't pay $20 for another full-circuit ticket. Just take the Metro to the Arlington Cemetery station, walk the short distance to the visitor center, buy the cemetery-only ticket, and save a few bucks. Finally, bathrooms are located in the visitor center. But don't come to Arlington Cemetery when you're hungry—there's no place to eat.

OTHER THINGS TO DO NEARBY The 9/11 Pentagon Memorial (currently under construction) and the Air Force Memorial are not far but require a car. The Iwo Jima Memorial and the Netherlands Carillon are about a 20-minute walk from Arlington House (down Custis Walk and through Weitzel Gate). The nearest restaurants via the Metro are in Rosslyn and Pentagon City.

Arts and Industries Building (*a Smithsonian museum*)
Closed for renovation.

Basilica of the National Shrine of the Immaculate Conception ★

APPEAL BY AGE	PRESCHOOL ★	GRADE SCHOOL ★	TEENS ★
YOUNG ADULTS ★	OVER 30 ★		SENIORS ★★

Location **Fourth Street and Michigan Avenue NE, on the campus of the Catholic University of America;** Nearest Metro station **Brookland-CUA;** ☎ **202-526-8300; www.nationalshrine.com**

Type of attraction The largest Catholic church in the U.S. and the seventh-largest religious structure in the world (guided and self-guided tours). **Admission** Free. **Hours** November 1–March 31, daily 7 a.m.–6 p.m.; until 7 p.m. the rest of the year. Guided tours are conducted Monday–Saturday, 9–11 a.m. and 1–3 p.m.; Sunday, 1:30–4 p.m. **When to go** Anytime. **Special comments** It's a huge cathedral—sterile and cold—and it requires a lot of walking. **How much time to allow** 1 hour.

DESCRIPTION AND COMMENTS A huge, blue-and-gold onion dome lends Byzantine overtones to this massive cathedral, as does the wealth of colorful mosaics throughout its interior. Yet the architecture is lean and stark, and many of the figures in the mosaics and stained-glass windows look cartoonish. It's not in the same league with the awe-inspiring National Cathedral across town. Sure is big, though.

TOURING TIPS Skip the guided tour, which stops in every one of the dozens of chapels. Instead, grab a map at the information desk on the ground (crypt) level and enter Memorial Hall, which is lined with chapels. Then go up the stairs (or elevator) to the Upper Church.

OTHER THINGS TO DO NEARBY The Franciscan Monastery is a brisk, 20-minute walk away: continue past the Metro station on Michigan Avenue to Quincy Street, turn right, and walk about four blocks. The Pope John Paul II Cultural Center, an interactive museum open to all faiths, is nearby. Call ☎ 202-635-5400 for hours and directions. A free shuttle service to the center operates from the Brookland-CUA Metro station on weekends. The Basilica has a small cafeteria on the ground level; a better bet is the Pizza Hut on Michigan Avenue.

The Arthur M. Sackler Gallery (*a Smithsonian Museum*) ★ ★ ★

APPEAL BY AGE	PRESCHOOL ★	GRADE SCHOOL ★★	TEENS ★★
YOUNG ADULTS ★★★	OVER 30 ★★★		SENIORS ★★★

Location 1050 Independence Avenue SW, on the Mall near the Castle (the Smithsonian Institution Building); Nearest Metro station Smithsonian; ☎ 202-633-4880 or 202-357-1729 (TDD); www.asia.si.edu

Type of attraction A museum dedicated to Asian art from ancient times to the present (self-guided tour). **Admission** Free. **Hours** Daily, 10 a.m.–5:30 p.m.; closed Christmas Day. **When to go** Anytime. **Special comments** A quiet respite when other Mall attractions are jammed with visitors. Fabulous and exotic art. **How much time to allow** 1 hour.

DESCRIPTION AND COMMENTS Descend through a granite-and-glass pavilion to view a collection of Asian (mostly Chinese) treasures, many of them made of gold and encrusted with jewels. The Sackler is full of exotic stuff that will catch the eye of older children, teens, and adults. Barring a strong interest in the Orient, however, first-time visitors on a tight schedule should visit the Sackler another time.

TOURING TIPS Stop at the information desk and ask about the guided tours offered throughout the day. The gift shop is an exotic bazaar featuring paintings, textiles, ancient games, Zen–rock garden kits, and plenty of other Asian-influenced items. Free walk-in tours are offered daily (except Wednesday) at 11 a.m.

OTHER THINGS TO DO NEARBY The Sackler is connected with its twin, the Museum of African Art, below ground, so that's the logical next stop—especially if it's rainy or blazingly hot outside. A new underground corridor connects the Freer Gallery to the Sackler. None of these museums offers a cafeteria, but the cafes at American Indian and National Gallery are not far.

The Brewmaster's Castle ★★★
(also known as The Christian Heurich House Museum)

APPEAL BY AGE	PRESCHOOL —	GRADE SCHOOL ★	TEENS ★★
YOUNG ADULTS ★★★	OVER 30 ★★★		SENIORS ★★★

Location 1307 New Hampshire Avenue NW (2 blocks south of Dupont Circle); Nearest Metro station Dupont Circle; ☎ 202-429-1894; www.Heurichhouse.org

Type of attraction The lavish home of a wealthy turn-of-the-century Washington businessman (guided tour). **Admission** $5 per person; suggested donation. **Hours** Wednesday–Friday, 11:30 a.m. and 1 p.m.; Saturday, 11:30 a.m., 1 and 2 p.m.; Sunday 1 and 2:30 p.m. Group tours are by reservation only and can be made by calling ☎ 202-429-1894. **Special comments** It has an outrageous Gilded Age interior, so don't be put off by the grimy exterior. **How much time to allow** 1 hour.

DESCRIPTION AND COMMENTS It's doubtful that any amount of money could re-create what wealthy brewer Christian Heurich built in the early 1890s: a regal 31-room mansion full of richly detailed mahogany and oak woodwork, elaborate plaster moldings, and a musician's balcony that lets live music be heard throughout the first floor. It may be the most opulent home open to the public in Washington. While most first-time visitors to Washington shouldn't feel obligated to spend time here, it's worth a look on a later trip. People who love decorative arts should put it on their "A" list.

TOURING TIPS The small garden behind the museum is a popular spot for a brown-bag lunch. The Victorian Garden is open spring through fall, on weekdays 10 a.m. to 4 p.m., weather permitting; enter in at 1921 Sunderland Place.

OTHER THINGS TO DO NEARBY Walk to Dupont Circle for a whiff of Washington's bohemian side: trendy cafes, shops, bookstores, and restaurants crowd Connecticut Avenue. Expect to be panhandled about every 50 feet in fair weather; the street merchants crowding around the Metro entrances suggest a Middle Eastern bazaar.

kids Bureau of Engraving and Printing ★ ★

APPEAL BY AGE	PRESCHOOL ★ ★	GRADE SCHOOL ★ ★ ★ ★	TEENS ★ ★ ★ ★
YOUNG ADULTS ★ ★ ★ ★		OVER 30 ★ ★ ★ ★	SENIORS ★ ★ ★ ★

Location Raoul Wallenberg Place (formerly 15th Street) and C Street SW (2 blocks south of the Mall); Nearest Metro station **Smithsonian;**
☎ **202-874-3019 or 202-874-3188 for a recording**

Type of attraction The presses that print U.S. currency and stamps (guided tour) Be aware that when the Department of Homeland Security raises the level to code Orange, the BEP is closed to the public. **Admission** Free. **Hours** Monday–Friday, 10 a.m.–2 p.m. and (May–August only) 5–7 p.m.; closed on federal holidays and weekends. The ticket office, located on Raoul Wallenberg Place, opens at 8 a.m. First come, first served and tickets are usually gone by 9 a.m. No tickets are required October–February. A valid ID is required. No book bags, backpacks, or any sharp objects are allowed. Go to the 14th Street side of the building to enter. **When to go** The earlier, the better. During peak season, try to arrive by 8 a.m. (or earlier) and pick up tickets at the ticket office; they are often gone by 9 a.m. **Special comments** Small children may have trouble looking over the ledge and down into the press rooms below. When the Department of Homeland Security level is elevated to code Orange, all general public tours are cancelled. After the novelty of seeing all that cash fades, it's just a printing plant. **How much time to allow** About an hour when the ticket system is in effect. In the early fall, when the line snakes out the front door and up 14th Street, figure on at least 2 hours. Count on about 15 minutes for every 100 people in line ahead of you.

DESCRIPTION AND COMMENTS This is a 35- to 45-minute guided tour through the rather cramped glass-lined corridors that go over the government's immense money and stamp printing plant. Visitors look down and gape at the printing presses that crank out the dough and at pallets of greenbacks in various stages of completion. The sign some wag hung on a press, however, says it all: "You have never been so close yet so far away." Kids love this place, so it's a tourist site families should plan on hitting, even if you're only in town for a short period.

TOURING TIPS Arrive early—this is one of D.C.'s most popular attractions. In early spring and summer, get to the ticket booth before 8 a.m. to avoid disappointment. The ticket office distributes about 80 tickets for every tour starting at 15-minute intervals between 9 and 10:45 a.m., and 12:30 and 2 p.m. When all tickets are gone, the ticket office closes. After picking up your tickets, come back for your tour and meet near the ticket office on Raoul Wallenberg Place, where you will be escorted into the building. You have about a 30-minute grace period if you're running late. For a unique souvenir, check out the bags of shredded money for sale in the visitor center at the end of the tour. For a VIP guided tour, contact your congressperson's office at least two months before your trip. The VIP tours are conducted at 8:15 and 8:45 a.m., Monday through Friday. Bathrooms are located inside the building where the tour begins.

OTHER THINGS TO DO NEARBY As you exit the building on Raoul Wallenberg Place, the Tidal Basin is a short walk to the left: benches, tables, a lot of greenery, and the calming effect of water make it a great spot to unwind or eat lunch—or rent a paddleboat. And there's a great view of the Jefferson Memorial. Other sights close at hand are the Holocaust Memorial Museum, the Washington Monument, the new National World War II Memorial, and the seven-and-a-half-acre memorial to President Franklin D. Roosevelt. The $52-million series of gardens, sculptures, and granite walls are located between the Lincoln and Jefferson memorials along the Potomac River and the Tidal Basin. There aren't a lot of places to eat nearby, however.

Corcoran Gallery of Art ★ ★ ★

APPEAL BY AGE	PRESCHOOL —	GRADE SCHOOL ★	TEENS ★ ★
YOUNG ADULTS ★ ★ ★	OVER 30 ★ ★ ★		SENIORS ★ ★ ★

Location 17th and E streets NW, a half block west of the White House; Nearest Metro stations Farragut West and Farragut North; ☎ 202-639-1700 or 888-CORCORAN; www.corcoran.org

Type of attraction A museum that primarily features American art from the colonial period to the present (self-guided tour). **Admission** $8 for adults, $6 for seniors and students, $4 for students 13–18, and $12 for families. Free on Mondays and after 5 p.m. on Thursdays. **Hours** Wednesday–Monday, 10 a.m.– 5 p.m.; Thursday, 10 a.m.–9 p.m.; closed Tuesdays, Christmas Day, and New Year's Day. **When to go** Anytime; Sunday gospel brunch; Thursdays after 5 p.m. **Special comments** Free 45-minute tours are offered daily at noon, Thursdays at 7:30 p.m., and Saturdays and Sundays at 10:30 a.m. and 2:30 p.m. Art snobs will feel at home. **How much time to allow** 2 hours.

DESCRIPTION AND COMMENTS Frank Lloyd Wright called this Beaux Arts museum "the best designed building in Washington." Inside are works by John Singer Sargent, Mary Cassatt, and Winslow Homer, among others. There's also an abundance of cutting-edge contemporary art.

It's a big place with a wide range of periods and styles, so you're bound to see something you like.

TOURING TIPS Maybe it's because of the art school next door, but this museum has a distinctly serious atmosphere. (In fact, one reason that a long-planned expansion was abandoned was that many people considered the Frank Gehry–designed addition a bad and even more frivolous match.) It's not a place to drag little Johnny and Sally, who would rather be looking at dinosaur bones in the National Museum of Natural History. For a delightful Sunday museum excursion, take this Smithsonian staffer's suggestion: begin with brunch in the Corcoran's stunning cafe, which is

unofficial **TIP**
After 5 p.m. on Thursday the Corcoran is "pay what you feel."

accompanied by gospel music from a local choir. Afterward, take a leisurely tour of the art museum and then stroll over to the Renwick Gallery for more first-class art—and, perhaps, some shopping in the Renwick's excellent museum shop. It's a great, laid-back way to spend the day and you won't be battling the crowds besieging the megamuseums on the Mall. The Corcoran's cafe hours are 11 a.m. to 2 p.m. (and 8 p.m. on Thursdays). Reservations are suggested; call ☎ 202-639-1786.

OTHER THINGS TO DO NEARBY Duck into the Organization of American States and enter a rain forest: a courtyard filled with palm trees and the sound of falling water awaits you. Walk up the staircase and peek into the opulent Hall of the Americas. The Octagon, one of the earliest Federal-period houses in the United States, is a block to the east; Dolley Madison entertained there after the Brits burned the White House in 1814. For lunch, stroll up 17th Street toward Pennsylvania Avenue. Le Sorbet, around the corner on G Street, can supply a sandwich and drink for less than $5. Another block north is McDonald's.

Daughters of the American Revolution (DAR) Museum ★★★★

APPEAL BY AGE	PRESCHOOL —	GRADE SCHOOL ★	TEENS ★★★★
YOUNG ADULTS ★★	OVER 30 ★★★★		SENIORS ★★★★★

Location 1776 D Street NW, across from the Ellipse; Nearest Metro station **Farragut West;** ☎ **202-879-3241; www.dar.org**

Type of attraction The 33 period rooms are a cornucopia of decorative arts and antiques (self-guided museum tour and a guided tour). **Admission** Free. **Hours** Monday–Friday, 9:30 a.m.–4 p.m.; Saturday, 9:30 a.m.–5 p.m. The museum is closed on Sunday, federal government holiday weekends, and for the first 2 weeks in July. Guided tours of the period rooms are available Monday–Friday, 10 a.m.–2:30 p.m., and Saturday, 9 a.m.–4:30 p.m. Tours leave approximately every 45 minutes. **When to go** Anytime. **Special comments** Expect to do a lot of stair climbing on the tour. You can't enter the rooms, and only two or three visitors at a time can squeeze into doorways to peer inside. A must-see for lovers of antiques and decorative arts. **How much time to allow** 2 hours.

DESCRIPTION AND COMMENTS This beaux arts building, completed in 1910, is a knockout. The huge columns that grace the front of the building are solid marble; a special railroad spur was built to transport them to the building site. The DAR Museum, predictably enough, emphasizes the role of women throughout American history and includes fine examples of furniture, ceramics, glass, paintings, silver, costumes, and textiles. It's a small museum filled with everyday items out of America's past. From the interior of a California adobe parlor of 1850, to a replica of a 1775 bedchamber in Lexington, Massachusetts, to the kitchen of a 19th-century Oklahoma farm family, the period rooms display objects in a context of both time and place. Kids will get a kick out of the four-sided mousetrap that guillotines rodents, the foot-controlled toaster, and the sausage stuffer that looks like an early-19th-century version of a NordicTrack machine.

To make the museum more attractive to children accompanying parents, docents drop kids off at the Touch Area on the third floor. While their parents tour nearby period rooms, kids can play with authentic 18th- and 19th-century toys and objects, including miniature Chippendale tables and chairs, real powder horns, butter molds, candle snuffers, and flags. The museum and period rooms are sleepers that a lot of visitors to Washington overlook. But for lovers of antiques and decorative arts, the rooms provide an opportunity to view beautiful objects in authentic period settings.

TOURING TIPS Finding the entrance is a bit tough, although the DAR building itself is easy enough to find. At D and 17th (across from the Ellipse), walk about half a block down D Street; the museum-and-tour entrance is on the side of the building. During the busy spring and summer, the period-room tours can get crowded, especially on Saturday, so try to arrive before noon.

OTHER THINGS TO DO NEARBY Walk up the marble steps and into the national headquarters of the American Red Cross, next door on 17th Street. A grand staircase leads to the second-floor ballroom, which holds three 25-foot stained-glass Memorial Windows, reputed to be the largest suite of Tiffany panels still in their original location (except in churches). The three were donated to the Red Cross by Union and Confederate nursing agencies, and their theme is ministry to the sick and wounded. Next door to DAR, the lobby of the Organization of American States building is a bit of a tropical paradise; around back is the Art Museum of the Americas, a small gallery featuring art from Latin America and the Caribbean (open Tuesday through Saturday, 10 a.m. to 5 p.m.; admission is free). Head up 17th Street toward Pennsylvania Avenue to find a large selection of restaurants.

Decatur House ★ ★ ★

APPEAL BY AGE	PRESCHOOL ★	GRADE SCHOOL ★	TEENS ★
YOUNG ADULTS ★★	OVER 30 ★★		SENIORS ★★★

Location 748 Jackson Place NW, across from Lafayette Park;
Nearest Metro stations Farragut West, Farragut North; ☎ 202-842-0920;
www.decaturhouse.org

Type of attraction One of Washington's earliest surviving important residences (guided tour). **Admission** Free. **Hours** Tuesday–Saturday, 10 a.m.–5 p.m.; Sunday, noon–4 p.m.; closed Mondays and Thanksgiving and Christmas days. **When to go** Anytime. **Special comments** An interesting yet narrow slice of early Americana; the tour involves descending a steep, curving staircase. **How much time to allow** 1 hour.

DESCRIPTION AND COMMENTS Stephen Decatur was a naval war hero who defeated the Barbary pirates off the shores of Tripoli (ring a bell?) during the War of 1812. If he hadn't been killed in a duel, some say he might have been president. No doubt he built this house in 1819 with presidential aspirations in mind: it's close to the White House. The first floor is decorated in authentic Federalist style and displays Decatur's furnishings and sword. The formal parlors on the second floor reflect a later Victorian restyling. Famous statesmen who resided in the building include Henry Clay, Martin Van Buren, and Edward Livingston.

TOURING TIPS If you're on a tight schedule, this isn't the place to be blowing your time. But it's an okay rainy-afternoon alternative that gives insight into the early days of Washington.

OTHER THINGS TO DO NEARBY The Renwick Gallery is around the corner on Pennsylvania Avenue; next to it is Blair House, where foreign dignitaries stay. Decatur House faces Lafayette Park, frequent site of political demonstrations, once home to many homeless, and predictably filled with statues. Across the street is the White House.

Dumbarton Oaks and Gardens ★★★★

| APPEAL BY AGE | PRESCHOOL — | GRADE SCHOOL ★ | TEENS ★★★ |
| YOUNG ADULTS ★★★★ | OVER 30 ★★★★ | | SENIORS ★★★★ |

Location 1703 32nd Street NW, between R and S streets, in Georgetown; ☎ 202-339-6400; www.doaks.org

Type of attraction A mansion/museum and a beautiful terraced garden (self-guided tour). **Admission** $1 donation suggested for adults for the museum; $7 fee for adults, $5 for seniors and children for the gardens March 15–October; free admission for the rest of the year. **Hours** Museum hours are Tuesday–Sunday, 2–5 p.m. The garden is open (weather permitting) November–March 14, Tuesday–Sunday, 2–5 p.m. and until 6 p.m. the rest of the year. Both the museum and gardens are closed on federal holidays, Christmas Eve, and Mondays. The gardens area is also closed during inclement weather. **When to go** Anytime. **Special comments** Don't be put off by the hushed surroundings—this is one of the best museums in Washington, intimate and gorgeous. However, there is no eatery, and picnics are not allowed. **How much time to allow** 2 hours.

DESCRIPTION AND COMMENTS Most people associate Dumbarton Oaks with the conference held here in 1944 that led to the formation of the United Nations. Today, however, it's a research center for Byzantine and pre-Columbian studies owned by Harvard University. The Byzantine collection is one of the world's finest, featuring bronzes, ivories, and jewelry. The exquisite pre-Columbian art collection is housed in eight interconnected, circular glass pavilions lit by natural light. It's a knockout of a museum. Dumbarton Oaks Gardens is located around the corner on R Street. The terraced ten-acre garden is rated one of the top gardens in the United States, featuring an orangery, a rose garden, wisteria-covered arbors and, in the fall, a blazing backdrop of trees turning orange, yellow, and red. Dumbarton Oaks isn't the kind of museum with much appeal to small children, and some adults may not find much of interest in the collection due to its narrow focus. But combined with the adjacent gardens, it's a worthwhile place to visit when in Georgetown.

TOURING TIPS Because Dumbarton Oaks doesn't open its massive doors until 2 p.m., combine your visit with a morning trip to Georgetown. If it's raining the day you plan to visit, try to rearrange your schedule so you can come on a nice day; the gardens are terrific. Or make reservations to get into Tudor Place, the 1805 home of Martha Washington's granddaughter at 1644 31st Street NW; ☎ 202-965-0400.

OTHER THINGS TO DO NEARBY Oak Hill Cemetery at 30th and R streets boasts a gothic revival chapel designed by James Renwick and fabulous 19th-century funeral sculptures. (Mt. Zion Cemetery and Female Union Band Cemetery at 27th and O streets are parts of a free black internment site going back to 1842.) Also look into Dumbarton House, a showcase of Federal-period architecture, furniture, and decorative arts (2715 Q Street NW; ☎ 202-337-2288).

kids Federal Bureau of Investigation (*closed for renovations and scheduled to reopen in 2007*)

Location Tenth Street NW at Pennsylvania Avenue; visitor's entrance is at Ninth and E streets NW; ☎ 202-324-3447; www.fbi.gov

Type of attraction FBI headquarters.

Ford's Theatre/Petersen House ★ ★ ★

APPEAL BY AGE	PRESCHOOL ★	GRADE SCHOOL ★★	TEENS ★★
YOUNG ADULTS ★★★	OVER 30 ★★★		SENIORS ★★★

Location 511 Tenth Street NW; Nearest Metro station Metro Center, 11th Street exit; ☎ 202-426-6924; *Ford's Theatre:* www.fordstheatre.org; *Petersen House:* www.nps.gov/foth/hwld.htm

Type of attraction The restored theater where Abraham Lincoln was shot, and the house across the street, where he died (self-guided tour). **Admission** Free. **Hours** Daily, 9 a.m.–5 p.m.; closed Christmas Day. **When to go** Anytime. **Special comments** The theater (but not the museum) is closed to visitors on Thursday and Sunday afternoons, when matinees are in progress. It may also be closed on other afternoons when rehearsals are in progress. An interesting but small museum; the theater is a reconstruction of the original interior. **How much time to allow** 1 hour.

DESCRIPTION AND COMMENTS Don't miss the recently updated Lincoln Museum in the basement of the theater, featuring the clothes Lincoln was wearing the night he was shot and the derringer used to kill him. Across the street, Petersen House offers a glimpse of 19th-century Washington. Ford's Theatre, both the museum and where Lincoln was shot, is small. Unless you're a history buff, this is mostly a fill-in stop, at least for first-time visitors.

TOURING TIPS Start with the theater, then view the museum in the basement before crossing the street to Petersen House.

OTHER THINGS TO DO NEARBY The International Spy Museum, the National Portrait Gallery, and the American Art Museum are all close. For lunch, it's four or five blocks to Chinatown, two blocks to the Old Post Office Pavilion, or just down the street to the Hard Rock Cafe.

Franciscan Monastery and Gardens ★ ★

APPEAL BY AGE	PRESCHOOL —	GRADE SCHOOL ★★★	TEENS ★★
YOUNG ADULTS ★★		OVER 30 ★★	SENIORS ★★

Location **1400 Quincy Street NE; Nearest Metro station Brookland-CUA; from the station exit, turn left, walk up to Michigan Avenue, turn left, and walk over the bridge; continue on Michigan Avenue to Quincy Street, turn right, and walk 4 blocks;** ☎ **202-526-6800**

Type of attraction A working monastery (guided tour). **Admission** Free. **Hours** Guided tours on the hour Monday–Saturday, 9 a.m.–4 p.m. (except at noon daily and 9 a.m. on Tuesday); Sunday, 1–4 p.m. **When to go** Anytime. **Special comments** The tour involves negotiating many narrow, steep stairs and low, dark passageways. A limited number of wheelchairs are available for touring the church and upper grounds. Beautiful architecture, peaceful grounds—and kind of spooky. **How much time to allow** 1 hour.

DESCRIPTION AND COMMENTS Built around 1900 and recently restored, this monastery has everything you'd expect: quiet, contemplative formal gardens; a beautiful church modeled after the Hagia Sophia in Istanbul; and grounds dotted with replicas of shrines and chapels found in the Holy Land. What's really unusual is the sanitized crypt beneath the church, which is more Hollywood than Holy Land. (You almost expect to run into Victor Mature wearing a toga.) It's a replica of the catacombs under Rome and is positively—if inauthentically—ghoulish. As you pass open (but phony) grave sites in the walls, the guide narrates hair-raising stories of Christian martyrs eaten by lions, speared, stoned to death, beheaded, and burned at the stake. Shudder.

TOURING TIPS If you're driving, parking is easy. Two parking lots are located across from the monastery on 14th Street. If you're visiting Washington in the spring, the beautiful gardens alone are worth the trip.

OTHER THINGS TO DO NEARBY The Basilica of the National Shrine of the Immaculate Conception—let's catch our breath—is just past the Metro station on Michigan Avenue. For lunch, a Pizza Hut is conveniently located near the Metro.

Frederick Douglass National Historic Site ★★★★

APPEAL BY AGE	PRESCHOOL ★	GRADE SCHOOL ★★	TEENS ★★★
YOUNG ADULTS ★★★	OVER 30 ★★★★		SENIORS ★★★★

Location 1411 W Street SE, in Anacostia; ☎ 202-426-5961 or 800-365-2267 for reservations; www.nps.gov/frdo/freddoug.html

Type of attraction Cedar Hill, the preserved Victorian home of abolitionist, statesman, and orator Frederick Douglass (guided tour by reservation only). At press time, portions of the house were closed for renovation. **How to get there** Drive; Anacostia is unsafe for pedestrians day or night. From the Mall, take Independence Avenue east past the U.S. Capitol to Second Street SE, where it is intersected by Pennsylvania Avenue. Bear right onto Pennsylvania Avenue, go to 11th Street SE, and turn right. Cross the 11th Street Bridge and go south on Martin Luther King Jr. Avenue to W Street SE. Turn left and go 4 blocks to the visitor center parking lot on the right. **Admission** $2 per person. **Hours** October–April, daily, 9 a.m.–4 p.m.; May–October, daily, 9 a.m.–5 p.m. Tours are hourly, except noon. Closed Thanksgiving, Christmas, and New Year's days. **When to go** Anytime. While not required, it's a good idea to call and make reservations for the house tour. **Special comments** Do not take the Metro to Anacostia. The entire area is unsafe; Cedar Hill, administered by the National Park Service, is safe. **How much time to allow** 1 hour.

DESCRIPTION AND COMMENTS   This lovely Victorian home on a hill overlooking Washington remains much as it was in Douglass's time. The former slave, who among other achievements became U.S. ambassador to Haiti, spent the final 18 years of his life in this house. Douglass lived here when he wrote the third volume of his autobiography, *Life and Times of Frederick Douglass.* For people interested in the history of the civil rights movement and genteel life in the late 1800s, Cedar Hill is a find. Our well-informed guide provided a detailed commentary on Douglass's life and times. Look for Douglass's barbells on the floor next to his bed. Most children, however, may find it dull.

TOURING TIPS   A late-afternoon visit is almost like stepping back into the 19th century, because the house is preserved as it was when Douglass died in 1895: there's no electricity, and the gathering shadows in the house evoke the past. Be sure to see "The Growlery," a small, one-room structure behind the main house that Douglass declared off-limits to the household so he could work alone.

OTHER THINGS TO DO NEARBY   The Anacostia Museum is a short drive. However, Anacostia, Washington's first suburb and an area rich in black history, is economically distressed and crime ridden. It's okay to drive during daylight, but it's not a part of town to visit on foot or at night.

 ## Folger Shakespeare Library ★★½

APPEAL BY AGE	PRESCHOOL –	GRADE SCHOOL ★	TEENS ★★
YOUNG ADULTS ★★	OVER 30 ★★		SENIORS ★★

Location 201 East Capitol Street SE; Nearest Metro stations **Capitol South, Union Station;** ☎ **202-544-4600; www.folger.edu**

Type of attraction A museum and library dedicated to the Bard (self-guided tour). **Admission** Free. **Hours** Monday–Saturday, 10 a.m.–4 p.m.; tours at 11 a.m. daily, and 11 a.m. and 1 p.m. on Saturday; closed on federal holidays. The Reading Room is open Monday–Friday, 8:45 a.m.–4:45 p.m., and Saturday, 9 a.m.–noon and 1–4:30 p.m. Garden is open April–October on every third Saturday of each month. There are tours at 10 a.m. and 11 a.m.; call ☎ 202-675-0395 for group tours. **When to go** Anytime. **Special comments** Parts of the library are available only to accredited scholars. **How much time to allow** 1 hour.

DESCRIPTION AND COMMENTS The Folger House is the world's largest collection of Shakespeare's printed works, as well as a vast array of other rare Renaissance books and manuscripts—one of its treasures, a copy of one of the First Folios, published in 1616, is on permanent display at the east end, open to the title page. (The Folger actually owns 79 copies of the First Folio, about a third of those in existence.) Stroll the Great Hall featuring hand-carved, oak-paneled walls and priceless displays from the museum's collection. You may also visit the three-tiered Elizabethan theater, with walls of timber and plaster and carved oak columns. The Folger is an incongruous attraction that holds appeal only for people with a love of language, Merrie Olde England, and the theater. But it's worth a peek on a second or third trip to Capitol Hill.

TOURING TIPS Guided tours of the building, exhibits, and the Elizabethan garden are conducted daily at 11 a.m. Special tours of the garden, featuring herbs and flowers grown in Shakespeare's time, are held every third Saturday from April through October at 10 and 11 a.m. The theater there, a miniature Globe, still hosts concerts, readings, and some theatrical performances, although the major productions have moved to the Shakespeare Theatre downtown. At the west end of the building, a statue of Puck from *A Midsummer Night's Dream* generally presides over a fountain and pool. The Folger doesn't have much of interest for kids, unless yours have a fondness for gardens or exhibits on Elizabethan England.

OTHER THINGS TO DO NEARBY The Folger is directly behind the Library of Congress, which sits in front of the U.S. Capitol. The Supreme Court is less than a block away. Walk south on Second Street SE to find a wide array of restaurants and cafes. The sixth-floor cafeteria in the Library of Congress's Madison Building is a cheap lunch option.

Franklin Delano Roosevelt Memorial ★ ★ ★ ★

APPEAL BY AGE	PRESCHOOL ★ ★ ★	GRADE SCHOOL ★ ★ ★	TEENS ★ ★ ★
YOUNG ADULTS ★ ★ ★	OVER 30 ★ ★ ★ ★	SENIORS ★ ★ ★ ★

Location West Potomac Park, between the Tidal Basin and the Potomac River; Nearest Metro station **Smithsonian (Independence Avenue exit) is about a brisk 30-minute walk away;** Other Metro stations **Even less convenient are Foggy Bottom–GWU and Arlington Cemetery (across Memorial Bridge in Virginia);** ☎ **202-426-6841; www.nps.gov/fdrm**

Type of attraction A 7.5-acre, open-air memorial to the 32nd president of the United States (self-guided tour). **Admission** Free. **Hours** Staffed daily, 8 a.m.–midnight, except on Christmas Day. **When to go** Anytime, except during inclement weather; the FDR Memorial is not enclosed. It's especially nice in cherry blossom season. **Special comments** Folks old enough to have voted for FDR and disabled people may find it difficult to visit the memorial; nearby parking is scarce and the walk from the nearest metro station is about a mile. One hundred and sixty unmetered parking spaces are located along Ohio Drive SW eastbound, and three lots with a total of 247 spaces are in East Potomac Park under the 14th Street bridges. Five handicapped spaces and one van space are located at the main entrance to the memorial on West Basin Drive. Except at off-peak times (before noon on weekdays and evenings), competition for the spaces is fierce. Other options for reaching the memorial include cabs and a water taxi. Washington's newest presidential memorial successfully blends history, texture, drama, nostalgia, landscaping, and flowing water. The result is a dramatic and inspiring memorial to America's best-loved 20th-century leader. **How much time to allow** 30 minutes to 1 hour.

DESCRIPTION AND COMMENTS   Unlike the nearby imposing marble edifices to Lincoln and Jefferson, the $52-million FDR Memorial on the Tidal Basin tells a story: in four open-air, interconnected "rooms" ("enclaves" or "tableaus" might be better words) that represent each of Roosevelt's four terms, his words are carved on granite walls, bronze images depict the alphabet-soup of programs and agencies he created to help millions of Americans devastated by the Depression, and statues depict the average citizens whose lives he touched. One shows a man listening intently to a radio, evoking the days before television—and a time when FDR's strong and vibrant voice gave hope to Americans in his "fireside chats."

Roosevelt himself is represented in the third room in a larger-than-life bronze statue. The president is seated, his body wrapped in a cape, his face lined with weariness as he approaches the final year of his life. His Scottish terrier Fala is at his feet. The fourth room features a statue of Eleanor Roosevelt, widely regarded as America's greatest first lady for her services as a delegate to the United Nations and as a champion for human rights. This is the first memorial to honor a presidential wife.

Many elements work in harmony to make the memorial a success. Textures of South Dakota granite, brick, rough wood, and falling water combine with ornamental plantings and shade trees to create the ambience of a secluded garden rather than an imposing structure. This is not a "hands off" memorial: the slightly-larger-than-life figures of FDR and Mrs. Roosevelt, as well as statues of five men in an urban bread line and a rural couple outside a barn door, are placed at ground level. Visitors can easily drape an arm around the first lady, sit in Franklin's lap as he delivers a fireside chat, or join the men in line for a souvenir snapshot. The memorial's many waterfalls (FDR considered himself a Navy man) attract splashers with stepping stones while kids enjoy climbing on giant, toppled granite blocks inscribed with the words "I hate war." As a result, visitors to the new memorial, both young and old, seem to enjoy themselves.

TOURING TIPS While you can enter the memorial (dedicated in May 1997) from either end, try to start your tour at the official entrance so you can stroll through the outside rooms in chronological order. That's not a problem if you're walking to the memorial from the Lincoln Memorial. But folks trekking from 14th Street and the Jefferson Memorial should resist the temptation to enter the memorial by continuing along the Tidal Basin and entering at the information center and bookstore. Restrooms are located at both entrances. The memorial is a nice spot for an impromptu picnic by the water, so bring a lunch.

OTHER THINGS TO DO NEARBY The Lincoln, Korean War, and Jefferson memorials are relatively close; just wear comfortable walking shoes and keep in mind that distances along the Tidal Basin and Mall can be deceiving. The Bureau of Engraving and Printing and the Holocaust Memorial Museum are located on Raoul Wallenberg Place, on the east side of the Tidal Basin just beyond the Jefferson Memorial; both require picking up time tickets during the spring and summer (year-round at the Holocaust Museum). Hungry? Pack a lunch. The Holocaust Museum has a small cafe with a limited selection and is the closest place to grab something to eat; or you can head the other way to the Georgetown waterfront. During warm weather, paddleboats are available for rent on the east side of the Tidal Basin, and a water taxi service shuttles tourists along the Potomac River from 11 a.m. to 6 p.m. daily. Clean, modern restrooms are available at the National World War II Memorial, between the Washington Monument and the Lincoln Memorial.

Freer Gallery of Art (*a Smithsonian museum*) ★ ★ ★ ★

APPEAL BY AGE	PRESCHOOL ★	GRADE SCHOOL ★ ★	TEENS ★ ★ ★
YOUNG ADULTS ★ ★ ★	OVER 30 ★ ★ ★ ★		SENIORS ★ ★ ★ ★

Location Jefferson Drive at 12th Street SW, on the Mall; Nearest
Metro station **Smithsonian; ☎ 202-357-4880 or 202-357-1729 (TDD);**
www.asia.si.edu

Type of attraction A museum featuring Asian and American art (self-guided tour). **Admission** Free. **Hours** Daily, 10 a.m.–5:30 p.m.; closed Christmas Day. **When to go** Anytime. **Special comments** This 70-year-old gallery reopened in 1993 after a 4½-year, $26-million renovation. Gorgeous art on a human scale in a setting that's not overwhelming. **How much time to allow** 1–2 hours.

DESCRIPTION AND COMMENTS Well-proportioned spaces, galleries illuminated by natural light, and quiet serenity are the hallmarks of this newly renovated landmark on the Mall. And the art? It's an unusual blend of American paintings (including the world's most important collection of works by James McNeill Whistler) and Asian paintings, sculpture, porcelains, scrolls, and richly embellished household items. Charles Lang Freer, the wealthy 19th-century industrialist who bequeathed this collection to the Smithsonian, saw similarities of color and surface texture in the diverse assemblage. Surrender to the gallery's tranquility and you may, too.

TOURING TIPS An underground link to the nearby Arthur M. Sackler Gallery creates a public exhibition space, as well as convenient passage between the two museums. Don't miss the Peacock Room, designed by James McNeill Whistler; it's widely considered to be the most important 19th-century interior in an American museum. Once the dining room of a Liverpool shipping magnate, it was installed in the Freer Gallery after Freer's death. The ornate room was painted by Whistler to house a collection of blue and white Chinese porcelains. Following a restoration that removed decades of dirt and grime, the room has been restored to its original splendor. Free walk-in tours of the Freer are available daily (except Wednesday) at 11 a.m.

OTHER THINGS TO DO NEARBY The Sackler Gallery, the National Museum of African Art, and the Enid A. Haupt Garden are within a few steps of the Freer Gallery. Directly across the Mall are the National Museum of American History and the National Museum of Natural History. Walk up the Mall toward the Capitol to reach the Arts and Industries Building (closed for renovation), the Hirshhorn Museum, and the National Air and Space Museum.

Gunston Hall ★★★

APPEAL BY AGE	PRESCHOOL ★½	GRADE SCHOOL ★★	TEENS ★★
YOUNG ADULTS ★★½		OVER 30 ★★★	SENIORS ★★★

**10709 Gunston Road, Mason Neck, VA (just off I-95 and Route 1);
☎ 202-338-3552 or 877-337-3050; www.gunstonhall.org**

Type of attraction Historic home of George Mason, 20 minutes south of Washington. **Admission** $8 adults, $5 students grades 1–12, and $7 seniors 60 and older. **Hours** Open daily, 9:30 a.m.–5 p.m., except Thanksgiving, Christmas, and New Year's days; 45-minute guided house tours every half hour. **When to go** During the week if possible. Occasionally the museum also hosts concerts. **Special comments** An underrated destination, the home is of interest to architecture and gardening fans as well as history buffs. **How much time to allow** 2 hours.

DESCRIPTION AND COMMENTS Mason is a fascinating character whose role, like those of several other early activists, has only in recent years been fully appreciated. He was highly influential in the years leading up to the American Revolution: he cowrote, with George Washington, the protest instruments later known as the Virginia Association and the Fairfax County Resolutions, and many of the provisions he constructed for the Virginia Declaration of Rights were adopted by Thomas Jefferson for the Declaration of Independence, including these: "that all men are born equally free and independent, and have certain inherent natural Rights . . . among which are the Enjoyment of Life and Liberty, with the Means of acquiring and possessing Property, and pursuing and obtaining Happiness and Safety." After the revolution, however, as a delegate to the Constitutional Convention, Mason came to feel that the Constitution as drafted was deeply flawed. He urged the inclusion of a Bill of Rights, opposed the extension of slave importation, and disagreed on various fine points (such as majority versus two-thirds votes). Ultimately, despite the resulting vilification, he was unable to bring himself to put aside his principles and sign.

The complex includes Mason's house, a first-class example of Georgian Colonial architecture constructed 1755–1760 and replete with elaborate interior carvings; gardens and grounds where archaeological programs are uncovering slave quarters, fences, and other elements; outbuildings such as a kitchen, dairy, laundry, and smokehouse; and a variety of farm animals. (It's the animals, and the occasional chance to "dig in" to the older ruins, that really get kids involved.) The museum shop has a nice collection of handblown glass, hand-turned wooden accessories from the plantation's 200-year-old boxwoods, scented soaps, silver and jewelry, and books.

TOURING TIPS Check the museum's Web site, which often has discount admission coupons.

OTHER THINGS TO DO NEARBY Mount Vernon is only about 12 miles away, with Woodlawn Plantation and the Pope-Leighey House only a few miles farther, so history buffs could make a day of it.

Hillwood Museum and Gardens ★ ★ ★ ★ ★

APPEAL BY AGE	PRESCHOOL —	GRADE SCHOOL —	TEENS ★ ★
YOUNG ADULTS ★ ★ ★	OVER 30 ★ ★ ★ ★ ★		SENIORS ★ ★ ★ ★

Location 4155 Linnean Avenue NW; Nearest Metro station Van Ness–UDC; For a pleasant 20-minute walk, go south on Connecticut Avenue past the *Star Trek*–y Intelsat complex on the right, then turn left on Upton Street. Follow Upton to Linnean, turn right, and walk about a block to the estate entrance—or grab a cab; ☎ 202-686-8500 or (877) HILLWOOD; ☎ 202-686-5807 for reservations; www.hillwoodmuseum.org

Type of attraction A mansion housing fabulous art treasures (guided or self-guided tours) and formal gardens on a 25-acre estate (guided and self-guided tours). **Admission** $12 for the house tour; $10 seniors 65+, $5 children ages 6–18, and $7 for full-time students; no children under age 6 permitted. Reservations required. **Hours** Tuesday–Saturday, 9 a.m.–5 p.m.; closed Sunday, Monday, the month of January, and most federal holidays. **When to go** Spring is the most beautiful season to tour the house and gardens. But these are popular destinations for garden clubs, so you must secure reservations well in advance. Because of Hillwood's wooded location in Rock Creek Park, it's always five degrees cooler here in D.C.'s hot and humid summers. **Special comments** Self-guided audio tours are offered from 9:30 a.m. to noon and from 2 to 5 p.m. A docent-led tour is offered daily from 12:30 to 2 p.m.; specify your preference when making reservations. A children's audio tour is also available ($5). **How much time to allow** 2 hours. The guided tour itself is over an hour but doesn't include the formal gardens and auxiliary buildings.

DESCRIPTION AND COMMENTS She was a girl from Michigan who inherited two things from her father: good taste and General Foods. That, in a nutshell, is the story of Marjorie Merriweather Post, who bought this Rock Creek Park estate in 1955. She remodeled the mansion and filled it with exquisite 18th- and 19th-century French and Russian decorative art. *Fabulous* is the word required to describe the collection of Imperial Russian objects on display. Mrs. Post was married to the U.S. ambassador to Russia in the 1930s—a time when the communists were unloading "decadent" pre-Revolution art at bargain prices. Mrs. Post bought literally warehouse-loads of stuff: jewels, dinner plates commissioned by Catherine the Great, Easter eggs by Carl Fabergé, and chalices and icons. She then had the loot loaded onto her yacht, *Sea Cloud* (the largest private ship in the world), for shipment home. The very best of the booty is on display here. The tour provides a glimpse into Mrs. Post's lavish lifestyle.

TOURING TIPS Call at least two months in advance for a spring tour, although you may luck into a cancellation by calling a day or two before your planned visit. Children under age 6 are not admitted on the tour. Plan your visit so that you have enough time to stroll the gardens. The estate also has a cafe that serves lunch and tea, a gift shop, and a greenhouse you can tour. A "Behind the Scenes" tour is offered Wednesdays at 3 p.m., June through March (except the first Wednesday of the month; $10 per person). Visitors get a glimpse of Hillwood as it was run when Mrs. Post lived here, by touring the fallout shelter, the massage room, the silver-polishing room, and other places not seen on the regular house tour. Reservations are suggested for the small cafe.

OTHER THINGS TO DO NEARBY Intelsat, near the Van Ness–UDC Metro station, looks like a building out of the late 21st century. That's no surprise, since the firm is an international conglomeration that produces satellites. The lobby features models and prototypes of its products hanging from the ceiling. The garden cafe offers a formal tea as well as light fare.

Hirshhorn Museum and Sculpture Garden ★★★★★
(*a Smithsonian museum*)

APPEAL BY AGE	PRESCHOOL ★	GRADE SCHOOL ★★	TEENS ★★★
YOUNG ADULTS ★★★★	OVER 30 ★★★★★		SENIORS ★★★★★

Location **Seventh Street and Independence Avenue SW, on the Mall;**
Nearest Metro stations **Smithsonian, L'Enfant Plaza; ☎ 202-633-4674;**
hirshhorn.si.edu

Type of attraction A museum of modern art (self-guided tour). **Admission** Free.
Hours Daily, 10 a.m.–5:30 p.m.; closed Christmas Day. Sculpture Garden open from 7:30 a.m. until dusk daily. **When to go** Anytime. **Special comments** The Hirshhorn is a lot of people's favorite art museum on the Mall; an outrageous collection of 20th-century art—don't miss it. **How much time to allow** 2 hours.

DESCRIPTION AND COMMENTS The art found inside is often as bizarre as the circular building that houses it. Works by modern masters such as Rodin, Winslow Homer, Mary Cassatt, and Henry Moore line the easy-to-walk galleries. The outdoor sculpture garden (set below Mall level) contains works by Rodin, Giacometti, and Alexander Calder, among many others. The sculpture offers a refreshing contrast to the marble palaces that line the Mall. If you visit only one modern-art gallery on your visit, make it the Hirshhorn.

TOURING TIPS Guided tours of the Hirshhorn are offered at 10:30 a.m. and noon, Monday through Friday, and at noon and 2 p.m. on weekends. During the summer months, additional docent-led tours are sometimes added. The museum's outdoor cafe is open for lunch during the summer only.

OTHER THINGS TO DO NEARBY Two nearby museums, Arts and Industries (closed for renovations) and Air and Space, offer startling contrasts to the Hirshhorn's treasures (both internally and architecturally). A less jarring experience may be the National Gallery of Art's East Wing, also featuring modern art, as well as several lunch options.

House of the Temple ★

APPEAL BY AGE	PRESCHOOL —	GRADE SCHOOL ★	TEENS ★
YOUNG ADULTS ★	OVER 30 ★		SENIORS ★

**Location 1733 16th Street NW; Nearest Metro station Dupont Circle;
☎ 202-232-3579; www.srmason-sj.org/web/temple.htm**

Type of attraction A Masonic temple modeled after one of the Seven Wonders of the World (guided tour). **Admission** Free. **Hours** Guided tours Monday–Friday, 8 a.m.–3:30 p.m. **When to go** Anytime. **Special comments** Unless you have an abiding interest in freemasonry, the tour is way too long; spectacular but cold. **How much time to allow** 2 hours (less if you're willing to fib to the tour guide; see below).

DESCRIPTION AND COMMENTS The walls are 8 feet thick; the exterior is surrounded by 33 massive columns that support a magnificent pyramidal roof; and, inside, the Temple Room features a soaring 100-foot ceiling and 1,000-pipe organ. Unfortunately, with the exception of the exterior, you have to take an excruciatingly boring guided tour to see these goodies. You're guaranteed to be bored silly by displays of bric-a-brac and memorabilia belonging to long-dead Masonic leaders. There is one slightly bizarre treat: the J. Edgar Hoover Law Enforcement Room, a shrine to the Mason and lifelong FBI chief. But unless you're a rabid fan of J. Edgar, after about two minutes you'll be . . . bored.

TOURING TIPS Arrive around 1 p.m. on a quiet afternoon and tell the tour guide you've got to catch a train at 2:30. Then plead for an abbreviated tour, which he may grudgingly provide if there aren't any other tourists on hand for a tour. But even reduced to an hour, the tour is too long.

OTHER THINGS TO DO NEARBY The House of the Temple is on the edge of a marginally safe neighborhood, so make a beeline toward Dupont Circle, where you'll find plenty to do. Six blocks west on S Street are the Textile Museum and the Woodrow Wilson House.

kids International Spy Museum ★ ★ ½

APPEAL BY AGE	PRESCHOOL ★	GRADE SCHOOL ★★★	TEENS ★★★
YOUNG ADULTS ★★★		OVER 30 ★★★	SENIORS ★★★★

Location 800 F Street NW; Nearest Metro station **Gallery Place–Chinatown;**
☎ **866-779-6873 or 202-654-0944; www.spymuseum.org**

Type of attraction The history and gadgetry of espionage housed in one of Washington's newest museums (self-guided tour). **Admission** $15 for adults ages 12–64; $14 for seniors 65+, active-duty military, and community and college students; $12 for children ages 5–11. **Hours** Daily, April–August, 9 a.m.– 8 p.m.; August–October, 10 a.m.–8 p.m.; October–March, 10 a.m.–6 p.m.; closed Thanksgiving, Christmas, and New Year's days. Check the Web site to confirm hours for when you want to go. **When to go** After the spook museum opened in the summer of 2002, lines stretched around the block throughout the day, signaling a minimum wait in line of 45 minutes (from the middle of the block on Ninth Street) or longer. Either arrive at least a half-hour before 9 a.m. or plan to visit around 5 p.m. weekdays, when there's usually no wait. **Special comments** Spycraft meets Austin Powers: the museum is slick, manipulative, and dodges some important moral questions (and historical failures) of U.S. intelligence operations. Otherwise, it's fun in an empty-headed sort of way (and located in a city full of world-class museums, most of them free). There's a long, steep flight of stairs to descend about halfway through the museum. **How much time to allow** 90 minutes to 2 hours.

DESCRIPTION AND COMMENTS   Since CIA headquarters across the Potomac in Langley isn't offering tours, this $40-million privately owned museum offers the next best thing: a look at the secret world of intelligence. More than 400 artifacts are on display, ranging from items dating from Biblical times to the modern age of terror. What you'll see: tools of the trade such as a lipstick pistol developed by the KGB, an Enigma cipher machine used by the Allies to break German secret codes during World War II, an Aston Martin DB 5 sports car decked out like the one used by James Bond in Goldfinger, and tributes to celebrity spies such as dancer Josephine Baker (who worked for the French resistance) and late TV chef Julia Child (who worked for the OSS). What you won't see: any mention of spectacular failures of U.S. intelligence, including how the CIA, NSA, DIA, and other alphabet-soup spy agencies missed the fall of the Soviet Union and the Shah of Iran or helped overthrow elected governments around the world. Alas, the museum's us-versus-them mentality spares visitors from the moral ambiguity of intelligence gathering. To get that insight, skip the museum and curl up with a novel by John le Carré (a former spy).

TOURING TIPS   This is one of those museums where visitors are herded into an elevator, taken to the second floor, and everyone negotiates their way through narrow corridors—making it difficult to linger or backtrack against the human current. Keep that in mind as you tour.

The National Portrait Gallery and the Smithsonian American Art Museum are across the street; the Verizon Center, the main downtown sports and music venue, is across the street. Ford's Theatre/Petersen House (where Lincoln was assassinated and died) are a block over on Tenth Street NW. The booming downtown area is teeming with new restaurants.

Islamic Center ★ ★

APPEAL BY AGE	PRESCHOOL ★	GRADE SCHOOL ★ ★	TEENS ★ ★
YOUNG ADULTS ★ ★ ★		OVER 30 ★ ★	SENIORS ★ ★

Location 2551 Massachusetts Avenue NW; Nearest Metro station Dupont Circle; ☎ 202-332-8343

Type of attraction A mosque (self-guided tour). **Admission** Free. **Hours** Monday–Saturday, 10 a.m.–5 p.m., and Sunday, 10 a.m.–2 p.m.; closed Fridays to non-Muslims between 1 and 2:30 p.m. **When to go** Anytime. Call ahead for a guided tour. **Special comments** The mosque enforces a strict dress code: Visitors must remove their shoes to go inside, and no shorts or short dresses are allowed. Women must cover their heads and wear long-sleeved clothing. **How much time to allow** 15 minutes.

DESCRIPTION AND COMMENTS A brilliant white building and slender minaret mark this unusual sight on Embassy Row. Visitors must remove their shoes before stepping inside to see the Persian carpets, elegantly embellished columns, decorated arches, and huge chandelier. Alas, with America's focus on the Middle East and things Islamic, we were disappointed on our visit to the Islamic Center: it fell a little short on giving any useful insight into that troubled part of the world. The small bookstore next to the mosque was filled with Arabic texts and translations of the Koran, but no one was behind the counter to answer our questions. Though close to other tourist sights, the mosque seems to have missed an opportunity to educate D.C. visitors about Islam. Those with a strong interest in the Middle East should call a week in advance for the one-hour guided tour.

TOURING TIPS Make this small, exotic building a part of a walk down Embassy Row. But unless you have an interest in Islam, it's not worth going out of the way to see.

OTHER THINGS TO DO NEARBY Take a short walk and tour the Textile Museum and the Woodrow Wilson House. On Tuesday through Saturday afternoons, the opulent Anderson House is open. The Phillips Collection is an intimate modern-art museum that's a refreshing change of pace from huge Mall museums.

Jefferson Memorial ★ ★ ★

APPEAL BY AGE	PRESCHOOL ★	GRADE SCHOOL ★ ★	TEENS ★ ★ ★
YOUNG ADULTS ★ ★ ★		OVER 30 ★ ★ ★	SENIORS ★ ★ ★

Location Across the Tidal Basin from the Washington Monument; Nearest Metro stations L'Enfant Plaza, Smithsonian; ☎ 202-426-6841; www.nps.gov/thje

---

Type of attraction A classical-style monument to the author of the Declaration of Independence and the third U.S. president (self-guided tour). **Admission** Free. **Hours** Always open; staffed 8 a.m.–11:45 p.m., except on Christmas Day. **When to go** For the best views, go at night or when the cherry trees along the Tidal Basin are in bloom. **Special comments** The view from the steps and across the Tidal Basin is one of the best in Washington. A favorite at night, but not convenient. **How much time to allow** 30 minutes.

DESCRIPTION AND COMMENTS The neoclassical, open-air design of this monument reflects Jefferson's taste in architecture. Because it's somewhat off the tourist path, it's usually less crowded than the monuments on the Mall.

TOURING TIPS Park interpreters staffing the monument frequently give talks and can answer questions about Jefferson and the monument. Visitors can walk to the memorial along the rim of the Tidal Basin from Independence Avenue or along 14th Street SW.

OTHER THINGS TO DO NEARBY The Bureau of Engraving and Printing and the Holocaust Memorial Museum are both on 14th Street. In 1997, a $52-million memorial to President Franklin D. Roosevelt opened on a 7.5-acre site located between the Lincoln and Jefferson memorials. The Tidal Basin is great for paddleboating. It's not a long walk to the waterfront fish market, where you can grab a crab (or sandwich).

John F. Kennedy Center for the Performing Arts ★ ★

APPEAL BY AGE	PRESCHOOL ★	GRADE SCHOOL ★	TEENS ★
YOUNG ADULTS ★★		OVER 30 ★★★	SENIORS ★★★

Location New Hampshire Avenue NW and F Street; Nearest Metro station Foggy Bottom–GWU; ☎ 202-416-8340 or 202-416-8524 (TTY); www.kennedy-center.org

---

Type of attraction Both presidential memorial and D.C.'s performing-arts headquarters (guided tour for groups only). **Admission** Free. **Hours** Daily, 10 a.m.–midnight. **When to go** Free tours begin every 15 minutes; Monday–Friday, 10 a.m.–5 p.m., and on Saturday and Sunday, 10 a.m.–1 p.m. **Special comments** So-so art, a huge building, and a great view (without a show ticket). The leisurely tour lasts about 45 minutes but is easy on the feet: the Kennedy Center is well carpeted. **How much time to allow** 1 hour.

DESCRIPTION AND COMMENTS The white rectilinear Kennedy Center facility boasts four major stages, a film theater, and a sumptuous interior shimmering with crystal, mirrors, and deep-red carpets. The Grand Foyer is longer than two football fields. Nations from around the world contributed art and artifacts on display in halls and foyers, such as African art, Beame porcelain, tapestries, and sculptures. If rehearsals aren't in progress, the tour includes peeks inside the intimate Eisenhower Theater, the Opera House (featuring a spectacular chandelier), and the Concert Hall, which seats 2,750. Admirers of JFK and culture vultures will love the tour, while kids will probably get bored. But you don't have to take the tour to enjoy the view; take the elevators to the roof terrace.

TOURING TIPS While the guided tour is leisurely and informative, the best way to visit the Kennedy Center is to attend a concert, play, or film. Before or after the event, go up to the seventh floor and stroll the roof terrace—the view at night is terrific. Free round-trip shuttle service from the Foggy Bottom Metro station is offered daily from 10 a.m. to midnight every 15 minutes. Also, don't miss the free performance given every day at 6 p.m. in the Grand Foyer.

OTHER THINGS TO DO NEARBY You can lunch or snack at the KC Cafe without securing a second mortgage on your house, but the Roof Terrace Restaurant is expense-account priced. The infamous Watergate project is across G Street from the Kennedy Center and features expensive shops and restaurants, but you won't find any memorial to a certain burglary that occurred there in 1972. A biking and jogging path along the Potomac River is just below the Kennedy Center; follow it upriver to Thompson's Boat Center, which rents canoes and bikes. A little farther is Washington Harbour, an upscale collection of shops, restaurants, and condominiums, featuring life-size and lifelike sculptures of tourists, joggers, workers, and artists that add a bit of whimsy to scenic al fresco dining along the river. Hard-core walkers can continue up Wisconsin Avenue and enter a world of trendy shops, restaurants, and crowded sidewalks. Before you walk too far, remember that Georgetown lacks a Metro station to get you back to where you started.

Kenilworth Park and Aquatic Gardens ★ ★ ★

APPEAL BY AGE	PRESCHOOL ★	GRADE SCHOOL ★ ★	TEENS ★ ★
YOUNG ADULTS ★ ★ ★	OVER 30 ★ ★ ★		SENIORS ★ ★ ★

Location 1900 Anacostia Drive NE, across the Anacostia River from the National Arboretum; ☎ 202-426-6905; www.nps.gov/kepa

Type of attraction A national park devoted to water plants (self-guided tour). **How to get there** Drive. Go south on Kenilworth Avenue from its intersection with New York Avenue. Exit at Eastern Avenue and follow signs to the parking lot off Anacostia Avenue. **Admission** Free. **Hours** Daily, 7 a.m.–4 p.m.; closed Thanksgiving, Christmas, and New Year's days. **When to go** June and July to see hardy water plants; July and August to see tropical plants and lotus. On the third Saturday in July a water-lily festival is held. Year-round it's a great place for bird-watching. **Special comments** The gardens are located in a dangerous neighborhood. Don't take public transportation. **How much time to allow** 1 hour.

DESCRIPTION AND COMMENTS In addition to pools filled with water lilies, water hyacinth, lotus, and bamboo, the gardens teem with wildlife such as opossum, raccoon, waterfowl, and muskrats. It's an amazing place to visit on a clear summer morning.

TOURING TIPS Come in the morning, before the heat closes up the flowers. Don't take public transportation; the surrounding neighborhood is unsafe. Drive or go by cab.

OTHER THINGS TO DO NEARBY The National Arboretum is only a few minutes away by car.

Korean War Veterans Memorial ★ ★ ★

APPEAL BY AGE	PRESCHOOL ★ ★	GRADE SCHOOL ★ ★ ½	TEENS ★ ★ ½
YOUNG ADULTS ★ ★ ★	OVER 30 ★ ★ ★ ½		SENIORS ★ ★ ★ ★

Location Between the Lincoln Memorial and the Tidal Basin, across the lawn from the Vietnam Veterans Memorial; Nearest Metro stations Smithsonian, Foggy Bottom–GWU; ☎ 202-426-6841; www.nps.gov/kowa

Type of attraction A three-dimensional freeze-frame sculpture of troops crossing a battlefield. **Admission** Free. **Hours** Always open; unstaffed, but rangers at the nearby Jefferson and Lincoln memorials are on duty from 8 a.m. to 11:45 p.m., except on Christmas Day. **When to go** Anytime, but it's particularly striking at night. **Special comments** Perhaps a few too many elements put together, but all are effective. A good companion piece to the Vietnam Veterans Memorial. **How much time to allow** 20–30 minutes.

DESCRIPTION AND COMMENTS The memorial consists of several distinct parts, though it's not particularly large as a whole. The most obvious elements are sculptor Frank Gaylord's 19 larger-than-life steel statues of soldiers. Each is seven feet, three inches tall, with deliberately outsized hands and heads. Represented are 14 Army troops, 3 Marines, 1 Navy recruit, and 1 Air Force serviceman; 12 are white, 3 are black, 2 are Hispanic, 1 is Asian, and 1 is Native American. All are heavily laden with packs and weapons and covered in ponchos; their attire and boots suggest it is winter, an impression that is even stronger at night, when the statues are individually illuminated and seem to move. (Three are a little ways off in the woods, so the sense of the company emerging from cover is very realistic.)

The second major component is a black granite wall. The design complements that of the Vietnam Veterans Memorial, which is almost directly across the Mall (though not visible from this point); instead of names, however, this wall is covered with images: 2,400 of them, created from 15,000 photos. Etched into the wall are guns, rescue helicopters, ambulances, bridges being built, mines being defused, doctors operating. Combined with the reflections of onlookers, the effect is as if you were looking through a window. The wall is made up of 38 panels, symbolizing both the 38th Parallel—the original boundary between North and South Korea—and the 38 months of the war's duration.

The wall alongside the walkway lists the names of the countries that sent troops; a small garden is planted with Rose of Sharon hibiscus, the national flower of South Korea. The memorial was dedicated

July 27, 1995, by President Clinton and South Korean President Kim Young Sam.

TOURING TIPS It's interesting to view this memorial and the Vietnam Veterans Memorial one after another; clearly, Maya Lin's striking wall has made a strong impression on other architects and designers, even if some members of the public have been slow to appreciate it.

OTHER THINGS TO DO NEARBY The memorial is in the middle of the west half of the Mall; there's a monument, and a monumental view, on every side.

Koshland Science Museum   ★ ½

APPEAL BY AGE	PRESCHOOL ★	GRADE SCHOOL ★★	TEENS ★★
YOUNG ADULTS ★★		OVER 30 ★★	SENIORS ★★

Location **Sixth and E streets NW; Nearest Metro station Gallery Place–Chinatown, Judiciary Square; ☎ 202-334-1201; www.koshland-science-museum.org**

Type of attraction A small museum aimed at teenagers and adults focusing on biologic and environmental scientific research (self-guided tour). **Admission** $5 adults, $3 seniors and students. **Hours** Daily, 10 a.m.–6 p.m.; closed on Tuesday. **When to go** Anytime. **Special comments** Surprisingly small and boring, with all exhibits on one level. **How much time to allow** 30 minutes.

DESCRIPTION AND COMMENTS Operated by the National Academy of the Sciences, this museum is slick and high-tech, with many interactive and touchy-feely exhibits. It's also narrowly focused on environmental and biologic science—and the perfect place for the budding DNA or global-warming researcher who has exhausted all the (free) science exhibits on the Mall. Others, be warned.

TOURING TIPS Make this a fill-in spot before or after lunch downtown, but at least be sure to look up at the building; a huge gyroscope is parked up there.

OTHER THINGS TO DO NEARBY The National Building Museum, the Law Enforcement Memorial, the International Spy Museum, the Portrait Gallery–American Art Museum complex, and Ford's Theatre are all close. Downtown has a wide variety of places to eat.

Kreeger Museum   ★★★

APPEAL BY AGE	PRESCHOOL ½	GRADE SCHOOL ★	TEENS ★★
YOUNG ADULTS ★★		OVER 30 ★★★	SENIORS ★★★

Location **2401 Foxhall Road NW, Georgetown; Nearest Metro station Tenleytown; ☎ 202-338-3552 or 877-337-3050; www.kreegermuseum.org**

Type of attraction Collection of 19th- and 20th-century art in Philip Johnson–designed mansion. **Admission** $8 adults, $5 students and seniors age 65 and older. **Hours** 90-minute guided tours Tuesday–Friday, 10:30 a.m. and 1:30 p.m. for ages 12 and up, by reservation only. Open Saturday, 10 a.m.–4 p.m. with guided tours all afternoon, no age restrictions or reservations required. Closed in August and around December holidays. **When to go** During the week if possible. Occasionally the museum also hosts concerts. **Special comments** A must-see third stop for modern-art fans (after the Hirshhorn and Phillips Collection) or architecture students. A fine and relatively quiet museum. **How much time to allow** 2 hours.

DESCRIPTION AND COMMENTS Philanthropist David Lloyd Kreeger and his wife, Carmen, began collecting art in the early 1950s and over the next 15 years acquired works from the 1850s to the 1970s, including Monet (nine paintings), Picasso (pieces from his entire career), Renoir, Cézanne, Chagall, Gauguin, van Gogh, Kandinsky, Miró, Calder, Noguchi, Moore, David Smith, and Gene Davis. In addition to arts fans, anyone interested in modern architecture should be certain to see this museum. The building, which was designed (in 1963, and completed in 1967) to serve as a residence, museum, and recital hall in one, is an architectural book of quotations: though definitively postmodernist, it alludes to Byzantine domes, Egyptian tombs, classical travertine facades, Middle Eastern window screens, and the Roman "modular system," with all spaces in some variation of 22 by 22 by 22 feet.

TOURING TIPS The main level of the museum, the sculpture terrace, and the restrooms are wheelchair accessible; you must take a staircase to lower galleries.

 Library of Congress ★ ★ ★ ★

APPEAL BY AGE	PRESCHOOL —	GRADE SCHOOL ★	TEENS ★ ★
YOUNG ADULTS ★ ★ ★	OVER 30 ★ ★ ★ ★		SENIORS ★ ★ ★ ★

Location First Street SE, on Capitol Hill; Nearest Metro station Capitol South; ☎ 202-707-8000; www.loc.gov

Type of attraction The world's largest library (guided and self-guided tours). **Admission** Free. **Hours** Exhibition areas in the newly restored Jefferson Building are open Monday–Saturday, 10 a.m.–5:30 p.m. The library is closed Sundays, federal holidays, and Christmas and New Year's days. The Visitors Theater in the Jefferson Building shows a free 12-minute film on the library's mission. Free guided tours are offered Monday–Friday at 10:30 a.m., 11:30 a.m., 1:30 p.m., 2:30 p.m., and 3:30 p.m., and Saturdays at 10:30 a.m., 11:30 a.m., 1:30 p.m., and 2:30 p.m. Groups are limited to 50 people; sign up for any tour (for that day only) at the Information Desk located in the visitor center (on the ground floor on the west side of the Jefferson Building). Pick up your tickets 10 minutes before the tour begins. **When to go** Anytime. **Special comments** A trip to the library might not be on most folks' vacation itineraries, but consider making an exception in this case. Impressive and informative. **How much time to allow** 1 hour for the guided tour and another hour to browse the exhibits.

DESCRIPTION AND COMMENTS Three huge structures make up the Library of Congress: the Jefferson, Madison, and Adams buildings. To understand what goes on here, take one of the guided tours. (To get the most out of the tour, first see the 12-minute video about the varied workings of the library.) After the tour, which lasts about an hour, you can look at other exhibits in the Jefferson and Madison buildings on your own. Who should go? The Library of Congress holds strong appeal for folks interested in books, academic research, American history, and antiquities. On the other hand, because it's a lecture tour, it is not suitable for young children, and most first-time visitors on a tight schedule shouldn't waste their valuable touring time here. But you should at least go in to admire the building; it's an art gallery in itself.

In the spring of 1997 a permanent exhibit called "American Treasures of the Library of Congress" marked the reopening of the Thomas Jefferson Building, under renovation since 1984. The rotating exhibition in the Great Hall features 200 of the library's rarest and most significant items, such as Thomas Jefferson's rough draft of the Declaration of Independence, Abraham Lincoln's first and second drafts of the Gettysburg Address, Wilbur Wright's telegram to his father announcing the first heavier-than-air flight, and Bernard Hermann's manuscript score for the film classic *Citizen Kane*.

TOURING TIPS Although the Library consists of three buildings, visitors enter at the Jefferson Building on First Street. The tour, with its well-informed guide, is the way to go if you have the time and interest. *Note:* The tours are extremely popular, and it's a good idea to arrive early during the spring and summer to sign up for a tour later in the day. Tickets are available for that day only. Special tours can be arranged for a group of 10 to 60 people through reservation only; the tour must occur Monday through Friday and to begin as early as 9 a.m. or as late as 1 p.m.

A permanent exhibit on copyright located on the fourth floor of the Madison Building features the original Barbie and Ken dolls, Dr. Martin Luther King Jr.'s "I Have a Dream" speech, and the statue of the Maltese Falcon used in the famous film of the same name. More temporary exhibits are located on the sixth floor. Library materials available here go way beyond books. For instance, the Library of Congress has an extensive collection of recorded music, broadcast material, and films. While ostensibly these research materials are for "serious" researchers only, almost anyone with a strong interest in, say, the recordings of Jimmy Durante can find valuable information and hear rare recordings. For musical material, go to the Recorded Sound Reference Center, located on the first floor of the Madison Building, where helpful librarians are ready to assist.

OTHER THINGS TO DO NEARBY The U.S. Capitol, Supreme Court, and Folger Library are all within a block or two. Capitol Hill abounds with nearby lunch spots. The sixth-floor cafeteria in the Madison Building is popular with congressional staffers, and it's a good deal for visitors, who can grab a bite to eat here from 12:30 p.m. to 3 p.m.

Lincoln Memorial ★★★

APPEAL BY AGE	PRESCHOOL ★★	GRADE SCHOOL ★★★	TEENS ★★★
YOUNG ADULTS ★★★		OVER 30 ★★★	SENIORS ★★★

Location At the west end of the Mall; Nearest Metro stations
Smithsonian, Foggy Bottom–GWU; ☎ **202-426-6841; www.nps.gov/linc**

Type of attraction A classical-style memorial to the 16th American president (self-guided tour). **Admission** Free. **Hours** Always open. Rangers on duty 8 a.m.– 11:45 p.m., except Christmas Day. **When to go** For the best views, visit in the early morning, at sunset, or at night. **Special comments** At night, facing west across the Potomac River, you can see the eternal flame at John F. Kennedy's grave. Both solemn and scenic. **How much time to allow** 30 minutes.

DESCRIPTION AND COMMENTS To see what the Lincoln Memorial looks like, just pull out a penny. Yet a visit to this marble monument inspires awe. Historic events took place on the steps: Black soprano Marian Anderson sang here in 1939 after being barred from Constitution Hall; Martin Luther King Jr. gave his "I Have a Dream" speech here in 1963. The Lincoln Memorial anchors the Mall and should be on anyone's must-see list.

TOURING TIPS The Legacy of Lincoln museum in the memorial's basement is worth a peek. You'll find exhibits about demonstrations held at the memorial and a video recounting the building's history. The Lincoln Memorial's location at the west end of the Mall near the river, however, puts this marble edifice at a distance from any lunch spots except for overpriced Mall hot-dog vendors, so eat first. Bathrooms are located on the memorial's ground level.

OTHER THINGS TO DO NEARBY The Vietnam Veterans Memorial and the Reflecting Pool are directly across from the Lincoln Memorial. The Korean War Veterans Memorial is between Lincoln and the Tidal Basin, on the way to the FDR Memorial. The Martin Luther King Jr. Memorial, now under development, is on the bank of the Tidal Basin closest to the Lincoln Memorial.

Meridian International Center ★★★

APPEAL BY AGE	PRESCHOOL ★	GRADE SCHOOL ★★	TEENS ★★
YOUNG ADULTS ★★		OVER 30 ★★	SENIORS ★★★

Location 1624 and 1630 Crescent Place NW; Nearest Metro station
Woodley Park–Zoo/Adams-Morgan; ☎ **202-939-5568; www.meridian.org**

Type of attraction 2 mansions designed by John Russell Pope; art exhibitions displayed in beautiful galleries; handsome gardens and a grove of linden trees (guided and self-guided tours). **Admission** Free. **Hours** Wednesday–Sunday, 2–5 p.m.; closed Mondays, Tuesdays, and federal holidays. The cafe is open Monday–Friday, noon– 2 p.m. **When to go** Anytime. **Special comments** Call ahead of time or check Friday's "Weekend" section of the *Washington Post* to make sure the center isn't closed (due to a conference) and to find out what's on display in the galleries. Grand architecture and a glimpse into the world of diplomacy. **How much time to allow** 1 hour.

DESCRIPTION AND COMMENTS Two side-by-side mansions designed by John Russell Pope (architect of the Jefferson Memorial, the National Gallery of Art building, and other Washington treasures) make up the Meridian International Center, a nonprofit organization that promotes conferences, symposiums, lectures, and seminars and provides services to international visitors, diplomats, scholars, politicians, and others.

The 45-room Meridian House (1921) reflects an 18th-century French Louis XVI style of architecture, while the White-Meyer House (1911) is a salmon-colored-brick Georgian-style mansion. Visitors are welcome to tour the ground floors of the gorgeous—though lightly furnished—buildings and the surrounding gardens. About five art exhibits a year rotate through the galleries of the White-Meyer House. The three-acre site, set off from the city by high, elegant walls, takes up an entire city block.

TOURING TIPS While folks who enjoy grand architecture won't need additional encouragement to visit these two distinguished buildings, others should plan on coming in the spring when the gardens are in bloom and an art exhibition is on display in the elegant galleries. A small cafe in the basement of the Meridian House (which recently underwent a two-year, $1.8-million restoration) offers coffee, tea, and lunch. For a guided tour of the property, just ask at the front desk in either building.

OTHER THINGS TO DO NEARBY Adams-Morgan, an eclectic multicultural neighborhood renowned for its ethnic eateries, is only two blocks away on 18th Street NW.

 ## Mount Vernon Estate and Gardens ★ ★ ★ ★ ★

APPEAL BY AGE	PRESCHOOL ★ ★	GRADE SCHOOL ★ ★ ★ ★	TEENS ★ ★ ★
YOUNG ADULTS ★ ★ ★ ★ ★	OVER 30 ★ ★ ★ ★ ★		SENIORS ★ ★ ★ ★ ★

Location 16 miles south of Washington in Mount Vernon, VA;
☎ **703-780-2000; www.mountvernon.org**

Type of attraction George Washington's 18th-century Virginia plantation on the Potomac River (self-guided tour). **How to get there** To drive from Washington, cross the 14th Street Bridge into Virginia, bear right, and get on the George Washington Memorial Parkway south. Continue past National Airport into Alexandria, where the parkway becomes Washington Street. Continue straight; Washington Street becomes the Mount Vernon Memorial Parkway, which ends at Mount Vernon. Tourmobile offers 4-hour narrated bus tours to Mount Vernon daily, June 15 through Labor Day. Departure is at noon. Tickets are $27 for adults and $13 for children ages 3–11. The price includes admission to Mount Vernon. Call Tourmobile at ☎ 202-554-5100 for more information. Gray Line offers 4-hour coach trips to Mount Vernon and Old Town Alexandria that depart from Union Station daily at 8:30 a.m. October 23–March 31, and 2 p.m. June 19–October 22. No tours are scheduled on Thanksgiving, Christmas, and New Year's days. Fares are $37 for adults and $18 for children. For more information, call Gray Line at ☎ 202-289-1995 or visit **www.grayline.com. Admission** Estate and

Gardens: $13 adults, $12 seniors 62+, $6 children ages 6–11, free age 5 and under. Gristmill: adults and seniors, $2 additional to Estate and Gardens tickets or $4 purchased alone; children (6–11), $1.50 additional or $2 purchased alone; free ages 5 and under. **Hours** All are open daily, including Christmas Day. Estate and Gardens: April–August, 8 a.m.–5 p.m.; November–February, 9 a.m.–4 p.m.; March, September, and October, 9 a.m.–5 p.m. Gristmill: 10 a.m.–5 p.m.; closed November–March. **When to go** Generally before 10 a.m., especially in hot weather. But sometimes tour and school buses arrive before the gates open, creating a line to buy tickets and tour the mansion. Come around 3 p.m. and you're sure to avoid the buses—and the lines. When longer hours are in effect, you must clear the grounds by 5:30 p.m. **Special comments** Mount Vernon is probably the only major D.C. attraction that opens at 8 a.m., making it a prime place to hit early in hot weather—if you have a car to get you there. During Christmas, the decorated mansion's seldom-seen third floor is open to the public. **How much time to allow** 2 hours.

DESCRIPTION AND COMMENTS Folks on a quick trip to Washington won't have time to visit Mount Vernon, but everyone else should. The stunning view from the mansion across the Potomac River is pretty much the same as it was in Washington's day. Unlike most historic sites in D.C., Mount Vernon gives visitors a real sense of how 18th-century rural life worked, from the first president's foot-operated fan chair (for keeping flies at bay while he read) to the rustic kitchen and outbuildings. Historic interpreters are stationed throughout the estate and mansion to answer questions and give visitors an overview of the property and Washington's life.

Mount Vernon is more than just a big house. Special 30-minute landscape and garden tours leave at 11 a.m., 1 p.m., and 3 p.m., April through October. "Slave Life at Mount Vernon" is a 30-minute walking tour to slave quarters and workplaces that starts at 10 a.m., noon, 2 p.m., and 4 p.m. daily, April through October. There's no additional charge for either tour.

Mount Vernon has opened several new attractions on the 30-acre plantation to help diffuse huge crowds that throng the mansion. The newest is a four-acre colonial farm site where visitors can view costumed interpreters using 18th-century farm methods and tools. Hands-on activities are available March through November, and wagon rides are offered on Fridays, Saturdays, and Sundays.

During the summer months, a "Hands-on History" area lets children handle 18th-century objects, play games such as rolling hoops, and learn about early American life; hours are 10 a.m. to 1 p.m. daily from Memorial Day through Labor Day. The estate's Web site, **www.mountvernon.org,** offers a historical primer for your visit. Forty-minute narrated cruises on the Potomac are offered May through August, Tuesday through Sunday and weekends in April and September; $9 adults and $5 children.

TOURING TIPS Mount Vernon is *very* popular, and tourists pull up by the busload in the spring and summer months—sometimes before the grounds even open. During the high tourist season, Monday, Friday, and Sunday mornings before 11 a.m. are the least busy periods. If you want to avoid big crowds, go around 3 p.m., but you have to leave the grounds by 5:30 p.m. When crowds are small in the winter, visitors are frequently given guided tours of the mansion in groups of 20 to 30 people.

OTHER THINGS TO DO NEARBY Mount Vernon offers a snack bar, two gift shops, a post office, a sit-down restaurant, and more in the vast new visitors center. Restrooms can be found near the museum on the grounds or between the gift shop and snack bar near the entrance. Visit Old Town Alexandria on your way to or from Mount Vernon. To stop at Gadsby's Tavern is appropriate, because that's what George Washington used to do.

NASA/Goddard Space Flight Visitor Center ★ ★ ★

APPEAL BY AGE	PRESCHOOL ★	GRADE SCHOOL ★ ★ ★	TEENS ★ ★ ★
YOUNG ADULTS ★ ★ ★		OVER 30 ★ ★ ★	SENIORS ★ ★ ★

Location Greenbelt, MD; ☎ 301-286-9041; www.gsfc.nasa.gov

Type of attraction NASA's 1,100-acre campuslike facility in suburban Maryland, including a small museum and other buildings (self-guided and guided tours). **How to get there** Drive. From downtown Washington, drive out New York Avenue, which becomes the Baltimore-Washington Parkway (I-295). Take the MD 193 East exit, just past the Capital Beltway. Drive about 2 miles past the Goddard Space Flight Center's main entrance to Soil Conservation Road and turn left. Follow signs to the visitor center. **Admission** Free. **Hours** July–August: Tuesday–Saturday, 10 a.m.–5 p.m.; closed Sunday and Monday. September–June 30: Tuesday–Friday, 10 a.m.–3 p.m.; Saturday–Sunday, 12–4 p.m.; closed Thanksgiving, Christmas, and New Year's days. **When to go** Anytime. **Special comments** Informative but not convenient for most visitors. **How much time to allow** 1 hour for the tours, 2 hours for the Sunday bus tours.

DESCRIPTION AND COMMENTS The small museum inside the visitor center is loaded with space hardware, including a space capsule kids can play in, space suits, and real satellites; think of it as a mini–National Air and Space Museum. Outside, some real rockets used to put the hardware into outer space are on display. While most folks will get their fill and then some of spacecraft at the museum on the Mall, a visit to NASA's Greenbelt facility is the icing on the cake for hard-core space cadets.

TOURING TIPS The small gift shop offers interesting NASA-related items such as postcards, 35mm color slides, posters, and publications. One-hour tours are given weekdays at 10 a.m., noon, and 2 p.m. On the first and third Saturdays of the month, model rocket launches are held on center grounds. Call the curator for details, ☎ 301-286-9041.

OTHER THINGS TO DO NEARBY Drive through the adjacent Agricultural Research Center, a collection of farms where the U.S. Department of Agriculture studies farm animals and plants. The roads are narrow and quiet—it's a rural oasis in the heart of Maryland's suburban sprawl. The

National Wildlife Visitor Center off nearby Powder Mill Road features nature displays and hiking paths.

National Air and Space Museum
(a Smithsonian Museum) ★ ★ ★ ★ ★

APPEAL BY AGE	PRESCHOOL ★ ★ ★ ★	GRADE SCHOOL ★ ★ ★ ★ ★	TEENS ★ ★ ★ ★ ★
YOUNG ADULTS ★ ★ ★ ★ ★		OVER 30 ★ ★ ★ ★ ★	SENIORS ★ ★ ★ ★

Location On the south side of the Mall near the U.S. Capitol; Nearest Metro stations Smithsonian, L'Enfant Plaza; ☎ 202-357-2700 or 202-357-1729 (TDD); www.nasm.edu

Type of attraction A museum that chronicles the history of manned flight (self-guided tour). **Admission** Free. **Hours** 10 a.m.–5:30 p.m.; closed Christmas Day. Depending on the shape of the federal budget, hours may be extended during the summer. **When to go** Before noon or after 4 p.m. Because of metal detectors and baggage checks, waits of up to 20 minutes can occur, especially at opening. If there's a long line at the Mall entrance, you *could* try the Independence Avenue entrance—but it's a long walk around this huge building (and may not be worth the effort because the line could be just as long). **Special comments** If you want to get tickets for the five-story-high IMAX theater, make the box office on the main floor your first stop. Some special exhibits require passes; check with the information desk in the main lobby. Absolutely not to be missed. **How much time to allow** 2 hours minimum—and you still won't see it all. If possible, try to spread your tour of the museum over 2 or more visits.

DESCRIPTION AND COMMENTS This museum is the most visited in the world, drawing about 9 million visitors a year. Entering from the Mall, visitors can touch a moon rock and gaze up at the Wright Brothers' plane and the *Spirit of St. Louis,* which Lindbergh flew across the Atlantic in 1927. Everywhere you look is another full-size wonder. The only drawback to this museum is its size—going to every exhibit becomes numbing after a while. If your length of stay allows it, try to split your time here into at least two visits. But it's a must-see for virtually anyone—not just airplane buffs and space cadets. The newly remodeled ground floor has new flight simulators. Five are tied to exhibits in the museum, giving visitors the chance to fly a World War I plane flown by Eddie Rickenbacker, Amelia Earhart's Lockheed Vega, and more. At the Einstein Planetarium, the starry sky has been replaced by digital projectors, which transport images from space and cast them out onto the 70-foot dome.

TOURING TIPS If you don't have an unlimited amount of time to wander around, try this strategy: After leaving the main lobby, work your way over to Space Hall, where you can tour Skylab and check out the Apollo-Soyuz spacecraft. For more insight into the exhibits, take one of the free, one-hour guided tours starting at 10:30 a.m. and 1 p.m. daily, beginning at the welcome center in the main lobby. You can avoid a few major bottlenecks by staying away from Skylab, the moon rock, and the cafeteria around lunchtime. Three exhibits also worth hitting early to avoid lines: "How Things Fly" (an interactive gallery that teaches the basic principles of flight), "Space Race" (examines the Cold War competition for outer space between the United States and the former Soviet Union), and "Beyond the Limits" (computers in aviation and space). *Note:* If you're seriously intrigued by this museum, but crowd-averse, you might consider the museum's other branch, the Steven F. Udvar-Hazy Center at Dulles International Airport, with more than 80 more aircraft and dozens of space artifacts including the Space Shuttle *Enterprise,* and the *Gemini VII* space capsule, as well as flight simulators, an IMAX theater, and airtraffic observation tower.

OTHER THINGS TO DO NEARBY To escape the worst of the crowds, try a stroll through the fragrant U.S. Botanic Garden, located a block east of the National Air and Space Museum. For lunch, the on-site cafeteria and restaurant feature a great view of the Capitol but run-of-the-mill dining. Best bet on weekdays: L'Enfant Plaza, where you can dine elbow-to-elbow with Washington bureaucrats in an underground mall with a wide range of eateries. The entrance is south of the Mall on Tenth Street SW, between D and E streets. On weekends and holidays, the cafe at the Museum of the American Indian, Capitol Hill (with its wide array of restaurants, bars, and cafes) and the Old Post Office Pavilion are good bets.

kids National Aquarium ★★

APPEAL BY AGE	PRESCHOOL ★★★★	GRADE SCHOOL ★★★★	TEENS ★★★
YOUNG ADULTS ★★		OVER 30 ★★	SENIORS ★★

Location **In the basement of the Department of Commerce building on 14th Street NW; Nearest Metro station Federal Triangle; ☎ 202-482-2826 or 202-482-2825 (recording); www.nationalaquarium.com**

Type of attraction The oldest aquarium in the United States (self-guided tour). **Admission** $5 adults, $4 seniors and military, $2 for children ages 2–10. **Hours** Daily, 9 a.m.–5 p.m.; closed Christmas Day. **When to go** Anytime. **Special comments** A cool, dark oasis on a sweltering summer afternoon. A basement full of fish tanks. **How much time to allow** 1 hour.

DESCRIPTION AND COMMENTS Essentially a long room lined with big fish tanks in the basement of an office building, this aquarium is not in the same league with other, newer fish-and-dolphin emporiums that are springing up all over (such as the one in Baltimore). But children will love it. Small and lacking crowd-pleasing sea mammals, the aquarium figures as a minor exhibit for filling in the odd hour or to escape from a sweltering afternoon. Otherwise, spend your valuable touring time elsewhere.

TOURING TIPS Sharks get fed at 2 p.m. on Monday, Wednesday, and Saturday; the piranhas get their meals at 2 p.m. on Tuesday, Thursday, and Sunday; and alligators on Friday. Adopt an animal for a year, including a shark ($100).

OTHER THINGS TO DO NEARBY The Washington Monument, the National Museum of American History, and the Old Post Office Pavilion are within a few minutes' walk. The Commerce Department cafeteria, open

Monday through Friday from 9 a.m. to 2 p.m., offers good, cheap fare: a soup and salad bar, pizza and pasta, a grill, a deli, and hot entrees.

National Archives ★★★

APPEAL BY AGE	PRESCHOOL ★	GRADE SCHOOL ★★	TEENS ★★★
YOUNG ADULTS ★★★	OVER 30 ★★★		SENIORS ★★★

**Location Seventh Street and Constitution Avenue NW, on the Mall;
Nearest Metro station Archives; ☎ 202-501-5205; www.archives.gov**

Type of attraction The magnificent rotunda where the Big Three of American government—the Declaration of Independence, the U.S. Constitution, and the Bill of Rights—are displayed (self-guided tour). Reservations required 6 weeks in advance for guided tours. **Admission** Free. **Hours** April 1–Memorial Day weekend, Exhibition Hall open weekdays, 10:15 a.m.–5:30 p.m.; Memorial Day weekend through Labor Day weekend, weekdays 10:15 a.m. through 7:30 p.m.; September–March 31, weekdays 10:15 a.m.–4 p.m.; closed Christmas Day. **When to go** Before noon or after 4 p.m. during spring and summer. If you happen to be in Washington on July Fourth, you can catch costumed patriots reading the Declaration aloud on the steps. **Special comments** Small children may need a lift to see the documents; skip it if the line is long. Use the entrance on Constitution Avenue. **How much time to allow** 30 minutes. **Average wait in line per 100 people ahead of you** 20 minutes.

DESCRIPTION AND COMMENTS In addition to trying to decipher the faint and flowing script on the sheets of parchment mounted in bronze and glass cases, visitors can stroll through a temporary exhibit of photos and documents covering various aspects of Americana. Most visitors seem as fascinated by the written description of the elaborate security system that lowers the sacred documents into a deep, nuclear-explosion-proof vault each night as they are by seeing the charters themselves—and you can't even see the contraption. The 75-foot-high rotunda is an impressive backdrop for our founding documents, but most people are surprised at how little there is to see inside this huge building. In fact, there *is* a lot more to see—but you've got to call in advance to arrange a tour. If the line to get in is long, skip it and come back later. It's really not worth the wait.

TOURING TIPS Some visitors say the documents on display in the exhibition areas outside the rotunda are more interesting—and certainly easier to read—than the better-known parchments under the big dome. For a behind-the-scenes view of the workings of the National Archives, arrange to take a reserved tour. During spring and summer, four weeks' notice is recommended. Or take a chance and show up at the Pennsylvania Avenue entrance (across from Eighth Street NW) at tour time. If there's a cancellation or a no-show, you're in. The reserved tours begin at 9:45 a.m. Monday through Friday and last about an hour. On the reserved tour, visitors take a tour of the building, including the stacks, microfilm viewing rooms, and exhibits and models that show how researchers preserve documents. The tour ends at the Rotunda. Oh, and don't miss the gift shop, where the best-selling item is a photograph of President Nixon and Elvis Presley embracing. It's a scream.

OTHER THINGS TO DO NEARBY Pick a Smithsonian museum you haven't seen yet and dive in. The cafe is open weekdays 10 a.m. through 4 p.m., and there are plenty of restaurants across Pennsylvania Avenue.

National Building Museum ★ ★ ★ ★ ★

APPEAL BY AGE	PRESCHOOL ★ ★	GRADE SCHOOL ★ ★ ★	TEENS ★ ★ ★
YOUNG ADULTS ★ ★ ★ ★		OVER 30 ★ ★ ★ ★	SENIORS ★ ★ ★ ★

Location **401 F Street NW; Nearest Metro station Judiciary Square;**
☎ **202-272-2448; www.nbm.org**

Type of attraction A museum dedicated to architecture and the construction arts that's an architectural marvel in its own right (self-guided and guided tours). **Admission** Free; suggested donation of $5 for adults. **Hours** Monday–Saturday, 10 a.m.–5 p.m.; Sunday, 11 a.m.–5 p.m.; closed Thanksgiving, Christmas, and New Year's days. **When to go** Anytime. **Special comments** The Great Hall is eye-popping. Tours are given Monday–Wednesday at 12:30 p.m., Thursday–Saturday at 11:30 a.m., 12:30 p.m., and 1:30 p.m., and on Sunday at 12:30 p.m. and 1:30 p.m. **How much time to allow** 45 minutes.

DESCRIPTION AND COMMENTS The ideal way to visit this museum would be to walk in blindfolded, then have the blindfold removed. Rather unimposing on the outside, the Pension Building (as this museum is better known to Washingtonians) offers one of the most imposing interiors in Washington, if not the world. The Great Hall measures 316 feet by 116 feet, and at its highest point the roof is 159 feet above the floor. Eight marbleized Corinthian columns adorn the interior. It's a must-see, even if all you do is poke your head inside the door.

TOURING TIPS The exhibits in the museum are on the thin side: the main attraction is the building itself. But if you're interested in architecture and building construction, check out the permanent and temporary exhibits on the first and second floors. The Courtyard Café is open weekdays, 9 a.m. to 4 p.m.; Saturday, 10 a.m.–4 p.m.; and Sunday, 11 a.m.–4 p.m.

OTHER THINGS TO DO NEARBY The three-acre National Law Enforcement Officers Memorial is directly across from the National Building Museum's entrance on F Street. Engraved on blue-gray marble walls are the names of 12,500 law enforcement officers who died in the line of duty throughout U.S. history. Four groups of striking statues, each showing a lion protecting her cubs, adorn the parks.

The Lillian and Albert Small Jewish Museum, at 701 Third Street NW, offers a glimpse into Washington's historic Jewish presence. The museum features temporary exhibits about the city's Jewish life, while the Adas Israel Synagogue on the second floor is listed in the National Register of Historic Places. Open Sunday through Thursday, noon to 4 p.m. Closed Saturdays and all major Jewish holidays; phone ☎ 202-789-0900 for more information. Chinatown and a large selection of restaurants are only two blocks away.

National Cryptologic Museum   ★ ½

APPEAL BY AGE	PRESCHOOL —	GRADE SCHOOL ★	TEENS ★★
YOUNG ADULTS ★★	OVER 30 ★★		SENIORS ★★

Location The National Security Agency, on the grounds of Fort George G. Meade, about 30 minutes north of Washington and east of Laurel, MD (Route 32 and the Baltimore-Washington Parkway); ☎ 301-688-5849; www.nsa.gov/museum/index.cfm

Type of attraction A small museum offering a glimpse into the secret world of spies, national defense, and ciphers (self-guided tour). **Admission** Free. **Hours** Weekdays, 9 a.m.–4 p.m.; the first and third Saturdays of each month, 10 a.m.–2 p.m.; closed federal holidays and Sundays. **When to go** Anytime. **Special comments** Gee, a real World War II German Enigma ciphering machine. Yet this tiny museum's greatest appeal may be its very existence: the National Security Agency (NSA) is the nation's largest spy organization—and its most secretive. **How much time to allow** 1 hour.

DESCRIPTION AND COMMENTS Tourists are barred from Central Intelligence Agency headquarters in Langley, across the river from Washington in suburban Virginia. Yet all is not lost for visitors lusting for a peek into the world of cloaks and daggers. The ultra-hush-hush National Security Agency operates this tiny museum dedicated to codes, ciphers, and spies in a former motel overlooking the Baltimore-Washington Parkway.

All the displays are static; they include items such as rare books dating from 1526, Civil War signal flags, KGB spy paraphernalia, and the notorious Enigma, a German cipher machine (it looks like an ancient Underwood on steroids) whose code was "broken" by the Poles and British during World War II. (*Spies,* a film on code breaking during World War II, tells the story continuously on a TV in a small theater in the museum.)

TOURING TIPS Don't miss the "bugged" Great Seal of the U.S. that hung in Spaso House, the U.S. ambassador's residence in Moscow (the microphone-equipped seal was uncovered in 1952). The new high-tech room features spy devices used to guard against computer hackers. Outside, you get a glimpse of the huge NSA headquarters complex from Route 32. NSA is called "The Puzzle Palace" for its secretiveness and worldwide electronic eavesdropping capability. The agency's budget, by the way, is a secret.

OTHER THINGS TO DO NEARBY South on the Baltimore-Washington Parkway are the National Wildlife Visitor Center and the NASA/Goddard Space Flight Center (Powder Mill Road exit).

National Gallery of Art: *East Building*   ★ ★ ★ ★ ★

APPEAL BY AGE	PRESCHOOL ★	GRADE SCHOOL ★★	TEENS ★★★
YOUNG ADULTS ★★★★★	OVER 30 ★★★★★		SENIORS ★★★★★

Location Fourth Street and Constitution Avenue NW, on the Mall; Nearest Metro stations Archives, Judiciary Square, Smithsonian; ☎ 202-737-4215; www.nga.gov

Type of attraction A museum housing 20th-century art and special exhibitions (self-guided tour). **Admission** Free. **Hours** Monday–Saturday, 10 a.m.–5 p.m.; Sunday, 11 a.m.–6 p.m.; closed Christmas and New Year's days. **When to go** Anytime. **Special comments** Even the building, usually referred to as the "East Wing" of the National Gallery, is a great work of art. Visitors with disabilities may park in available spaces in front of the building. Introductory tours are offered daily and last about an hour; for times, call ☎ 202-842-6247. No luggage, backpacks, book bags, or other personal bags allowed. **How much time to allow** 2 hours.

DESCRIPTION AND COMMENTS Both the interior and exterior of this I. M. Pei–designed building are spectacular, so it's worth a visit even if you hate modern art. Outside, the popular 1978 building consists of unadorned vertical planes. Inside, it's bright, airy, and spacious. Look for art by modern masters such as Picasso, Matisse, Mondrian, Miró, Magritte, Warhol, Lichtenstein, and Rauschenberg. The exhibits change constantly, so there's no telling which of these is on display.

TOURING TIPS Occasionally, temporary exhibits (such as a Van Gogh show) are extremely popular and may require a free "time ticket" that admits you on a certain day at a specific hour. You may pick up such tickets in advance; tickets are available as much as a month before a show opens. If you don't have a ticket on the day you visit the East Wing, you're not completely out of luck: a number of tickets are set aside every day for distribution that day only. If you want one, arrive at the ticket counter on the main floor by noon (or 2 p.m. during the week). Then come back later to see the exhibit. When you exit the museum, turn left and check out the high, knife-edge exterior corner wall of the gallery, near the Mall—it's almost worn away from people touching their noses to it.

The new, more than six-acre National Gallery Sculpture Garden opened in the spring of 1999 on the Mall adjacent to the West Building. Works from the gallery's permanent collection, as well as temporary exhibits, grace the symmetrical garden, its central pool, and the circle of linden trees. A variety of shade trees provide welcome relief in the summer, and there's free jazz on Friday evenings; while the central pool serves as a public ice-skating rink in the winter.

OTHER THINGS TO DO NEARBY The West Wing, with its more traditional European art, is connected to the East Building by an underground concourse. The Capitol and the U.S. Botanic Garden are close by, as well as the National Archives. The Cascade Café/Buffet, a cafeteria along the concourse, and the Sculpture Garden's Pavilion Café are good bets.

National Gallery of Art: *West Building*   ★ ★ ★ ★ ★

APPEAL BY AGE	PRESCHOOL ★	GRADE SCHOOL ★ ★ ★	TEENS ★ ★ ★
YOUNG ADULTS ★ ★ ★ ★	OVER 30 ★ ★ ★ ★ ★		SENIORS ★ ★ ★ ★ ★

Location Sixth Street and Constitution Avenue NW, on the Mall;
Nearest Metro station Archives; ☎ 202-737-4215; www.nga.gov

Type of attraction Museum featuring European and American art from the 13th through the 19th centuries (self-guided and guided tours). **Admission** Free.

Hours Monday–Saturday, 10 a.m.–5 p.m.; Sunday, 11 a.m.–6 p.m.; closed Christmas and New Year's days. **When to go** Anytime. **Special comments** Art with a capital "A." Introductory tours are offered daily and last about an hour. For times, call ☎ 202-842-6247. It's usually referred to as the "West Wing" of the National Gallery. **How much time to allow** 2 hours for a light skimming, but you could spend a week.

DESCRIPTION AND COMMENTS   This is where you find the heavy hitters: Dutch masters such as Rembrandt and Vermeer, plus Raphael, Monet, and Jacques-Louis David, just to name a few. And it's all housed in an elegant neoclassical building designed by John Russell Pope. It's a world-class art museum; first-time visitors should make at least one stop.

The Micro Gallery, 13 computer stations featuring high-tech computers and 20-inch touchscreen color monitors, provides visitors with images and information on about 1,700 paintings, sculptures, and decorative arts; 650 artists; and more than 530 art-related subjects. Modeled after a similar system at the National Gallery in London, the Micro Gallery lets visitors with little or no computer experience expand their appreciation of the gallery's permanent collection. You can even create a personal tour of the museum and print a map showing the locations of works of art you've selected. The Micro Gallery is located on the main floor near the Mall entrance.

TOURING TIPS   Most of the museum's paintings are hung in many small rooms, instead of a few big ones, so don't try to speed through the building or you'll miss most of them. When museum fatigue begins to set in, rest your feet in one of the atriums located between the museum's many galleries. If you plan on dragging kids through this massive place, try bribing them with a later trip to the National Zoo.

Some temporary exhibits require a free "time ticket" that admits you on a certain day at a specific hour. You may pick up such tickets in advance; they are available as much as a month before a show opens. If you don't have a ticket on the day you want to visit the West Wing, you're not completely out of luck: a number of tickets are set aside every day for distribution that day only. If you want one, arrive at the ticket counter on the main floor by noon (or 2 p.m. on a weekday). Then come back later to see the exhibit.

OTHER THINGS TO DO NEARBY   Take the connecting corridor (an underground concourse) to the gallery's East Building. The Air and Space Museum is directly across the Mall, while the National Archives are in the other direction, across Constitution Avenue. One of the more attractive museum cafeterias on the Mall is located along the concourse, and the more elegant (and quiet) Garden Court near the museum shop often has special menus to complement exhibits—Provençal fare for the Cézanne show, for instance. The Pavilion Café at the National Gallery's Sculpture Garden (located next door, across from the National Archives) has indoor and outdoor seating.

kids National Geographic Society's Explorers Hall ★★

APPEAL BY AGE	PRESCHOOL ★★★	GRADE SCHOOL ★★★★	TEENS ★★★★
YOUNG ADULTS ★★★		OVER 30 ★★	SENIORS ★★

Location 17th and M streets NW, 4 blocks north of the White House; Nearest Metro stations Farragut North, Farragut West; ☎ 202-857-7588; www.nationalgeographic.com/museum

Type of attraction A small, high-tech exhibition that delights children (self-guided tour). **Admission** Free. **Hours** Monday–Saturday and holidays, 9 a.m.–5 p.m.; Sunday, 10 a.m.–5 p.m.; closed Christmas Day. **When to go** Anytime. **Special comments** Well-done exhibits that aren't overpowering and sometimes engrossing. The downtown exhibit is handy in an area that's spotty on entertaining things for kids. **How much time to allow** 1 hour.

DESCRIPTION AND COMMENTS It's like walking through a couple of National Geographic TV specials. Located on the first floor of the National Geographic Society's headquarters, this small collection of exhibits showcases weather, geography, astronomy, biology, exploration, and space science. Temporary exhibits range from huge scale models of Crusades-era castles under siege, to imaginary monsters and manipulated photographs. The society also hosts concerts, films, and ethnic cultural events.

TOURING TIPS Don't miss the extensive sales shop that offers books, videos, maps, and magazines. The courtyard on M Street, a great spot for a brown-bag lunch, is filled with whimsical animal sculptures. Free films are shown on Tuesdays at noon.

OTHER THINGS TO DO NEARBY The *Washington Post* is two blocks away on 15th Street NW, between L and M; call ☎ 202-334-7969 to arrange a free tour. The still-imposing Russian embassy is around the corner on 16th Street; you can't go in, but check out the array of antennas on the roof.

National Museum of African Art ★★
(a Smithsonian museum)

APPEAL BY AGE	PRESCHOOL ★	GRADE SCHOOL ★★	TEENS ★★
YOUNG ADULTS ★★★		OVER 30 ★★★	SENIORS ★★★

Location 950 Independence Avenue SW, on the Mall near the Castle (the Smithsonian Institution Building); Nearest Metro station Smithsonian; ☎ 202-633-4600 or 202-357-4814 (TDD); www.nmafa.si.edu

Type of attraction A museum specializing in the traditional arts of Africa (self-guided tour). **Admission** Free. **Hours** Daily, 10 a.m.–5:30 p.m.; closed Christmas Day. **When to go** Anytime. **Special comments** Provides a quiet respite when other Mall attractions are jam-packed; an excellent museum shop. Exquisite sculpture and fascinating household items. **How much time to allow** 1 hour.

DESCRIPTION AND COMMENTS This relatively new subterranean museum, which opened in 1987, is paired with the Sackler Gallery, a museum of

Asian art, and separated by an above-ground garden. Inside is an extensive collection of African art in a wide range of media, including sculpture, masks, household and personal items, and religious objects. Intellectually, this museum transports museum-goers far away from the Mall. It's an okay destination for older children, teens, and adults looking for some non-European cultural history and art. This museum is a great alternative on hot or crowded days in Washington.

TOURING TIPS One-hour guided tours are given at 1:30 p.m. Monday through Thursday and at 11 a.m. and 1 p.m. on weekends. And don't miss the excellent museum shop, where you'll find textiles, jewelry, scarves and sashes, wood carvings, and a wide selection of African music on tape, CD, and video.

OTHER THINGS TO DO NEARBY This museum is twinned with the Arthur M. Sackler Gallery, and even connects with it below ground—a nice feature on a sweltering Washington afternoon. If the weather's mild, stroll the Enid A. Haupt Garden, which separates the two museums at ground level. Neither museum has a cafeteria; check the options at the National Gallery or Museum of the American Indian.

kids National Museum of American History ★★★★
(a Smithsonian museum) closed for renovation

APPEAL BY AGE	PRESCHOOL ★★★	GRADE SCHOOL ★★★★	TEENS ★★★★★
YOUNG ADULTS ★★★★★		OVER 30 ★★★★★	SENIORS ★★★★★

Location **14th Street and Constitution Avenue NW, on the Mall; Nearest Metro stations Smithsonian, Federal Triangle; ☎ 202-633-1000 or 202-357-1729 (TDD); www.americanhistory.si.edu**

Type of attraction An extensive collection of artifacts reflecting the American experience—historical, social, and technological (self-guided tour). **Admission** Free. **Hours** Daily, 10 a.m.–5:30 p.m.; extended summer hours depend on budget restraints; closed Christmas Day. **When to go** To avoid the worst crowds, visit before noon and after 3 p.m. **Special comments** A collection of national treasures; don't miss it. The immensity of this museum almost demands that visitors try to see it in more than one visit. **How much time to allow** 2 hours on a first pass; it would take a week to see it all.

DESCRIPTION AND COMMENTS Three exhibit-packed floors feature such treasures as the original Star-Spangled Banner (one of the prime inspirations for the renovation and atrium-opening of the museum), steam locomotives, a Model T Ford, a pendulum three stories high that shows how the earth rotates, a collection of ball gowns worn by First Ladies, and Archie Bunker's chair. If you can't find something of interest here, you may need mouth-to-mouth resuscitation. For a lot of people, this ranks as their favorite Mall museum. No wonder—it offers viewers a dizzying array of history, nostalgia, technology, and culture. And kids love it. It's a must-see for virtually all visitors.

TOURING TIPS At most museums, you look at *stuff*, but a lot of the collection at American History is arranged so that viewers can learn about *people* in the context of their times. To see what we mean—and to help you organize yourself in this bewilderingly large museum—make it a point to see these exhibits: the First Ladies' Inaugural Gown Exhibition; uniforms and arms from the American wars; and a collection of objects about television that includes Archie Bunker's chair, Fonzie's jacket, one of Mr. Rogers' sweaters, Oscar the Grouch (of *Sesame Street* fame), and for baby boomers, some items from the *Howdy Doody Show*. Check at the information desk for a schedule of tours (usually at 10 a.m. and 1 p.m. daily), demonstrations, concerts, lectures, films, and other activities put on by the museum staff. Some final hints: A lot of people touring the museum on their own overlook the Hall of Transportation in the museum's east wing, which features an excellent collection of cars, trains, and motorcycles. Car aficionados will love it. Kids (and most adults) enjoy the Science in American Life exhibit, the Hands-on Science Center, and the Hands-on History Room.

OTHER THINGS TO DO NEARBY Within a short walk are the Washington Monument, the National Aquarium, the Old Post Office Pavilion, and the National Museum of Natural History. Almost directly across the Mall are the Freer and Sackler Galleries and the National Museum of African Art. And, yes, the American History Museum has a cafeteria and an ice-cream parlor.

National Museum of the American Indian
(*a Smithsonian museum*) ★ ★ ★

| APPEAL BY AGE | PRESCHOOL ★ | GRADE SCHOOL ★ ★ | TEENS ★ ★ |
| YOUNG ADULTS ★ ★ ★ | OVER 30 ★ ★ ★ | | SENIORS ★ ★ ★ |

Location Fourth Street and Independence Avenue SW (on the Mall between the Air and Space Museum and the U.S. Botanic Gardens); Nearest Metro stations Federal Center, L'Enfant Plaza; ☎ 202-633-1000 or 202-357-1729 (TDD); www.americanindian.si.edu

Type of attraction One of the largest and most diverse collections of Indian art and artifacts in the world (self-guided tour). **Admission** Free. **Hours** Daily, 10 a.m.–5:30 p.m.; closed Christmas Day. Fabulous setting and expensive shop. **How much time to allow** 1–1½ hours.

DESCRIPTION AND COMMENTS The Smithsonian's newest museum on the Mall (which opened in September 2004) cost $219 million and features four levels and 250,000 square feet of exhibition space. One of the most striking buildings in Washington, it was designed to honor traditional methods of worship and natural conservation as well as to showcase arts and traditional crafts. Here the term "American Indian" means much more than those of the United States; it also includes indigenous tribes from Canada, Alaska, Mexico, and Central and South America (though less heavily). The exhibits are relatively small, but the shop is one of the most alluring—silver and turquoise, wood carvings, feather masks, fine pottery and glass, and ivory and stone carvings—and the cafe is a popular draw. The museum sits on a 4.25-acre site with natural rock formations and native plants set in a forest, wetlands, meadow-lands, and croplands.

TOURING TIPS Officials expect the museum to attract a record numbers of vis-itors. Unless you're visiting in the winter, plan to arrive at the ticket office at least 30 minutes before it opens at 10 a.m. (the earlier the better).

OTHER THINGS TO DO NEARBY The Air and Space Museum and U.S. Botanic Garden are next door and the National Gallery of Art is across the Mall. The Mitisam cafe here is one of the best and most unusual on the Mall, offering the foods of several different regions and ranging from venison to grilled salmon to bison to tacos.

National Museum of Health and Medicine ★ ★

| APPEAL BY AGE | PRESCHOOL — | GRADE SCHOOL ★ ★ | TEENS ★ ★ ★ |
| YOUNG ADULTS ★ ★ ★ | | OVER 30 ★ ★ ★ | SENIORS ★ ★ ★ |

Location On the grounds of Walter Reed Army Medical Center, located between 16th Street and Georgia Avenue NW, near Takoma Park, MD; Nearest Metro station Takoma; if you have a car, drive; ☎ 202-782-2200; nmhm.washingtondc.museum

Type of attraction A medical museum (self-guided tour). **Admission** Free. **Hours** Daily, 10 a.m.–5:30 p.m.; closed Christmas Day. Docent-led tours are offered on the second and fourth Saturdays of the month at 1 p.m. **When to go** Anytime. **Special comments** Some excellent exhibits, but a bit unsettling. Though not as gruesome as it used to be, it's still not a place for the squeamish. Unless you're a health professional or harbor an intense interest in the history of medicine, this small but fascinating museum is simply too difficult to get to. Wait a few years until it relocates to the Mall. **How much time to allow** 1 hour.

DESCRIPTION AND COMMENTS Excellent exhibits on the human body make this museum a worthwhile destination. Although there are still plenty of bottled human organs, skeletons, and graphic illustrations of the effects of disfiguring diseases, the emphasis has shifted from the bizarre to education. Exhibits on medicine in the Civil War and an extensive microscope collection (including huge electron microscopes) will prob-ably have more appeal to physicians, scientists, and other health professionals. We're glad to report that the museum has improved the quality of its exhibits and its overall appearance since our first visit.

TOURING TIPS Finding this place can be tough. By subway, it's a brisk 15-minute walk to the museum from the Takoma Metro station. As you exit the sta-tion, turn right and walk under the railroad tracks, then turn right at Blair Road. Walk one block to Dahlia Street and turn left. Walter Reed is about six blocks straight ahead. The museum is directly behind the large white hospital building; you can walk around it on the left. If you're driving, enter the Walter Reed complex through the Dahlia Street gate on Georgia Avenue. The museum is located in the south end of Building 54 (behind the large white hospital building). There's a small parking lot next to the museum.

OTHER THINGS TO DO NEARBY Nothing recommended due to lackluster location.

 National Museum of Natural History
(*a Smithsonian museum*) ★★★★★

APPEAL BY AGE PRESCHOOL ★★★★ GRADE SCHOOL ★★★★★ TEENS ★★★★★
YOUNG ADULTS ★★★★★ OVER 30 ★★★★★ SENIORS ★★★★★

Location On the Mall at Tenth Street NW and Constitution Avenue;
Nearest Metro stations Smithsonian, Archives, Federal Triangle;
☎ **202-633-1000 or 202-357-1729 (TDD); www.mnh.si.edu**

Type of attraction America's treasure chest of the natural sciences and human culture (self-guided tour). **Admission** Free; IMAX admission is $8 adults and $6.50 for seniors and children under age 17. **Hours** Daily, 10 a.m.–5:30 p.m.; open until 8 p.m. during the summer months; closed Christmas Day. **When to go** Before noon and after 4 p.m. Free weekday highlight tours are offered Monday–Friday at 10:30 a.m. and 1:30 p.m (except July and August). Meet in the rotunda. **Special comments** In the recently renovated Discovery Room, kids ages 4 years and up can touch nearly everything. **Hours** Tuesday–Friday, noon–2:30 p.m.; weekends, 10:30 a.m.–3:30 p.m. Make the popular Discovery Room your first stop and pick up free time tickets; tour the rest of the museum and return at the time stamped on your ticket. The displays of huge dinosaur fossils and the world's best known gem make this museum a classic. **How much time to allow** 2 hours is enough time to see the really cool stuff, but you could easily spend an entire day here.

DESCRIPTION AND COMMENTS Distinguished by its golden dome and the towering bull elephant in the rotunda, the Museum of Natural History is a Washington landmark. It's also a bit old-fashioned, with long halls filled with dioramas, display cases, and hanging specimens that reflect the Victorian obsession with collecting things. This museum, along with Air and Space across the Mall, is immensely popular with families, and for a good reason—folks of all ages and tastes will find fascinating things to see here.

In September 1997, the Janet Annenberg Hooker Hall of Geology, Gems, and Minerals opened, showcasing the museum's world-class gem-and-mineral collection. It's part of a still-ongoing $8.5-million museum renovation, which includes an IMAX theater specializing in nature films. The gem hall features interactive computers, animated graphics, film and video presentations, and hands-on exhibits. In addition to the 45.52-carat Hope Diamond, the space features meteorites, emeralds, a 23,000-carat topaz, crystals, a walk-through mine, a re-creation of a cave, and a plate tectonics gallery showing how the earth's surface shifts.

A new mammal hall premiered in 2003, with state-of-the-art dioramas explaining mammalian evolution, and hands-on activities that hold kids' interests. Another huge renovation, the 23,000-square-foot Ocean Hall, is scheduled to open in fall of 2008, combining oceanographic, sea life, and weather exhibits.

TOURING TIPS After entering through the big doors at the Mall entrance, bear right to see the dinosaur skeletons. Then ascend to the second floor to gaze upon the supposedly cursed Hope Diamond and to explore the gem hall. If you're not put off by crawling critters, stop by the Insect Zoo, which features a wide array of (live) bugs. Special exhibits are located on the ground level (Constitution Avenue entrance).

OTHER THINGS TO DO NEARBY The National Museum of American History (closed for renovation) is next door; across the Mall are the Hirshhorn Museum, the Arts and Industries Building (closed for renovation), the Museum of African Art, and the Sackler and Freer galleries; the National Archives is across Constitution Avenue. A convenient choice for lunch is the Old Post Office Pavilion, about a block away on 12th Street, or the Pavilion Café, located in the National Gallery Sculpture Garden. The fast-food kiosk in front of the museum on the Mall is overpriced: if you crave a hot dog, walk over to Constitution Avenue, find a street vendor, and save a buck.

National Museum of Women in the Arts ★ ★ ★ ★

APPEAL BY AGE	PRESCHOOL ★	GRADE SCHOOL ★ ★	TEENS ★ ★ ★
YOUNG ADULTS ★ ★ ★		OVER 30 ★ ★ ★ ★	SENIORS ★ ★ ★ ★

Location **1250 New York Avenue NW; Nearest Metro station Metro Center;**
☎ **202-783-5000 or 800-222-7270; www.nmwa.org**

Type of attraction The world's single most important collection of art by women (self-guided tour). Admission $8 for adults; $6 for seniors 60+ and students; free for ages 18 and under. Hours Monday–Saturday, 10 a.m.–5 p.m.; Sunday, noon–5 p.m.; closed Thanksgiving, Christmas, and New Year's days. When to go Anytime. Special comments Unfortunately, this beautiful museum is a little off the beaten path. Both the building and the art are superb. How much time to allow 1–2 hours.

DESCRIPTION AND COMMENTS This relatively new museum has a permanent collection of paintings and sculpture that includes art by Georgia O'Keeffe, Frida Kahlo, and Helen Frankenthaler, as well as art by women from the 16th century to the present. From the outside, it looks like any other office building along crowded New York Avenue. But inside the former Masonic Grand Lodge are striking architectural features such as a crystal chandelier, a main hall and mezzanine, and the Grand Staircase. The second-floor balcony hosts temporary exhibits; the third floor is where you'll find the permanent collection. Next door, a new annex that opened in the fall of 1997 allowed the museum to expand the amount of artwork on display, including sculpture and contemporary works by lesser-known women artists. While this beautiful museum well off the beaten path deserves to be seen by more people, first-time visitors can wait and enjoy it on a later trip.

TOURING TIPS Take the elevator to the fourth (top) floor and work your way down. The Mezzanine features an attractive cafe offering light fare, and there's a gift shop on the ground floor.

OTHER THINGS TO DO NEARBY A block away is the old Greyhound Bus Station, now a fully restored Art Deco masterpiece; take a peek inside. The Capitol City Brewing Company brews beer on the premises and serves hearty fare like burgers to go with it.

National Portrait Gallery–Smithsonian American Art Museum ★ ★ ★ ★

APPEAL BY AGE	PRESCHOOL ★	GRADE SCHOOL ★★	TEENS ★★½
YOUNG ADULTS ★★★½	OVER 30 ★★★★		SENIORS ★★★★

Location **Eighth and F streets NW;** Nearest Metro station
Gallery Place–Chinatown or Archives–Navy Memorial–Penn Quarter;
☎ **202-633-1000; www.reynoldscenter.org**

Type of attraction Two major American art collections joined in one beautifully restored building. **Admission** Free. **Hours** Open daily, 11:30 a.m.–7 p.m.; closed Christmas Day. **When to go** Anytime. **Special comments** The museums are housed in a beautiful historic space. A great collection, both modern and traditional. **How much time to allow** 2 hours.

DESCRIPTION AND COMMENTS After a six-year, $283-million renovation, these twin institutions—now collectively known as the Donald W. Reynolds Center for American Art and Portraiture, in honor of the philanthropist whose donations made the renovation possible—are housed in one of Washington's great buildings: the 1836 Patent Office, which in Pierre L'Enfant's plan for the city marks the central point between the White House and Capitol building. The original architect, Robert Mills, had studied with Jefferson, designed the Washington Monument, and took much of his inspiration from the Parthenon.

After decades of ill-advised additions, including false ceilings, walls and window barriers, linoleum, fluorescent lights, and the like, the structure has been elegantly returned to its airy self, with vaulted ceilings, dozens of skylights, a huge central courtyard (to be covered by a glass ceiling), and cantilevered double staircases.

In its time, the building has housed the Declaration of Independence, Ben Franklin's printing press, Matthew Perry's Japanese mementos, and various inventions of the times (such as false teeth and sewing machines), along with several presidential inaugural balls. But in 1863, it was turned into a Union Army hospital, where volunteer nurse Walt Whitman tended the wounded and dying and wrote letters for them and poems about them. In 1877, it suffered a catastrophic fire that destroyed some 87,000 patent models (and led to a somewhat rococo Victorian redressing). Eventually it housed the Department of the Interior offices and the Civil Service Commission, and was very nearly demolished in 1853 until preservationists prevailed.

TOURING TIPS The museum complex is so centrally located, and so near a subway stop, that it's a good refuge on a rainy or very hot day; also, since it's open later than most museums, it can become your afternoon destination. Limited but nice, the cafe has been hosting "Take Five" evenings—live jazz and five new acquisitions—on second Thursdays under the magnificent ceiling of the Luce Center, a series of art "drawer" galleries on the third floor.

OTHER THINGS TO DO NEARBY The International Spy Museum is directly across the street, as is the Monaco Hotel, which was built in 1839 to house the city's first general post office. Covering an entire city block and copied from a Roman palazzo, complete with marble columns and facia, the hotel has been beautifully restored; the restaurant has a nice open-air bar and lounge that make for a restful break.

National Postal Museum
(a Smithsonian Museum) ★ ★ ★

APPEAL BY AGE	PRESCHOOL ★ ★	GRADE SCHOOL ★ ★ ★	TEENS ★ ★
YOUNG ADULTS ★ ★	OVER 30 ★ ★ ★		SENIORS ★ ★ ★

Location Washington City Post Office building, 2 Massachusetts Avenue NE, next to Union Station; Nearest Metro station **Union Station;** ☎ **202-633-5555 or 202-633-9849 (TDD); www.postalmuseum.si.edu**

Type of attraction Displays from the largest philatelic collection in the world and exhibits about the social, historical, and technological impact of the U.S. postal system (self-guided tour). **Admission** Free. **Hours** Daily, 10 a.m.–5:30 p.m.; closed Christmas Day. **When to go** Anytime. **Special Comments** Nifty. And the building that houses the museum is stunning. **How much time to allow** 1–2 hours.

DESCRIPTION AND COMMENTS It's more interesting than it sounds—even if you're not one of America's 20 million stamp collectors. Kids will love the real airplanes hanging from the ceiling in the atrium, plus hands-on fun like the chance to sort mail on a train and track a letter from Kansas to Nairobi. Exhibits are arranged so that children and adults are entertained while they're in relative proximity to each other. Themes focus on the history of mail service, how the mail is moved, the social importance of letters, and the beauty and lore of stamps. Serious collectors can call in advance for appointments to see any stamp in the museum's world-class collection or to use the extensive library.

TOURING TIPS Due to its small size (at least when compared to museums on the Mall), it's easy to whiz through it in a half-hour or so. And because it's right across the street from Union Station, many folks will find it convenient to drop in while waiting for a train. Docent-led "drop-in" tours are available at 11 a.m. and 1 p.m. daily.

OTHER THINGS TO DO NEARBY The Capital Children's Museum is only a few blocks away, making a full day of kid-oriented museum-hopping a distinct possibility—without going near the Mall. Union Station's food hall can satisfy any food craving.

kids **National Wildlife Visitor Center** ★ ★ ★

APPEAL BY AGE	PRESCHOOL ★★★★	GRADE SCHOOL ★★★★	TEENS ★★★
YOUNG ADULTS ★★★		OVER 30 ★★★	SENIORS ★★★

Location Off Powder Mill Road, 2 miles east of the Baltimore-Washington Parkway, south of Laurel, MD; ☎ 301-497-5760; patuxent.fws.gov/vcdefault.html

Type of attraction A museum featuring wildlife research exhibits located in a 13,000-acre national wildlife refuge about 30 minutes north of Washington (self-guided tour). **Admission** Free. **Hours** Daily, March–November, 10 a.m.–5:30 p.m.; closed Christmas Day. **When to go** Anytime. Weekends are busier than weekdays. **Special comments** You'll need a car to get here. Call ahead if you'd rather avoid large groups of schoolchildren on field trips. And there's no restaurant or snack bar on the premises. Static exhibits and stuffed animals, but a tranquil setting in the heart of the hectic Washington-Baltimore corridor. **How much time to allow** 1–2 hours.

DESCRIPTION AND COMMENTS This large, airy museum operated by the U.S. Department of the Interior is filled with attractive exhibits—dioramas, mostly—focusing on a wide range of wildlife and environmental topics. While the static displays won't accelerate the pulse rates of adults weary from traipsing through Smithsonian edifices on the Mall, children are fascinated by this place. Large dioramas on pollution, overpopulation, forest and ocean degradation, wildlife habitats, wolves, whooping cranes, and other endangered species demonstrate the value of wildlife research.

TOURING TIPS A "viewing pod" equipped with spotting scopes and binoculars lets youngsters (and adults) observe wildlife through a picture window overlooking acres of pond and natural wildlife habitat. If it's a nice day, enjoy the sights and sounds of real wildlife by taking a stroll on paved trails through woods and around ponds populated by geese, ducks, and other animals that find refuge on the refuge. Thirty-minute narrated tram rides with a wildlife interpreter are offered on weekends in the spring and fall and daily from the end of June through August. The cost is $3 for adults, $2 for seniors, and $1 for children. On weekends documentary wildlife films are shown in the center's movie theater.

OTHER THINGS TO DO NEARBY The NASA/Goddard Space Flight Center in Greenbelt, Maryland, is only a few miles away; follow signs posted on Powder Mill Road near the Baltimore-Washington Parkway.

Folks looking for additional outdoor enjoyment and the opportunity to see more wildlife can drive a few miles north to the North Tract of the Patuxent Research Refuge; take the Baltimore-Washington Parkway north two exits to Route 198 east, drive one mile, and turn right onto Bald Eagle Drive to the Visitor Contact Station. The 8,100-acre tract features forest, wetlands, a wildlife viewing area (with an observation tower), and eight miles of paved roads for car touring and bicycling. There are another ten miles of graded gravel roads for hiking, mountain biking, and horseback riding. For more information, call ☎ 301-776-3090.

The National Cryptologic Museum is located next to the huge National Security Agency complex near the intersection of Baltimore-Washington Parkway and Route 32; drive north on the parkway a few miles and follow the signs. For a large selection of fast-food options, take the parkway north a few miles to Route 197.

National World War II Memorial ★ ★ ★

APPEAL BY AGE	PRESCHOOL ★	GRADE SCHOOL ★ ★	TEENS ★ ★
YOUNG ADULTS ★ ★ ★	OVER 30 ★ ★ ★		SENIORS ★ ★ ★ ★ ★

Location At 17th Street NW and the Mall, between the Washington Monument and the Lincoln Memorial; Nearest Metro station Smithsonian; www.wwiimemorial.com and www.nps.gov/nwwm

Type of attraction A memorial on the National Mall to the 16 million Americans who served in uniform during World War II (self-guided tour). **Admission** Free. **Hours** Park rangers on site each day except Christmas Day. The monument may be closed during July 4th celebrations. **When to go** Anytime (except during inclement weather). **Special comments** Clean, modern restrooms are located behind the visitor center. A limited number of handicapped parking spaces are available. Impressive, but a little stodgy, not in the same ballpark as the FDR Memorial. **How much time to allow** 30 minutes to an hour.

DESCRIPTION AND COMMENTS The "greatest generation" gets its due in this new memorial, dedicated in May 2004, for its contributions in winning the most devastating war in human history (it killed 50 million people). Two 43-foot arches, a 17-foot pillar for each state and territory, and 4,000 gold stars honor the more than 400,000 soldiers who died in the conflict. The assemblies of white granite surround a large pool, fountains, and a piazza located in a spectacular setting.

TOURING TIPS In the summer, go in the morning or evening to avoid the worst heat of the day. Clean, modern, and air-conditioned restrooms—a scarce commodity on the Mall—are located behind the visitor center (on the Pacific pavilion side of the memorial).

OTHER THINGS TO DO NEARBY You're in the heart of tourist Washington. The Lincoln Memorial, the Washington Monument, and the Vietnam Veterans Memorial are close by, as are the Martin Luther King Jr. Memorial (under construction) and the Korean War Veterans Memorial. The Smithsonian museum complex is on the other side of the Washington Monument. The Bureau of Engraving and Printing and the National Holocaust Memorial are on 15th Street, south of the Washington Monument. The FDR Memorial is on the Tidal Basin, across Independence Avenue (to the south).

kids National Zoological Park
(part of the Smithsonian Institution)   ★ ★ ★ ★ ★

APPEAL BY AGE PRESCHOOL ★★★★★   GRADE SCHOOL ★★★★★   TEENS ★★★★
YOUNG ADULTS ★★★★   OVER 30 ★★★★   SENIORS ★★★★

Location 3001 Connecticut Avenue NW; Nearest Metro stations Woodley Park–Zoo/Adams-Morgan, Cleveland Park; ☎ 202-673-4800 (24-hour recording) or 202-673-7800 (TDD); www.nationalzoo.si.edu

Type of attraction The Smithsonian's world-class zoo (self-guided tour). **Admission** Free. **Hours** April 2–October 28: grounds are open 6 a.m.–8 p.m. and buildings are open 10 a.m.–6 p.m.; October 29–March 10: grounds are open 6 a.m.–6 p.m. and buildings are open 10 a.m.–4:30 p.m. The Pollinarium and the invertebrate exhibits are closed Tuesdays. The park is closed Christmas Day only. **When to go** Anytime. In the summer, avoid going during Washington's sweltering afternoons. In the spring, avoid visiting between 10 a.m. and 2 p.m. weekdays, when many school buses full of children arrive. **Special comments** Many sections of the paths winding through the Zoo's 163 acres are steep. A first-rate operation in a beautiful setting. **How much time to allow** 2 hours just to see the most popular attractions; a whole day to see it all. Better yet, see the Zoo over several visits.

DESCRIPTION AND COMMENTS   The National Zoo emphasizes natural environment, with many animals roaming large enclosures instead of pacing in cages. And it's all found in a lush woodland setting in a section of Rock Creek Park. Two main paths link the many buildings and exhibits: Olmstead Walk, which passes all the animal houses, and the steeper Valley Trail, which includes all the aquatic exhibits. They add up to about two miles of trail. The Zoo's nonlinear layout and lack of sight lines make a map invaluable; pick one up at the Education Building near the entrance for a buck. The most popular exhibits include the elephants; the great apes; the white tiger; the cheetahs; and the giant pandas, Tian Tian and Mei Xiang (their famously photogenic cub, Tai Shaw, will have to be returned to China when he turns two), in their new habitat.

   For diversity and a good chance of seeing some animal activity, check out the Small Mammal House, the invertebrate exhibit (kids can look through microscopes), and the huge outside bird cages (the condors look the size of Volkswagens). If your visit to Washington is long enough to include forays away from the Mall, make this beautiful park part of your itinerary. Aside from a wide variety of wildlife on view, the wooded setting is a welcome relief from viewing too much marble downtown.

TOURING TIPS   Plan to visit either early or late in the day. Animals are more active, temperatures are cooler—and crowds are thinner. During busy periods, some exhibits are subject to "controlled access" to prevent crowding; in other words, you may have to wait in line. If it is rainy, most of the indoor exhibits can be found along Olmstead Walk. Feedings and demonstrations occur throughout the day at the cheetah, elephant, seal, and sea-lion exhibits; check at the Education Building for times.

Don't miss three permanent exhibits: Pollinarium, Think Tank, and the Amazonia Science Gallery. Pollinarium, a lush garden housed in a 1,250-square-foot greenhouse, features hundreds of zebra long-wing butterflies that flutter around as visitors get a firsthand look at animal pollinators, plants, and the process of pollination. A glass-enclosed beehive gives an up-close glimpse of the activities of thousands of honeybees.

Think Tank, a 15,000-square-foot exhibit that opened in late 1995, attempts to answer the question, "Can animals think?" Scientists conduct demonstrations on language, tool use, and social organization. Displays, artifacts, graphics, and videos cover topics such as problem-solving ability, brain size, and language. Four animal species are featured in the exhibit: orangutans, Sulawesi macaque monkeys, hermit crabs, and leaf-cutter ants.

The Amazonia Science Gallery explores the biological diversity of the Amazon rain forest; a biodiversity demonstration lab is equipped with a working electron microscope and with displays of living beetles, frog eggs, tadpoles, and boas. The two-meter-diameter "Geosphere" globe uses projectors, satellite imagery, and computer data to show seasonal changes, weather and land cultivation patterns, population distribution, and other factors that affect life on earth.

The two newest attractions are the 12,000-square-foot Giant Panda Habitat, complete with Chinese-style "mist" and rocky landscapes; and the nearby Asia Trail, stocked up with sloth bears, giant Japanese salamanders, and the endangered clouded leopards.

OTHER THINGS TO DO NEARBY If you've done the Zoo justice, your feet will hurt and your energy level will be too depleted for much else: go back to your room. Lunch spots abound three blocks north on Connecticut Avenue; from there it's a short walk to the Cleveland Park Metro. But if you've got feet of steel, take the half-hour hike to the National Cathedral.

The Octagon ★★★

APPEAL BY AGE	PRESCHOOL ★	GRADE SCHOOL ★★	TEENS ★★
YOUNG ADULTS ★★★	OVER 30 ★★★		SENIORS ★★★

Location 1799 New York Avenue NW; Nearest Metro station Farragut West; ☎ 202-638-3221; www.archfoundation.org/octagon

Type of attraction One of the first great homes built in Washington; a museum showcasing American architecture and historic preservation (guided tour). **Admission** $5 adults; $3 students and seniors. **Hours** Tuesday–Sunday, 10 a.m.–4 p.m.; closed Mondays, Thanksgiving, Christmas, and New Year's days. **When to go** Anytime. **Special comments** One long staircase leads to the second-floor exhibition galleries. Another interesting, yet narrow, slice of early Washington history. **How much time to allow** 1 hour.

DESCRIPTION AND COMMENTS This elegant building is where President James Madison and First Lady Dolley Madison took up temporary residence after the British burned the White House during the War of 1812. Built in 1801 (when Washington was mostly swamp), this early Federalist building recently underwent a $5-million, six-year renovation; it's owned by the American Architectural Foundation. Period rooms on the first floor offer visitors a glimpse of how the upper crust lived in the early days of Washington; the coal stoves in the entrance hall are original. The former bedrooms upstairs are now galleries displaying temporary exhibits on architecture and design.

TOURING TIPS Interpreters give half-hour tours of the building that provide additional glimpses into the past—and tell fascinating anecdotes about the building and the city's early days. For example, President Madison signed the Treaty of Ghent, which ended the war that had driven him from the White House, in the upstairs parlor. Later the building served as a girls' school and was subdivided into ten apartments before it was acquired by the American Architectural Foundation in 1899.

OTHER THINGS TO DO NEARBY The Corcoran Gallery of Art is a block away. The Renwick Gallery and the White House are also close by.

kids Old Post Office Tower and Pavilion ★ ★ ★ ★

APPEAL BY AGE	PRESCHOOL ★ ★ ★	GRADE SCHOOL ★ ★ ★ ★	TEENS ★ ★ ★ ★
YOUNG ADULTS ★ ★ ★		OVER 30 ★ ★ ★	SENIORS ★ ★ ★

Location 12th Street and Pennsylvania Avenue NW; Nearest Metro station Federal Triangle; ☎ 202-289-4224 or 202-606-8691 for the tower; www.nps.gov/opot

Type of attraction A multiethnic food court in a spectacular architectural setting; home of the second-best view in Washington; trendy shops (guided tour of the tower). **Admission** Free. **Hours** During the summer, retail stores are open Monday–Saturday, 10 a.m.–9 p.m., and Sunday, noon–7 p.m. In the winter, stores are open Monday–Saturday, 10 a.m.–7 p.m., and Sunday, noon–6 p.m. Summer food court hours are Monday–Saturday, 10 a.m.–9 p.m., and Sunday, noon–8 p.m.; the food court closes an hour earlier the rest of the year. From Easter Sunday through Labor Day, the tower is open 8 a.m.–10:45 p.m.; the rest of the year it's open 10 a.m.–5:45 p.m. **When to go** Anytime to take the glass elevator up the clock tower; beat the worst of the crowds in the food court after 1 p.m. **Special comments** This is the place to come when they run out of time tickets at the Washington Monument. The food court is a favorite stop for tour buses, making it difficult at times to find a table. A great view and a lifesaver for tourists who hate the overpriced, crummy food served in most museums. **How much time to allow** 1 hour for the clock tower.

DESCRIPTION AND COMMENTS This fine old building, a Pennsylvania Avenue landmark, was slated for demolition, but preservationist groups intervened to save it. Today, the 315-foot clock tower offers a spectacular view of Washington, while the multiethnic-food court occupies a stunning glass-roofed architectural space ten stories high. It offers a complete tourist experience for people of all ages: a view to kill for (through large plate glass windows, not tiny windows like at the Washington Monument), great food, and a shopping mall. And with its proximity to the Mall and White House, the Pavilion is a convenient place to visit for a quick lunch or snack.

TOURING TIPS It's elbow-to-elbow in the small elevator to the observation deck. Beware of clumps of screaming teenagers in the food court—it's a popular destination for school groups. To reach the glass-enclosed elevators to the observation deck, go to the patio area in the food court. The National Park Service rangers on duty in the tower are a great source of advice about D.C. touring. Ask one to show you the lay of the land from the observation deck. Or, if you want to get out and about, check the kiosks for bike and Segway rental.

OTHER THINGS TO DO NEARBY Make faces at the groupers in the National Aquarium, stop by the International Spy Museum, or visit Ford's Theatre. If you can't find anything good to eat in the food court, walk a couple of blocks to the Hotel Washington on 15th Street; its rooftop bar has an equally stunning view, and the advantage of a liquor license.

Old Town Alexandria ★ ★ ★ ★

APPEAL BY AGE	PRESCHOOL ★ ★	GRADE SCHOOL ★ ★ ★	TEENS ★ ★ ★
YOUNG ADULTS ★ ★ ★ ★ ★	OVER 30 ★ ★ ★ ★ ★		SENIORS ★ ★ ★ ★ ★

Location **In suburban Virginia, 8 miles south of Washington;** Nearest Metro station **King Street; For more information on Old Town, call the Alexandria Convention and Visitors Association at ☎ 800-388-9119 or 703-838-4200; Press 4 for a recording of special events that's updated regularly**

Type of attraction A restored colonial port town on the Potomac River, featuring 18th-century buildings on cobblestone streets, trendy shops, bars and restaurants, parks, and a huge art center (guided and self-guided tours). **Admission** Some historic houses charge $4 for admission. Admission to the Torpedo Factory Art Center, the Lyceum, and the George Washington Masonic National Memorial is free. Tickets that get you into three historic sites for $9 ($6 for children ages 11–17) are sold at Ramsay House, the main visitor center on King Street. **Hours** Historic houses, shops, and the Torpedo Factory Art Center open by 10 a.m. and remain open through the afternoon. **When to go** Anytime. **Special comments** The most scenic spot for a brown-bag lunch are the picnic tables located at the foot of First Street, on the Potomac River. A satisfying contrast to awesome D.C. **How much time to allow** At least half a day. If it's the second half, stay for dinner; Old Town Alexandria has a great selection of restaurants.

DESCRIPTION AND COMMENTS Alexandria claims both George Washington and Robert E. Lee as native sons, so history buffs have a lot to see. Topping the list are period revival houses that rival those in Georgetown, another old port up the river; **Gadsby's Tavern Museum** (131 North Royal Street; ☎ 703-545-4242); **Christ Church,** where Washington attended services (118 North Washington Street; ☎ 703-544-5883); the **Lee-Fendall House** (614 Oronoco Street; ☎ 703-548-1789); and the newly restored four-story **Stabler-Leadbetter Apothecary Museum**

old town alexandria

0   0.125 mile
0   100 meters

To National
Airport and
Washington, D.C.

Montgomery St.

Madison St.

Wythe St.

Pendleton St.

Oronoco St.

Princess St.

Queen St.

Cameron St.

King St.

Prince St.

Duke St.

Wolfe St.

Wilkes St.

Gibbon St.

Franklin St.

← To I-95 and 1

← From I-95 and 1

To Mount Vernon,
Woodlawn, &
Gunston Hall

Henry St. (Rte. 1 South)
Patrick St. (Rte. 1 North)
Alfred St.
Columbus St.
Washington St.
St. Asaph St.
Pitt St.
Royal St.
Fairfax St.
Lee St.
Union St.

CANAL
CENTER PLAZA

Potomac River

FOUNDERS
PARK

Quay St.

WATERFRONT
PARK

WASHINGTON,
D.C.
Arlington
VIRGINIA
Alexandria
MARYLAND
Area of detail
0   5 mi
0   5 km

● ATTRACTIONS
1. Alexandria Black History
   and Resource Center
2. The Athenaeum
3. Carlyle House
4. Christ Church
5. Friendship Firehouse
   Museum

6. Gadsby's Tavern Museum
7. Gunston Hall
8. Lee-Fendall House
9. The Lyceum
10. Market Square
11. Mt. Vernon
12. Old Presbyterian
    Meeting House

13. Ramsay House
    Visitors Bureau
14. Stabler-Leadbetter
    Apothecary Museum
15. Torpedo Factory/
    Alexandria
    Archaeology

(105–107 South Fairfax Street; ☎ 703-836-3713), where in 1859 Lt. J. E. B. Stuart, then at the U.S. Army, handed Col. Robert E. Lee—then also an officer in the national force—his orders to quell John Brown's insurrection at Harper's Ferry. This hip, revitalized city on the Potomac is crammed with exotic restaurants (Thai, Indian, Lebanese, Greek) and shops (art, jewelry, children's books, antiques, Persian carpets). And, unlike those in Georgetown, the eating and drinking establishments in Old Town aren't overrun by suburban teenagers on weekends.

TOURING TIPS As you exit the King Street Metro station, either board a DASH bus for a quick trip down King Street to Old Town (85 cents), or walk to your left and turn right onto King Street for a pleasant 15-minute stroll toward the river. The closest visitor center is at the Lyceum, where two exhibition galleries and a museum of the area's history are featured; from King Street, turn right onto Washington Street and walk a block. There's also a small museum featuring prints, documents, photographs, silver, furniture, and Civil War memorabilia. Farther down King Street on the left is Ramsay House, built in 1724 and now Alexandria's official visitor center, open daily from 9 a.m. to 5 p.m., except Thanksgiving, Christmas, and New Year's days. Ramsay House makes a good starting point for a walking tour of Old Town Alexandria. The Torpedo Factory Art Center at the foot of King Street features more than 150 painters, printmakers, sculptors, and other artists and craftspeople. Visitors can watch artists at work in their studios housed in the former munitions factory. If you drive to Alexandria, park your car in a two-hour metered space, feed it a nickel or a dime, and go to a visitor center to pick up a pass that lets you park free for 24 hours in any two-hour metered zone inside Alexandria city limits (renewable once); you'll need your vehicle's license plate number. But parking is scarce and the King Street Metro is conveniently located.

OTHER THINGS TO DO NEARBY About a mile west of the center of Alexandria is the George Washington National Masonic Memorial. A free tour features a view from the 333-foot tower, Washington memorabilia, a 370-year-old Persian rug valued at $1 million, and more information about masonry than you probably want. The tours are given Monday through Saturday on the half hour in the mornings and on the hour in the afternoons; the memorial is open daily, 9 a.m. to 5 p.m. Mount Vernon, George Washington's plantation on the Potomac, is eight miles downriver.

Phillips Collection ★ ★ ★ ★

APPEAL BY AGE	PRESCHOOL —	GRADE SCHOOL ★	TEENS ★★
YOUNG ADULTS ★★★★	OVER 30 ★★★★		SENIORS ★★★★

Location 1600 21st Street NW; Nearest Metro station Dupont Circle;
☎ **202-387-2151; www.phillipscollection.org**

Type of attraction The first museum dedicated to modern art in the United States (self-guided tour). **Admission** Weekends: $12 adults, $10 seniors 62+ and full-time students; varying charges for special exhibitions. No charge for visitors 18 and under. Admission to the permanent collection is free during the week, but the museum suggests contributions at the same level. **Hours** Tuesday–Saturday, 10 a.m.–5 p.m.; Sunday, noon–7 p.m. (5 p.m. June–September). Open Thursday until 8:30 p.m. Closed Mondays, New Year's Day, Martin Luther King Jr.'s birthday, Presidents Day, Memorial Day, Fourth of July, Labor Day, Columbus Day, Thanksgiving, and Christmas days. **When to go** Anytime. **Special comments** With lots of carpeting and places to sit, the Phillips Collection is a very comfortable museum to tour. The cafe is closed temporarily as the museum undergoes renovation and expansion. One of the best art museums in Washington. **How much time to allow** 2 hours.

DESCRIPTION AND COMMENTS Founded by Duncan Phillips, grandson of the founder of the Jones and Laughlin Steel Company, the Phillips Collection is set in the family's former mansion, which helps explain its intimate and comfortable feeling. The collection is too large for everything to be on display at once, so the art is constantly rotated. Expect to see works by Monet, Picasso, Miró, Renoir, and Van Gogh, among other modern masters. The large and ornate Music Room is as spectacular as the art hanging on its walls. Over the past several years, the Phillips has expanded twice into adjoining town houses to allow for larger visiting exhibits, and the cafe is expanding as well. If you've seen the Hirshhorn and the National Gallery of Art's East Wing, this should be on your agenda. It's a classy museum on a human scale.

TOURING TIPS The kids would probably prefer a trip to the zoo. Take advantage of the free 45-minute guided tours given Saturdays at 2 p.m. The well-informed guides do a good job of giving a context for the paintings and sculptures, the building, and its founder's taste in modern art.

OTHER THINGS TO DO NEARBY Cross Massachusetts Avenue and see another eye-popping mansion, the Anderson House (open Tuesday through Saturday from 1 to 4 p.m.)

Renwick Gallery (*a Smithsonian museum*) ★ ★

APPEAL BY AGE	PRESCHOOL ★	GRADE SCHOOL ★ ★	TEENS ★ ★
YOUNG ADULTS ★ ★	OVER 30 ★ ★ ★		SENIORS ★ ★ ★

Location 17th Street and Pennsylvania Avenue NW (diagonally across from the White House); Nearest Metro station **Farragut West;** ☎ **202-633-2850 or 202-357-1729 (TDD);** **www.americanart.si.edu/renwick**

Type of attraction A museum dedicated to American crafts and decorative arts (self-guided tour). **Admission** Free. **Hours** Daily, 10 a.m.–5:30 p.m.; closed Christmas Day. **When to go** Anytime. **Special comments** Don't expect an exhibition of hand-woven baskets: the museum features a wide array of mixed-media sculptures, tapestries, and constructions by major contemporary artists, which makes for an especially attractive museum shop. An elegant setting, yet a bit dull. **How much time to allow** 1 hour.

DESCRIPTION AND COMMENTS This branch of the American Art Museum is named for the building's architect, James Renwick, who also designed the Smithsonian's whimsical Arts and Industries Building (and St. Patrick's Cathedral in New York City). Both the art and the Second Empire architecture of the mansion make this Smithsonian museum worth a stop when you're near the White House. Works on display are constructed in glass, ceramics, wood, fiber, and metal. But folks on a first-time visit to Washington or with children should skip it.

TOURING TIPS Glide up the Grand Staircase to enter the elegant Grand Salon, now an art gallery featuring floor-to-ceiling oil paintings, velvet curtains, and traditional furniture. On the same floor is the elegant Octagon Room, which faces the street and is used as exhibition space. The first floor hosts temporary exhibits.

OTHER THINGS TO DO NEARBY Next door is Blair House, where visiting foreign dignitaries stay; you can't get in, but look for Secret Service agents and diplomatic limos. A plaque on the wrought-iron gates honors a guard who saved President Truman from a would-be assassin. Around the corner on 17th Street is the closest McDonald's to the White House, the one that used to lure President Clinton off his jogging route.

 ## Smithsonian Institution Building　★ ★ ★ ★

APPEAL BY AGE	PRESCHOOL —	GRADE SCHOOL ★ ★	TEENS ★ ★
YOUNG ADULTS ★ ★ ★	OVER 30 ★ ★ ★ ★	SENIORS	★ ★ ★ ★

Location **1000 Jefferson Drive SW, on the Mall;** Nearest Metro station **Smithsonian; ☎ 202-633-1000 or 202-357-1729 (TDD); www.si.edu**

Type of attraction Information desks and displays, and a continuously running movie that introduces visitors to the vast number of Smithsonian museums. **Admission** Free. **Hours** Daily, 9 a.m.–5:30 p.m.; closed Christmas Day. **When to go** Anytime. **Special Comments** A must for first-time Mall visitors. **How much time to allow** 30 minutes.

DESCRIPTION AND COMMENTS This redbrick building—you can't miss it—contains no exhibits. Also known as "the Castle," it serves as an information center that will help you save time and trouble and reduce the frustration that comes from visiting the Smithsonian's large and perplexing museum complex. Step into one of the two theaters to see the 20-minute film. It's a bit long but gives a good idea of what each museum has to offer. Then you can talk to someone at the information desk for specific directions and advice (including multilingual assistance). A nifty map exhibit on the east wall lights up the location of each of the museums on the Mall, as well as other popular D.C. sights, when you press the corresponding button.

Society of the Cincinnati Museum at Anderson House　★ ★ ★ ★

APPEAL BY AGE	PRESCHOOL ★	GRADE SCHOOL ★ ★	TEENS ★ ★
YOUNG ADULTS ★ ★	OVER 30 ★ ★ ★ ★	SENIORS	★ ★ ★ ★

Location **2118 Massachusetts Avenue NW;** Nearest Metro station **Dupont Circle;** ☎ **202-785-2040; www.thesocietyofthecincinnati.addr.com**

Type of attraction A combination mansion and Revolutionary War museum (self-guided tour). **Admission** Free. **Hours** Tuesday–Saturday, 1–4 p.m.; closed national holidays. **When to go** Anytime. **Special comments** Robber-baron decadence. Children will love the Revolutionary War figurines fighting battles; older folks will marvel at the opulence. **How much time to allow** 1 hour.

DESCRIPTION AND COMMENTS This mansion along Embassy Row is a real sleeper that few visitors ever see. Built in 1906 by Larz Anderson, a diplomat, it's a reflection of fabulous turn-of-the-century taste and wealth. The two-story ballroom is a stunner; tapestries line the crystal chandeliered dining room; and paintings by Gilbert Stuart and John Trumbull hang in the billiard room. Anderson was a member of the Society of the Cincinnati, whose members are descendants of French and American officers who served in the Revolutionary Army. After his death, his widow donated the mansion to the society. Today the building serves the society as both headquarters and museum. Even first-time visitors to D.C. should make the effort to see this spectacular mansion, which is located a block or so from Dupont Circle.

TOURING TIPS The first floor contains displays of Revolutionary War artifacts. On the second floor, the mansion remains as it was originally furnished, with 18th-century paintings, 17th-century tapestries from Brussels, and huge chandeliers.

OTHER THINGS TO DO NEARBY Take a walk along Embassy Row or browse the shops around Dupont Circle. Other sights within walking distance include the Phillips Collection (modern art), the Christian Heurich Mansion, the Textile Museum, and the Woodrow Wilson House.

Textile Museum   ★ ★

APPEAL BY AGE	PRESCHOOL —	GRADE SCHOOL ★	TEENS ★ ★
YOUNG ADULTS ★ ★ ★	OVER 30 ★ ★ ★		SENIORS ★ ★ ★

Location 2320 S Street NW; Nearest Metro station **Dupont Circle;** ☎ **202-667-0441; www.textilemuseum.org**

Type of attraction A museum dedicated to textile arts (self-guided tour). **Admission** Free; $5 donation suggested. **Hours** Monday–Saturday, 10 a.m.–5 p.m.; Sunday, 1–5 p.m.; closed federal holidays and December 24. **When to go** Anytime. **Special comments** The museum is wheelchair accessible but not barrier free. Call ahead if you have special needs. Introductory tours are offered Wednesdays and weekends at 1:30 p.m., September through May. Interesting, but small and esoteric. **How much time to allow** 1 hour.

DESCRIPTION AND COMMENTS Cloth, a mass-produced commodity in the West, no longer enjoys much prestige as an art form. But it's a different story in the rest of the world. The museum's collection ranges from countries as diverse as India, Indonesia, and China to Mexico, Guatemala, and Peru. Intricate designs and rich colors grace more than 14,000 textiles and 1,400 carpets dating from ancient times to the present day. Because the items can't be exposed to light for long periods of time, the exhibits are constantly rotated. This museum is much more interesting than it sounds—the rich colors derived from natural dye processes and elaborate details in the fabrics are subtly beautiful. Definitely for distinct tastes, but not to be missed if it appeals to you.

TOURING TIPS In the new second-floor Textile Learning Center, visitors can touch, feel, and examine textiles close up. It's an opportunity to get a better grip on how and why textiles are cultural carriers that reveal a lot about how people live. Don't miss the pleasant garden behind the museum. The gift shop is chock-full of books and items related to textiles and rugs.

OTHER THINGS TO DO NEARBY The Woodrow Wilson House is next door. The Islamic Center is around the corner on Massachusetts Avenue. In the other direction, S Street crosses Connecticut Avenue, where you can shop and dine to your heart's content.

Union Station ★★★★

APPEAL BY AGE	PRESCHOOL ★	GRADE SCHOOL ★★	TEENS ★★★
YOUNG ADULTS ★★★★		OVER 30 ★★★★	SENIORS ★★★★

Location Massachusetts Avenue and North Capitol Street NE; Nearest **Metro station Union Station; ☎ 202-289-1908; www.unionstationdc.com**

Type of attraction A spectacular interior space housing a transportation hub, upscale shops, a cineplex, and a food court. **Admission** Free. **Hours** Shops open Monday–Saturday, 10 a.m.–9 p.m.; Sunday, noon–6 p.m. **When to go** Anytime. **Special comments** A beaux-arts palace and a great lunch stop. The food court's fare is on the expensive side, but the vast selection justifies the extra cost; a handy rainy-day destination. **How much time to allow** 1 hour to wander; longer for shopping or eating.

DESCRIPTION AND COMMENTS The Main Hall, with a 90-foot barrel-vaulted ceiling, is breathtaking. Shops run the gamut: chic clothing stores, The Great Train Store, bookstores, Brookstone, the Nature Company—130 stores altogether. In the food court you'll find everything from sushi to ribs, while a nine-screen cinema complex offers solace on a rainy day. There are also seven restaurants for dining or private functions, an international currency exchange, three sightseeing companies and three rental car companies on-site. First-time visitors to D.C. shouldn't miss this magnificent structure. With more than 25 million visitors a year, Union Station is the most-visited tourist attraction in Washington (the National Air and Space Museum is number two).

TOURING TIPS Union Station is a great jumping-off point for touring Washington. Capitol Hill is a few blocks away (step out the front and walk toward the big dome), and Tourmobile, Gray Line, and Old Town Trolley tours stop in front. Monday through Friday, Maryland commuter trains (called MARC) regularly shuttle between D.C. and Baltimore, stopping at points between (a round-trip from Baltimore is $14). Virginia Railway Express shuttles commuters and day-trippers from Fredericksburg, Manassas, and points in between to Union Station weekdays. To top it off, there's a Metro station in the basement. It's hard to believe that Washington functioned before Union Station's rebirth (at a cost of more than $100 million) in 1988.

OTHER THINGS TO DO NEARBY Kids will love it, but either walk in a group or take a cab: the neighborhood is marginal. The Postal Museum is next door to Union Station; the U.S. Capitol, the Supreme Court, and the Library of Congress are close.

U.S. Botanic Garden ★ ★ ★

APPEAL BY AGE	PRESCHOOL ★	GRADE SCHOOL ★ ★	TEENS ★ ★
YOUNG ADULTS ★ ★ ★	OVER 30 ★ ★ ★		SENIORS ★ ★ ★ ★

Location **100 Maryland Avenue SW (on the Mall near the U.S. Capitol); Nearest Metro station Federal Center SW; ☎ 202-225-8333; www.usbg.gov**

Type of attraction A permanent collection of tropical, subtropical and desert plants housed in a stunning, fully renovated, 38,000-square-foot greenhouse (self-guided tour). **Admission** Free. **Hours** Daily 10 a.m.–5 p.m. **When to go** Anytime. **Special comments** Skip it on a sweltering summer afternoon. An excellent and comprehensive collection of plant life. **How much time to allow** 30 minutes.

DESCRIPTION AND COMMENTS The Conservatory, a building that reflects the grand manner of Victorian architecture (even though it was constructed in the 1930s), houses a living museum on the Mall. The central jungle depicts an abandoned plantation in a tropical rain forest under a dome that rises to 93 feet. Other sections display orchids, ferns, cacti, and other types of plants in naturalistic settings. While people with green thumbs will want to put these gardens on their first-visit itinerary, most folks will just want to know it's nearby for a quiet break from more hectic sights along the Mall. You can sit down here, relax, read a book—or just do nothing in a magnificent setting.

TOURING TIPS Before or after strolling though this giant greenhouse, visit Frederic Bartholdi Park (open from dawn until dusk), located across Independence Avenue from the Conservatory and named for the designer of the Statue of Liberty. The park features displays of bulbs, annuals, and perennials. The focal point is Bartholdi Fountain, originally exhibited at the 1876 Centennial Exhibition in Philadelphia.

OTHER THINGS TO DO NEARBY The National Air and Space Museum and the Hirshhorn Museum and Sculpture Garden are close, as is the U.S. Capitol (although to tour the building requires time tickets handed out early each morning). L'Enfant Plaza, about five blocks away, has a shopping mall loaded with restaurants and fast-food outlets.

U.S. Capitol ★★★★★

Location East end of the Mall; Nearest Metro station Capitol South, Union Station; ☎ 202-225-6827 for a recording or 202-225-3121 for the Capitol switchboard; www.aoc.gov

Type of attraction The building where Congress meets (guided tours only). **Admission** Free. **Hours** The building is open Monday–Saturday, 9:30 a.m.– 8 p.m. (March–August) and 9 a.m.–4:30 p.m. (September–February); closed Thanksgiving and Christmas. Pick up free tickets at the Capitol Guide Service kiosk on the curving sidewalk southwest of the Capitol (the Mall side, near the U.S. Botanic Garden). Ticket distribution begins at 9 a.m.; if you want one of the 450 tickets (good for that day only), arrive by 8 a.m. **Special comments** After closing to the public after September 11, the Capitol reopened (to guided tours only) in December 2001. A shuttle is available from the ticket kiosk to the Capitol. Prohibited items include knives, pointed objects, pepper spray, duffel bags, backpacks, aerosol cans, bottles, food, and beverages. A Visitor's Center is under construction underground on the east side, which will have a cafeteria, gift shop, and restrooms, as well as exhibit spaces. Interesting and beautiful. **How much time to allow** 1 hour for the tour.

DESCRIPTION AND COMMENTS The U.S. Capitol manages to be two things at once: an awesome monument to democracy and one of the most important places in the world, as the frequent presence of reporters and film crews outside attests. The rather brief public tour, however, takes visitors through only a small part of the Capitol: the Rotunda and a few other rooms, which may include Statuary Hall, the House or Senate chambers (when they're not in session), and the low-ceilinged crypt. From the soaring Rotunda to the opulent rooms where the House and Senate meet, the Capitol is both physically beautiful and packed with historical significance. For first-time visitors, the tour is both awe-inspiring and relatively quick (after you've picked up tickets).

TOURING TIPS If your plans include viewing a session of Congress, don't make the time-consuming mistake thousands of other visitors make: coming to the Capitol without a gallery pass. Go first to the office of your senator or representative to pick one up. (Don't forget to ask for maps and other helpful touring goodies while you're there.) Don't know the name of your representative or of your senators? Then call ☎ 202-224-3121 for help locating an office. The free tour is heavy on the history of the building, but if your group makes it to either the House or Senate chambers, you'll get a good run-down on how Congress operates. (Stick close to the guide if you expect to hear the entire spiel.)

OTHER THINGS TO DO NEARBY Explore the rest of Capitol Hill: The Supreme Court and Library of Congress face the Capitol's east front. On the other side, the east end of the Mall features the U.S. Botanic Garden and the East Wing of the National Gallery of Art. Capitol Hill is famous for its bars and restaurants. To find them, walk toward Constitution Avenue and past the Library of Congress's Madison Building, located between Independence Avenue and C Street NE.

U.S. Department of the Interior   ★ ½

APPEAL BY AGE	PRESCHOOL ★	GRADE SCHOOL ★★	TEENS ★
YOUNG ADULTS ★	OVER 30 ★		SENIORS ★

Location 1849 C Street NW between 18th and 19th streets; Nearest Metro station Farragut West; ☎ 202-208-4743; www.doi.gov

Type of attraction A museum located inside a square-mile chunk of government bureaucracy (self-guided tour). **Admission** Free; adults must show a photo ID to enter. **Hours** Monday–Friday, 8:30 a.m.–4:30 p.m., and every third Saturday, 1–4 p.m.; otherwise, closed weekends and federal holidays. **When to go** Anytime. **Special comments** Boring. Go on a rainy day. **How much time to allow** 45 minutes.

DESCRIPTION AND COMMENTS This six-wing, seven-story limestone edifice includes 16 acres of floors and two miles of corridors—along with an old-fashioned museum. Dioramas of mines and geothermal power plants, Native American artifacts, and a historical exhibit of the National Park Service crowd the rather dark and quiet exhibition hall. This is definitely a rainy-day kind of a museum, unless you have a strong interest in national parks.

TOURING TIPS Outdoors people and map lovers shouldn't miss the U.S. Geological Survey map store, located off the lobby on the E Street side of the building. You can also load up on brochures on any (or all) U.S. national parks at the National Park Service office here. The Indian Craft Shop, across from the museum entrance, sells turquoise and silver jewelry, baskets, and other handicrafts made by Native Americans. The basement cafeteria can seat 1,200 people (open weekdays, 7 a.m. to 2:45 p.m.).

OTHER THINGS TO DO NEARBY The DAR Museum and the Corcoran Gallery of Art are around the corner on 17th Street; the Mall is about two blocks south. The Octagon, one of Washington's earliest and most elegant homes, is half a block north on 18th Street. For places to eat, head north up any numbered street toward Pennsylvania Avenue.

U.S. Department of State Diplomatic Reception Rooms   ★ ★ ★ ★ ★

APPEAL BY AGE	PRESCHOOL –	GRADE SCHOOL –	TEENS ★★★★
YOUNG ADULTS ★★★★	OVER 30 ★★★★★		SENIORS ★★★★★

Location 2201 C Street NW; Nearest Metro station Foggy Bottom–GWU; ☎ 202-647-3241; fax ☎ 202-736-4232; 202-736-4474 (TDD); www.state.gov/m/drr

Type of attraction The rooms where visiting foreign dignitaries are officially entertained (guided tour). **Admission** Free. **Hours** Tours are given Monday–Friday at 9:30 a.m., 10:30 a.m., and 2:45 p.m. by reservation only, which should be made 4 weeks in advance. **Special comments** See what $90 million in decorative arts can buy. Children under age 12 are not permitted on the tour, nor are strollers, briefcases, or backpacks. Reservations are accepted up to 90 days in advance of your visit. A short, optional public affairs tour is offered after the main tour. Although most tourists miss this, you shouldn't. **How much time to allow** 1 hour.

DESCRIPTION AND COMMENTS While the State Department goes about its important work in a building with architecture best described as "early airport," the interiors on the eighth floor are something else entirely: A fabulous collection of 18th- and early-19th-century fine and decorative arts fills stunning rooms that are used daily to receive visiting heads of state and foreign dignitaries. This is a tour for almost anyone: antique and fine arts lovers, history buffs, and just casual visitors. It's also a sight that the overwhelming majority of D.C. tourists miss. First-time visitors should make the effort to get reservations well in advance of their trip. Then forget about visiting the White House.

TOURING TIPS By guided tour only; reservations are required and should be made at least four weeks in advance of your visit. Restrooms are located near the waiting room and can be visited before and after the tour.

OTHER THINGS TO DO NEARBY The Lincoln Memorial and Vietnam Veterans Memorial are a short walk away, down 23rd Street to the Mall. The closest places to eat are a few blocks up 23rd Street, away from the Mall.

U.S. Holocaust Memorial Museum ★ ★ ★ ½

APPEAL BY AGE	PRESCHOOL —	GRADE SCHOOL ★★	TEENS ★★
YOUNG ADULTS ★★★	OVER 30 ★★★★		SENIORS ★★★★

Location 100 Raoul Wallenberg Place SW (formerly 15th Street), near the Mall between the Washington Monument and the Bureau of Engraving and Printing; Entrances are on Raoul Wallenberg Place and 14th Street; Nearest Metro station Smithsonian (Independence Avenue exit); ☎ 202-488-0400; www.ushmm.org

Type of attraction A museum and memorial presenting the history of the persecution and murder of 6 million Jews and others by Nazi Germany during World War II (self-guided tour). **Admission** Free. **Hours** Daily, 10 a.m.–5:30 p.m.; closed Christmas Day and Yom Kippur. **When to go** After favorable publicity generated large crowds following its opening in the spring of 1993, the Holocaust Museum went to a time-ticket system to eliminate long lines at its permanent exhibits. While the ticket office opens at 10 a.m., plan on getting in line no later than 9 a.m. to be sure of getting a ticket (which are given out for that day only). If you want to be sure of getting on a morning tour during the busy spring and summer months, get in line by 8:30 a.m. For advance tickets, call ☎ 800-400-9373. **Special comments** According to Holocaust Museum officials, the main exhibit is inappropriate for children under age 11—and we agree. In fact, almost everyone can pinpoint the spot where their throat begins to feel tight. However, a special exhibit on the museum's first floor, "Daniel's Story: Remember the Children," is designed for visitors ages 8 and older. It gives a child's perspective on the Holocaust, but without the shocking graphics of the permanent exhibit. No tickets are required for the special, nonpermanent exhibitions. Tickets can also be ordered in advance through Tickets.com. Call ☎ 800-400-9373, or order online at **www.tickets .com.** As its designers intended, the Holocaust Museum is ugly, forbidding, and grim—and it delivers a stern message about the evils of racial persecution. It also packs an emotional punch that may not fit some folks' vacation plans. **How much time to allow** 1½–2 hours.

DESCRIPTION AND COMMENTS This $168-million museum utilizes stunning, high-tech audiovisual displays, advanced computer technology, and a model of a Nazi death camp to deliver a message about one of the darkest periods in human history. But that's not all. As part of the museum experience, museum-goers are cast as "victims" of Nazi brutality. Visitors receive an identity card of a real Holocaust victim matched to their sex and age—a demographic double. The building attacks the emotions of visitors in other, more subtle ways. The interior of the museum, while spotless, is relentlessly industrial and forbidding—pipes are exposed and rough surfaces of brick and concrete are cold and unwelcoming. Diagonal walls in the exhibition areas create a disorienting effect. Ghostly shapes pass overhead on glass-bottomed walkways, suggesting Nazi prison guards patrolling a camp. (Actually, they are visitors walking on footbridges linking the permanent exhibit spaces.) Every moment spent inside the museum is orchestrated to impart the horror of Nazi persecution. In fact, the primary, and essential, difference between this museum and the Holocaust Museum in New York is that in Manhattan, the mood is "We will survive." This says, "We will never forget."

While many exhibits focus on Jewish life prior to the Holocaust and the political and military events surrounding World War II, the most disturbing displays are graphic depictions of Nazi atrocities. Large TV screens scattered throughout the exhibits present still and motion pictures of Nazi leaders, storm troopers rounding up victims, and life inside Jewish ghettos. Some of the TV screens are located behind concrete barriers to prevent younger (and, inadvertently, shorter) visitors from seeing them. They show executions, medical experiments on Jewish prisoners, and suicide victims. It's very strong, grim stuff.

TOURING TIPS Given the unrelenting horror of its subject matter, the Holocaust Museum is at best sobering and, at worst, depressing. There's no bright gloss to put on a museum chronicling the systematic murder of 6 million people . . . and anyone visiting the Holocaust Museum during a vacation should keep that in mind before placing it on his or her touring agenda, especially if traveling with small children.

OTHER THINGS TO DO NEARBY The Holocaust Memorial Museum occupies some prime real estate near the Mall, the Bureau of Engraving and Printing, the Washington Monument, the Tidal Basin, the FDR Memorial, and the Jefferson Memorial, so finding things to do before or after a tour of the museum is easy. The Museum Annex on Raoul Wallenberg

Place has a small deli/cafe that offers vegetarian and some prepackaged and certified kosher fare.

U.S. National Arboretum ★★★

Location 3501 New York Avenue NE; **Nearest Metro station** None nearby; ☎ 202-245-2726; www.usna.usda.gov

Type of attraction A 444-acre collection of trees, flowers, and herbs (self-guided tour). **How to get there** Drive. Take New York Avenue from downtown and enter on the service road on the right just past Bladensburg Road. **Admission** Free. **Hours** Daily, 8 a.m.–5 p.m. The information center is open weekdays, 8 a.m.–4:30 p.m.; the gift shop is open weekdays, March–mid-December, 10 a.m.–3 p.m. The National Bonsai and Penjing Museum is open daily, 10 a.m.–3:30 p.m. Closed on Christmas Day. **When to go** In the spring, fields of azaleas are in bloom. The world-class bonsai collection is a treat all year. Late July and August feature blooming aquatic plants. For more information on what's in bloom visit **www.ars-grin.gov/na.** **Special comments** The arboretum is mobbed in the spring; the rest of the year is usually tranquil. Though interesting and beautiful, it is hard to get to. **How much time to allow** 1 hour to half a day.

DESCRIPTION AND COMMENTS With nine miles of roads and more than three miles of walking paths, the U.S. National Arboretum offers visitors an oasis of quiet and beauty for a drive or a stroll. Even people without green thumbs will marvel at the bonsai collection, whose dwarf trees are more like sculptures than plants. One specimen, a Japanese white pine, is 350 years old. Folks with limited time who aren't gardening enthusiasts, however, shouldn't spend their valuable touring hours on a visit.

TOURING TIPS Flowering dogwood and mountain laurel bloom well into May. The rest of the year, it's a fine place to go for a long walk. The surrounding neighborhoods aren't safe, so either drive or take a cab.

OTHER THINGS TO DO NEARBY The Kenilworth Aquatic Gardens are only a few minutes away by car.

U.S. Supreme Court ★★★★

Location One First Street NE, across from the east front of the U.S. Capitol; **Nearest Metro stations** Union Station, Capitol South; ☎ 202-479-3211; www.supremecourtus.gov

Type of attraction The nation's highest court (self-guided tour). **Admission** Free. **Hours** Monday–Friday, 9 a.m.–4:30 p.m. Free lectures are offered every hour on the half-hour between 9:30 a.m. and 3:30 p.m. when the court isn't in session. Closed Saturdays, Sundays, and federal holidays. **When to go** Anytime to tour the building. To see the Court in session, the public may attend oral arguments held Mondays, Tuesdays, and Wednesdays, 10 a.m. to 2 p.m., in 2-week intervals from October through April; check the "A" section of the *Washington Post*. **Special comments** Seeing an oral argument here is probably your best chance of witnessing one of the 3 major branches of the government in operation while in D.C. Extremely interesting and enlightening. **How much time to allow** 1 hour to tour the building; plan on at least 2 hours total to see an oral argument.

DESCRIPTION AND COMMENTS   This magnificent faux Greek temple is where the nine-member Supreme Court makes final interpretations of the U.S. Constitution and laws passed by Congress. When the Court's not in session, visitors may enter the stunning courtroom and hear a short lecture on its workings. An excellent 20-minute film explains the workings of the Supreme Court in more detail. On the ground floor is a small museum, a gift shop, a cafeteria, and a snack bar. A visit to the Supreme Court is a must for anyone interested in how the federal government works, or how the law works in general. Others should pass it up, although the building itself is impressive.

TOURING TIPS   To see an oral argument, plan on arriving no later than 9 a.m. to get in line. Two lines form: a regular line, for those wishing to hear an entire argument (an hour), and a three-minute line, for folks who just want to slip in for a few moments. Bring quarters: you will have to place personal belongings like backpacks and cameras in coin-operated (quarters only) lockers. Security here is no-nonsense: visitors pass through *two* X-ray machines before entering the courtroom, where very serious-looking security people patrol the aisles. Small children are not allowed in the courtroom during oral arguments.

OTHER THINGS TO DO NEARBY   The U.S. Capitol, the Library of Congress, the National Postal Museum, and the Folger Shakespeare Library are all close by. The comfortable cafeteria on the ground level of the Supreme Court is one of the better government eateries. It's open for breakfast from 7:30 to 10:30 a.m. and for lunch from 11:30 a.m. to 2 p.m. except at noon and 1 p.m. when only Court employees may enter. Capitol Hill is renowned for its many bars and cafes, many of which are a short walk up Second Street SE.

Vietnam Veterans Memorial   ★ ★ ★ ★

APPEAL BY AGE	PRESCHOOL ★	GRADE SCHOOL ★★	TEENS ★★
YOUNG ADULTS ★★★	OVER 30 ★★★★	SENIORS ★★★★	

Location On the west end of the Mall near the Lincoln Memorial; Nearest Metro station Foggy Bottom–GWU; ☎ 202-426-6841; www.thewall-usa.com

Type of attraction A memorial to U.S. soldiers who died in Vietnam. **Admission** Free. **Hours** Daily 8 a.m.–11:45 p.m.; closed Christmas Day. **When to go** Anytime. **Special comments** At night this memorial is especially moving as people light matches to search for names inscribed on the wall. Deeply moving. **How much time to allow** 30 minutes to 1 hour.

DESCRIPTION AND COMMENTS "The Wall," as it is known, is a black, V-shaped rift in the earth, nearly 494 feet long and ranging from 8 inches tall at its outer edges to 10 feet tall at its center. The design competition for the memorial, which was open to the public, was won by Maya Lin, then a 21-year-old in her third year at Yale. Both her concept and her inexperience were the subject of great controversy; to placate those veterans and their families who thought it too severe and abstract, an additional sculpture depicting three soldiers was also commissioned. The Wall was dedicated on Veterans Day (November 13), 1982. Fredrick Hart's *Three Servicemen* sculpture, which now dominates the entrance to the memorial (and, in our opinion, compromises the concept visually), was dedicated two years later, also on Veterans Day. Tucked more inconspicuously to one side is a tribute to the women who served in Vietnam, sculpted by Glenna Goodacre and dedicated on Veterans Day in 1993.

TOURING TIPS At both ends of the Wall, visitors will find books that list the inscribed names and panel numbers to help them locate an inscription.

OTHER THINGS TO DO NEARBY The Lincoln Memorial, the Reflecting Pool, the $18-million Korean War Veterans Memorial, and Constitution Gardens are close by. Across from the Mall, the National Academy of Sciences features science exhibits and a statue of Albert Einstein with a lap that's large enough to sit in for picture-taking. For food, walk up 23rd Street toward Foggy Bottom and an assortment of restaurants and carryouts.

Voice of America ★ ★ ★

APPEAL BY AGE	PRESCHOOL —	GRADE SCHOOL ★	TEENS ★
YOUNG ADULTS ★ ★	OVER 30 ★ ★		SENIORS ★ ★

Location Tours meet at the C Street entrance between Third and Fourth streets SW; Nearest Metro station **Federal Center SW;** ☎ **202-619-3919; www.voa.gov**

Type of attraction The U.S. Government's overseas radio broadcasting studios (guided tour). **Admission** Free; reservations are required and no groups larger than 20 people are allowed. **Hours** The 45-minute tours are Monday–Friday at 10:30 a.m., 1:30 p.m., and 2:30 p.m., except holidays. **Special comments** A "must" for news junkies. Fascinating and informative. **How much time to allow** 45 minutes.

DESCRIPTION AND COMMENTS After a short video about the VOA, the knowledgeable tour guide walks you through some of the agency's 34 studios, where you see and hear radio announcers reading newscasts in languages such as Arabic, Estonian, and Urdu. Worldwide, the VOA operates more than 100 shortwave radio transmitters, and all broadcasts originate in this building. You'll also see some murals painted by noted artist Ben Shahn in the 1940s. But mostly this is a tour for people interested in media and world events; it would bore most children silly.

TOURING TIPS You should call to reserve a place on a tour, but individuals and small groups won't have trouble joining a tour by just showing up a few minutes before a scheduled departure.

OTHER THINGS TO DO NEARBY The U.S. Botanic Garden is around the corner on Maryland Avenue SW, and the Mall is two blocks away. For lunch, try the L'Enfant Plaza underground shopping mall, which on weekdays is usually jammed with bureaucrats looking for good, cheap food—and finding it. But don't go on weekends: most of the restaurants are closed, and the place is dead. Capitol Hill has a wide assortment of restaurants and cafes; another good choice for off-the-Mall eating is the Old Post Office Pavilion.

kids Washington Monument ★ ★ ★ ★ ★

APPEAL BY AGE   PRESCHOOL ★ ★ ★ ★   GRADE SCHOOL ★ ★ ★ ★ ★   TEENS ★ ★ ★ ★ ★
YOUNG ADULTS ★ ★ ★ ★ ★   OVER 30 ★ ★ ★ ★ ★   SENIORS ★ ★ ★ ★ ★

Location On the Mall between 15th and 17th streets NW; Nearest Metro station Smithsonian; ☎ 202-426-6841; www.nps.gov/wamo

Type of attraction A monument to the first U.S. president. Admission Free. Hours Daily 9 a.m.–4:45 p.m. The monument may be closed in thunderstorms and during periods of sustained high winds (not out of fear that the giant obelisk will tumble, but to protect visitors waiting in line on this exposed hilltop). In addition, the grounds surrounding the monument may be closed during security alerts; use the 15th Street entrance. The ticket kiosk is open from 8 a.m. to 4:30 p.m.; it's better to get there early as it's on a first-come, first-served basis. When to go At 7:30 a.m. to pick up a time ticket. Special comments Skip this one in bad weather—the views can be lousy. No food, drinks, or large bags are allowed into this monument. The Park Service operates a time-ticket system to eliminate the long lines that used to wrap three times around the base of the monument. Pick up the free tickets (a maximum of six per person) at the kiosk located on 15th Street on the edge of the monument grounds. Then return at the time stamped on your ticket for the trip up the elevator later that day; kiosk hours are 8 a.m. until all 1,400 tickets run out. Show up 5 minutes before the time printed on your ticket. With only 150 tickets given out per half hour, all the tickets are usually gone by 9:30 a.m. on busy days and by 1:30 p.m. on slow days; early-morning tickets go first. Tickets can be reserved in advance for a fee by calling ☎ 800-967-2283 or online at www.reservations.nps.gov. There's a $2 service charge per ticket . . . and if it's raining or the view's socked in by clouds, too bad. Refunds are given only if the monument is closed. Obligatory for first-time visitors. How much time to allow Once you make it to the top, 30 minutes on the cramped observation deck can seem like an eternity.

DESCRIPTION AND COMMENTS At the top you're 500 feet up, and D.C.'s absence of other tall buildings (it's a law) guarantees a glorious, unobstructed view of Washington—if it's not raining. For most people, a first-time trip to Washington isn't complete without an ascent of this famous landmark. Yet most of them are surprised when they reach the cramped observation deck: you almost have to elbow your way to the tiny windows to see anything. The view, however, is great. Nobody's ever disappointed once they see it.

TOURING TIPS The new, year-round time-ticket system eliminates three-hour waits in line for the elevator trip to the top of the monument, which reopened in the summer of 2000 after renovations. (The wait in line is now reduced to about half an hour for most visitors.) Bathrooms are located behind the outdoor amphitheater on the monument grounds and the snack bar near the ticket kiosk, but use them only in desperate situations: they are usually dirty. A nearby snack bar is over-priced; during the week, try the the food courts in the Old Post Office Pavilion which, as it happens, offers an even better view—and the Ronald Reagan Building.

OTHER THINGS TO DO NEARBY You're at the heart of tourist Washington: at hand are the Bureau of Engraving and Printing, the Holocaust Memorial Museum, the National Museum of American History, and the National Aquarium. At one end of the Mall is the Lincoln Memorial; the U.S. Capitol is at the other. If it's a nice day and you're museumed out, explore the stretch of the Mall between the Washington Monument and the Lincoln Memorial. Much of it is tree-lined, tranquil, and not nearly as crowded as the east end of the Mall (toward the U.S. Capitol).

Washington National Cathedral ★ ★ ★ ★ ★

APPEAL BY AGE	PRESCHOOL ★	GRADE SCHOOL ★ ★	TEENS ★ ★ ★ ★
YOUNG ADULTS ★ ★ ★ ★ ★		OVER 30 ★ ★ ★ ★ ★	SENIORS ★ ★ ★ ★

Location Massachusetts and Wisconsin avenues NW; Nearest Metro station The Woodley Park–Zoo/Adams-Morgan station is about a half-hour walk; drive or take a cab; ☎ 202-537-6200 or 202-537-5596 for guided-tour information; 202-364-6616 for touring conflict info or special events; www.cathedral.org/cathedral

Type of attraction The sixth-largest cathedral in the world (guided and self-guided tours). **Admission** Free; suggested donations are $3 adults, $2 seniors, and $1 children. **Hours** Monday–Friday: 10 a.m.–5:30 p.m., tours 10–11:30 a.m. and 12:45–3:30 p.m.; Saturday: 10 a.m.–4:30 p.m., tours 10–11:30 a.m. and 12:45–3:30 p.m.; Sunday 8 a.m.–6:30 p.m., tours 12:45–2:30 p.m. Summer hours: open weekdays until 8 p.m. **When to go** Anytime. **Special comments** A Gothic masterpiece. Take the optional 30- to 45-minute, docent-led tour. **How much time to allow** 1 hour.

DESCRIPTION AND COMMENTS If you've been to Europe, you'll experience déjà vu when you visit this massive Gothic cathedral. It's a tenth of a mile from the nave to the high altar; the ceiling is 100 feet high. Don't miss the Bishop's Garden, modeled on a medieval walled garden, or the Pilgrim Observation Gallery and a view of Washington from the highest vantage point in the city. Small children may not enjoy being dragged around this huge cathedral, but just about anyone else will enjoy its magnificent architecture and stone carvings.

TOURING TIPS Docent-led tours are offered on weekdays. While the tours are free, suggested donations are $3 for adults and $1 for children. Remember to wear comfortable shoes. Try to catch the free organ demonstration given Wednesdays 1:15 to 3:15 p.m. Carillon recitals are given on Sundays; times vary so call ahead. You can also visit the grave of Woodrow Wilson, the only president buried in Washington. The Cathedral isn't well served by public transportation, but walking there takes you through safe, pleasant neighborhoods that are home to Washington's elite: it's about a half-hour stroll up Cathedral Avenue from the Woodley Park–Zoo/Adams-Morgan Metro.

OTHER THINGS TO DO NEARBY The National Zoo is about a half-hour walk from the National Cathedral, or take a cab. For lunch, walk two blocks north on Wisconsin Avenue to Cleveland Park and choose among Thai, Chinese, Mexican, and pizza restaurants. The best deals are at G. C. Murphy's, which features gyros, pita sandwiches, mini-pizzas, subs, pastries, and Italian coffee. Most items on the menu are under $5.

kids Washington Navy Yard ★ ★ ★

APPEAL BY AGE	PRESCHOOL ★	GRADE SCHOOL ★ ★ ★ ★	TEENS ★ ★ ★
YOUNG ADULTS ★ ★		OVER 30 ★ ★	SENIORS ★ ★ ★

9th and M streets SE, on the waterfront; Nearest Metro station Navy Yard. Because this is an unsafe neighborhood any time of day, we recommend that visitors either drive (parking is available inside the gate) or take a cab. Navy Museum, ☎ 202-433-4882; Marine Corps Historical Museum, 202-433-3534; Navy Art Gallery, 202-433-3815; *USS Barry*, 202-433-3377; www.ndw.navy.mil/NavyYard/History.html

Type of attraction Three military museums and a U.S. Navy destroyer (self-guided tours by reservation only; call ☎ 202-433-6897). **Admission** Free; reservations required for nonmilitary personnel. **Hours** Monday–Friday, 9 a.m.–4 p.m.; closed weekends and all federal holidays. Marine Corps Historical Museum closed Tuesdays; Navy Art Gallery open until 5 p.m. in the summer and until 4 p.m. in the winter; closed Monday and Tuesday. **When to go** Anytime. But unless you have military ID, advance reservations are required. **Special comments** A nice contrast to the look-but-don't-touch Mall museums. Hands-on fun for kids; informative for adults. **How much time to allow** 2 hours.

DESCRIPTION AND COMMENTS Exhibits in the Navy Museum include 14-foot-long model ships, undersea vehicles *Alvin* and *Trieste,* working sub periscopes, a space capsule that kids (and wiry adults) can climb in, and, tied up at the dock, a decommissioned destroyer to tour. The Marine Corps Historical Museum is less hands-on, featuring exhibit cases and Marine Corps mementos. The Navy Art Gallery is a small museum with paintings of naval actions painted by combat artists. A strong interest in the military is a prerequisite for making the trek to the Washington Navy Yard, and it's not a side trip that many first-time visitors make. But kids will love it. For current exhibition information visit **www.history .navy.mil** and click on "The Navy Museum."

TOURING TIPS Don't make our mistake—jumping off at the Metro's Navy Yard station and walking ten scary blocks to the Navy Yard entrance;

drive or take a cab. It's too bad these museums are so far off the beaten path, because there's a lot here to see and do.

OTHER THINGS TO DO NEARBY Nothing recommended.

 The White House ★ ★

APPEAL BY AGE	PRESCHOOL ★ ★	GRADE SCHOOL ★ ★ ★	TEENS ★ ★ ★ ★
YOUNG ADULTS ★ ★ ★ ★		OVER 30 ★ ★ ★ ★	SENIORS ★ ★ ★ ★

Location 1600 Pennsylvania Avenue NW; Nearest Metro station Federal Triangle; ☎ 202-456-7041 or 202-456-2121 (TDD); www.whitehouse.gov

Type of attraction The official residence of the president of the United States (self-guided tour). **Special comments** Public tours of the White House are available for groups of 10 or more people, but requests must be submitted through one's member of Congress and are accepted up to 6 months in advance. These free, self-guided tours are scheduled Tuesday through Saturday (excluding federal holidays) 7:30 a.m. to 12:30 p.m., and are scheduled on a first-come, first-served basis approximately one month in advance of the requested date. You should submit your request as soon as possible since there are only a limited number of tours available. *Note:* White House tours may be subject to last-minute cancellation. All visitors should call the 24-hour Visitors Office information line at ☎ 202-456-7041 to determine if any last-minute changes have been made in the tour schedule. During high tourist season, the tour requires too much time and effort for this 15-minute experience even with the additional exhibits and videos at the White House Visitors Center at 15th and E streets NW. **How much time to allow** Block out an entire morning, even though there's time to do something else (like eat breakfast) before your scheduled tour.

DESCRIPTION AND COMMENTS First things first: you have absolutely zero chance of seeing the president on this tour of the White House. The all-too-quick tour passes through the ubiquitous metal detectors and into the East Wing lobby; look out the window into the Rose Garden. Then it's up the stairs to the East Room, the Green Room, the Blue Room, the Red Room, and the State Dining Room—and you're done! It's hard to dispute the emotional pull of the presidential residence or its sumptu-ous beauty, but if you're on a first-time visit to Washington and on a limited schedule, consider visiting the White House on another trip, preferably in the fall or winter.

The visitor center is large and attractive, featuring lots of carpeting, places to sit, nice restrooms (but no food concessions), static displays on the White House, a gift shop, and a video tour of the mansion for those who didn't crawl out of bed before dawn to get in line for a ticket.

TOURING TIPS Check the White House Web site to see if your visit coincides with one of the occasional Garden Tours.

OTHER THINGS TO DO NEARBY Across from the White House on Lafayette Square is St. John's Episcopal Church, known as "The Church of the Pres-idents," because every president since Madison has attended services here. Step inside the small church to view its simple design; on most Wednesdays at noon there's an organ recital. Behind the White House

the white house area

Area of detail

GEORGETOWN

The White House

Union Station

ARLINGTON

VIRGINIA

The Capitol

0 ___ 1 mi

0 ___ 1 km

DUPONT CIRCLE

N. St.

Dupont Circle
Red Line

M. St.

National Geographic Society

L. St.

Connecticut Avenue

Farragut North
Red Line

K. St.

19th St.

18th St.

17th St.

16th St.

15th St.

I. St.

Farragut West
Blue & Orange Lines

Decatur House

Veteran's Administration

McPherson Square
Blue & Orange Lines

14th St.

Pennsylvania Avenue

H. St.

K St.

LAFAYETTE SQUARE

New York Avenue

13th St.

Renwick Gallery

G. St.

G. St.

W. Executive Ave.

E. Executive Ave.

Metro Center
Red, Blue, & Orange Lines

Executive Office Building

The White House

Treasury Department

F. St.

F. St.

General Services Administration

Octagon House

Federal Triangle
Blue & Orange Lines

Corcoran Gallery of Art

State Pl.

Treasury Pl.

Pennsylvania Avenue

19th St.

E. St.

Red Cross

South Executive Ave.

White House Visitor Center

E. St.

District Building

Old Post Office Tower

Interior Department

18th St.

Zero Milestone

15th St.

Virginia Avenue

DAR Museum

D St.

Constitution Hall

C. St.

THE ELLIPSE

Commerce Department

Ronald Reagan Building and International Trade Center

Bureau of Indian Affairs

OAS Annex

Organization of American States (OAS)

National Aquarium

Labor Department

Constitution Avenue

FOGGY BOTTOM

CONSTITUTION GARDENS

17th St.

National Museum of American History

Reflecting Pool

National World War II Memorial

Washington Monument

14th St.

Madison Drive

Sylvan Theater

Jefferson Drive

John Paul Jones statue

Independence Avenue

Independence Avenue

Kutz Bridge

15th St.

U.S. Holocaust Museum

Department of Agriculture

0 ___ 0.125 miles

0 ___ 100 meters

Tidal Basin

Bureau of Engraving and Printing

Phone

Restrooms

stands the Washington Monument, another D.C. edifice that requires time tickets. Pick them up at the kiosk on 15th Street. Coming in 2007: the Newseum, the world's first interactive museum of news. Formerly located in Arlington, Virginia, the museum will reopen in a new 600,000-square-foot facility at Sixth Street and Pennsylvania Avenue, between the White House and the U.S. Capitol.

Woodrow Wilson House ★★★★

APPEAL BY AGE	PRESCHOOL ★	GRADE SCHOOL ★★	TEENS ★★★
YOUNG ADULTS ★★★	OVER 30 ★★★★		SENIORS ★★★★

**Location 2340 S Street NW; Nearest Metro station Dupont Circle;
☎ 202-387-4062; www.woodrowwilsonhouse.org**

Type of attraction The final home of the 28th U.S. president (guided tour). **Admission** $5 adults; $4 seniors 62+; $2.50 students; free ages 6 and under. **Hours** Tuesday–Sunday, 10 a.m.–4 p.m.; closed Mondays and national holidays. **When to go** To avoid a crowded tour during spring and summer, arrive before noon. **Special comments** Interesting and informative. Lots of stairs, including a steep, narrow descent down a back staircase. **How much time to allow** 1–2 hours.

DESCRIPTION AND COMMENTS After Woodrow Wilson left office in 1921, he became the only former president to retire in Washington, D.C.—and he did so in this house. The tour starts with a 25-minute video narrated by Walter Cronkite that puts this underrated president in perspective and fires you up for the tour. Ninety-six percent of the items in this handsome Georgian Revival town house are original, so visitors get an accurate picture of aristocratic life in the 1920s. On the tour you'll see Wilson's library (his books, however, went to the Library of Congress after his death), his bedroom, his old movie projector, and beautiful furnishings.

TOURING TIPS The basement kitchen is virtually unchanged from Wilson's day, with original items such as an ornate wooden icebox and a coal and gas–fired stove. Peek inside the pantry, still stocked with items from the 1920s such as Kellogg's Corn Flakes ("wonderfully flavored with malt, sugar, and salt"). This is another tour that gives visitors the feeling they've been somewhere special and off the beaten tourist track.

OTHER THINGS TO DO NEARBY The Textile Museum is next door. Embassy Row is around the corner on Massachusetts Avenue, and in the other direction, Connecticut Avenue bustles with shops and restaurants.

VIRGINIA SUBURBS

NOT SURPRISINGLY, the northern Virginia suburbs are filled with historical sites, many that would be of special interest to families or veterans. Just off I-395 south on West Braddock Road is **Fort Ward** (☎ 703-838-4848; **www.fortward.org**), a well-preserved Civil War fort and living-history museum with frequent reenactments and exhibits portraying Washington and Alexandria in wartime.

Often overlooked in the Mount Vernon hoopla, in spite of its close connections (and collections, some of which came from Mount Vernon), is **Woodlawn Plantation** (9000 Richmond Highway/Route 1, Alexandria; ☎ 703-780-4000; **www.woodlawn1805.org**). Constructed in 1800–1805 for Major Lawrence Lewis (George Washington's nephew and social secretary) and his wife, Nelly Custis Lewis (Martha Washington's granddaughter), the estate is only about three miles from Mount Vernon. The Lewises were married at Mount Vernon on Washington's last birthday, in 1799, and he gave them 2,000 acres from the Mount Vernon estate on which to build a home (and engaged the architect of the U.S. Capitol to design it). The Palladian mansion, with a two-story central block and one-and-a-half-story wings, was sheathed in brick baked by slaves on the plantation grounds. A second major attraction at Woodlawn is the **Pope-Leighey House** (☎ 703-780-4000; **www.popeleighey1940.org**), an intact Frank Lloyd Wright Usonian home, built in 1941 and moved from Falls Church to Woodlawn when highway construction threatened its preservation. It is complete with all the furniture Wright designed for it and is constructed entirely of cypress, brick, glass, and concrete. The complex is open from March to December.

The **Claude Moore Colonial Farm at Turkey Run** in McLean (6310 Georgetown Pike; ☎ 703-442-7557; **www.1771.org**) is a living-history museum that re-creates a low-income tenant family farm just before the Revolutionary War. Staff dressed in period costumes answer questions as they work the land and do the chores, tend the turkeys and hogs, and do the mending. Visitors are encouraged to pitch in or to dress the part.

If you head toward the big Leesburg Outlet Malls and the historical town of Leesburg, stop by **Oatlands Historic House and Gardens** (20850 Oatlands Plantation Road, Leesburg; ☎ 703-777-3174 or **www .oatlands.org**), an early-19th-century wheat plantation and stuccoed-brick Greek Revival mansion with an octagonal family room, half-octagonal interior stairs at either end, and a grand portico (the mansion is closed to the public January through March).

The new **National Museum of the Marine Corps,** near the Marine Corps base in Quantico and dedicated in November 2006 by President George W. Bush, has a striking design that echoes the famous Iwo Jima flag-raising memorial, only in abstract, angular steel. The 210-foot "mast" also evokes the image of a sword half-pulled from its sheath, cannons poised for firing, and aircraft takeoffs—all scenarios familiar to members of the 239-year-old corps. Exhibits range from a World War II Curtiss Jenny to a supersonic jet and Persian Gulf tanks to target ranges and flight simulators, plus a cold-air room that recalls the wintry environment of the Korean War. The museum will also incorporate artifacts from the former Marine Corps Center at the Washington Navy Yard and the Marine Corps Air-Ground Museum at Quantico.

PART EIGHT

DINING *and* RESTAURANTS

EXPERIENCING WASHINGTON CUISINE

THE NEW WASHINGTON COOKERY

IN THE LAST 15 YEARS, and even more rapidly over the past seven or eight years, Washington has evolved from an extremely predictable restaurant town, one in which dining out was more a matter of convenience and expense account than pleasure, to one of the top ten culinary centers in the country—a city where it's really fun to be a restaurant critic.

The sorts of heavy French and Italian and Continental dishes to which a generation of Washingtonians was inured have been replaced by market-fresh, innovative, and even nutritionally informed recipes, many of them combining elements of the older classic cuisines (often lumped together as "modern eclectic" and a strong influence in the development of what is, for lack of a better term, described as "modern American"). Beyond those are the scores of Vietnamese, Japanese, Indian, Middle Eastern, Chinese (of all regions), Central and South American (of many regions), and Ethiopian establishments in the area, not just first-generation mom-and-pop immigrant eateries but professional, critically acclaimed restaurants. And the greater quantity of choices in all styles means better quality as well: the most recent boom, the one in Thai food, has—like the successive explosions in other ethnic fare—educated diners to the delicacy as well as the potency of that cuisine, and chased many of the quickie, unauthentic kitchens out of business.

The ethnic-fare boom is almost certain to continue: national surveys show that younger consumers, Generations X and Y, as marketers call them, are developing tastes for a variety of ethnic flavors early in life, and consider them as much a part of the American buffet

washington, d.c., dining

```
0        0.125 mi
0        125 m
```

Q St.

Church St.

Dupont
Circle
Red Line

P St.

Logan
Circle

19

Scott Circle

Farragut
North
Red Line

Thomas
Circle

M St.

9

McPherson Square

L St.

15

21

7

Washington
Circle

K St.

Franklin
Square

Foggy Bottom–GWU
Blue &
Orange Lines

13

Farragut
Square

10

I St.

14

20

8

McPherson
Square
Blue &
Orange Lines

George
Washington
University

FOGGY BOTTOM

H St.

G St.

18
3

Kennedy
Center

F St.

White
House

E St.

C St.

Constitution Ave.

Lincoln
Memorial

Washington
Monument

Arlington
Mem. Bridge

*Tidal
Basin*

Jefferson
Memorial

◆ DINING	
1. Austin Grill	13. Kaz Sushi Bistro
2. Bistro Bis	14. Kinkead's
3. Butterfield 9	15. Marcel's
4. Café Atlántico/	16. Montmartre
Minibar	17. Oceanaire Seafood
5. CityZen	Room
6. Corduroy	18. Old Ebbitt Grill
7. D.C. Coast	19. Tabard Inn
8. Equinox	20. Taberna del
9. Galileo	Alabardero
10. Gerard's Place	21. Teatro Goldoni
11. IndeBleu	22. TenPenh
12. Jaleo	23. Tosca
	24. Zaytinya

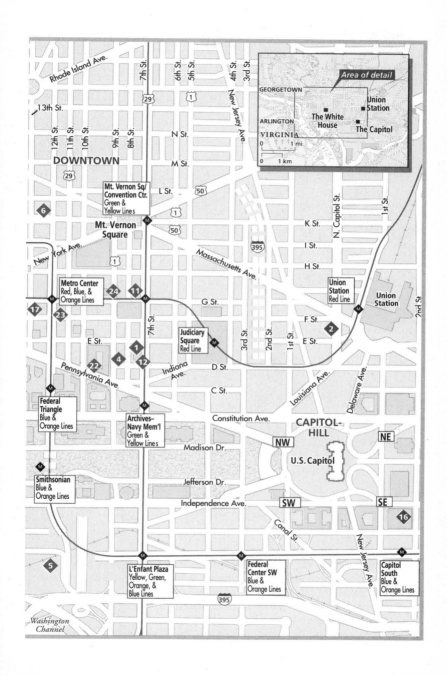

Rhode Island Ave.

7th St.

6th St.

5th St.

4th St.

3rd St.

New Jersey Ave.

29

1

13th St.

12th St.

11th St.

10th St.

9th St.

8th St.

N St.

M St.

DOWNTOWN

29

Mt. Vernon Sq/
Convention Ctr.
Green &
Yellow Lines

L St.

50

1

6

Mt. Vernon
Square

50

K St.

N. Capitol St.

1st St.

New York Ave.

1

Massachusetts Ave.

I St.

H St.

395

Metro Center
Red, Blue, &
Orange Lines

24

11

G St.

Union
Station
Red Line

Union
Station

17

23

Judiciary
Square
Red Line

2nd St.

E St.

Pennsylvania Ave.

22

4

1

12

3rd St.

2nd St.

1st St.

F St.

E St.

2

Indiana
Ave.

D St.

Louisiana Ave.

Delaware Ave.

Federal
Triangle
Blue &
Orange Lines

Archives–
Navy Mem'l
Green &
Yellow Lines

C St.

Constitution Ave.

**CAPITOL-
HILL**

NW

NE

Madison Dr.

Smithsonian
Blue &
Orange Lines

U.S. Capitol

Jefferson Dr.

Independence Ave.

SW

SE

16

Canal St.

New Jersey Ave.

5

L'Enfant Plaza
Yellow, Green,
Orange, &
Blue Lines

Federal
Center SW
Blue &
Orange Lines

Capitol
South
Blue &
Orange Lines

395

Washington
Channel

Area of detail

GEORGETOWN

Union
Station

ARLINGTON

The White
House

VIRGINIA

The Capitol

0   1 mi

0   1 km

dupont circle dining

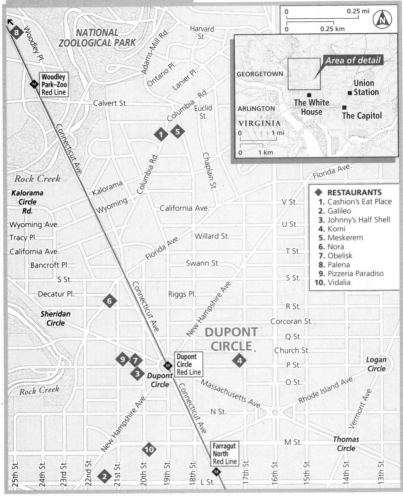

as the Italian, Mexican, and Chinese—meaning Cantonese, primarily—
older diners tend to stick to. And continued immigration naturally means
greater cultural diversity, which is why there are increasing numbers of
African and Russian restaurants in this country.

The Washington palate has become demanding enough (and, to
be frank, the expense accounts have expanded sufficiently) to inspire

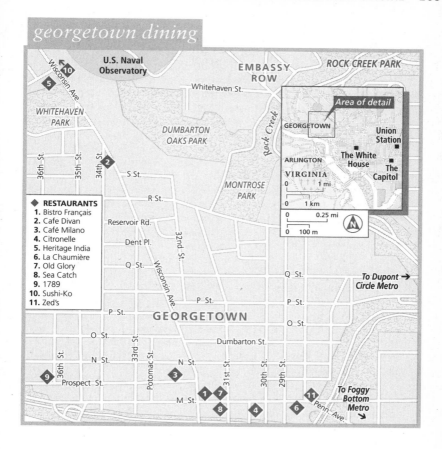

georgetown dining

RESTAURANTS
1. Bistro Français
2. Cafe Divan
3. Café Milano
4. Citronelle
5. Heritage India
6. La Chaumière
7. Old Glory
8. Sea Catch
9. 1789
10. Sushi-Ko
11. Zed's

a surprising number of restaurants from other dining capitals to open branches in the nation's capital, from New York's ultra-haute Lespinasse (closed since the sale of the St. Regis Hotel chain) and super–steak houses **Charlie Palmer Steak, Bobby Van's, BLT Steak,** and **Smith & Wollensky** to Boston's **Olives;** L.A.'s haute-haute **Citronelle** (now Michel Richard's home base); Miami's **Ortanique;** and—albeit one step removed—California's landmark French Laundry, thanks to the hiring of its longtime chef de cuisine, Eric Ziebold, at the Mandarin Oriental Hotel's ambitious **CityZen** restaurant. Strasbourg's three-Michelin-star chef Antoine Westerman created, and frequently checks in on, **Cafe 15** at the Suite L. And although he won't be packing his bags permanently, New York star chef Eric Ripert of the famed Le Bernadin has agreed to oversee the creation of a top-flight restaurant at the Ritz-Carlton downtown.

Though it's a 90-minute drive, Washingtonians gladly claim pride of place for the five-star **Inn at Little Washington** ("Little" because it's in Washington, Virginia), whose chef, Patrick O'Connell, has been admired in print in every culinary journal of note.

And a different sort of Washington generation, a host of chefs who grew up in the kitchens of star chefs Roberto Donna, Jean-Louis Palladin, Mark Miller, O'Connell, and Yannick Cam, as well as the better hotel restaurants and those same old-time classicists, have kitchens and restaurants of their own. More collegial than contentious, these young chefs are developing a style that plays up regional flavors: Chesapeake Bay seafoods; Virginia, West Virginia, and Maryland game; and the wealth of organic produce and herbs being raised for this market. Organic-cooking maven Nora Pouillon may not be able to claim all the credit for the number of menus with additive-free or heart-healthy entries, but as founder of a national organic network, the Chefs Collective, she has inspired many other chefs to demand the freshest ingredients. (And, of course, Washington is the home of the Center for Science in the Public Interest, the folks who went right on and told you that fettuccine Alfredo was just as bad for you as you always knew it was.)

That an increasing number of these young chefs are choosing to remain in the D.C. area is itself proof of the audience's sophistication. Among them are Todd Gray of **Equinox,** Jacques Ford of **Matisse,** Damien Salvatore of **Persimmon,** Eric McCoy of **Café Bethesda,** Jason Tepper of **La Miche,** Jonathan Krinn of **2941,** Johnny Monis of **Komi,** and Barbara Black of **Addie's.**

Even more intriguing is the number of chefs who, like Ziebold, have been lured away from big-name eateries in Manhattan to positions in the nation's capital. Frank Morales, formerly of New York's Union Pacific, is now at **Zola,** in the very hot new-downtown MCI Center district. Jamie Leeds, a veteran of such Manhattan hot spots as Tribeca Grill and Union Square Cafe, created **15 ria** in the Washington Terrace Hotel (1515 Rhode Island Avenue NW; ☎ 202-742-0015). Gray Koonz protégé Jon Mathieson left Lespinasse to open **Poste Moderne** in the Hotel Monaco and Mina Newman, formerly of Layla, created a menu of hilariously irreverent recipes at Restaurant in Tysons Corner (though both have since moved on). Just to name a few.

New Restaurant Districts

Along with the awakening of the Washington palate has come a rearrangement of the dining map. While **Georgetown** remains a busy shopping and nightlife area, it is no longer the dominant restaurant strip. The revitalized downtown arts and entertainment district from the Verizon Center at Seventh Street west to about Tenth Street north of Pennsylvania Avenue, known as **Penn Quarter;** the ongoing renaissance of its near-neighbor, the **midtown region** from about Tenth to 20th Streets between F and K; the ethnically mixed **Adams-Morgan** and cutting-edge **U Street/Logan Circle** neighborhoods; and the north-west suburbs—particularly the Asian-polyglot neighborhoods of **Wheaton** and **Bethesda** in Maryland, with their "golden triangles" of restaurants—have all emerged as livelier locations, with **Gaithers-burg** and **Germantown** hot on their heels. At the same time, restaurant dining has become so diversified that one no longer needs to go to the "Little Saigon" neighborhood around Clarendon for very good Viet-namese cooking or to Chinatown for dim sum; the "older" Little Ethiopia of Adams-Morgan has given way to a second, more lively neighborhood around 14th and U streets. In fact, it's hard to imagine that anyone living in the Washington metropolitan area is more than a mile from five or six different ethnic restaurants.

Not surprisingly, given its long lobbying habits, Washington has also rediscovered the big steak and big-ticket business meals, and put the two together at the 21st-century version of the saloon, the platinum-card chophouse. These are now so popular, and their formats so similar—prime beef, creamed spinach, Caesar salad, and hefty wine lists—that we have simply listed the biggest cow palaces and their wine menus later in this chapter, under "The Best . . .," so that you can browse by location.

No (Or Some) Butts About It

They said it couldn't be done—that restaurants couldn't survive no-smoking bans—but New York City, and more pointedly the next-door-neighboring suburbs of Maryland, including restaurant centers Bethesda, Rockville, Wheaton, Silver Spring, and so on—have proved "them" wrong. As of New Year's Day 2007, more than good resolutions are putting cigarettes into the trash: the District of Columbia's no-smoking regulations now cover restaurants and night-clubs, and even many bars. And, as mentioned in Part Four, Arriving and Getting Oriented, the ban also covers the public transportation you may be planning to take to the restaurant. (Be alert: dedicated smokers often snatch out and light cigarettes on the escalators of the Metro.) The ban also covers most restrooms, so you'll likely have to step outdoors for a smoke.

There is no such regulation in the Virginia suburbs, but many restaurants are already moving to restrict smoking. The general trend has been to try to limit smoking to the lounge areas of restaurants or establishing separate nonsmoking dining rooms, but if you prefer to avoid any secondhand chemicals (or aromas), it would be a good idea to call ahead.

Industry Trends

With the slowing of the 1990s stock market and a few hints of eco-nomic "correction," Washington's restaurant industry took a hit from customer efforts to economize. Several of the finer establish-ments, caught between the pincers of exorbitant rent and declining expense-account business—most notably Lespinasse and its successor, Timothy Dean's; Provence; and Aquarelle—closed, and several have had to take advantage of Chapter 11 or similar restructuring.

Nevertheless, the first time since the late Jean-Louis Palladin was in his **Watergate** heyday, Washington is home to first-rank creative chefs who are continually rethinking and reconstructing food, notably José Andrés (**Café Atlántico/Minibar, Jaleo, Zaytinya,** and now **Oyamel**), Fabio Trabocchi (**Maestro**), Marou Outtawa of **Farrah Olivia** (600 Franklin Street, Old Town Alexandria; ☎ 703-778-2233), Eric Ziebold (**City Zen**), and Michel Richard of **Citronelle.** There are still plenty of expensive menus, though, from which to choose, and some of the most influential chefs in the area have opened what might be called "off-the-rack" restaurants (cafes, bistros, even pizzerias) in addition to their designer menus—sometimes inside the same rooms. Roberto Donna of **Galileo** has both a more upscale section, the **Laboratorio del Galileo,** and a less formal **Osteria del Galileo** inside the restaurant plus an outdoor grill in summer (all currently under renovation). **Restaurant Eve** has a "tasting room," its own seasonal outdoor grill, and a bistro, with separate menus; **Palena** has a bar menu distinct from its main list, as do Butterfield 9, Le Paradou, and Marcels, among others.

And even beyond that, these chefs are creating second restaurants to exploit the less formal bistro craze: Michel Richard has opened **Michel Richard Central** on Pennsylvania Avenue; Robert Wiedmaier of Marcel's is opening **Beck's** on K Street in spring 2007; Cathal Armstrong of Restaurant Eve has opened a Dublin-style fish-and-chippery called **Eamonn's** in Old Town Alexandria; and Roberto Donna has opened **Bebo** in Crystal City.

The 100 or so restaurant profiles that follow are intended to give you a sense of the atmosphere and advantages of a particular establishment as well as its particular cuisine. None should be taken as gospel, because one drawback of Washington's new appetite for adventure is that restaurants open and close—and promising chefs play musical kitchens—with breathtaking speed. This also means that we have for the most part profiled only restaurants that have been in operation for at least a year, or that have chefs with such strong track records that they are of special interest. Some very promising restaurants have been omitted because they were just opening at press time (see page 275); other rather well-known ones may not have come up to scratch. (We tend to avoid chain restaurants, though it's not a hard-and-fast rule.) We have also in some cases given preference to establishments with easy subway or cab access, since we realize that the majority of visitors to Washington stay (if not with family or friends) in the major business or tourist areas.

And, blame it on yuppie consciousness, gourmet magazine proliferation, or real curiosity, the increased interest in the techniques of cooking has also produced a demand for variety, constantly challenging presentations, and guaranteed freshness. Consequently, many of the fancier restaurants change their menus or some portion thereof every day, and many more change seasonally, so the specific dishes recommended at particular places may not be available on a given night. Use these critiques as a guide, an indication of the chef's interests and strengths, rather than a hard-and-fast ordering chart. And truth to tell, the wait staff often has pretty good advice, if you ask sincerely.

The Hotel-dining Scene

When it comes to hotel dining rooms, Washington contradicts the conventional wisdom that hotel restaurants are not worth seeking out. In D.C. many of the better chefs are working in hotels. This is a mutually beneficial arrangement, allowing the chefs to concentrate on managing a kitchen, not a business, and providing an extra attraction to potential clients. Since Washington's hotels count on a great deal of expense-account business, they generally offer menus on the expensive side. In addition to the restaurants profiled, we recommend those at the Willard Inter-Continental (**Willard Room**), the Hay-Adams Hotel (**Lafayette**), the Four Seasons (**Seasons**), **Jefferson Hotel,** the Madison Hotel (**Palette**), One Washington Circle (**Circle Bistro**), the River Inn (**Dish**), **Café Mozu** and **CityZen** at the Mandarin Oriental, the Hyatt Regency in Reston (**Market Street Grill**), Sofitel (**Café 15**), Washington Terrace (**15 ria**), the Hotel Monaco (**Poste Moderne Brasserie**), Henley Park (**Coeur de Lion**), the Ritz-Carlton in Georgetown (**Fahrenheit**), the Fairmont (**The Bistro**), and the Mayflower (**Café Promenade**), as well as those noted in "The New Downtown Dining" (page 272).

The Inns and Outs

The Washington area is also blessed with some very fine country inns within a couple hours' drive. We have actually profiled only the nationally famous **Inn at Little Washington** in this edition, but in addition, if you're taking a longer vacation and want to see the countryside (or perhaps are gliding around the wineries of Civil War battlefields), we would recommend looking into such restaurants as **Antrim 1844** in Taneytown, **Willow Grove** in Orange, **Foti's** in Culpeper, the **Turning Point Inn** in Urbana, **Four and Twenty Blackbirds** in Flint Hill, the **Hermitage Inn** in Clifton, and the **Ashby Inn** in Paris. And the Goose Run restaurant at the luxurious **Salamander Inn and Spa,** opening in summer 2007, will be run by executive chef Todd Gray, chef-owner of Equinox (profiled later).

Diners' Special Needs

The following profiles attempt to address the special requirements of diners who use wheelchairs or leg braces. Because so many of Washington's restaurants occupy older buildings and row houses, options for wheelchair users are unfortunately limited. In most cases, wheelchair access is prevented right at the street, but many restaurants offering easy entrance to the dining room keep their restrooms up or down a flight of stairs. In either case, we list them as having "no" disabled access. "Fair" access suggests that there is an initial step or small barrier to cross, or that passage may be a bit tight, but that once inside the establishment, dining is comfortable for the wheelchair user. Again, hotel dining rooms are good bets—the same wide halls and ramps used for baggage carts and deliveries serve wheelchair users as well. Newer office buildings and mixed shopping and entertainment complexes have ramps and elevators that make them wheelchair accessible; the ones above subway stations even have their own elevators.

We have not categorized restaurants as offering vegetarian or other restricted diets because almost all Washington restaurants now offer either vegetarian entrees on the menu or will make low-salt or low-fat dishes on request, although some are particularly amenable to doing this, and we have said so. Use common sense: a big-ticket steak house is unlikely to have many nonmeat options (though many have become accustomed to making veggie plates), but since few countries in the world feature as much meat in their cuisine as America, most ethnic cuisines are good bets for vegetarians.

PLACES TO SEE FACES

WASHINGTON MAY NOT REALLY BE HOLLYWOOD on the Potomac (so many movie stars come to town to lobby for their pet causes, it's getting close), but there are celebrity faces aplenty. Consequently, out-of-towners often list "famous people" right after the Air and Space Museum on the required-viewing list. Since being seen is part of the scene—and getting star treatment is one of the perks of being famous—celebrities tend to be visible in dependable places, particularly at lunch.

In the past several years, **Café Milano** in Georgetown has emerged as probably the single most celeb- and socialite-centric restaurant, with politicians, diplomats, royals, and even media-types. Ditto performers—the new décor is based on the best-known roles of regular Placido Domingo (that was before the maestro invested in Zengo, but he's still a good customer). However, with all the sports and big-arena concerts at Verizon Center, and the equally hot competition for restaurant buzz in the Penn Quarter, celeb spotting is easy there: see "The New Downtown Dining," page 272.

In this town, at least, politics not only makes strange bedfellows, it makes strange dining partners. Which may be why it wasn't all that odd that Democratic bad boy James Carville and his Republican-commentator wife, Mary Matalin, tried opening their own neo-Southern restaurant, West 24 (it didn't get enough bipartisan support). Top Democratic lobbyist Tommy Boggs and former GOP heavy Haley Barbour have more expertise in getting along; and their flagrantly pork-barrel sort of steak house, the **Caucus Room** (Ninth and D streets; ☎ 202-393-1300), is a hit. Café Milano also gets bipartisan support; you might spot Vice President Dick Cheney to one side, and FOB Terry McAuliffe up front, and Senator John Kerry on the patio. (On the other hand, in restaurants as in politics, it's the PR, stupid; a spate of stories tagging lobbyist Jack Abramoff brought a swift end to his upscale steak-and-sushi bar Signatures.)

The venerable steak-and-lobster **Palm** (1225 19th Street NW; ☎ 202-293-9091), with its wall-to-wall caricatures of famous customers and its bullying waiters, is still a popular media and legal-eagle hangout. **The Capital Grille** (601 Pennsylvania Avenue NW; ☎ 202-737-6200) is particularly well located; only a short stroll from the Capitol grounds, it serves as both boardroom and back room for the GOP. After the party's 1995 gala, a couple hundred of the black-tie guests dropped by the Grille for drinks and cigars. Only a few nights before, when a clutch of budget-crunching Republican senators had peeked in after last call, the general manager had rolled up his sleeves and grilled a couple dozen strategic burgers. The Grille gets its share of odd couples, too: back in more collegial times, then-Senators Lauch Faircloth, a right-leaning Republican, and liberal intellectual Senator Pat Moynihan (now deceased) arrived for dinner, Faircloth announcing the pair to staff as "the redneck and the aristocrat."

Galileo, the flagship restaurant of Washington's *capo di tutti capi* chef Roberto Donna, has its opposing political icons, Ted Kennedy and Bob Dole. **Nora** was an early favorite of the Clintons and Gores; **Bistro Bis,** near Union Station (and the Senate office buildings) is another power-broker hangout (15 E Street, NW; ☎ 202-661-2700); especially look out at breakfast and lunch. The old-clubby **Monocle** (107 D Street NE; ☎ 202-546-4488), the unofficial transfer point between the Senate and its office buildings, draws the Republican money men (815 Connecticut Avenue, NW; ☎ 202-659-3727).

The elegant Raj-redux **Bombay Club** across the street from the White House attracts politico-turned-commentator George Stephanopoulos and John Glenn. Senator Frank Lautenberg of New Jersey (who wrote the bill banning smoking on airlines), Stephanopoulos, D'Amato, and former senator Bob Kerrey (new president of New School University in New York) have taken the steak-and-stogie course at **Les Halles** (1201 Pennsylvania Avenue NW; ☎ 202-347-6848).

Pol-watchers should also check out **Two Quail** (320 Massachusetts Avenue NE; ☎ 202-543-8030) for congresswomen or **La Colline** for committee staffers. **Bullfeathers** is full of national committee staffers from both parties (410 First Street SE; ☎ 202-543-5005). **The Hay-Adams** (One Lafayette Square NW; ☎ 202-638-6600) is where the power breakfast was born, starring White House staff and federal bureaucrats.

Treasury and White House staffs crowd the neighboring **Old Ebbitt Grill,** ☎ 202-347-4801, the **Occidental Grill** (1475 Pennsylvania Avenue

NW; ☎ 202-783-1475), and **Georgia Brown's.** And, among the low-profile politicians and working press who frequent the **Market Inn,** especially in shad roe season, are rumored to be CIA and other professionals incognito (200 E Street SW; ☎ 202-554-2100).

World Bank and OAS suits lunch at **Taberna del Alabardero;** corporate write-offs go to the **Prime Rib** (☎ 2020 K Street NW; ☎ 202-466-8811) and the midtown **Morton's** (L Street and Connecticut; ☎ 202-955-5997).

Oceanaire Seafood Room (see profile, page 324) draws plenty of media faces, including CNN anchor Bernard Shaw and talk-show host Larry King, a number of ABC News staffers, including John Cochran, commentator George Stephanopoulos, Sam Donaldson, and Chris Wallace; radio antihero Oliver North, as well as a number of pro athletes. (The downtown restaurants being so near the Verizon Centre, any of them may sport a jersey or two.)

Tosca has become a sort of unofficial Democratic hangout: regulars include many younger pros from the Kennedy-Shriver-Townsend clan as well as Senator Edward Kennedy (who prefers dining in the kitchen); and longtime presidential alter ego Martin Sheen of NBC's *The West Wing;* and power couple NBC reporter Andrea Mitchell and former Federal Reserve Chairman Alan Greenspan.

THE NEW DOWNTOWN DINING

THE REVIVAL OF THE AREA BETWEEN the power poles of the Capitol and the White House, with the new Convention Center and the Verizon Centre sports arena in between, has produced an astonishing restaurant boom in the downtown area; after all, with all those lobbyists, politicians and sports fans, how could it miss?

Among the best new entries into the downtown dining scene are: **Zaytinya,** an upscale Middle Eastern tapas restaurant from the folks who brought you Jaleo and Café Atlántico; **Zola,** next to the International Spy Museum; the luxe **Le Paradou;** the whimsical **Minibar** at Café Atlántico; **Tosca;** the Nuevo Latino **Oyamel, Butterfield 9, IndeBleu, Oceanaire Seafood Room,** and **Matchbox,** some profiled later. Others include **Finemondo** (1319 F Street NW; ☎ 202-737-3100), a sort of kebab house on the big-steak-house model and offering whole lambs on a day's notice; **Ella's Wood-Fired Pizza** (901 F Street NW; ☎ 202-638-3434); **Chef Geoff's** (1301 Pennsylvania Avenue NW; ☎ 202-464-4461); **Ceiba** (721 14th Street NW; ☎ 202-393-3983), a sort of retro Havana cafe; the New Orleans–homesick **Acadiana** (901 New York Avenue, NW; ☎ 202-408-8848); **Poste Moderne Brasserie** in the Hotel Monaco (555 Eighth Street, NW; ☎ 202-783-6060); the French-Indian **Rasika** (633 D Street NW; ☎ 202-637-1222); and the Latin-Asian **Zengo** (781 Seventh Street NW; ☎ 202-393-2929).

With the influx of boutique hotels has come also the boutique lounges, mostly named simply after the hotels themselves but often serving rather more upscale fare than the traditional bar bites. Longtime local chef John Wabeck was briefly executive chef for three of these (almost too hip) scenes at once, although he gave them slightly different personalities: the more Asian-fusion **Topaz Bar** (1722 N Street NW; ☎ 202-393-3000); the Nuevo Latino–accented **Bar Rouge** (1315 16th Street NW; ☎ 202-232-8000); and **Helix** (1430 Rhode Island Avenue NW; ☎ 202-462-9001). Wabeck has now settled the group's fourth venture in several months, the **Firefly Restaurant** alongside the Hotel Madera (1310 New Hampshire Avenue NW; ☎ 202-861-1310). Actually, it's the fifth venture, as these four all belong to the same group that owns the Hotel Monaco. And despite its periodic changing of the kitchen guard, the restaurant—actually, the fireside parlor, the courtyard, and the several small dining rooms—at the **Tabard Inn** (1739 N Street, NW; ☎ 202-331-8528) remains justifiably popular.

THE RESTAURANTS

OUR FAVORITE WASHINGTON RESTAURANTS

WE HAVE DEVELOPED DETAILED PROFILES for the most interesting and reliable restaurants (in our opinion) in town. Each profile features an easily scanned heading that allows you, in just a second, to check out the restaurant's name, overall star rating, cuisine, cost, quality rating, and value rating.

OVERALL STAR RATING The star rating is an overall rating that encompasses the entire dining experience, including style, service, and ambience in addition to the taste, presentation, and quality of the food. Five stars is the highest rating possible and connotes the best of everything. Four-star restaurants are exceptional, and three-star restaurants are well above average. Two-star restaurants are good. One star is used to indicate an average restaurant that demonstrates an unusual capability in some area of specialization—for example, an otherwise unmemorable place that has great barbecued chicken.

CUISINE This is actually less straightforward than it sounds. A couple of years ago, for example, "pan-Asian" restaurants were generally serving what was then generally described as "fusion" food—Asian ingredients with European techniques, or vice versa. Since then, there has been a pan-Asian explosion in the area, but nearly all specialize in what would be street food back home: noodles, skewers, dumplings, and soups. Modern American sounds pretty broad, and it is—part "new continental," part "regional," and part "new eclectic." Like art, you know it when you see it. Where there are major subdivisions of cuisine, we have tried to put it in the most obvious place; **Marcel's** is Belgian-French, while **Le Mannequin Pis** is definitely Belgian. And Nuevo Latino is distinctly different from traditional Spanish or South American. Again, though, experimentation and "fusion" is ever more common, so don't hold us, or the chefs, to too strict a style.

COST To the right of the cuisine type in the ratings bar is an expense description that provides a comparative sense of how much a complete meal will cost. A complete meal for our purposes consists of an entree with vegetable or side dish and choice of soup or salad. Appetizers, desserts, drinks, and tips are excluded.

Inexpensive	$14 and less per person
Moderate	$15–$30 per person
Expensive	More than $30 per person

QUALITY RATING The food quality is rated on a five-star scale, five being the best rating attainable. The quality rating is based solely on the food served, taking into account taste, freshness of ingredients, preparation, presentation, and creativity. There is no consideration of price. If you want the best food available, and cost is not an issue, look no further than the quality ratings.

★★★★★	Exceptional value; a real bargain
★★★★	Good value
★★★	Fair value; you get exactly what you pay for
★★	Somewhat overpriced
★	Significantly overpriced

VALUE RATING If, on the other hand, you are looking for both quality and value, then you should check the value rating, also expressed in stars. The value ratings are defined as follows:

PAYMENT We've listed the type of payment accepted at each restaurant using the following code: AMEX equals American Express (Optima), CB equals Carte Blanche, D equals Discover, DC equals Diners Club, MC equals MasterCard, JCB equals Japan Credit Bank, T equals Transmedia, and VISA is self-explanatory.

WHO'S INCLUDED Because restaurants are opening and closing all the time in Washington, we have tried to confine our list to establishments with a proven track record over a fairly long period of time. Franchises and national chains are rarely included, although local "chains," restaurant groups of three or four, may be. Newer or changed establishments that demonstrate staying power and consistency will be profiled in subsequent editions. Also, the list is highly selective. Noninclusion of a particular place does not necessarily indicate that the restaurant is not good, but only that it was not ranked among the best in its genre. Detailed profiles of individual restaurants follow in alphabetical order at the end of this part.

UP *and* COMING *at* PRESS TIME

- **Acadiana** 901 New York Avenue NW; ☎ 202-408-8848
- **Agraria** 3000 K Street NW (Washington Harbour); ☎ 202-298-9192
- **Bastille DC** 1201 North Royal Street, Old Town Alexandria, VA; ☎ 703-519-3776
- **Bebo** 2250-B Crystal Drive, Crystal City, VA; ☎ 703-412-5076
- **Beck's** 1101 K Street NW (opening spring 2007)
- **Central Michel Richard** 1101 Pennsylvania Avenue NW; ☎ 202-625-2150
- **D'Acqua** 801 Pennsylvania Avenue NW; ☎ 202-783-7712
- **Farrah Olivia by Morou** 600 Franklin Street, Old Town Alexandria, VA; ☎ 703-778-2233
- **Indigo Landing** 1 Marina Drive, Alexandria, VA; ☎ 703-548-0001
- **PS7** 777 I Street NW; ☎ 202-742-8550
- **Willow** 4301 North Fairfax Drive, Arlington, VA; ☎ 703-465-8800

THE BEST . . .

The Best Afternoon Teas

- **Four Seasons Hotel** 2800 Pennsylvania Avenue NW; ☎ 202-342-0444
- **The Hay-Adams Hotel** One Lafayette Square NW; ☎ 202-638-6600
- **Henley Park Hotel** 926 Massachusetts Avenue NW; ☎ 202-638-5200
- **Jefferson Hotel** 1200 16th Street NW; ☎ 202-347-2200
- **Mandarin Oriental Hotel** 1330 Maryland Avenue SW; ☎ 202-787-6868
- **Park Hyatt Hotel** 24th and M streets NW; ☎ 202-789-1234
- **Ritz-Carlton Hotel** 1150 22nd Street NW; ☎ 202-965-7627
- **The Tea Cozy** 119 South Royal Street, Alexandria, VA; ☎ 703-836-8181
- **Teaism** 400 Eighth Street NW; ☎ 202-638-6010
  2009 R Street NW; ☎ 202-667-3827
- **Willard Inter-Continental** 1401 Pennsylvania Avenue NW; ☎ 202-637-7440

The Biggest Beef Steak Houses

- **Blackie's** 1227 22nd Street NW; ☎ 202-333-1100
- **BLT Steak** 1625 I Street NW; ☎ 202-689-8999
- **Bobby Van's** 809 15th Street NW; ☎ 202-589-0060
- **Capital Grille** 601 Pennsylvania Avenue NW; ☎ 202-737-6200
- **Caucus Room** Ninth and F streets NW; ☎ 202-393-1300

Restaurants by Cuisine, then Star Ratings

CUISINE AND NAME	OVERALL RATING	PRICE RATING	QUALITY RATING	VALUE RATING
AMERICAN (SEE ALSO MODERN AMERICAN AND SOUTHERN)				
Old Ebbitt Grill	★★	Mod	★★½	★★★
BARBECUE				
Old Glory	★★	Mod	★★½	★★★
BELGIAN				
Le Mannequin Pis	★★★	Mod	★★★	★★★½
BURMESE				
Burma	★★½	Inexp	★★½	★★★
CHINESE				
Mark's Duck House	★★½	Inexp	★★★	★★★
ETHIOPIAN				
Meskerem	★★★	Inexp	★★★	★★★½
Zed's	★★	Inexp	★★★	★★★
FRENCH				
Citronelle	★★★★	Very Exp	★★★★	★★
Marcel's	★★★★	Exp	★★★★	★★★
Le Paradou	★★★	Very Exp	★★★½	★★½
L'Auberge Chez François	★★★	Very Exp	★★★½	★★★★
Bistro Bis	★★★	Exp	★★½	★★½
Montmartre	★★★	Mod	★★★½	★★★½
Bistro Français	★★½	Mod	★★½	★★★
Gerard's Place	★★½	Exp	★★★	★★★
La Chaumière	★★½	Mod	★★★	★★★
La Miche	★★½	Mod	★★★	★★½
Tabard Inn	★★½	Mod	★★½	★★★
FRENCH-ASIAN FUSION				
IndeBleu	★★★	Exp	★★★★	★★★
INDIAN				
Indique	★★★	Inexp	★★★½	★★★
Heritage India	★★★	Mod	★★★	★★★
ITALIAN				
Maestro	★★★★★	Very Exp	★★★★	★★★★
Galileo	★★★½	Exp	★★★★	★★★

CUISINE AND NAME	OVERALL RATING	PRICE RATING	QUALITY RATING	VALUE RATING
ITALIAN (CONTINUED)				
Obelisk	★★★½	Exp	★★★★½	★★★★
Tosca	★★★½	Mod	★★★★	★★½
Café Milano	★★½	Exp	★★★	★★
Teatro Goldoni	★★½	Mod	★★★	★★★
JAPANESE				
Sushi-Ko	★★★★½	Mod	★★★★½	★★★★
Kaz Sushi Bistro	★★★½	Mod	★★★★	★★★
Makoto	★★★½	Very Exp	★★★½	★★★½
Tako Grill	★★★½	Inexp	★★★½	★★★
Murasaki	★★★	Mod	★★★	★★★
KOREAN				
Woo Lae Oak	★★★	Mod	★★★½	★★★★
MIDDLE EASTERN				
Zaytinya	★★★½	Mod	★★★½	★★★½
MODERN AMERICAN				
The Inn at Little Washington	★★★★★	Very Exp	★★★★★	★★★★★
CityZen	★★★★	Very Exp	★★★★	★★★
Palena	★★★★	Exp	★★★★½	★★★
Restaurant Eve	★★★★	Very Exp	★★★★	★★★
Komi	★★★½	Very Exp	★★★★	★★★
2941	★★★½	Mod	★★★	★★★★
Vidalia	★★★½	Mod	★★★½	★★★
Butterfield 9	★★★	Very Exp	★★★★	★★★
Colvin Run Tavern	★★★	Exp	★★★½	★★★
Corduroy	★★★	Exp	★★★	★★★
Equinox	★★★	Mod	★★★½	★★★
Grapeseed	★★★	Exp	★★★	★★★
1789	★★★	Exp	★★★★	★★★
Addie's	★★½	Mod	★★★	★★★★
D.C. Coast	★★½	Mod	★★★	★★★
Geranio	★★½	Mod	★★★	★★★
Nora	★★½	Exp	★★★½	★★★
Persimmon	★★½	Mod	★★★★	★★★
Old Angler's Inn	★★	Exp	★★★	★★½

Restaurants by Cuisine/Star Ratings (continued)

CUISINE AND NAME	OVERALL RATING	PRICE RATING	QUALITY RATING	VALUE RATING
NUEVO LATINO				
Café Atlántico/Minibar	★★★★	Mod	★★★★	★★★★
Jaleo	★★★	Mod	★★★	★★★
PAN-ASIAN				
TenPenh	★★½	Mod	★★½	★★½
PIZZA				
Pizzeria Paradiso	★★½	Inexp	★★★	★★★★
PORTUGUESE				
Tavira	★★½	Mod	★★★	★★½
SEAFOOD				
Black's Bar & Kitchen	★★★	Mod	★★★★	★★★★
Kinkead's	★★★	Exp	★★★	★★½
Johnny's Half-Shell	★★½	Inexp	★★½	★★★
Oceanaire Seafood Room	★★	Exp	★★★	★★½
Sea Catch	★★	Mod	★★★	★★½
SOUTHERN				
Cashion's Eat Place	★★★½	Exp	★★★	★★★
Georgia Brown's	★★	Mod	★★★	★★

The Biggest Beef Steak Houses (continued)

- **Charlie Palmer Steak** 101 Constitution Avenue NW; ☎ 202-547-8100
- **Don Shula's** 8028 Leesburg Pike, Tysons Corner, VA; ☎ 703-506-3256
- **Fleming's Steakhouse & Wine Bar** 1960 Chain Bridge Road, Tysons Corner, VA; ☎ 703-442-8384
- **J. Gilbert's** 6903 Old Dominion Drive, McLean, VA; ☎ 703-893-1034
- **Morton's of Chicago** 3251 Prospect Street NW; ☎ 202-342-6258
  8075 Leesburg Pike/Route 7, Tysons Corner, VA; ☎ 703-883-0800
  1050 Connecticut Avenue NW; ☎ 202-955-5997
  1631 Crystal Square Arcade, Arlington, VA; ☎ 703-418-1444
  One Freedom Square, Reston Town Center, Reston, VA; ☎ 703-796-0128
- **Palm** 1225 19th Street NW; ☎ 202-293-9091
  1750 Tysons Boulevard, Tysons Corner, VA; ☎ 703-917-0200
- **Prime Rib** ☎ 2020 K Street NW; ☎ 202-466-8811

CUISINE AND NAME	OVERALL RATING	PRICE RATING	QUALITY RATING	VALUE RATING
SPANISH				
Taberna del Alabardero	★★★	Very Exp	★★★	★★★
TEX-MEX				
Austin Grill	★★	Inexp	★★½	★★★
THAI				
Busara	★★★	Mod	★★★	★★★
Bangkok Garden	★★★	Inexp	★★★	★★★★
Thai Farm	★★★	Inexp	★★★	★★★★
Benjarong	★★½	Inexp	★★★	★★★
Tara Thai	★★	Inexp	★★½	★★★
TURKISH				
Cafe Divan	★★½	Inexp	★★½	★★★★
VIETNAMESE				
Four Sisters (Huong Que)	★★★	Inexp	★★★	★★★★
Green Papaya	★★½	Inexp	★★★	★★
Taste of Saigon	★★	Inexp	★★½	★★★

- **Ruth's Chris Steakhouse** 1801 Connecticut Avenue NW; ☎ 202-797-0033
  724 Ninth Street NW; ☎ 202-393-4488
  7315 Wisconsin Avenue, Bethesda, MD; ☎ 301-652-7877
  2231 Crystal Drive, Crystal City, VA; ☎ 703-979-7275
- **Sam & Harry's** 1200 19th Street NW ☎ 202-296-4333
  8240 Leesburg Pike, Tysons Corner, VA; ☎ 703-448-0088
- **Smith & Wollensky** 1112 19th Street NW; ☎ 202-466-1100

The Freshest Beers (Brewed On-site)

- **Capitol City Brewing Co.** 1100 New York Avenue NW; ☎ 202-628-2222
  2 Massachusetts Avenue NE; ☎ 202-842-2337
  2700 South Quincy Street, Arlington, VA; ☎ 703-578-3888
- **DuClaw Brewing Co.** 16-A Bel Air South Station Parkway, Bel Air, MD;
  ☎ 410-515-3222

Restaurants by Location

AREA AND NAME	OVERALL RATING	PRICE RATING	QUALITY RATING	VALUE RATING	CUISINE
THE NATIONAL MALL					
CityZen	★★★★	V. Exp	★★★★	★★★	Modern American
CAPITOL HILL					
Johnny's Half Shell	★★½	Inexp	★★½	★★★	Seafood
Montmartre	★★	Mod	★★★½	★★★½	French
DOWNTOWN					
Austin Grill	★★	Inexp	★★½	★★★	Tex-Mex
Bistro Bis	★★★	Exp	★★½	★★½	French
Burma	★★½	Inexp	★★½	★★★	Burmese
Butterfield 9	★★★	V. Exp	★★★★	★★★	Modern American
Café Atlántico/Minibar	★★★★	Mod	★★★★	★★★★	Nuevo Latino
Corduroy	★★★	Exp	★★★	★★★	Modern American
D.C. Coast	★★½	Mod	★★★	★★★	Modern American
Equinox	★★★	Mod	★★★½	★★★	Modern American
Georgia Brown's	★★	Mod	★★★	★★	Southern
Gerard's Place	★★½	Exp	★★★	★★★	French
IndeBleu	★★★	Exp	★★★★	★★★	Fr.-Asian Fusion
Jaleo	★★★	Mod	★★★	★★★	Nuevo Latino
Oceanaire Seafood Room	★★	Exp	★★★	★★½	Seafood
Old Ebbitt Grill	★★	Mod	★★½	★★★	American
Le Paradou	★★★	V. Exp	★★★½	★★½	French
Taberna del Alabardero	★★★	V. Exp	★★★	★★★	Spanish
Teatro Goldoni	★★½	Mod	★★★	★★★	Italian
TenPenh	★★½	Mod	★★½	★★½	Pan-Asian
Tosca	★★★½	Mod	★★★★	★★½	Italian
Zaytinya	★★★½	Mod	★★★½	★★★½	Middle Eastern
FOGGY BOTTOM					
Kaz Sushi Bistro	★★★½	Mod	★★★★	★★★	Japanese
Kinkead's	★★★	Exp	★★★	★★½	Seafood
GEORGETOWN					
Austin Grill	★★	Inexp	★★½	★★★	Tex-Mex
Bistro Français	★★½	Mod	★★½	★★★	French
Busara	★★★	Mod	★★★	★★★	Thai
Cafe Divan	★★½	Inexp	★★½	★★★★	Turkish
Café Milano	★★½	Exp	★★★	★★	Italian

AREA AND NAME	OVERALL RATING	PRICE RATING	QUALITY RATING	VALUE RATING	CUISINE
GEORGETOWN (CONTINUED					
Citronelle	★★★★★	V. Exp	★★★★	★★★★	French
Heritage India	★★★	Mod	★★★	★★★	Indian
La Chaumière	★★½	Mod	★★★	★★★	French
Old Glory	★★	Mod	★★½	★★★	Barbecue
Pizzeria Paradiso	★★½	Inexp	★★★	★★★★	Pizza
Rocklands	★½	Inexp	★★½	★★★	Barbecue
Sea Catch	★★	Mod	★★★	★★½	Seafood
1789	★★★	Exp	★★★★	★★★	Modern American
Sushi-Ko	★★★★½	Mod	★★★★½	★★★★	Japanese
Zed's	★★	Inexp	★★★	★★★	Ethiopian
DUPONT CIRCLE/ADAMS-MORGAN					
Cashion's Eat Place	★★★½	Exp	★★★	★★★	Southern
Galileo	★★★½	Exp	★★★★	★★★	Italian
Heritage India	★★★	Mod	★★★	★★★	Indian
Komi	★★★½	V. Exp	★★★★	★★★	Modern American
Marcel's	★★★★	Exp	★★★★	★★★	French
Meskerem	★★★	Inexp	★★★	★★★½	Ethiopian
Nora	★★½	Exp	★★★½	★★★	Modern American
Obelisk	★★★½	Exp	★★★★½	★★★★	Italian
Pizzeria Paradiso	★★½	Inexp	★★★	★★★★	Pizza
Tabard Inn	★★½	Mod	★★½	★★★	French
Vidalia	★★★½	Mod	★★★½	★★★	Modern American
UPPER NORTHWEST					
Indique	★★★	Inexp	★★★½	★★★	Indian
Makoto	★★★½	V. Exp	★★★½	★★★½	Japanese
Murasaki	★★★	Mod	★★★	★★★	Japanese
Palena	★★★★	Exp	★★★★½	★★★	Modern American
MARYLAND SUBURBS					
Addie's	★★½	Mod	★★★	★★★★	Modern American
Austin Grill	★★	Inexp	★★½	★★★	Tex-Mex
Bangkok Garden	★★★	Inexp	★★★	★★★★	Thai
Benjarong	★★½	Inexp	★★★	★★★	Thai
Black's Bar & Kitchen	★★★	Mod	★★★★	★★★★	Seafood
Grapeseed	★★★	Exp	★★★	★★★	Modern American
Jaleo	★★★	Mod	★★★	★★★	Nuevo Latino

Restaurants by Location (continued)

AREA AND NAME	OVERALL RATING	PRICE RATING	QUALITY RATING	VALUE RATING	CUISINE
MARYLAND SUBURBS (CONTINUED)					
La Miche	★★½	Mod	★★★	★★½	French
Le Mannequin Pis	★★★	Mod	★★★	★★★½	Belgian
Old Angler's Inn	★★	Exp	★★★	★★½	Modern American
Persimmon	★★½	Mod	★★★★	★★★	Modern American
Tako Grill	★★★½	Inexp	★★★½	★★★	Japanese
Tara Thai	★★	Inexp	★★½	★★★	Thai
Taste of Saigon	★★	Inexp	★★½	★★★	Vietnamese
Tavira	★★½	Mod	★★★	★★½	Portuguese
Thai Farm	★★★	Inexp	★★★	★★★★	Thai
VIRGINIA SUBURBS					
Austin Grill	★★	Inexp	★★½	★★★	Tex-Mex
Busara	★★★	Mod	★★★	★★★	Thai
Colvin Run Tavern	★★★	Exp	★★★½	★★★	Modern American

The Freshest Beers (Brewed On-site) (continued)

- **Franklin's Restaurant and Brewpub** 5123 Baltimore Avenue, Hyattsville, MD; ☎ 301-927-2740
- **Hops** 3625 Jefferson Davis Highway, Alexandria, VA; ☎ 703-837-9107
- **Gordon Biersch Brewery Restaurant** 900 F Street NW; ☎ 202-783-5454
- **John Harvard's Brewhouse** 1299 Pennsylvania Avenue NW; ☎ 202-783-2739
- **Rock Bottom Restaurant & Brewery** 7900 Norfolk Avenue, Bethesda, MD; ☎ 301-652-1311
- **Growlers** 227 East Diamond Avenue, Gaithersburg, MD; ☎ 301-519-9400
- **Sweetwater Tavern** 14250 Sweetwater Lane, Centreville, VA; ☎ 703-449-1100
- **Virginia Beverage Co.** 607 King Street, Alexandria, VA; ☎ 703-684-5397

The Best Burgers

- **The Brickskeller** 1523 22nd Street NW; ☎ 202-293-1885 810 Seventh Street NW; ☎ 202-289-2030
- **Old Ebbitt Grill** 675 15th Street NW; ☎ 202-347-4801
- **RFD** 810 Seventh Street NW; ☎ 202-289-2030
- **Union Street Public House** 121 South Union Street, Alexandria, VA; ☎ 703-548-1785

AREA AND NAME	OVERALL RATING	PRICE RATING	QUALITY RATING	VALUE RATING	CUISINE
VIRGINIA SUBURBS (CONTINUED)					
Four Sisters (Huong Que)	★★★	Inexp	★★★	★★★★	Vietnamese
Geranio	★★½	Mod	★★★	★★★	Modern American
The Inn at Little Washington	★★★★★	V. Exp	★★★★★	★★★★★	Modern American
Jaleo	★★★	Mod	★★★	★★★	Nuevo Latino
L'Auberge Chez François	★★★	V. Exp	★★★½	★★★★	French
Maestro	★★★★★	V. Exp	★★★★	★★★	Italian
Mark's Duck House	★★½	Inexp	★★★	★★★	Chinese
Restaurant Eve	★★★★	V. Exp	★★★★	★★★	Modern American
Tara Thai	★★	Inexp	★★½	★★★	Thai
Taste of Saigon	★★	Inexp	★★½	★★★	Vietnamese
2941	★★★½	Mod	★★★	★★★★	Modern American
Woo Lae Oak	★★★	Mod	★★★½	★★★★	Korean

The Most Entertaining Décor

- **Busara** 2340 Wisconsin Avenue NW; ☎ 202-337-2340
  8142 Watson Street, McLean, VA; ☎ 703-356-2288
- **Firefly** 1310 New Hampshire Avenue NW; ☎ 202-861-1310
- **Mie N Yu** 3125 M Street NW; ☎ 202-333-6122
- **Pizzeria Paradiso** ☎ 2029 P Street NW; ☎ 202-223-1245
- **Ristorante Filomena** 1063 Wisconsin Avenue NW; ☎ 202-338-8800
- **Tara Thai** 226 Maple Avenue West, Vienna, VA; ☎ 703-255-2467
  4828 Bethesda Avenue, Bethesda, MD; ☎ 301-657-0488
  2071 Rockville Pike (Montrose Crossing), Rockville, MD; ☎ 301-231-9899
  7501-C Leesburg Pike, Tysons Corner, VA; ☎ 703-506-9788
  9811 Washingtonian Boulevard (Rio Centre), Gaithersburg, MD;
  ☎ 301-947-8330
- **Teatro Goldoni** 1909 K Street NW; ☎ 202-955-9494

The Best Family Dining

- **Café Deluxe** 1800 International Drive, Tysons Corner, VA; ☎ 703-761-0600
  4910 Elm Street, Bethesda, MD; ☎ 301-656-3131
- **Guapo's** 4515 Wisconsin Avenue NW; ☎ 202-686-3588
  8498 Centreville Road, Manassas Park, VA; ☎ 703-393-9449
  9811 Washingtonian Boulevard (Rio Centre), Gaithersburg, MD;
  ☎ 301-977-5655

The Best Family Dining (*continued*)

- **Hard Rock Cafe** 999 E Street NW; ☎ 202-737-ROCK
- **Olney Ale House** 2000 Sandy Spring Road (Route 108), Olney, MD; ☎ 301-774-6708
- **Radio Free Italy** 5 Cameron Street (Torpedo Factory), Alexandria, VA; ☎ 703-683-0361

Best Museum Restaurants on the Mall

- **National Air & Space Museum Wright Place Food Court** Sixth Street and Independence Avenue NW; ☎ 202-357-2700 (best for kids)
- **National Gallery of Art Sculpture Garden Pavilion Café** Ninth Street and Constitution Avenue NW; ☎ 202-289-3360
- **National Gallery of Art West Building Garden Court** Sixth Street and Constitution Avenue NW; ☎ 202-216-2480
- **National Museum of American History Ice Cream Parlor** 14th Street and Constitution Avenue NW; (closed for renovation)
- **National Museum of the American Indian Mitsitam Cafe** Fifth Street and Independence Avenue NW; ☎ 202-633-7044
- **National Museum of Natural History Fossil Cafe** Tenth Street and Constitution Avenue NW; ☎ 202-357-2700 (best for kids)
- **United States Holocaust Museum Cafe** 100 Raoul Wallenberg Place (15th Street NW); ☎ 202-488-6151 (vegetarian, kosher)

The Best Pizza

- **Ella's Wood-Fired Pizza** 901 F Street NW; ☎ 202-638-3434
- **Matchbox** 1713 H Street NW; ☎ 202-289-4441
- **Pizzeria Paradiso**
  2029 P Street NW; ☎ 202-223-1245
  3282 M Street NW, Georgetown; ☎ 202-337-1245
- **Potomac Pizza** 19 Wisconsin Circle, Chevy Chase, MD; ☎ 301-951-1127
- **Primi Piatti** 2013 I Street NW; ☎ 202-223-3600
- **Two Amys** 3715 Macomb Street and Wisconsin Avenue NW; ☎ 202-885-5700
- **Zio's** 9083 Gaither Road, Gaithersburg, MD; ☎ 301-977-6300

The Best Raw Bars

- **Black's Bar & Kitchen** 7750 Woodmont Avenue, Bethesda, MD; ☎ 301-652-6278
- **Blue Point Grill** 600 Franklin Street, Alexandria, VA; ☎ 703-739-0404
- **Kinkead's** 2000 Pennsylvania Avenue NW; ☎ 202-296-7700
- **McCormick & Schmick's**
  11920 Democracy Drive, Reston, VA; ☎ 703-481-6600
  7401 Woodmont Avenue, Bethesda, MD; ☎ 301-961-2626
  1652 K Street NW; ☎ 202-861-2233
  8484 Westpark Drive, Tysons Corner, VA; ☎ 703-848-8000

901 F Street NW ☎ 202-639-9330
- **Oceanaire Seafood Room** 1201 F Street NW; ☎ 202-347-BASS
- **Old Ebbitt Grill** 675 15th Street NW; ☎ 202-347-4801
- **Sea Catch** 1054 31st Street NW; ☎ 202-337-8855

The Best Serious Bar Food

- **Butterfield 9** 600 14th Street NW; ☎ 202-289-8810
- **Citronelle** 3000 M Street NW (in the Latham Hotel); ☎ 202-625-2150
- **Marcel's** 2401 Pennsylvania Avenue NW; ☎ 202-296-1166
- **Palena** 3529 Connecticut Avenue NW; ☎ 202-537-9250
- **Restaurant Eve** 110 South Pitt Street, Old Town Alexandria, VA; ☎ 703-706-0450
- **Restaurant Kolumbia** 1801 K Street NW; ☎ 202-331-5551
- **Teatro Goldoni** 1909 K Street NW; ☎ 202-955-9494

The Best Sunday Brunches

- **Bombay Club** 815 Connecticut Avenue NW; ☎ 202-659-3727
- **Café Atlántico** 405 Eighth Street NW; ☎ 202-393-0812 (Saturday only)
- **The Four Seasons Hotel Garden Terrace** 2800 Pennsylvania Avenue NW; ☎ 202-342-0444
- **Firefly** 1310 New Hampshire Avenue NW; ☎ 202-861-1310
- **Georgia Brown's** 950 15th Street NW; ☎ 202-393-4499
- **The Irish Inn at Glen Echo** MacArthur Boulevard and Clara Barton Parkway, Glen Echo, MD; ☎ 301-229-6600
- **Jaleo** 480 Seventh Street NW; ☎ 202-628-7949
  7271 Woodmont Avenue, Bethesda, MD; ☎ 301-913-0003
  2250-A Crystal Drive, Arlington, VA; ☎ 703-413-8181
- **The Kennedy Center Roof Terrace** Virginia and New Hampshire avenues NW; ☎ 202-416-8555
- **Kinkead's** 2000 Pennsylvania Avenue NW; ☎ 202-296-7700
- **Melrose** 24th and M streets NW (Park Hyatt Hotel); ☎ 202-955-3899
- **New Heights** 2317 Calvert Street NW; ☎ 202-234-4110
- **Old Angler's Inn** 10801 MacArthur Boulevard, Potomac, MD; ☎ 301-299-9070
- **Old Ebbitt Grill** 675 15th Street NW; ☎ 202-347-4801

The Best Sushi Bars

- **Chopsticks** 1073 Wisconsin Avenue NW; ☎ 202-338-6161
- **Ginza** 1009 21st Street NW; ☎ 202-833-1244
- **Ha Ku Ba** 706 Center Point Way, Gaithersburg, MD; ☎ 301-947-1283
- **Hama Sushi** 2415 Centreville Road, Herndon, VA; ☎ 703-713-0088
- **Kaz Sushi Bistro** 1915 I Street NW; ☎ 202-530-5500
- **Miyagi** 6719 Curran Street, McLean, VA; ☎ 703-893-0116

The Best Sushi Bars (*continued*)

- **Momo Taro** 16051 Frederick Road/Route 355, Rockville, MD;
  ☎ 301-963-6868
- **Murasaki** 4620 Wisconsin Avenue NW; ☎ 202-966-0023
- **Niwano Hana** 887 Rockville Pike (Wintergreen Plaza), Rockville, MD;
  ☎ 301-294-0553
- **Sakana** ☎ 2026 P Street NW; ☎ 202-887-0900
- **Sake Club** 2635 Connecticut Avenue NW; ☎ 202-332-2711
- **Sushi-Ko** 2309 Wisconsin Avenue NW; ☎ 202-333-4187
- **Sushi Taro** 1503 17th Street NW; ☎ 202-462-8999
- **Tachibana** 6715 Lowell Avenue, McLean, VA; ☎ 703-847-1771
- **Tako Grill** 7756 Wisconsin Avenue, Bethesda, MD; ☎ 301-652-7030
- **Tono Sushi** 2605 Connecticut Avenue NW; ☎ 202-332-7300
- **Yoko** 2946-J Chain Bridge Road, Oakton, VA; ☎ 703-255-6644
- **Yosaku** 4712 Wisconsin Avenue NW; ☎ 202-363-4453

The Best with Tables in the Kitchen

- **Bistro Bis** 15 E Street NW; ☎ 202-661-2700
- **Charlie Palmer Steak** 101 Constitution Avenue NW; ☎ 202-547-8100
- **Citronelle** 3000 M Street NW (Latham Hotel); ☎ 202-625-2150
- **Galileo** 1110 21st Street NW; ☎ 202-293-7191 (closed for renovation)
- **The Kennedy Center Roof Terrace** Virginia and New Hampshire avenues NW;
  ☎ 202-416-8555
- **Maestro** 1700 Tysons Boulevard (Ritz-Carlton), Tysons Corner, VA;
  ☎ 703-821-1515
- **Melrose** 24th and M streets NW (Park Hyatt Hotel); ☎ 202-955-3899
- **Nora** 2132 Florida Avenue NW; ☎ 202-462-5143

The Best Views

- **CityZen** 1330 Maryland Avenue NW (Mandarin Oriental Hotel);
  ☎ 202-787-6006
- **Hotel Washington Roof** 515 15th Street NW; ☎ 202-638-5900
- **Lafayette** 16th and H streets NW (Hay-Adams Hotel); ☎ 202-638-2570
- **New Heights** 2317 Calvert Street NW; ☎ 202-234-4110
- **Perry's** 1811 Columbia Road NW; ☎ 202-234-6218
- **Indigo Landing** 1 Marina Drive, Alexandria, VA; ☎ 703-548-0001
- **Sequoia** 3000 K Street NW; ☎ 202-944-4200

The Best Wine Lists

- **Blue Duck** 24th and M streets NW (Park Hyatt Hotel); ☎ 202-419-6755
- **Charlie Palmer Steak** 101 Constitution Avenue NW; ☎ 202-547-8100
- **Citronelle** 3000 M Street NW (Latham Hotel); ☎ 202-625-2150
- **Colvin Run Tavern** 8045 Leesburg Pike, Tysons Corner, VA; ☎ 703-356-9500

- **Corduroy**   1201 K Street NW (Sheraton Four Points Hotel);
  ☎ 202-589-0699
- **D.C. Coast**   1401 K Street NW; ☎ 202-216-5988
- **Fiore di Luna**   1025-I Seneca Road (Seneca Square), Great Falls, VA;
  ☎ 703-444-4060
- **Galileo**   1110 21st Street NW; ☎ 202-293-7191 (closed for renovation)
- **Gerard's Place**   915 15th Street NW; ☎ 202-737-4445
- **Grapeseed**   4865-C Cordell Avenue, Bethesda, MD; ☎ 301-986-9592
- **The Inn at Little Washington**   Middle and Main streets, Washington, VA;
  ☎ 540-675-3800
- **Jaleo**   480 Seventh Street NW; ☎ 202-628-7949
  7271 Woodmont Avenue, Bethesda, MD; ☎ 301-913-0003
  2250-A Crystal Drive, Arlington, VA; ☎ 703-413-8181
- **Kinkead's**   2000 Pennsylvania Avenue NW; ☎ 202-296-7700
- **L'Auberge Chez François**   332 Springvale Road, Great Falls, VA;
  ☎ 703-759-3800
- **Le Paradou**   678 Indiana Avenue NW; ☎ 202-347-6780
- **Maestro**   1700 Tysons Boulevard (Ritz-Carlton), Tysons Corner, VA;
  ☎ 703-821-1515
- **Obelisk**   2029 P Street NW; ☎ 202-872-1180
- **Paya Thai**   8417 Old Courthouse Road, Vienna, VA; ☎ 703-883-3881
- **Sam and Harry's**   1200 19th Street NW; ☎ 202-296-4333
- **Seasons**   2800 Pennsylvania Avenue NW (Four Seasons Hotel);
  ☎ 202-944-2000
- **Taberna del Alabardero**   1776 I Street NW; ☎ 202-429-2200
- **2941**   2941 Fairview Park Drive, Falls Church; ☎ 703-270-1500
- **Vidalia**   1990 M Street NW; ☎ 202-659-1990
- **Zola**   800 F Street NW; ☎ 202-654-0999

RESTAURANT PROFILES

Addie's   ★★½

MODERN AMERICAN	MODERATE	QUALITY ★★★	VALUE ★★★★

**11120 Rockville Pike, Rockville; ☎ 301-881-0081;
www.addiesrestaurant.com**   Maryland Suburbs

Reservations Not available Saturday and Sunday. **When to go** Late lunch, midweek. **Entree range** $9–$27. **Payment** VISA, MC, AMEX, DC. **Service rating** ★★★½. **Friendliness rating** ★★★★. **Metro** Grosvenor-Strathmore. **Parking** Free lot. **Bar** Beer and wine. **Wine selection** Good. **Dress** Casual, informal. **Disabled access** Good. **Customers** Locals, area business. **Hours Lunch:** Monday–Friday, 11:30 a.m.–2:30 p.m.; Saturday, noon–2:30 p.m. **Dinner:** Monday–Thursday, 5:30–9:30 p.m.; Friday, 5:30–10 p.m.; Saturday 5–10 p.m.; Sunday 5–9 p.m.

SETTING AND ATMOSPHERE   This is a simple suburban house turned into a cartoon fantasy, a family dine-in kitchen of the future past: rooms brightly painted primary blue, red, and yellow; collections of oddball clocks; plastic place mats; doorknobs mounted as coat hooks; and antique stoves as serving tables. And the simple white oval platters actually come as a pleasant surprise in this era of florid china.

HOUSE SPECIALTIES   Playful tastes starring the likes of grilled marinated quail and goat cheese (appetizer or entree-sized); seared scallops in mango sauce or black olive couscous and pesto; soft-shell crabs over linguini; duck confit with baby beets and parsnips; crab cakes over polenta; ostrich with onion compote; cornmeal-crusted oysters with roasted corn and prosciutto; seared tuna with shrimp wontons.

OTHER RECOMMENDATIONS   Variations of pescado Andalucia, fish (halibut, bass, or rockfish) with mussels, potatoes, and merguez sausage stew; updated duck cassoulet; shrimp taco salad; grilled vegetables with real flavor.

ENTERTAINMENT AND AMENITIES   Outdoor seating (though with a close view of Rockville Pike traffic).

SUMMARY AND COMMENTS   Owners Jeff and Barbara Black are simply having fun with food, and it shows: the menu is trendy and smart without being overly showy; flavorings are distinctive but not overwhelming; salt is carefully considered. When the urge for comfort food strikes one of them, it's apt to be roast chicken or pork chops. Lunch is much simpler, geared to the working/shopping crowds from White Flint Mall across the street—sandwiches (including a fried-oyster sandwich), chili, and salads. The Blacks actually have a sort of family empire now, including Blacks Bar and Kitchen (profiled); Black Salt, a combination fish market and seafood restaurant; and the eclectic Victorian bistro Black Market.

Austin Grill   ★★

TEX-MEX	INEXPENSIVE	QUALITY ★★½	VALUE ★★★

750 E Street NW, Downtown; ☎ 202-393-3776
2404 Wisconsin Avenue NW, Georgetown; ☎ 202-337-8080
7278 Woodmont Avenue, Bethesda, MD; ☎ 301-656-1366
8430-A Old Keene Mill Center, West Springfield, VA; ☎ 703-644-3111
801 King Street, Old Town Alexandria, VA; ☎ 703-684-8969
www.austingrill.com

Reservations For parties of 10+. **When to go** Late afternoon, late night. **Entree range** $7–$18. **Payment** VISA, MC, AMEX, D, DC. **Service rating** ★★★. **Friendliness rating** ★★★. **Metro** *E Street:* Metro Center; *Woodmont Avenue:* Bethesda. **Parking** Street. **Bar** Full service. **Wine selection** Fair. **Dress** Casual. **Disabled access** Poor; all bathrooms are upstairs. **Customers** Local, student. **Hours Brunch:** Saturday and Sunday, 11 a.m.–3 p.m. **Lunch/dinner** Monday, 11:30 a.m.–10:30 p.m.; Tuesday–Thursday, 11:30 a.m.–11 p.m.; Friday and Saturday, 11 a.m.–midnight; Sunday, 11 a.m.–10:30 p.m.

SETTING AND ATMOSPHERE   Hot adobe pastels, Crayola-colored tile, buffalo and lizard stenciling, angular art-joke graphics, and Tex-Mex pun art and T-shirts in funky vinyl-booth roadhouse settings. Great Texas music on the PA. If not a mom-and-pop joint, it's a friends' franchise: one of the original prep cooks who started at age 19 in Georgetown became the head chef in Bethesda.

HOUSE SPECIALTIES Carnitas (braised pork marinated with garlic, oranges grilled with peppers and onions); chicken enchiladas with tomatillo sauce; grilled steak taco; hand-rolled chicken tamales with Texas chili; grilled fish of the day; real all-beef chunky chili; "Austin special enchilada" with three sauces; grilled fish.

OTHER RECOMMENDATIONS Margaritas; chile-flavored ribeye; fajita platters; lime-marinated chicken breast; barbecued brisket.

SUMMARY AND COMMENTS The perfect antidote for designer chili cuisine (not that these are plain-Jane spots; in fact, they're corporate cousins of the slick-chic Jaleo). The original Georgetown branch made its first friends just from the smell of the smoker out back. The hot-hot sauces—choose from four—were the local endorphin addict's drugs before chiles were cool, so to speak. Incidentally, the Springfield location has been experimenting with serving breakfast, but a fairly straight version.

Bangkok Garden ★★★

THAI	INEXPENSIVE	QUALITY ★★★	VALUE ★★★★

4906 St. Elmo Avenue, Bethesda; ☎ 301-951-0670;
www.bkkgarden.com   Maryland Suburbs

Reservations Accepted on weekends. **When to go** Anytime. **Entree range** $6–$15. **Payment** VISA, MC, AMEX, D. **Service rating** ★★★½. **Friendliness rating** ★★★★. **Metro** Bethesda. **Parking** Street, free lot after 7 p.m.; valet Thursday through Saturday. **Bar** Full service. **Wine selection** House. **Dress** Casual. **Disabled access** Fair. **Customers** Local, ethnic. **Hours** Sunday–Thursday, 11 a.m.–10:30 p.m.; Friday and Saturday, 11 a.m.–11 p.m.

SETTING AND ATMOSPHERE Small, cheery, and so crowded with brass and plaster animals—giraffes, elephants, temple Foo dogs, peafowl, deer—that the enshrined young Buddha resembles a Thai St. Francis of Assisi. Enlarged and framed colorful Thai currency and portraits of the royal family are also prominent.

HOUSE SPECIALTIES A rich, skin-and-fat duck in five-flavor sauce; fat "drunken" noodles with beef; *hoy jawh* (a crispy pork-and-crab appetizer cake); squid with basil and chile (unusual, almost purely squid and scarce vegetable filler); the tangy rather than searing seafood combination.

OTHER RECOMMENDATIONS Soft-shell crabs in one of five sauces, including one very light version with asparagus and oyster sauce; steamed crab dumplings; shrimp in chile oil.

SUMMARY AND COMMENTS Though relatively low-profile amid the Thai boom—with Americans, that is; it's very popular within the Thai community—this family-run restaurant rewards regular attendance and obvious interest because some of the best dishes aren't on the English menu, but are available to anyone who knows to ask. A particularly delicious example is the

"Thai steak tartare," a beef version of a Thai pork classic that is rich with garlic, cilantro, and basil and served with a steaming basket of "sticky rice" intended to be used as the utensil: take a pinch of rice—about a tablespoon—slightly flatten it and grasp a bite of meat with it and pop the whole morsel into your mouth. At $8, it's a steal of a meal.

Benjarong   ★★½

| THAI | INEXPENSIVE | QUALITY ★★★ | VALUE ★★★ |

885 Rockville Pike (Wintergreen Plaza), Rockville; ☎ 301-424-5533; www.benjarongrestaurant.com   Maryland Suburbs

Reservations Suggested. **When to go** Anytime. **Entree range** $9–$14. **Payment** VISA, MC, AMEX, D, DC. **Service rating** ★★★. **Friendliness rating** ★★★★. **Metro** None nearby. **Parking** Free lot. **Bar** Full service. **Wine selection** House. **Dress** Informal. **Disabled access** Good. **Customers** Local, ethnic. **Hours** Monday–Thursday, 11:30 a.m.–10 p.m.; Friday and Saturday, 11:30 a.m.–10:30 p.m.; Sunday, 5–10 p.m.

SETTING AND ATMOSPHERE A simple but soothing room decorated with off-white grass wallpaper, pink linens, black lacquer chairs, and a few Thai carvings and figurines.

HOUSE SPECIALTIES Duck with asparagus (in season); spicy duck and coriander salad; mussels steamed in lemongrass and spices; sliced beef filet in red-wine sauce; fresh squid sautéed with chiles and basil; and the best *pra pla mug*—a sort of squid ceviche with lime juice and chiles—even in this Thai-smart town.

OTHER RECOMMENDATIONS Steamed whole snapper with delicate scallions and ginger sauce or crispy fried flounder; spicy shrimp in red curry sauce; red curry duck; seafood combination chow foon noodles; a rattle-shaped chicken-drummette appetizer stuffed with ground chicken and pork; soft-shell crabs in a choice of sauces; and a sort of barbecue beef in chile paste with scallions.

SUMMARY AND COMMENTS Benjarong (the name refers to a type of multi-colored Thai porcelain) is closed awaiting new digs, but the kitchen staff used the hiatus for a trip to Thailand to sharpen their skills. Many of the dishes here are Southern Thai, meaning the curries are creamier and there's a good pork satay on the menu. There are also several good vegetarian choices, including a delicately peppery sautéed watercress. If you're uncertain of spice levels, inquire; this is a hospitable and accommodating establishment.

Bistro Bis   ★★★

| FRENCH | EXPENSIVE | QUALITY ★★½ | VALUE ★★½ |

15 E Street NW; ☎ 202-661-2700; www.bistrobis.com   Downtown

Reservations Recommended. **When to go** Late lunch, early or late dinner. **Entree range** $31–$50. **Payment** VISA, MC, AMEX, D, DC. **Service rating** ★★★. **Friendliness rating** ★★★½. **Metro** Union Station. **Parking** Valet after 5:30, pay lot. **Bar** Full service. **Wine selection** Good. **Dress** Business, informal. **Disabled access** Good. **Customers** Political/media biz, food trendies. **Hours** **Breakfast:**

Every day, 7–10 a.m. **Brunch:** Saturday and Sunday, 11:30 a.m.–2:30 p.m. **Lunch:** Monday–Friday, 11:30 a.m.–2:30 p.m. **Dinner:** Every day, 5:30–10:30 p.m.

SETTING AND ATMOSPHERE Its name is short for "bistro," and like that offhand joke, it's sleek, chic, and a touch oblique, its long space divided into a series of step-down semi-detached dining "suites" off a hallway. The dark old Tiber Creek Pub has been transformed into a very blond-wood and etched-glass complex that somehow makes you feel that your companions may be billing you by the hour: zinc-topped bar, cigar-bar mezzanine with lobbylike chairs, and an almost voyeuristic display of exposed-steel kitchen countertop. Even the fireplace has changed from London pubby to L.A. clubby.

HOUSE SPECIALTIES Intriguingly idiosyncratic semiclassic French fare: tangy steak tartare topped with cornichon fans and served on super-crisp garlic potato chips (appetizers); pan-roasted monkfish wrapped in cured ham with apples and Calvados; rabbit with mustard sauce; braised veal short ribs; huge and tender scallops; and the more traditional bistro-esque steak 'n' fries, sweetbreads, duck confit, etc.

OTHER RECOMMENDATIONS Roast poultry, in generous portions—a half hen even at lunchtime. Game specials are carefully tended, too.

SUMMARY AND COMMENTS "Bis" can also mean an encore, but while this may be the second fine production from the team of Sallie and Jeff Buben of Vidalia (see later in this section), it resembles that neo-Southern favorite only in its refusal to see traditional fare as limiting. The quantity of food is not so unusual in this business-expense era, but the delicacy of seasoning and the staff's light hand with rich sauces make it hard to leave much on the plate. The all-French wine list has some fine bargains on it, especially for those willing to look beyond the warhorse burgundy or chablis labels.

Bistro Français ★★½

FRENCH	MODERATE	QUALITY ★★½	VALUE ★★★

3124 M Street NW; ☎ 202-338-3830; www.bistrofrancaisdc.com
Georgetown

Reservations Recommended. **When to go** Pre- or post-theater. **Entree range** $15–$26 Brunch $20. **Payment** VISA, MC, AMEX, DC. **Service rating** ★★★. **Friendliness rating** ★★★. **Metro** Foggy Bottom–GWU. **Parking** Street (validated parking for 2 hours). **Bar** Full service. **Wine selection** House. **Dress** Casual. **Disabled access** Good. **Customers** Local, ethnic. **Hours** Every day, 11 a.m.–3 a.m.; Friday and Saturday until 4 a.m. **Brunch:** Sunday, 11 a.m.–3 p.m.

SETTING AND ATMOSPHERE This old reliable hasn't changed much since the word "bistro" was new to Washington—hanging pots, rotisserie spits, frankly well-used flatware, and clanking trays. In other words, just right.

HOUSE SPECIALTIES This is the sort of place where as nice as the menu is—especially Dover sole, coq au vin, its signature spit-roasted chicken—the daily specials are even better: for instance, duck confit, roast game birds, or lamb with artichokes.

OTHER RECOMMENDATIONS   The steak 'n' fries here is probably the standard against which all others should be measured. And there are fixed-price lunch, $15, and pre-theater fixed dinner menus for $20, including wine.

SUMMARY AND COMMENTS For all its many pleasures—its famous late-night service and the especially telling fact that many local chefs eat here after-hours—it sometimes seems as if this old favorite gets the Rodney Dangerfield treatment from the fashionable crowds, and is feeling a little bedraggled in response.

Black's Bar & Kitchen ★★★

SEAFOOD	MODERATE	QUALITY ★★★★	VALUE ★★★★

**7750 Woodmont Avenue, Bethesda; ☎ 301-652-6278;
www.blacksbarandkitchen.com**   Maryland Suburbs

Reservations Recommended. **When to go** Anytime. **Entree range** $16–$29. **Payment** VISA, MC, AMEX, DC. **Service rating** ★★★. **Friendliness rating** ★★★½. **Metro** Bethesda. **Parking** Pay lot, street meters, valet. **Bar** Full service. **Wine selection** Good house list. **Dress** Business, casual. **Disabled access** Yes. **Customers** Local, business. **Hours Lunch:** Monday–Friday, 11:30 a.m.–2:30 p.m.; Sunday brunch, 11 a.m.–2:30 p.m. **Dinner:** Monday–Thursday, 5:30–10 p.m.; Friday and Saturday, 5–11 p.m.; Sunday 5:30– 9:30 p.m. Closed Tuesday.

SETTING AND ATMOSPHERE Following an extensive, and expensive ($2 million), renovation, this formerly funky fish house is a stunning, upscale grill with sleek patio and pond, black glass facade with "Hell's Kitchen" red logo, burgundy glass dividers in the bar, and Tuscan-mural dining room with a wine cellar as its centerpiece, an advertisement for the 250-plus label wine list. The oyster bar and communal table are hot happy-hour properties.

HOUSE SPECIALTIES Twice-cooked chicken (poached, then deep-fried); sesame-crusted oysters; Portuguese-style roasted cod with chorizo and kale; Addie's steamed mussels; a South-Med take on tuna with fennel, olives, tomato, artichoke, and lemon oil over polenta.

OTHER RECOMMENDATIONS Any of a half-dozen wood-grilled options, including rockfish, spice-crusted duck, lamb loin, and a double pork chop the size of a small cleaver.

SUMMARY AND COMMENTS Jeff Black (see listing for Addie's, page 287) and executive chef Mallory Buford have abandoned some culinary fashion frills in favor of a bold, not-quite-retro take on comfort food; who could resist corn cakes with green tomato jam? Light fare is available at the bar all afternoon.

Burma ★★½

BURMESE	INEXPENSIVE	QUALITY ★★½	VALUE ★★★

740 Sixth Street NW, Suite 200 (upstairs); ☎ 202-638-1280   Downtown

Reservations Accepted. **When to go** Anytime. **Entree range** $6–$8. **Payment** VISA, MC, AMEX, D, DC. **Service rating** ★★★½. **Friendliness rating** ★★★. **Metro** Gallery Place–Chinatown. **Parking** Lot. **Bar** Beer and wine. **Wine selection**

House. **Dress** Casual, informal. **Disabled access** Yes, but call ahead. **Customers** Ethnic South Asian, local, tourist. **Hours Lunch:** Monday–Friday, 11 a.m.–3 p.m. **Dinner:** Every day, 6–10 p.m.

SETTING AND ATMOSPHERE A modest and unobtrusive second-floor warren with only a handful of native art on the walls to advertise its ethnicity.

HOUSE SPECIALTIES *Kaukswe thoke,* a tangy noodle dish with ground shrimp, cilantro, red pepper, and peanuts; pickled green tea–leaf salad, a slightly sour, spicy slaw with caramelized onions and peanuts dressed in a green tea pesto; squid with ham and scallions; a chile-spiked tofu-and-shrimp stir-fry; and an almost soul-food version of mustard greens with shrimp, pork, or chicken.

OTHER RECOMMENDATIONS Gold fingers, strips of squashlike calabash in a peppery dipping sauce; chile- and mango-flavored pork; a macrobiotic delight of substantial dried tofu with cruciferous veggies; roast duck (requires 24 hours' notice).

SUMMARY AND COMMENTS Using familiar ingredients found at any Asian grocery, this Burmese holdout manages to turn out flavors surprisingly distinct from its near relatives: not so "fishy" (no fermented fish sauce or soy) or seafood-conscious as Vietnamese, less purely peppery and more sour-tangy than Thai, and with the concentrated tea and smoke background of classic Chinese and Japanese cuisine. Disabled patrons should call ahead to make sure the elevator is unlocked. Incidentally, this place is a remarkable bargain: prices haven't changed in years. And it's fast—one of the best pre-concert stops in the MCI Centre/Shakespeare Theatre circuit.

Busara ★★★

THAI	MODERATE	QUALITY ★★★	VALUE ★★★

2340 Wisconsin Avenue NW, Georgetown; ☎ 202-337-2340;
8142 Watson Street, McLean, VA; ☎ 703-356-2288; www.busara.com

Reservations Recommended. **When to go** Before 7:30 p.m. or after 9:30 p.m. **Entree range** $7–$17; market price higher. **Payment** VISA, MC, AMEX, D, DC. **Service rating** ★★★½. **Friendliness rating** ★★★. **Metro** None nearby. **Parking** Street, lot, valet after 6 p.m. **Bar** Full service. **Wine selection** Fair. **Dress** Informal. **Disabled access** No. **Customers** Local, ethnic. **Hours Lunch:** *Georgetown and McLean:* Monday–Friday, 11:30 a.m.–3 p.m.; Saturday and Sunday, 11:30 a.m.– 4 p.m. **Dinner:** *Both locations:* Sunday–Thursday, 5–10:30 p.m.; Friday and Saturday, 5–11 p.m.

SETTING AND ATMOSPHERE These Thai siblings are aggressively and cheekily modern. The décor of molded hard black rubber, brushed steel, slate, and heavily lacquered flame-streaked tabletops looks as if it were created by a former hot rod customizer—not to mention the ice-blue neon overhead (*busara* means "blue topaz") and post-Pop art. Outside, a partially covered patio curves around a miniature, but elegant, Japanese garden with a fountain. The Tysons Corner branch is even brighter.

HOUSE SPECIALTIES Kanom Jeeb (steamed pork, crabmeat dumplings served with a Thai soy sauce), crispy fried soft-shell crabs topped with a choice of chile and garlic, black beans and mushrooms, or celery, onion and curry; roasted quail with asparagus and oyster sauce; cellophane noodles with three kinds of mushrooms; marinated pork satay with both a tomato-peanut sauce and a chile-spiked vinegar dip; duck in red curry; Thai bouillabaisse in coconut milk; country-style lamb curry.

OTHER RECOMMENDATIONS Tiger shrimp grilled over watercress; vegetarian pad thai; soft-shell crabs and whole flounder. The Tysons branch has a grill that turns out chicken, lean pork, and assorted fresh fish and shellfish as well.

SUMMARY AND COMMENTS These are Siamese grins with the emphasis on presentation as much as preparation and a lightened-up attitude toward greens and veggies that makes them crisp and filling. A wide variety of spicing is represented (the chile-pod symbols next to menu items are fairly reliable for gauging heat; the Tysons branch sticks to the more familiar stars), and extra sauces or peppers are easy to obtain. Even nicer, there is no MSG in anything.

Butterfield 9 ★★★

MODERN AMERICAN	VERY EXPENSIVE	QUALITY ★★★★	VALUE ★★★

600 14th Street NW; ☎ 202-289-8810; www.butterfield9.com Downtown

Reservations Recommended. When to go Anytime. Entree range $22–$37; fixed price, $35–$65. Payment VISA, MC, AMEX, DC. Service rating ★★★★. Friendliness rating ★★★½. Metro Metro Center or Gallery Place. Parking Valet, lots, street. Bar Full service. Wine selection Very good. Dress Business casual. Disabled access Good. Customers Locals, business, pre-theater. Hours Lunch: Monday–Friday, 11:30 a.m.–2:30 p.m. Dinner: Sunday–Thursday, 5:30–10 p.m.; Friday–Saturday, 5:30–11 p.m.

SETTING AND ATMOSPHERE Cool, buttery interior with multiple levels that offer semiprivate sensation; nice mezzanine.

HOUSE SPECIALTIES Multicourse meals with several amuse-bouches, including vegetarian and seafood menus (plus upscale bar fare). Specific dishes of note include butter-poached baby lobster with fennel purée and cherry jus; scallop-crusted halibut with sweet-and-sour endive; asparagus soup with lemon crème fraîche; farro risotto with tempura squash blossom; creamy clam-and-scallop seviche with yuzu vinaigrette.

OTHER RECOMMENDATIONS Seared escolar (white tuna); ricotta gnocchi with baby peas and pea vines; ostrich dusted with ground Szechuan peppercorns.

SUMMARY AND COMMENTS This good-looking restaurant has had a checkered career, but under Chef Michael Harr it seems to have finally settled into a three-star (and promising more) groove. The combinations are freshly conceived and precisely balanced, and while portions initially seem small, even the five-course meals come with one or two amuse-bouches and sweets.

Café Atlántico/Minibar ★★★★

NUEVO LATINO	MODERATE	QUALITY ★★★★	VALUE ★★★★

405 Eighth Street NW; ☎ 202-393-0812; www.cafeatlantico.com
Downtown

Reservations Recommended. **When to go** Anytime. **Entree range** $9–$25; *Minibar:* fixed price, $95. **Payment** VISA, MC, AMEX, DC. **Service rating ★★★**. **Friendliness rating ★★★**. **Metro** Archives, Gallery Place. **Parking** Street; valet at dinner, $10. **Bar** Full service. **Wine selection** Renowned. **Dress** Casual. **Disabled access** Good. **Customers** Local, ethnic. **Hours Lunch:** Monday–Friday, 11:30 a.m.– 2.30 p.m.; Saturday, 11:30 a.m.–1:30 p.m. **Dinner:** Sunday–Thursday, 5–10 p.m.; Friday and Saturday, 5–11 p.m.; *Minibar:* Seatings at 6 and 8:30 p.m. only.

SETTING AND ATMOSPHERE A very stylish salon, like the living room of an art collector: brilliant fabrics, large and vibrant paintings, loftlike balconies and windows, mosaics, and richly oiled wood. The clientele tends to match the décor—very vibrant, very "on," and frequently very loud.

HOUSE SPECIALTIES Foie gras soup with floating corn and chanterelle "island"; seared salmon with cauliflower and quinoa; scallops with coconut rice, ginger and squid; duck confit with baby spinach, pepitas, and passion fruit. Upstairs at the Minibar, it's a chef's tasting menu that may top 30 items.

OTHER RECOMMENDATIONS The Saturday "Latino dim sum" brunch, with 25–30 tapas-sized dishes from $1.95 to $9 (deluxe); or pre-theater dinner, $22.

SUMMARY AND COMMENTS Café Atlántico is riding two waves at once: location and cuisine. In the heart of the arts-intelligentsia neighborhood around the Shakespeare Theatre and Lansburg Building, it's also the first major restaurant in this area to specialize in *cocina nueva*, the Latin version of New Continental—lighter fare, more fashionably presented, and, depending on your perspective, less homey and more expensive than the Central and South American originals. Founding chef José Andrés, winner of numerous culinary awards, has designed the menus for Jaleo, Zaytinya, and the new Oyamel as well. This is really two restaurants in one: the four-star rating should be read as a three-star for Café Atlántico and a five-star for Minibar—if you're into the most playful cooking. Inspired by his mentor, New Catalonian star chef Ferran Adria, Andreas and executive chef Katsuya Fukushima have designed, or, rather, decon- structed, such chemistry-set wizardry as hot-and-cold foie gras soup; "cappuccino" wrapped in cotton candy; feta-water linguini; splinter-sized fried fish in a London-style cone the size of your little finger; test-tube mojitos; gazpacho "poppers;" and cherry tomatoes on a needle of mozza- rella cream to be shot into your mouth. Though Minibar's seating is currently limited to six, meaning that advance reservations are essential, plans are underway to expand. Meanwhile, Fukushima is carrying a little more of the Minibar fun to the downstairs menu.

Cafe Divan ★★½

TURKISH	INEXPENSIVE	QUALITY ★★½	VALUE ★★★★

1834 Wisconsin Avenue NW; ☎ 202-338-1747; www.cafedivan.com
Georgetown

Reservations Recommended. **When to go** Thursdays for whole marinated rotisserie. **Entree range** $5–$16. **Payment** VISA, MC. **Service rating** ★★★★. **Friendliness rating** ★★★★. **Metro** None nearby. **Parking** Street. **Bar** Full service. **Wine selection** Many Turkish bottlings. **Dress** Business, casual. **Disabled access** Good. **Customers** Locals, homesick Middle Eastern diplomats. **Hours** Monday–Friday, 11 a.m.–10:30 p.m.; Saturday and Sunday, 11 a.m.–11 p.m.

SETTING AND ATMOSPHERE A remarkably (and unusually) bright and sunny triangular corner, with windows winging out on both sides, with polished Brazilian cherry flooring, Turkish tile, and pomegranate accents.

HOUSE SPECIALTIES Eggplant-smothered lamb shank; the *meze* platter of feta, hummus, taramasalata, and stuffed grape leaves. *Doner kebab,* thin-sliced layers of marinated lamb and veal alternately rolled on a spit and grilled, is a weekend special at most Turkish restaurants, but here it's available at every meal.

OTHER RECOMMENDATIONS *Slahmacun* (Turkish flatbread pizza) topped with chopped lamb and tomatoes or a variety of other toppings; *manti* (the beef-stuffed and yogurt-topped dumplings common to Eastern Asia); a lamb-and-chicken-kebab combo.

SUMMARY AND COMMENTS While not the most accessible in terms of location—the busy stretch of upper Georgetown is rife with restaurants and diners (and residents) struggling for parking—Cafe Divan has made itself a neighborhood favorite by dint of cheery service and Turkish fare far beyond the oily standards.

Café Milano ★★½

ITALIAN	EXPENSIVE	QUALITY ★★★	VALUE ★★

3251 Prospect Street NW; ☎ 202-333-6183; www.cafe-milano.com
Georgetown

Reservations Strongly suggested. **When to go** Late lunch, late dinner. **Entree range** $14–$37. **Payment** VISA, MC, AMEX, DC. **Service rating** ★★★½. **Friendliness rating** ★★★½. **Metro** None nearby. **Parking** Street, pay lots. **Bar** Full service. **Wine selection** Good. **Dress** Business, hip informal. **Disabled access** Through rear entrance. **Customers** Local, embassy. **Hours Lunch:** Every day, 11:30 a.m.–4 p.m. **Dinner:** Monday, Tuesday, and Sunday, 4–11 p.m.; Wednesday–Saturday, 4 p.m.–midnight. **Brunch:** Sunday, 11 a.m.–3 p.m.

SETTING AND ATMOSPHERE A cross between a haute couturier's salon and a Milan disco, with a subway map painted on the ceiling—and new a portrait of Placido Domingo as El Cid, too (all of which makes for interesting philosophical speculation on the direction Italian interests have taken since the days of the Sistine Chapel). At Bice, where owner Franco Nuschese was manager, the shadowboxes held wallpaper samples; here they frame the even hip-jokier designer ties—presumably from his closet, as he never seems to be wearing one—and limited-edition scarves. And the pastas are named after designers. There's a terrace for warm-weather dining and a prettier-than-usual long bar.

HOUSE SPECIALTIES   Ravioli Cavalli (veal-and-spinach-stuffed ravioli in a butter sage sauce with shaved porcini mushroom); zucchini-and-basil-filled half-moon pasta with fresh tomato air-dried ricotta cheese; assorted grilled seafood, calamari, Mediterranean cuttlefish, shrimp and turbot with lemon, olive oil, and arugula; and for the big boys, steaks and chops with real Italian flavor, no Chicago nakedness. There are even light little pizzas, and lighter courses are available late.

Cashion's Eat Place   ★★★½

NEW SOUTHERN	EXPENSIVE	QUALITY ★★★	VALUE ★★★

1819 Columbia Road NW; ☎ 202-797-1819; www.cashioneatplace.com
Dupont Circle/Adams-Morgan

Reservations Recommended. **When to go** Anytime. **Entree range** $19–$35. **Payment** VISA, MC, AMEX. **Service rating** ★★★. **Friendliness rating** ★★★★. **Metro** Woodley Park–Zoo/Adams-Morgan. **Parking** Valet $5. **Bar** Full service. **Wine selection** Good. **Dress** Business, casual. **Disabled access** Not wheelchair accessible. **Customers** Locals, foodies. **Hours Brunch:** Sunday, 11:30 a.m.–2:30 p.m. **Dinner:** Tuesday and Sunday, 5:30–10 p.m.; Wednesday–Saturday, 5:30–11 p.m.

SETTING AND ATMOSPHERE   A deliberately low-key, upscale family-style cafe (see the black-and-white photos of partners Ann Cashion and John Fulchino) in a multiethnic neighborhood that draws its clientele from far and wide (and young and old), even though it's a little pricey for the area (which, admittedly, is rapidly yuppifying).

HOUSE SPECIALTIES   Saddle of rabbit stuffed with veal, ham and truffles; braised pork with greens; duck confit; fried sweetbreads over spinach; duck with foie gras.

OTHER RECOMMENDATIONS   Roast free-range chicken; curried mussels; fried seafood; almost any pork dish.

SUMMARY AND COMMENTS   Ann Cashion, a Mississippi native, has made this Southern cuisine-at-the-crossroads establishment a showplace for new Southern fare, meaning that she sees it as the American version of an Italian trattoria: all regional produce, all seasonal, all straightforward, but Continental in terms of combining ingredients—the cornbread and wild mushrooms, the rabbit with truffles, and plenty of vegetables, a luxury oddly missing from many Washington plates. *Note:* The menu changes daily, so take "seasonal" seriously. Cashion is one of Washington's several regional James Beard Award winners.

Citronelle (aka Michel Richard Citronelle) ★★★★★

Latham Hotel, 3000 M Street NW; ☎ 202-625-2150; www.citronelledc.com Georgetown

Reservations Required. **When to go** Lunch, before 9 p.m. **Entree range** Lunch, $12–$38; prix-fixe dinner, $125. **Payment** VISA, MC, AMEX, D, DC, JCB, CB. **Service rating** ★★½. **Friendliness rating** ★★★★. **Metro** Foggy Bottom–GWU. **Parking** Valet. **Bar** Full service. **Wine selection** *Wine Spectator* Award. **Dress** Jackets at dinner. **Disabled access** Excellent. **Customers** Local, tourist, business. **Hours Breakfast:** Every day, 6:30–10:30 a.m. **Brunch:** 10:30 a.m.–3:30 p.m. on Easter, Mother's Day, and Thanksgiving. **Lunch:** Monday–Friday, noon–2 p.m. **Dinner:** Sunday–Thursday, 6:30–10 p.m.; Friday, 6:30–10:30 p.m.; Saturday, 6–10:30 p.m.

SETTING AND ATMOSPHERE Using a series of small level shifts and cutaway ceilings, the designers of this pretty but not showy establishment have made the space seem both intimate and expansive. The upstairs lounge is classic flannel grey and green; the downstairs rooms have a more classic look. Clearly, the star attractions are the exposed kitchen and its six chefs, two preppers, and salad chef—and the show does go on, sometimes unreasonably slowly.

HOUSE SPECIALTIES Although listed as French because of Chef Michel Richard, this could just as well be called "Modern American," "eclectic," or simply flamboyant. Among his greatest inspirations have been a faux osso buco with veal cheeks and a potato "bone"; rabbit and foie gras–stuffed cannelloni; cuttlefish "fettuccine" with baby beets; sweetbread and foie gras sausage; a very nutrition-of-the-millennium fricassee of sweetbreads, snails, and soybeans; rabbit puzzle dishes mixing loin, limb, and rack of ribs; sautéed foie gras; braised veal in various forms.

SUMMARY AND COMMENTS L.A. star chef Michel Richard has now made this his flagship and he has become paterfamilias to Washington Big Five chefs (no physical insult intended), and in many ways his personal playground. Inspired by—and in turn inspiring—other creative and engaging chefs including Minibar's José Andrés and Maestro's Fabio Trabocchi, when it's good, it's very very good. Real food-mag addicts should go for the six-course tasting menu—if they can write off the tab. *Note:* At press time, Richard was preparing to open a less formal restaurant, Central Michel Richard, at 1101 Pennsylvania Avenue NW.

CityZen ★★★★

1330 Maryland Avenue NW, in the Mandarin Oriental Hotel; ☎ 202-787-6006; www.cityzenrestaurant.com The National Mall

Reservations Strongly recommended. **When to go** Anytime. **Entree range** Fixed-price menus, $75–$90; à la carte entrees, $21–$33. **Payment** VISA, MC, AMEX, D, DC. **Service rating** ★★★★. **Friendliness rating** ★★★. **Metro** Smithsonian. **Parking** Valet. **Bar** Full service. **Wine selection** Top flight. **Dress**

Business, dressy casual. **Disabled access** Very good. **Customers** Foodies, power brokers, arts benefactors, special-occasion couples, platinum-card business parties. **Hours** Tuesday–Thursday, 6–9:30 p.m.; Friday and Saturday, 5:30–9:30 p.m.; closed Sunday and Monday.

SETTING AND ATMOSPHERE The hotel bows to feng shui principles, so the name—half urban, half Zen—fits well. It's a very sleek and showy L-shaped space, with 20-foot-high ceilings; a wall of fire behind the bar; a long, exposed kitchen; and a cool stone- and putty-colored interior with tangerine lanterns and chocolate leather banquettes.

HOUSE SPECIALTIES The menu changes monthly, but the dash and push-the-envelope style are constants. Sometimes the trick is too cute (a *shabu-shabu* of foie gras in lukewarm stock) or the service illogically elaborate (the waiter offers a choice of black salt or *sel de mer* while already sprinkling the dish), but when the food is good, it's very, very good. There's a three-course tasting menu ($75), a five-course tasting menu ($90), and a five-course vegetarian menu ($80), but everything comes with extras such as *amuse-bouche;* the kitchen's signature miniature Parker House rolls, served in a box like fine tea; miniature truffles, and more. Look for organ meats such as lamb's brains and liver, grilled or pan-crisped seafood, and game birds such as quail meticulously stuffed with sweetbreads and chard. Most dishes have almost-iconoclastic condiments: grain-mustard *sabayon,* Manchego-cheese emulsion, celery root–horseradish tapenade, and the like, but always in supporting roles.

OTHER RECOMMENDATIONS Rabbit in any treatment (a recent trio plate combined a tiny rack, a spoonful of diced leg meat, and a slice of loin); rich but concise shoat belly; vegetarian choucroute with roasted baby cabbage and "melted" Brussels sprouts; and artisanal cheese.

SUMMARY AND COMMENTS A three-course menu is available in the bar or lounge for $45, although sometimes the staff seems reluctant to admit it. Some hungrier patrons feel the portions are a little small for the price, but the eventual total seems generous. Culinarily speaking, this is one of the city's star attractions.

Colvin Run Tavern ★★★

MODERN AMERICAN	EXPENSIVE	QUALITY ★★★½	VALUE ★★★

8045 Leesburg Pike, Tysons Corner, Vienna; ☎ 703-356-9500; www.colvinrun.com   Virginia Suburbs

Reservations Recommended. **When to go** Lunch, early dinner. **Entree range** $21–$37. **Payment** VISA, MC, AMEX, D, DC. **Service rating ★★★★. Friendliness rating ★★★★. Metro** None nearby. **Parking** Valet. **Bar** Full service. **Wine selection** Very good. **Dress** Business, Friday casual. **Disabled access** Good. **Customers** Local power-lunchers, business diners, platinum-card romantics. **Hours Lunch:** Monday–Friday, 11:30 a.m.–2:30 p.m. **Dinner:** Monday–Thursday, 5:30–10 p.m.; Friday and Saturday, 5:30–10:30 p.m.; Sunday, 5–9 p.m.

SETTING AND ATMOSPHERE This is something of a concept restaurant, where four regions—Nantucket, the Shenandoah, Charleston, and Maine—are each represented by décor areas and menu items. It's an unobtrusively good-looking restaurant, with a fireplace in the lounge and a gracious marble bar (which wraps around the wine room) and those "regional" touches (flagstone in the Shenandoah, etc.), but décor is background—a welcome relief, actually. This is a very busy neighborhood, so expect to adjust to peak hours.

HOUSE SPECIALTIES The menu changes almost constantly, but look for such offerings as squab with potato gnocchi; Zinfandel-braised short ribs; veal cheeks; stuffed leg of lamb rolled to the table and sliced; and similar cart service for venison, rack of veal, lamb, and so on, depending on the market.

OTHER RECOMMENDATIONS Pan-roasted rockfish; seared scallops with sherry-lemon; crispy sweetbreads; rabbit–foie gras terrine, and rabbit with sweetbreads. Menu changes daily or often.

SUMMARY AND COMMENTS A number of food and wine publications, in and outside the area, have taken note of Colvin Run as one of Washington's best newer restaurants, and with reason. It's the second child of chef Bob Kinkead of the eponymous Kinkead's downtown. And while he is not in the kitchen (and in fact the menu, under former Kinkead's sous-chef Jeff Gaetjen, is quite different, being in heavy carno-territory), he keeps a close eye on quality.

Corduroy ★★★

MODERN AMERICAN	EXPENSIVE	QUALITY ★★★	VALUE ★★★

Sheraton Four Points Hotel, 1201 K Street NW; ☎ 202-589-0699; www.corduroydc.com **Downtown**

Reservations Recommended. **When to go** Anytime. **Entree range** $16–$41. **Payment** VISA, MC, AMEX, D, DC. **Service rating** ★★★½. **Friendliness rating** ★★★★. **Metro** McPherson Square. **Parking** Street, pay lots, valet. **Bar** Full service. **Wine selection** Very good. **Dress** Business, Friday casual. **Disabled access** Good. **Customers** Business, food-conscious commuters. **Hours Breakfast:** Monday–Friday, 6:30–10:30 a.m.; Saturday and Sunday, 7–11 a.m. **Lunch:** Every day, noon–2:30 p.m. **Dinner:** Sunday–Friday, 5:30–10:30 p.m.; Saturday, 5:30–11 p.m.

SETTING AND ATMOSPHERE Dark and earthy—mahogany with wheat and egg-plant accents—but hospitable, with views of the kitchen and the bar to provide bustle.

HOUSE SPECIALTIES Goat cheese in potato-crust tarte over roasted-red-pepper coulis; pan-seared halibut with corn and chanterelles; buffalo with mushroom ravioli; wild striped bass with chanterelles and Chinese long beans.

OTHER RECOMMENDATIONS Soft-shell crabs and tangy unripe grapes; veal cheeks osso buco; roast duck breast with turnips, bok choy, and fig sauce.

SUMMARY AND COMMENTS Chef Tom Power has been through the kitchens of Citronelle and the Old Angler's Inn, but seems most at home with his own menu. He uses local and seasonal ingredients to good effect—thankfully, a growing movement in Washington—and even his more elaborate dishes have a becoming modesty of presentation, so they're easy for all comers to accept. For solo diners, the bar menu ranges from casual salads to a nice lobster salad sandwich and a few pastas. (Note that weekend lunch is bar menu only.)

D.C. Coast ★★½

MODERN AMERICAN	MODERATE	QUALITY ★★★	VALUE ★★★

1401 K Street NW; ☎ 202-216-5988; www.dccoast.com Downtown

Reservations A virtual necessity. **When to go** Late lunch, dinner. **Entree range** $14–$30. **Payment** VISA, MC, AMEX, D, DC, T. **Service rating** ★★★½. **Friendliness rating** ★★★★. **Metro** McPherson Square. **Parking** Valet after 5 p.m. ($5 minimum), pay lots. **Bar** Full service. **Wine selection** Very good. **Dress** Business, informal. **Disabled access** Good. **Customers** Business, tourists. **Hours Lunch:** Monday–Friday, 11:30 a.m.–2:30 p.m. **Dinner:** Monday–Thursday, 5:30–10:30 p.m.; Friday and Saturday, 5:30–11 p.m.; Sunday, closed.

SETTING AND ATMOSPHERE The restaurant's name is a sort of joke on chef Jeff Tunk's previous stints at Washington's "waterfront" River Club, New Orleans, and San Diego. The décor is a low-key pun to match, with a bronze mermaid, a gently rolling ceiling (the curl of which allows mezzanine diners a view of the bar and kitchen staff), fan-pleated sconces that could have been Neptune's cockle shells, and huge oval mirrors that make the reflected customers seem to swim in and out of your imagination.

HOUSE SPECIALTIES The menu is as Calypso as the mermaid—fresh half-shelled oysters topped with a sorbet of pickled ginger and sake; smoked lobster finished with a soy sauté; mushroom-crusted halibut; lobster bisque with lobster-stuffed dumplings; fresh tuna ravioli. The wine list is interesting and moderately priced, and the wines by the glass are blessedly unpredictable and refreshing.

OTHER RECOMMENDATIONS Soft-shell crabs and crab cakes; cornmeal-fried oysters. Pastry chef David Guas is one of DC's cleverest.

SUMMARY AND COMMENTS This-smart-but-not-showy restaurant is balanced between two booming neighborhoods—the revived downtown business district and the reviving Convention Center/MCI Centre area—and on the 14th Street "fault line" of eateries drawing trend-savvy young types with expense accounts. Even better, it's a light-and-light alternative to downtown's preponderance of rich sauces and big-beef chophouses. For a quick spiritual pick-me-up, caviar by the ounce is available at the bar. The same management team owns several other downtown hot spots, including the Havana-inspired Ceiba, the New Orleans–nostalgic Agraria, and the Asian-fusion TenPenh (see profile, page 337)—though each has its own style.

Equinox ★★★

MODERN AMERICAN	MODERATE	QUALITY ★★★ ½	VALUE ★★★

818 Connecticut Avenue NW; ☎ 202-331-8118;
www.equinoxrestaurant.com Downtown

Reservations Required for lunch and dinner. **When to go** Lunch. **Entree range** $18–$33. **Payment** VISA, MC, AMEX, DC. **Service rating** ★★★★. **Friendliness rating** ★★★★. **Metro** Farragut North or McPherson Square. **Parking** Valet, street. **Bar** Full service. **Wine selection** Good. **Dress** Business, casual. **Disabled access** Good. **Customers** Foodies, business. **Hours** **Lunch:** Monday–Friday, 11:30 a.m.–2 p.m. **Dinner:** Monday–Thursday, 5:30–10 p.m.; Friday and Saturday, 5:30–10:30 p.m.; Sunday, 5–9 p.m.

SETTING AND ATMOSPHERE The best thing about the décor at Equinox is its unobtrusiveness: smart tailored shades of charcoal and matte metal like a chalk-stripe suit. (Actually, it's a good metaphor for chef Todd Gray's polished and reticent technique.) The glass-walled sidewalk area is particularly popular, though better in the evening, after the rush-hour traffic slows.

HOUSE SPECIALTIES Barbecued salmon with roasted sweet corn, Spanish peppers, and backyard basil; sautéed spinach and shallots; foie gras with rhubarb compote; lamb shank paired with loin and pumpkin bread pudding; soft-shelled crabs over fresh vegetable julienne; peanut-crusted pork tenderloin with braised Rappahannock greens, sweet onion, and cider pork jus; grilled free-range chicken breast with caramelized artichoke hearts, preserved lemon, and niçoise olives; grilled quail.

OTHER RECOMMENDATIONS The dishes on the chef's six-course tasting meal were not on the menu, but they became such an open secret, and so popular, that Equinox now serves only fixed-price menus at dinner: three, four, or six courses for $55 to $85 without wines.

SUMMARY AND COMMENTS Chef-owner Todd Gray spent many years as the on-site chef at Galileo, and that kitchen's consistently excellent reputation depended heavily on his work (in fact, his leaving in part forced Galileo honcho Roberto Donna to rededicate himself to the art of cooking as well as restauranteering). It must be pointed out, however, that now that he has his own head, he's not cooking Italian (or French, which he performed under Jean-Louis Palladin), but what he calls mid-Atlantic regional, heavy on fresh seafood and updated Chesapeake Bay flavors. The menu changes frequently, but in general, expect vegetables to be incorporated into the recipes, not relegated to the side; light sauces based on reductions and natural flavors; and a fondness for contrasting sweet and sour or rich and acid within a single dish—see the examples above. Gray is also overseeing development of the tony Salamander Inn and Sheila Johnson resort complex in Middleburg, Virginia.

Four Sisters (Huong Que) ★★★

VIETNAMESE	INEXPENSIVE	QUALITY ★★★	VALUE ★★★★

6769 Wilson Boulevard, Falls Church; ☎ 703-538-6717
Virginia Suburbs

Reservations Recommended. **When to go** Late lunch–early dinner, anytime. **Entree range** $6–$25. **Payment** VISA, MC, AMEX. **Service rating** ★★★★. **Friendliness rating** ★★★★. **Metro** None nearby. **Parking** Free lot. **Bar** Beer and wine. **Wine selection** House. **Dress** Business casual, casual. **Disabled access** Good. **Customers** Area foodies, ethnic families, locals. **Hours** Sunday–Thursday, 10:30 a.m.–10 p.m.; Friday and Saturday, 10:30 a.m.–11 p.m.

SETTING AND ATMOSPHERE This may seem to be just one of the many Vietnamese establishments in the Eden Center, but it is first among peers, and its high percentage of Vietnamese customers proves it. It may be crowded, but it's incredibly cheery, with kids staring into the tanks of live fish and baby frogs and the tables bright with tree orchids.

HOUSE SPECIALTIES The classic Vietnamese banquet dish beef seven ways, including sliced rare beef salad, fondue and steamed meatballs; roast quail; a shredded vegetable salad with shrimp and pork; steamed baby clams with minced pork, lime and sesame crackers for scooping; whole steamed black cod, with that layer of fat to keep it moist.

OTHER RECOMMENDATIONS Unusually light spring rolls with herbs for wrapping instead of lettuce; sea bass in black beans; crisp stir-fried asparagus; lightly curried frog's legs in season; grilled beef in grape leaves; caramelized catfish; pork or squid with sour cabbage.

SUMMARY AND COMMENTS For years this was a foodies' insider favorite, the more so because the owners of the five-star Inn at Little Washington used to drive in every Monday, their night off, and have dinner here; but in fact it's just as hospitable to the non-famous. Nor does it condescend to non-ethnic diners by changing or dumbing down the recipes (they'll show you how to eat the trickier dishes). Despite the name, it's more than just the four sisters; it's their two brothers and their parents as well, a mom-and-pop joint to the max. The menu is almost intimidating, more than 200 entries long and a mix of more and less familiar dishes, but it's hard to go wrong; all the family is more than happy to advise you.

Galileo ★★★½

ITALIAN	EXPENSIVE	QUALITY ★★★★	VALUE ★★★

1110 21st Street NW; ☎ 202-293-7191; www.robertodonna.com
Dupont Circle/Adams-Morgan

Reservations Required. **When to go** Anytime. **Entree range** $15–$35. **Payment** VISA, MC, AMEX, D, DC, CB. **Service rating** ★★★★. **Friendliness rating** ★★★½. **Metro** Dupont Circle. **Parking** Free valet (dinner, except Sunday). **Bar** Full service. **Wine selection** *Wine Spectator* Award. **Dress** Dressy casual. **Disabled access** Good. **Customers** Locals, tourists, businesspeople, gourmet-mag groupies. **Hours Lunch:** Monday–Friday, 11:30 a.m.–2 p.m. **Dinner:** Monday–Thursday, 5:30–10 p.m.; Friday and Saturday, 5:30–10:30 p.m.; Sunday, 5–10 p.m.

Note: At press time, Galileo was closed for renovation; Chef Roberto Donna has opened an Italian trattoria called Bebo at 2250-B Crystal Drive in Crystal City; ☎ 703-412-5076.

Georgia Brown's ★★

SOUTHERN	MODERATE	QUALITY ★★★	VALUE ★★

950 15th Street NW; ☎ 202-393-4499; www.gbrowns.com Downtown

Reservations Suggested. **When to go** Anytime. **Entree range** $16–$23. **Payment** VISA, MC, AMEX, CB, DC, D. **Service rating** ★★★½. **Friendliness rating** ★★★½. **Metro** McPherson Square or Farragut North. **Parking** Street; valet (after 6 p.m.), $6. **Bar** Full service. **Wine selection** Very good. **Dress** Business, informal. **Disabled access** Good. **Customers** Business, local, tourist. **Hours Brunch:** Sunday, 10 a.m.–2:30 p.m. **Lunch/dinner:** Monday–Thursday, 11:30 a.m.–10:30 p.m.; Friday, 11:30 a.m.–11:30 p.m.; Saturday, 5:30–11:30 p.m.; Sunday, 5:30–9 p.m.

SETTING AND ATMOSPHERE An almost too-sophisticated take on Southern garden district graciousness, with vinelike wrought iron overhead, sleek wood curves, and conversation nooks; window tables are prime.

HOUSE SPECIALTIES Real Frogmore stew, with oysters, scallops, clams, shrimp, fish, and potatoes; fried (or grilled) catfish with black-eyed pea succotash; beautiful white shrimp, heads still on, with spicy sausage over grits; kitchen-sink sausage-chicken-shrimp gumbo. Look for unusual short-term specials such as squab and Australian yabbies.

OTHER RECOMMENDATIONS Sugar-and-spice-rubbed pork chop with maple-whipped mashed potatoes and sautéed green beans; grilled lamb chops marinated in garlic oil; southern fried chicken marinated in buttermilk and served with collard greens and mashed potatoes.

ENTERTAINMENT AND AMENITIES Live jazz at Sunday brunch.

SUMMARY AND COMMENTS This is not low-country cuisine (except perhaps for the high-octane planter's punch); it's haute country, updated versions of dishes you might have found in Charleston or Savannah. Presentation is distinctive without being showy, and portions are generous. Homesick Southerners can indulge in the fried chicken livers and the farm-biscuit-like scones and still look uptown. The wine list is all-American and fairly priced; barrel-aged bourbons and single-malt Scotches are available as well.

Geranio ★★½

MODERN AMERICAN	MODERATE	QUALITY ★★★	VALUE ★★★

722 King Street, Old Town Alexandria; ☎ 703-548-0088; www.geranio.net Virginia Suburbs

Reservations Recommended. **When to go** Anytime. **Entree range** $13–$25; market price higher. **Payment** VISA, MC, AMEX. **Service rating** ★★★★. **Friendliness rating** ★★★★. **Metro** King Street. **Parking** Street. **Bar** Full service. **Wine selection** Good. **Dress** Business, casual. **Disabled access** Not accessible. **Customers** Local. **Hours Lunch:** Monday–Friday, 11:30 a.m.–2:30 p.m. **Dinner:** Monday–Saturday, 6–10:30 p.m.; Sunday, 5:30–9:30 p.m.

SETTING AND ATMOSPHERE A classic Old Town Alexandria town house, the exposed brick is softened by richly-colored still lifes. Décor also includes the odd hanging implement (a huge old grain scale), majolica-look flooring, and plastered walls painted a soft flaxen that deepens through the evening to a sage green.

HOUSE SPECIALTIES Oven-roasted pork loin with creamy polenta, wilted spinach and crispy onions; braised veal cheeks with black-pepper spaetzle; osso buco with saffron risotto and broccoli rabe; lobster risotto with a half lobster or lobster over polenta; seared rare tuna.

OTHER RECOMMENDATIONS "Lasagna" of Atlantic salmon, smoked salmon, and creamed spinach in a crispy pasta; seared salmon; oven-roasted ribeye with sweet onions, zucchini, and pancetta over a baked potato cake.

SUMMARY AND COMMENTS Chef-owner Troy Clayton, who trained with Jean-Louis Palladin, has managed to maintain the neighborhood hospitality of this Old Town beauty while completely refreshing and upscaling the menu. Dishes are complex in pairings but without gratuitous frills; this is a restaurant that remains quiet only by choice.

Gerard's Place ★★½

| FRENCH | EXPENSIVE | QUALITY ★★★ | VALUE ★★★ |

915 15th Street NW; ☎ 202-737-4445 Downtown

Reservations Recommended (not available after 9:30 p.m.). **When to go** Monday. **Entree range** $24–$52. **Payment** VISA, MC, AMEX, CB, DC. **Service rating** ★★★. **Friendliness rating** ★★½. **Metro** McPherson Square. **Parking** Street; valet (evenings). **Bar** Full service. **Wine selection** Good. **Dress** Business, casual. **Disabled access** Very good. **Customers** Business, local, tourist. **Hours** Lunch Monday–Friday, 11:30 a.m.–2:30 p.m. **Dinner:** Monday–Thursday, 5:30–9 p.m.; Friday and Saturday, 5:30–9:30 p.m.

SETTING AND ATMOSPHERE A quietly powerful room, painted simply in charcoal and terra-cotta and studded with a series of stark pencil lithographs.

HOUSE SPECIALTIES The menu changes weekly, but look for any sweetbread or venison dish; perfectly poached lobster topped with a tricolor confetti of mango, avocado, and red bell pepper in lime-Sauternes sauce (Pangaud's signature dish); "foie gras of the sea" (known to sushi connoisseurs as ankimo or monkfish liver), lightly crusted and grilled rare, as rich as real foie gras but with a fraction of the calories and guilt; terrine of quail bound by quail liver; boned rabbit rolled and wrapped in Japanese seaweed; soft-shell crabs not with almonds but sweeter, unexpected hazelnuts.

OTHER RECOMMENDATIONS Hearty bistro-max dishes such as pot-au-feu of cured duck and savoy cabbage; cod cheeks; braised oxtail; breast of duck with shepherd's pie of the leg. Or you can try the tasting menu: five courses for $85 (without wine). A vegetarian tasting menu is also offered.

ENTERTAINMENT AND AMENITIES On Monday, Gerard's Place waives not only the corkage fee on wines but the markup as well.

SUMMARY AND COMMENTS Founder Gerard Pangaud whose establishment had earned two Michelin stars, has retired to head up the local

L'Académie du Cuisine, which bodes well for DC's dining future; but longtime sous-chef Ben Lefenfeld is keeping the flame alive.

Grapeseed ★★★

MODERN AMERICAN	EXPENSIVE	QUALITY ★★★	VALUE ★★★

4865-C Cordell Avenue, Bethesda; ☎ 301-986-9592; www.grapeseedbistro.com Maryland Suburbs

Reservations Recommended. **When to go** Early dinner, late on weekends. **Entree range** $20–$29. **Payment** VISA, MC, AMEX, D, DC. **Service rating** ★★★½. **Friendliness rating** ★★★. **Metro** Bethesda. **Parking** Pay lots, street meters, valet. **Bar** Full service. **Wine selection** Very good. **Dress** Business, casual chic. **Disabled access** Narrow. **Customers** Food trendies, locals, business **Hours** Monday–Thursday, 5–10 p.m.; Friday and Saturday, 5–11 p.m.; Sunday, 5–9 p.m.

SETTING AND ATMOSPHERE This sleek and unfussy space, with its removable front walls onto the sidewalk and its leggy distance to the partially exposed bar, makes two points immediately: the wine is up front, and the food goes right behind. Chef-owner Jeff Heineman has designed a modern tapas menu to match his impressive list of wines, all available by the glass, bottle, or even taste. Both "appetizers" and entrees, which can vary considerably in size and staying power, come listed as accompanying red wine or white, and the pairings are usually quite smart—unless the country's wine imports hit a snag, as they sometimes do. However, the staff is well prepared to make alternate recommendations.

HOUSE SPECIALTIES Ethereal sweetbreads; crisp and delicate cornmeal-fried oysters; spice-dusted red snapper; luxuriant braised veal cheeks; turkey breast stuffed with fontina, almonds, and green olives (and the Sangiovese recommendation is just right); a witty and robust pepper-crusted filet mignon with oxtail ragoût.

OTHER RECOMMENDATIONS Wild mushroom fricassee; "Portuguese stew" of clams, pork, shiitakes, and oranges; snails with hazelnuts; grilled rockfish with wild mushrooms and roasted corn; seared scallops with port; roast pork with white balsamic vinegar and grapes; seared duck with rosemary and lavender.

SUMMARY AND COMMENTS Allow some time to get the full impact of this menu. The list of dishes is so intriguing that it's difficult not to over-order, which won't at all bother your palate but may surprise you at check-out, especially as the wines can reach $10 a glass. Still, this is a delightful change of pace, a quick private seminar in new wines and forward thinking. It's almost certainly headed for a fourth star.

Heritage India ★★★

INDIAN	MODERATE	QUALITY ★★★	VALUE ★★★

1337 Connecticut Avenue NW, Dupont Circle/Adams-Morgan; ☎ 202-331-1414 2400 Wisconsin Avenue NW, Georgetown; ☎ 202-333-3120

Reservations Recommended. **When to go** Anytime. **Entree range** $9–$24. **Payment** VISA, MC, AMEX, DC. **Service rating** ★★. **Friendliness rating** ★★★. **Metro** *Connecticut Avenue:* Dupont Circle or Farragut North. **Parking** Street, pay lot. **Bar** Full Service. **Wine selection** Good. **Dress** Business, casual. **Disabled access** Good at Bethesda only. **Customers** Business, locals, ethnic. **Hours Brunch:** Saturday and Sunday, noon–4 p.m. **Lunch:** Monday–Friday, 11:30 a.m.–2 p.m. **Dinner:** Bistro, Monday–Saturday, 5:30–10 p.m.; Tasting Room, Tuesday–Saturday, 5:30–10 p.m.

SETTING AND ATMOSPHERE The Glover Park site is more traditional, with its saffron walls, romantic sepia-toned photos and Raj-era lithographs and fabric upholstery. The newer Dupont Circle branch is confidently new-generation-centric; the bar stretches nearly the length of the room.

HOUSE SPECIALTIES Heat freaks look to the lamb vindaloo, a real fire starter; moderately spicy choices include fish filets, any of a half-dozen tandoori dishes; a tangy but not too spicy dish of sliced grouper in green pepper and tomatoes.

OTHER RECOMMENDATIONS A soothing dish of baby eggplant in sesame sauce; okra and onions in dried mango powder; vegetable fritters; assorted breads.

SUMMARY AND COMMENTS This was one of the first new-age Indian kitchens, so to speak, in the Washington area, ranging into less familiar and more subtle regional fare, and its success has inspired a number of other kitchens to invest in complexity and upscale service. (It has a third "relative," for those staying in Bethesda: Passage to India, once called Heritage India and still, since the chef is the same, with a very similar menu.)

IndeBleu   ★★★

FRENCH-ASIAN FUSION   EXPENSIVE   QUALITY ★★★★   VALUE ★★★

707 G Street NW; ☎ 202-333-2538; www.bleu.com/indebleu
Downtown

Reservations Recommended. **When to go** Happy hour or late. **Entree range** $21–$50. **Payment** AMEX, MC, V, D. **Service rating** ★★★★. **Friendliness rating** ★★★. **Metro** Gallery Place. **Parking** Valet, street, lots. **Bar** Full service. **Wine selection** Good. **Dress** High style, business, couture, street smart. **Disabled access** Good. **Customers** Nightlife trendies, after-hours business parties, pre- and post–arena-goers. **Hours Lunch:** Monday–Friday, 11:30 a.m.–1:30 p.m. **Dinner:** Daily, 5:30 p.m.–2 a.m.

SETTING AND ATMOSPHERE A mini-Marrakesh of a lounge with a DJ booth and sleek minimalist bar downstairs, and two yin-yang dining rooms upstairs: one vivid in persimmon and pumpkin, the other coolly ivory with sheers. The tone is light and witty—the martini menu looks like a Metro-station map—and the chef's table, where up to six can enjoy Chef Vikram Garg's tasting menu, actually rotates so you can face the kitchen or not.

HOUSE SPECIALTIES Crispy Indian *dosa* filled with mixed wild mushrooms; lobster bisque with lobster brandad and caviar; veal-stuffed gnocchi with chanterelles and walnuts; pan-seared veal tenderloin topped with cardamom-infused sweetbreads; lacquered duck breast with pepper-dusted pomegranate and morel risotto.

OTHER RECOMMENDATIONS Oven-roasted sea bass paired with curried mussels; rabbit-stuffed samosas with apple chutney and rum-raisin sauce; cumin-dusted scallops with orange-braised chicory; *naan* du jour.

SUMMARY AND COMMENTS The difference in atmosphere from downstairs to up is fairly extreme, but what else can you expect from a group that also runs a hair salon and a dance studio? If the music isn't too loud or body-busy, the bar and lounge have fun light fare such as samosas, lamb-chop "lollipops," and tuna tartare on lentil crackers. Garg has worked in India (Bombay and Delhi), Dubai, and the British Virgin Islands, so his culinary sense of humor involves a tendency toward sweet-and-sour, crisp-and-melting contrasts.

Indique ★★★

INDIAN	INEXPENSIVE	QUALITY ★★★½	VALUE ★★★

3512–14 Connecticut Avenue NW; ☎ 202-244-6600; www.indique.com
Upper Northwest

Reservations Recommended. **When to go** Early dinner. **Entree range** $9–$18. **Payment** VISA, MC, AMEX. **Service rating** ★★★. **Friendliness rating** ★★★★. **Metro** Cleveland Park. **Parking** Street, pay lot. **Bar** Full service. **Wine selection** Good. **Dress** Business casual. **Disabled access** Good. **Customers** Locals, moviegoers, ethnics. **Hours Lunch:** Every day, noon–3 p.m. **Dinner:** Sunday–Thursday, 5:30–10:30 p.m.; Friday and Saturday, 5:30–11 p.m.

SETTING AND ATMOSPHERE A lovely indoor "courtyard" with a second story mezzanine, faux-aged murals, walls of tandoori-rub bronze, lattice-cut marble dividers and skylike inserts overhead.

HOUSE SPECIALTIES Steamed mussels in coconut broth; caramelized eggplant bangun bharta; spiced lamb shank; calamari Ullarthiyathi in a ginger, chile, and mustard-seed sauce; buttery chicken tikka makhani; shrimp wrapped with ginger, tomato, and spices and baked in a banana leaf.

OTHER RECOMMENDATIONS Shrimp Baruval with spicy onions and tomatoes; shrimp and scallop masala; and the appam stews, with slightly sour pancakes in sambal coconut sauce. A good variety of breads, stuffed or plain.

SUMMARY AND COMMENTS This upscale and wide-ranging restaurant, with its stunning presentations and carefully attended side dishes, is the jewel in the Bombay Bistro business crown, and one of a happily expanding number of serious Indian kitchens in Washington that look beyond the tandoori line. If possible, get in before 8 p.m., because it's very popular with the post-movie crowd. The same owners have opened Indique Heights, an equally stunning spot atop the Friendship Heights Metro station.

The Inn at Little Washington   ★★★★★

MODERN AMERICAN   **VERY EXPENSIVE**   **QUALITY ★★★★★**   **VALUE ★★★★★**

**Middle and Main streets, Washington, VA; ☎ 540-675-3800;
www.theinnatlittlewashington.com**   Virginia Suburbs

Reservations Required. **When to go** Anytime. **Entree range** Prix fixe: $138, Sunday–Thursday; $148, Friday; $168, Saturday. **Payment** VISA, MC. **Service rating** ★★★½. **Friendliness rating** ★★½. **Metro** None nearby. **Parking** Free lot. **Bar** Full service. **Wine selection** *Wine Spectator* Award. **Dress** Dressy, informal. **Disabled access** Fair. **Customers** Local, tourist. **Hours** Monday–Thursday, 6–9:30 p.m.; Friday and Saturday, seatings at 5:30, 6, 9, and 9:30 p.m.; Sunday, seatings at 4, 4:30, 7, 7:30, 8, and 8:30 p.m.; Tuesday, closed except during May and October.

SETTING AND ATMOSPHERE An elegantly appointed but unfussy frame build-ing with an enclosed garden (with many romantic seatings on the patio) and rich, hand-painted walls, velvet upholstery, and the clean glint of real crystal and silver in all directions.

HOUSE SPECIALTIES The menu changes continually, but look for dishes such as seafood and wild mushroom risotto; veal or lamb carpaccio; tender-loin of beef that reminds you why that's such a classic entree; home-smoked trout; sweetbreads with whole baby artichokes; baby lamb morsels with lamb sausage alongside. And although the dinner is purportedly four courses, here, as at several other top-flight restau-rants, there are apt to be extras along the way.

OTHER RECOMMENDATIONS Soft-shell crabs however offered (usually respect-fully simple); a signature appetizer of black-eyed peas and Smithfield ham topped with foie gras; that same ham, sliced thin as prosciutto, wrapped around fresh local figs; portobello mushroom pretending to be a filet mignon.

SUMMARY AND COMMENTS A culinary legend—it's been profiled in the *New Yorker* and selected by *Travel + Leisure* as the second-finest hotel in the U.S. and eighth-finest in the world—the Inn at Little Washington is the capital's most popular distant dining destination. Chef Patrick O'Connell is a name to make magic with in gourmet (and gourmand) circles all over the country. O'Connell's strength is a sense of balance: dishes are never overwhelmed or overfussy; local produce is empha-sized (which guarantees freshness); and a lot of fine ingredients are allowed to speak for themselves, which is sadly rare. Everyone remem-bers his or her first passion here—homemade white-chocolate ice cream with bitter-chocolate sauce—and for some Washingtonians, driving down to the other Washington becomes an addiction, a compulsion. It's the single biggest reason (besides horses, perhaps) for the boom in yuppie commuting to the hills. Incidentally, it was O'Connell who bought up the wine cellar when Le Pavillon (where Yannick Cam used to be chef) went bankrupt, and one can almost not regret it.

Jaleo ★★★

NUEVO LATINO	MODERATE	QUALITY ★★★	VALUE ★★★

480 Seventh Street NW, Downtown; ☎ **202-628-7949**
7271 Woodmont Avenue, Bethesda, MD; ☎ **301-913-0003**
2250-A Crystal Drive, Arlington, VA; ☎ **703-413-8181**
www.jaleo.com

Reservations 5–6:30 p.m only. **When to go** Early evening. **Entree range**
$15–$45. **Payment** VISA, MC, AMEX, D, DC. **Service rating** ★★★. **Friendliness rating** ★★★. **Metro** *Downtown:* Archives–Navy Memorial; *Bethesda:* Bethesda; *Arlington:* Crystal City. **Parking** Street; valet after 5 p.m except on Sunday, $8. **Bar** Full service. **Wine selection** Good. **Dress** Business, casual. **Disabled access** Good. **Customers** Local, tourist. **Hours Brunch:** Sunday, 11:30 a.m.–3 p.m. **Lunch/dinner:** Sunday and Monday, 11:30 a.m.–10 p.m.; Tuesday–Thursday, 11:30 a.m.–11:30 p.m.; Friday and Saturday, 11:30 a.m.–midnight.

SETTING AND ATMOSPHERE A combination tapas bar, chic competition, and piazza, with bits of wrought iron, a lush suedelike gray décor, and (in the original downtown branch) a partial copy of the John Singer Sargent painting from which it takes its name.

HOUSE SPECIALTIES Paella (in three versions), and tapas—bite-sized appetizers (four to a plate) meant to help wash down glasses of sangria and sherry and pass hours of conversation. Among the best regulars: orange-peel-marinated mussels; raw tuna with anchovy oil; Cadiz-style marinated fried shark; monkfish with eggplant and black olive oil; grilled quail; spinach with apples, pine nuts, and raisins; salmon with artichokes; eggplant flan with roasted peppers; serrano ham and tomatoes on focaccia; and miniature lamb chops. Chef José Andrés's daily specials and particularly seasonal rarities, frequently of shrimp or shellfish, are extremely good bets.

OTHER RECOMMENDATIONS Sausage with white beans; grilled portobello mushrooms (getting to be a local staple); lightly fried calamari; paella.

SUMMARY AND COMMENTS Jaleo has taken tapas, a late-blooming bar fad, and built an entire menu around them—there are five times as many tapas as whole entrees. If you're with three or four people, you can just about taste everything in sight. (In fact, the first time, you may want to go extra slow: the plates look so small, and the palo cortada goes down so smoothly, that you can overstuff yourself without realizing it.) The bar does a heavy business, too, especially pre- and post-theater. It's already so trendy that if you really want to celeb-spot, go off rush hour; they're ducking the crowds.

Johnny's Half Shell ★★½

SEAFOOD	INEXPENSIVE	QUALITY ★★½	VALUE ★★★

400 North Capitol Street; ☎ **202-737-0400; www.johnnyshalfshell.net**
Capitol Hill

Reservations Not accepted. **When to go** Pre- or post-rush. **Entree range**
$16–$24. **Payment** VISA, MC, AMEX. **Service rating** ★★★. **Friendliness rating**

★★★★. **Metro** Union Station. **Parking** Street, pay lots. **Bar** Full service. **Wine selection** Good. **Dress** Business, casual. **Disabled access** Not accessible. **Customers** Locals, business. **Hours Lunch:** Monday–Friday, 11:30 a.m.–2:30 p.m. **Dinner:** Monday–Saturday, 5–10 p.m.

SETTING AND ATMOSPHERE Intentionally low-key, it hearkens back to the New Orleans–style oyster bars and Gulf Coast fish houses: Naugahyde, a marble-topped pull-up bar, and a no-reservations policy.

HOUSE SPECIALTIES The New Orleans seafood gumbo and the Chesapeake seafood stew, one dark and dirty and the other light and sunny; an equally lighthearted take on Manhattan-style clam chowder; halibut over chanterelles; grilled squid over wilted arugula; soft-shell crabs with corn pudding; fried oyster po' boys (on bread flown in from New Orleans); barbecued shrimp and grits.

OTHER RECOMMENDATIONS Barbecued shrimp on cheese grits, a "dirtier" (spicier) version than the more genteel, creamy Lowcountry dishes elsewhere in town; roasted littleneck clams; decadent crab imperial.

SUMMARY AND COMMENTS Executive chef Ann Cashion and co-owner John Fulchino are old friends to Washington foodies (see profile of Cashion's Eat Place, page 297). This newly-relocated (and expanded) hangout, is a mini-getaway to the sort of old New Orleans bar that is becoming a rarity in the tourist-crazy Big Easy itself: fried oysters, frigid beer, and the sort of couture "comfort food" that Cashion is famous for.

Kaz Sushi Bistro ★★★½

JAPANESE	MODERATE	QUALITY ★★★★	VALUE ★★★

1915 I Street NW; ☎ 202-530-5500; www.kazsushibistro.com
Foggy Bottom

Reservations Recommended. **When to go** Anytime. **Entree range** $12–$20. **Payment** VISA, MC, AMEX, DC. **Service rating** ★★★. **Friendliness rating** ★★★. **Metro** Farragut West or Farragut North. **Parking** Pay lots. **Bar** Beer and wine. **Wine selection** Fair, several sakes. **Dress** Business, casual. **Disabled access** No. **Customers** Food trendies, business. **Hours Lunch:** Monday–Friday, 11:30 a.m.– 2 p.m. **Dinner:** Monday–Saturday, 6–10 p.m.

SETTING AND ATMOSPHERE A smart and savvy-funny room, with a mini–fountain wall in front, a smallish sushi bar in the rear, and abstract but oddly maguro-ish wallpaper.

HOUSE SPECIALTIES Sake-poached scallops; lobster salad; glazed grilled baby octopus; spicy broiled green mussels; foie gras infused with plum wine; "Japanese-style duck confit" in miso; salmon belly with fennel and yogurt sauce; the signature sea trout "napoleon" of chopped fish tossed with peanuts, cilantro, and soy-ginger dressing and layered on crispy wontons.

OTHER RECOMMENDATIONS Nontraditional sushi such as tuna with foie gras or with kalamata pesto; lobster with wasabi mayo; asparagus and roasted-red-pepper roll; portobello and sun-dried tomato roll.

SUMMARY AND COMMENTS Chef-owner Kaz Okochi earned many of his fans while working at Sushi-Ko, where he originated many of what he calls his "original small dishes." He is also fearless about mixing East and West, but not in the usual fusion forms, i.e., the tuna and foie gras. The quality of the more traditional sushi is first-rate, of course. But you can get good sushi in a number of places, as listed in the front of this chapter. So take Kaz's inventions for a spin. Note the number of intriguing vegetarian options as well.

Kinkead's ★★★

SEAFOOD	EXPENSIVE	QUALITY ★★★	VALUE ★★½

2000 Pennsylvania Avenue NW; ☎ **202-296-7700; www.kinkeads.com**
Foggy Bottom

Reservations Recommended (required for the dining room upstairs). **When to go** Anytime, Sunday brunch. **Entree range** $20–$40. **Payment** VISA, MC, AMEX, D, DC. **Service rating** ★★★. **Friendliness rating** ★★★. **Metro** Foggy Bottom–GWU or Farragut West. **Parking** Valet at dinner, pay lots, meters. **Bar** Full service. **Wine selection** Good. **Dress** Business, informal. **Disabled access** Good. **Customers** Business, local. **Hours Brunch:** Sunday, 11:30 a.m.–2:30 p.m. **Lunch:** Monday–Friday, 11:30 a.m.–2:30 p.m. **Dinner:** Sunday–Thursday, 5:30–10 p.m.; Friday and Saturday, 5:30–10:30 p.m.

SETTING AND ATMOSPHERE Pleasantly restrained, ranging over two floors and divided into a series of elevated or glass-enclosed areas. The kitchen staff is visible upstairs, as is commonplace these days; it's a little less common to see chef-owner Robert Kinkead on the consumer side of the glass wall, barking at his cooks via headset like a football coach talking to the booth.

HOUSE SPECIALTIES A melting chargrilled squid over polenta with tomato confit (appetizer); roast cod with crab imperial; seared sea scallops with a fennel tarte tatin; seared tuna with portobellos and flageolets; lobster specials; roast saddle of rabbit with crispy sweetbreads and fava bean–chanterelle ragoût; Brazilian-style pork with black beans; walnut-encrusted snapper.

OTHER RECOMMENDATIONS Ipswich-style fried soft-shell clams; crab and lobster cakes (appetizers); sautéed cod cheeks; Sicilian swordfish with fennel, olives, currants, and arugula.

ENTERTAINMENT AND AMENITIES Live jazz weeknights; nonsmoking raw bar.

SUMMARY AND COMMENTS This is a seafood restaurant for those still a little leery of fish–or rather, fishy flavors. Kinkead's style is simple and straightforward but not shrinking; his sauces are balanced but assured, designed to highlight the food, not the frills. Any available seafood can be ordered broiled or grilled, but "simply grilled" here is almost an oxymoron. And Kinkead, whose first fame came from his Nantucket restaurant, has installed a little home away from home downstairs by way of a raw bar–plus first-rate chowder, soups, and salads. It's been a little inconsistent recently, however.

Komi ★★★½

MODERN AMERICAN	VERY EXPENSIVE	QUALITY ★★★★	VALUE ★★★

1509 17th Street NW; ☎ 202-332-9200; www.komirestaurant.com
Dupont Circle/Adams-Morgan

Reservations Recommended. **When to go** Anytime. **Entree range** $27–$32; fixed price, $31–$71. **Payment** VISA, MC, AMEX, D, DC. **Service rating** ★★★. **Friendliness rating** ★★★★. **Metro** Dupont Circle. **Parking** Street. **Bar** Full service. **Wine selection** Good. **Dress** Business, dressy casual. **Disabled access** No. **Customers** Local foodies, after-work business partners. **Hours** Tuesday–Saturday, 6–9:30 p.m.

SETTING AND ATMOSPHERE Very cool and elegant but unfussy; classic town house upgrade.

HOUSE SPECIALTIES The five-course tasting menu is all that's offered on weekends; Tuesday through Thursday there are à la carte menu choices, too. Among the high points: roasted turbot on the bone; chestnut noodles with trumpet mushrooms and parsnips; wood-roasted venison paired with venison moussaka; guinea-hen saltimbocca with chanterelles.

OTHER RECOMMENDATIONS Pappardelle with goat ragù; fresh spaghetti with sardines and breadcrumbs.

SUMMARY AND COMMENTS Chef Johnny Monis, still well under 30, is one of Washington's rising stars (the whole crew looks like a college team), and good things come to those who don't even wait—the moment you're seated, you're likely to get your first little treat (say, warm dates stuffed with mascarpone and yogurt). There is a Greek flavor to the menu, but it's entirely original.

L'Auberge Chez François ★★★

FRENCH	VERY EXPENSIVE	QUALITY ★★★½	VALUE ★★★★

332 Springvale Road, Great Falls; ☎ 703-759-3800;
www.laubergechezfrancois.com   Virginia Suburbs

Reservations Required 4 weeks in advance. **When to go** Summer evenings in good weather for the terrace. **Entree range** $40–$50. **Payment** VISA, MC, AMEX, D, DC. **Service rating** ★★★★. **Friendliness rating** ★★★★. **Metro** None nearby. **Parking** Free lot. **Bar** Full service. **Wine selection** Very good. **Dress** Dressy, business (jacket required for men at night). **Disabled access** Very good. **Customers** Locals. **Hours** Tuesday–Thursday, 5:30–9:30 p.m.; Friday and Saturday, seatings at 5:30–6:30 p.m. or 9–9:30 p.m.; Sunday, 1:30–8 p.m.

SETTING AND ATMOSPHERE One of the most beloved and romantic dining sites in the area, a real country inn with exposed beams, a mix of views of Alsace (home of paterfamilias—executive chef Jacques Haeringer), only-a-family-could-love drawings, and a travel-brochure veranda. It's so widely known as an engagement and anniversary mecca that *Regrets Only,* Sally Quinn's semi–roman à clef about journalistic and political circles, included a rather improbable but dramatic tryst in the parking lot (in an MG with a stick shift, no less).

HOUSE SPECIALTIES Classics such as rack of lamb ($50 for one, $98 for two), Châteaubriand for two ($98), and duck foie gras either sautéed with apples or "plain"; the true choucroute royal garni, with Alsatian sauerkraut, sausages, smoked pork, duck, pheasant, and quail; game in season, such as medallions of venison and roast duck; veal kidneys in a rich, mustardy sauce; sweetbreads with wild mushrooms in puff pastry; roasted boneless duck breast paired with the stuffed leg and fruit-dotted rice; seafood fricassee with shrimp, scallops, lobster, rockfish, and salmon in Riesling.

OTHER RECOMMENDATIONS Various seafood and game pâtés; red snapper braised in beer; boneless rabbit stuffed with leeks and fennel; soft-shell crabs with extra crabmeat stuffed into the body; big scallops in a bright (but not overwhelming) tomato and bell pepper sauce.

SUMMARY AND COMMENTS What look like entrees on the menu are really whole dinners, and with salads, fancy appetizers, and dessert—not to mention bread and cheese and a bit of sorbet—this is a lot of food. Although the two-to-four weeks' notice rule still applies, competition has increased, along with cancellations: it may be worth it to call in the late afternoon, especially during the week. You can't make reservations for the outdoor terrace, incidentally; just call to make sure it's open (about May through September) and then show up.

La Chaumière ★★½

| FRENCH | MODERATE | QUALITY ★★★ | VALUE ★★★ |

2813 M Street NW; ☎ 202-338-1784; www.lachaumieredc.com
Georgetown

Reservations Recommended. **When to go** Anytime. **Entree range** $15–$50. **Payment** VISA, MC, AMEX, DC, , JCB, CB. **Service rating ★★★. Friendliness rating ★★★. Metro** Foggy Bottom–GWU. **Parking** Two-hour parking at Four Seasons Hotel (dinner). **Bar** Full service. **Wine selection** Good. **Dress** Business, informal. **Disabled access** Good. **Customers** Local, embassy, business. **Hours Lunch:** Monday–Friday, 11:30 a.m.–3:30 p.m. **Dinner:** Monday–Saturday, 5:30–10:30 p.m. Closed Sunday.

SETTING AND ATMOSPHERE After 25 years in the often tumultuous Georgetown culinary competition, the cooking in this big-beamed, in-town country inn, with its free-standing fireplace in the center and old iron tools on the wall, has a revived freshness, thanks to the new kitchen broom of chef Patrick Orange. And what goes around comes around: bistro fare of owner Gerard Pain's sort is suddenly booming around him.

HOUSE SPECIALTIES Oysters; seasonal specials of rabbit, choucroute, or venison (as uptown as medallions with chestnut purée or as down-home as potpie); seafood crêpes or jumbo shad roe; bouillabaisse; traditional tripe à la mode in Calvados. Here, as at the Bistro Français across the street (see listing), the daily specials are even more amazing; terrine of duck foie gras or fresh foie gras with cassis; ostrich loin wrapped in bacon; bison osso buco; seared sea bass with portobello-turnip risotto.

OTHER RECOMMENDATIONS Calf's liver or brains; sweetbreads with turnips and Jerusalem artichokes; medallions of ostrich with blood-orange sauce; quenelles of pike in lobster.

SUMMARY AND COMMENTS Part of La Chaumière's charm is its weekly treats: Wednesday it's couscous, and Thursday, cassoulet. This is family-style food, and most of its regulars are treated like family. Actually, "regulars" is a key word here; La Chaumière hearkens back to the time when Georgetown was more neighborhood than shopping mall, and a lot of its customers feel as if they graduated into adult dinner-dating here. The fireplace is one of the area's hottest soulful-gazing areas.

La Miche ★★½

FRENCH	MODERATE	QUALITY ★★★	VALUE ★★½

7905 Norfolk Avenue, Bethesda; ☎ 301-986-0707; www.lamiche.com
Maryland Suburbs

Reservations Recommended. **When to go** Anytime. **Entree range** Fixed price $35 and $50. **Payment** VISA, MC, AMEX, DC. **Service rating** ★★★. **Friendliness rating** ★★★½. **Metro** Bethesda. **Parking** Valet, street. **Bar** Full service. **Wine selection** Good. **Dress** Business, informal. **Disabled access** No. **Customers** Local, business. **Hours Brunch:** Sunday, 11:30 a.m.–2 p.m. **Lunch:** Tuesday–Friday, 11:30 a.m.–2 p.m. **Dinner:** Monday–Saturday, 6–9:45 p.m.; Sunday, 6–8 p.m.

SETTING AND ATMOSPHERE The tone is somewhere between an old French inn and an upscale bistro, with white lace curtains, gleaming wood, flowers, and soft, well-laundered linens.

HOUSE SPECIALTIES House-smoked salmon with celeriac; veal chop; nicely viscous frog's legs; braised lamb shank or rabbit; duck confit or grilled duck or almost any duck presentation.

SUMMARY AND COMMENTS La Miche was a magnet in Bethesda long before the restaurant boom of the 1990s, and new chef-owner Jason Tepper knows better than to shake off all the old standbys; he's just shaking them out. The dishes are classically "provincial" in the best, as-you-like-it fashion, but not weighty or cloying. Look for the likes of duck liver and foie gras, cassoulet, snails, medallions of venison, etc., depending on the season.

Le Mannequin Pis ★★★

BELGIAN	MODERATE	QUALITY ★★★	VALUE ★★★½

18064 Georgia Avenue, Olney; ☎ 301-570-4800   Maryland Suburbs

Reservations Recommended. **When to go** Early dinner or after 9 p.m. on weekends. **Entree range** $15–$25. **Payment** VISA, MC, AMEX, D. **Service rating** ★★½. **Friendliness rating** ★★★. **Metro** None nearby. **Parking** Free lot. **Bar** Full service. **Wine selection** Fair. **Dress** Suburban casual, business. **Disabled access** Good. **Customers** Food-trend saveurs, locals. **Hours** Tuesday–Thursday, 5–9:30 p.m.; Friday and Saturday, 5–10:30 p.m.; Sunday, 5–9 p.m.

SETTING AND ATMOSPHERE Named for the famously rude statue in Brussels (the one of the little boy relieving himself into the fountain), this is a combination 1950s rec room, bistro, and coquette's salon, with tacked-up plywood, sponged egg-yolk walls, heavy red drapes, and stunning abstract paintings by chef Bernard Dehaene's mother. One other thing: whenever the light in the men's room is turned on, the statue "tinkles."

HOUSE SPECIALTIES Mussels, done a half-dozen ways (try the beer, leeks, and goat cheese broth); classic Belgian fries (called *pommes pailles,* or potato straws); endive salads; wood-roasted sea bass with capers, balsamic vinegar, and braised Belgian endive; oysters au gratin in Champagne; veal chop with escargot; roast pork with salty-sour pickled figs and spinach; salmon medallions with red cabbage and leeks. The daily specials are especially intriguing; split yabbies (Australia crawfish) spread with Cognac-anchovy butter; foie gras; Flemish-ized osso buco with caramelized onions and beer.

OTHER RECOMMENDATIONS Side dishes of braised endive and mini-saucepans of Brussels sprouts; rich Belgian beers; fish of the day; rump steak with a choice of sauces.

SUMMARY AND COMMENTS Like its décor, and its unapologetically economical location in an unprepossessing strip mall, Le Mannequin Pis can be delightfully iconoclastic or bafflingly headstrong, especially when the very short staff gets overwhelmed by a full dining room. Occasional lapses in kitchen temper are not unknown (they were a hallmark of original chef-owner Bernard Dehaene), but it's of a piece with the restaurant's personality. Less entertaining are the infrequent lapses in kitchen performance, but they're becoming rare. Now if Montgomery County would just keep up its end on the beer list . . .

Le Paradou ★★★

FRENCH	VERY EXPENSIVE	QUALITY ★★★½	VALUE ★★½

678 Indiana Avenue NW; ☎ 202-347-6780; www.leparadou.net
Downtown

Reservations Strongly recommended. **When to go** Lunch, after rush dinner. **Entree range** Fixed price, $70–$145; à la carte menu in the lounge only, $24–$27. **Payment** VISA, MC, AMEX, DC, JCB, CB. **Service rating** ★★★½. **Friendliness rating** ★★½. **Metro** Navy Memorial–Archives–Penn Quarter or Judiciary Square. **Parking** Street, pay lot, valet at dinner. **Bar** Full service. **Wine selection** Very good. **Dress** Business, office casual. **Disabled access** Lounge only. **Customers** Business, expense account T&E, foodies. **Hours Lunch:** Monday–Friday, 11:45 a.m.–2:15 p.m. **Dinner:** Monday–Thursday, 6–10:30 p.m.; Friday and Saturday, 5:30–11:30 p.m.

SETTING AND ATMOSPHERE This sleek and cool two-level site has had several tenants, but its looks remain relatively similar to its opening as part of the Bice line: wide open and airy, all cream paint and blond wood and white linen (like a mega–corporate conference room) livened by overhead fiber-optic "stars" and big dramatic, floral arrangements. The private dining room is an old-fashioned gem with a huge crystal chandelier.

HOUSE SPECIALTIES An almost transparent lobster purse with ginger-carrot jus; truffle-studded *boudin blanc* on puréed fennel; oysters with caviar and sea urchin; foie gras (in a variety of sauces); veal chop with chanterelles and baby turnips; mini-bouillabaisse; lamb chop with tomato confit and olives with potato ravioli.

OTHER RECOMMENDATIONS Dover sole with scallop-stuffed zucchini blossoms; lobster-truffle risotto; squab with cumin and dates; classic coquilles St. Jacques.

ENTERTAINMENT AND AMENITIES Ornate amuse-bouches such as caviar and seafood mousse in a blown-out egg shell.

SUMMARY AND COMMENTS This is not a place to cut corners, even on a bar bill ($9 martinis, etc.); the wine list is heavily marked up and bar appetizers start at $8. But then, chef Yannick Cam has never hesitated to go whole hog. His style is concentrated, intense, and self-consciously sophisticated. But an occasional flightiness in the kitchen—grit in an otherwise ethereal sea urchin flan, greasy foie gras under seasoned lamb or pedestrian steak in the presumably less influential bar—at those prices keeps it below dependable four- (or five-) star standing as yet. His first Washington restaurant, Le Pavillon, was a sensation, and really a revelation of nouvelle cuisine in what was then a pretty heavy Continental cream-sauce town; he's since been in and out of a series of Provençal, Brazilian, Catalonian-Spanish and French-country inn establishments—and that's the second big caveat. Cam is notoriously restless, and might well head off again before he celebrates many anniversaries. Still, there's no denying that when he's good, he's very, very good.

Maestro ★★★★★

| MODERN ITALIAN | VERY EXPENSIVE | QUALITY ★★★★ | VALUE ★★★ |

Ritz-Carlton Hotel, 1700 Tysons Boulevard, Tysons Corner;
☎ **703-821-1515** **Virginia Suburbs**

Reservations Highly recommended. **When to go** Anytime. **Entree range** $30–$70; Prix fixe, Tuesday–Thursday, $85–$145; Friday $110–$135; Saturday, $135–$155. **Payment** VISA, MC, AMEX, D, DC. **Service rating** ★★★★½. **Friendliness rating** ★★★★. **Metro** None nearby. **Parking** Valet. **Bar** Full service. **Wine selection** *Wine Spectator* Award. **Dress** Business, dressy. **Disabled access** Very good. **Customers** Local expense accounters, special occasions, hotel patrons. **Hours Breakfast:** Monday–Friday, 6:30–11 a.m. **Brunch:** Sunday, 10:30 a.m.–2:30 p.m. **Dinner:** Tuesday–Thursday, 6–9 p.m.; Friday, 6–9:30 p.m.; Saturday, 5:30–10 p.m.

SETTING AND ATMOSPHERE This is a classic luxury hotel dining room—white linen, brocade upholstery, heavy silver, huge flowers, and charming silver animal centerpieces—but with an almost equally huge open kitchen, where prodigal chef Fabio Trabocchi and a bustling supporting cast prepare (and polish) the ornate presentations and send them out with old-fashioned European flourish.

HOUSE SPECIALTIES Seared foie gras with blood-orange sorbet; lobster ravioli with half-lobster tails; sweetbreads Milanese; hay-smoked potato gnocchi; a veg–non-veg pairing of tofu and Kobe carpaccio; osso buco–stuffed agnolotti; gratin of sea urchin; a reconception of tournedos Rossini as foie gras–stuffed filet and "bones" of celeriac filled with bone marrow mousse; panfried scallops wrapped in focaccia with chanterelles and salsa verde; monkfish liver-stuffed ravioli with periwinkles; wild turbot baked over fragrant saltwater hay; Dungeness crab and chanterelle ravioli; scallops in the shell with Jerusalem artichoke julienne; grilled baby lobster with black truffles.

OTHER RECOMMENDATIONS A dry-aged veal chop in Amarone; roast squab with figs; any sea urchin presentation.

SUMMARY AND COMMENTS Chef Fabio Trabocchi, just hitting his stride at 30, is a genius—and a playful one, like his friends Michel Richard and José Andrés, presenting pseudo-sushi with tweezers instead of chopsticks. There are actually several menus (which are perhaps a little much of a muchness, but impressive): more traditional Italian, very mod-Italian, and three tasting menus of various sizes. While the cooking is sometimes a little erratic—paradoxically, when the room is less busy, which perhaps suggests the chef is less inspired—it's never less than elaborate, and when it's good, which admittedly is most of the time, it's truly stunning. And, Maestro has another master at hand: sommelier Vincent Feraud, the dean of Washington wine stewards.

Makoto ★★★½

JAPANESE	VERY EXPENSIVE	QUALITY ★★★½	VALUE ★★★½

4822 MacArthur Boulevard NW; ☎ 202-298-6866 **Upper Northwest**

Reservations Recommended. **When to go** Anytime. **Entree range** Tasting menu, $60–$70. **Payment** VISA, MC. **Service rating** ★★★★½. **Friendliness rating** ★★★. **Metro** None nearby. **Parking** Street. **Bar** Full service. **Wine selection** House. **Dress** Business, casual. **Disabled access** No. **Customers** Ethnic Japanese, locals, businesspeople. **Hours Lunch:** Tuesday–Saturday, noon–2:30 p.m. **Dinner:** Tuesday–Sunday, 6–10:30 p.m.

SETTING AND ATMOSPHERE A secret Japanese garden of a spot, hidden behind two wood doors (with a stone garden between where you exchange your shoes for bedroom slippers) and only two lines of diners long. The kitchen is, in effect, the décor: slightly sunken behind what is now the sushi counter, the chefs busily stir, fry, and slice over the restaurant equivalent of a Pullman stove.

HOUSE SPECIALTIES A fixed-price omakase (chef's choice) dinner based on the market and featuring courses of two to six bites each, but extraordinarily generous: up to seven courses of sashimi; sushi (perhaps four different pieces, like a tray of fine miniature desserts); grilled marinated filet of fish (a choice); such delicate morsels as ankimo (monkfish liver) or rare duck breast with asparagus tips and sesame seeds; salmon with Chinese broccoli; large bowls of wheat-noodle soup; and sherbet.

OTHER RECOMMENDATIONS Limited à la carte sushi, such as *uni* (sea urchin), *toro,* or fresh sardines; yakitori, skewer-grilled marinated chicken.

SUMMARY AND COMMENTS This is a tiny establishment—perhaps 30 seats, even counting the new sushi bar—which explains how the chefs are able to produce such exquisite and imaginative meals. For the greatest pleasure, order the tasting menu and experience *kaiseki* cuisine, the formal, Zen-derived technique that salutes both nature and art by using only fresh, seasonal ingredients and a variety of colors, textures, and cooking techniques. Be sure to show your appreciation by admiring each carefully presented dish as it arrives. Note that none of the seats have backs—they're just boxes with removable tops for storing purses, jackets, and cushion lids—and there is no separate nonsmoking area. Though unrelated, the sushi bar upstairs, Kotobuki, is a popular stop.

Marcel's ★★★★

FRENCH-BELGIAN	EXPENSIVE	QUALITY ★★★★	VALUE ★★★

2401 Pennsylvania Avenue NW; ☎ 202-296-1166; www.marcelsdc.com
Dupont Circle/Adams-Morgan

Reservations Recommended. **When to go** Pre-theater. **Entree range** $26–$39; Pre-theater 3-course, $48. **Payment** VISA, MC, AMEX, DC. **Service rating** ★★★. **Friendliness rating** ★★★. **Metro** Foggy Bottom–GWU. **Parking** Valet, street meters, lots. **Bar** Full service. **Wine selection** Very good. **Dress** Business, dressy casual. **Disabled access** Very good. **Customers** Business, foodies **Hours** Monday–Thursday, 5:30–10 p.m.; Friday and Saturday, 5:30–11 p.m.; Sunday, 5:30–9:30 p.m.

SETTING AND ATMOSPHERE Much of the sunniness—yellow paint, weathered wood, wrought iron, stone facades, flowers—of the former Provençal décor remains, though a little more restrained. The long marble bar is a showpiece, and the partially exposed (and elevated) kitchen is not so intrusive as elsewhere.

HOUSE SPECIALTIES The boudin blanc is a signature dish, and a don't miss. Game dishes in season, such as breast of squab on truffled risotto; pheasant and foie gras in white bean ragoût with winter vegetables; or roulade of rabbit stuffed with sausage over caramelized cabbage. Also crispy duck breast with duck confit; panfried skate; coriander-seed-crusted salmon; and foie gras–duck liver mousse.

OTHER RECOMMENDATIONS Seared scallops with lardons of applewood bacon; duck consommé with sweetbreads; and coriander salmon, lobster sauce, and caviar. The "brasserie" bar menu offers more rustic fare at about $10 a plate.

ENTERTAINMENT AND AMENITIES Pre-theater menu $48 (including limo to the Kennedy Center), outdoor tables in good weather; live piano music nightly except Sunday.

SUMMARY AND COMMENTS Chef-owner Robert Weidmaier, formerly of Café on M and Aquarelle, has consistently gotten bolder, cleaner—and better. Though the menu is French, he gives his menu a Belgian touch that provides a rootier flavor: confits, root vegetables (including the various endives, of course), artichokes, and flavorful but not heavy sausages. The service is very attentive, though at times a trifle "educational." Marcel, incidentally, is the owner's young son—and a second son, Beck, was the inspiration for a second, less formal restaurant at 1101 K Street NW.

Mark's Duck House ★★½

CHINESE	INEXPENSIVE	QUALITY ★★★	VALUE ★★★

6184-A Arlington Boulevard, Falls Church; ☎ 703-532-2125; www.marksduckhouse.com Virginia Suburbs

Reservations Helpful. **When to go** Late lunch, late dinner. **Entree range** $7–$15; whole duck, $24. **Payment** VISA, MC. **Service rating** ★★★. **Friendliness rating** ★★★. **Metro** None nearby. **Parking** Valet. **Bar** Newly licensed. **Wine selection** Basic. **Dress** Casual. **Disabled access** Yes. **Customers** Mostly Asian, but food-savvy types from all over. **Hours** Sunday–Thursday, 10 a.m.–midnight; Friday, 10 a.m.–1 a.m.; Saturday 10 a.m.–2 a.m.

SETTING AND ATMOSPHERE Pig's heads, swags of roasted ducks, tanks of live (for the moment, anyway) seafood—maybe this should be called Mark's Menagerie Diner: after all, there are some 400 items on the dinner menu, not to mention the 70 kinds of dim sum available every day from 10 a.m. to 3 p.m. On the other hand, it does sell as many as 100 ducks on a busy night—mostly Peking duck to non-Chinese customers and Cantonese roast duck, which is similar but with more of a fat layer—a Chinese delicacy—to the ethnic crowd.

HOUSE SPECIALTIES Aside from the ducks: roast pork; stir-fried greens; black cod; spicy quail; noodle soups with seafood, duck, or pork; eggplant with bean curd and shrimp paste; chive dumplings; barbecued pork buns.

OTHER RECOMMENDATIONS For those who enjoy offal and organs, there's plenty here, and often on the specials board: knuckles, tripe, tongues (duck and pork), kidneys, etc. Also look for whole frogs, not just the legs; small birds such as squab and quail; sea cucumber; steamed sea bass.

SUMMARY AND COMMENTS When this place is jumping, which is most of the time—in fact, the Chinese sign actually translates as "Great Crowded Restaurant"—the cacophony from large family groups can be deafening, and the service a little less patient than its usual high style; but these are noises of great satisfaction. Don't go to Mark's for pedestrian dishes you can get elsewhere; experiment and enjoy. Eel is great stuff.

Meskerem ★★★

ETHIOPIAN	INEXPENSIVE	QUALITY ★★★	VALUE ★★★½

2434 18th Street NW; ☎ 202-462-4100; www.meskeremonline.com Dupont Circle/Adams-Morgan

Reservations Suggested. **When to go** Anytime. **Entree range** $9–$13. **Payment** VISA, MC, AMEX, DC. **Service rating** ★★★. **Friendliness rating** ★★★. **Metro** Woodley Park–Zoo/Adams-Morgan. **Parking** Street. **Bar** Full service. **Wine selection** Minimal. **Dress** Casual. **Disabled access** Good. **Customers** Locals, tourists. **Hours** Sunday–Thursday, noon–midnight; Friday and Saturday, noon–1 a.m.

SETTING AND ATMOSPHERE Simple but cheerful, with "skylight" rays painted blue and white, and Ethiopian-style seating (for the limber) on leather cushions at balcony basket-weave tables.

HOUSE SPECIALTIES *Kitfo* (tartare with chile sauce, but it can be ordered lightly cooked, or you can have a similar hot chopped-beef stew called *kay watt*); lamb *tibbs* (breast and leg meat sautéed with onions and green chiles); shrimp watt; beef or lentil and green chile *sambusa* (fried pastries).

OTHER RECOMMENDATIONS Chicken *alicha* for the spice-intimidated; a honey-wine version of *kitfo* called *gored-gored*.

SUMMARY AND COMMENTS There are three things novices need to know about Ethiopian food: first, it's eaten with the hands, using a spongy pancake called *injera* as plate, spoon, and napkin all in one; second, *alicha* is the name of the milder stew or curry preparation; and third, *watt* is the spicier one. Washington's many Ethiopian restaurants (there may be a dozen in Adams-Morgan alone) offer similar menus, in some cases without much distinction between stews, but Meskerem is one of the best. If you want a sampler—a tray-sized injera palette—order the *mesob* for $7.25. *Meskerem,* incidentally, is the first month of the 13-month Ethiopian calendar, the one that corresponds to September, which in Ethiopia is the end of the rainy season and thus is akin to springtime.

Montmartre ★★

FRENCH	MODERATE	QUALITY ★★★½	VALUE ★★★½

327 Seventh Street NW; ☎ 202-544-1244   Capitol Hill

Reservations Recommended. **When to go** Early or late dinner. **Entree range** $16–$25. **Payment** VISA, MC, AMEX, DC. **Service rating** ★★★★. **Friendliness rating** ★★★★. **Metro** Eastern Market. **Parking** Street. **Bar** Full service. **Wine selection** Short but good. **Dress** Casual, business. **Disabled access** Fair. **Customers** Local. **Hours Lunch:** Tuesday–Friday, 11:30 a.m.–2:30 p.m. **Dinner:** Tuesday–Thursday, 5:30–10 p.m.; Friday and Saturday, 5:30-10:30 p.m.; Sunday, 5:30–9 p.m.

SETTING AND ATMOSPHERE This is the sort of place that makes *cozy* seem like part of the word *cafe,* a single sunny-sponged room of about 50 seats with a tiny bar at the back, lively views of the sidewalk to the front and the kitchen to the rear, and elbow-to-elbow tables.

HOUSE SPECIALTIES The signature dish here is slow-braised rabbit leg with olives and wide egg noodles in cream sauce, and it's hard to beat. Otherwise, look for hangar steak (onglet); a very Parisian salad of frisée with fried gizzards and bacon lardons; cream of cauliflower soup with mussels; shrimp and lemon risotto; mussels with Ricard; sautéed monkfish over potato cake with anchovy butter.

OTHER RECOMMENDATIONS Daily specials such as venison rib chops with braised endive and a guinea hen confit with Jerusalem artichokes.

SUMMARY AND COMMENTS This is one of the beneficiaries of the shake-up at Bistrot Lepic (the other is Petits Plats in Woodley Park), as the owners are alums of that hospitable cafe and of the longtime Provençal hang-out, Lavandou in Cleveland Park. Its success as a neighborhood favorite is attested to by the fact that there are frequently crowds winding out the door. It has also allowed them to open a second bistro, Montsouris, in Dupont Circle.

Murasaki ★★★

JAPANESE	MODERATE	QUALITY ★★★	VALUE ★★★

4620 Wisconsin Avenue NW; ☎ 202-966-0023; www.murasaki.com
Upper Northwest

Reservations Helpful. **When to go** Anytime. **Entree range** $10–$28; market price higher. **Payment** VISA, MC, AMEX, D, DC. **Service rating** ★★★★. **Friendliness rating** ★★★★. **Metro** Tenleytown-AU. **Parking** Street. **Bar** Beer and Wine. **Wine selection** Limited. **Dress** Business, casual. **Disabled access** Good. **Customers** Ethnic Japanese, business. **Hours Lunch:** Monday–Friday, 11:30 a.m.–2:30 p.m; Saturday and Sunday, noon–2:30 p.m. **Dinner:** Monday–Thursday, 5:30–10 p.m.; Friday and Saturday, 5:30–10:30 p.m; Sunday, 5:30–9 p.m.

SETTING AND ATMOSPHERE *Murasaki* means "purple," but there isn't much of that hue in this elegantly spare room, which tends instead to a clean, partially Deco and only slightly "Asian" look using wood framing, cream walls, and a pleasant side patio. The grill and sushi bars, which run a long L around the rear of the room, are the focal points.

HOUSE SPECIALTIES The real specialties (occult parts of sea creatures, delicate baked dishes, etc.) are not printed on the menu, since novice diners too often order dishes they then dislike, so Japanese connoisseurs should consult with the chef about favorite items. On the other hand, even lobster sashimi and lobster miso soup can tickle the trend-addicted. Also look for eggplant dengaku, soft-shell crabs tempura, miso-marinated sea bass; white tuna and uni sushi—in fact, any sushi here.

OTHER RECOMMENDATIONS An assortment of seafood tempura that puts all Maine fisherman's platters to shame; and for unregenerate carnivores, pork teriyaki and (seared) beef sushi.

SUMMARY AND COMMENTS The chefs here are among the most respected by their peers, and the restaurant's proximity to the Japanese Embassy is probably no accident; large tables of Japanese diners and even wedding parties often crowd the dining room. Should Murasaki be booked, there is a very likeable, though more predictable, Japanese restaurant just down the street called Yosaku that should please (4712 Wisconsin Avenue NW; ☎ 202-363-4453).

Nora ★★½

MODERN AMERICAN	EXPENSIVE	QUALITY ★★★½	VALUE ★★★

2132 Florida Avenue NW; ☎ 202-462-5143; www.noras.com
Dupont Circle/Adams-Morgan

Reservations Recommended. **When to go** Anytime. **Entree range** $25–$32; tasting menu, $58–$64; vegetarian, $58. **Payment** VISA, MC, AMEX, personal checks. **Service rating** ★★★½. **Friendliness rating** ★★★★. **Metro** Dupont

Circle. **Parking** Street, valet. **Bar** Full service. **Wine selection** Good. **Dress** Business, casual. **Disabled access** No. **Customers** Locals. **Hours** Monday–Saturday, 5:30–10:30 p.m.; Sunday, closed.

SETTING AND ATMOSPHERE A pretty corner town house with exposed brick walls and a gallery of handicrafts, quilt pieces, and faux näif art in the dining rooms; an enclosed greenhouse balcony in the rear is the prettiest area.

HOUSE SPECIALTIES The menu changes frequently, but look for sautéed calf's liver, salmon, and more imaginative vegetarian platters than elsewhere.

SUMMARY AND COMMENTS Nora, the neighborhood hangout of the Dupont Circle A and B lists, was haute organic before organic was chic: chef-owner Nora Pouillon was a prime mover in the slow food and renewable crops forces, and is still on the board of the Chef's Collaborative. The back of the menu, which changes daily, lists the specific farms where the meat, produce, dairy products, and eggs—naturally low in cholesterol, according to the supplier—are raised. Nora's own all-edible flower and herb garden alongside the restaurant is indicative. The cost of acquiring such specialized ingredients is passed on, but not unreasonably. Nora was also ahead of the crowd by introducing alternative grains and pastas, and it was the first restaurant to make lentils that didn't taste like a Zen penance. Its only drawback is an odd tendency to weightiness—the meals sometimes feel heartier than they taste.

Obelisk ★★★½

ITALIAN	EXPENSIVE	QUALITY ★★★★½	VALUE ★★★★

2029 P Street NW; ☎ 202-872-1180   Dupont Circle/Adams-Morgan

Reservations Recommended. **When to go** Anytime. **Entree range** Prix fixe, 5-course, $65. **Payment** VISA, MC, DC. **Service rating** ★★★★. **Friendliness rating** ★★★½. **Metro** Dupont Circle. **Parking** Street. **Bar** Full service. **Wine selection** Good. **Dress** Business, informal. **Disabled access** No. **Customers** Local, business. **Hours** Tuesday–Saturday, 6–10 p.m.; closed Sunday and Monday.

SETTING AND ATMOSPHERE A cozy room that's elegant and good-humored; the customers, staff, and accoutrements—not only the room's floral centerpiece and silver chest but the astonishingly light breadsticks and bottles of grappa—work intimately elbow to elbow.

HOUSE SPECIALTIES Chef Peter Pastan has figured out the cure for overlong, overrich menus—he offers a fixed-price menu, four to five courses with only three or maybe four choices per course. Among typical antipasti: marinated anchovies and fennel; artichokes with goat cheese; caramel-soft onion and cheese tart; crostini; a thick soup; quail terrine; crispy fried cheese; polenta with gorgonzola; potato or rice balls. The *primi* course is apt to be seafood or pasta (red pepper noodles with crab and pungent chive blossoms; gnocchi with pesto; wheat noodles with rabbit ragoût) or soup; the *secondi,* veal (particularly tenderloin prepared with artichokes or chanterelles); fish (pompano with olives; black sea bass with artichokes; grilled shrimp with herb purée); or perhaps game birds or a mixed grill. After that comes a fine bit of cheese, with or without a dessert course following. Whatever the price—it varies with the daily menu—it's a quality bargain in this town.

SUMMARY AND COMMENTS Pastan's hand is so deft he doesn't need to overdress anything; sauces are more like glazes, and pungent ingredients—olives, pine nuts, garlic, and greens—are perfectly proportioned to their dish. Above all, it shows the value of letting a chef who knows exactly what he likes do as he likes. Pastan, who also owns Pizzeria Paradiso next door, knows the value of a really good bread dough, more than one in fact.

Oceanaire Seafood Room ★★

SEAFOOD	EXPENSIVE	QUALITY ★★★	VALUE ★★½

1201 F Street NW; ☎ 202-347-BASS; www.theoceanaire.com   Downtown

Reservations Recommended. **When to go** Anytime. **Entree range** $20–$80. **Payment** VISA, MC, AMEX, D. **Service rating** ★★★. **Friendliness rating** ★★★. **Metro** Metro Center. **Parking** Valet, pay lots. **Bar** Full service. **Wine selection** Very good. **Dress** Business, dressy casual. **Disabled access** Good. **Customers** Local business, boutique finance types, lobbyists. **Hours** Monday–Thursday, 11:30 a.m.–10 p.m.; Friday, 11:30 a.m.–11 p.m.; Saturday, 5–11 p.m.; Sunday, 5–9 p.m.

SETTING AND ATMOSPHERE Inspired by the great ocean liners of the 1930s, the room is full of curved surfaces, gleaming cherry- and etched-wood dividers, brass-studded leather booths and heavy silver. The music is Big Band, the condiment tray includes oyster crackers, and the raw bar, with its leather-topped stools and great piles of oysters, is a trip in itself. So are the retro cocktails: side cars, Singapore slings, cosmopolitans, etc.

HOUSE SPECIALTIES Oysters (up to a dozen varieties a day); even more kinds of fresh fish flown in daily from all directions (Arctic char, Hawaiian spearfish, North Atlantic cod), all available simply grilled; crab- and shrimp-stuffed gray sole; lobsters by the pound; a huge chilled seafood platter or, for fried seafood fans, the old-fashioned fisherman's platter. If the sushi-grade black grouper is available, head straight for it.

OTHER RECOMMENDATIONS Crab cakes; a "cocktail" of rock lobster–sized shrimp; Ipswich clam or oyster pan roast.

ENTERTAINMENT AND AMENITIES The relish tray of pickled herring, carrot sticks, olives, radishes, giant capers, etc. This even comes with oysters, making a dozen at the bar the steal meal of the new century. In fact, if we were only rating on the oyster bar, Oceanaire would be five stars.

SUMMARY AND COMMENTS This is the seafood chain of the 21st century, the logical outcome (given the ever-increasing size of the portions, steak houses and expense accounts) of the hefty surf-vs.-turf wars. Everything is huge, easily shared, and that goes double for desserts. (The retro look and retro extravagance partly explain some of the retro entrees, such as baked Alaska and oysters Rockefeller.) The asparagus is fat, the frills are a little excessive, and you definitely pay for the quality—even some chophouse veterans might blink at the $22-per-pound tag on the lobsters—and some of the staff can be showily informative, but for a seafood fan, it really is a luxury liner. And for those tired of only a swordfish option at the steak palace, it's funny to see the "not seafood" list hidden at the bottom: one chicken option, a filet mignon, or a cheeseburger.

Old Angler's Inn ★★

MODERN AMERICAN	EXPENSIVE	QUALITY ★★★	VALUE ★★½

10801 MacArthur Boulevard, Potomac; ☎ 301-299-9097; www.oldanglersinn.com Maryland Suburbs

Reservations Required. **When to go** Summer for brunch outside. **Entree range** $24–$36. **Payment** VISA, MC, AMEX, DC, JCB, CB. **Service rating** ★★★. **Friendliness rating** ★★★. **Metro** None nearby. **Parking** Free lot. **Bar** Full service. **Wine selection** Brief. **Dress** Dressy, business, jacket and tie. **Disabled access** No. **Customers** Locals. **Hours Brunch:** Sunday, noon–2:30 p.m. **Lunch:** Tuesday–Saturday, noon–2:30 p.m. **Dinner:** Tuesday–Sunday, 6–9 p.m.; closed Monday.

SETTING AND ATMOSPHERE A beautiful, old-fashioned inn above the river, with a blazing fireplace in the parlor bar downstairs and a huddle of small dining rooms up a narrow, iron spiral staircase (and bathrooms out of the servants' quarters). The stone terrace and gazebo levels are open in good weather.

HOUSE SPECIALTIES The menu changes seasonally, but frequently includes ostrich, foie gras, venison, and lobster. Also look for squab or duck dishes, caviar (either as an ingredient or in classic service), and fresh fish.

OTHER RECOMMENDATIONS Ask for the chef's-choice menu (for the whole table only), which can be requested as vegetarian or seafood-only if you like.

SUMMARY AND COMMENTS This has always been a beautiful site, but its familiar weaknesses—haphazard service and hit-or-miss food—still threaten it occasionally, and the wine list's range doesn't keep up with its price range. The crowd, too, has changed a little: dressing down more, treating it more as a neighborhood restaurant than a special occasion "inn"—which may be the direction it's headed. A new outdoor bar with occasional live music in warm weather is a welcome addition.

Old Ebbitt Grill ★★

AMERICAN	MODERATE	QUALITY ★★½	VALUE ★★★

675 15th Street NW; ☎ 202-347-4801; www.ebbitt.com Downtown

Reservations Recommended. **When to go** Sunday brunch, after work for power-tripping. **Entree range** $9–$25. **Payment** VISA, MC, AMEX, DC, D. **Service rating** ★★★. **Friendliness rating** ★★★. **Metro** Metro Center or McPherson Square. **Parking** Pay lots (validated after 6 p.m. and all day Sunday). **Bar** Full service. **Wine selection** Good; corkage fee, $15. **Dress** Business, informal. **Disabled access** Very good (through G Street atrium). **Customers** Business, feds, locals, tourists. **Hours Breakfast:** Monday–Friday, 7:30–11 a.m. **Brunch:** Saturday and Sunday, 8:30 a.m.–4 p.m. **Lunch/dinner:** Monday–Friday, 11 a.m.–midnight; Saturday and Sunday, 4 p.m.–midnight; late-night menu every day, midnight–1 a.m.

SETTING AND ATMOSPHERE An updated old-boys' club, but with equal opportunity hospitality: a few horsey accoutrements (bridles, snaffles) in front, lots of greenery and etched-glass dividers in the main room, and a classic oyster bar.

HOUSE SPECIALTIES Linguine with shrimp, basil, and fresh tomatoes; pork chops with homemade applesauce; black pepper–rubbed leg of lamb with papaya relish; old-fashioned pepper-pot beef; steamed mussels; smoked salmon (a company signature) and smoked bluefish when available. Annually, during the brief halibut season in Alaska, the Old Ebbitt and its Clyde's cousins have a halibut celebration that is a command performance for seafood lovers. For brunch, fat old-style French toast and corned beef hash.

ENTERTAINMENT AND AMENITIES Occasional piano music at happy hour.

SUMMARY AND COMMENTS This is one restaurant whose whole experience is somehow better than the food might indicate by itself. The Old Ebbitt—actually, the new Old Ebbitt for those who remember the fusty Back Bay–style original around the corner and its stuffed owls and scuffed bar rails—takes its White House neighborhood location seriously, but not too seriously. That is, it gives out pagers to patrons waiting for tables, but the staff democratically seats the ties and T-shirts side by side.

Old Glory ★★

BARBECUE	MODERATE	QUALITY ★★½	VALUE ★★★

3139 M Street NW; ☎ 202-337-3406; www.oldglorybbq.com
Georgetown

Reservations Parties of 6 or more only, for lunch or weekday dinner. **When to go** Afternoon. **Entree range** $9–$25. **Payment** VISA, MC, AMEX, DC, D. **Service rating** ★★½. **Friendliness rating** ★★★. **Metro** Foggy Bottom. **Parking** Pay lots, street. **Bar** Full service. **Wine selection** Minimal. **Dress** Casual, informal. **Disabled access** Good. **Customers** Local, tourist. **Hours Brunch:** Sunday, 11 a.m.–3 p.m. **Lunch/dinner:** Monday–Thursday, 11:30 a.m.–2 a.m.; Friday and Saturday, 11:30 a.m.–3 a.m.; Sunday, 11 a.m.–2 a.m.; late-night menu available every day, 11:30 p.m. until closing.

SETTING AND ATMOSPHERE A chic and cheeky take on roadhouse diner décor with a sort of Six Flags theme: the state colors of Tennessee, Texas, Georgia, Kentucky, Kansas (which used to be Arkansas), and the Carolinas hang overhead, while each table is armed with bottles of six different barbecue sauces—mild, sweet, vinegary, multichilied, mustardy, tomatoey—named for the same seven states. A mix of old and new country and honky-tonk music plays on the PA.

HOUSE SPECIALTIES Pork ribs or beef spareribs; "pulled" (shredded rather than chopped) pork shoulder; jerk-rubbed, roasted chicken; slow-smoked leg of lamb; smoked ham; various combinations or sandwich versions thereof. Daily specials often include pit-fired steaks or fresh seafood.

OTHER RECOMMENDATIONS Pit-grilled burgers with cheddar and smoked ham; marinated and grilled vegetables; marinated, wood-grilled shrimp.

SUMMARY AND COMMENTS This trendy finger-lickers' stop is surprisingly good, particularly when it comes to the sort of Southern side dishes that rarely travel well. The biscuits are fine (the cornbread isn't), and the hoppin' John—black-eyed peas and rice—is better than authentic. It's neither mushy nor greasy.

Palena ★★★★

MODERN AMERICAN	EXPENSIVE	QUALITY ★★★★½	VALUE ★★★

3529 Connecticut Avenue NW; ☎ 202-537-9250; www.palenarestaurant.com Upper Northwest

Reservations Recommended. **When to go** Anytime **Entree range** $11–$31; 3-course, $55; 4-course, $62; 5-course, $69. **Payment** VISA, MC, AMEX, D, DC. **Service rating** ★★★½. **Friendliness rating** ★★★½. **Metro** Cleveland Park. **Parking** Street, pay lot. **Bar** Full service. **Wine selection** Good. **Dress** Business, casual. **Disabled access** Good. **Customers** Local up-and-comers; connected out-of-towners. **Hours** Monday–Saturday, 5:30–10 p.m.

SETTING AND ATMOSPHERE Deceptively low-key from the sidewalk, this is a long, lean, easy, cream-colored space leading back from a chic front lounge to a subtle garden that provides a pleasant light over the banquets. This is another dual-menu restaurant: the less formal front room is á la carte and lots of fun (try the half-roast chicken and the real cheeseburger on house-made brioche, one of the best $10 meals in town); dinner is either three, four, or five fixed-price courses.

HOUSE SPECIALTIES The menus are seasonal, and also market driven, but among examples of the kitchen's work: daring and generally delightful presentations such as lobster and beet salad; rabbit rolled around a quail egg with greens stuffing; venison loin paired with braised short ribs or veal cheeks with sweetbreads; sautéed skate, pan-roasted lamb loin, or pig's ears en croquette (which points out the chef's unusually broad repertoire).

OTHER RECOMMENDATIONS Carefully tended duck breast or sometimes sweet-gamy squab; red snapper in a Thai-inflected broth; meaty crab salad. Ravioli stuffed with oxtail, almonds, raisins and spinach; house-made pasta with duck ragù. And in this case, the desserts are the equal of the entrees.

SUMMARY AND COMMENTS Chef and co-owner Frank Ruta has one of D.C.'s most impressive kitchen resumes, starting at the White House (three administrations) and working through the River Club, Obelisk, and Provence—hence the free eclecticism of his combinations. He and his co-owner, the equally prominent pastry chef Ann Amernick, whom he met at the White House, bought what had been one of the previous Greenwood sites and actually upscaled the food while somehow smoothing the atmosphere, replacing personality with repose. (Both, of course, are desirable in dining circles.)

Persimmon ★★½

MODERN AMERICAN	MODERATE	QUALITY ★★★★	VALUE ★★★

7003 Wisconsin Avenue, Chevy Chase; ☎ 301-654-9860;
www.persimmonrestaurant.com Maryland Suburbs

Reservations Recommended. **When to go** Weeknights. **Entree range** $17–$25. **Payment** VISA, MC, AMEX, DC. **Service rating** ★★½. **Friendliness rating** ★★★½. **Metro** Bethesda. **Parking** Street (metered), pay lots. **Bar** Beer and wine. **Wine selection** Small but good. **Dress** Business, informal. **Disabled access** Good. **Customers** Older suburban couples, young conservative professionals. **Hours Lunch:** Monday–Saturday, 11:30 a.m.–2 p.m. **Dinner:** Monday–Saturday, 5:30–10 p.m.; Sunday, closed.

SETTING AND ATMOSPHERE A real storefront, which has survived various incarnations with its pressed-tin ceiling remarkably intact, now exotically sponged to match its ruby-ripe name and given a "brocade" glitter with clusters of gilt-frame mirrors.

HOUSE SPECIALTIES A trio of tartares: tuna, salmon, and ceviche; barbecue chicken pot stickers with mango salsa and black beans; wasabi-fried oysters; duck confit with frageolets; mushroom-and-blue-cheese-stuffed ravioli; crab cakes; pecan-crusted rack of lamb; shiitake-and-hoisin-crusted salmon.

OTHER RECOMMENDATIONS That retro favorite, roast chicken with mashed potatoes and vegetable ragoût; grilled pork porterhouse with fried plantains; bouillabaisse, crab cakes and fish in general.

ENTERTAINMENT AND AMENITIES A homemade pâté with the bread basket.

SUMMARY AND COMMENTS This simple but smart little eclectic American bistro—actually more mod/Med/fusion—might well fill the Georgetown-chic gap in Bethesda. Chef-owner Damian Salvatore is another Washington chef whose cooking gets more assured and more interesting all the time. And the kitchen (which seems to run more smoothly than in early years) is extremely presentation savvy.

Pizzeria Paradiso ★★½

PIZZA	INEXPENSIVE	QUALITY ★★★	VALUE ★★★★

2029 P Street NW, Dupont Circle/Adams-Morgan; ☎ 202-223-1245
3282 M Street NW, Georgetown; ☎ 202-337-1245
www.eatyourpizza.com

Reservations Not accepted. **When to go** Anytime, except around 8–10 p.m. **Entree range** $9–$17. **Payment** VISA, MC, DC. **Service rating** ★★★. **Friendliness rating** ★★★. **Metro** P Street: Dupont Circle. **Parking** Street, pay lot. **Bar** Beer and wine. **Wine selection** Limited. **Dress** Casual. **Disabled access** No. **Customers** Local, tourist, student. **Hours** Monday–Friday, 11:30 a.m.–11 p.m.; Saturday, 11 a.m.–midnight; Sunday, noon–10 p.m.

SETTING AND ATMOSPHERE As tiny as this upper room is, it's hilariously decorated, with trompe l'oeil stone walls opening at the "ruined roof" to a blue sky; columns with capitals of papier-mâché veggies; a woodburning stove painted like a smokestack; and semi-Impressionistic painted cardboard pizzas like Amish hexes around the walls (a sly comment on the mass-market competition, perhaps?).

HOUSE SPECIALTIES Pizzas with four cheeses, or the Atomica, with salami, black olives, and hot peppers; zucchini, eggplant, peppers, and fresh buffalo mozzarella; mussels (surprisingly, yes); and potato with pesto sauce and Parmesan.

OTHER RECOMMENDATIONS Thick sandwiches made with focaccia, including roast lamb and roasted veggies; multimeat Italian subs; pork with hot peppers.

SUMMARY AND COMMENTS It may seem extravagant to give such high marks to a pizzeria, but pizza this good—shoveled in and out of the deep oven, with a splash of extra-virgin olive oil and a handful of cheese tossed on at the last moment—makes most American takeout blush. It's almost a redefinition of pizza. This restaurant also has real attitude—not commercial camp, just an irresistible New Wave nonchalance. The Georgetown branch has a great beer bar, Bierria Paradiso, below stairs. There is also a family-business connection to Two Amys pizzeria at 3715 Macomb Street NW; ☎ 202-885-5700.

Restaurant Eve ★★★★

| MODERN AMERICAN | VERY EXPENSIVE | QUALITY ★★★★ | VALUE ★★★ |

110 South Pitt Street, Old Town Alexandria; ☎ 703-706-0450; www.restauranteve.com Virginia Suburbs

Reservations Strongly recommended. **When to go** Early for quiet, late for energy. **Entree range** Bistro, $25–$34; fixed-price, $95–$125. **Payment** VISA, MC, AMEX, D, DC. **Service rating** ★★★★. **Friendliness rating** ★★★★. **Metro** King Street. **Parking** Public garage, street. **Bar** Full service and unusually inventive. **Wine selection** Top flight. **Dress** Business, nice casual. **Disabled access** Good. **Customers** Destination-no-issue foodies, Old Town professionals, cocktail trendies, wine lovers, late-night indulgers. **Hours Lunch:** Monday–Friday, 11:30 a.m.–2:30 p.m. **Dinner:** Monday–Saturday, 5:30–10 p.m. (bistro), 5:30–9:30 p.m. (tasting room); Monday–Friday, 11:30 a.m–10:30 p.m., Saturday, 5–11 p.m. (lounge).

SETTING AND ATMOSPHERE Simple, elegant, intimate-sized Federal town house with exposed brick, polished wood floors, and soft background music.

HOUSE SPECIALTIES From the bistro menu: homemade garlic veal sausage with salsify and oyster mushrooms; confit of house-cured pork belly with cannellini beans; potato-crusted halibut with morels and ramps; roast monkfish with oven-dried tomatoes, chorizo, and olives. Among the tasting-room dishes: hog's head "bangers"; butter-poached lobster; foie gras with Meyer-lemon marmalade; braised beef tripe with *merguez* and roasted cipollini onions; pan-roasted sweetbreads; lamb's tongue with anise and orange; olive oil–poached escolar with smoked-ham vinaigrette. Among the surprises: morsels of porcini beignet; deviled quail's egg with caviar.

SUMMARY AND COMMENTS Chef Cathal Armstrong, one of *Food & Wine* magazine's top chefs of 2006, is Irish by nature, French by nurture—he spent his childhood summers in France—and has cooked Latino fusion, French bistro, modern Southern, and Italian. But this ambitious kitchen is all-American, heavy on Virginia produce, artisanal cheeses, organic meats, and sustainable seafood. Eve is actually two (or three) restaurants in one: the formal tasting room and the more casual, but still upscale, à la carte bistro, plus a bar and lounge. (Coming soon: Eve's Bar-Kitchen, another lounge on the second floor.)

The tasting-room menu comprises five or nine courses: "Creation" (appetizers), "Ocean" (seafood), "Earth and Sky" (meats and poultry), "Age" (cheeses), and "Eden" (desserts). And that doesn't count the couple of preliminary treats. Sommelier and passionately creative bartender Todd Thrasher, who makes his own quinine tonic for gin and tonics, makes the bar a fun scene: Eve's will be his exhibition kitchen, so to speak. The bar and lounge is open all afternoon and late at night. In addition, Armstrong and manager-wife Meshelle have opened Eamonn's, a Dublin-style fish-and-chips shop named after their son (Eve is their daughter), at 728 King Street, and the knock-and-enter retro "speakeasy" PX above that.

Sea Catch ★★

SEAFOOD	MODERATE	QUALITY ★★★	VALUE ★★½

1054 31st Street NW; ☎ 202-337-8855; www.seacatchrestaurant.com
Georgetown

Reservations Recommended. **When to go** Early. **Entree range** $10–$32, market price higher. **Payment** VISA, MC, AMEX, D, DC. **Service rating** ★★★. **Friendliness rating** ★★½. **Metro** Foggy Bottom. **Parking** Validated for 3 hours. **Bar** Full service. **Wine selection** Good. **Dress** Casual, business. **Disabled access** Good. **Customers** Local, business. **Hours Lunch:** Monday–Saturday, noon–3 p.m. **Dinner:** Monday–Saturday, 5:30–10 p.m.; Sunday: Brunch 11 a.m. to 3 p.m.; Dinner 5:30 p.m.–9 p.m.

SETTING AND ATMOSPHERE Sleekly elegant, with a white marble raw bar, polished-wood dining room with fireplace, and, in good weather, a balcony overlooking the Chesapeake & Ohio Canal.

HOUSE SPECIALTIES Jumbo lump crab cakes with vegetable slaw; poached lobster linguine; seared tuna au poivre; chef Shively's Louisiana seafood gumbo; grilled rainbow trout, flounder, mahi mahi, chilean sea bass, swordfish and always whole fish of the day.

OTHER RECOMMENDATIONS A personal "off the menu" favorite is the lobster sashimi, which is only available when the raw bar isn't too busy. Fresh stone crab claws flown in from Maine are another seasonal treat. Also check for happy hour specials.

SUMMARY AND COMMENTS This is an underrated seafood establishment particularly ideal for people who suffer from fear of frying. The key here is balance: Chef Jeff Shively likes to play with his presentations, but not to the point where the quality or texture of the shellfish is obscured. Those who prefer the straighter stuff may order lobster steamed, grilled, broiled, baked, or poached; a variety of fresh fish (there is no freezer in the kitchen, proof of the chef's dedication to freshness) brushed with oil and grilled; or an updated surf-and-turf of tenderloin and crab-stuffed mushrooms. Ask for guidance with the wine list—it's much more interesting than the usual fish grill's selection. However, for dedicated carnivores, the Thai-marinated roast chicken or the steaks are very dependable. There is also a steamed lobster and shellfish dinner for $30.

1789 ★★★

MODERN AMERICAN	EXPENSIVE	QUALITY ★★★★	VALUE ★★★

1226 36th Street NW; ☎ 202-965-1789; www.1789restaurant.com
Georgetown

Reservations Recommended. **When to go** Anytime. **Entree range** Prix fixe, $35; $23–$38. **Payment** VISA, MC, AMEX, D, DC. **Service rating** ★★★. **Friendliness rating** ★★★. **Metro** None nearby. **Parking** Valet. **Bar** Full service. **Wine selection** Good. **Dress** Jacket required. **Disabled access** No. **Customers** Local, business, tourist. **Hours** Monday–Thursday, 6–10 p.m.; Friday, 6–11 p.m.; Saturday, 5:30–11 p.m.; Sunday, 5:30–10 p.m.

SETTING AND ATMOSPHERE A meticulously maintained Federal town house with blazing fireplaces, polished silver, and historic poise; a certain formality is implied rather than expressed. Coat and tie still required, but there are a few extras on hand.

HOUSE SPECIALTIES Branzino with clams and roasted peppers; sweet snails in pastry and parsley sauce; lamb tongue salad; steak tartare with quail egg; caramelized Kurobuta pork chop with house-cured bacon, sorrel, and honey.

OTHER RECOMMENDATIONS Rack of lamb with Cheddar potatoes; rabbit-stuffed rabbit.

SUMMARY AND COMMENTS This menu, inspired by seasonal availability, showcases regional game and seafood with care and respect. The kitchen aims to re-create and reclaim classic dishes—grilled quail with oysters and bacon, venison medallions, rack of lamb—and update them rather than invent novel treatments. In other words, it's more of a culinary tender of the flame than an innovator, which suits its old-money clientele. However, under the direction of new chef Nathan Beauchamp, the kitchen is moving with increasing confidence into a middle ground, still classic but fresh. Beachamp's "seasonal" menus change eight times a year, not four.

Sushi-Ko ★★★★½

JAPANESE	MODERATE	QUALITY ★★★★½	VALUE ★★★★

2309 Wisconsin Avenue NW; ☎ 202-333-4187; www.sushiko.us
Georgetown

Reservations Recommended. **When to go** Anytime. **Entree range** $15–$23. **Payment** VISA, MC, AMEX. **Service rating** ★★★. **Friendliness rating** ★★★. **Metro** None nearby. **Parking** Street, valet (dinner only). **Bar** Full service. **Wine selection**

Good, particularly French. **Dress** Business, casual. **Disabled access** No.
Customers Local, ethnic. **Hours Lunch:** Tuesday–Friday, noon–2:30 p.m.
Dinner: Monday–Thursday, 6–10:30 p.m.; Friday, 6–11 p.m.; Saturday, 5:30–
11 p.m.; Sunday, 5:30–10 p.m.

SETTING AND ATMOSPHERE   A sleek twist on classic sushi-bar décor downstairs,
carefully unfrilly; more obviously modern—i.e., non-tradition-bound—
upstairs.

HOUSE SPECIALTIES   Any of the seasonal "small dishes," either traditional or
contemporary, from Chef Koji Terano, involving and often combining
fish, both cooked and raw, with seaweeds, wild greens, grains, herbs,
caviar, and sometimes unexpected American touches. If you want to see
what he can do, order the four-course ($40) or six-course ($65) tasting
menu: you'll be full but not stuffed.

OTHER RECOMMENDATIONS   Sushi, especially seasonal dishes such as ankimo
(monkfish liver) and toro (fatty tuna); broiled eel; soft-shell crabs; octopus salad; grilled fish; spring for real wasabi.

SUMMARY AND COMMENTS   Thanks to its unusual seasonal dishes, Sushi-Ko
attracts a broad, generally knowledgeable, and fairly affluent crowd.
This has made it possible for owner Daisuke Utagawa and his team to
offer a more flexible style of cooking, both traditional and improvisational—that is, based on market availability and traditional seasonal
factors. However, while the "ordinary" sushi is reasonable, those specials can make dinner somewhat more pricey than a meal at most other
sushi bars, so don't waste it on someone who's happy with a grocery-
store California roll. Utagawa is also intrigued with the notion of
matching French wines and Japanese food, and offering higher-quality
sakes. At press time, an offshoot of Sushi-Ko was under construction
next to the luxury shops of the Collection at Chevy Chase, near the
Friendship Heights Metro Station.

Tabard Inn   ★★½

FRENCH/ITALIAN	MODERATE	QUALITY ★★½	VALUE ★★★

1739 N Street NW; ☎ 202-785-1277; www.tabardinn.com
Dupont Circle/Adams-Morgan

Reservations Recommended. **When to go** Anytime. **Entree range** $10–$32.
Payment VISA, MC, AMEX, D, DC. **Service rating** ★★★. **Friendliness rating**
★★★★. **Metro** Farragut North or Dupont Circle. **Parking** Street. **Bar** Full
service. **Wine selection** Good. **Dress** Business, informal. **Disabled access** No.
Customers Business, locals. **Hours Breakfast:** Monday–Friday, 7–10 a.m.;
Saturday and Sunday, 7–9:30 a.m. **Brunch:** Saturday, 11 a.m.–2:30 p.m.; Sunday,
10:30 a.m.–2:30 p.m. **Lunch:** Monday–Friday, 11:30 a.m.–2:30 p.m. **Dinner:**
Sunday–Friday, 6–10 p.m.; Saturday, 6–10:30 p.m.

SETTING AND ATMOSPHERE   This almost theatrically old-English jumble of
rooms has a courtyard at its heart (as all good English country inns
should), a series of small dining rooms with surprisingly light-hearted

décor (a garden-path mural up the stairs, for example), and a wood-lined library with couches and a fireplace, ideal for a winter afternoon, cocktail before dinner, or after-dinner cordial.

HOUSE SPECIALTIES Grilled rare tuna; wild mushroom and fava bean lasagna; grilled marinated ostrich steak; roasted cod; seafood stew; grilled scallops with fettuccine; smoked mozzarella tomatoes and caramelized-Vidalia-onion tart; baby-spinach salad.

SUMMARY AND COMMENTS Although it's currently in a sort of hearty eclectic bistro style, the Tabard has gone through a series of chefs, and so the tone and quality is a little erratic; but it's still a favorite spot thanks to its picturesque setting.

Taberna del Alabardero ★★★

| SPANISH | VERY EXPENSIVE | QUALITY ★★★ | VALUE ★★★ |

1776 I Street NW (entrance on 18th Street); ☎ 202-429-2200; www.albardero.com Downtown

Reservations Recommended. **When to go** Anytime for tapas, lunch for fixed-price meals. **Entree range** Lunch, $18–$24 and dinner, $27–$37; daily vegetarian menu, $65; chef's tasting menu, $85; fixed-price lunch and dinners, $42–$55. **Payment** VISA, MC, AMEX, D, JCB, DC. **Service rating** ★★★★. **Friendliness rating** ★★★. **Metro** Farragut West or Farragut North. **Parking** Free next door. **Bar** Full service. **Wine selection** Very good. **Dress** Jacket and tie suggested. **Disabled access** Good. **Customers** Local, embassy, ethnic. **Hours Lunch:** Monday–Friday, 11:30 a.m.–2:30 p.m. **Dinner:** Monday–Thursday, 5:30–10:30 p.m.; Friday and Saturday, 5:30–11 p.m.; Sunday, closed.

SETTING AND ATMOSPHERE Lace curtain and velvet old-world elegance, with ornate moldings and a magnificent private room (like a chapel) in the center.

HOUSE SPECIALTIES Luscious lobster paella at night, as well as traditional and wild mushroom paellas; squid in its own ink, roast leg of lamb; veal chop with red wine sauce; octopus with peppers; baked meat pies.

OTHER RECOMMENDATIONS Daily specials, particularly game, and at least a half-dozen seafood specials every day; quail or pheasant; halibut with mussels. There are fixed-price menus at lunch ($42) and dinner ($55).

SUMMARY AND COMMENTS This is a very old-world-style restaurant and quite dignified. One alternative is to dabble in Taberna's riches via the tapas menu, a selection of a dozen smaller-sized dishes (and you can linger as long as you like). There is also a list of a dozen sherries by the glass and red or white sangria. And it's also getting into the special-events trend, with wine dinners and imported guest chefs who show off Spanish regional cuisine with monkfish in saffron ragoût, cream of pumpkin porcini soup, etc. With the departure of both longtime chef Josu Zubikarai and his assistant-successor Enrique Sanchez, the menu and ratings may be up for review.

Tako Grill ★★★½

JAPANESE	INEXPENSIVE	QUALITY ★★★½	VALUE ★★★

7756 Wisconsin Avenue, Bethesda; ☎ 301-652-7030; www.takogrill.com
Maryland Suburbs

Reservations Recommended. **When to go** Before 7 p.m. **Entree range** $6–$17.
Payment VISA, MC, AMEX. **Service rating** ★★★★. **Friendliness rating** ★★★.
Metro Bethesda or Medical Center. **Parking** Street, public garages, free lot
(dinner only). **Bar** Wine and beer. **Wine selection** House. **Dress** Casual,
informal. **Disabled access** Very good. **Customers** Local, business. **Hours Lunch:**
Monday–Saturday, 11:30 a.m.–2 p.m. **Dinner:** Monday–Thursday, 5:30–10 p.m.;
Friday and Saturday, 5:30–10:30 p.m.; Sunday, 5–9:30 p.m.

SETTING AND ATMOSPHERE A cool, hip, very 21st-century-Tokyo room, a
study in white, black, and scarlet, but with deft artistic touches (the
flower arrangements) and almost hallucinatory "script" versions of
Japanese verses hung on the walls. (The chefs, particularly the younger
ones, are very Tokyo stylish, too—check out the bleached and reddened
hair.) The adjoining sake bar (where you may order food as well) is
particularly smart.

HOUSE SPECIALTIES Soft-shell-crab tempura fried and chopped into hand
rolls; grilled teriyaki king salmon; broiled freshwater eel on rice; *sushi
bar:* sushi assortment of tuna, yellowtail, salmon, flounder, crab stick,
shrimp, seawater eel and shad roe; grilled whole red snapper or rainbow trout; glazed grilled eel; tiny candied whole octopus.

SUMMARY AND COMMENTS Of the four best Japanese restaurants in the
area, each has a different slant: Makoto's (a very small hideaway on
Macarthur Boulevard) is classic; Sushi-Ko's cutting-edge; Kaz's influenced
by the deconstruction movement; and Tako's cool—especially thanks to
the addition of the sake bar. In addition to some of the best and freshest
sushi and sashimi in the area, Tako has a hot-stone grill called a robotai, on
which whole fish, large shrimp, and a variety of fresh vegetables are
cooked. The line of customers waiting to get in—two recent expansions
notwithstanding—is the surest evidence of Tako's quality. Weekday lunches
are a business special: soup, salad, rice, and a daily entree (orange roughy,
chicken teriyaki, ginger pork), plus six pieces of rolled sushi for $9. And
since often several of the waitresses are vegetarian or vegan, Tako is especially well equipped to satisfy customers with special diets.

Tara Thai ★★

THAI	INEXPENSIVE	QUALITY ★★½	VALUE ★★★

4828 Bethesda Avenue, Bethesda, MD; ☎ 301-657-0488
12071 Rockville Pike (Montrose Crossing), Rockville, MD; ☎ 301-231-9899
4001 North Fairfax Drive, Ballston, VA; ☎ 703-903-4999
7501-C Leesburg Pike, Tysons Corner, VA; ☎ 703-506-9788
226 Maple Avenue West, Vienna, VA; ☎ 703-255-2467

Reservations Helpful. **When to go** Weekdays. **Entree range** $10–$14. **Payment** VISA, MC, AMEX, D, DC. **Service rating** ★★★. **Friendliness rating** ★★★½. **Metro** *Bethesda:* Bethesda; *Rockville:* Twinbrook. **Parking** Free lot. **Bar** Full service. **Wine selection** House. **Dress** Informal, casual. **Disabled access** Fair. **Customers** Ethnic, local. **Hours Lunch:** Monday–Friday, 11:30 a.m.–3 p.m.; Saturday and Sunday, noon–3:30 p.m. **Dinner:** Sunday–Thursday, 5–10 p.m.; Friday and Saturday, 5–11 p.m.

SETTING AND ATMOSPHERE "Tara" has nothing to do with the Old South. It means "blue," and these charming restaurants are marine blue and swimming in fantastical creatures and lacquered tables. The original Vienna branch is quite small, but so friendly that it seems cheerfully crowded rather than annoyingly so. The Bethesda branch draws a more mixed 20- and 30-something crowd to its cheeky murals, window-box bar, and chrome touches. The newest is the big Rockville branch—the gold-and-glitter look.

HOUSE SPECIALTIES Whole fish, either fried with chile sauce or steamed in banana leaves with black mushrooms and ginger; soft-shell crabs; "wild" lamb curry; red curry beef; green eggplant curry with chicken.

OTHER RECOMMENDATIONS *Nua sawan* (thin dried but tender beef, fried and served with slaw—sort of a Thai barbecue); honey-glazed duck. For a light meal or shared appetizer, try the "heavenly wings" (chicken drummettes scraped back into rattle shapes, stuffed with crab and green onion, then battered and fried).

SUMMARY AND COMMENTS Too much success is a two-edged sword: while the fare at the Vienna and Bethesda branches remains consistently good, some of the other branches, notably Rockville, are more erratic. The group also owns the promising Tara Asian, near the Rockville Metro, which serves pan-Asian fare.

Taste of Saigon ★★

VIETNAMESE	INEXPENSIVE	QUALITY ★★½	VALUE ★★★

410 Hungerford Drive, Rockville, MD; ☎ **301-424-7222**
8201 Greensboro Drive, McLean, VA; ☎ **703-790-0700;**
www.tasteofsaigon.com

Reservations Accepted. **When to go** Anytime. **Entree range** $8–$15. **Payment** VISA, MC, AMEX, D, DC, CB. **Service rating** ★★★. **Friendliness rating** ★★★★. **Metro** *Rockville:* Rockville; *McLean:* None nearby. **Parking** Free lot. **Bar** Full service. **Wine selection** Limited. **Dress** Informal. **Disabled access** Good. **Customers** Local, business, ethnic. **Hours** Monday–Saturday, 11 a.m.–11 p.m.; Sunday, 11 a.m.–9:30 p.m.

SETTING AND ATMOSPHERE An intriguingly angular, sleek, gray-and-black-lacquer room slyly tucked into the back of a plain office building.

HOUSE SPECIALTIES Steamed whole rockfish served with rice crêpes and vegetables for rolling up; choice of seafoods—whole live lobster (up to four pounds), soft shells, scallops, or shrimp—in a house special black-pepper sauce.

OTHER RECOMMENDATIONS Cornish hen stuffed with pork; boneless roast quail; pho and other noodle soups in appetizer or entree sizes; rich venison curry.

ENTERTAINMENT AND AMENITIES Patio dining in good weather.

SUMMARY AND COMMENTS The specials here are interesting dishes; it's as if the kitchen were as intrigued as the diners. The beef dishes are only fair, but the seafood and game bird entrees are particularly good. Some of the sauces are quite heavy, but if you stick to the steamed fish or bountiful soup choices, a Vietnamese dinner can be a dieter's dream.

Tavira ★★½

PORTUGUESE	MODERATE	QUALITY ★★★	VALUE ★★½

8401 Connecticut Avenue, Chevy Chase; ☎ 301-652-8684; www.tavirarestaurant.com Maryland Suburbs

Reservations Recommended. **When to go** Anytime. **Entree range** $15–$30. **Payment** AMEX, VISA, MC, DC. **Service rating** ★★★. **Friendliness rating** ★★★. **Metro** None nearby. **Parking** Free lot. **Bar** Full service. **Wine selection** Fair. **Dress** Business, casual. **Disabled access** Good. **Customers** Locals, businesspeople. **Hours Lunch:** Monday–Friday, 11:30 a.m.–2:30 p.m. **Dinner:** Monday–Thursday, 5:30–10 p.m.; Friday and Saturday, 5:30–11 p.m.

SETTING AND ATMOSPHERE Named for a medieval fortress town (a good pun, considering it's in the basement of a bank, like a dungeon), it's made bright by sunny paint, a fireplace, heavy artisan pottery, and glass sconces—a sort of indoor patio with bar.

HOUSE SPECIALTIES A tureen of mussels with tomato-sweet pepper broth; veal chops with sherry; clams with chorizo and prosciutto; grilled lamb chops. Don't miss the "French fries," really more like homemade potato chips.

OTHER RECOMMENDATIONS Roasted red peppers stuffed with goat cheese; seafood stew; traditional salt cod shredded with straw potatoes, onions, and egg; spicy grilled chicken piri-piri; paella-like *arroz valenciana.*

SUMMARY AND COMMENTS Although not terribly visible to traffic, Tavira is making itself indispensable in a neighborhood hungry for good food and a city ready for its mix of traditional Mediterranean and navy-trade fare. It's also a good place to test out *vinho verde,* the "green wine" of Portugal, so called for its light, youthful (i.e., green) quality, and a fine complement to the sometimes oil- and garlic-strong food.

Teatro Goldoni ★★½

ITALIAN	MODERATE	QUALITY ★★★	VALUE ★★★

1909 K Street NW; ☎ 202-955-9494; www.teatrogoldoni.com Downtown

Reservations Recommended. **When to go** Lunch; late dinner. **Entree range** $16–$36. **Payment** VISA, MC, AMEX, DC. **Service rating** ★★★. **Friendliness rating** ★★★. **Metro** Farragut West or Farragut North. **Parking** Valet, pay lots. **Bar** Full service. **Wine selection** Very good. **Dress** Business, dressy, dressy casual. **Disabled access** Good. **Customers** Business, foodies. **Hours Lunch:**

Monday–Friday, 11:30 a.m.–2 p.m. **Dinner:** Monday–Thursday, 5:30–10 p.m.; Friday and Saturday, 5–11 p.m.

SETTING AND ATMOSPHERE Take the word "teatro" seriously: this is a theatrical setting for a culinary performance. Mini-spots are trained on the plates like klieg lights on stars; the huge mirror over the bar reveals the show behind you; and the tables and booths are on their own "stages." And you'd better be dressed for the part: not only are the other customers watching you, but the eyeholes of the masks on the wall and those of the photographed models (like the rest of the décor, half commedia dell'arte, half carnival) seem to be evaluating you. In other words, it's either exhilarating or over-the-top, depending on your mood.

HOUSE SPECIALTIES Look for earthy but not heavy flavors: roasted veal chop served with fingerling potatoes and wild mushroom sauce; lobster risotto; braised lamb shank served over a cannellini bean purée; pan seared tuna "rare" served with sautéed zucchini and carrots, and topped with balsamic-vinegar sauce. In colder weather, expect comfort dishes, again more rich than weighty: braises, stews, ragùs, chicken and morel "casserole."

OTHER RECOMMENDATIONS If roasted veal is on the specials, go straight for it. Also expect interesting risottos and good vegetarian options such as the penne pasta with wild mushrooms, arugula, truffle oil, and shaved Parmesan cheese.

SUMMARY AND COMMENTS Chef-owner Fabrizio Aielli is on his third eponymous restaurant, and that after years at Galileo with Roberto Donna. However, his particular accent is Venetian, and the squid and fried-seafood dishes, such as the *fritto misto,* are among his personal prides. His flamboyance opens Teatro up to some inconsistencies; but even the errors are interesting.

TenPenh ★★½

PAN-ASIAN	MODERATE	QUALITY ★★½	VALUE ★★½

1001 Pennsylvania Avenue NW; ☎ 202-393-4500; www.tenpenh.com
Downtown

Reservations Recommended. **When to go** Early dinner or bar. **Entree range** $13–$28. **Payment** VISA, MC, AMEX, D, JCB, DC, CB. **Service rating ★★★★. Friendliness rating ★★★. Metro** Federal Triangle or Archives–Navy Memorial–Penn Quarter. **Parking** Valet, pay lots. **Bar** Full service. **Wine selection** Very good. **Dress** Business, casual, dressy. **Disabled access** Very good. **Customers** Business, food trendies, media, pols. **Hours Lunch:** Monday–Friday, 11:30 a.m.–2:30 p.m. **Dinner:** Monday–Thursday, 5:30–10:30 p.m.; Friday and Saturday, 5:30–11 p.m.

SETTING AND ATMOSPHERE This is a famous old law-firm office building, and it looks it outside, but inside, TenPenh is like one of those simple Asian jewelry boxes that opens to reveal the subdued glitter of saffron and gold silk, patinaed Buddhas, hammered-bronze flatware, teak lamps, curio trays as dessert buffets, incense coils dangling from the ceiling, and bamboo place mats. And no wonder: the owners took a three-week shopping trip to Bangkok, Hong Kong, Ho Chi Minh City, Macao, and Singapore to hand-pick $40,000 worth of furnishings.

HOUSE SPECIALTIES Peking duck roll; Hong Kong-style crispy catfish; curried lump crab cakes; steamed shrimp–scallion dumplings; spicy wok-seared calamari; a sort of tempura-fried California roll (all appetizers); grilled yellow fin tuna; udon noodle shrimp stir-fry with coconut milk; five spice/pecan-crusted halibut with port-ginger sauce; the signature Chinese smoked lobster with crispy fried spinach; red Thai curry prawns with pineapple.

OTHER RECOMMENDATIONS Oysters with sake-pickled ginger granita (another signature); house-smoked salmon and wonton "Napoleon"; panko crusted soft-shell crab ravioli; crispy fish of the day.

ENTERTAINMENT AND AMENITIES Great amuses-bouche, such as the Thai-spiked gazpacho.

SUMMARY AND COMMENTS The executive chef here is Jeff Tunks, also of D.C. Coast, assisted by Clift Wharton; and his fearless handling of seafood is at the heart of this fun-fare bazaar. Both the appetizer and entree lists run the gamut from simple to ornate, mild to spicy, light to heavy; it's really like dining in Bangkok, where the outdoor stalls are like a giant progressive dinner, only sitting in a mogul's tent. Not only is the wine list thoughtful, unusual, and affordable, there are several fine sakes to try as well.

Thai Farm ★★★

THAI	INEXPENSIVE	QUALITY ★★★	VALUE ★★★★

800 King Farm Boulevard, No. 125, Rockville; ☎ 301-258-8829; www.thaifarmrestaruant.com **Maryland Suburbs**

Reservations Helpful but not essential. **When to go** Anytime. **Entree range** $7–$15. **Payment** VISA, MC, AMEX. **Service rating** ★★★. **Friendliness rating** ★★★★. **Metro** None nearby. **Parking** Street, free lot. **Bar** Full service. **Wine selection** House. **Dress** Casual. **Disabled access** Good. **Customers** Families, locals. **Hours** Monday–Thursday, 11:30 a.m.–10 p.m.; Friday and Saturday, 11:30 a.m.–10:30 p.m.; Sunday, 5–10 p.m.

SETTING AND ATMOSPHERE A sort of three-dimensional panorama of Thai farming—a pun in itself, as the restaurant is in the King Farm development which was until recently a working farm—with murals of farming on the walls and tabletops lacquered with grasses and rice.

HOUSE SPECIALTIES *Yum* watercress (quick-fried leaves tossed with chicken, shrimp, squid, and cashews in lime-chile sauce); fried calamari (scored, not ring-sliced); Pattaya seafood in red curry; panang sauces that are peanutty without being overwhelming; chile-spiked *hoy pow* mussels; whole fish.

OTHER RECOMMENDATIONS Green curry vegetables; *gang ped yang;* duck in panang sauce; steamed dumplings; spicy meat salad.

SUMMARY AND COMMENTS Chef Vilai Chivavibul, who was the original chef at Benjarong (profiled previously), has a remarkably light, clean hand with both spices and curries and with frying, but her handling of seafood, especially scallops and squid (which many chefs tend to overcook), is particularly admirable.

Tosca ★★★½

ITALIAN	MODERATE	QUALITY ★★★★	VALUE ★★½

1112 F Street NW; ☎ 202-367-1990; www.toscadc.com   Downtown

Reservations Recommended. **When to go** Lunch, late dinner **Entree range** $18–$32. **Payment** VISA, MC, AMEX, D, DC. **Service rating** ★★★½. **Friendliness rating** ★★★½. **Metro** Metro Center or Gallery Place–Chinatown. **Parking** Street, pay lots, valet. **Bar** Full service. **Wine selection** Good. **Dress** Business, Friday casual. **Disabled access** Good. **Customers** Business (especially power lunchers), pre-theater, young trendy. **Hours Lunch:** Monday–Friday, 11:30 a.m–2:30 p.m. **Dinner:** Sunday–Thursday, 5:30–10:30 p.m.; Friday and Saturday, 5:30–11 p.m.

SETTING AND ATMOSPHERE This is décor so cool many people find it cold—stony shades of gray and beige with only splashes of cream and teal—but it does have the effect of making the dishes themselves seem more vivid. If you are hungry for sensation, go for the tasting menu, five or six courses for $85, vegetarian for $45.

HOUSE SPECIALTIES Octopus salad with fennel and artichokes; heirloom tomato ravioli; fresh thyme taglierini with roasted lobster and green peas; Milanese-style breaded chicken cutlet with arugula and Parmesan cheese salad with oven-dried tomatoes; fettuccine with veal and duck-liver ragoût; lamb shanks with buckwheat polenta; black sea bass roasted under fresh porcinis.

OTHER RECOMMENDATIONS Roasted lamb with marinated eggplant and red onions; crab cake with sautéed green peas, caramelized Vidalia onions and pine-nut sauce; fresh pea and house-made pork-sausage risotto; choice of fresh grilled seafoods.

SUMMARY AND COMMENTS Even in this newly-bustling restaurant neighborhood, Tosca stands out. D.C is rich in chefs who started out in the Galileo galley, and Cesare Lanfranconi is another; this especially shows in his combinations but he has a uniquely Lombard accent. Lunch is expensive but elaborate enough to be the meal of the day; try the fast pre-set lunch for $25. There is also a chef's table in the kitchen, which is particularly popular with Senator Ted Kennedy, among others, so reserve early and often.

2941 ★★★½

MODERN AMERICAN	MODERATE	QUALITY ★★★	VALUE ★★★★

2941 Fairview Park Drive, Falls Church; ☎ 703-270-1500; www.2941.com Virginia Suburbs

Reservations Strongly recommended. **When to go** Lunch, anytime **Entree range** $23–$28. **Payment** VISA, MC, AMEX, DC, JCB, CB. **Service rating** ★★★. **Friendliness rating** ★★★½. **Metro** None nearby. **Parking** Free lot, valet at night. **Bar** Full service. **Wine selection** Very good. **Dress** Business, casual. **Disabled access** Very good. **Customers** Business, locals, foodies, special occasion diners. **Hours Lunch:** Monday–Friday, 11:30 a.m–2 p.m. **Dinner:** Monday–Saturday, 5:30–10 p.m.; Sunday, 5–10 p.m. **Brunch:** Sunday, 11 a.m.–1:30 p.m.

SETTING AND ATMOSPHERE Extremely handsome, despite its apparently staid office building address: a three-story atrium, huge glass windows and doors and even glass sculptures, Zen-like fish ponds with stone patio, lake and fountain view to boot. Inside it sparkles with warm wood (and sometimes firelight from the two hearths), Floribbean blue and tangerine linens and a vast U-shaped marble bar.

HOUSE SPECIALTIES Foie gras crusted with pistachios (among other treatments); salmon with sorrel; signature meat pairings such as steak with braised beef cheeks, lamb tenderloin and roast leg, and veal tenderloin with wiener schnitzel or sweetbreads. And here bread is a specialty, too, thanks to the chef's dad, ophthalmologist-turned-baker Mal Krinn: usually a half-dozen in the basket, from Parmesan to sage to fennel, pumpernickel to sourdough.

OTHER RECOMMENDATIONS Hot tempura-like seafood puffs; caramelized scallops with mushroom ragù; quail with apples and blue cheese; Alaskan black cod with honey and soy. Vegetables get unusually close attention here.

ENTERTAINMENT AND AMENITIES Palate cleansers between courses; the bill comes out "sweetened" with cotton candy, chocolates, and house-made marshmallows.

SUMMARY AND COMMENTS This may be, along with the Minibar, the most fun fine restaurant in Washington. Chef and co-owner Jonathan Krinn is originally a local boy—his partner is his former teacher, L'Académie de Cuisine director Pascal Dionot—but with New York's prestigious Gramercy Tavern and Union Pacific on his resume as well as Gerard's Place (see page 305) with Michelin stars Gerard Pangaud and Alain Ducasse and Michel Rostang in France. It shows in his style, too, which is stylish and just a little showy, (his ginger- and sake-seared tuna skewered like "lollipops" and sided with tuna tartare) but never silly. Remarkably, Krinn is his own pastry chef, too.

Vidalia ★★★½

MODERN AMERICAN	MODERATE	QUALITY ★★★½	VALUE ★★★

1990 M Street NW; ☎ 202-659-1990; www.bistrobis.com
Dupont Circle/Adams-Morgan

Reservations Recommended. **When to go** Anytime. **Entree range** $12–$32. **Payment** VISA, MC, AMEX, D. **Service rating** ★★★★. **Friendliness rating** ★★★. **Metro** Dupont Circle or Farragut North. **Parking** Street, garage, valet (dinner). **Bar** Full service. **Wine selection** Very good. **Dress** Business, dressy, casual. **Disabled access** Good. **Customers** Business, local, tourist. **Hours Lunch:** Monday–Friday, 11:30 a.m.–2:30 p.m. **Dinner:** Sunday–Thursday, 5:30–10 p.m.; Friday and Saturday, 5:30–10:30 p.m.

SETTING AND ATMOSPHERE To celebrate its tenth anniversary, owners Jeff and Sallie Buben gave it a million-dollar face-lift, and although this is actually a below-stairs establishment (disabled access is through the office lobby elevators), it's remarkably bright for a basement and as new–Southern Revival as *Southern Living* magazine: buttermilk walls, elegant green and blue upholstery, and displays of silk magnolias and bold ceramics.

HOUSE SPECIALTIES Depending on the season, the flavors are hearty or light, but the juxtapositions are always intriguing. Veal sweetbreads with a crisp lobster roll, veal cheeks over cheese grits; mustard seed–crusted tuna, pan-seared; pan-roasted monkfish with a crayfish-rice fritter, tasso ham, mâche salad, and étouffée sauce; a Provençal-style round-bone lamb steak with artichokes, olives, and pork rib chop panfried with sweet potato soufflé, smothered onions, turnip greens, fried apples, and lemon-orange whiskey sauce at dinner, and a spiced-pork sandwich slow-cooked and served open-face with toasted cornbread, avocado, and black bean–relish at lunch.

OTHER RECOMMENDATIONS Shrimp and grits is the signature dish; pan-roasted hen with fingerling potatoes; at lunchtime, cornmeal-crusted catfish with succotash of butterbeans, pearl onions, corn, bacon, and dumpling squash; buttermilk-fried chicken breast with black-pepper gravy, fingerling potatoes, and green bean and butter pea salad.

ENTERTAINMENT AND AMENITIES Complimentary wine tastings, Tuesday, 5–7 p.m.; amuses-bouches such as mushroom bouillon.

SUMMARY AND COMMENTS Executive Chef Jeff Buben and longtime on-site chef Peter Smith have just shaken up their menu, picking native American ingredients based on flavor rather than tradition. Though the name is Southern, the menu is fused with broader tastes. The luxuriant sauces aren't necessarily low-cal, but they're served with a light touch.

Woo Lae Oak ★★★

KOREAN	MODERATE	QUALITY ★★★½	VALUE ★★★★

1500 South Joyce Street, Arlington, VA; ☎ 703-521-3706
8240 Leesburg Pike, Tysons Corner, VA; ☎ 703-827-7300
www.woolaeoak.com

Reservations Accepted, suggested on weekends. **When to go** Anytime. **Entree range** $10–$20. **Payment** VISA, MC, AMEX. **Service rating** ★★★★. **Friendliness rating** ★★★. **Metro** *Arlington:* Crystal City; *Tysons Corner:* None nearby. **Parking** Free lot. **Bar** Full service. **Wine selection** Fair. **Dress** Casual, informal. **Disabled access** No. **Customers** Ethnic, local. **Hours** Every day, 11:30 a.m.–10:30 p.m.

SETTING AND ATMOSPHERE The Arlington location is California Asian and is a big, curving slice of a room on stilts, with modernized versions of traditional wood-slat-and-rice-paper décor. The Tyson's Corner site is more trendy, with abstract art and a mood wall, and it has a busy bar scene. All tables have barbecue grills built in.

HOUSE SPECIALTIES *Shin sun ro* (a fancy hot pot—like Japanese *shabu-shabu*—that requires 24 hours' notice); saeng sun jun (battered and grilled fish);

bulgolgi (the familiar sweet-soy beef barbecue); spicy fish stew in a pot; *yook hwe bibimbap* (marinated raw sirloin strips with spinach, bean sprouts, zucchini, etc., in sesame oil); boneless short-rib cubes.

OTHER RECOMMENDATIONS *Paijun,* a scallion seafood crêpe; sliced raw fish and vegetables on rice with a hot pepper–chile paste on the side; broiled red snapper; scallion, seafood, and green-pepper pancake; panfried meatballs coated with egg and flour.

SUMMARY AND COMMENTS Woo Lae Oak is widely considered the first name in Korean cuisine in the Washington area. Part of a small but international chain (Seoul, New York, Chicago, L.A.), even the older, less splashy branch in Arlington serves 150,000 meals a year. And for good reason: this is not food to eat alone. The fun is barbecuing (or in the case of the many hot-pot dishes, dipping) with friends. Besides, many of the dishes are made for two, and the sashimi appetizer is so big—about 24 pieces, and cut Korean-style, meaning large—that it's either a meal or a first course for several. Many dishes cost less at lunch. The one real disappointment about this restaurant for non-Asian diners is that staffers frequently either doubt that you know what you're ordering or don't take it seriously; for example, even with the 24 hours' notice, it can be hit-or-miss whether you get your *shin sun ro.*

Zaytinya ★★★½

MIDDLE EASTERN	MODERATE	QUALITY ★★★½	VALUE ★★★½

701 Ninth Street NW; ☎ 202-638-0800; www.zaytinya.com **Downtown**

Reservations Available 5–6:30 p.m. only. **When to go** Late lunch–early dinner; late dinner. **Entree range** $17–$23. **Payment** VISA, MC, AMEX. **Service rating** ★★★½. **Friendliness rating** ★★★½. **Metro** Gallery Place–Chinatown or Metro Center. **Parking** Street, pay lot, valet at dinner. **Bar** Full service. **Wine selection** Good. **Dress** Business, casual. **Disabled access** Good. **Customers** Business, foodies, young bar trendies, pre-MCI Center crowds. **Hours** Sunday and Monday, 11:30 a.m.–10 p.m.; Tuesday–Thursday, 11:30 a.m.–11:30 p.m.; Friday and Saturday, 11:30 a.m.–midnight.

SETTING AND ATMOSPHERE A big, high, and airy but almost modern art–minimalist room, white and angular with a soaring atrium-style ceiling, cut-through shelving walls stocked with lit candles, a long (and very busy) bar, half-hidden dining nooks and niches, a fireplace and a mezzanine overlooking the Manhattan-style communal table in the center of the main dining room.

HOUSE SPECIALTIES Lamb mini-meatballs with cinnamon oil and dried fruit; beer and cracked-wheat tartare; feta- and tomato-stuffed quail with fingerling potatoes; crab cakes with shaved fennel; flaming cheese with oyster, shiitake, and cremini mushrooms.

OTHER RECOMMENDATIONS Pork and orange-rind sausage; braised rabbit with lentils; fried mussels with pistachios; giant favas with tomatoes and red onions; meat-stuffed *manti* dumplings; squid in a variety of treatments.

SUMMARY AND COMMENTS Not Middle Eastern in the usual sense, Zaytinya—

which means "olive oil" in Turkish—is specifically Eastern Mediterranean. 2004 *Bon Appétit* Chef of the Year José Andrés, already racking up stars with the Minibar at Café Atlántico, launched this smart and sophisticated Greek/Turkish/Lebanese *meze* restaurant in between his Spanish tapas kitchens (Jaleo) and his latest, the Cuban Oyamel. The range is boggling, and the Middle Eastern wine list is unusually intriguing.

Zed's ★★

ETHIOPIAN   **INEXPENSIVE**   **QUALITY** ★★★   **VALUE** ★★★

1201 28th Street NW; ☎ 202-333-4710; www.zeds.net Georgetown

Reservations Accepted. **When to go** Anytime. **Entree range** $10–$16. **Payment** VISA, MC, AMEX, D, DC. **Service rating** ★★★. **Friendliness rating** ★★★. **Metro** Foggy Bottom–GWU. **Parking** Street, pay lots. **Bar** Full service. **Wine selection** House. **Dress** Casual, business. **Disabled access** Not accessible. **Customers** Ethnic, local. **Hours** Every day, 11 a.m.–11 p.m.

SETTING AND ATMOSPHERE A deceptively simple Georgetown row house outside, its whitewashed exterior gives way to a cool, shadowy world of wood screens and white linen, fresh flowers, formally dressed staff, musical instruments, and artifacts of Ethiopian culture.

HOUSE SPECIALTIES Classic Ethiopian fare such as the chicken–hard-boiled-egg stew called *doro watt;* the spicy steak tartare called *kitfo;* the many vegetarian stews: carrots and cabbage, eggplant, and tomatoes; string beans and cauliflower; lentils; etc. Zed also offers some less familiar dishes, such as a whole fried fish in moderately spicy sauce, a purée of spiced roasted flaxseeds; and a soul food–style mix of collard greens and beef.

OTHER RECOMMENDATIONS Sautéed chicken strips; bulgur wheat; spicy lamb stew; a condiment of dried cottage cheese. Everything is preservative free.

SUMMARY AND COMMENTS Zed Wondemu is the first name in Washington's Ethiopian establishments: Her original site, several blocks to the west, was the first Ethiopian establishment to break out of the Adams-Morgan alley, and it made converts of many local diners. Her cooking is notable for the quality of its *injera,* the sourdough-ish pancake that is platter and utensil in one (see the profile for Meskerem, page 320, for more details), and for the number of veggie dishes made with oil rather than the traditional clarified butter, making them vegan friendly.

PART NINE

SHOPPING *in* WASHINGTON

◼ MALL SHOPPING

IT SHOULD COME AS NO SURPRISE that Washington, with one of the highest median household incomes in the nation and an increasingly diverse population, offers a wide variety of shopping opportunities. You can quite literally shop until you drop—virtually malled to death. On Saturday afternoons, roads leading to the shopping centers are as congested as commuter routes during rush hour. The stretch of I-95 south of Washington around the **Potomac Mills** factory outlet complex in Dale City—which has now surpassed even Colonial Williamsburg as the number-one tourist attraction in Virginia—is nearly always backed up (see "Bargains" in the "Specialty Shops" section later in this part). **Tysons Corner,** just west of the Beltway, is so large it helped inspire one of the catch phrases of 1990s development, the "edge city." Tysons is a Siamese twin mall now, the original Tysons and the Galleria at Tysons II, and has its own brewpub, appropriately named the Edge City Brewery. The newer **Leesburg Corner Premium Outlets** on Route 7 west of Tysons Corner and the vast **Arundel Mills,** from the same folks who brought you Potomac Mills, are spreading the name-brand wealth around the region. See more on these megacenters on pages 356–357.

SUBURBAN MALLS

MOST OF THE SMALLER SUBURBAN MALLS are probably similar to what you have back home with a few easily accessible by subway. (And for those serious shopaholics, the good news is that a Metro extension to Tyson's Corner is at last in the works, though it will take a couple of years.) One is **The Fashion Centre** (☎ 703-415-2400) at Pentagon City in Arlington, Virginia—a beautiful conservatory-style building filled with 160 primarily high-end retailers: **Crate and Barrel,** the **Wizards of the Coast, Macy's,** and **Nordstrom,** the Seattle-based clothing retailer renowned for its service and selection. It also opens onto the Ritz-Carlton Hotel, where you can have a very refreshing elegant meal or high tea. The Pentagon City Metro stop, on the Blue Line, deposits shoppers right into the mall. The **Chevy Chase Pavilion** (☎ 202-686-5335), at the very north end of the District of Columbia on the border of Maryland, and the **Mazza Gallerie** across the street (☎ 202-966-6114) are two corners of the burgeoning Chevy Chase shopping neighborhood served by the Friendship Heights station: See "Great Neighborhoods for Window-Shopping," page 348.

White Flint Mall (☎ 301-468-5777), north of Washington, also has a subway stop, although it's a block or so away; shuttle bus service is continuous. It houses **Bloomingdale's, Ann Taylor, Lord & Taylor, Eurostyle Imports, the Limited,** a **Cheesecake Factory** restaurant (which hands out silent "beepers" so you can keep shopping while waiting for a table), as well as a better-than-average food court and a huge, three-story **Borders Books & Music. Dave & Buster's,** a vast virtual-reality sports/billiard/parlor/bar/restaurant complex, dominates the top floor (see its profile on page 387 in Part Ten, Entertainment and Nightlife). There is also a European-style day spa, **Roxsan,** which offers everything from hairstyling to ornately painted (real or false) nails, mud baths, massages, and all-natural facials.

Montgomery Mall (☎ 301-469-6000) does not have subway access, but for serious shoppers, it's only a ten-minute cab ride from **White Flint** and the mall shuttle from the White Flint Metro via the 96 Ride-On bus is only 35 cents. It's anchored by a **Nordstrom, Sears,** and **Macy's,** and includes **A/X Armani Exchange, Eileen Fisher, J. Crew, J. Jill, Banana Republic, Evans fur salon, and Rosendorf.** It also has a food court with a full-sized **Legal Seafood** and a **California Pizza Kitchen** and a **three-screen cineplex** for bored kids. The formerly dowdy **Wheaton Mall** (a block from the Wheaton Metro) received a financial and name-branch transfusion a couple of years ago (it's a corporate sibling to Montgomery Mall) and now offers 250 or so mostly mid-priced stores, shops, and kiosks, including **Express, Victoria's Secret, Ann Taylor Loft, Guess?, Old Navy, Helzberg Diamonds, Lane Bryant,** and **Nine West,** plus its own grocery store, food court, **Ruby Tuesday,** cineplex, and **Bally's Total Fitness** club.

Though public transportation is still years away from it, **Tysons Corner** (☎ 703-893-9400) offers nearly 400 shops in two large arcades, including **Nordstrom, Lord & Taylor, Bloomingdale's, Brooks Brothers, Hilfiger, Burberry, Movado, Talbots for Women,** and the **Washington Redskins'** official store. (The "Corner" fills up the neighborhood between Routes 7 and 123.) Just across the way is **Fairfax Square** (☎ 703-448-1830), a sort of mini-mall of superlabel shops (**Tiffany, Gucci, Hermès, Louis Vuitton**) that whet your appetite for the platinum-card eateries such as **Morton's of Chicago** and the old-guard white linen **Ritz-Carlton Hotel**'s four-star Italian restaurant, **Maestro.**

MALLS IN D.C.

THERE ARE FEWER MALLS WITHIN CITY LIMITS. **Georgetown Park** (☎ 202-298-5577), near the intersection of M Street and Wisconsin Avenue, is the most extravagant, featuring a lush Victorian design and some popular retailers: **Abercrombie & Fitch, Papillon, Anthropologie, H&M, Ann Taylor, J. Crew, and Sharper Image.** It also includes a **Benihana** Japanese steak house with sushi bar, the original **Clyde's of Georgetown,** and a food court. Georgetown Park now sort of melds into the M Street shopping scene; see "Great Neighborhoods for Window-shopping" on the next page.

Two Washington landmarks have lately been reborn as shopping centers: the **Old Post Office Pavilion** and **Union Station.** The **Pavilion,** on Pennsylvania Avenue just north of the Smithsonian, is the place for stocking up on souvenirs; it also has a tower with a view that rivals the Washington Monument but with a fraction of the waiting line. Union Station, the city's restored train station on Massachusetts Avenue, is a grand beaux arts building whose glory is undiminished by its two-story arcade of shops, including **Ann Taylor** and **Nine West** (handy for travelers who arrive short of clothes or shoes). Be sure to wander into the East Hall, which has kiosks selling one-of-a-kind jewelry, ethnic Russian and Afrocentric crafts, and other merchandise. The lowest level is a bustling food court, and there's more just outside the train track waiting areas. It also has a branch of the New York neo-soul food restaurant **B. Smith's,** a **Pizzeria Uno, Thunder Grill** for Mexican, **America** (a restaurant that claims to have dishes from all 50 states), a couple of elevated-view bars, and a multiplex cinema. The Pavilion is very near the Federal Triangle Metro stop; Union Station's Metro stop is an escalator-ride down.

And although it's a couple of blocks from the Metro Center stations, most tourists will want to look into the **Shops at National Place** (F Street SW, between 13th and 14th streets; ☎ 202-662-1250), which has **Banana Republic, Victoria's Secret,** and a couple of cafes. For free, you get to watch for political and media celebrities while you window-shop; the building also houses the National Press Club.

FLEA MARKETS

WASHINGTON IS NOT A GREAT FLEA MARKET town in the way that New York City is, but it does have a few dependable gatherings, and browsing flea markets for bargain-hunters is like grazing for goodies. The best or at least the most likely to yield a fancy find, is the Georgetown **Flea Market** (Wisconsin Avenue and S Street NW), open Saturdays and Sundays 8 a.m. to 4 p.m.; *Lonesome Dove* author Larry McMurty, who used to run a second-hand bookstore in the neighborhood, based his novel *Cadillac Jack* on the market. It's currently in exile at 2100 Clarendon Boulevard, near the courthouse Metro stop in Arlington (☎ 703-528-6748).

Other good spots include the **Bethesda Flea Market** (7155 Wisconsin Avenue in Bethesda), which is accessible by subway and open Wednesday, Saturday, and Sunday, 7 a.m. to 5 p.m.; and the flea market at **Eastern Market** (Seventh Street between Pennsylvania Avenue and North Carolina Avenue), which is also accessible by the subway and open Sunday 10 a.m. to 5 p.m. Both the Bethesda and Eastern Market gatherings have extra attractions; Bethesda sets up around the old **Farm Women's Co-op,** so there's usually good food, flowers, and preserves inside; and the Eastern Market hosts a neighborhood crafts and street fair most Saturdays as well. (But use good judgment; in bad weather the vendors stay home.)

GREAT NEIGHBORHOODS *for* WINDOW-SHOPPING

IF MALLS MAKE YOU CRAZY, Washington has a number of neighborhoods made for window-shopping.

GEORGETOWN

GEORGETOWN, THE CITY'S LARGEST walk-and-shop district, has spread out like a half-covered super-mall with a combination of chains, independents, and boutique shops. To name a few: **Hu's Shoes** (3005 M Street; ☎ 202-342-0202), **Commander Salamander** (1420 Wisconsin Avenue NW; ☎ 202-337-2265), **BCBG Max Azria** (3210 M Street NW; ☎ 202-333-2224), **Kate Spade** (3061 M Street NW; ☎ 202-333-8302), **Barney's Co-op** (3040 M Street NW, ☎ 202-350-5832), the upscale baby boutique **K Baby** (3112 M Street NW; ☎ 202-333-3939), **Ralph Lauren** (1245 Wisconsin Avenue; NW ☎ 202-965-0905), **Coach** (3259 M Street NW; ☎ 202-333-3005), **Club Monaco** (3235 M Street NW; ☎ 202-956-2118), **Hugo Boss** (1517 Wisconsin Avenue NW; ☎ 202-625-2677), **Rugby by Ralph Lauren** (1065 Wisconsin Avenue NW; ☎ 202-298-5928), **Urban Chic** (1626 Wisconsin Avenue NW; ☎ 202-338-5398), **Miss Sixty/Energie** (1239 Wisconsin Avenue NW; ☎ 202-965-6430), the neo-preppy **Sherman Pickey** (1647 Wisconsin Avenue NW; ☎ 202-333-4212), **Zara** (1238 Wisconsin Avenue NW; ☎ 202-944-9797), **Sassanova** (1641 Wisconsin Avenue NW; ☎ 202-471-4400), **Betsey Johnson** (1319 Wisconsin Avenue NW; ☎ 202-338-4090), the vintage-couture collection at **Annie Creamcheese** (3279 M Street NW; ☎ 202-298-5555), plus the now-ubiquitous **Banana Republic** (3200 M Street NW; ☎ 202-333-2554), **H&M** (3222 M Street NW; ☎ 202-298-6792), **Benetton** at the intersection of Wisconsin Avenue NW and M Street NW (☎ 202-625-0443), **Urban Outfitters** (3111 M Street NW; ☎ 202-342-1012), and one of only five **Adidas Originals** retro-repro boutiques (1251 Wisconsin Avenue NW; ☎ 202-625-8501).

It's a corporate two-fer at the corner of 31st and M: **Pottery Barn** downstairs and **Smith and Hawken** upstairs.

Thanks to the crowds of teens and 20-somethings that hang out on Georgetown's sidewalks on weekends, many of these keep late hours for impulse shopping. These are also the two main restaurant strips. Shops for antiques, both formal and more offbeat, stretch up Wisconsin past R Street, interspersed with collections of artwork, books, and shoes; see the section on "Antiques" in the "Specialty Shops" section, page 343.

Georgetown also has more than a few shops specializing in one-of-a-kind crafts—including art glass at **Maurine Littleton** (1667 Wisconsin Avenue NW; ☎ 202-333-9307), ceramics at **American Studio Plus** (2906 M Street NW; ☎ 202-965-3273), antique garden ornaments and furniture at **Cote Jardin** (3218 O Street NW; ☎ 202-333-3067), and jewelry and wooden crafts at **Appalachian Spring** (1415 Wisconsin Avenue NW; ☎ 202-337-5780). **A Mano** (1677 Wisconsin; ☎ 202-298-7200) lays out fine French linens, faïence, and majolica plates for the fanciest breakfast in bed ever.

Thos. Moser Cabinetmakers has opened one of only five shops at 3300 M Street NW (☎ 202-338-4292), which opens into the **Cady Alley** complex, home to a number of high-end furnishings stores (**Gore Dean, Random Harvest, Contemporaria**), clothing boutiques, such as the designer-heavy **Relish,** luxury bath fitters, kitchen specialists, and even antique marble floors from the Holy Land. Across the street is the vast showroom of **Artefacto** (3333 M Street NW; ☎ 202-338-3337), whose collection reflects both the style and the natural materials of Brazil. And inside Georgetown Tobacco (3144 M Street NW; ☎ 202-338-5100) is a treasure trove of elaborate hand-painted carnival masks to make the Phantom of the Opera change his tune. But the specialty collector fascinated by late-19th- and early-20th-century decorative arts will find a paradise on M Street; see "Decorative Arts," page 358.

ADAMS-MORGAN, U STREET, AND LOGAN CIRCLE

HISTORICALLY, ADAMS-MORGAN and U Street (or the "New U" neighborhood, as it's known now) had little connection. Adams-Morgan began as a wealthy white residential area adjoining the still-exclusive Kalorama but, with "white flight" to the suburbs after the unrest of the 1960s, emerged as the heart of the Hispanic and then Ethiopian communities. Over the past 15 or 20 years, it has developed into an eclectic nightlife and dining area, especially along 18th Street. U Street, though at the north end of the Shaw neighborhood, was the closest thing Washington had to a Harlem, thanks to its national-circuit jazz and vaudeville venues and the proximity of Howard University. An even more direct victim of the riots, it had sadly deteriorated and only began to revive a decade ago, thanks partly to some timely government investment and partly to a wave of young couples willing to invest in renovating the old town houses as restaurants and small businesses.

In recent years, these two ethnically heterogenous areas have become increasingly popular with younger, hip, and international crowds. Three even more encouraging developments—the emergence of 14th Street as a center for small theaters and of U Street for nightclubs; the opening of the U Street-Cardozo subway station; and the commercial ripple effects from the construction of the Verizon Center sports and entertainment arena and the new Convention Center to the south—have increased that area's visibility and pedestrian traffic even more. And thanks to their hip, entrepreneurial habitués, Adams-Morgan and U Street are becoming intriguing window-shopping destinations as well.

Although the two neighborhoods have not completely met in the middle, they are beginning to send out tendrils of development toward one another. (However, the area can still be somewhat edgy late at night.)

Among the best and brightest clothing boutiques are the designer-sample-grazing center **Kaur Three** (2102 18th Street NW; ☎ 202-299-0404) and the self-described "girlie" shop, **Daisy** (4940 St. Elmo Avenue NW; ☎ 301-656-2280), haute-accessory central. A few doors up is **All About Jane** (2839 Clarendon Boulevard; ☎ 703-243-4424), stocking T-shirts for the too-too trendy.

In between Adams-Morgan's melting pot of restaurants (and its quite serious and expensive antique stores) are African and Hispanic (and Rasta) clothing stores and craft boutiques, racks of Mexican wedding dresses, religious icons, and perhaps a medicinal herb or two.

For architectural remnants—mantels, stained and leaded-glass windows, chandeliers, door handles, and columns—check out the **Brass Knob** (2311 18th Street NW; ☎ 202-332-3370); the **Brass Knob Backdoors Warehouse** a parking lot away (2329 Champlain Street NW; ☎ 202-265-0587), which holds the clawfoot tubs, radiators, and sinks; and the innovative furnishings at the four-story **Skynear & Co.** (2122 18th Street NW; ☎ 202-797-7160), which stocks hand-painted pillows, repro armoires and red China cabinets, whimsical wrought iron, acrobatic light fixtures, and the like. (The Gen-X, smart-set stuff is in the basement.) **Dada Decorative Arts** (1814 Adams Mill Road; ☎ 202-387-3232) has an oversized sense of the absurd that suits the name.

And although it's a little south of the main drag, **Simply Home** (1811-B 18th Street NW; ☎ 202-986-8607) is anything but the suburban catalog shop it sounds; it's a Thai family business, and the direct Bangkok-to-D.C. wares include silk throws, bamboo rice bowls, ceramics, chopsticks, and even cabinets.

Four blocks east of Simply Home are **Home Rule** (1807 14th Street NW; ☎ 202-797-5544), one of those shops that has figured out that home accessories don't have to be humorless; **Vastu** (1829 14th Street NW; ☎ 202-234-8344), a gallery of limited-edition furniture; **Go Mama Go!** (1809 14th Street NW; ☎ 202-299-0850), which stocks smaller-scale but eye-catching ethnically flavored furnishings perfect for the chic dorm room, condo, or loft; and **Muleh** (1831 14th Street NW; ☎ 202-667-3440), stocked with eco-friendly furnishings from Indonesia and the Philippines. A block north, **Ruff & Ready** (1908 14th Street NW; ☎ 202-667-7833) is an old-fashioned neighborhood antique store with great finds hidden all the way to the back, and which also offers increasingly desirable garden antiques.

The heaviest concentration of stores along U Street is between 16th and 13th streets, near the entrance to the subway. **Urban Essentials** (1330 U Street NW; ☎ 202-299-0640) puts the emphasis on "urban," as in cool: a soft-drink-machine-turned-CD rack, modular storage containers, mod-design home office pieces, etc. **Good Wood Inc.** (1428 U Street NW; ☎ 202-986-3640), on the other hand, says "country," specializing in 19th-century American furniture, including arts and crafts, andirons, and stained glass, but at Sunday auction prices. And down at **Dragonfly** (1457 Church Street NW; ☎ 202-265-3359), the tags read Tibet, China, Thailand, and Myanmar (Burma).

Habitat (1510 U Street NW; ☎ 202-518-7222) deals in primarily Mexican crafts and jewels. The African and African American decorative arts and accessories, sculpture, and ceremonial items at **Zawadi Gallery** (1524 U Street NW; ☎ 202-232-2214) range from the fine and expensive to the simply attractive and affordable. **Millennium Decorative Arts** (1528 U Street NW; ☎ 202-483-1218) is one of several retro-kitsch shops (and eateries) in new-U, mixing Waring blenders and fondue pots with the real retro stuff such as Eames chairs and a Saarinen pedestal table.

Fans of vintage clothing and accessories in the 1950s–1970s range should cruise the three stories at **Meep's** and **Aunt Neensie's** (2104 18th Street; ☎ 202-265-6546). Vintage accessory addicts should head for **Nana** (1528 U Street NW; ☎ 202-667-6955). And **Wild Women Wear Red** specializes in what it calls "funky, functional footwear for women," striking but well-made shoes, sandals, and boots at affordable prices (1512 U Street NW; ☎ 202-387-5700).

Note than some of the shops in the U Street neighborhood are open only on weekends or toward the latter part of the week.

CHEVY CHASE

A NEW HYBRID D.C.–MONTGOMERY COUNTY NEIGHBORHOOD— and a commercial gold mine—has been emerging around the Friendship Heights Metro station for several years. At the intersection of Western and Wisconsin avenues, which also serves as the boundary between the two jurisdictions (and the multiexit Friendship Heights Metro station), there are now two substantial shopping malls, a stand-alone **Bloomingdale's,** several trendy new restaurants, and a complex containing some of the most luxe shops in Washington.

Mazza Gallerie, which is undergoing a face-lift, is home to **Neiman Marcus, Saks Fifth Avenue for Men, Ann Taylor, House of Villeroy and Boch, Harriet Kassman, Pampillonia Jewelers, Williams-Sonoma,** and a branch of **Filene's Basement** as well as a cineplex to park the kids. **Chevy Chase Pavilion,** which has its own **Embassy Suites Hotel** and **Washington Sports Club,** also houses **J.Crew, Talbots, Stein Mart, Ann Taylor Loft, World Market,** and **Pottery Barn** plus a food court, **Cheesecake Factory,** and **Maggiano's Little Italy.**

Lord and Taylor and **Saks Fifth Avenue** are on Western just around the corner, along with a **Brooks Brothers.**

But cross Western Avenue into Chevy Chase, and you might well believe you're at the corner of Fifth Avenue and 55th in Manhattan. **Ralph Lauren**'s two-story boutique—which looks like a European prince's hunting lodge downstairs and a Hollywood starlet's bedroom upstairs—rubs structural shoulders with **Jimmy Choo, Louis Vuitton, Christian Dior, Barney's Co-Op, MaxMara, Gucci,** and the combined forces of **Tiffany & Co., Bulgari,** and **Cartier,** along with the local diamond powerhouse **Merviso.** Across the street are **MicMac Bis,** a mini–designer boutique specializing in Issey Miyake, Yohji Yamamoto, DKNY, and so on; **Everett Hall,** a men's store popular with local newscasters and politicians; and a **Banana Republic, Gap,** and **Chico's** (for those on a budget).

Not surprisingly, perhaps, there are also several trendy restaurants (**Indique Heights, Lia, Famoso, Sushi-Ko,** and the more midstream but dependable **Clyde's**) and a whole city's worth of spas (**Cultura, Renu**), salons (**Elizabeth Arden, Georgette Klinger**), and so on.

Hint: The Friendship Heights Metro station is on the Washington side, so if you have to take a taxicab from downtown instead of the subway, make sure the driver lets you out in D.C.—at Neiman Marcus, for instance. Similarly, if you're coming from the north (and again, it's only one stop from the Bethesda Metro), ask to get off in Maryland; specify the Dior building.

DUPONT CIRCLE

DUPONT CIRCLE IS FOR SHOPPERS LOOKING TO enrich the mind—it's full of art galleries, espresso bars, and bookstores (see "Specialty Shops," page 354). Most of these are on the north side of the circle: the art galleries are generally clustered along R Street in the two blocks just west of Connecticut Avenue (leading you gently toward the **Phillips Collection**). The **Chao Phraya Gallery** (2009 Columbia Road, a half-block east of Connecticut Avenue; ☎ 202-745-1111), showing Chinese and Southeast Asian art and antiques, is a few blocks north.

West of the circle near the Phillips Collection is the **Geoffrey Diner Gallery** (1730 21st Street NW; ☎ 202-483-5005), which specializes in

American and British Arts and Crafts furniture, including Stickley and Mission, and Deco and Nouveau pieces. **Affrica** (2129 Florida Avenue; ☎ 202-745-7272) offers African textiles, masks, figurines, and currency. **Marston-Luce** (1651 Wisconsin Avenue; ☎ 202-333-6800) is a Francophile's dream but open by appointment only. (Their Georgetown store at 1651 Wisconsin Avenue is open to the public.)

South of the circle, on Connecticut Avenue NW, between N and K streets, are high-end retailers such as **Ralph Lauren Polo, Burberry, Hugo Boss, Betsy Fisher, Thomas Pink,** and **Rizik's,** a prominent local women's shop; and **Pampillonia Jewelers,** which specializes in antique and estate pieces. There is also a fine estate jewelry shop called the **Tiny Jewel Box,** and just over at 18th and M is **Alan Marcus & Co.** (1200 18th Street NW, 10th floor; ☎ 202-331-0671), which discounts big-name watches, pens, crystal, and silver. And for designer pieces, look into **I. Gorman** at 20th and L streets (☎ 202-775-8544).

BETHESDA

BETHESDA, MARYLAND, WHICH IS JUST BEYOND Chevy Chase, has become not only one of the major restaurant centers in the Washington area but also a magnet area for fine rugs, art and antiques, books, tobacconists, vintage and consignment clothing (which, in an area as prosperous as this, means everything from faux pearls to furs), and trendy home furnishings. **Urban Country** (7801 Woodmont Avenue; ☎ 301-654-0500) is crammed with painted, faux-distressed, and gilded furniture, desktop accessories, ceramics, linens, glass, and flatware; they also custom-upholster. At **Tone on Tone** (7920 Woodmont; ☎ 240-497-0800), the Scandinavian antiques with their pale distressed finish evoke a gentler era. **Cattycorner** at 7766 Woodmont is a branch of **Random Harvest** (☎ 301-280-2777), a dependable but more predictable store. **Bartley Tile Concepts** (6931 Arlington Road; ☎ 301-913-9113) sells hand-painted tiles, marble, and slate, both new and salvaged. **Lomay-Schnitzel Antiques** (6826 Wisconsin Avenue; ☎ 301-656-1911) is an old and respected source of English, French, and continental pieces, both original and fine reproduction. And **Sansar** (4805 Bethesda Avenue; ☎ 301-652-8676) is a showcase of hand-crafted glass, wood, silver, metal, and textiles; you could fill the whole house with livable art. Just cattycorner down is **Artsy Fartsy** (4836 Bethesda Avenue; ☎ 301-652-0110), which pushes the whimsy envelope.

But these days, the Bethesda boomers, like those in Adams-Morgan, are generally looking East. Just down the street from Urban Country is the San Francisco–based **Design Within Reach** (4828 St. Elmo Avenue, Bethesda; ☎ 301-215-7200). **Muleh** (4731 Elm Street; ☎ 301-941-1174) offers both real and reproduction antiques from Africa, Southeast Asia, and the Middle East. **Asian Home Furnishings** (4715 Cordell Avenue; ☎ 301-656-0400) is another direct-from-the-Thai-in-laws operation. **Grant Antiques** (4835 Cordell Avenue; ☎ 301-215-9292) is as much fun to shop in as to bargain-hunt; it's like a stage set. **Pasha Home Fashion** (4865 Cordell; ☎ 301-657-1120) sells Indonesian mahogany, Italian leather, and Peruvian jewelry.

Among art galleries are **Allyson Louis** (12250 Rockville Pike; ☎ 301-656-2877), **Capricorn Galleries** (10236 River Road; ☎ 301-765-5900), and **Marin-Price** (7022 Wisconsin Avenue; ☎ 301-718-0622). Particularly fine art glass is available—one might almost say on exhibit—at the **Glass Gallery** (4720 Hampden Lane; ☎ 301-657-3478). **ZYZYX** mixes and matches art glass and ceramics with better production pieces (10301-A Old Georgetown Road; ☎ 301-493-0297).

CAPITOL HILL

ON CAPITOL HILL MOST SHOPS ARE in the vicinity of the **Eastern Market**—an actual market where vendors set up tables selling produce, baked goods, and flea market bric-a-brac—located on Seventh Street between Pennsylvania and Independence avenues SE. There, amid the restaurants and bars, are secondhand clothing shops and first-rate crafts stores, and a weekend flea market. Around the old Eastern Market building on Eighth just north of Pennsylvania Avenue, you can browse through a variety of antiques stores and boutiques, as well as farmers' produce and fresh poultry stands. There's a pottery co-op upstairs at the Market itself. Otherwise, the major shopping center of the hill is **Union Station,** which has dozens of name chains. There are also a few stores in the blocks around the Library of Congress side of the Capitol. **Art and Soul** (225 Pennsylvania Avenue, NW; ☎ 202-548-0105) hangs out garden party and retro-hippie chic.

OLD TOWN ALEXANDRIA

OLD TOWN ALEXANDRIA, VIRGINIA, is a walker's delight, too, with shops clustered up, down, and around King Street, most of them selling antiques, crafts, and home furnishings. **Traditions of France** (1113 King Street; ☎ 703-836-5340) is piled high with high-end reproductions manufactured in Provence—real French fakes you might say. **Wayne Fisher American Design** (114 South Royal Street; ☎ 703-836-6043) specializes in charming old toys, pottery, tools, and painted wood ornaments as well as furniture. This trendy indoor-outdoor look is spotlighted at **Egerton Gardens** (1117 King Street; ☎ 703-548-1197).

Other good poking-around spots include **Random Harvest** (810 King Street; ☎ 703-548-8820), the **Old Colony Shop** (222-B South Washington Street; ☎ 703-548-8008), and **Robert Bentley Adams** (405 South Washington Street; ☎ 703-549-0650).

SPECIALTY SHOPS

Antiques

Serious antique-seekers get out of town—driving an hour or more to the countryside of Maryland, Virginia, West Virginia, or Pennsylvania for the bargains. Frederick, Maryland, about an hour north of Washington, is particularly popular with area antiquers. The biggest single group is at the 125-dealer **Emporium Antiques** (112 East Patrick Street, Frederick; ☎ 301-662-7099), though walking the Main Street neighborhood and the streets just off it will turn up plenty of others. But you will find treasures—though few bargains—in and around Washington. The largest concentration of such shops is on **"Antique Row"** in Kensington, Maryland, about four miles from the D.C. line. There are more than 50 antique dealers on **Howard Avenue,** with smaller shops east of Connecticut Avenue and larger warehouses west of Connecticut. **Marco Polo's Treasures** is an oasis of various Asian imports, including furniture, jewelry, even gods and saints (4263 Howard; ☎ 301-530-3420). **Sparrows** (4115 Howard Avenue; ☎ 301-530-0175) specializes in late-18th- to early-19th-century French and French Revival pieces, including fine Deco and Nouveau. **Paris-Kensington** specializes in smaller bronze figurines, clocks, silver, and porcelain. **Huret Antiques** (4106 Howard Avenue; ☎ 301-530-7551) takes the formal approach which helpfully explains its periods, rules, epochs, and styles for less practiced customers. **J'antiques** (10429 Fawcett Street; ☎ 301-942-0936) offers silver flatware and filigree, fine estate jewelry, and Limoges. Not surprisingly, there's even a restaurant called **Café Monet.**

In Georgetown and Alexandria, you'll find a variety of shops selling collectibles from the past three centuries. Among Georgetown's best (in geographically ascending order) are **Darrell Dean** (1524 Wisconsin Avenue NW; ☎ 202-333-6330), **Space** (1625 Wisconsin Avenue NW; ☎ 202-333-0140), **David Bell Antiques** (1655 Wisconsin Avenue NW; ☎ 202-965-2355), and **Miller & Arney** (1737 Wisconsin Avenue NW; ☎ 202-338-2369). **Susquehanna Antique Company** (3216 O Street NW; ☎ 202-333-1511) specializes in fine dining and gaming tables. One Georgetown favorite is **Christ Child Opportunity Shop** (1427 Wisconsin Avenue NW; ☎ 202-333-6635), where, on the second floor, you'll find silver, china, paintings, and other cherishables on consignment from the best Georgetown homes. (See the neighborhood profiles earlier in this part.)

The best antiques in Alexandria are in Old Town along Washington Street and in the 4000 block of King Street: check out **Studio Antiques & Fine Art** (524 North Washington Street; ☎ 703-548-5253) and **Washington Square Antiques** (689 South Washington Street; ☎ 703-836-3214).

Art

One of Washington's most concentrated selections of art for sale—traditional, modern, photographic, and ethnic—can be found around **Dupont Circle.** The best shops are centered on a sort of crossroads of Connecticut Avenue and R Street and spread a couple of blocks in each direction—especially R Street around 20th and 21st streets, where there are a dozen galleries within two blocks. Gallery openings are generally on the first Friday of the month.

However, a renaissance of independent artists and co-ops has made the Seventh Street area just north of Pennsylvania Avenue the SoHo of D.C. Among the important stops are the **Zenith Gallery** (413 Seventh Street NW; ☎ 202-783-2963), which specializes in photography, new art, and neon; and the **Touchstone Co-op** (406 Seventh Street NW; ☎ 202-347-2787). The Seventh Street neighborhood opens every third Thursday of the month for a free gallery crawl that covers a dozen shops; meet in the lobby of the **Goethe-Institut** (812 Seventh Street NW; ☎ 202-289-1200) at 6:30 p.m.

The newly united **Galleries of the 14th Street Arts Corridor**— a group around the P Street District, including the **Adamson Gallery, Curator's Office, Transformer, G Fine Art, Hemphill,** and **plan b**—has irregular late hours.

Similarly, the art galleries of **Canal Square** in Georgetown stay open late every third Friday, with jazz and hors d'oeuvres and wine for patrons. Another popular source for art is the **Torpedo Factory Art Center** in Old Town Alexandria (105 North Union Street; ☎ 703-838-4565), where 150 artists in a range of media—painting, sculpture, jewelry, and more—have set up studios. You can buy their work, or simply watch them create.

Bargains

Washington may have its million-dollar houses, expense-account restaurants, and pricey private schools, but it also has a surprising number of discount outlets. Savvy shoppers hardly ever pay full price for their Coach bags, their Lancôme cosmetics, or their Polo dress shirts.

Nowadays, even the relatively affluent D.C. area is surrounded by big-name, bargain-price supermalls. To the south is **Potomac Mills Mall** in Dale City, Virginia—one of the world's largest outlet malls. Just 45 minutes south of D.C., off I-95, this 250-store mall (☎ 800-VA MILLS) gets more visitors each year than any other Virginia tourist attraction—even more than Colonial Williamsburg. It's nearly impossible to hit all of the stores, which include the popular Swedish home-furnishings store **IKEA** and outlets for **Nordstrom, Eddie Bauer, Guess, Ann Taylor, Saks Off Fifth, Gap, Polo,** and **Brooks Brothers.**

To the west, perhaps 15 or 20 minutes past the various Tysons Corner malls at the intersection of Route 7 and the Route 15 Bypass, is the **Leesburg Corner Premium Outlets** (241 Fort Evans Road NE; ☎ 703-737-3071), a closet-heavy complex whose more famous designer names include **BCBG Max Azria, Cole Haan, Geoffrey Beene, Tommy Hilfiger, Polo Ralph Lauren, Kenneth Cole, Greg Norman, Perry Ellis, Kasper,** and **Liz Claiborne**, along with **Jones New York, Barneys, Saks Off Fifth, Burberry's, Movado,** and **Seiko**.

And northeast of town, off the Baltimore-Washington Parkway or Route 110 east of I-95, is **Arundel Mills** (7000 Arundel Mills Circle, Hanover, Maryland; ☎ 410-540-5100). More than a million square feet of name brands that echo the other two but trump them with a 24-theater cinema you can park the kids at and a full-sized **Bass Pro Shops Outdoor World,** where you can exhaust them on the rock climbing wall.

If you can't make it to the suburbs except by Metro, Washington now has its first inside-the-Beltway off-price mall, **City Place** in Silver Spring, Maryland (☎ 301-589-1091). At the intersection of Colesville Road (Route 29) and Fenton Street, three blocks north of the Silver Spring Metro (Red Line), City Place's best assets are Marshalls and its shoe outlets.

Bookstores

It's little wonder Washingtonians are well read: almost everywhere you look, there is a bookstore. There are general-interest chains like **B. Dalton** and **Borders,** but the majority are small independents, many with narrow specialties such as art, travel, Russian literature, or mystery.

If you're in a book-browsing mood, you might take the red line to Dupont Circle or the Orange Line to Farragut West. Between these two Metro stops, along and just off Connecticut Avenue between S and I streets, are some of the city's best bookstores. Walking south from S Street NW, toward Dupont Circle, you'll hit the **Newsroom,** with an exhaustive stock of foreign-language periodicals (1803 Connecticut Avenue NW; ☎ 202-332-1489); **Lambda Rising,** a gay/lesbian bookshop (1625 Connecticut Avenue NW; ☎ 202-462-6969); and **Kramerbooks,** a bookstore and cafe that's quite the scene on weekends, when it's open 24 hours (1517 Connecticut Avenue NW; ☎ 202-387-1400). Right off the circle on P Street you'll find **Second Story Books,** a terrific source for used books (2000 P Street NW; ☎ 202-659-8884); and **Backstage,** which sells scripts and performing-arts books (545 Eighth Street SE; ☎ 202-544-5744). Down side streets you can seek out **Olsson's Books and Records,** the city's most beloved general-interest book source, with a selective but broad inventory (1307 19th Street NW; ☎ 202-785-1133). One of the **Books-a-Million** stores is also on Dupont Circle between New Hampshire Avenue and P Street at about one o'clock (☎ 202-319-1374); it discounts the current *New York Times* hard- and paperback bestsellers at 30 percent off retail price.

Over by Farragut West you'll find volumes on the visual arts at **Franz Bader** (1911 I Street NW; ☎ 202-337-5440) and travel guides at **The ADC Map Store** (1636 I Street NW; ☎ 202-628-2608). There is a fairly large **Borders** on L Street at 19th Street, though not as overwhelming as the flagship store in White Flint Mall; and a three-decker **Barnes and Noble** store, one of several recently opened in the Washington area, in Georgetown at M and 21st streets.

And even Washingtonians tend to overlook the **Government Printing Office Bookstore,** which carries more than 15,000 books, pamphlets, and CD-ROMs as well as books of photographs—and sometimes the real things—from the Library of Congress (710 North Capitol Street; ☎ 202-512-0132).

Another specialty bookstore can be found farther north. **Politics & Prose** specializes in psychology, politics, and the works of local authors—and hosts many of their book-signing parties (5015 Connecticut Avenue NW; ☎ 202-364-1919). And although it's not widely advertised, the **Shops at Mount Vernon** claim to have the largest bookstore in the country dedicated to George Washington (see "Museum Shops," right). Collectors of serious comic books and graphic novels should head to **Big Planet Comics,** with branches in Georgetown (3145 Dumbarton Street NW; ☎ 202-342-1961), Bethesda (4908 Fairmont Avenue; ☎ 301-654-6856), and Vienna (426 Maple Avenue; ☎ 703-242-9412).

Decorative Arts

The south side of M Street between 28th and 30th streets NW in Georgetown offers a staggering array of antiques and decorative arts, particularly rich in Art Deco, Art Nouveau, and Moderne pieces. At **Justine Mehlman** (2824 Pennsylvania Avenue; ☎ 202-337-0613), you'll find silver, pewter and glass, and ceramic vases, the majority of them attributed, from Liberty Arts and Crafts and Nouveau artists; plus fine Victorian rings and earrings, enamel, intaglio, and even Bakelite.

The display rooms of jewelry designer to the stars (and the pols) **Ann Hand** swings around the corner of 29th and M (2900 M Street; ☎ 202-338-7710) with racks of pearls (in an array of colors) thick as Fort Knox. **Grafix** (2904 M Street NW; ☎ 202-342-0610) sells vintage posters—including Art Nouveau and Deco examples, antique hand-tinted maps, and collectible prints and illustration plates. A partitioned town house at 2918 M Street NW features **Michael Getz** (☎ 202-338-3811) and **Cherub Gallery** (☎ 202-337-2224) and gathers a collection of works by such artists and studios as Tiffany, Lalique, Daum, and Icart. Here you can find heavy wrought irons, ivory-handled fish services and magnifying glasses, cream pitchers and perfume bottles, elegant cocktail shakers, nymphic candelabra, and ornate photo frames. In the back room is the largest collection of silver napkin rings outside a melting pot. **Keith Lipert** (2922 M Street NW; ☎ 202-965-9736) also displays art, glass, and silver, but its emphasis is on enamelware, ceramics, and heavier pieces.

Designer Clothing

In the free-spending 1980s, couture clothiers couldn't open shops fast enough in the Washington area. While the 1980s may be gone, most of the boutiques remain. And most are in "Gucci Gulch"—a row of chic shops extending from the 5200 to 5500 blocks of Wisconsin Avenue. To an extent, though, this strip has been surpassed by the new, loosely jointed Chevy Chase shopping neighborhood described on page 351.

Insider Shops

Although the White House, the House of Representatives, and even Camp David have monogrammed and souvenir merchandise, it's available only to special staff. Outsiders who want to look like Washington insiders do have a few options, however.

The **NASA Exchange** gift shop (300 E Street SW; ☎ 202-358-0162) is for astronaut wannabes. It is open Monday to Friday, 8:15 a.m. to 4 p.m (closed during lunch, 1 to 2 p.m.).

A different sort of insider store is the **Counter Spy Shop** (1027 Connecticut Avenue NW; ☎ 202-887-1717), which has tiny cameras, bugging and taping trackers, night-vision scopes, and protective clothing. Just look mysterious.

Museum Shops

Some of Washington's greatest finds are in its museum gift shops. A museum's orientation is a good guide to its shop's merchandise—prints, art-design ties, and art books fill the **National Gallery of Art** shop; model airplanes and other toys of flight are on sale at the **Air and Space Museum.** The largest Smithsonian shops are at the **Museum of American History,** which sells toys, clothing, musical instruments, and recordings from countries highlighted in the exhibits; although all the museums have some items reflecting the collection. (Unfortunately, it's currently closed for renovation.) And the hippest gifts are currently on view—sort of—at the **International Spy Museum** store (☎ 202-654-0950), which stocks video and CD copies of old spy TV shows and themes, pens disguised as lipsticks, disguises for people, and miniature cameras.

Some good museum shops are often overlooked by tourists. Among the best are the **National Building Museum** shop (☎ 202-272-2448), which sells design-related books, jewelry, architecturally inspired greeting cards, and gadgets; the **Arts and Industries** shop (☎ 202-357-2700), a pretty, Victorian setting stocked with Smithsonian reproductions; the **National Museum of the American Indian** (☎ 202-275-1231) with its turquoise and silver jewelry, Zuni pottery, hand carvings, and rugs; the **Textile Museum** (☎ 202-67-0441), stocked with silk saris, shawls, brocade bags, and quilts; the **National Museum of African Art** shop (☎ 202-633-4600), a bazaar filled with colorful cloth, Ethiopian crosses, and wooden ceremonial instruments such as hand drums and tambourines; the **Arthur M. Sackler Gallery** shop (☎ 202-633-4880), with cases full of brass Buddhas, Chinese lacquerware, jade and jasper jewelry, feng shui kits, and porcelain; the **Renwick Gallery,** which stocks unusual art jewelry; the Shakespeare-lovers' treasure trove at the **Folger Shakespeare Library** (☎ 202-544-4600); and the newly expanded shop at the **John F. Kennedy Center for the Performing Arts** (☎ 202-467-4600), stocked with videos, opera glasses, and other gifts for performing-arts lovers.

The **Hillwood Museum** (☎ 202-686-8510) has jewelry and ornaments inspired by Marjorie Merriweather Post's famous collection of Fabergé and Russian porcelains. The **Stephen Decatur House Museum** (☎ 202-842-1856) has patriotic souvenirs emphasizing American history and architecture, and the expanded shop at **Mount Vernon** (☎ 703-799-6301) offers reproductions of Martha's cookbook, George's key to the Bastille, and period china and silver patterns.

Oriental Rugs

Washington, D.C., offers the broadest selection of handmade Oriental rugs available in the United States. In fact, there is so much competition here that prices are forced below what you would expect to pay for comparable quality in other American cities. Though shops are sprinkled all around the greater Washington area, the biggest concentration of reputable stores is located on Wisconsin Avenue from Friendship Heights to Bethesda.

Political Memorabilia

If you're a serious collector, no doubt you already know about stores selling political buttons and ribbons, autographed letters and photos, and commemorative plates and pens. If you're not a collector, these shops can be as fun to browse through as museums, except that you can touch things, buy them, and take them home. Two such shops, within walking distance of one another, are **Capitol Coin and Stamp** (1001 Connecticut Avenue NW; ☎ 202-296-0400) and **Political Americana** (1331 Pennsylvania Avenue NW; ☎ 202-737-7730), which also has a branch inside Union Station. **The Honest Abe Souvenir Company** (F and Tenth streets NW; ☎ 202-347-1021) has all sorts of Washingtonia, from tiny busts of Martin Luther King Jr. to D.C. snow globes and Georgetown T-shirts.

Prints and Photography

Although most dealers in fine photos are in Georgetown, one of the most prominent is the **Kathleen Ewing Gallery** (1609 Connecticut Avenue NW, Suite 200; ☎ 202-328-0955). Otherwise, visit the **Robert Brown Gallery** (2030 R Street NW; ☎ 202-483-4383); the **Ralls Collection** (1516 31st Street NW; ☎ 202-342-1754); and the **Govinda Gallery** (1227 34th Street NW; ☎ 202-333-1180), which specializes in photographs of and by rock 'n' rollers, from Annie Leibovitz to onetime Beatle-turned-artist Stu Sutcliffe and his photographer girlfriend Astrid Kirchherr. For prints and works on paper, visit the **Georgetown Gallery of Art** (3235 P Street NW; ☎ 202-333-6308), **Hemphill Fine Arts** (1515 14th Street NW; ☎ 202-342-5610), and the **Spectrum Gallery** (1132 29th Street NW; ☎ 202-333-0954). For antique maps, botanical prints, and vintage cartoons, try the **Old Print Gallery,** also in Georgetown (1220 31st Street NW; ☎ 202-965-1818).

Salon Products

Although it seems as if every mall now has a **Body Shop** and several imitators, for the good stuff think about Georgetown: **Aveda** has a huge new spa/salon/store around the corner (1325 Wisconsin Avenue NW; ☎ 202-965-1325), offering body products from toners to massage oils, all made of only plant products—no artificial scents or coloring and no animal testing—and scented with the likes of rosemary, cinnamon, sesame, and almond oils. Soaps, bath salts, and oils are available by the ounce or bottle, not to mention facials, scrubs, and massages. There's sort of a "triptych" of cosmetic stores on M Street, starting with the very hot French chain **Sephora,** where you can try on nearly a hundred brands of lipstick (3065 M Street; ☎ 202-338-5644); **MAC** (3067 M Street NW; ☎ 202-944-9771); and **Blue Mercury** (3059 M Street NW; (202) 965-1300), which is both a spa and a Merle Norman for the new millennium, stocked with custom creams, exotic oils, and lipsticks named for film stars. And across the street are the Provençal-based **L'Occitane** (3106 M Street NW; ☎ 202-337-6001) and the all organic London-based **Lush** (3066 M Street NW; ☎ 202-333-6950).

Watches

Washington's answer to Tourneau is **Alan Furman & Co.,** which offers up to 50% off on Rolex, Patek Philippe, and Cartier, plus Lalique and Baccarat crystal and Montblanc pens (12250 Rockville Pike; ☎ 202-331-0671).

Wine and Gourmet Foods

Georgetown has a branch of New York's famed **Dean & Deluca** (3276 M Street NW; ☎ 202-342-2500), complete with cafe. **Mayflower Wines** joined forces with the **Sutton Place Gourmet** shops in 1992 to provide one-stop, fine-food shops in the greater Washington area. Each shop offers an excellent selection of wines and an impressive variety of gourmet and ethnic foods. The wine buyers travel abroad each year to select the stores' wine inventory and are particularly tuned in to Italian reds. Visitors to the stores from outside the District, Virginia, and Maryland can buy wine and have it shipped home. If you do not have time to shop in person, the **Sutton Place Gourmet** publishes a newsletter describing highly touted (and reasonably priced) wines. The newsletter also includes recipes. To receive the free newsletter call ☎ 301-564-3100.

Another fine wine store, which invests in wine futures and offers a strong catalog, is **MacArthur Liquors** (4877 MacArthur Boulevard NW; ☎ 202-338-1433) in the Palisades neighborhood west of Georgetown. It's worth remembering that because of tax laws, wine for consumption is less expensive in stores like this within the District than in stores just over the border in Maryland or Virginia. Originally owned by the well-liked purveyor Addy Bassin, MacArthur is still often called "Bassin's" by Washington natives.

Writing Implements

Fahrney's Pens (1317 F Street NW; ☎ 202-628-9525) has all the write stuff: for more than 70 years, Fahrney's has sold nothing but beautiful pens, including Watermans and Montblancs.

PART TEN

ENTERTAINMENT *and* NIGHTLIFE

WASHINGTON NIGHTLIFE:
More Than Lit-up Monuments

WASHINGTON AFTER-HOURS USED TO BE AN OXYMORON. Public transportation set its clock by the bureaucracy, commuters had too far to go (and come back the next morning) to stay out late, and big expense-account money was lavished on restaurants and buddy bars. Besides, Washingtonians suffered from a persistent cultural inferiority complex that had them running to buy tickets to see touring theatrical companies while not-so-benignly neglecting homegrown troupes.

Nowadays, though, the joke about "Washington after hours" being an oxymoron is just that: a joke. It's not that there's too little nightlife around, it's that there's too much. Or too many. Washington is a hodgepodge of big-city bustlers, bureaucrats, yuppies, journalists, diplomats, artists, immigrants, CEOs, and college students; and every one of these groups is trying to create, and then integrate, their own circles. The fact that many overlap, and others evolve, means you can dabble in a little of everything.

Washington's legitimate theatrical community is underestimated but excellent; ballet, Broadway, and cabaret are almost constant presences, opera less so but increasingly frequent. At least some of the racetracks are open year-round; there are major- and minor-league sports teams at play in every season (see the "Spectator Sports" section). And nightclubs come in as many flavors as their patrons: discos and dance halls, live-music venues, comedy showcases, salsa bars, specialty bars, sports bars, espresso bars, gay bars, singles scenes, and "second scenes" for re-entering singles. There are even a couple of strip joints around for boys'-night sentimentalists and plenty of brewpubs for beer connoisseurs.

Just in the last couple of years, a kind of nightclub renaissance has revitalized whole neighborhoods, a shift that has been particularly visible downtown in areas that once were nearly deserted after rush hour, or at least after cocktail hour. The Verizon Center has sparked a development boom downtown in what is now called **Penn Quarter;** there many of the hippest restaurants also have the hottest bar scenes. The **"New U"** corridor that originally centered on 14th and U streets NW (and which now stretches to Ninth or Tenth) has begun to merge with the small-theater strip, adding balance and interest. **Adams-Morgan** has regained vitality, thanks in part to the shift from Eurotrash posing to mambo-savvy swingers. The H Street NE neighborhood between 12th and 15th streets, famously hard-hit by riots after the assassination of Rev. Martin Luther King Jr. and left desolate for nearly 30 years thereafter, has become one of the most idiosyncratic and entertaining nightlife areas in town—nicknamed the **Atlas District,** after the newly restored cinema–turned–multispace performing-arts center. Curiously, **Georgetown,** once a nightlife mecca, has only a handful of hot spots left, including **Blues Alley** and **Blue Gin,** both profiled later, and such décor-heavy bars as **Mie N Yu** at 3125 M Street NW.

Among the more important musical addresses in the New U are the **9:30** club, the **Chi-Cha Lounge,** and the **Black Cat** (all profiled); the up and coming **Velvet Lounge** (915 U Street NW; ☎ 202-462-7625); the North African-Arabic **Cafe Nema** (1334 U Street NW; ☎ 202-462-2640); **Bohemian Caverns** (2001 11th Street NW; ☎ 202-299-0800); **Cada Vez** (1438 U Street NW; ☎ 202-667-0785); or for jazz swingers, **UTopia** (1418 U Street NW; ☎ 202-483-7669); **HR-57** (1610 14th Street NW; ☎ 202-667-3700); and on concert nights, the **Lincoln Theatre** (1215 U Street NW; ☎ 202-328-6000). For being-scenery, there are **Bar Nun** (1326 U Street NW; ☎ 202-667-6680), with its soul and funk music but quiet storm alcoves; the **Saint** (1520 14th Street NW; ☎ 202-234-0886); the **Saloon** (1207 U Street NW; ☎ 202-462-2640); and **Republic Gardens** (1355 U Street NW; ☎ 202-232-2710).

Adams-Morgan is a movable feast, starting with **Rumba Café** (2443 18th Street NW; ☎ 202-588-5501) and moving toward the **Green Island Cafe** (2327 18th Street NW; ☎ 202-667-4355); the multi-purpose restaurant-lounge **Felix** (2406 18th Street NW; ☎ 202-483-3549); jazzy **Columbia Station** (2325 18th Street NW; ☎ 202-462-6040); the multilevel **Reef,** with its enormously popular rooftop bar (2446 18th Street NW; ☎ 202-518-3800); **Chloe,** with its minimalist warehouse-chic (2473 18th Street NW; ☎ 202-256-6592); the deep-dive **Dan's Café** (2315 18th Street NW; ☎ 202-265-9241); the 1950s gas station–look **Toledo Lounge** (2435 18th Street NW; ☎ 202-986-5416); the aptly named coffeehouse-bar-hookup-hangout **Tryst** (2459 18th Street NW; ☎ 202-232-5500); **Anzu Downstairs** (2436 18th Street NW; ☎ 202-462-8844); **Bossa Bistro** (2463 18th Street; ☎ 202-667-0088); **Madam's Organ,** with live blues, R&B, or bluegrass nightly (2461 18th Street NW; ☎ 202-667-5370); salsa classroom **Latin Jazz Alley** (1721 Columbia Road NW; ☎ 202-328-6190); the quintessential beer hall–basement-rec-room goof **Chief Ike's Mambo Lounge,** which also attracts one of the most mixed crowds (age, sex, and race) in town (1725 Columbia Road NW; ☎ 202-332-2211); **Pharmacy Bar** (2337 18th Street NW; ☎ 202-483-1200); **Habana Village** (1834 Columbia Road NW; ☎ 202-462-6310); and many others. Actually, you might end up back at the bottom end for late-night refueling at the **Duplex Diner** (18th and U streets NW; ☎ 202-265-7828).

Nearly as impressive is the millennial revival of downtown **Connecticut Avenue,** long a strictly commercial-business area, and one that regularly defeated attempts to push the expense-account-restaurant envelope. These days, the five-star intersection at Connecticut, M, Jefferson and 18th streets NW, just above Farragut North, marks the junction of **MCCXXIII** (pronounced "twelve twenty-three"); the underground "fly me" aero-look **Fly** (1802 Jefferson Place NW; ☎ 202-828-4433); and **Ozio** (all profiled); the swank all-white and sushi-chic (and smoker-friendly) hybrid dance hall **Dragonfly** (1215 Connecticut Avenue NW; ☎ 202-331-1775); the Moroccan casbah bar **Andalu** (1214 18th Street NW; ☎ 202-785-2922); and its neighbor **Lucky Bar** (1221 Connecticut Avenue NW; ☎ 202-331-3733); **Club Five** (1214-B 18th Street NW; ☎ 202-331-7123); **Toka** (1140 19th Street NW; ☎ 202-429-8652); **Ooh La La Restaurant** (1800 M Street; ☎ 202-785-1177); and the outwardly low key **18th Street Lounge** (1212 18th Street NW; ☎ 202-466-3922), the grandfather of the lounge neighborhood. There are even a couple of neo-hip strip joints (see "The Sex Thing," page 378). And if all that's too much for you, just turn up the street to the intentionally retro beer-bar **Big Hunt** (1345 Connecticut Avenue NW; ☎ 202-785-2333); or the tapas-and-pajama-party sofa lounge **Cloud** (1 Dupont Circle; ☎ 202-872-1122), both within eyeshot of the Dupont Circle Metro.

The new **Atlas District,** a three-block stretch of H Street NE centered around the new **Atlas Performing Arts Center,** is suddenly ablaze with neon signs. Among the dozen-plus clubs are sports bars, such as the **Argonaut** at 1433 H Street NE (☎ 202-397-1416); retro-cocktail chic bars; the **H Street Martini Lounge** (1236 H Street NE; ☎ 202-397-3333); and the weird and wonderful **Showbar Presents the Palace of Wonders** (1210 H Street NE; ☎ 202-398-7469), which is as much bar as carnival, literally: one of the owners spent years collecting old sideshow memorabilia such as the nine-foot Peruvian mummies and eight-legged goat that are featured in the second-floor gallery. Showbar even imports carny-style entertainment: sword swallowers (including one of the bartenders), burlesque-style dancers, daredevils, and arm-wrestlers.

The more usual live entertainment can be found at the **Rock and Roll Hotel** (1353 H Street NE; ☎ 202-388-7625; **www.rockandroll hoteldc.com**), a funeral home renovated not as an overnighter but as a midsized (capacity 400) rock venue with VIP suites and pool tables upstairs; and **The Red and the Black** (1212 H Street NE; ☎ 202-399-3201), a New Orleans–looking (and cooking) bar with more acoustic bands. Go-go, a local variant on funk, may have disappeared from the music charts, but longtime Washington go-go heroes Sugar Bear (frontman for the genre's most famous act, Experience Unlimited, which had a hit single with "Da Butt" in the late 1980s) and Little Benny are still holding court at **Rose's Dream Bar and Lounge** (1370 H Street NE, upstairs; ☎ 202-398-5700).

For theatrical performances, check the **H Street Playhouse** (1365 H Street NE; ☎ 202-396-2125), which has survived incarnations as a garage, roller rink, furniture store, and diner to become a 100-seat theater and home to several small area companies; and the newly opened **Atlas Performing Arts Center** itself (1333 H Street NE; ☎ 202-399-7993), a former Art Deco cinema that has been renovated to house one fixed-stage venue seating 275 and a second, nearly as large flexible-seating black-box theater. Among the companies that will call Atlas their home base are the Washington Performing Arts Society, the Levine School of Music, Joy of Motion, Washington Savoyards, the Capital City Symphony, Step Afrika, and Forum Theatre and Dance.

The Atlas District isn't near a subway stop—there are plans to lay tracks for a streetcar line along H Street, though there's no firm construction date—and a cab from Union Station is about $10 for two without tip, but several of the venues, including the Argonaut, The Red and the Black, Showbar, and Rock and Roll Hotel, have joined to provide a free shuttle back to Union Station on Friday and Saturday nights between 10 p.m. and 2:30 a.m.

Live entertainment in Washington can be divided into three categories: legitimate theater, comedy, and live rock/pop/jazz/country music. The club profiles that follow focus on live music, comedy clubs, discos/dance clubs, and noteworthy after-hours scenes because they generally require no advance planning. (In some cases, live music venues might sell out particular performances, so call ahead.) Nightly schedules of live music clubs, comedy clubs, and theatrical productions, as well as listings of piano rooms, opera companies, movie showtimes, etc., are printed in the *Washington Post* Friday "Weekend" section and the free *Washington City Paper*.

LEGITIMATE THEATER

WASHINGTON BOASTS MORE THAN A DOZEN major theatrical venues (not even counting the Kennedy Center's five stages separately) and more than a half-dozen smaller residential and repertory companies, plus university theaters, small special-interest venues, and itinerant troupes (see the Atlas Performing Arts Center, above). The "big six" are where national touring companies, classical musicians, and celebrity productions are most apt to show up, and they have the most complete facilities for handicapped patrons. They are also likely to be the most expensive. But Washington is in a performing arts boom, and the "small" theaters are rapidly getting bigger, and better.

On any given night at the **Kennedy Center for the Performing Arts,** you might see the resident National Symphony Orchestra under Leonard Slatkin or a visiting philharmonic in the 2,500-seat **Concert Hall,** a straight drama or classic farce in the 1,100-seat **Eisenhower Theater,** and a Broadway musical, kabuki spectacular, or premier cru ballet company in the 2,300-seat Opera House—that is, when the Washington Opera, under general director Placido Domingo, is not in residence. The two smaller arenas, **Terrace Theater** and **Theater Lab,** share the third floor with the restaurant (which has a nice view if you can get it) and archives. Philip Johnson's steeply canted and gracious Terrace, a gift from the nation of Japan, houses experimental or cult-interest productions, specialty concerts, and showcases; in the Theater Lab, designed to accommodate the avant and cabaret, the semi-improvised murder farce *Shear Madness* is halfway through its second decade. Most remarkable, however, is the Kennedy Center's gift to Washington music lovers: the **Millennium Stage,** which provides national and top local acts in an indoor venue—and patrons a free show—at 6 p.m. every day of the year. The Kennedy Center is at Virginia and New Hampshire avenues NW, next to the Watergate; the closest subway station is Foggy Bottom, and the Center operates a free shuttle from the station. For tickets and information, call ☎ 202-467-4600 or visit **www.kennedy-center.org.**

Penn Quarter, the neighborhood just north of Pennsylvania Avenue between Fourth and 12th streets NW, has become a lively complex of restaurants, bars and sports bars, dance clubs, art galleries, and theaters. It's so busy, in fact, that "Penn Quarter" has been added to the name of the Archives–Navy Memorial Metro station. Among the most important is the **Shakespeare Theatre,** which moved in 1992 from its beloved but cramped home at the Folger Shakespeare Library into new digs in the grandly renovated Lansburg Building. It now seats about 450; but it is now constructing a second, larger theater around the corner at 620 F Street that will offer jazz, dance, film and chamber music, as well as theatrical productions. Each season it produces four classic plays, three by Shakespeare, and regularly corrals a few major stage and screen stars to headline. It also puts on free Shakespeare at the **Carter-Barron Amphitheater** every summer. The Shakespeare Theatre is at 450 Seventh Street NW, near the Gallery Place and Archives–Navy Memorial–Penn Quarter subway stops; for information, ☎ 202-547-1122; TTY ☎ 202-638-3863; **www.shakespearetheatre.org.**

There is still Shakespeare at the **Folger Shakespeare Library,** a handful of productions in an intimate setting that suggests a nobleman's banquet hall (201 East Capitol Street; ☎ 202-544-7077).

Woolly Mammoth, which had been borrowing performance space from its neighbors in the 14th and U corridor, has new digs at Seventh and D, ☎ 202-393-3939. The off-off-style **Warehouse Theater** is a few blocks north at 1017 Seventh, ☎ 202-783-3933. **Ford's Theatre,** where the balcony box in which Abraham Lincoln was shot remains draped in black (and spectrally inhabited, according to rumor), is a smallish (750-seat) but comfy and newly renovated venue that hosts three or four productions a year, but is best known for the annual production of Dickens's *A Christmas Carol.* Ford's is at 511 10th Street NW (Metro Center subway); ☎ 202-418-4808; **www.fordstheatre.org.**

The **Warner Theatre,** which survived a two-year restoration marathon, is now a rococo delight, complete with a few special boxes with food service. Although it is emphasizing more legitimate theatrical bookings and musicals, it still occasionally harks back to the days when it was one of the nicer small-concert venues for popular music (the reclusive Brian Wilson, for instance, chose the Warner for his "Smile" and final "Pet Sounds" tours). The Warner is at 13th and E streets NW, near Federal Triangle or Metro Center; for information, call ☎ 202-783-4000 or go to **www.warnertheatre.com.**

The **National Theatre,** which was thoroughly, if a little showily, restored in Miami-bright pastels a few years ago, is managed by the Shubert Organization, which not only books its touring Broadway productions there but more and more often uses it for pre-Broadway tryouts. The National is at 1321 Pennsylvania Avenue NW, near the Federal Triangle or Metro Center subway stop. For information, call ☎ 202-628-6161; for tickets, call ☎ 800-447-7400 or visit **www.nationaltheatre.org.**

The tripartite **Arena Stage** is the most prestigious of Washington resident companies and was a prime factor in the rebirth of American regional theater. The **Fichandler** theater-in-the-round seats a little over 800; the **Kreeger** holds more than 500; and the tiny, pubbish **Old Vat Room** seats fewer than 200. Though it likes to show off its versatility (such as a dizzying reenactment of the Marx Brothers' *The Cocoanuts* or the Flying Karamazov Brothers acting in *The Brothers Karamazov*), the Arena is dedicated and fearless, producing Athol Fugard and August Wilson, as well as Tennessee Williams and Eugene O'Neill. The Arena is at Sixth Street and Maine Avenue SW, on the waterfront, which is also the Metro station; call ☎ 202-488-3300 or visit **www.arena-stage.org.**

Although many of these professional productions can be pricey and often sell out, the **Ticket Place** office, also down in Penn Quarter and right down from Shakespeare Theatre and Woolly Mammoth at 407 Seventh Street NW, sells half-price tickets (plus a service charge amounting to 10% of the face value) for same-day shows and concerts. Cash, travelers' checks, and debit cards are accepted. The Ticket Place is open Tuesday through Saturday from 11 a.m. until 6 p.m.; tickets for Sunday and Monday shows are sold on Saturday when available; call

☎ 202-842-5387 for a list of available tickets. The Kennedy Center also sells a limited number of same-day tickets at half price and offers half-price tickets for students, seniors, military, fixed-income families, and those with permanent disabilities. For more information, call ☎ 202-467-4600. A limited number of standing-room passes at reduced prices and occasional returned seats may be available as well. (Several other ticket vendors in the area such as **Top Centre** sell tickets to area concerts and sporting events, but they usually impose a large service charge.)

unofficial **TIP**
Discount drama? Check day-of-show specials.

Washington's "off-Broadway" theaters are clustered around the revitalized 14th Street NW neighborhood, specializing in new and cutting-edge works. Among the most intriguing are **1409 Playbill Café** (1409 14th Street NW; ☎ 202-265-3055); **Arena Stage** at 14th and T streets NW; and the **Studio Theatre** (14th and P streets NW; ☎ 202-332-3300), which is unveiling a three-stage expansion. The Jewish-interest **Theater J** is just a few blocks away (1529 16th Street NW; ☎ 202-518-9418). On the Green Line, a Metro station (called U Street/African-American Civil War Memorial) is located nearby at 14th and U streets.

The theater-building boom is not limited to downtown, either. One of the strongest "small" theaters is **Signature Theatre** in Arlington, which has received strong national reviews, especially of its Sondheim productions (3806 South Four Mile Run Drive; ☎ 800-955-5566); Signature is also building a new space, yet another two-stage space that will seat nearly three times its current 135. **The Center for the Arts at George Mason University** (☎ 703-993-ARTS), in Fairfax, also hosts a varied program of arts and letters, as well as performances.

In the past few years, a number of impressive performance venues have been developed in the Maryland suburbs, several accessible by subway. One, the new **Music Center at Strathmore Hall** in North Bethesda, has a dedicated pedestrian overpass from the Grosvenor-Strathmore Metro station. The original Strathmore Hall already hosted tea-time concerts on Tuesdays and Wednesdays, along with summertime concerts and family-fare films on the lawn; it also has art galleries and crafts shows; for information on programs, call ☎ 301-530-0540. The Music Center, which seats 2,000, books national classical and pop singers, visiting symphony orchestras, and folk and blues society shows.

On the same Metro line, just across the street from the Bethesda station, is one of two performance stages belonging to the **Round House Theatre** company (East-West Highway and Waverly Street, Bethesda; ☎ 240-644-1099).

Farther out the Red Line, near the Rockville Metro stop, is Montgomery College and the **Robert E. Parilla Performing Arts Center** (for the box office call ☎ 301-279-5301), which brings in European ballet and symphony orchestra, and such family-oriented touring acts as

Mickey Rooney, Smokey Robinson, and old Broadway shows. There is no shuttle, but bus or cab service is available from the station.

In addition, Maryland now boasts one of the area's most impressive performance arts complexes. The recently completed **Clarice Smith Performing Arts Center at Maryland,** on the College Park campus of the University of Maryland, offers as many venues as the Kennedy Center (and in several cases, even more cutting-edge acoustical and recording technology): the 1,100-seat **Dekelboum Concert Hall,** the 180-seat **Dance Theatre,** the 650-seat proscenium **Kay Theatre,** the 300-seat **Gildenhorn Recital Hall,** the intimate 100-seat **Laboratory Theatre,** and the 200-seat "black box"–style **Kogod Theatre.** Also on campus, but not actually in the Smith complex, is the **Tawes Theatre,** a 1,350-seat Broadway-style proscenium, which has been for many years the home of the prestigious William Kapell Piano Competition.

Recent Smith Center offerings have ranged from Chinese opera and the Shanghai Traditional Orchestra, to Phillip Glass and the Bang on a Can All-Stars, to the Merce Cunningham Dance Company, to the theater department's production of *The Trojan Women,* to the Guarneri String Quartet in open rehearsal. The Clarice Smith Center is at University Boulevard and Stadium Drive in College Park; you can take the Green Line subway to the College Park Station and take one of two free shuttles to the Stamp Student Union or the campus "Circuit" shuttle directly to the complex. For more information, call ☎ 301-405-2787.

And although they require cars (or friends), there are two other prominent venues in Montgomery County: the **Olney Theatre** (2001 Olney-Sandy Spring Road, Olney; ☎ 301-924-3400) and the increasingly popular **BlackRock Center for the Arts** in Germantown (12901 Town Commons Drive; ☎ 301-528-2260). With its three venues— a 210-seat main stage, a 130-seat dance theater, and an outdoor performance stage for theatrical productions, festivals, concerts, and outdoor family films—plus exhibition galleries and classrooms, Black-Rock is one of the best examples of "new town" community centers. Among recent artists booked there are the Marcus Roberts Trio, the Baltimore Symphony Orchestra Chamber Players, Richie Havens, Janis Ian, local rockabilly and soul faves Ruthie and the Wranglers and Mary Ann Redmond, and indie filmmakers and storytellers.

In addition, several of the downtown public buildings frequently hold concerts of classical, jazz, pop, or folk music, and even some medieval consorts, among them the Washington National Cathedral, the National Gallery of Art, the Library of Congress, and the National Museum of Natural History, which on Thursdays hosts Jazz at the IMAX. For information on these, plus the handful of smaller theaters and itinerant companies, check the "Guide to the Lively Arts" in the *Washington Post* Friday "Weekend" or Sunday "Show" sections or the free *City Paper* handout.

In general, Washington audiences have loosened their ties when it comes to theater attire. To some extent, the more serious a production is, the dressier the crowd, although jeans have become ubiquitous, particularly at the smaller, avant-garde companies. Opening nights are often black tie (or "creative black tie"), but you can go as you are. And incidentally, many of the nicer restaurants near the big-ticket venues offer pre-theater menus at fixed (and bargain) prices; be sure to inquire.

COMEDY IN WASHINGTON

WASHINGTON IS FULL OF JOKES—and that's the first one. Capital comedians divide very roughly into three generations and styles: the cabaret performers (those "Washington institutions" whose satires are usually musical and relatively gentle); the sketch and improvisational troupes from the post-Watergate *Saturday Night Live* era; and the stand-up artists who are the anti-establishment baby-busters—in some cases, the urban guerrillas. The first two groups are almost unavoidably political; the stand-up comedians range from political podium to locker room.

The most famous of the cabaret comedians is PBS irregular **Mark Russell,** whose residency at the Omni Shoreham lasted about four senatorial terms and who still plays several weeks at a time at Ford's Theatre every year (online at **www.markrussell.net**).

The most loyal opposition is offered by the **Capitol Steps,** a group of former and current Hill staffers who roast their own hosts by rewriting familiar songs with pun-ishing lyrics. In addition to entertaining at semi-official functions (which may be one reason why their barbs are a tad blunted compared to some more outspoken satirists'), the Capitol Steps are a popular tourist attraction and perform every Friday and Saturday at the Ronald Reagan International Trade Building at 13th Street and Pennsylvania Avenue NW; call ☎ 202-312-1555; **www.capsteps.com.** The Metro stop is Federal Triangle.

After a few years' hiatus, **Comedy Sportz** has reformed and plays its *Whose Line Is It Anyway?*–style games Thursdays through Saturdays on the third floor of the Metro-connected Ballston Common Mall (☎ 703-294-5233).

Gross National Product (reservations at ☎ 202-783-7212), an underground resistance movement that went above ground after Reagan's election, is now a national act and is in residence in New York or Los Angeles at various times. Politics, especially the executive power structure, is its obsession: it skewers snoops, creeps, and veeps with gusto and, despite its long tenure, a hint of childish glee. Revues have titles like "Clintoons: The First Hundred Daze" and "A Newt World Order." Shows are about 90 minutes long, and since topicality is the name of the game, skits rise and fall with the state of the world. (At press time, "Son of a Bush" was playing Saturday nights at Warehouse

Theater). GNP also operates one of Washington's more unique tour services, **Scandal Tours,** which takes sightseers past such political landmarks as Gary Hart's town house; the Jefferson Hotel, where political gun-for-hire Dick Morris simultaneously sucked a prostitute's toes and directed the Democrats' campaign strategy; and Fanne Foxe's impromptu swimming pool, the Tidal Basin—an event retold by sex scandal veteran "Bob Packwood." Scandal Tours depart from the Old Post Office Pavilion Saturdays at 1 p.m. (reservations at ☎ 202-783-7212; information at **www.gnpcomedy.com**).

The overbooking and overbuilding that made comedy shops the fast-food entertainment of the 1980s is giving way to more exclusive (or at least better-budgeted) clubs. The most reliable are the downtown franchise of the star-circuit **Evening at the Improv** (profiled) and the cable-comic showcase's **Wiseacres** (8401 Westpark Drive in the Tysons Westpark Hotel; ☎ 877-947-3227 or 703-734-2800). Hip gay and straight comedians of both sexes—Kate Clinton, Paula Poundstone, Dennis Miller, Judy Tenuta—do so well in Washington that many are regularly booked not into clubs but into midsized theatrical venues and colleges. Many nightclubs and restaurants offer comedy one night a week; check newspapers for specific listings.

In general, all clubs now follow a standard lineup: the opener, usually a local beginner who patters about ten minutes and also serves as emcee (and who, especially on open-mike night, may mean the difference between a smooth production and a free-for-all); the "featured act," either an experienced journeyman or perhaps a second-rank national or cable TV performer, who does about 30 minutes; and the headliner, usually somebody with Letterman or Leno credits or at least a cable special, who performs about an hour.

LIVE POP, ROCK, AND JAZZ

ALTHOUGH IT ISN'T WIDELY ADVERTISED, for some reason, Washington is a haven for music lovers of all types, and in the summer especially an astonishing amount of music is free to the public. From classical to college-radio rock, from hole-in-the-wall to the Washington Mall, you can hear it all. Credit for the rise in live-music clubs in the Washington area is split between the booming third-world community, used to later hours and different music styles; the large college and 20-something population looking for entertainment, along with the 30-somethings who started looking ten years ago; the increasing number of those 20- and 30- and even 40-somethings who live in the suburbs and don't want to go downtown for a good time; the more assertive gay and faux-prole communities seeking accommodation; and the fair number of stubborn musicians and underground entrepreneurs who have established venues and support networks for themselves and one another.

Jazz, of course, has a long history in Washington—in the 1930s and 1940s the U Street/Howard Theatre corridor was known as the "Black Broadway" and rivaled Harlem. And after years of declining audiences and bankrupted clubs, jazz is reviving all around the area, and the number of young jazz musicians, black and white, classical and contemporary, is remarkable. In fact, the **Lincoln Theatre** (not far from the U Street/African-American Civil War Memorial Metro at 1215 U Street NW; ☎ 202-328-6000), which used to be one of the most popular stops for top performers, has been restored to its Georgian Revival glory and is beginning to feature jazz and pop shows again.

Among the best places to hear jazz are **Blues Alley** and **Takoma Station Tavern** (profiled); **Twins** (1344 U Street; ☎ 202-234-0072 and 5516 Colorado Avenue NW; ☎ 202-882-2523); the **Ritz-Carlton Pentagon City** (1250 South Hayes Street, Arlington, Virginia; ☎ 703-415-5000); the **Basin Street Lounge/219 Restaurant** (219 King Street, Alexandria, Virginia; ☎ 703-549-1141); **The Ice House Café** (760 Elden Street, Herndon, Virginia; ☎ 703-437-4500); **Bangkok Blues,** a fine Thai restaurant in its own right (926 West Broad Street, Falls Church, Virginia; ☎ 703-534-0095); **Columbia Station** (2325 18th Street NW; ☎ 202-462-6040); **U-Topia** (1418 U Street NW; ☎ 202-483-7669); **Ellington's on Eighth** (424-A Eighth Street SE; ☎ 202-546-8308); and **Bohemian Caverns,** like the Lincoln Theatre, an old club rediscovered.

The mega–rock-concert venues tend to be sports arenas doing double duty: the 20,000-plus-seat **Verizon Center** downtown, home to the Washington Bullets basketball and Washington Wizards hockey teams; the 50,000-seat **RFK Stadium,** erstwhile home of the Redskins football team (which has the advantage of being accessible by Metro to the Stadium-Armory stop); and the all-purpose 10,000-seat **Patriot Center** college arena at George Mason in Fairfax, which also tends to carry the big-name country concerts. Tickets for these shows are usually available by phone from **Ticketmaster** at ☎ 202-397-SEAT (or online at **www.ticketmaster.com**), but beware: "service charges" and handling fees have been known to reach $4.50 per ticket—not per order.

The most popular outdoor commercial venue is **Wolf Trap Farm Park** off Route 7 in Vienna, Virginia, which offers almost nightly entertainment—pop, country, jazz and R&B, MOR (middle-of-the-road) rock, and even ballet and Broadway musical tours—and picnicking under the stars during the summer at its **Filene Center** amphitheater. During the winter season, Wolf Trap shifts to its small but acoustically great **Barns,** literally two rebuilt barns; among its best concerts are the annual Folk Masters series coordinated with the Smithsonian. Wolf Trap has started its own phone service called **ProTix,** which charges lower fees than Ticketmaster (and thus has not incurred the wrath of any popular rock group); log on to **www.wolftrap.org** or call ☎ 703-255-1900 for Wolf Trap shows. On summer nights, the Metro operates a $5 round-trip shuttle service from the West Falls Church station to the Filene

Center, but watch your watch: the return shuttle leaves either 20 minutes after the final curtain or at 11 p.m., whichever is earlier, in order to ensure that riders don't miss the Metro.

The recently upgraded **Merriweather Post Pavilion** in Columbia, Maryland, has the busiest pop/rock outdoor arena and mixes old-favorite rock and pop tours with younger-draw and cult acts (Norah Jones, Kid Rock, even Incubus and Béla Fleck); but it is some distance from Washington and can only be reached by car. (It also uses the ProTix network; see newspapers for current listings.) However, it has a new rival around the other side of the Beltway: the **Nissan Pavilion** outside Manassas, Virginia, which has 10,000 covered seats, and lawn seating for another 15,000 people. Operated by Cellar Door Productions, the largest booking agency on the east coast (and owners of the **Bayou** nightclub in Georgetown), the Nissan Pavilion is currently booking many of the same acts as MPP; both use the Ticketmaster network (☎ 202-397-SEAT; **www.nissanpavilion.com**). Like Merriweather Post, however, it can only be reached by car.

The more progressive rock acts, which draw strong college and postgrad audiences, tend to be booked into college auditoriums such as George Washington University's **Lisner Auditorium or Smith Center.** National acts with limited audiences—R&B, gospel, soul, folk—are often booked into **DAR Constitution Hall** alongside the Ellipse. Check the newspaper listings for entertainers and phone numbers while you're in town. **George Mason University Center for the Arts,** which adjoins the Patriot Center, is a lovely new midsized venue for classical and jazz music and drama. Tickets available at ☎ 800-955-5566 or **www.tickets.com.**

You will also find concerts at many Washington churches, including the **National Cathedral** and depending on the time of year, inside museums and galleries.

There are several fine outdoor music venues in the area, including **Freedom Plaza** at 14th and Pennsylvania Avenue near the White House, home to numerous free music and ethnic festivals during the summer, particularly the annual **DC World Jazz Fest** held during the Fourth of July celebrations. **Carter-Barron Amphitheatre** in Rock Creek Park hosts gospel, soul, jazz, and R&B concerts on summer weekends. Several other smaller city parks, museums, and federal building plazas stage concerts that are listed in the newspapers.

The Mall between the U.S. Capitol and the Washington Monument is the site of many festivals during the year, especially on such holidays as Memorial Day, the Fourth of July, and Labor Day, when the National Symphony Orchestra headlines family concerts. The Smithsonian's annual **Festival of American Folklife,** which features three or four different ethnic groups every year, also has music and dance parties every night; it runs from the weekend before the Fourth of July through the holiday itself.

The most important clubs booking national alternative-rock acts are the **9:30** club and the **Black Cat** (see profiles for both venues on pages 393 and 384, respectively).

For folk, country, and bluegrass music, the landmark venue is the **Birchmere** in Alexandria, Virginia (profiled), which boasts Mary Chapin Carpenter as a favorite daughter. One of the increasingly important venues both for local and national bookings, plus the rare eccentric, country, or cult oldie, is the **State Theatre** in Falls Church, a great vintage movie theater turned restaurant/bar/concert venue (220 North Washington Street; ☎ 703-237-0300). Piano bars are legion, but the best and most accomplished jazz is played at **Circle Bistro** (One Washington Circle; ☎ 202-293-5390).

The best bets for acoustic, folk-rock, modern pop, or original music on just any old night are **Iota** (profiled), which is especially popular with local progressive pop/rock writers; **Jammin' Java,** also booking second-level national and local acts nightly (profiled); **Austin Grill** (919 Ellsworth Avenue, Silver Spring, Maryland; ☎ 240-247-8969); **Whitlow's on Wilson** (2854 Wilson Boulevard, Arlington, Virginia; ☎ 703-276-9693); the **Clarendon Grill** (1101 North Highland Street, Arlington, Virginia; ☎ 703-524-7455); and the **Rhodeside Grill** (1836 Wilson Boulevard, Arlington, Virginia; ☎ 703-243-0145); all in the hot new Clarendon neighborhood. The last of the area's once-plentiful bluegrass spots is the **Tiffany Tavern** in Alexandria, Virginia (1116 King Street; ☎ 703-836-8844). Art-indie rockers are likely to show up at **Galaxy Hut,** owned by popular edge-cutter Alice Despard (2711 Wilson Boulevard, Arlington, Virginia; ☎ 703-525-8646). "Coffeehouses" are flourishing (the folk-music variety, not the cappuccino type, though they're booming, too), but many coffeehouse acoustic-music events occur only monthly in area churches or schools; check the papers.

Old-style blues has lost some of its best venues in recent years, but there are still the **New Vegas Lounge** (1415 P Street NW; ☎ 202-483-3971); the **Sunset Grill** (7250 Columbia Pike NW, Annandale, Virginia; ☎ 703-658-0928); **Fat Tuesday's** (10673 Braddock Road, Fairfax, Virginia; ☎ 703-385-8660); and **J.V.'s** (6666 Arlington Boulevard, Falls Church, Virginia; ☎ 703-241-9504).

Irish bars do a flourishing business in Washington with the help of a resident community of performers. Among the pubs with live music—and almost always at least one fireplace—are the **Dubliner** (profiled); **Ireland's Four Provinces** (by the Cleveland Park Metro at 3412 Connecticut Avenue NW; ☎ 202-244-0860); **Irish Times** (14 F Street NW; ☎ 202-543-5433); **Nanny O'Brien's** across the street (3319 Connecticut Avenue NW; ☎ 202-686-9189); **Fado Irish Pub** (808 Seventh Street NW; ☎ 202-789-0066); the **Old Brogue** (760-C Walker Road, Great Falls, Virginia; ☎ 703-759-3309); and **Ireland's Own** (111 North Pitt Street, Alexandria, Virginia; ☎ 703-549-4535).

Washington is also home to one other type of band: the **armed-services bands.** From about Memorial Day to Labor Day, ensembles from the four branches perform Monday, Tuesday, Wednesday, and Friday at 8 p.m. at the east or west side of the Capitol; Tuesday, Thursday, Friday, and Sunday at 8 p.m. at various locations; and Tuesday at 8 p.m. at the Navy Memorial at 7th and Pennsylvania Avenue NW. Call ☎ 703-696-3399 or visit **www.army.mil/armyband** for details. Programs include patriotic and martial numbers, country, jazz, pop, and some classical music. You're welcome to bring brown bags, but alcohol is not permitted.

SWING YOUR PARTNER

COUNTRY AND DISCO DANCING HAVE BEEN BIG for years in Washington, but ethnic and folk dancing—klezmer, polka, contra, Cajun—as well as swing dance and big-band boogie are also popular, especially in the suburbs. Their venues are also nonthreatening and hospitable spots for singles, even novices, since many have pre-dance "workshops" for learning the steps, and all seem well supplied with tolerant and deft "leaders."

For swing dancing, the best bets are the **Washington Swing Dance Committee,** which holds Saturday night dances in all but the coldest weather at the grand deco Spanish Ballroom in the old Glen Echo amusement park in Bethesda, Maryland (information at ☎ 301-340-9732); the **Clarendon Ballroom** (3185 Wilson Boulevard, Arlington, Virginia; ☎ 703-469-2244); **Chevy Chase Ballroom** (5207 Wisconsin Avenue NW; ☎ 202-363-8344); **Hollywood Ballroom** in Silver Spring, Maryland (2126 Industrial Parkway; ☎ 301-622-5494). The America branch in Union Station sometimes hosts bands, too; call ☎ 202-682-9555. Various restaurants around town are experimenting with martini-lounge swing nights during the week; check the local listings. For folk, Cajun, and contra dances contact the **Folklore Society of Greater Washington** at ☎ 202-546-2228 or **www.fsgw.org.**

You can polka (and pile on the bratwurst) to your heart's content any Friday, Saturday, or Sunday at **Blob's Park,** a Bavarian-fantasy beer hall and polka pavilion in Jessup, Maryland, that holds 1,000 revelers and a five-man oompah band; for information, call ☎ 410-799-0155 or visit **www.blobspark.com.**

For country, try **Nick's** in Alexandria, Virginia (642 South Pickett Street; ☎ 703-751-8900) or **Spurs** (2106 Crain Highway, Waldorf, Maryland; ☎ 301-843-9964).

For Latin dancing, try **Bravo Bravo** (1001 Connecticut Avenue NW; ☎ 202-223-5330); **Cuzco** (5831 Columbia Pike, Falls Church, Virginia; ☎ 703-845-1661); **Habana Village** in Adams-Morgan, which has salsa lessons on Wednesday through Friday (1834 Columbia Road NW; ☎ 202-462-6310); **Café Citron** (1343 Connecticut Avenue NW; ☎ 202-530-8844); or **Latin Alley,** also in Adams-Morgan, for lessons and dance Wednesday through Saturday (1721 Columbia Road NW; ☎ 202-328-6190). For Washington's longest-running 1980s dance party, check out the regular Thursday gig at **Heaven/Hell** in Adams-Morgan (2327 18th Street NW; ☎ 202-667-4355).

The 20-to-40 crowd that's into Top 40 disco tends to hang out at **MCCXXIII** and **Platinum** (both profiled); the **Edge** (56 L Street SE; ☎ 202-488-1200); and **Home Nightclub** (911 F Street NW; ☎ 202-638-4663). Internationals head to **Dream** and **Zanzibar** (profiled). And the new indie-rock, Brit, and "electroclash" club, booking live and spinning simultaneously, is **DC 9** (1940 Ninth Street NW; ☎ 202-483-5000), a double-wide complex of bars, faux bedrooms, and DJ booms.

ESPRESSO AND EIGHT-BALL

THE TWO BIGGEST TRENDS IN WASHINGTON are coffee bars and billiards parlors. At either you can spend not merely hours but whole evenings, and in a few cases, hang out virtually around the clock.

Many of the espresso bars are tiny walk-ins; some are mere service windows. And of course, there's a familiar brand name— or two—on nearly every corner. But a couple are among the most interesting after-hours hangouts in the city, even if the patrons are the only "entertainment." Check out **Tryst** in Adams-Morgan (2459 18th Street NW; ☎ 202-232-5500), **Busboys and Poets** in new-U (2201 14th Street NW; ☎ 202-387-7638), **Kirsten's Cafe** in Silver Spring, Maryland (9326 Georgia Avenue; ☎ 301-495-9686), or **Shimba Hills Coffee** in the Penn Quarter (601 F Street NW; ☎ 202-393-0065).

The biggest Metro-accessible billiards parlors around are **Dave & Buster's** and **Buffalo Billiards** (both profiled); **Orange Ball Billiards and Cafe**, with 28 tables and nearly twice that many TVs (430 Hungerford Drive, Rockville; ☎ 301-309-6440), which serves food late and even has a DJ. **Winston Billiards** (1776 East Jefferson Street, Rockville, Maryland; ☎ 301-231-4949), which also serves food until 1 a.m. Sunday through Thursday, and until 3 a.m. on Friday and Saturday; **CarPool** (4000 North Fairfax Drive, Arlington, Virginia; ☎ 703-532-7665), at the Ballston station; **Townhouse Tavern** (near the Dupont Circle stop at 1637 R Street NW; ☎ 202-234-5747); **Galaxy Billiards** (near the Silver Spring station at 8661 Colesville Road; ☎ 301-495-0081); **Continental Billiards** (1911 North Ft. Myer Drive; ☎ 703-465-7675) close to the Rosslyn Metro; **Cue Bar** (1115 U Street NW; ☎ 202-332-7665, near U Street/African-American Civil War Memorial), which mixes pool and Ping Pong; **Atomic Billiards** (3427 Connecticut Avenue NW, at the Cleveland Park Metro; ☎ 202-363-7665); and **Bedrock Billiards** (1841 Columbia Road NW; ☎ 202-667-7665), a short walk from the Woodley Park–National Zoo/Adams-Morgan Metro station.

TRUE BREWS

WASHINGTON HAS ALSO DISCOVERED ANOTHER FRESH BREW—
beer. In fact, the entire Washington-Baltimore region has gone silly
for suds. A boom in brewpubs and microbreweries has made it possible to support your local craft brewers in style and also to taste a
huge number of recipes, from pilsners and lagers to stouts, porters,
wheat ales, fruit beers, bocks, and seasonals. And most offer at least
informal tours of the works, if you're intrigued.

Among the downtown brewpubs are the **Capital City Brewing Co.**
branches near the Washington Convention Center (11th and H streets
NW; ☎ 202-628-2222), in the Village at Shirlington (2700 South
Quincy Street, Arlington, Virginia; ☎ 703-578-3888), and in the Postal
Museum building (2 Massachusetts Avenue NW; ☎ 202-842-2337),
which are as much beer temples as singles scenes. **R.F.D.** (810 Seventh
Street NW; ☎ 202-289-2030), offshoot of the Brickskeller in Dupont
Circle (profiled), doesn't brew, but carries 300 beers. **John Harvard's
Brewhouse** is a branch of a Cambridge, Massachusetts, favorite (13th
Street and Pennsylvania Avenue NW; ☎ 202-783-2739). In Bethesda,
the latest outpost of the Cap City group goes mug to mug with **Rock
Bottom Brewery** at Old Georgetown Road and Woodmont Avenue
(☎ 301-652-1311). Among other popular spots where vats are on view
are **Growlers Station** in Gaithersburg, Maryland (227 East Diamond
Avenue; ☎ 301-519-9400); **Dr. Dremo's Taphouse** (2001 Clarendon
Boulevard, Arlington, Virginia; ☎ 703-528-4660); or **Old Dominion
Brewing Co.** in Ashburn, Virginia (44633 Guilford Drive; ☎ 703-724-
9100), which is also the area's most successful microbrewing company.

For more Washington suds stops, check the "Freshest Beers"
restaurant list on page 279.

THE SEX THING

WASHINGTON IS NOT THE SINGLES CAPITAL OF THE WORLD, but
it does have many of the ingredients for a busy meat-market scene:
frequent turnovers in power, a dozen colleges and universities, a con-
tinual influx of immigrants and corporate hires, and what until
recently was considered a recession-proof economy.

The singles bars around Washington are relatively benign. Many
of them are dance clubs as well, so there's something to do besides
discuss astrological incompatibilities. The sports-bar habitués tend
to be a little more flagrant in their appraisals of fresh talent, as are
those in bars that cater to the 40-something crowd.

The District has been home to a strong gay community for
decades, and most nightclubs and bars attract at least a slightly
mixed, albeit unobtrusive crowd; several mainstream lounges host
particular gay nights once a week or so. However, there are many
well-established gay nightspots, especially around Dupont Circle and
Capitol Hill. Among the most popular accessible clubs are the preppy

JR's (1519 17th Street NW; ☎ 202-328-0090) near Dupont Circle, which has long been known as the "gay Cheers"; **Halo** (1435 P Street NW; ☎ 202-797-9730), a swanky retro-mood cocktail lounge; the white-collar **Green Lantern** downstairs and the lumberjack-shirt **Toolshed** upstairs at 1335 Green Covet NW (☎ 202-347-4533) near McPherson Square; the pointy-toe and big-buckle **Remington's** (near the Eastern Market station at 639 Pennsylvania Avenue SE; ☎ 202-543-3113); the new **BeBar** (1318 Ninth Street NW; ☎ 202-232-4533); the lesbian billiards hall **Phase One** (525 Eighth Street SE; ☎ 202-544-6831); and the soft-core leather-with-rhythm **DC Eagle** (both near the Mount Vernon Place–Convention Center Metro at Seventh and M streets NW; ☎ 202-347-6025).

Several of the hottest gay/lesbian/straight-but-not-narrow dance clubs are clustered around Dupont Circle, the traditional heart of D.C.'s gay culture. Among them are **Cobalt/30 Degrees** (17th and R streets NW; ☎ 202-232-6569); **Chaos** (1633 Q Street NW; ☎ 202-232-4141), with its Saturday and Sunday-brunch drag-diva revues; and **Apex** (1415 22nd Street NW; ☎ 202-296-0505), which has semisteamy videos to go with the marathon mixes and occasional "drag king" shows. The ladies' version of *Saturday Night Fever* is Liquid Ladies at Apex, and there's Sunday-morning "Mass" at the mixed gay-straight **Five** (1214-B 18th Street NW; ☎ 202-331-7123), nominated by the *Washington Post* as best dance club in the District.

Ziegfeld's is the most flamboyant of the outer hangouts, featuring uproarious and often astonishingly polished drag shows Thursday through Sunday (1345 Half Street SE; ☎ 202-554-5141). Although it's not in the safest neighborhood, Ziegfeld's will call you a cab when you're ready to leave. Ironically, the neighborhood is on the verge of a major upscaling thanks to Major League Baseball, which will likely mean the end of the club scene.

For those staying in Crystal City, **Freddy's Beach Bar** is the hangout of choice, with nightly karaoke and Sunday night drag shows (555 South 23rd Street; ☎ 703-685-0555).

If you can't dance but hate to eat alone, try **Annie's Paramount Steak House** (1609 17th Street NW; ☎ 202-232-0395) or **Perry's** (1811 Columbia Road NW; ☎ 202-234-6218), home of the most straight friendly drag brunch ever.

Finally, although the onetime red-light district around 14th Street was officially eradicated by redistricting and redevelopment, old habits die hard. North and east of the White House, and especially in the blocks around 13th and L, prostitutes not only parade past and proposition pedestrians but take advantage of traffic lights and stop signs to accost drivers. Periodically the police crack down on the scene, which is signalled by the overnight closing of streets in the neighborhood; but it makes only a temporary dent. The business also takes advantage of public transportation: many of the hotel bars

Nightclubs by Neighborhood

NIGHTCLUB | DESCRIPTION | COVER

THE NATIONAL MALL
Hard Rock Cafe | Themed bar and grill with memorabilia | None
Zanzibar | Upscale world-music disco | $10

CAPITOL HILL
Dubliner | Traditional Irish pub | None

DOWNTOWN
The Improv | Pro-circuit comedy dinner club | $10–$25
Ozio | Trendy martini and cigar lounge | None
Platinum | Lavish four-floor dance club | $15–$20

GEORGETOWN
Blues Alley | National-circuit jazz dinner club | $18–$75
Blue Gin | Trend-victim-décor disco/martini lounge | $10

DUPONT CIRCLE/ADAMS-MORGAN
Black Cat | Live rock/pop venue with some DJs | $5–$20
Brickskeller | Vast beer selection and pub fare | None
Buffalo Billiards | Singles bar with $6-per-hour pool | None

along the Metro are hangouts for soliciting singles—and humorously, they seem to prefer the Red Line, as if in tribute to red-light districts.

A few reminders: Although most prostitutes try to protect themselves from disease, both drug use and AIDS are pervasive. Second, many dates are actually bait, fronts for drug dealers who can more immediately endanger your health and safety. Besides, District police are fully familiar with the tricks of the trade, so we don't advise that you get involved. If you must look, don't touch—and keep your car doors locked.

For a somewhat less hands-on experience, there are a couple of relatively sedate strip joints downtown, including **Archibald's,** which is on the ground floor of the Comedy Café building off MacPherson Square (1520 K Street NW; ☎ 202-737-2662); **Camelot,** just off Connecticut Avenue at 1823 M Street NW (☎ 202-887-5966); **Nexus** (900 First Street SE; ☎ 202-488-3666); and the gay **Ziegfeld's/Secrets** (1345 Half Street SE; ☎ 202-554-5141). **Good Guys,** above Georgetown, is an old favorite (2311 Wisconsin Avenue NW; ☎ 202-333-0128). And for the safest fantasy trips around, drop by Georgetown's funny-sexy boutique the **Pleasure Place** (1063 Wisconsin Avenue NW;

NIGHTCLUB	DESCRIPTION	COVER
DUPONT CIRCLE/ADAMS-MORGAN (CONTINUED)		
Chi-Cha Lounge	Relaxed Latino-jazz/cigar bar	None
MCCXXIII	Pricey three-story hipster lounge	$15
UPPER NORTHWEST		
9:30	Big-name alternative and punk venue	$35–$40
Takoma Station	Upscale jazz bar	$5
NORTHEAST		
Love	Four-story cocktail lounge and dance hall	$10
SOUTHEAST		
Nation	Multiroom dance club	$10–$30
MARYLAND SUBURBS		
Dave & Buster's	Adult game-room bar	$5 weekends
VIRGINIA SUBURBS		
Birchmere	Live folk and rockabilly bar and brewery	$15–$45
Iota	Tavern with live pop and roots rock	varies
Jammin' Java	All-ages alt-rock coffeehouse to the max	$5–$20

☎ 202-333-8570), which offers videos, X-rated birthday cards, T-shirts, fishnet stockings, and the like.

MORE ON THE SAFETY THING

THERE IS ONLY ONE SAFETY TIP TO REMEMBER: there is no guaranteed neighborhood in the area. In fact, we have left some otherwise deserving and successful clubs off the list because they're in questionable territory, even for savvy residents. The suburbs are generally okay, but even the ostensibly upscale areas of the District, such as Georgetown and Dupont Circle, are not immune to crime. It's best to leave nightclubs, especially after midnight, in company. Attach yourself to a group or ask the club management for an escort. It's also wiser to call a cab than to walk more than a block or so. (Mace, incidentally, is now legal in Maryland, Virginia, and the District of Columbia.)

And a final tip: if you believe in helping out the homeless (the staggering number of which you may find one of the less inspiring monuments to modern life in Washington), try stashing dollar bills or change in an outside pocket so that you can reach them without opening your wallet or purse.

Nightclubs by Type

NIGHTCLUB | DESCRIPTION | NEIGHBORHOOD | TYPICAL COVER

BAR AND GRILLS/BUFFETS

Dave & Buster's | Adult game-room bar | Maryland Suburbs | $5 weekends
Hard Rock Cafe | Bar and grill with memorabilia | National Mall | None

CIGAR BARS

Chi-Cha Lounge | Relaxed Latino-jazz/cigar bar | Dupont Circle/Adams-Morgan | None
Ozio | Trendy martini and cigar lounge | Downtown | None

COCKTAIL LOUNGES

Blue Gin | Trend-victim-décor disco and martini lounge | Georgetown | $10
MCCXXIII | Pricey, three-story hipster lounge | Dupont Circle/Adams-Morgan | $15

COMEDY CLUBS

The Improv | Pro-circuit comedy dinner club | Downtown | $10–$25

DANCE CLUBS

Love | Four-story lounge and dance hall | Northeast | $10
Nation | Multiroom dance club | Southeast | $10–$30
Platinum | Lavish four-floor dance club | Downtown | $15–$20

PROFILES *of* CLUBS *and* NIGHTSPOTS

Birchmere

LIVE FOLK, NEW ACOUSTIC, NEWGRASS, HIP ROCKABILLY/OUTLAW, LIGHT JAZZ AND COUNTRY, AND OCCASIONAL OFF-PEAK POP MUSIC

3701 Mt. Vernon Avenue, Alexandria; ☎ 703-549-7500; www.birchmere.com Virginia Suburbs

Who goes there Gracefully aging boomers and a few recalcitrant rednecks; unreconciled folkies; local musicians. **Cover** Varies with entertainment; roughly $15–$45. **Minimum** None. **Mixed drinks** $3–$8. **Wine** $5.50–$7.50. **Beer** $4.75–$5.65. **Dress** A few suits, a lot of flannels, universal jeans, neo-farm country wear and boots of all sorts—cowboy, hiking, motorcycle. **Food available** After years of getting by on potato chips, Birchmere patrons can now get serious

NIGHTCLUB | DESCRIPTION | NEIGHBORHOOD | TYPICAL COVER

DANCE CLUBS (CONTINUED)
Zanzibar | Upscale world-music disco | National Mall | $10

LIVE JAZZ/BLUES
Blues Alley | National-circuit jazz dinner club | Georgetown | $18–$75
Takoma Station | Upscale jazz bar | Upper Northwest | $5

LIVE POP/ROCK
Birchmere | Live folk and rockabilly bar and brewery | Virginia Suburbs | $15–$45
Black Cat | Live rock/pop venue with some DJs | Dupont Circle/Adams-Morgan
$5–$20
Iota | Tavern with live pop/roots rock | Virginia Suburbs | varies
Jammin' Java | All-ages alt-rock coffeehouse to the max | Virginia Suburbs
$5–$20
9:30 | Big-name alternative/punk venue | Upper Northwest | $5–$40

PUBS/BILLIARDS BARS
Brickskeller | Vast beer selection and pub fare | Dupont Circle/Adams-Morgan
None
Dubliner | Traditional Irish pub | Capitol Hill | None
Buffalo Billiards | Part biz-whiz pool party, part singles bar (over 21 only)
Dupont Circle/Adams-Morgan | None

tavern fare, including barbecue, burgers, and hot nibbles, from the folks at Union Street Pub and King Street Blues. **Hours** Every day, 6–11:30 p.m. Shows start at 7:30 p.m. **Metro** None nearby.

WHAT GOES ON This is one of the major clubs in town, the biggest for new acoustic and country acts especially, such as Rosanne Cash and hometown heroine Mary Chapin Carpenter, plus cult regulars Jerry Jeff Walker and Delbert McClinton; old folk Tom Paxton and John Stewart; new femme fronters Kristin Hersh, Christine Lavin, and Maria Muldaur.

SETTING AND ATMOSPHERE The long-awaited new home for this venerable club has jumped from old-fashioned to newfangled: not only a much more spacious 500-seat main stage but a cigar-martini bar (for the expected influx of trendy patrons?), a 150-seat side stage/cafe, a microbrewery on-site, and "real" pub food.

IF YOU GO Go early: parking is tight (but free); the line is long; and seating is first-come, closest-in. If you're trying to eat light, eat elsewhere. Remember to take off your big hat so the folks behind you can see. And take thankful note of the sign that asks for quiet during performances: this really is a listening club. Visit **www.birchmere.com** for a schedule.

TOURING TIP At press time, the Birchmere was developing a sister venue in Silver Spring near the AFI and Round House Theaters.

Black Cat

MAJOR LIVE ROCK-POP VENUE WITH DJS FOR BACKUP

1811 14th Street NW; ☎ 202-667-7960; www.blackcatdc.com
Dupont Circle/Adams-Morgan

Who goes there 20–40; locals and tourist music fans. **Cover** Varies with entertainment, $5–$20. **Minimum** None. **Mixed drinks** $5–$8. **Wine** $5–$7. **Beer** $3.50–$5. **Dress** Ranges from grungy to nightclub-hip, depending on the act. **Food available** Vegan and vegetarian fair from the now-defunct Food for Thought menu. **Hours** Sunday–Thursday, 8 p.m.–2 a.m.; Friday and Saturday, 7 p.m.– 3 a.m. **Metro** U Street/African-American Civil War Memorial/Cardozo.

WHAT GOES ON A mix of hot regional and early-national alternative rock, funky-punk, and high-ticket camp (El Vez, the "Mexican Elvis," etc.).

SETTING AND ATMOSPHERE The larger room holds 600, the rear room (aka the "Backstage") only about 100, so that's sometimes turned over to dance club on the weekends, with a mix of synth pop, film, Brit-indie, and even some mod and cult garage.

IF YOU GO A who's-who of indie rock has passed through the Black Cat— and more recently, some rediscoveries, such as the Little Steven- inspired revival tour of the Zombies, Fleshtones, et al—so buy advance tickets for major concerts, and expect some sweating crowds at the louder acts.

Blue Gin

EURO-CHIC, RETRO-LOUNGE-LIZARD, SLEEK, DESIGNER MARTINI FACTORY

1206 Wisconsin Avenue NW; ☎ 202-965-5555   Georgetown

Who goes there "New Georgetowners"; interns and suits; *Apprentice* wannabes; fashionistas; and circuit drinkers. **Cover** $10 after 10 p.m. on Friday and Saturday. **Minimum** No drink minimum, $300 bottle service. **Mixed drinks** $5–$12. **Wine** $6–$12. **Beer** $6–$9. **Dress** Officially only no-sneakers/no-tanks rule, but in practice, dress for success (or for dancers, bling to swing). **Food available** Slightly pricey nibblies tricked out as tapas. **Hours** Tuesday–Thursday, 6 p.m.–2 a.m.; Friday and Saturday, 6 p.m.–3 a.m. **Metro** Foggy Bottom–GWU.

WHAT GOES ON Although nominally a dance club downstairs ('tronic, hip- hop, house and retro club), this is more bar than nightclub, and when we say "designer martinis," we mean it. Much of the cocktail menu was created for Blue Gin by London celeb bartender Antonia Andrasi, and the $10 specialty "martinis" run to such ingredients as elderflower syrup and rose water, blood oranges and watermelon, lychee nuts and passion fruit (but all liquor brands are premium). The wine list doesn't yet measure up, but a serious upscaling is promised.

SETTING AND ATMOSPHERE Downstairs is a sort of Zen disco den, with Asian-looking stools and candlelight; upstairs is a serious-business bar with leather sofas and banquettes, projection DVDs (on the building wall next door) and red walls—as Diana Vreeland might say, the new black.

IF YOU GO It's best to arrive unfashionably early, not only to escape the cover charge but because the upstairs fills up (and the bouncer bars the door) well before the witching hour. Or use it as midweek warmup. Fans of even more elaborate fantasy décor should walk down to Mie N Yu at 3125 M Street, where every room has a different dreamscape.

Blues Alley

NATIONAL-CIRCUIT JAZZ DINNER CLUB

1073 Wisconsin Avenue NW (in the alley); ☎ 202-337-4141; www.bluesalley.com Georgetown

Who goes there 20–60; locals and tourists; other jazz pros; neo-jazz fans. **Cover** Varies with entertainment; $18–$75. **Minimum** Two drinks or $10 food. **Mixed drinks** $6–$9.50. **Wine** $4.50–$7. **Beer** $5–$7. **Dress** Jacket over jeans, business attire, musician chic. **Food available** Full menu of semi-Creole food: gumbo, chicken, steak. **Hours** Every day, 6 p.m.–12:30 a.m. **Metro** Foggy Bottom–GWU.

WHAT GOES ON When the big-name jazz performers come to town, this is where they play. And although many customers grumble about ticket prices, they pay anyway—partly because the acts require high guarantees, partly because Georgetown rents are high, and partly because so many other jazz clubs have folded.

SETTING AND ATMOSPHERE A fairly simple lounge, with exposed brick walls, a platform at one end and the bar at the other, and smallish dinner tables scattered between.

IF YOU GO Get there early; the line often goes around the block, and seating is first-come and squeeze-'em-together, even with reservations. The old and cramped restrooms that are barely accessible upstairs are one drawback, and the ventilation can be another, but the acoustics are very good.

Brickskeller

ENCYCLOPEDIC BEER RATHSKELLER

1523 22nd Street NW; ☎ 202-293-1885; www.thebrickskeller.com; www.lovethebeer.com Dupont Circle/Adams-Morgan

Who goes there 21–45; students; former students; home brewers; beer fanatics. **Cover** None. **Minimum** None. **Mixed drinks** $4.75–$8. **Wine** $4.50–$6.50. **Beer** $5–$8.50. **Dress** Jackets, jeans, khakis. **Specials** Special drafts upstairs Friday and Saturday after 7 p.m. **Food available** The house specialty is buffalo; good pub food in general, and the kitchen stays open almost as long as the bar. **Hours** Monday–Thursday, 11:30 a.m.–2 a.m.; Friday, 11:30 a.m.–3 a.m.; Saturday, 6 p.m.–3 a.m.; Sunday, 6 p.m.–2 a.m. **Metro** Dupont Circle.

WHAT GOES ON Almost half a century ago, Maurice Coja put 50 kinds of beer, mostly bottled, in the basement of the Marifex Hotel and opened for business. Twenty years later, he had to give up kegs because room was so tight, and now, with 1,000 beers from all over the world offered at the same time, including over 100 microbrews, brands and cans are stuffed into every corner. The Brickskeller used to offer live music of the folk-rock variety but eventually realized the beer was sufficient entertainment. There are dart boards and a jukebox instead.

SETTING AND ATMOSPHERE A rabbit warren of rooms, with the main bar in the front and scuffed and hard-working tables snaking around between the dart boards. Feel free to strike up a conversation; the Brickskeller is unpretentious, college-bar friendly, and lively.

IF YOU GO Don't be shy; consult the staff. Beer is serious business here and you can learn a lot if you go slowly. Start light and work your way up to Samiclaus, a potent by-the-fireside beer of 14 % alcohol. (The good news is the kitchen is open late, and the Metro is nearby.) Skip the mixed beer cocktails, or beer-tails; they're more novelty act than revelation.

Buffalo Billiards

PART BIZ-WHIZ POOL PARTY, PART SINGLES BAR (OVER 21 ONLY)

1330 19th Street NW; ☎ 202-331-7665; www.buffalobilliards.com
Dupont Circle/Adams-Morgan

Who goes there Junior associates; postgrads; bar pros. **Cover** None. **Minimum** None for bars or people-watching; to play, $6 per player per hour. **Mixed drinks** $3.25–$6. **Wine** $3.50–$4. **Beer** $3.25–$6.50. **Dress** Mix of office wear and jock chic; as many lace-ups as high-rises. **Specials** Happy hour 4–8 p.m. weekdays; 1–7 p.m. Saturday; 4–7 p.m. Sunday, with beer specials and wine and rail drinks for $2.50. **Food available** Mostly small plates—nachos, buffalo wings (of course), sandwiches—but also some fairly serious entrees such as tuna steak and trout. **Hours** Monday–Thursday, 4 p.m.–2 a.m.; Friday, 4 p.m.–3 a.m.; Saturday, 1 p.m.–3 a.m.; Sunday, 4 p.m.–1 a.m. **Metro** Dupont Circle.

WHAT GOES ON Parties circulate, singles practice their shots, and couriers wait for assignments.

SETTING AND ATMOSPHERE This is just one of a half-dozen upscale, all-the-modern-indulgences pool halls all over the area (see the section "Espresso and Eight-ball" on page 367), but it's one of the busiest and largest, the flagship of its owners' half-dozen parlors, with two entire rooms (one smoking, one nonsmoking) and vibrators to alert waiting customers to their tables. It's woodyish—*Buffalo Bill*-iards, get it?—but not too gadget-happy. And it's one level down from the street, which gives it a sort of old-fashioned speakeasy quality.

IF YOU GO Don't worry about your pool skills particularly, unless you're hoping to shark someone; a lot of the patrons are pleasure-seekers, not pros, and they won't be looking over your shoulder. The main thing is to watch where you're going: don't knock someone else's cue or back into the player at the next table, and if that player lines up a shot first, it's his/her right of way, so to speak.

Chi-Cha Lounge

PART NEIGHBORHOOD CAFE, PART LATINO-CHIC JAZZ AND CIGAR LOUNGE WITH A FEW "EXOTIC" TOUCHES

1624 U Street NW; ☎ 202-234-8400   Dupont Circle/Adams-Morgan

Who goes there 20–30-something regulars; Latino internationals. **Cover** None. **Minimum** One drink or menu item. **Mixed drinks** $4–$9. **Wine** $4–$6.50. **Beer** $3–$5. **Dress** Business, light cocktail, and nice casual; see below. **Specials** Ask a server. **Food available** "Modern Andean" fare, mostly tapas-sized snacks. **Hours** Sunday–Thursday, 5:30 p.m.–2 a.m.; Friday and Saturday, 5:30 p.m.–3 a.m. **Metro** U Street/African-American Civil War Memorial/Cardozo.

WHAT GOES ON   This offbeat but endearing hangout, the "hacienda" of local entrepreneur Mauricio Fraga-Rosenfeld (Ozio, Gazuza, etc.), offers a few exotic indulgences to homesick internationals, such as the *arguileh* (hookahlike water pipes for smoking fruit-cured tobacco) for Middle Easterners, popped giant corn kernels and glasses of the eponymous chi-cha, a spicy fruit-and-rice alcohol traditional in Latin America.

SETTING AND ATMOSPHERE   Sort of rec-room casbah. "Couch potato" here means a little *tamal* snack on the sofa. The music is frequently live and ranges from flamenco guitar to Latin jazz to Euro-jazz standards; visiting pros such as the Gipsy Kings and Buena Vista Social Club have been known to drop in after their shows.

IF YOU GO   The dress code is pretty much the formal standard nowadays: no hats for men, no athletic wear, no printed T's, no tanks, "no attitudes"— but no neckties, either, as per the owner's own preferences.

Dave & Buster's

ADULT ENTERTAINMENT À LA SPIELBERG–PART HIGH-TECH, PART RETRO-REGRESSIVE

White Flint Mall, Bethesda; ☎ 301-230-5151; www.daveandbusters.com Maryland Suburbs

Who goes there Late-20s couples bored with disco; traveling salesmen nostalgic for Vegas; some computer geeks and groups of mixed-sex hangers-on looking for post-movie action. **Cover** $5 weekends after 10 p.m. **Minimum** None. **Mixed drinks** $5–$7. **Wine** $3.50–$5.75. **Beer** $2.75–$5.25. **Dress** Upper shopping mall–quality: casual, but no tanks, cutoffs, etc. **Specials** Half-price rail drinks and beer specials at happy hour. **Food available** A full range of familiar upscale suburban fare: from artichoke dip and stuffed jalapeños to pastas, grilled salmon, Santa Fe chicken pizza, and ribs and rib-eyes. **Hours** Sunday–Wednesday, 11:30 a.m.–midnight; Thursday–Saturday, 11:30 a.m.–1 a.m.; Sunday, 11:30 a.m.–midnight. **Metro** White Flint.

WHAT GOES ON   This is a carnival of the business animals: a half-dozen pocket billiard tables, pinball and video games, a couple of simulated "19th hole" golf games, shuffleboard, and four full-size virtual-reality pods, interlinked for games and sports simulation. There are also casino games, with fully trained blackjack dealers and tables—but the poker chips are "on loan" only. No actual gambling is allowed. Everything is played by token in fact, except the virtual-reality pods. On Fridays and Saturdays, it's murder mystery dinner theater.

SETTING AND ATMOSPHERE This is unabashedly a bar as well as a playroom, with two sideline bars: the double-sided, 40-foot bar that partners the "midway" (a stretch of interactive video and carny attractions); and the elevated, square "Viewpoint" bar (not to mention the private "showroom" with its own stage, bar, dining tables, and even audiovisual equipment, which is bound to become the status CEO party room of D.C.).

IF YOU GO This is Dave & Buster's ninth such complex around the country, and they've got it down smooth. Besides offering nearly every sort of game, it has polished service, fairly strict rules about drinking and dressing, and even stricter rules about under-21-year-olds being with an adult. Even better in this cigar-crazed era, smoking is extremely limited (even cigarettes only where allowed).

Dubliner

CLASSIC IRISH PUB

520 North Capitol Street NW; ☎ 202-737-3773; www.dublinerdc.com
Capitol Hill

Who goes there Hill workers, both upwardly mobile (staffers) and established (senators and lobbyists). **Cover** None. **Minimum** None. **Mixed drinks** $3.25–$6; Dubliner coffee is an Irish coffee with Bailey's added. **Wine** $4–$5.50. **Beer** $3–$4. **Dress** No cutoffs or tank tops. **Specials** Reduced light-fare prices, 11 p.m.–1 a.m.; daily specials Monday–Friday for lunch and dinner. **Food available** Irish-pub classics, from stew to hot sandwiches. **Hours** Monday–Thursday, 7 a.m.–1:30 a.m.; Friday and Saturday, 7 a.m.–2:30 a.m.; Sunday, 7:30 a.m.–1:30 a.m. **Metro** Union Station.

WHAT GOES ON This is not the oldest Irish bar in town, but it has become the clan leader—centrally located, pol-connected, and providing the training ground for founders of a half-dozen other bars, including the semi-sibling-rival Irish Times next door. Fittingly, the Dubliner also has one of the most colorful histories, filled with romantic intrigue, boom-and-bust bank troubles, and riotous St. Patrick's week parties.

SETTING AND ATMOSPHERE Now part of the pricey and hunt-country gracious Phoenix Hotel complex, the Dubliner is filled with antiques, such as the 1810 hand-carved walnut bar in the back room. The front bar is louder and livelier, often populated by the surviving members of the Dubliner's Irish football and soccer teams; the snug is a discreet heads-together, take-no-names hideaway in the finest tradition; and the parlor is where the tweeds gather.

IF YOU GO Be sure to have at least one Guinness on draft: The Dubliner pours an estimated quarter-million pints a year. Drop by the Irish Times next door for a breather (the high ceilings carry smoke away) and the *Finnegans Wake* crazy quilt of literary and political conversation, and interns' rave downstairs. Then call a cab. Please.

Hard Rock Cafe

SOUVENIR SHOP DISGUISED AS BARBECUE BAR

999 E Street NW; ☎ 202-737-7625   The National Mall

Who goes there 12–55; tourists and locals; Hard Rock memorabilia collectors; air-guitar experts. **Cover** None. **Minimum** None. **Mixed drinks** $7–$18. **Wine** $6–$15. **Beer** $3–$7. **Dress** To be seen: pony-print leather, denim, sports or rock-and-roll tour jackets, business attire, creative black tie, Bermuda shorts (on tourists). **Food available** Surprisingly good. **Hours** Sunday–Thursday, 11 a.m.–11 p.m.; Friday and Saturday, 11 a.m.–12 a.m. **Metro** Metro Center.

WHAT GOES ON Despite the name, this is not actually a club—nor does it rock. One of 100 Hard Rocks around the world, each of which takes its nickname from the site, this is the "Embassy" and sometimes the "Smithsonian of Rock 'n' Roll," taking its turn rotating the nearly 7,000 pieces of music history in the HRC collection. The souvenir shop, with its signature T-shirts, is as busy as the bar, which is often stand-in-line packed—a doorman passes judgment on the hopeful.

SETTING AND ATMOSPHERE This is ersatz nostalgia for the second Rolling Stone generation, with a bar designed like a piano, half of a pink Cadillac (sort of a franchise signature) hanging from the ceiling, and a lot of fed suits from nearby buildings trying to look cool. Hard Rock also makes a point of being Lollapalooza-era PC, supporting the Walden Project and nuclear freezes and hosting radio-chic benefits and post-concert VIP receptions, usually without the star.

IF YOU GO Pick up the guidebook, formally known as the "Hard Rock Cafe Self-Motivating Non-Nuclear-Powered Memorabilia Tour of the World's Foremost Rock 'n' Roll Museum" and start circling the balcony. Look for such treasures as Bo Diddley's first jerry-rigged electric guitar, Michael Jackson's glittering kneepad, and a stained-glass triptych featuring Elvis, Jerry Lee Lewis, and Little Richard.

The Improv

NATIONAL-CIRCUIT COMEDY CLUB

1140 Connecticut Avenue NW; ☎ 202-296-7008; www.dcimprov.com
Downtown

Who goes there Visiting business types; 30ish suburbanites; 25–45 midlevel managers. **Cover** $10–$25, according to performer. **Minimum** Two items. **Mixed drinks** $4–$8. **Wine** $5–$7. **Beer** $3–$4. **Dress** T-shirts with jackets, suits, casual yup attire. **Specials** Tuesday, free admission to anyone wearing an Improv T-shirt ($12 in the lobby). **Food available** Full menu described as available before the 8:30 p.m. show, but light fare available whenever; standard one-size-fits-all menu with chicken cordon bleu, prime rib, catch of the day, Caesar salad, etc. **Hours** Tuesday–Thursday, 7–11 p.m.; Friday and Saturday, 6:30 p.m.–12:30 a.m. Shows Tuesday through Thursday at 8:30 p.m. and Sunday at 8 p.m. **Metro** Farragut North or Dupont Circle.

WHAT GOES ON Standard Improv franchise fare: a short opening act, often local; a semi-established feature act; and a headliner from the national club/cable showcase circuit. However, like many comedy clubs, the Improv is increasingly dependent on extended bookings of more theatrical comics such as Rob "The Caveman" Becker or Jack Gallagher, who perform alone for 90 minutes or so.

SETTING AND ATMOSPHERE Again, this goes with the franchise—a "brick wall" stage sentimentally recalling the original no-frills Improvisation, and the black-and-white checkerboard floor and trim that is practically a logo design. TV screens hang overhead for those with obscured views, but they're not big enough to be terribly useful. The wait staff wear tux-material Bermuda shorts.

IF YOU GO Don't bother to come early, at least on weeknights, when being seated in order of arrival isn't apt to be a problem. Since latecomers are usually seated amongst the diners, you have no real reason to seek early reservations. Besides, nibbling through the appetizers list is a more satisfying experience than sitting down to dinner and then sitting through the show. The Improv, though below sidewalk level, has wheelchair access via the elevator in the building lobby.

iota

NEIGHBORHOOD JOINT WITH SMART CONVERSATION AND LIVE NEW-POP ROOTS ROCK

2832 Wilson Boulevard, Arlington; ☎ 703-522-8340; www.iotaclubandcafe.com   Virginia Suburbs

Who goes there Messengers; students; 30-something T-shirts; microbrew-savvy beer buddies; other musicians. **Cover** Varies, some shows free. **Minimum** None. **Mixed drinks** $3–$10. **Wine** $4.50–$8.50. **Beer** $3–$7. **Dress** Jeans, with or without bolo; hog leathers; baggy athletic wear; and frayed button-down collars. **Specials** Happy hour 5–8 p.m., $1 off rail and draft prices. **Food available** Freestyle, eclectic pub food but far better than most: Asian spicy beef, tuna steak, black pepper–doused French fries. **Hours** Every day, 5 p.m.–2 a.m. **Metro** Clarendon or Courthouse.

WHAT GOES ON On a regular basis, this has the best lineup of acoustic rock, neo-roots, soft psychedelic, and eclectic melodic rock in town, and it's the quality of the people who run the shows, both before and behind the scenes, that makes it so. Steve Hagedorn holds the open mike on Wednesdays. When he's in town, this is where you're likely to find hometown favorite Kevin Johnson hosting songwriters' nights.

SETTING AND ATMOSPHERE In a time when a lot of Washington bars have an intentionally mismatched rec-room random look, Iota's décor is unusual but intelligent—murals, geometric eye-catchers chiseled into the exposed brick walls, and beams that show the age of the neighborhood (especially nice, since there's so little of it left otherwise). The room used to be only half this size, but giving the performers some extra elbowroom has not made either the musicians or their audiences self-conscious.

IF YOU GO This is a good place to strike up a conversation at the bar before the music gets loud: you run into crossword-puzzle freaks, novelists, doctoral candidates, musicians, roadies, and ponytails of the friendly sort. It's the sort of bar that makes hanging out a pleasure.

Jammin' Java

ALL-AGES ALT-ROCK COFFEEHOUSE TO THE MAX, WITH ROCK, A LITTLE PUNK, COUNTRY, FOLK, AND BLUES, AND EVEN THE ODD JUG BAND

227 Maple Avenue, East Vienna; ☎ 703-255-1566; www.jamminjava.com
Virginia Suburbs

Who goes there Unreconstructed hard-folk boomers; family diners; midlife musical hopefuls; eclectic-minded 20-somethings. **Cover** $5–$20, according to performer. **Wine** $7. **Beer** $4–$5. **Dress** Easy listening, mostly jean therapy but also softball mom and Land's End men's jeans. **Food available** Wraps and sandwiches, "gourmet chilis" and salads, plus espresso drinks. **Hours** Daily, 7 a.m.–midnight.

WHAT GOES ON Two or three sets of music per night, mostly local but with some good regional and college-circuit acts, cult favorites such as Marshall Crenshaw and the Kennedys, and open-mike Mondays.

SETTING AND ATMOSPHERE This is one of the area's most promising venues, a comfortably snug L-shaped room with bar and food counter in front with a handful of tables and the music room (also a recording studio) around the side. This is an all-ages, no-smoking, family-friendly version of a music club, and in fact it's owned by three brothers, the Brindleys, who are recording their own alt-country album there. Unfortunately, it's nowhere near a Metro station.

IF YOU GO There is somewhat limited seating in the music room, and the crowd is often SRO, but nobody's a stranger here; it's a nice mix. Since you can eat all day, it may be better to come early, eat (maybe grab a table), and save the espresso for the show.

Love

FOUR-STORY, MANHATTAN-STYLE SUPER-LOUNGE

1350 Okie Street NE; ☎ 202-347-5255; www.lovetheclub.com
Northeast

Who goes there *Friends, Sex and the City* sophisticates, Damon Wayans, and even Seinfeld are looking for love in all the lounge places. **Cover** $10; sometimes free with promotion. **Mixed drinks** $5–$8. **Wine** $5–$7. **Beer** $3–$5. **Dress** Trendy; they hosted an Armani fashion show. **Specials** Free cover early (before 11 p.m., give or take an hour). **Food available** Entrees like crab cakes and jerk chicken from Republic Gardens chef Lois Spencer. **Hours** Thursday, Friday, and Saturday, 9 p.m.–4 a.m. **Metro** Rhode Island Avenue.

WHAT GOES ON Thursdays is usually international night, and the crowd is very mixed and elegant. Weekends are a mix of soul/R&B, hip-hop, and even a little trance, as the yuppie (Fridays) and buppie (Saturdays) level rises and falls. Occasionally, it gets live music, and cutting edge at that: Ludacris, Busta Rhymes, and the Roots have all jammed here.

SETTING AND ATMOSPHERE This is somewhere between a post-millennial Studio 54 and a luxury liner on land: mahogany paneling, leather lounge chairs, plush carpeting, and ambient lighting. Besides the four dance halls, there's a billiard room, nearly wall-to-wall bars and a deck for cooling down. The fourth floor is even available for private parties for a mere $5,000.

IF YOU GO Seriously dress to impress here; even Sean "Diddy" Combs would have to shed the jeans at this door. No athletic wear. For $360, you and seven of your closest friends can jump the line; $200 goes toward your bar bill. This is a "revitalizing" neighborhood, but there is valet parking or shuttle service from nearby secured lots. Best bet: get the cell phone number from your cabbie. Better bet: hire a limo—you and those seven friends.

TOURING TIP The Brickskeller family also includes RFD—Regional Food and Drink—in the Penn Quarter neighborhood (810 Seventh Street NW; ☎ 202-289-2030).

MCCXXIII

GEN-X/GEN-TECHS VERSION OF CONSPICUOUS CHAMPAGNE CHIC

1223 Connecticut Avenue NW; ☎ 202-822-1800
Dupont Circle/Adams-Morgan

Who goes there Embassy/buppie/Euro slicks; white-collar/tie associates; ambitious committee staff, trust-fund babies; and the occasional Hollywood celeb. **Cover** None early, about $15 after 10 p.m. on event nights. **Minimum** 1 drink. **Mixed drinks** $6–$10. **Wine** $6–$8. **Beer** $4–$6. **Dress** One of the strictest dress codes around, with old-fashioned doormen to enforce it, so stalk the stalk as you talk the talk. **Food available** Happy hour 5–9 p.m. Tuesdays, Thursdays, and Fridays. **Hours** Tuesday–Thursday, 4 p.m.–2 a.m.; Friday, 4 p.m.–2 a.m.; Saturday, 6 p.m.–3 a.m.; Sunday, 8 p.m.–2 a.m. **Metro** Farragut North or Dupont Circle.

WHAT GOES ON Once the cocktail hour conventions are observed, the club goes showily swing-your-VIP, with a mix of disco, house, reggae, and even Top 40 music. Sunday night is gay-centric Lizard Lounge.

SETTING AND ATMOSPHERE Now a three-story complex, MCCXXXIII (cute-speak for 1223, the street address) is industrial chic for the titanium-card crowd: caviar-bar restaurant downstairs, Champagne lounge upstairs, catwalk to glide over, and now boudoir-style dance club-within-a-club on the third floor. You can even reserve your favorite couch. *Sleek* and *breezy* define the atmosphere, and that goes for the lit-within fabric dividers. The VIP level is definitely titanium-card material; a $500 minimum for 10 people.

IF YOU GO Definitely hit the ATM; you'll need lavish tip cash as well as your credit cards—unless you're in line early for the 6-8 p.m. "Flirt" night on Wednesdays, when drinks are on the house. Remember that this is only one of a half-dozen hot spots at this intersection, including the sub-terranean Fly and Andalu; see the description of the 18th Street nightlife intersection in the introduction to this chapter.

9:30

NATIONAL-NAME LIVE ALTERNATIVE, PROGRESSIVE, SEMI-PUNK RETRO AND ROCK MUSIC CLUB

815 V Street NW; ☎ 202-393-0930; www.930.com   Downtown

Who goes there 18–35; new music hopefuls; postgrads; young media and political types; couriers; cowpunks. **Cover** Varies with entertainment, from $5 to as much as $40. **Minimum** None. **Mixed drinks** $4–$5.25. **Wine** $4.50–$6.50. **Beer** $3.25–$4.25. **Dress** Grunge, imitation grunge, rhinestone cowboy, leftover business wear, knife-customized athletic wear, black jersey, black spandex, black denim, and black baggies. **Food available** Tex-Mex and barbecue fare. **Hours** Sunday–Thursday, 7:30 p.m.–until close; Friday and Saturday, 9 p.m.–until close. **Metro** U Street/African-American Civil War Memorial/Cardozo.

WHAT GOES ON "9:30" is the name, it used to be the address (before the former club moved into an old gospel-music hall and radio-broadcast site), and it used to be the showtime, but thanks to workday hang-overs, midweek music now starts at 8:30. This is arguably Washington's most important club, the loss-leader indulgence of major concert pro-moter Seth Hurwitz, who, with daring and eclectic booking of breaking acts, fosters loyalty from new bands as their reputations rise. Promis-ing local bands fight to get work as first acts here; a headliner contract is a real prize. In any given month, you might see Liz Phair, Five for Fighting, Joan Jett, Sergio Mendes, the BoDeans, or funk patriarch George Clinton.

SETTING AND ATMOSPHERE A slightly trendy mix of leftover cornices, pilasters, virtue-of-necessity exposed steel trusses, and dropped lighting—but still theatrically dark, with great sight lines. The balconies are fine, and there are several bars, including one "quiet room" and a nostalgic, grungier one downstairs.

IF YOU GO Find out who's playing: The crowd that pays up for Ice T isn't the same as the one for Marshall Crenshaw or Happy Mondays—or They Might Be Giants, or even Anthrax. Never accuse Hurwitz of lacking a sense of humor.

Ozio

TREND-HAPPY, NEOCON MARTINI AND CIGAR LOUNGE

**1813 M Street NW; ☎ 202-822-6000; www.oziodc.com
Downtown**

Who goes there Ash-kissing Standard & Poor's and Rat Pack–chic wannabes, but with only standard pickup lines and a limited grasp of the inside-the-Beltway gossip they dish; nouveau riche-makers. **Cover** None. **Minimum** None. **Mixed drinks** $6–$10. **Wine** $5–$9. **Beer** $5. **Dress** European-cut jackets and Nicole

Miller ties (especially the ones with martini glasses); imitation menswear or Eurotrash skinny-fits for women. **Food available** "American tapas" that are more like Middle Eastern crostini, but interesting; a short menu of entrees, primarily steaks and seafood. **Hours** Monday–Thursday, 5 p.m.–2 a.m.; Friday, 5 p.m.–3 a.m.; Saturday, 6 p.m.–3 a.m. **Metro** Farragut North or Dupont Circle.

WHAT GOES ON Posturing for fun and profit. The name is Italian slang for "the act of doing nothing"—hanging, in other words. The action starts in a lounge-lizard style, and gradually shifts into Euro-Latin and, on the highest levels (that's the third and fourth floors to you), hip-hop, house, and trance.

SETTING AND ATMOSPHERE This is actually what a cigar-and-martini lounge ought to look like: Tuscan red sponged walls; a sleek, glass-walled, walk-in cigar vault; lots of low, row cocktail tables for noshing and ashing, set off with recycled wrought-iron fencing and Deco-ish light fixtures designed to suggest the Paris Métro. It is, in fact, downstairs from the sidewalk, which makes even more atmospheric sense. Ozio is trying out late-night jazz on Monday through Wednesday nights, even more Parisian electric guitar.

IF YOU GO Bring your gold and platinum cards: the martinis are long and strong and cost between $8 and $10 (except Thursdays from 9:30 to 11 p.m., when ladies drink Champagne free, and cheap Grand Marnier Saturdays after 10 p.m.), while the cigars run $8 to $50. There is one smoke-free dining room. And carry a lot of business cards, too: this is turning into a network center for up-and-coming lobbyists and credit card sharks.

Platinum

DISCO BALL GLITTERING IN THE MAIN HALL, LATIN SHARKSKIN GLITTERING IN THE BASEMENT

915 F Street NW; ☎ 202-393-3555; www.platinumclubdc.com
Downtown

Who goes there Younger internationals. **Cover** Free early, then $15–$20. **Minimum** None. **Mixed drinks** $4–$8. **Wine** $5–$7. **Beer** $3–$5. **Dress** Trendy. **Specials** Vary. **Food available** Sushi (what else?). **Hours** Thursday–Sunday, 10 p.m.–3 a.m. **Metro** Metro Center.

WHAT GOES ON Despite changing names a couple of times (Fifth Column, the Bank), this may have survived to become the grande dame of D.C. neo-discos, and is traditionally the entry-level club for would-be sophisticates. Thursday is College Night (ID gets you a discount), Friday is old-fashioned Ladies' Night 18 and up (Cinderellas get in free till 11 p.m.), Saturday is just a trancy free-for-all. Tuesday and Sunday are heavier, with hip-hop the dominant beat.

SETTING AND ATMOSPHERE A former bank, Platinum still has the prosperous look, with a lavish chandelier and marble flooring, and a sound system to match. Four floors counting the VIP lounge *con* fireplace, and balconies to be seen in. Concessions sell candy and cigars to both girls and guys.

IF YOU GO Dress code here, as with most the better clubs these days, so college studio or congressional aide, dump the faux-cool for the fashion chic. Get in before the witching hour to save money and shoe time outside. If the line's too long, check out the nearby Home Nightclub at 911 F Street NW (☎ 202-638-4663; www.homenightclub.net), a new and very promising weekends-only annex from the same management.

Takoma Station

CLASSICALLY MINDED BUPPIE JAZZ BAR

6914 Fourth Street NW; ☎ 202-829-1999; www.takomastation.com
Upper Northwest

Who goes there 25–55; mixed media types; yuppies; buppies; other musicians. **Cover** $5. **Minimum** None. **Mixed drinks** $4–$8.50; their Long Island iced tea is strong enough to make you confuse your geography. **Wine** $3.50–$7. **Beer** $3–$5. **Dress** Suits and nice dresses; jeans, but with a jacket; no cutoffs; no tennis shoes. **Specials** Happy hour 4–8 p.m. weekdays. **Food available** Southern-style fried chicken, greens, meat loaf, ribs. **Hours** Sunday, 6:30 p.m.–2 a.m.; Monday through Friday, 4 p.m.–2 a.m; Saturday, 6:30 p.m.–3 a.m. **Metro** Takoma.

WHAT GOES ON Cocktail conversation here is loud, but once the performers—high-profile area pros and often national-rank musicians passing through who drop in to jam—begin, the attention level is pretty good. A true neighborhood joint owned by the taciturn Bobby Boyd, this bar was one of the nightspots that helped revitalize the untrendy side of Takoma Park without changing its character.

SETTING AND ATMOSPHERE This building, a former boxing gym, wears its age gracefully, with exposed brick, see-through room dividers that make the bar an integral part of the stage area, and just a handful of hanging plants.

IF YOU GO Don't be demonstrative, especially if you arrive early; the Boyds live on the nightside schedule and like to start mellow. Don't gawk at the media types who come in after production hours. Sunday is change-up night, with live reggae and a slightly younger crowd.

Zanzibar

WORLD-BEAT DISCO

700 Water Street SW; ☎ 202-554-9100   The National Mall

Who goes there 23–45 set; trade-law, embassy, and import reps; buppies, West African entrepreneurs, and Latin chic-sters. **Cover** $5 before 10 p.m. on Wednesday and Thursday, $10 after 10 p.m.; $10 before 11 p.m. on Friday, $20 after 8 p.m.; $10 before 9 p.m. on Saturday (ladies free), $20 after 9 p.m. **Minimum** None. **Mixed drinks** $4–$8.50. **Wine** $4.75–$6. **Beer** $4–$5. **Dress** Dress to impress or advertise success: European lapels, dresses with hip flounces, aerobic wear disguised as cocktail spandex; no T-shirts, jeans, or sneakers allowed. **Specials** Free admission and hors d'oeuvres at happy hour, 5–7 p.m. Fridays and 9–10 p.m. Saturdays. **Food available** Full West African menu. **Hours**

Wednesday, 5 p.m.–1 a.m.; Thursday, 5 p.m.–2 a.m.; Friday, 5 p.m.–3 a.m.; Saturday, 9 p.m.–4 a.m.; closed Sunday–Tuesday. **Metro** Maine Avenue.

WHAT GOES ON Salsa, soca, soukous, samba salsa, reggae, and even go-go take turns—mostly on the turntable, but occasionally with live bands. This is an expansively, expensively stylish singles bar, with potentially valuable networking as the undertone. The serious action starts after midnight; the visiting amateurs tend to turn pumpkin at 12.

SETTING AND ATMOSPHERE A sometime bureaucrats' business lunch spot, this is a long, underground wood-and-brick conference-room setup divided into larger and smaller areas, with a mahogany bar facing both and a lighted patio fountain outside the window.

IF YOU GO Be prepared to dance if you want to meet people; there's very little chatter at the bar unless you prove yourself (or are extremely well dressed). The downstairs is mostly restaurant, with great water views; the upstairs is nearly all dance floor. To go with the flow, move up and down both sides of the room; there is an unspoken tidal wave of unattached partners. *Note:* To simplify life, the tips are built into the drink prices, which makes them something more of a bargain.

PART ELEVEN

EXERCISE *and* RECREATION

■ WORKING OUT

MOST OF THE FOLKS ON OUR *Unofficial Guide* research team work out routinely. Some bike, some run, some lift weights or do aerobics. While visiting Washington during the hot summer months, it didn't take long to figure out that exercising in the city's fearsome heat and humidity presented some problems.

Washington is also prone to high levels of allergens, especially in spring and fall; and of pollution, especially in the summer. On those days, local authorities may declare Code Red days, during which anyone with respiratory problems should limit exertion and even outdoor exposure (and when some of the smaller bus systems are free, so as to encourage fewer drivers); or Code Orange, a milder warning. Ask the hotel concierge or check news reports.

The best months for outdoor exercise are March through June and September through December. In July and August, you must get up very early to beat the heat. January and February can bring quite cold weather, although snow usually isn't a problem. During the summer months, unless you get up very early, we recommend working out inside.

WALKING

WITH ITS WIDE-OPEN SPACES, Washington is made for walking. Security is very good along the Mall and Potomac Park, making for a safe walking environment at all hours of the day and night.

A long walk down the Mall and through **East and West Potomac Parks** offers grand views of the **Lincoln, Jefferson,** and **FDR memorials** and the **Washington Monument,** as well as the **Tidal Basin** and the **Potomac River.** For a really long excursion, cross Arlington Memorial Bridge and explore **Arlington National Cemetery.** You can also walk north along the river past the **Kennedy Center** and the **Thompson Boat Center** and into **Georgetown.**

North of the Mall, in what is now called the **Penn Quarter** neighborhood (see description in "New Restaurant Districts" on page 266 in Part Eight, Dining and Restaurants), there's plenty to see, but unless you get out early, you'll find the traffic and the traffic lights make sustained walking a little difficult. The Georgetown Waterfront, combined with M Street, and the portions of the Chesapeake and Ohio Canal Towpath that parallel the Potomac River are very popular. North of the White House, **Connecticut Avenue** offers unlimited window-shopping at the city's ritziest shops. South of the Capitol, **Fort McNair** is open to anyone who would like to stroll through well-kept grounds on a narrow peninsula where the Washington Channel and the Anacostia River meet the Potomac: take the Metro to the Waterfront Station and walk straight down Fourth Street SW to Fort McNair (not recommended after dark). Afterwards, you can stroll the waterfront marinas on **Maine Avenue.**

Although you must drive to get there, the **U.S. National Arboretum** in Northeast Washington offers walkers three and a half miles of easy trails winding through 444 acres of trees and flowers. In late April and May, fields of azaleas, flowering dogwood, and mountain laurel are in bloom.

The Mall and its surrounding areas are fairly flat, and distances can be deceiving there, making it easy to overextend yourself. Carry enough money to buy refreshments en route and for cab or Metro fare back to your hotel in case you get too tired to walk back.

RUNNING

WASHINGTON'S WEALTH OF PARKS OFFERS plenty of options to both casual and serious joggers. Most of the better running areas are relatively flat but visually stunning. Many of the best paths are centrally located, close to major in-town hotels and other attractions, making either a morning or late afternoon run easy to fit into a busy business or touring schedule. We don't recommend jogging at night except perhaps along the better-lit sections of the Mall; see the section on "How to Avoid Crime and Keep Safe in Public Places" on page 104 in Part Four. Check with the hotel concierge for maps or directions to the closest trains.

The heart of Washington and its most popular running location is the **Mall,** featuring packed-dirt paths. Nearby, the **Ellipse** (behind the White House) and the **Tidal Basin** offer paved pathways to run on.

Tree-shaded **Rock Creek Park** is a better bet during hot weather. A good starting point is where Connecticut Avenue crosses over Rock Creek Parkway in Northwest Washington. Run north to **Pierce Mill** and retrace your steps for a four-mile jog.

In Georgetown, the **Chesapeake & Ohio (C&O) Canal Towpath** offers what is probably the best running surface in town. Runners, cyclists, and hikers love this wide, dirt-pack trail that runs for miles between the scenic Potomac River and the canal. The river views are spectacular in

rock creek park

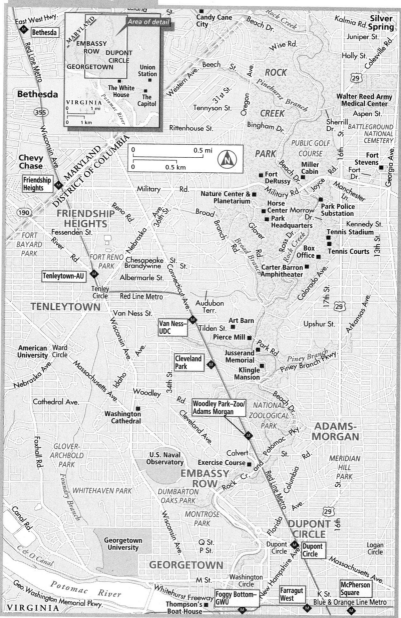

East West Hwy.
Bethesda

Area of detail

MARYLAND

EMBASSY ROW DUPONT CIRCLE
GEORGETOWN
Union Station
The White House
The Capitol
VIRGINIA
0   1 mi
0   1 km
Potomac River

Bethesda

Chevy Chase

Friendship Heights

MARYLAND

DISTRICT OF COLUMBIA

Candy Cane City
Beech Dr.
Rock Creek
Wise Rd.
Kalmia Rd. Silver Spring
Juniper St.
Holly St.
Colesville Rd.
29

Military Rd.

Western Ave.
31st St.
Tennyson St.
Rittenhouse St.
Oregon Ave.
Pineburst Branch
Bingham Dr.
ROCK CREEK PARK
Sherrill Dr.
Walter Reed Army Medical Center
Aspen St.
BATTLEGROUND NATIONAL CEMETERY

0   0.5 mi
0   0.5 km

PUBLIC GOLF COURSE
16th St.
Fort Stevens
Fort Dr.
Georgia Ave.

Reno Rd.
36th St.
Broad
Branch Rd.
Glover Rd.
Ross Dr.
Rock Creek
Broad Branch Rd.

Military Rd.
Fort DeRussy
Miller Cabin
Beach Dr.
Nature Center & Planetarium
Horse Center Morrow Dr.
Park Headquarters
Park Police Substation
Kennedy St.
Tennis Stadium
Box Office
Tennis Courts
13th St.
Carter Barron Amphitheater
Colorado Ave.

FRIENDSHIP HEIGHTS
Fessenden St.
190
FORT BAYARD PARK
River Rd.
FORT RENO PARK
Chesapeake St.
Brandywine St.
Albermarle St.
Tenleytown-AU
Tenley Circle
Red Line Metro
Van Ness St.

Nebraska Ave.

TENLEYTOWN

Connecticut Ave.

Audubon Terr.
Van Ness–UDC
Tilden St.
Pierce Mill
Art Barn

17th St.
29
Upshur St.
Arkansas Ave.

American University
Ward Circle
Nebraska Ave.
Cathedral Ave.
Wisconsin Ave.
Idaho Ave.
Woodley
34th St.
Cleveland Park
Jusserand Memorial
Klingle Mansion
Park Rd.
Piney Branch
Piney Branch Pkwy.

Washington Cathedral

Massachusetts Ave.

Woodley Park–Zoo/ Adams Morgan

Cleveland Ave.
NATIONAL ZOOLOGICAL PARK
Beach Dr.
ADAMS-MORGAN

GLOVER-ARCHBOLD PARK

Foxhall Rd.
Foundry Branch

U.S. Naval Observatory
EMBASSY ROW
Calvert St.
Exercise Course
Rock Creek and Potomac Pkwy.
Columbia Rd.
MERIDIAN HILL PARK
16th St.

WHITEHAVEN PARK
DUMBARTON OAKS PARK
MONTROSE PARK
Wisconsin Ave.

Red Line Metro

Florida Ave.
DUPONT CIRCLE
29

Canal Rd.
C & O Canal
Geo. Washington Memorial Pkwy.

Georgetown University
Q St.
P St.
GEORGETOWN
M St.
Washington Circle
Whitehurst Freeway
Thompson's Boat House

Dupont Circle
Dupont Circle
Logan Circle
Massachusetts Ave.

New Hampshire Ave.
Farragut West
K St.
McPherson Square
Blue & Orange Line Metro

Potomac River
VIRGINIA
Foggy Bottom–GWU

c&o canal towpath trail

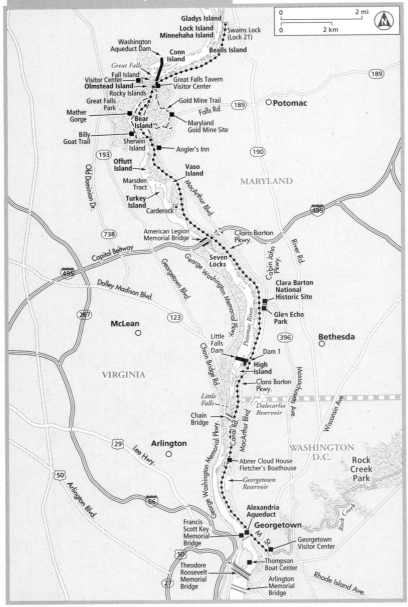

mount vernon trail

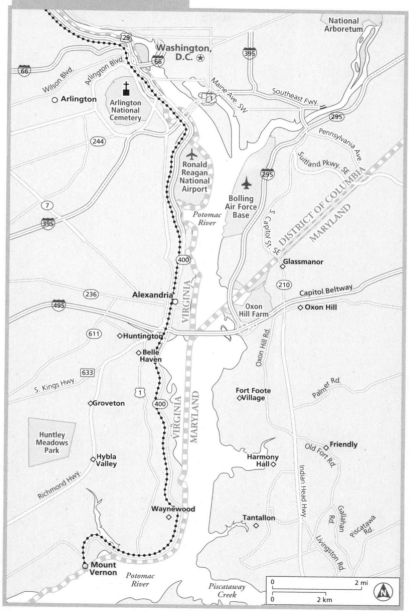

washington and old dominion railroad regional park

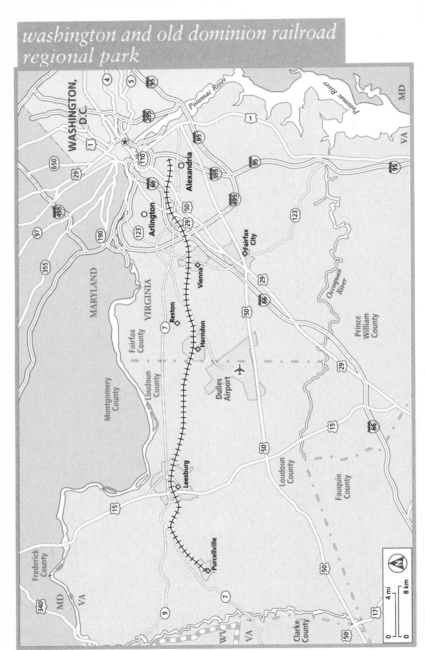

places; the placid canal reflects the greenery alongside; and historic lockhouses and locks appear at regular intervals. Mileposts along the towpath keep you informed of your distance. Farther up, in Maryland, the enormous cataract at **Great Falls** attracts hikers and picnickers.

There's now a second route from Georgetown that follows the **C&O Towpath** for several miles but then turns east toward Bethesda and Silver Spring. The **Capitol Crescent Trail,** based on the old Baltimore and Ohio Railroad right-of-way, has both a wide biking trail and in many places a separate parallel-running path. From Georgetown to Bethesda—where the trail emerges at a convenient restaurant neighborhood—is about seven miles; the second leg to Silver Spring is another four; but you can catch the Metro at either place if you aren't up to the return trip.

Another river route is the **Mount Vernon Trail,** a paved path that starts near the Lincoln Memorial, crosses Arlington Memorial Bridge, and goes downriver on the Virginia side of the Potomac for about 16 miles to Mount Vernon. Unless you're a marathoner, cut this run in half: run to Ronald Reagan National Airport and back, about seven and a half miles. In blustery fall, winter, and early spring weather, runners and cyclists will find that the better-protected **C&O Canal Towpath** offers more protection from strong winds coming off the river. Closer to downtown and the Mall, **West Potomac Park** is the best route in the spring, when the Japanese cherry trees are blooming around the Tidal Basin. Start near the Jefferson Memorial, head down Ohio Drive, and make the loop at the end of the park; if you've got any energy left, continue past the Jefferson Memorial and loop around the Tidal Basin. Go early in the morning to beat the crowds.

SWIMMING

LOCAL WATERS ARE POLLUTED to one degree or another, so stick to your hotel swimming pool or to the several nice aquatic centers. There's a year-round pool on Capitol Hill, the **Rumsey Aquatic Center,** at 635 North Carolina Avenue SE, very near the Eastern Market Metro station (☎ 202-724-4495); another near the White Flint station, the **Montgomery Aquatic Center** (5900 Executive Boulevard, North Bethesda; ☎ 301-468-4211); and many seasonal pools; again, the hotel concierge can direct you to the nearest pool or gym.

The closest saltwater beach is **Sandy Point State Park** in Maryland, about an hour's drive east on US 50 on the shores of the Chesapeake Bay. Atlantic Ocean beaches are a minimum three-hour drive; traffic tie-ups on summer weekends are horrendous as beachgoers funnel into the twin Chesapeake Bay bridges, where multihour backups are routine.

FITNESS CENTERS AND AEROBICS

ALMOST ALL OF THE MAJOR HOTELS have a spa or fitness room with weight-lifting equipment. For an aerobic workout, most of the fitness rooms offer a stationary bicycles, a StairMaster, or an elliptical trainer.

Many Washington fitness centers are members-only and don't offer daily or short-term memberships. The few exceptions are all coed. **The Fitness Company** (**www.thefitnesscompany.com**), features free weights, fixed weights, a full range of aerobic exercise equipment including a StairMaster, rowing and cycling machines, and a full schedule of aerobics classes. **Vida Fitness** (601 F Street NW; ☎ 202-393-8432) in the Verizon Center has the arena's sporting events on its TV screens, so if you can't get tickets, at least you can work out with the team.

There are a dozen or so **Bally Total Fitness Clubs** in the Washington area (about $15 for a day pass; **bally.know-where.com**) and two dozen **Sport & Health Clubs** some with golf and tennis facilities (**www.sportandhealth.com**).

Washington Sports Club, at 1835 Connecticut Avenue NW (across from the Hilton near Dupont Circle), offers much the same activities and services as The Fitness Company. The daily rate is $25. For more information, call ☎ 202-332-0100.

TENNIS

WASHINGTON'S THREE PUBLIC TENNIS CLUBS are popular, making it difficult to get a court during peak hours without a reservation. The **Rock Creek Tennis Center,** which is home to an ATP pre–U.S. Open Tournament every August that draws many of the sport's bigger stars (Andre Agassi was a five-time champion), has 25 total courts—10 hard and 15 clay; it's located at 16th and Kennedy streets in Upper Northwest. Five more indoor courts are heated during the winter. The club accepts reservations up to a week in advance. The club is open from 7 a.m. to 11 p.m. (on summer weekends till 8 p.m.). Call ☎ 202-722-5949 or go to **www.rockcreektennis.com** for more information.

The **East Potomac Tennis Club,** located on Ohio Drive in East Potomac Park, features 10 clay and 14 hard courts. Reservations for prime-time hours go fast, and you need to make reservations a week in advance. Players have a good chance of getting a court without reservations weekdays between 10 a.m. and 3 p.m. Rates range from $8 to $17 an hour. A credit-card deposit is required; open daily, 7 a.m.–10 p.m. Call ☎ 202-554-5962 for more information.

Pierce Mill, a small tennis center located in Rock Creek Park, offers clay courts. Call ☎ 202-554-5962 for more information.

ROCK CLIMBING

The new **Earth Treks Rockville,** four blocks south of the Rockville Metro station in the Marlo Furniture building (725 Rockville Pike; ☎ 340-283-9942), has 40-foot walls, teaching areas, and more than 100 top-rope climbs. A day pass is $16.

RECREATIONAL SPORTS:
Biking, Hiking, Kayaking, and So On

BICYCLING

WASHINGTON OFFERS BOTH ON- AND OFF-ROAD cyclists a wide variety of bicycling, from flat and easy cruises along paved bike paths and the C&O Canal Towpath, to challenging terrain in the rolling countryside of nearby Virginia and Maryland.

Fall is the best season for cycling around Washington, with cool, crisp weather and a riot of color as the leaves turn in mid- to late October. Even in winter, Washington's mild climate offers at least a few days a month that are warm enough to induce cyclists to jump on their bikes.

A variety of bicycles are available for rent at **Thompson Boat Center** (one-speed bikes are $4 an hour or $15 a day, and hybrid bikes are $8 an hour or $25 a day; ☎ 202-333-4861; **www.thompsonboat center.com**), open daily from 8 a.m. to 5 p.m.; bikes must be returned by 6 p.m. The center is located between the Kennedy Center and Georgetown on the Potomac. **Fletcher's Boathouse,** above Georgetown on Canal Road, also rents out bikes ($6 per hour for up to four hours or $25 a day; ☎ 202-244-0461).

Bike the Sites rents comfort mountain bikes (as well as strollers, mobility scooters, and wheelchairs) from its offices behind the Old Post Office Pavilion (☎ 202-842-2453; **www.bikethesites.com**). A second kiosk at the Rosslyn Metro Center rents bicycles only.

Road Biking

In downtown Washington, bicycling is better left to couriers. Unrelenting traffic congestion, combined with absent-minded tourists preoccupied with monuments and finding a cheap parking space, makes riding a bike on Washington's streets a brutal experience for all but the most hardened urban cyclists. Luckily, Washington features a network of bike paths that takes the terror out of riding a skinny-tired bike in—and out of—the city.

In terms of great scenery and enough distance to really get a workout, the **Mount Vernon Trail** is Washington's premier bike path. In addition to pedaling the 16 paved miles to Mount Vernon, cyclists can make side trips to Dyke Marsh wildlife habitat, explore fortifications at Fort Hunt, and see a 19th-century lighthouse at Jones Point Park.

Another good out-and-back ride is the **Washington and Old Dominion Railroad Regional Park (W&OD),** a 45-mile-long paved linear bikeway that connects with the Mount Vernon Trail upriver of Arlington Memorial Bridge on the Virginia side of the Potomac. The trail intersects with a series of "bubble" parks in urban Northern Virginia *covered bridge bicycle tour*

Key
.... Bicycle route
←🚲→ Direction of travel
🏠 Covered Bridge

Thurmont

Graceham

Rocky Ridge Rd.

Main St.

Moser Rd.

Blue Mtn.

Blue Mtn. Rd.

Frederick Rd.

Black Mill Rd.

Hessons Bridge Rd.

Old Frederick Rd.

MARYLAND

Angleberger Rd.

Lewistown

Old Frederick Rd.

Woodsboro

Powell Rd.

Mountaindale Rd.

Ulica Rd.

Monocacy River

Putman Rd.

Bethel Rd.

To
Frederick, MD
and
Washington, DC

Clover Hill

Frederick Community College
start and finish of bicycle tour

Opossumtown Pike

0   1 mi
0   1.6 km

sugarloaf mountain bicycle tour

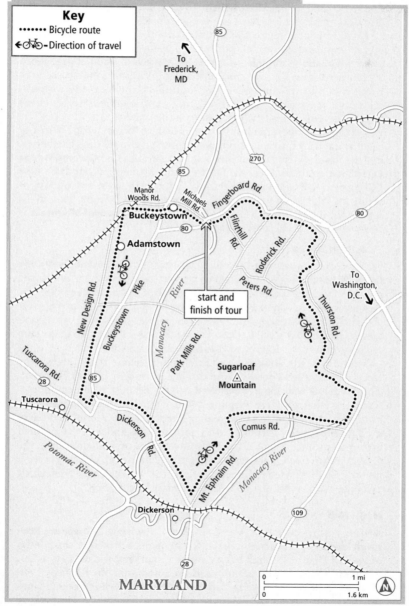

Key
• • • • • • Bicycle route
←🚲— Direction of travel

To Frederick, MD

85

270

Manor Woods Rd.
Michaels Mill Rd.
Fingerboard Rd.

Buckeystown
80

Flinthill Rd.
Roderick Rd.

80

Adamstown

New Design Rd.

Buckeystown Pike

Monocacy River

start and finish of tour

Peters Rd.

To Washington, D.C.

Thurston Rd.

Park Mills Rd.

Sugarloaf Mountain

Tuscarora Rd.
28

Tuscarora

85

Dickerson Rd.

Comus Rd.

Monocacy River

Potomac River

Mt. Ephraim Rd.

Dickerson

109

28

MARYLAND

0 _____ 1 mi
0 _____ 1.6 km

N

and provides access to the rural Virginia countryside beyond the Capital Beltway. Both the Mount Vernon Trail and the W&OD trail are easily reached from Washington by bicycle by riding across the Arlington Memorial Bridge, at the Lincoln Memorial.

Road riders itching to see beautiful countryside outside the Washington metropolitan area (but within a day's drive) should go to either **Middleburg, Virginia,** or **Frederick, Maryland.** Middleburg, about 30 miles west of D.C., is in the heart of Virginia's horse country. Beautiful rolling countryside in the foothills of the Blue Ridge Mountains and low-traffic roads bordering thoroughbred horse farms make this area a fantastic place to spin the cranks.

Frederick, is about an hour's drive north of Washington. North of town along US 15, covered bridges, narrow back roads, fish hatcheries, and mountain vistas evoke images of Vermont. The **Covered Bridge Cycle Tour** starts at Frederick Community College. From D.C. take I-270 north to Frederick and get on US 15 north; then exit on Opposumtown Pike going north to the college, about a mile on the left. To the south of Frederick, a 25-mile loop around **Sugarloaf Mountain** is a favorite with local road cyclists.

Mountain Biking

Fat-tired cyclists can ride 184 miles one-way on the **Chesapeake & Ohio Canal Towpath,** beginning in Georgetown then following along the Potomac River upstream to **Cumberland, MD.** The hardpacked dirt surface gives the illusion of being flat all the way; actually, the trip upriver is slightly uphill. Because of floods in the winter and spring, it's a good idea to call the National Park Service at ☎ 301-739-4200 to make sure the section you're planning to ride is open to cyclists.

Hammerheads looking for challenging single-track and some steep climbing have to do some driving to find it, but it's worth it. The **Frederick Municipal Watershed** offers the best technical single-track this side of West Virginia—and it's a lot closer. Located an hour's drive from Washington near Frederick, MD, the 6,000-acre mountaintop forest is riddled with narrow trails and well-maintained dirt roads. Since there are hardly any signs or trail markers, the Catoctin Furnace Quadrangle topographic map and a compass are a must. Local knowledge helps, too; call the Wheel Base, Frederick's pro bike shop, at ☎ 301-663-9288 for maps and advice.

HIKING

WHILE ONLY ABOUT 15 MINUTES from downtown, **Theodore Roosevelt Island** is a wilderness oasis offering hikers a little over three miles of wide, flat paths through forests, swampy marshes, and rocky beaches. The park is located on the Potomac River across from the Kennedy Center and can be reached by car. Park in the area off the northbound lanes of the George Washington Memorial Parkway on the Virginia side of the river. A footbridge connects the Virginia shore to the island.

The **C&O Canal,** which begins in Georgetown, features a hard-packed dirt path that follows the Potomac River north for 184 miles (see "Running," page 398). Along the way are river views, forest, and wildlife. At **Great Falls Park,** north of Washington on the Virginia side of the river, the Potomac roars over a series of steep, jagged rocks and flows through a narrow gorge. It's a dramatic scene and worth the trip. Hiking trails follow the river and offer views of **Mather Gorge. Rock Creek Park** in Northwest Washington offers 15 miles of hiking trails, plus bridle trails you can hike. Maps are available at the park headquarters, 5163 Williamsburg Lane NW (☎ 202-895-6070).

For a more extensive guide to hikes in the area, check out author Paul Elliott's *60 Hikes within 60 Miles: Washington, D.C.*, published by Menasha Ridge Press (**www.menasharidge.com**).

CANOEING AND KAYAKING

Canoes and rowboats are available for rent on the C&O Canal and the Potomac River at **Thompson Boat Center,** located between the Kennedy Center and Georgetown (☎ 202-333-4861). Single kayaks are $8 an hour or $24 a day, double kayaks are $10 an hour or $30 a day, and canoes are $10 per hour or $30 a day. **Fletcher's Boat House,** located at Canal and Reservoir Roads above Georgetown (☎ 202-244-0461; **www.fletchersboathouse.com**), has canoes for rent at $11 an hour or $22 a day. **Jack's Boats,** located on K Street in Georgetown (☎ 202-337-9642), has canoes and kayaks for rent at $15 for one hour, $25 for two hours, or $35 a day. Pedal boats can be rented at the **Tidal Basin** (☎ 202-484-0206): a two-passenger rental is $8 an hour and a four-passenger rental is $16 an hour.

Whitewater enthusiasts need go only a few miles north of the Capital Beltway to find excellent Class I through Class VI rapids year-round on the **Potomac.** Local boaters boast that it's the best urban whitewater experience in the United States, featuring a very remote, wilderness feel; some Olympic hopefuls have trained here. One of the most popular trips is the Class II Seneca rapids section. The put-in is at **Violets Lock,** located on River Road (MD 190), north of Potomac, MD. Violets Lock is also the take-out, meaning you don't have to run a shuttle: it's a round-trip that lets you return to your starting point by paddling up the C&O Canal, about one and a half miles below Violets Lock. Below the Seneca rapids, the river is very scenic, featuring many islands and no rapids. But you must make the next take-out on the left bank at Maryland's Great Falls National Park or become another statistic as the river drops through Great Falls.

Seasoned paddlers may want to try running the Class II/III+ rapids that start below Great Falls and end at the Old Angler's Inn. As with Seneca rapids, no shuttle is required: park across the road from the Old Angler's Inn on MacArthur Boulevard on the Maryland side of the Potomac and follow the trail to the put-in. Paddle upstream on the C&O Canal to below Great Falls (at least 100 yards) for the return leg.

ICE SKATING

THERE ARE A FEW YEAR-ROUND ICE RINKS in the Washington area, but the two that would be the most fun for out-of-towners are seasonal: one on the Mall and the other at the heart of official Washington within sight of the White House.

Come skating weather—generally mid-November through mid-March—the **Sculpture Garden of the National Gallery of Art** at Seventh or Ninth Street and Constitution or Madison Avenue (☎ 202-289-3360; **www.nga.gov/ginfo/skating.shtm**) is transformed into a fantasy ice rink in the middle of the Mall, with the U.S. Capitol and all the Smithsonian museums lit up as a backdrop. It's open from 10 a.m. to 9 p.m. Monday through Thursday, from 10 a.m. until a romantic 11 p.m. Fridays and Saturdays, and from 11 a.m. to 9 p.m. on Sundays. A two-hour session is $7 for adults or $6 age 50 and over, age 12 and under, and students with ID; skate rental is $3, and locker rental is 50¢ (but with a $5 refundable deposit).

The **Pavilion Cafe,** a lovely retro-Deco glass-sided eatery alongside the garden, stays open late during the skating season, serving sandwiches, pizzas, salads, hot chocolate, coffee and tea, and wine and beer until 8 p.m. Sundays and weekdays and until 9 p.m. Fridays and Saturdays.

A few blocks away, **Pershing Park,** just east of the Treasury Building and the White House at 14th Street and Pennsylvania Avenue NW, with a view of the Washington Monument and many federal buildings, also gets a wintertime coat of ice. It's lit and late, too, so that you can skate from 11 a.m. to 9 p.m. on weekdays and until 11 p.m. on Fridays and Saturdays. Skate rental is $2.50, and a two-hour ticket is $6.50 for adults and $5.50 for ages 12 and under; there are often early-bird discounts, too. For more information, call ☎ 202-737-6938 or visit **www.pershingparkicerink.com.**

Several public rinks are accessible by Metro—and at Metro developments, in fact. The plaza atop the **Bethesda Metro** is iced during winter, as is the outdoor-cafe area at the **Shops at Pentagon Row,** part of the Pentagon City complex; and **Reston Town Center.** For hockey fans, however, the most intriguing facility might be the new **Arlington Ice Skating Center,** atop a seven-story office building at Ballston Common Mall (at the Ballston Metro) in Arlington; it's also the practice rink for the NHL Washington Capitals.

SKIING

MODERATELY GOOD DOWNHILL SKI SLOPES are within a couple hours' drive from Washington and offer dependable, machine-made snow and night skiing from November through March. **Whitetail,** a $25-million ski area in nearby Pennsylvania, features a vertical drop of almost 1,000 feet, 14 trails, and plenty of lift capacity. Call ☎ 717-328-9400 for information on ski packages, lodging, and lift rates.

Jointly owned **Ski Roundtop** and **Liberty Mountain Resort,** also located in south-central Pennsylvania, are about a two- to three-hour drive from Washington. Both offer 600-foot verticals, 13 trails, and 100-percent snowmaking. Call Ski Roundtop at ☎ 717-432-9631 and Liberty Mountain Resort at ☎ 717-642-8282 for lift rates, hours, and directions.

HORSEBACK RIDING

THE ROCK CREEK PARK HORSE CENTER offers guided rides on the equestrian trails located in Rock Creek Park. Rates are $30 for an hour; reservations are required. Children must be at least 30 inches tall for the guided rides. Rock Creek also offers pony rides for $20. The center, which is open all year, is located at Military and Glover Roads in Northwest Washington. The hours are Tuesday through Friday, noon to 6 p.m.; Saturday and Sunday, 9 a.m. to 5 p.m. Call ☎ 202-362-0117 or visit **www.rockcreekhorsecenter.com** for more information. For indoor riding, the **Potomac Horse Center** in Gaithersburg (1411 Quince Orchard Road; ☎ 301-208-0200) has several indoor as well as trail facilities and hosts kids' pony parties as well as dressage and hunter-jumper training.

GOLF

WASHINGTON HAS THREE PUBLIC GOLF COURSES operated on National Park Service land and open from dawn to dusk. Fees are $9 to $17 for 9 holes and $19 to $22 for 18 holes weekdays; weekends, the rates range from $11 to $27, respectively. Reservations are not accepted. All three courses feature snack bars, pro shops, rental clubs, and gas cars. For more information, visit **www.golfdc.com.**

East Potomac Golf Course, located in East Potomac Park across from Washington's waterfront area, offers one 18-hole course, two 9-hole courses, and an 18-hole miniature golf course. It's the busiest of the National Park Service courses; plan to arrive at dawn on weekends if you don't want to wait. East Potomac has wide-open fairways, well-kept greens, and great views of surrounding monuments. The park also offers tennis, outdoor pool, playground, bathroom, and picnic facilities, so it's a good choice for family outings. Call ☎ 202-554-7660 for more information.

Langston Golf Course, at 28th Street and Benning Road NE (near RFK Stadium), features an 18-hole course, including newly remodeled back-9 holes, and a driving range. Langston, the only public course with water holes, is located along the Anacostia River. For more information, call ☎ 202-397-8638.

Rock Creek Golf Course is located at 16th and Rittenhouse streets NW, four-and-a-half miles north of the White House on 16th Street. It offers duffers a hilly and challenging 18-hole course through rolling hills and wooded terrain. Call ☎ 202-882-7332 for more information.

SPECTATOR SPORTS

AFTER WAITING MORE THAN 30 YEARS, our nation's capital has a new Major League Baseball team, the **Washington Nationals.** America's national pastime returned to D.C. on a professional level when the former Montreal Expos moved here and began their first season at RFK Stadium (at the Stadium-Armory Metro station) in spring of 2005. An elaborate new stadium complex is under construction with views of the Anacostia River and the federal monuments; it's scheduled to be ready for the 2008-2009 season, and will also be Metro accessible.

In the decades between teams, however, many Washingtonians developed a fierce devotion to the **Baltimore Orioles,** only an hour north. Visitors to D.C. can make the trek by train to catch the Birds playing at home, Oriole Park at Camden Yards, near Baltimore's downtown Inner Harbor. Check the sports section of the *Washington Post* for information on both teams' home games and tickets.

If you're one of the growing number of fans of **minor-league baseball,** Washington is worth a minitour. The Class A **Frederick Keys** (named in honor of Francis Scott Key, a rural Maryland native) play in the historic town of Frederick, MD, about an hour to the northeast (☎ 301-662-0013). The Class A **Potomac Nationals,** a farm team for the New Nats, play just outside Fairfax County; call ☎ 703-590-2311 for details.

The closest option for baseball is Prince George's County Stadium, where the **Bowie Baysox,** a Class AA team belonging to the same group as the Keys, have been steadily building a crowd. Both teams are associated with the Orioles, so they're sentimental favorites. Baysox tickets run only $12 for box seats, $15 for field box, $9 for adults, and $6 for children, seniors, and active military. Call ☎ 301-464-4865 for information.

For **professional basketball,** the **Washington Wizards** and the WNBA's **Mystics** (the league's highest-attendance team in 2002) play out of the Verizon Center, located downtown (right above the Gallery Place Metro). For schedules and tickets, call ☎ 202-661-5050 or visit the teams' respective Web sites: **www.nba.com/wizards** and **www.wnba.com/mystics.**

The **University of Maryland Terrapins** offer topflight **college basketball** at Comcast Center on the school's campus in suburban College Park. Call ☎ 301-314-7070 for information. **Georgetown University** plays its home games at Verizon Center; for ticket information call ☎ 202-687-HOYA.

The **George Mason University Patriots** who made it into the NCAA Final Four in 2006, play on their college campus in Fairfax, but tickets may be hard to come by (☎ 703-993-3270). The **George Washington University Colonials** (☎ 202-944-6050) have many devoted fans (including newscasters Tim Russert and Wolf Blitzer); the team's Smith Center home is near the Foggy Bottom–GWU Metro stop.

D.C.-AREA HORSE TRACKS

Harness:	Rosecroft Raceway—Fort Washington, MD; ☎ 301-567-4000
Thoroughbred:	Bowie Race Course—Bowie, MD; ☎ 301-262-8111
	Charles Town Raceways—Charles Town, WV; ☎ 304-725-7001
	Laurel Race Course—Laurel, MD; ☎ 301-725-0400
	Maryland Jockey Club—Baltimore, MD; ☎ 410-542-9400

Lots of luck getting tickets to see professional football in Washington: the **Washington Redskins** have sold out stadiums for years, and the team holds the reputation as the hardest ticket to acquire in pro sports. Still interested? Scalpers regularly charge three and four times the regular ticket price—and higher, if the 'Skins are playing Dallas.

In 1997, the Redskins moved from RFK Stadium to what is now FedEx Field in Landover. The stadium has nearly 92,000 seats, so tickets are slightly easier to obtain. On the other hand, they're among the most expensive in the NFL; parking alone will run you $35. Following suit, Baltimore built a new football stadium for the Ravens, née Cleveland Browns. For Redskins schedule and ticket information, call ☎ 301-276-6800 or visit **www.redskins.com.** For the Ravens, call ☎ 410-261-RAVE or visit **www.baltimoreravens.com.**

College football is another matter. The **Maryland Terrapins** play in Byrd Stadium at College Park (☎ 301-314-7070). **The Naval Academy** in Annapolis, Maryland, and **Howard University** in Washington also field teams; check the *Post* for home game information.

Washington's **professional hockey** team, the **Washington Capitals,** shares partial ownership with the Wizards and Mystics, and also plays at the Verizon Center in downtown D.C. near Gallery Place. For information, call ☎ 202-628-3200.

Pro soccer comes to Washington when the **D.C. United** play 16 home games each season (March through September) at RFK Stadium. Tickets for evening and Sunday afternoon games range from $22 to $55. For schedule information, call ☎ 202-587-5000. The **Washington Bayhawks** (nee Baltimore Bayhawks) pro-lacrosse team, which won two league championships and four division titles in the MLL's six-year history, now plays at Georgetown University's multisports facility (☎ 866-99-HAWKS).

Horse racing is available at a number of tracks around Washington; while Pimlico is farthest from the city, it is home to the Preakness Stakes, the middle contest of thoroughbred racing's Triple Crown, and the third Saturday in May is part of a huge celebration there. Check the *Washington Post* to see which track is in season during your visit. Bus service from the city is usually available.

ACCOMMODATIONS INDEX

RESTAURANT INDEX

Note: Page numbers of restaurant profiles are in **boldface** type.

SUBJECT INDEX

Unofficial Guide Reader Survey

If you'd like to express your opinion about traveling in Washington, D.C., or this guidebook, complete the following survey and mail it to:

Unofficial Guide Reader Survey
P.O. Box 43673
Birmingham, AL 35243

Inclusive dates of your visit:_____

Members of your party:

	Person 1	Person 2	Person 3	Person 4	Person 5
Gender:	M F	M F	M F	M F	M F
Age:					

How many times have you been to Washington? _____
On your most recent trip, where did you stay? _____

Concerning your accommodations, on a scale of 100 as best and 0 as worst, how would you rate:

The quality of your room? The value of your room?
The quietness of your room? Check-in/checkout efficiency?
Shuttle service to the airport? Swimming pool facilities?

Did you rent a car?_____ From whom?_____

Concerning your rental car, on a scale of 100 as best and 0 as worst, how would you rate:
Pickup-processing efficiency?____ Return processing efficiency?___
Condition of the car?____ Cleanliness of the car?____
Airport shuttle efficiency?____

Concerning your dining experiences:
Estimate your meals in restaurants per day? _____
Approximately how much did your party spend on meals per day? ____

Favorite restaurants in Washington: _____
_____

Did you buy this guide before leaving? _____ While on your trip?_____

How did you hear about this guide? (check all that apply)

☐ Loaned or recommended by a friend ☐ Radio or TV
☐ Newspaper or magazine ☐ Bookstore salesperson
☐ Just picked it out on my own ☐ Library
☐ Internet

What other guidebooks did you use on this trip? _____

_____

_____

_____

On a scale of 100 as best and 0 as worst, how would you rate them?

_____

_____

_____

Using the same scale, how would you rate the *Unofficial Guide*(s)?

_____

Are *Unofficial Guides* readily available at bookstores in your area? _____

Have you used other *Unofficial Guides*? _____

Which one(s)? _____

_____

_____

Comments about your Washington trip or the *Unofficial Guide*(s):

_____

_____

_____

_____

_____

_____

_____

_____

_____

_____

_____

_____

_____

_____

_____

_____

_____

_____

_____

_____